Developing Web Applications with Perl, memcached, MySQL® and Apache

Developing Web Applications with Perl, memcached, MySQL® and Apache

Patrick Galbraith

WILEY

Wiley Publishing, Inc.

Developing Web Applications with Perl, memcached, MySQL® and Apache

Published by
Wiley Publishing, Inc.
10475 Crosspoint Boulevard
Indianapolis, IN 46256
www.wiley.com

Copyright © 2009 by Wiley Publishing, Inc., Indianapolis, Indiana

Published simultaneously in Canada

ISBN: 978-0-470-41464-4

Manufactured in the United States of America

10 9 8 7 6 5 4 3 2 1

For general information on our other products and services please contact our Customer Care Department within the United States at (877) 762-2974, outside the United States at (317) 572-3993 or fax (317) 572-4002.

Library of Congress Control Number: 2009927343

Wiley also publishes its books in a variety of electronic formats. Some content that appears in print may not be available in electronic books.

To my wonderful wife, Ruth, whom I have known for 27 years and who has stood by me while writing this book, even when I couldn't give her the time she deserved. Also, to my dear friend Krishna, who gave me inspiration every day.

Credits

Acquisitions Editor
Jenny Watson

Project Editor
Maureen Spears

Technical Editor
John Bokma

Production Editor
Rebecca Coleman

Copy Editor
Sara E. Wilson

Editorial Manager
Mary Beth Wakefield

Production Manager
Tim Tate

Vice President and Executive Group Publisher
Richard Swadley

Vice President and Executive Publisher
Barry Pruett

Associate Publisher
Jim Minatel

Project Coordinator, Cover
Lynsey Stanford

Proofreader
Corina Copp, Word One

Indexer
Robert Swanson

About the Author

Patrick Galbraith lives up in the sticks of southwestern New Hampshire near Mt. Monadnock with his wife, Ruth. Since 1993, he has been using and developing open source software. He has worked on various open source projects, including MySQL, Federated storage engine, Memcached Functions for MySQL, Drizzle, and Slashcode, and is the maintainer of DBD::mysql. He has worked at a number of companies throughout his career, including MySQL AB, Classmates.com, OSDN/Slashdot. He currently works for Lycos. He is also part owner of a wireless broadband company, Radius North, which provides Internet service to underserved rural areas of New Hampshire. His web site, which comes by way of a 5.8GHz Alvarion access unit up in a pine tree, is `http://patg.net`.

About the Technical Editor

John Bokma is a self-employed Perl programmer and consultant from the Netherlands. He has been working professionally in software development since 1994, moving his primary focus more and more toward the Perl programming language. John and his wife, Esmeralda, currently live in the state of Veracruz, Mexico, with their daughter Alice. John's other two children, Jim and Laurinda, live with their mother in New Zealand. For more information or to contact John, visit his web site at `http://johnbokma.com/`.

Acknowledgments

One weekend in 1993, I had the chance to go on a getaway to San Diego. Instead, I opted to stay home and download, onto 26 floppies, Slackware Linux, which I promptly installed onto my Packard Bell 386. I could never get the built-in video card to work with X, so I ended up buying a separate video card and had to edit my XConfig file to get it to work. How much more interesting this was to do than editing a config.sys and an autoexec.bat! From then on, I was hooked. I worked at Siemens Ultrasound Group in Issaquah, Washington, at the time. An engineer there named Debra, when asked what was a good thing to learn, said something I'll never forget: "Learn Perl." Debra — you were right!

I always wanted to be a C++ graphics programmer. That didn't happen because of this thing called the World Wide Web. I remember Ray Jones and Randy Bentson of Celestial Software showing me a program called Mosaic, which allowed you to view text over the Internet. Images would be launched using XV. Everywhere I worked, I had to write programs that ran on the Web, which required me to write CGI in Perl. So much for my goal of being a C++ programmer — but I consider this a great trade for a great career. (I did eventually get to write C++ for MySQL!)

I would first like to thank my editor, Maureen Spears, who is not only a great editor, but also a friend. She gave me much-needed encouragement throughout the writing of this book.

A special thanks goes to John Bokma for his meticulous attention to detail and great knowledge of Perl — particularly with regard to Perl programming style and convention that I didn't realize had changed over the last several years. I was somewhat set in my ways!

Thank you to Jenny Watson, who gave me the opportunity to write this book in the first place!

Thanks to Monty Widenius for creating MySQL and for being a mentor as well as a good friend, and thanks, Monty, for looking over Chapters 1, 2, and 3! Thanks also to Brian Aker for being another great mentor and friend, as well as being a software-producing machine with a scrolling page full of open source software projects that he's created, including Drizzle and libmemcached. Thanks to Sheeri Kritzer for her encouragement and for listening to me — she finished her book not too long before I finished mine, so she understood completely what I was going through.

I'd like to thank my friend, Wes Moran, head of design for Sourceforge, for providing the nice, clean, simple HTML design I used for many of the examples in this book.

Thanks to Eric Day for his excellent input and review of chapters pertaining to Gearman.

A special thanks to Joaquín Ruiz of Gear 6, who provided a lot of input on Chapter 1, as well as Jeff Freund of Clickability and Edwin Desouza and Jimmy Guerrero of Sun, who put me in touch with others and were great sources of memcached information.

I would like to thank my current colleagues at Lycos, and former colleagues at Grazr and MySQL, as well as the team members of Drizzle, for their part in my professional development, which gave me the ability to write this book. Thanks also to anyone I forgot to mention!

Acknowledgments

Finally, I would like to thank the entire Open Source community. My life would not be the same without open source software.

There's a verse in an ancient book, the Bhagavad Gita, that aptly describes how people like Monty Widenius, Linus Torvalds, Larry Wall, Brian Aker and other leaders within the Open Source community inspire the rest of us:

"Whatever action a great man performs, common men follow. And whatever standards he sets by exemplary acts, all the world pursues."

Contents

Contents

Contents

Contents

Contents

Contents

Contents

Contents

Foreword

Over a decade ago I walked into an office in Seattle on a Saturday to do an interview. The day before I had had the worst interview of my life. I had spent an entire day wandering through the halls of a large Seattle-based company answering asinine questions. I was not in a particularly good mood and doing an interview on a Saturday was not really what I wanted to be doing.

The interview was not done in the normal one-on-one fashion, but instead it was being done with me talking to about seven developers at once. I was being asked all sorts of questions about databases, web servers, and more general stuff about how programming languages work. There was this one particular guy who kept asking me these oddball questions that just seemed to come out of nowhere. For a while I kept thinking to myself, "Where is this stuff coming from?" It all seemed random at first, and then I figured out why he was asking the questions.

He was putting together a bigger picture in his head and was asking questions in order to learn how to put together entire systems. The questions had nothing to do with the trivial corners of any particular technology but instead dealt with how to build systems. He was using the opportunity to learn.

Patrick is an amazing fellow. Of all of the people I have worked with over the years, he has been the one who has always been the person who asked the questions. He is obsessed with learning and, unlike most engineers, he has no fear of divulging that he doesn't know something about a particular topic. He will ask any question and read any book that he must in order to learn how something works. He asks questions in the most humble of manners and I have never seen him shy away from even the most heated of personalities in his quest for answers.

The book you hold in your hands is the result of that curiosity. There is no web related system you could not build given the tools this book provides. Queues, webservers, caching, and databases. You can build the world we have created in the Internet with these tools.

Brian Aker

Introduction

Web Application development has changed a lot in the past ten years. Now there are so many new technologies to choose from when implementing a web application, and so many ways to architect an application to get the most optimal performance.

One of those technologies is memcached, a high-performance, distributed memory object caching system that you can use as a front-end cache for your applications to store data you would otherwise have to access from a database. This has been a great boon to numerous companies looking for ways to gain performance without having to spend a king's ransom — now affordable commodity hardware can be used to run memcached to simply provide more memory for application caching. Before, the focus would have been on how to get more power (hardware) for database servers.

Then there is MySQL, the world's most popular open source database and a full-fledged relational database management system. MySQL has advanced greatly in the past ten years, providing many fine features that you, as a web developer, can take advantage of. MySQL came into being during the advent of the World Wide Web and, in fact, was the database of choice for many web applications. Thus, it was a major factor in the very growth of the World Wide Web. Both MySQL and Linux evolved and became popular because of the Internet and were innately well suited for web application development.

A technology that isn't so new but is still very pertinent is Perl. Perl is an incredibly versatile programming language that doesn't get the fanfare of many of the new languages now available; Perl quietly and dutifully provides the functionality that powers many web sites and applications. Such is the burden of a mature and stable technology. However, Perl has *much* to be excited about. There is a legacy of more than two decades of developers solving many problems, and a plethora of CPAN modules for just about everything you could ever need to do programmatically. There are also new features and frameworks for Perl, such as Moose, and the eventual release of Perl 6. It has been long coming, but that's probably because Perl 5 works so well. Also, writing Perl programs is incredibly enjoyable!

Other new technologies include:

❏   Ajax, which has made it possible to create rich and interactive web applications that are on par with traditional desktop applications. This will continue to transform the Web in a fundamental way.

❏   Gearman, a system to farm out work to other machines. This is a new system that makes it possible to implement distributed computing/MapReduce.

❏   Sphinx, a powerful, full-text search engine that integrates well with MySQL.

The goal of this book is to cover each of these technologies separately to help you gain an in-depth understanding of each of them, and then to put the pieces together to show you how you can use these technologies to create web applications. This book will also introduce you to new technologies that no other book has yet covered in such detail, as well as the idea of the LAMMP stack — Linux, Apache, memcached, MySQL, and Perl.

Who This Book Is For

To understand much of what is shown in this book, you should have at least an intermediate level of Perl or another programming language, the ability to perform some common system administrative tasks, and a basic understanding of what a database is.

The target of this book is the intermediate programmer, though this can be a broad group. There are some Perl application developers who are Perl experts but who might avoid becoming intimately acquainted with the database, and then there are others who are database administrators who can write some Perl utilities but who have not made the leap to writing web applications in Perl. This book is intended as a bridge between the two skill sets, to help either of the "intermediate" groups to learn something new.

What This Book Covers

This book will cover each component in the LAMMP stack separately, so you can gain an understanding of each in isolation. It will then put all the pieces together to show how you can effectively use them for developing web applications. This isn't the typical web application programming book! It's written by an author who has had to fulfill many different roles in (usually) small organizations, where necessity dictated that he wear the various hats of a database administrator, systems administrator, and even a Perl application coder! This is also not a web application design book. The web applications presented in this book use as simple a design as possible to get the point across.

How This Book Is Structured

This book covers the following topics:

- ❑ **Chapter 1:** How web application development has changed over the years and an overview of the new technologies this book will cover.
- ❑ **Chapters 2–3:** Basic and then more advanced MySQL usage and concepts, including introductions to writing MySQL User Defined Functions and to the Sphinx full-text search engine.
- ❑ **Chapter 4:** A refresher on Perl programming.
- ❑ **Chapter 5:** A refresher on object-oriented Perl.
- ❑ **Chapter 6:** Programming with Perl and MySQL, covering DBI.
- ❑ **Chapter 7:** A simple command-line Perl contact list application using MySQL.
- ❑ **Chapter 8:** An introduction to memcached and writing Perl database applications using memcached as a caching layer.
- ❑ **Chapter 9:** A discussion of libmemcached, a memcached client library written in C that offers more features and performance as well as a Perl interface.
- ❑ **Chapter 10:** An introduction to the Memcached Functions for MySQL (UDFs).
- ❑ **Chapter 11:** A complete guide to Apache installation and configuration.
- ❑ **Chapter 12:** A simple contact list CGI application written in Perl that shows the use of MySQL and memcached together.

❑ **Chapter 13:** A mod_perl overview.

❑ **Chapter 14:** Using mod_perl handlers, this chapter shows you some basic mod_perl handlers and demonstrates the power of mod_perl.

❑ **Chapter 15:** More mod_perl, showing you how to convert the application from Chapter 12 to a mod_perl application, as well as some other mod_perl application examples, such as handling cookies, sessions, and templating systems.

❑ **Chapter 16:** How to write Ajax mod_perl web applications.

❑ **Chapter 17:** The crown jewel of this book puts all previous technologies together, presenting a search engine application using mod_perl, memcached, MySQL, Gearman, and Sphinx!

❑ **Appendix A:** MySQL installation.

❑ **Appendix B:** MySQL configuration, backups, and monitoring.

What You Need to Use This Book

This book is targeted for Unix operating systems, but also makes a good attempt at showing you how to install MySQL, Apache, and mod_perl on Windows. So it's entirely possible to use Windows for the examples presented in this book.

The code examples in this book were tested to make sure they work. Some things were changed, though verified, during the editing phase.

The components you will need for this book are:

❑ MySQL version 5.1 or higher, though 5.0 should work

❑ Apache 2.2

❑ Modperl 2.0

❑ Perl 5.8 or higher, though earlier versions should work

❑ memcached 1.2.6 or higher

❑ Sphinx 0.9.8 or higher

❑ libmemcached 0.25 or higher

Conventions

To help you get the most from the text and keep track of what's happening, we've used a number of conventions throughout the book.

> **Boxes like this one hold important, not-to-be forgotten information that is directly relevant to the surrounding text.**

Notes, tips, hints, tricks, and asides to the current discussion are offset and placed in italics like this.

As for styles in the text:

- ❑ We *highlight* new terms and important words when we introduce them.
- ❑ We show keyboard strokes like this: Ctrl+A.
- ❑ We show file names, URLs, and code within the text like so: `persistence.properties`.
- ❑ We present code in two different ways:

```
We use a monofont type with no highlighting for most code examples.
We use gray highlighting to emphasize code that's particularly important
in the present context.
```

Source Code

As you work through the examples in this book, you may choose either to type in all the code manually or to use the source code files that accompany the book. All of the source code used in this book is available for download at `http://www.wrox.com`. Once at the site, simply locate the book's title (either by using the Search box or by using one of the title lists) and click the Download Code link on the book's detail page to obtain all the source code for the book.

Because many books have similar titles, you may find it easiest to search by ISBN; this book's ISBN is 978-0-470-41464-4.

After you download the code, just decompress it with your favorite compression tool. Alternately, you can go to the main Wrox code download page at `http://www.wrox.com/dynamic/books/download.aspx` to see the code available for this book and all other Wrox books.

Errata

We make every effort to ensure that there are no errors in the text or in the code. However, no one is perfect, and mistakes do occur. If you find an error in one of our books, like a spelling mistake or faulty piece of code, we would be very grateful for your feedback. By sending in errata, you may save another reader hours of frustration and at the same time you will be helping us provide even higher quality information.

To find the errata page for this book, go to `http://www.wrox.com` and locate the title using the Search box or one of the title lists. Then, on the book's details page, click the Book Errata link. On this page you can view all errata that has been submitted for this book and posted by Wrox editors. A complete book list, including links to each book's errata, is also available at `www.wrox.com/misc-pages/booklist.shtml`.

If you don't spot "your" discovered error on the Book Errata page, go to `www.wrox.com/contact/techsupport.shtml` and complete the form there to send us the error you have found. We'll check the information and, if appropriate, post a message to the Book's Errata page and fix the problem in subsequent editions of the book.

p2p.wrox.com

For author and peer discussion, join the P2P forums at p2p.wrox.com. The forums are a Web-based system for you to post messages relating to Wrox books and related technologies and interact with other readers and technology users. The forums offer a subscription feature to email you topics of interest of your choosing when new posts are made to the forums. Wrox authors, editors, other industry experts, and your fellow readers are present on these forums.

At http://p2p.wrox.com you will find a number of different forums that will help you not only as you read this book, but also as you develop your own applications. To join the forums, just follow these steps:

1. Go to p2p.wrox.com and click the Register link.
2. Read the terms of use and click Agree.
3. Complete the required information to join as well as any optional information you wish to provide and click Submit.
4. You will receive an email with information describing how to verify your account and complete the joining process.

You can read messages in the forums without joining P2P, but to post your own messages, you must join.

After you join, you can post new messages and respond to messages other users post. You can read messages at any time on the Web. If you would like to have new messages from a particular forum emailed to you, click the Subscribe to this Forum icon by the forum name in the forum listing.

For more information about how to use the Wrox P2P, be sure to read the P2P FAQs for answers to questions about how the forum software works as well as for many common questions specific to P2P and Wrox books. To read the FAQs, click the FAQ link on any P2P page.

1

LAMMP, Now with an Extra *M*

How things have changed in the last decade! The Internet is no longer a luxury. It is now a necessity. Every day, more and more commerce is conducted over the Internet, more businesses are built around the Internet, and more people use the Internet for their primary source of entertainment, communication, and social networking. To provide all this functionality, more and more web applications and services are available and required. These applications and services are replacing traditional desktop applications and legacy ways of doing things; the local computer focus is now Internet-centric. Sun Microsystems' motto, "The network is the computer," truly has become a reality.

The way today's web sites are developed and how the underlying architecture is implemented have also changed. With Web 2.0, web applications are much more dynamic than ever and offer rich, desktop-like functionality. Web applications that once ran exclusively on servers and produced HTML output for web browser clients are now multitiered, distributed applications that have both client components like AJAX (Asynchronous JavaScript and XML), JavaScript, and Flash, as well as server components like mod_perl, PHP, Rails, Java servlets, etc. These new web applications are much richer in features, and users now expect them to behave like desktop applications. The result is a satisfying and productive user experience.

The architecture that is required to support these applications has also changed. What used to be a simple database-to-web-application topography now comprises more layers and components. Functionalities that were formerly implemented in the web application code are now spread out among various services or servers, such as full-text search, caching, data collection, and storage. The concept of "scale-out versus scale-up" has become a given in web development and architecture. This is the case now more than ever before with *cloud computing*, which offers dynamically scalable services, either virtualized or real, over the Internet.

One component in all of these changes is caching. In terms of web applications, *caching* provides a means of storing data that would otherwise have to be retrieved from the database or repeatedly regenerated by the application server. Caching can significantly reduce the load on these back-end databases, allowing for better web application performance overall. Also, a database isn't the only point of origin for information. Other sources of information could include remote service calls, search index results, and even files on disk — all of which can benefit greatly by caching.

Originally, there really was no easy way to provide good caching. There was a kind of caching using tricks like IPC::Sharable, global/package variables, database session tables, even simply files, but nothing offered real, centralized caching of the type that is available now.

This is where the extra *M* in this chapter's title comes in. It stands for memcached. memcached is a high-performance, distributed memory object caching system that provides caching for web applications. Along with covering the other letters of the LAMMP acronym — Linux, Apache, MySQL, and Perl — this book will also cover how you can leverage memcached in your web application development.

The object of this book is to show you everything you would need to know about MySQL, memcached, Perl, and Apache, as well as many other great technologies including Gearman, Sphinx, AJAX, and JavaScript, in order to take advantage of each for writing feature-rich, useful, and interesting web applications. This book also covers a lot of material that will expand your skill set to help you become a well-rounded web developer.

Linux

Linux is the world's most popular open-source operating system and the operating system on which a significant percentage of web servers run. Linux, originally created by Linus Torvalds starting in 1991, is itself a term given to the operating system, which includes numerous programs, utilities, and libraries around the core Linux kernel.

Linux was developed on and freely distributed over the Internet by a growing group of developers. It matured along with the Internet, emerging with the same principle of open development and communication that the Internet is known for. This open development concept, known as *open source*, or free software, is a model that allows developers to see the source code of a program and make modifications such as bug fixes and enhancements to the code. This model allowed for developers all over the world to contribute to Linux. This even included development to the kernel itself, as well as to the utilities and programs bundled along with the Linux kernel. Programs included compilers, interpreters, web servers, databases, desktop environments, mail servers, and many other tools that meant people could install an operating system that had everything they needed for implementing a web server, along with dynamic web applications.

Many programs that were available (and still are available) were made possible by the GNU Project. Initiated by Richard Stallman in 1984 along with the Free Software Foundation, GNU had the goal of creating a UNIX-like operating system with the philosophy that *"people should be free to use software in all the ways that are socially useful."* These tools, particularly the compiler GCC, were crucial to the development of Linux. Also crucial to Linux's adoption was the GPL (GNU Public License), which also came from the GNU Project. This license allowed developers to contribute to projects, knowing that their work would remain open and free to the benefit of the world.

Apache, Perl, PHP, and MySQL were developed to run on a number of operating systems. They also ran well on Linux, and with the same concept of open development, they allowed developer contributions to their advancement and maturation.

Originally, Linux was dismissed by many a pundit as being a "toy" operating system, or at best a "hobbyist" operating system. Nevertheless, system administrators, who quickly became Linux enthusiasts, quietly deployed Linux to run an increasing number of services across the tech world. Ironically, many of the critical articles written by these skeptical pundits were probably being served at the time on web servers running Linux.

Today, Linux is considered a serious operating system. You can now buy hardware with Linux pre-installed from all major server vendors. Most interestingly, even big vendors who sell their own Unix variants also sell and support Linux on their servers — Sun, IBM, and HP are examples.

Without question, when a web server is installed and launched today, there isn't much thought as to whether Linux should be used — just as a desktop operating system is most of the time assumed to be Windows, a web server operating system can often now be assumed to be Linux. For several years now, even personal computers have been available with Linux preinstalled.

Although this book's target operating system is Linux (the *L* in LAMP), the author has attempted not to leave Windows Apache MySQL Perl (WAMP) developers out in the cold. Where possible, installation instructions and other configuration parameters are made available for Windows.

Apache

Another open-source project that had its genesis around the same time as Linux is the Apache HTTP Web Server. Developed by the Apache Software Foundation, the Apache HTTP Web Server is the world's most popular web server. Therefore it is also the web server that this book covers. Apache was originally released in 1994, around the same time that Linux was coming into popularity. Apache was most often bundled along with Linux in various Linux distributions, so setting up a Linux server usually meant you were also setting up Apache.

The pie chart in Figure 1-1 shows the market share of the Apache web server as used by the million busiest web sites, as of March 2009.

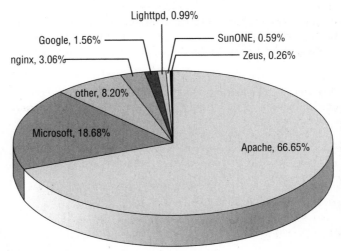

Figure 1-1
Netcraft, http://news.netcraft.com/

With a running Apache server, you had at your disposal a full-fledged web server that allowed you to build web sites — both static pages and dynamic web applications using CGI (Common Gateway Interface). Since then, Apache has evolved even further, becoming much more modular. The number of programming languages available for building web applications with Apache has also increased: You now have a choice of using CGI, mod_perl, PHP, Ruby, Python, C/C++, and others. For Java web application development, the Apache Software Foundation has developed Apache Tomcat, a JSP and Java servlet engine that can talk HTTP. So there are many choices for developing web sites, depending on what you prefer and where your expertise lies.

This book will focus on Apache web development using Perl, and in particular, mod_perl. Since Apache is very modular, it allows for developing various modules to extend its functionality, as well as providing access to the server to run various interpreted languages such as Perl, PHP, Python, ASP, and Ruby. This is in contrast to how CGI worked, which was running programs externally to the web server.

MySQL

Another of the open-source hatchlings is the MySQL database. MySQL was originally developed on Solaris but soon switched to be developed under Linux as Linux became more stable and more popular. MySQL grew, along with Linux, to become the default database of choice for web application development on Apache. This was because MySQL is fast, reliable, easy to install and administer. Also, it didn't cost a fortune (whether free or at the various support level pricings), and had various client application APIs and drivers, including Perl.

As far as web applications go, one change made during the last decade was MySQL's prevalence as the de facto database for open-source database development. Already quite popular a decade ago, MySQL has since advanced greatly in capacity, features, and stability to become the world's most popular open-source database. Most Linux distributions make it extremely easy to install MySQL (as well as PostgreSQL) during operating system installation, so you can have a fully functioning relational database system (RDBMS) that you can readily use for your web applications in no time.

Many popular web sites and customers use MySQL for a number of purposes. Figure 1-2, shows a list of the 20 most popular web sites that run MySQL.

Other sites and organizations that run MySQL include:

- ❑ Slashdot.org
- ❑ LiveJournal
- ❑ Craig's List
- ❑ Associated Press
- ❑ Digg.com
- ❑ NASA – JPL
- ❑ U.S. Census Bureau

This book shows you much more than previous web application development books. You will see just how powerful, yet how easy, it is to use MySQL. The author hopes this will give you a reason for making MySQL your database of choice, if it isn't already so. In this book, you will see:

❏   How to install and configure MySQL

❏   How to use MySQL's various utility and client programs

❏   How to use MySQL. This book starts out with simple usage examples for those who aren't familiar with databases and progresses to more advanced usage examples, showing you how to write useful triggers and stored procedures.

❏   How to use MySQL storage engines and what each engine is designed and best suited for

❏   How to set up dual-master replication — something you'll want to know if you are a web developer at a smaller start-up company. You can trust the author that this is a possibility in this industry!

❏   How to write a user defined function (UDF). Yes, this will be implemented in the C programming language, even though this book is targeted to Perl developers. Even if you are a true Perl geek, you'll probably find this interesting — possibly even enough to make you want to write your own. It's always good to expand your horizons a bit!

Figure 1-2
Sun Microsystems

memcached

memcached is a newer project, the new kid on the block, that came into being later than Linux, Apache, MySQL, or Perl. However, memcached has become just as much an integral component to the overall LAMP stack — which is the reason LAMP should now be referred to as LAMMP! Perhaps no one has thought of this yet because memcached is so simple to run and just works, or because it's so ubiquitously used that it almost goes without saying that it's now the de facto caching solution for horizontal web application development. That being said, memcached deserves some focus and appreciation for how it can benefit your web application platform, and likewise deserves a letter up on the LAMMP sign on the mountaintop above Hollywood.

memcached is a high-performance, distributed memory object caching system developed by Danga Interactive to reduce the database load for the extremely busy web site LiveJournal.com, which was at the time handling over 20 million dynamic page views per day for 1 million users. memcached solved for LiveJournal.com the problem that many other sites also have — how to reduce read access to the database.

A typical way to improve the throughput of a site is to store all query results from the database into memcached. Then, before fetching new data from the database, first check to see if it exists in memcached.

Using memcached, LiveJournal.com reduced their database load to literally nothing, allowing them to improve user experience. Because memcached was developed and released to the world as open-source software, Danga's creation has benefited thousands upon thousands of web developers, system administrators, and the wallets of numerous organizations due to hardware cost savings. Now it has become possible to utilize commodity hardware to act as simple memory servers. Some memcached success stories are discussed in the following sections.

Gear6

Gear6 is a company that built a business around scalable memcached solutions for superior site scaling, enabling their customers to scale their dynamic sites. Gear6 allowed these sites to increase their use of memcached (in some cases growing from about 100 gigabytes to 3 terabytes in only six months!) without using more rack space. memcached also helped Gear6 grow its customer base because of its wide use, as shown in the following table:

Type of Site	memcached Function
Social networking sites	To store profile information
Content aggregation sites	To store HTML page components
Ad placement networks	To manage server-side cookies
Location-based services	To update content based on customer location
Gaming sites	To store session information

Clickability

Clickability is a company that provides SaaS (Software-as-a-Service) web content management platform products. Their services include content management, web site publishing and delivery, search, web analytics, and newsletter delivery. They use memcached as a layer-2 cache for application servers to store content objects as serialized Java objects. They now run multiple instances of memcached, which are regularly cleared and versioned for cache consistency. They also use multicast messaging to cache objects across multiple memcached servers, as well as a messaging queue used for sending a clearing message to application servers. They originally did not use memcached, but were able to implement it into their architecture within a couple of days after deciding to take advantage of memcached's benefits. Because of memcached, particularly how it provides a caching layer to web applications to prevent excessive hits to the database, they now serve 400 million page-views a month!

GaiaOnline

GaiaOnline is the leading online hangout web site (with seven million visitors per month and a billion posts), geared toward young people for making friends, playing games, trading virtual goods, watching movies and interacting in an online community. A user can also create a virtual personality, referred to as an *avatar*. memcached has been a crucial tool in allowing GaiaOnline to grow their site from serving originally 15,000 to 20,000 users at a time to now being able to serve 100,000 users simultaneously.

How memcached Can Work for You

Gear6, Clickability, and GaiaOnline aren't the only memcached success stories. Some other sites that also use memcached extensively include: LiveJournal, Slashdot, Craigslist, Facebook, Wikipedia, Fotolog, Flickr, and numerous others.

In fact, Figure 1-3 shows that 80 percent of the top sites use memcached.

- LiveJournal
  - 20M dynamic page views/day
- Facebook
  - 80S memcached
- Fotolog
  - 40 memcached vs. 140 DS Serv. and 70 Web Serv.
- Flickr
  - 14 memcached vs. 144 DS Serv. and 244 Web Serv.
- Wikipedia
  - 79 memcached vs. 30 DS Serv.

1.Yahoo	11.Orkut
2.Google	12.Rapidshare
3.Youtube	13.Baidu
4.Live	14.Microsoft
5.MSN	15.Google.in
6.MySpace	16.Google.de
7.Wikipedia	17.QQ.com
8.Facebook	18.eBay
9.Blogger	19.Hi5
10.Yahoo.co.jp	20.Google.fr

Source: Alexa Top Sites - 08.05.16

80% of these web sites use Memcached!!!

Figure 1-3
Sun Microsystems

Indeed, memcached is a now primary component to the LAMMP stack. This book will attempt to show you why. Things you will learn in this book include:

- ❑ How memcached works
- ❑ What read-through and write-through caches are and can do
- ❑ Caching issues you should be aware of
- ❑ How to set up and configure memcached
- ❑ How to write Perl programs that use memcached
- ❑ The new libmemcached client library, which gives you even more performance for writing Perl programs that use memcached
- ❑ The Memcached Functions for MySQL, which are user-defined functions (UDFs) written by the author. These functions allow you to interface with memcached from within MySQL. You will see how you can use these convenient functions with MySQL:
  - ❑ From within your Perl code
  - ❑ With triggers

❑   With handy SQL queries that perform a simple read-through cache

❑   How you can modify your Perl applications to use these functions instead of using the Perl client to memcached

❑   Some simple caching strategies with memcached

Perl

The Perl programming language is the eldest of all the open-source siblings in the LAMMP stack. Created by Larry Wall — a linguist, musician, programmer, and all-around nice guy — in 1987, Perl was first developed for report processing and text manipulation. With the advent of the World Wide Web, Perl became a natural choice for developing web applications because of its innate ability to process and parse data. Implementing the functional equivalent of regular expressions or other Perl string manipulations, which are easy using Perl, takes many more lines of code and longer development time if implemented in other programming languages. This, as well as not having to worry about things like memory management, means relatively rapid development in Perl. You could write a fully functional Perl web application in a fraction of the time it would have taken to implement the equivalent application in the other programming languages available at the beginning of the World Wide Web. This is one of the many reasons Perl became popular for web development.

Originally, Perl web applications were written as CGI programs, which meant Perl programs were run by an external Perl interpreter. Drawbacks to this included a lack of persistence with running web applications; and running external programs could also adversely affect performance.

Then, in 1996, Gisle Aas developed and released the first version of mod_perl, which is a Perl interpreter embedded into Apache. Doug MacEachern, Andreas Koenig, and many contributors soon took the lead in developing mod_perl and released subsequent versions, such as version 1.0.

mod_perl now made it possible for Perl web applications to have persistence that was previously unavailable using CGI. Additionally, mod_perl gave Perl developers the ability to write Apache modules in Perl, because mod_perl is much more than CGI with persistence — it provides the Perl developer access to the entire Apache life cycle, including all phases of the HTTP request cycle.

A decade later we find that mod_perl is still being used extensively. The buzz and excitement may be over several new web development technologies and languages — and some would say Perl web development is passé — however, Perl is a more mature technology and it just works well — as is usually case with something that's been around a while. People are always excited about newer things, but there's still a lot to be excited about when you use Perl for web applications and development!

mod_perl 2.0, released in May 2005, provided many new and exciting changes, including support for threads, integration into Apache 2.0 (which itself had attractive new features and enhancements), the same great ability to write mod_perl handlers for any part of the Apache life cycle, and the added feature of writing mod_perl filter handlers for Apache 2.0's filter interface.

Certainly, other languages and web application development paradigms have some features over mod_perl. PHP has an application deployment model that has facilitated a bonanza of PHP web applications, such as Wordpress, Drupal, Joomla, Mediawiki, and many others, and particularly those with the APS (Application Packaging Standard) used in applications such as Plesk for web site hosting services. This makes PHP application installation and deployment even simpler. Why has Perl/mod_perl not developed an equivalent of this? Perhaps it is because mod_perl already does give you as much control over the Apache life cycle and because it has a higher level of complexity (it's not solely focused on the HTTP response phase).

Also, you do have to have some ability to modify the Apache configuration if you use mod_perl handlers as your method of web application development. The answer is to use ModPerl::Registry, with which you can run CGI programs in mod_perl with very little modification to the application and still have all the benefits that a mod_perl handler has. Configuring Apache to run ModPerl::Registry is no more difficult for a web site administrator than loading mod_php to run PHP applications. So, where are all the applications? Well, we, as Perl web application developers, need to write them.

Here are some other reasons you might want to develop web and other applications using Perl:

- ❑ **Code is fun to write and free-flowing.** You can solve any number of problems in infinite ways while focusing on application development and implementation (the problem you're trying to solve) rather than on the language itself.

- ❑ **The Perl data structures work.** Both hashes and arrays are very easy when you go to organize data, navigate, and iterate. Try the equivalent in C, and you will see!

- ❑ **CPAN (Comprehensive Perl Archive Network).** You have a choice of modules for anything you could ever possibly want. So much functionality already exists that you don't have to reinvent the wheel. Every other day, the author finds an existing module that already does something he spent hours implementing!

- ❑ **Perl is a dynamically typed language.** For those who don't like to feel constrained, it's perfect. You can just write your program without referencing a document or web site to know how objects interface. Just code it!

- ❑ **Perl supports object-oriented programming.**

- ❑ **Perl clients exist for just about any type of server.** To name a few: MySQL, memcached, Apache, Sphinx, Gearman, and numerous others.

- ❑ **Perl has an XS (eXternal Subroutine) interface.** This allows you to write glue code and to use C code, if you need something to run faster than it would if it were written purely in Perl. This is what the MySQL Perl driver DBD::mysql uses for working with MySQL's client library.

- ❑ **Perl supports all the new exciting technologies, such as AJAX.**

- ❑ **There are numerous templating options.** You have various ways to tackle the site content versus application functionality.

- ❑ **You can even write Perl stored procedures for MySQL.** You do this using external language stored procedures, developed by Antony Curtis and Eric Herman.

Now, one claim you may have heard needs to be addressed: "Perl is great for prototyping, but you should develop the implementation in another 'real' language." This is a nonsensical statement that enthusiasts of other languages, having no experience in Perl development, have often said. Millions of dollars have been wasted completely reimplementing a perfectly good Perl web application to run in another language. Consider that many extremely busy web sites are running in Perl — Slashdot and LiveJournal are two such sites. The irony is that you will often see similar untrue statements ignorantly posted on the Slashdot forum — a forum that Perl provides so that opinions can be heard!

This book shows you numerous things you can do in Perl, including:

❏ A Perl primer for those of you who might be rusty

❏ A Perl object-oriented programming refresher

❏ Not just Perl web applications, but also writing utilities and command line programs

❏ Useful snippets of code that you can integrate into your Perl lexicon

You will also see how easy it is to use Perl to work with the other components of the LAMMP stack, for example:

❏ MySQL and memcached for data storage

❏ Apache mod_perl handlers

❏ Sphinx for full-text search (including the implementation of a simple search engine application)

❏ Gearman, which allows you to farm out work to other machines

It's the author's hope that this book will reinvigorate your fondness for Perl, or give you even more justification and enthusiasm for wanting to develop web and other applications using Perl.

Other Technologies

This book will also introduce you to other new technologies, namely Sphinx and Gearman. It will show you how to use these as additional components in the LAMMP stack to build truly useful and interesting applications.

Sphinx

Sphinx is a full-text search engine developed by Andrew Aksyonoff in 2001. It is an acronym for *SQL Phrase Index*. It is a standalone search engine, although it integrates nicely with MySQL and other databases for fetching the data that it then indexes. Sphinx is intended to provide fast, efficient, and relevant search functions to other applications. It even has a storage engine for MySQL so that you can utilize MySQL alone to perform all your searches. Sphinx also has various client libraries for numerous languages, including a Perl client library written by Jon Schutz, Sphinx::Search.

Sphinx also allows you to have multiple Sphinx search engines to provide distributed indexing functionality. This is where you would have an index defined that actually comprises a number of indexes running on other servers.

This book will not only introduce you to Sphinx, it will also show you a simple search engine application implemented using Sphinx, as well as a basic Sphinx configuration with a delta index that you could use for any number of applications that require a full-text search engine. You will also be shown how you can replace MySQL's full-text search with Sphinx for a better full-text searching functionality.

Gearman

Gearman is a project originally created (in Perl) by Brad Fitzpatrick of Danga, who is also known for creating both memcached and the social web site LiveJournal. Gearman is a system that provides a job server that assigns jobs requested by clients to various named worker processes. A *worker process* is basically a program that runs as a client and awaits an assignment from the Gearman job server, which it then performs. You split up your processing over various machines tasked for whatever requirements your applications need. This spreads out functionality, which is implemented in programs known as workers that might otherwise have been implemented in application code. This can also be used for MapReduce: distributing the processing of large data sets across numerous machines (for a great description of the MapReduce framework, see http://labs.google.com/papers/mapreduce.html).

This new functionality means web application developers and system architects can completely rethink how things have traditionally been done, using commodity machines to run some of these tasks.

Eric Day recently rewrote the Gearman job server, referred to as gearmand, in C for performance reasons, along with client and worker libraries in C. He has also written a package of new Gearman MySQL user defined functions based on the C library, and is working other developers for new and improved language interfaces. Another feature being developed is persistence and replication for jobs, which is one of the main things people ask about when first looking at Gearman for reliable job delivery.

This book will cover these new projects and you will see how to use them to implement automated data retrieval and storage, as well as Sphinx indexing through Gearman workers. This book also gives you one idea of how you can use Gearman to pique interest in Gearman.

The New Picture

Yes, things have changed in the last decade. And they probably will change more in the future.

Figure 1-4 represents how it is architecturally possible to implement the various tools and technologies that are discussed in this book. The architecture includes:

❑ memcached and MySQL, where a web application would retrieve its data: either durable data not cached from MySQL, or anything that needs to be cached within memcached.

❑ memcached objects, which are kept up to date to represent the state of the durable data in MySQL. This is done either by the application code or from within MySQL using the Memcached Functions for MySQL (UDFs), which would provide read-through and/or write-through caching.

❑ Sphinx, which can be run on a number of servers, provides the full-text indexing to the web application using the Sphinx::Search Sphinx Perl client module or through MySQL using the Sphinx storage engine. Sphinx has as its data source a query that returns a result set from MySQL that it in turn uses to create its full-text indexes.

❑ Gearman, which in this case is shown running on two different Gearman job servers (although it can run on any number of servers). Gearman is a job server for the Gearman clients — either clients implemented within the application code, cron jobs, or clients in the form of the Gearman MySQL UDFs — to assign jobs to the Gearman workers. In turn, the workers can perform any number of tasks on all the other components, such as storing and retrieving data to and from memcached to MySQL, indexing Sphinx, or any other functional requirement for the web applications.

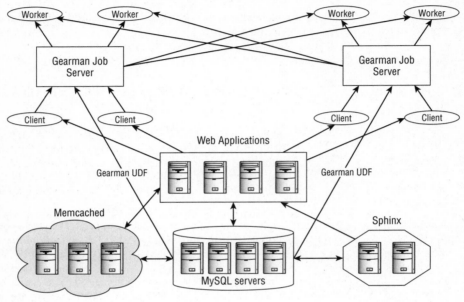

Figure 1-4

Variations on the theme that Figure 1-4 shows are infinite and limited only by your imagination. And this book hopes to provide some fodder for your imagination in this regard! Depending on your application or architecture requirements, your own version of Figure 1-4 will differ.

The Future of Open-Source Web Development and Databases

What does the next ten years hold for web development and the Internet in general? What features will MySQL, Perl, memcached, and Apache have implemented by then? Some things now are showing trends that are sure to continue:

❑ Open source is a proven development model and will continue to be the one of the major sources of innovation of new technology.

❑ MySQL has proven itself as a great back-end database for web applications and will continue to increase its market share, particularly because of its power, ease of use, and low or free cost, especially important given current economic conditions.

❑ Web applications will continue to evolve, developing more in number and variety of features. People will use many of these new applications in place of desktop applications.

❑ Cloud computing will increasingly become a preferred method on which businesses develop and deploy their web applications. This will depend on economic conditions, which may cause businesses to seek ways of cutting costs — hardware and hosting service costs traditionally being one of the largest expenses.

❑ SaaS (Software-as-a-Service), a new way of deploying software to customers as an on-demand service, will continue to grow. SaaS goes hand in hand with cloud computing.

❑ *Multitenancy* — users using the database at the same time — will work better and there may be development in this as a shared environment.

Projects to Watch!

The following are particular projects worth mentioning. These are projects that you will want to keep an eye on!

❑ **Drizzle:** Drizzle is a fork of MySQL version 6.0 that has the goal to become "A Light-weight SQL Database for Cloud and Web." The idea of Drizzle is to create a very efficient, lightweight, modular database that is specifically targeted toward the Web and cloud computing. Many features of MySQL have been removed for efficiency's sake, although some will eventually be reimplemented as long as their reintroduction doesn't affect Drizzle's goal of remaining lightweight and efficient.

❑ **MariaDB and Maria Storage Engine:** Maria is the next-generation storage engine based on MyISAM that provides transactional support, crash recovery, and the benefit of the speed for which MyISAM is known. MariaDB is a branch of the MySQL server that Monty Widenius and his team have released. It uses the Maria Storage Engine as the default storage engine. The goal of MariaDB is to keep up with MySQL development and maintain user compatibility, but also to keep improving the database and adding more features while engaging the open-source community in this effort.

❑ **Gearman:** With MapReduce becoming a household word, Gearman will increasingly play a significant role in distributed computing.

❑ **Apache Hadoop:** Similar to Gearman, this is a Java-based framework for distributed computing.

❑ **Perl:** Perl 6 will be released!

❑ **Percona:** Watch out for the great efforts of Percona. They are focused on providing their own high-performance branch of MySQL.

❑ **Hypertable:** A high-performance distributed data storage system, modeled after Google's BigTable project.

Summary

This chapter introduced you to the topics and recent technological developments that this book will cover and it offered some observations about how much things have changed within the last decade. The suggestion was made that the LAMP stack needs to have an extra *M* added to it (to become LAMMP) because memcached has both benefited horizontal web application development and become a major component for so many web application deployments throughout the Internet — it is just as important a component as Linux, Apache, MySQL, and Perl. Also, this chapter offered some thoughts on what the next ten years may hold for open-source databases and web application development.

The author hopes you have fun reading this book. He had fun writing it.

2

MySQL

The purpose of this chapter is to give web developers the necessary knowledge to understand and use MySQL for developing dynamic web applications. It contains the following discussions:

❑   The "About MySQL" section is a MySQL primer, and provides a brief overview, description and history of MySQL.

❑   The "Installing and Configuring MySQL" section guides you through installation and configuration to get a MySQL server running and includes database creation, setting up privileges, and setting up replication.

❑   The "Database Planning" section gives information on how to design an optimal database schema, set database server settings for performance, and provides simple tips to remember when developing the database architecture of a web application.

❑   The "Using MySQL Functionality" section covers some of the most useful components of MySQL such as triggers, functions and procedures, storage engine types, user defined functions (UDFs), as well as external language stored procedures.

How CGI and PHP Changed the Web Dramatically

In the beginning of the World Wide Web, all web site content was static. To allow for web servers to provide search functionality, the original web server code was modified. This was cumbersome and it proved difficult to provide the ability to add new functionality.

Then two specifications came into being; CGI and PHP changed the world wide web dramatically.

The CGI (Common Gateway Interface) is a standard protocol specification that was developed by a group of developers who included Rob McCool, John Franks, Air Lutonen, Tony Sanders, and George Phillips in 1993. Shortly, thereafter, PHP followed. PHP is a scripting language originally developed by Rasmus Lerdorf, which originally stood for Personal Home Page because he developed PHP to replace Perl scripts he used to manage his home page; PHP then became an entire scripting language.

Both CGI/Perl and PHP now allowed web site developers to write dynamic web applications without having to modify the web server. At that time, developers who wrote CGI programs often depended on flat files for data storage, making storage difficult to maintain and resulting in performance issues. There were databases available for use with web applications. However, these were too expensive for the average web developer to afford, as well as being much too difficult to set up and administer, requiring a DBA (database administrator). These database also ran only on expensive server hardware. Most importantly, they were not designed for the web because they were often slow to connect to.

With the release of mSQL (Mini SQL), which although not free, was inexpensive, there was finally a choice for web development that wasn't cost-prohibitive and was also easy to use.

With the release of databases such as MySQL (in 1995) and PostgreSQL (in 1996, though evolving from Postgres and before that Ingres, which came about in the 1980s), along came even more choices of databases for web developers to use that were easy to install and administer, did most of everything that they needed, ran on inexpensive hardware and operating systems, and were free. Commodity database systems such as MySQL and PostgreSQL allowed web development to take off and for dynamic data to easily be put online and maintained.

Not only that, these databases used SQL which is easy to embed or run from within web applications. It's also easier to read what data is being written to or read from the database, which further added to these databases gaining in popularity. In fact, Monty Widenius at the time had written a program called "htmlgenerator" that parsed SQL out of HTML files and ran embedded queries from those HTML files in MySQL, results in the HTML being generated at HTML tables.

Today, databases are the main source of data for web applications. This can include page content, user information, application meta-data, and any data that allows for a dynamic web application to have full, useful functionality. Without data, there's not much that an application can do.

About MySQL

Since May 23, 1995, MySQL has been a popular, open-source relational database system (RDBMS) that millions of users and developers have downloaded. It's also one of the core components of this book.

MySQL's basic functionality can be explained as this:

1. A query is entered via a client program such as the MySQL command line tool `mysql`.
2. The parser parses this query into a data structure internally, known as an item tree, which represents the query fragments.
3. The tables that are used by the query are opened through the table handler interface.
4. For the SELECT statement only, the optimizer examines this item/parse tree, determining in which order the query fragments will be executed, and computes the execution path.

5. The execution path is essentially how the server will retrieve the data.

6. The main server coder makes read, write, update, or delete calls to the table handler interface depending on the query type.

7. The storage engine, through inheritance (from the table handler), runs the appropriate methods to act upon the read or write of the data from the underlying data source.

8. MySQL sends the results back to the client. In case of a SELECT, this is the result data. For other queries, such as INSERT, it's an OK packet that contains, among other things, how many rows were affected by the query.

Netbas begat REG800 begat Unireg begat MySQL

In 1980, a then 17-year-old Monty Widenius and Kaj Arno took the Red Viking Line ferry from Finland to Sweden (tax-free Vodka!) to buy 16KB of memory for their Z80-based processor, the ABC 80 processor (manufactured by DIAB, a Swedish hardware company), from Allan Larsson's computer store in Stockholm and eventually formed a relationship with Allan. At that meeting Monty also met Lars Karsson, founder of DIAB, which manufactured the ABC 80. Three years later, Allan convinced Monty to write a generic database for the ABC microcomputers. Only weeks later, Monty delivered a working prototype. Around this time Monty developed a friendship and working relationship with David Axmark, with whom he later founded MySQL. Later, Monty worked for Tapio Laakso Oy, a Finnish company where he converted COBOL programs to TRS80 Basic and from TRS80 Basic to ABC Basic. While doing this, Monty found redundancies that he discussed with Allan. They considered the market for developing a system to manage data more efficiently. Hence came Netbas, which begat REG800, which begat DataNET, which begat Unireg, which finally begat MySQL.

MySQL's genesis from Unireg was the result of Monty and David's realization that the SQL language was well suited, in terms of being used with web application technologies such as CGI programs written in Perl, for the task of web development (as well as for non-web Perl programs). One primary reason for Monty to develop MySQL was how cumbersome it was to use Unireg for Web development. It took Monty about nine months to code the upper layer of MySQL and it released in October 1996. Thirteen years and millions of downloads later, MySQL is now the world's most popular open source database. Thousands upon thousands of web sites use MySQL.

David had tried to convince Monty for years to write an SQL layer on top of Unireg. It was, however, when Allan Larsson started to use Unireg's report generator to generate web pages that Monty was convinced something had to be done; he thought what Allan did was a creative hack and he didn't want to ever have to maintain the resulting web page code.

It's important to reflect on Monty's genius: His ability to develop copious lines of code that are amazingly efficient. It's been observed that he can look at numerous lines of code and find a way to reduce them to a tenth their original size! The core developers

Continued

of MySQL are of the same caliber and possess the same dedication that Monty is known for.

Monty adheres to the philosophy that having a good code base is a prerequisite to succeed. He feels the major reason for MySQL's popularity is that MySQL was free to use for most people and that he and his team spent a major part of their time helping MySQL users. As way of example, for the first 6 years, Monty personally sent out more than 30,000 emails helping people with MySQL-related issues. This attitude of selflessness and charity, together with a good documentation, was what made MySQL stand out among the all the other databases.

MySQL is written in C and C++, and some of the core API functions are written in assembly language for speed, again lending to MySQL's efficiency. For the curious observer, because MySQL is open-sourced, the source is entirely viewable and a great way to see the inner workings of a complex and powerful system. Also, because the source is freely available, anyone can contribute enhancements, bug fixes, or add new functionality to MySQL.

So what are MySQL's important features? They are as follows:

- ❑ **MySQL is very fast, easy to use, and reliable.** One of the primary reasons MySQL was adopted for web applications was that it is easy to install and "just works." Originally, MySQL's simplicity contributed to quick processing of the type of data that web sites commonly required. It's more complex now, but still retains its fast nature.

- ❑ **MySQL has documentation.** Documentation is available online in various formats and in its entirety. Gratis. You don't have to pay for MySQL's manuals like other RDBMS (or for the system itself, unless you want support!).

- ❑ **MySQL is multi-threaded.** This allows more connections with less memory because with threading, you have each thread sharing the same memory versus a model such as forking, where each child is a copy of the parent, including the memory of the parent.

- ❑ **MySQL supports features such as replication and clustering.** Its robust replication supports a number of replication schemes depending on the application requirements. One example might be where you have a read/write master that handles all the DML (data-modification language) statements such as INSERTS, UPDATES, DELETES, etc., and a read-only slave that handles all the read queries.

- ❑ **MySQL supports transactions and has ACID-compliant Storage Engines** (InnoDB, Maria, Falcon). In addition to the commonly used InnoDB storage engine, MySQL is also developing two other transactional storage engines: Maria, which is based on MyISAM, and Falcon, which was developed from Jim Starkey's Netfrastructure database. There is also a publicly available, transactional storage engine developed by PrimeBase called PBXT. ACID compliance is implemented by the storage engine itself. *ACID* stands for *Atomicity, Consistency, Isolation, Durability*.

    - ❑ **Atomicity:** The transaction is atomic and none of the SQL statements within the transaction should fail, and if they do, the entire transaction fails.

    - ❑ **Consistency:** The execution of a transaction must occur without violating the consistency of the database.

❑ **Isolation:** When multiple transactions are executed simultaneously, they must not affect any of the other transactions, meaning that a transaction should complete before another one is started, and the data that a transaction may depend on is not affected by another.

❑ **Durability:** Once a transaction is committed, the data is not lost. A good example of durability is a recent test at a MySQL developer meeting against Maria where the server was unplugged in the middle of executing various statements, and when it was turned back on, the statements were completed and no data were lost.

❑ **MySQL has various client APIs for Perl, PHP, C/C++, Java, C#, ODBC, Ruby, etc.**

❑ MySQL runs on numerous operating systems and hardware platforms.

❑ MySQL has numerous installation options ranging from source compilation to various binary package formats.

❑ MySQL offers a number of storage engines depending on application requirements as well as a pluggable storage engine interface for anyone wanting to implement his or her own storage engine.

MySQL can be broken down into some core components, as shown in the following table:

Component	Description
Parser/Command Executor	This is the part of MySQL that processes a query that has been entered into a data structure known as an item tree.
Optimizer	The SELECT optimizer uses the item tree that was built by the parser to determine the least expensive execution plan for the query.
Table Handler	This is an abstract interface between the storage engines and the database server.

Now that MySQL is installed on your system (if it isn't, see Appendix A for instructions), you are probably anxious to get your feet wet and actually start using MySQL. The following sections show you how to use MySQL. This includes explaining what programs are packaged with MySQL, how to work with data — inserting, reading, updating, deleting, and other basic operations as well as showing how to use views, triggers, functions, and procedures. This section also covers what the different storage engines are and how you can write User Defined Functions (UDFs) and external-language stored procedures.

MySQL Programs

MySQL, in addition to the server itself, has many programs that are included with the MySQL installation. These programs include the MySQL server program, server manager programs, and scripts, clients, and various utilities. Some of these programs may or may not be included in every installation, depending on the operating system or the way the MySQL installation is packaged. For instance, the Windows MySQL installation doesn't include UNIX startup scripts, whereas RPM divides MySQL install packages between client and server.

Depending on the installation type, these programs are usually found in a directory with other executable files, or in some cases only the executable files that come with MySQL. The following table shows the directory structure that MySQL uses for various operating systems and platforms:

With the Installation Type . . .	. . . The Files Are Found in This Folder
Source installation of MySQL	`/usr/local/mysql/bin`
RPM and Ubuntu/Debian installs	`/usr/bin`
Windows	`C:\Program Files\MySQL\MySQL Server 5.1\bin`
UNIX, MySQL server program (depends on distribution)	`/usr/sbin`, `/usr/local/mysql/libexec`, or `/usr/libexec`

MySQL programs all have various flags or options, specified with a single hyphen (-) and a single letter (short options) or double hyphens (--) and a word. For instance, the MySQL client monitor program mysql has the hyphen question mark (-?) or the hyphen help (--help) options to print command-line option information for a given command. Some of the options are flags with no value, while some take values with the option. With the short options, the value is followed by the option. With long options there must be an equal sign and then a value. As an example, the *user* argument to the MySQL client program is either -u username or --user=username.

As mentioned above, if you need to know all available command-line arguments that any one of the MySQL programs accept, enter the name of the program followed by -? or --help. In addition to all the command-line options that are available, the current defaults for the given program will also be printed. Examples are:

```
mysql --help
```

. . . and for version:

```
mysql --version
```

. . . and for a full listing of options:

```
mysqld --help --verbose
```

This section covers some of the more common of these programs that you will use most often. Other sections in this chapter will cover some less commonly used programs.

Client Programs

There are several MySQL client programs that you will use to interact with the MySQL server and perform common tasks, such as an interactive shell where you enter SQL statements, create database backups, restore database backups, and perform administrative tasks. This section covers each of these.

mysql

This is the most common program you will use with MySQL. It is the MySQL client monitor as well as essentially an SQL shell. It's where you interactively type in SQL commands to manipulate both data and data definitions within the database, and it has history functionality built into it (stored in .mysql_history on UNIX systems). You can also use it to pipe the output of a query from a file into an output file in tabbed or XML format. It can alternatively be used to load data from a file such as a database dump into the database.

A simple example to use it as an interactive shell is:

```
shell> mysql --user root --password rootpass test
Reading table information for completion of table and column names
You can turn off this feature to get a quicker startup with -A

Welcome to the MySQL monitor.  Commands end with ; or \g.
Your MySQL connection id is 6
Server version: 5.1.20-beta-debug-log Source distribution

Type 'help;' or '\h' for help. Type '\c' to clear the buffer.
```

mysql>

The command line above used to run the client program mysql connects to the test schema as the user *dbuser*. The mysql> prompt is where you interact with the database.

To load a data file produced from a dump to load into the *test* schema, the usage is:

```
shell> mysql --user webuser --password=mypass webapp < backup.sql
```

mysqldump

You use this command to create backups of your database. mysqldump has many options allowing you to specify all or specific schemas and tables, output format, locking options, replication information, data and table creation information, data only, or table creation information only.

An example of using mysqldump to dump your webapps data and schema creation is:

```
mysqldump --user webuser --password=mypass webapps > webapps_dump.sql
```

This dumps everything in webapps and produces a file you can use to reload the webapps schema in its entirety — to its state at the time when the dump was performed.

If you want only the data of your webapps schema, and no CREATE TABLE statements (schema creation), use this:

```
shell> mysqldump --user webuser --no-create-info --password=mypass
webapps > webapps_data.sql
```

A common means of producing a nightly backup is to run as a cron job (UNIX) or Scheduled Tasks using taskmanager with Windows.

mysqladmin

This is a MySQL command-line administrative tool that performs a number of tasks such as creating and dropping databases and tables, displaying database system status, replicating slave control, granting table reloading, flushing of various components such as disks and system caches, shutting down the database, and other tasks.

An example of creating a new database and then dropping a database is:

```
shell> mysqladmin --user=root --password=-rootpass create webapps
```

```
shell> mysqladmin --user=root --password=rootpass drop pariahdb
```

... or chained:

```
shell> mysqladmin -user=root --password=rootpass create webapps drop parahdb
```

Another really useful thing you can do with mysqladmin to continually observe the status of MySQL:

```
shell> mysqladmin --sleep=1 processlist
```

... which will display the process list every second until you type Ctrl+C. Also:

```
shell> mysqladmin --sleep=1 --relative extended-status
```

mysqlimport

This utility is for importing data into MySQL from a text file. For example, you could have tab-delimited or comma-delimited data from another data source that you want to import into MySQL. This utility makes it simple and fast to import that data.

One example is if you have a text file with the following three entries:

```
1,Monty Widenius
2,David Axmark
3,Allan Larsson
```

And the table you intend to load this data into is:

```
mysql> CREATE TABLE t1 (id INT(3), name VARCHAR(32));
```

Then you issue the command.

```
shell> mysqlimport --fields-terminated-by=, -u webuser -p mypass webapps /tmp/t1.dat
```

The text file must be named the same as the table you intend to load the data into. Also, it must be available on the file system in a location that the MySQL server, which runs usually as the mysql *user, can read it. Though it should also be noted that if you can connect to a remote server and the file you want to load is only available from the client host you are connecting from, you can have the server read the data file using the* --local *option on the client, as well as requiring you to set the option* --local-infile *when you start the server.*

Now the data is imported:

```
mysql> select * from t1;
+------+----------------+
| id   | name           |
+------+----------------+
|    1 | Monty Widenius |
|    2 | David Axmark   |
|    3 | Allan Larsson  |
+------+----------------+
```

mysqlshow

This is a simple utility to display schemas of a database, the tables in those schemas, and columns and indexes of those tables. This utility is a convenient way to drill down and see what the organization of your database is. An example of this is:

```
shell> mysqlshow --user=username --password=pass rootpass


+--------------------+
|     Databases      |
+--------------------+
| information_schema |
| federated          |
| federated_odbc     |
| mysql              |
| remote             |
| test               |
| uc_2008            |
| webapps            |
+--------------------+
shell> mysqlshow -user=username --password=pass webapps
Database: webapps
+---------+
| Tables  |
+---------+
| history |
| t1      |
| users   |
+---------+
shell> mysqlshow --user=username --password=pass webapps t1
Database: webapps  Table: t1
+-------+-------------+------------------+------+-----+---------+----------------
-------------------------------+---------+
| Field | Type        | Collation        | Null | Key | Default | Extra          |
Privileges                     | Comment |
+-------+-------------+------------------+------+-----+---------+----------------
-------------------------------+---------+
| id    | int(3)      |                  | NO   | PRI |         | auto_increment |
select,insert,update,references |         |
| name  | varchar(32) | latin1_swedish_ci | NO  |     |         |                |
select,insert,update,references |         |
+-------+-------------+------------------+------+-----+---------+----------------
-------------------------------+---------+
```

Other useful examples of mysqlshow:

```
shell> mysqlshow --verbose mysql
Database: mysql
+---------------------------+----------+
|          Tables           | Columns  |
+---------------------------+----------+
| columns_priv              |        7 |
| db                        |       20 |
| func                      |        4 |
| help_category             |        4 |
| help_keyword              |        2 |
| help_relation             |        2 |
| help_topic                |        6 |
| host                      |       19 |
| proc                      |       16 |
| procs_priv                |        8 |
| tables_priv               |        8 |
| time_zone                 |        2 |
| time_zone_leap_second     |        2 |
| time_zone_name            |        2 |
| time_zone_transition      |        3 |
| time_zone_transition_type |        5 |
| user                      |       37 |
+---------------------------+----------+
```

... which shows a basic listing of each table in the mysql schema and now how many columns each table has:

```
shell> mysqlshow -vv mysql
database: mysql
+---------------------------+----------+------------+
|          Tables           | Columns  | Total Rows |
+---------------------------+----------+------------+
| columns_priv              |        7 |          0 |
| db                        |       20 |         22 |
| func                      |        4 |         30 |
| help_category             |        4 |         36 |
| help_keyword              |        2 |        395 |
| help_relation             |        2 |        809 |
| help_topic                |        6 |        466 |
| host                      |       19 |          0 |
| proc                      |       16 |         73 |
| procs_priv                |        8 |          0 |
| tables_priv               |        8 |          3 |
| time_zone                 |        2 |          0 |
| time_zone_leap_second     |        2 |          0 |
| time_zone_name            |        2 |          0 |
| time_zone_transition      |        3 |          0 |
| time_zone_transition_type |        5 |          0 |
| user                      |       37 |         29 |
+---------------------------+----------+------------+
17 rows in set.
```

Additionally showing you the total number of rows for each table:

```
shell> mysqlshow --status mysql
```

The last example displaying a full status of each table in the `mysql` schema (not shown for brevity).

Utility Programs

This section covers various utility programs that you use to perform tasks such as repairing tables and accessing replication logging information. It will also provide compilation information for building client programs for MySQL.

myisamchk

The `myisamchk` utility is for checking, repairing, optimizing, and describing tables created with the MyISAM storage engine. Because `myisamchk` acts upon the table files directly, you must either shut down MySQL or have the tables being checked locked. A simple example of checking the table `t1` is to issue a FLUSH TABLES command to flush any modifications to the table that are still in memory and to lock the tables as shown below:

```
mysql> FLUSH TABLES WITH READ LOCK;
```

Then enter the directory containing the actual data files for the table:

```
shell> ls
db.opt
history.ARZ
history.frm
t1.MYD
t1.MYI
t1.frm
users.frm

shell> myisamchk t1
Checking MyISAM file: t1
Data records:        0   Deleted blocks:        0
- check file-size
- check record delete-chain
- check key delete-chain
- check index reference
- check record links
```

Then unlock the tables:

```
mysql> UNLOCK TABLES;
```

In the unlikely case you have serious data corruption, you can use `myisamchk` (or for the Maria storage engine, `maria_chk`) to fix the problem using the following steps:

1. Make a backup of your data using `mysqldump`. If the fault is with the hard disk, copy the actual data files to another hard disk from which you'll run the repair.

2. Shut down MySQL.

3. Execute the following code:

```
cd mysql-data-directory
myisamchk --check --force --key_buffer_size=1G --sort-buffer-
size=512M */*.MYI
```

If using Maria, execute the following code:

```
maria_chk --check --force --page_buffer_size=1G --sort-
buffer-size=512M */*.MAI
```

The `--force` option will automatically repair any tables that were corrupted.

You can also use the `--recover` option instead of the `--check` option to optimize data usage in a table. One thing to keep in mind — if you have a lot of data in your table, this can take a long time!

mysqlbinlog

The `mysqlbinlog` utility is for reading the contents (SQL statements or events) of the binary log as text. The binary log is a log where all write statements — DML, or *data modification language*, statements (INSERT, UPDATE, DELETE, TRUNCATE) and DDL, *data definition language, statements* (DROP TABLE, ALTER TABLE, etc.) — are written. The master writes these statements to this binary log so that a slave can read and execute these statements. In addition to using `mysqlbinlog` to read events in the master's binary log, it can also read statements from the slave's relay log. The relay log is where the slave writes statements read from the master's binary log to then be executed. This will be covered in more detail in the "Replication" section of Chapter 3.

The binary log doesn't have to be used for replication or even be run on a master. It can also be used as a means of providing incremental backups to be used for recovery from a crash.

The output of this program provides information, such as the SQL statements that were executed and when they were executed.

An example of running `mysqlbinlog` to see what statements were executed from 11:52:00 to 12:00:00 would be:

```
shell> mysqlbinlog --start-datetime='2008-06-28 11:52:00'\
  --stop-datetime='2008-06-28 12:00:00' bin.000067

/*!40019 SET @@session.max_insert_delayed_threads=0*/;
/*!50003 SET @OLD_COMPLETION_TYPE=@@COMPLETION_TYPE,COMPLETION_TYPE=0*/;
DELIMITER /*!*/;
# at 4
#8628 11:51:5 server id 1  end_log_pos 106        Start: binlog v 4,
server v 5.1.20- # Warning: this binlog was not closed properly.
ROLLBACK/*!*/;
# at 212
#8628 11:53:14 server id 1  end_log_pos 318 Query
thread_id=4  exec_time=0
use webapps/*!*/;
SET TIMESTAMP=1214668394/*!*/;
```

```
SET @@session.foreign_key_checks=1, @@session.sql_auto_is_null=1,
@@session.unique_checks=1/*!*/;
SET @@session.sql_mode=0/*!*/;
SET @@session.auto_increment_increment=10,
@@session.auto_increment_offset=1/*!*/;
/*!\C latin1 *//*!*/;
SET @@session.character_set_client=8,@@session.collation_connection=8
insert into t1 values (5, 'Sakila')/*!*/;
DELIMITER ;
# End of log file
ROLLBACK /* added by mysqlbinlog */;
/*!50003 SET COMPLETION_TYPE=@OLD_COMPLETION_TYPE*/;
```

mysql_config

The mysql_config utility prints out the options with which MySQL was compiled. This is used to automatically produce compile flags when compiling programs for MySQL. For example, when you build the Perl driver for MySQL, DBD::mysql, the configuration for the driver uses mysql_config to derive the flags it needs to build the driver.

Here is an example of using mysql_config to obtain the library compile flags:

```
shell> mysql_config --libs
-L/usr/local/mysql/lib/mysql -lmysqlclient -lz -lm
```

MySQL Daemon and Startup Utilities

Finally, the MySQL distribution includes the actual server binary file, mysqld, as well as shell scripts for running this server — it can run a single server or multiple servers and can start and stop the server.

mysqld

The mysqld daemon is the server. It's a multi-threaded server that provides the functionality that makes MySQL a relational database. It can be issued with command-line options, or more often uses a configuration file for these options, my.cnf (my.ini for windows). It's also usually run using a utility such as mysqld_safe or mysqlmanager.

mysqld_safe

The mysqld_safe utility is a shell script to run mysqld on UNIX and Netware systems. It is the preferred means of running MySQL because it provides functionality to restart the server in case of a system error and logs any mysqld daemon errors to an error log.

mysql.server

The mysql.server is a shell script for System-V UNIX variants, used to start and stop mysqld using mysqld_multi. Using System-V run directories, this script starts or stops MySQL according to the run level being set.

An example of starting MySQL with mysql.server is:

```
/etc/init.d/mysql.server start
```

mysqld_multi

mysqld_multi is a utility to control the running state of multiple MySQL instances. In order to run multiple instances, the my.cnf file has to have each listed in a separate section named with the convention mysqld1, mysqld2, mysqldN. mysqld_multi can run mysqld or mysqld_safe to start MySQL. An example of a my.cnf file that can be used with mysqld_multi would be:

```
[mysqld_multi]
mysqld        = /usr/local/mysql/bin/mysqld_safe
mysqladmin    = /usr/local/mysql/bin/mysqladmin
user          = root

[mysqld1]
datadir              = /usr/local/mysql/var/data1
mysqld               = /usr/local/mysql/bin/mysqld_safe
user                 = mysql
port                 = 3306
socket               = /tmp/mysql1.sock

[mysqld2]
datadir              = /usr/local/mysql/var/data2
mysqld               = /usr/local/mysql/bin/mysqld_safe
user                 = mysql
port                 = 3307
socket               = /tmp/mysql2.sock
```

This specifies that there are two servers, one as mysqld1 and the other as mysqld2, running each on their own ports and sockets, using different data directories.

In the example, the actual servers run as the mysql user, compared to mysqld_multi, which runs as root. This is so mysqld_multi will have the necessary privileges to start and stop both servers.

Using mysqld_multi to start both servers, the command would be:

```
shell> mysqld_multi start 1,2
```

To stop server 2:

```
shell> mysqld_multi stop 2
```

Running multiple servers with mysqld_multi will be covered in more detail in the "Replication" section.

Working with Data

Now that post-installation tasks have been performed and the various programs that come with a MySQL distribution have been explained, you should be ready to start delving into database functionality.

This section guides you through creating a schema that will contain your database objects, creating tables, inserting, querying, modifying, and deleting data. After these basic concepts are demonstrated, more advanced database functionality will be explained.

Creating a Schema and Tables

In the section in Appendix A, "Post Installation," you created a webuser database user with privileges to the webapps schema. This is the schema, a container of database objects, that will be referred to throughout the course of this book. To create this schema, the mysqladmin command can be used, run as the *root* database user:

```
shell> mysqladmin --user=root --password=pass create webapps
```

With the webapps schema created, tables and other database objects can be created within this schema:

You could alternatively use the MySQL command-line client to do this as well:

```
mysql> CREATE DATABASE webapps;
```

Now you can connect to the new schema:

```
shell> mysql --user=webuser --password=pass webapps
shell> mysql -u webuser -ppassword webapps
```

This connects you to the MySQL server as the webuser account on the webapps schema. If you want to see a list of all the schemas within a database to which you have access rights, the command SHOW DATABASES gives this information, showing other schemas as well as the schema you just created:

```
mysql> SHOW DATABASES;
+--------------------+
| Database           |
+--------------------+
| information_schema |
| test               |
| webapps            |
+--------------------+
```

Now that you are connected, you can create two new tables. The following code snippet shows the creation of two tables:

```
mysql> CREATE TABLE users (
    -> uid INT(3) NOT NULL AUTO_INCREMENT,
    -> username VARCHAR(32) NOT NULL DEFAULT '',
    -> score DECIMAL(5,2) NOT NULL DEFAULT 000.00,
    -> age INT(3) NOT NULL DEFAULT 0,
    -> state_id INT(3) NOT NULL DEFAULT 0,
    -> PRIMARY KEY (uid),
    -> UNIQUE KEY username (username),
    -> KEY state_id (state_id));
Query OK, 0 rows affected (0.05 sec)

mysql> CREATE TABLE states (
    -> state_id INT(3) NOT NULL DEFAULT 0,
    -> state_name VARCHAR(25) NOT NULL DEFAULT '',
    -> PRIMARY KEY (state_id));
Query OK, 0 rows affected (0.02 sec)
```

The -> is printed by the command-line client when it needs more data. It will send the data once it gets a line that contains a semicolon (;).

Two tables now exist named *users* and *states*.

What Exactly Is (or Is Not) NULL?

NULL is something that you probably want to get a grip on when you work with databases — that is, if you can grip something that is missing and unknown!

If you've ever tried to use Roman numerals, they are pretty tedious and cumbersome for performing calculations. This is because there is no placeholder digit or zero. The Romans had no concept of zero or nothingness, nor did much of the West at that time. How could nothing be quantified?

The concept of zero is really key to modern mathematics and a prerequisite to computers ever having been invented. This concept of nothingness came from India, where Vedic and later Buddhist philosophies had an innate understanding of nothingness. Along with this philosophy there was also a system of mathematics at the time, rules for the use of zero in Indian philosopher Brahmagupta's book *Brahmasputha Siddhanta* (6th century). The Sanskrit word for nothingness or emptiness is *Sunya*, and this useful concept made its way to the West through use by the Arabs, from whom, in turn, the West adopted it.

This concept of nothingness or emptiness would seem to describe NULL, but in SQL NULL is not zero, nor is it an empty string. There's another Sanskrit word that might better describe NULL, *Maya*, which means "that which not is."

With MySQL, NULL means a missing, unknown value. NULL can also be described by its relation to those values that are NOT NULL. The table that follows shows the result of a value with a given operator, and NULL.

Value	Operator with NULL	Result value
1	= NULL	NULL
1	<> NULL	NULL
1	< NULL	NULL
1	> NULL	NULL
1	IS NULL	0
1	IS NOT NULL	1
0	IS NULL	0
0	IS NOT NULL	1
''	IS NULL	0
''	IS NOT NULL	1

As you can see, NULL compared, using any operator to any value in SQL is always NULL. Also, 1, 0, and empty strings are not NULLs. So there is some distinction between zero and NULL, and empty strings and NULL: both zero and empty strings are *known* values.

Column Data Types

The first table was created with five columns: uid, username, ranking, age, state_id. The first column, uid, is an INT(3) (synonym for INTEGER). The specification of (3) is for left-padding when printing from within the client and does not affect the range of this column. The NOT NULL flag was set to guarantee that NULL values cannot be inserted into this column (more about not allowing NULLs in a table for performance reasons is found in the "Performance" section). Also, the AUTO_INCREMENT flag was set. AUTO_INCREMENT is a unique feature of MySQL which automatically increments the value of the column for subsequent insertions into the table. This provides a convenient means of guaranteeing uniqueness of that column's value for each record inserted into the table.

The second column, username, is created as a VARCHAR(32) column. This means that the column is able to store up to 32 characters of text. A VARCHAR is named such because at the storage-engine level, only the space needed to store that column's value for a given record is allocated in the data file. There is a CHAR data type that will allocate exactly what is specified.

The third column, ranking, is a DECIMAL type column. The specification of (5,2) signifies precision and scale. This means that a number must have five digits and two decimals and that the range for *score* is -999.99 to 999.99. In other words, if you were to insert 1000.0 into this column, it would convert the number to 999.99 and if you inserted 998.999 it would convert the number to 999.00 (rounded).

Then there are the fourth and fifth columns, age and state_id, INT(3) types respectively.

Indexes

The indexes on *users* are on the columns uid, username and state_id. When you design your schema and determine which tables you will use for the data you need to store, you have to consider what columns you'll be using to find a given record. In this case, it's easy to imagine that you would want to look up a user by the user id or uid, his or her username, as well as what state he or she is from.

The index on uid (user id) is the PRIMARY KEY index. A primary key is a unique index — there can be no two identical values for this column in the table — and it is used to uniquely identify each row in a table. Because AUTO_INCREMENT is being specified, this will automatically provide the values for this column, so you don't have to worry about providing unique numeric values when inserting rows. Also, a table can have only one PRIMARY KEY index, hence the name PRIMARY.

The index on username is a UNIQUE index. Similar to a PRIMARY KEY index, there can be no two identical values for this column in the table, except with unique UNIQUE index, many NULL values are permitted. This is how you can guarantee that there is only one user with a given name in your user table. Unlike PRIMARY KEY indexes, a table can have more than one UNIQUE index.

The second table, *states*, is a simple table containing a state_id INTEGER column and a state_name VARCHAR column. The only index on this table is the PRIMARY KEY index on state_id.

You'll notice that *users* and *states* both have a state_id. This is done to indicate that there is a relationship between *users* and *states*, the state_id column being the common column between the two. You'll see after some data is inserted what the relationship means in terms of using an SQL query to return data.

Schema Information

One way to verify the definition of how you created your table is to use the command SHOW CREATE TABLE:

```
mysql> SHOW CREATE TABLE users\G
*************************** 1. row ***************************
       Table: users
Create Table: CREATE TABLE `users` (
  `uid` int(3) NOT NULL auto_increment,
  `username' varchar(32) NOT NULL default '',
  `score` decimal(5,2) NOT NULL default '0.00',
  `age` int(3) NOT NULL default '0',
  `state_id` int(5) NOT NULL default '0',
  PRIMARY KEY  (`uid`),
  UNIQUE KEY `username` (`username`),
  KEY `state_id` (`state_id`)
) ENGINE=MyISAM AUTO_INCREMENT=5 DEFAULT CHARSET=latin1
```

The output of some commands can contain a lot of formatting characters that make the output "stretch" far to the right. To view the output of a command without this formatting, use \G instead of a semicolon.

Another way to view the definition of a table is the DESCRIBE command:

```
mysql> DESCRIBE users;
+----------+--------------+------+-----+---------+----------------+
| Field    | Type         | Null | Key | Default | Extra          |
+----------+--------------+------+-----+---------+----------------+
| uid      | int(3)       | NO   | PRI | NULL    | auto_increment |
| username | varchar(32)  | NO   | UNI |         |                |
| score    | decimal(5,2) | NO   |     | 0.00    |                |
| age      | int(3)       | NO   |     | 0       |                |
| state_id | int(5)       | NO   | MUL | 0       |                |
+----------+--------------+------+-----+---------+----------------+
5 rows in set (0.00 sec)
```

To see what tables exist in a schema, you can issue the command SHOW TABLES:

```
mysql> SHOW TABLES;
+-------------------+
| Tables_in_webapps |
+-------------------+
| states            |
| users             |
+-------------------+
```

SHOW has a numerous options. You can use HELP SHOW in the command line client to get an extensive list of the different options available:

```
mysql> HELP SHOW;
```

Yet one more tool in your arsenal is the *information schema* which you can use to view all manner of information (refer to the MySQL reference manual). The information schema, which is named INFORMATION_SCHEMA, works just like any other database in MySQL, except it doesn't contain real tables. All the tables that provide information are views with the information generated when needed. An example of using INFORMATION_SCHEMA to give the equivalent of SHOW TABLES is:

```
mysql> SELECT TABLE_NAME,TABLE_TYPE,ENGINE FROM TABLES
    -> WHERE TABLE_SCHEMA = 'webapps';
+---------------------+------------+---------+
| TABLE_NAME          | TABLE_TYPE | ENGINE  |
+---------------------+------------+---------+
| states              | BASE TABLE | MyISAM  |
| users               | BASE TABLE | InnoDB  |
+---------------------+------------+---------+
```

Schema Modification

You will sometimes need to modify your schema, either adding or dropping a column to or from a table, changing the data type or definition of a column, adding an index to a table, or renaming a table. The ALTER TABLE statement is the means of doing this. The syntax for ALTER TABLE has numerous options described in full in the MySQL reference manual. The basic syntax for ALTER TABLE is:

```
ALTER TABLE [ONLINE | OFFLINE] [IGNORE] tbl_name alter_specification
[,alter_specification] ...
```

❑   OFFLINE | ONLINE pertain to how ALTER TABLE is performed on NDB Cluster tables.

❑   IGNORE pertains to how the ALTER statement will deal with duplicate values in columns that have a newly added constraint of unique. If IGNORE is not specified, the ALTER will fail and not be applied. If IGNORE is specified, the first row of all duplicate rows is kept, the reset deleted, and the ALTER applied.

❑   The alter_specification would be what you are changing — what columns or indexes you are adding, dropping, or modifying, or what constraints you are placing on columns.

This section offers a few examples to give the basic idea of how to use ALTER TABLE.

In the previous example you created the table *users* with several columns. If you now need to modify some of these columns — for example, if the *username* column isn't large enough to store some names and you want to change it from 32 characters maximum to 64 — the following ALTER TABLE would achieve this:

```
mysql> ALTER TABLE users MODIFY COLUMN username VARCHAR(64)
NOT NULL default '';
Query OK, 9 rows affected (0.01 sec)
Records: 9  Duplicates: 0  Warnings: 0
```

As the output shows, the nine existing records in the table are affected by this change, and the *users* table should now have a modified definition for the username column:

```
mysql> DESC users;
+----------+--------------+------+-----+---------+----------------+
| Field    | Type         | Null | Key | Default | Extra          |
+----------+--------------+------+-----+---------+----------------+
| uid      | int(3)       | NO   | PRI | NULL    | auto_increment |
| username | varchar(64)  | NO   | UNI |         |                |
| ranking  | decimal(5,2) | NO   |     | 0.00    |                |
| age      | int(3)       | NO   |     | 0       |                |
| state_id | int(5)       | NO   | MUL | 0       |                |
+----------+--------------+------+-----+---------+----------------+
```

Next, you realize that the column score isn't really the name you want for this column. What you really want is ranking, so you issue another ALTER TABLE statement:

```
mysql> ALTER TABLE users CHANGE COLUMN score ranking DECIMAL(5,2)
NOT NULL default '0.00';
```

Furthermore, you notice that both the *age* and *ranking* columns are columns that you will be either using for sorting or retrieving data and that they need indexes.

```
mysql> ALTER TABLE users ADD INDEX ranking(ranking);
```

```
mysql> ALTER TABLE users ADD INDEX age(age);
```

You can also perform multiple alterations in one statement (preferable, especially if your table is huge!):

```
mysql> ALTER TABLE users ADD INDEX ranking(ranking), ADD INDEX age(age);
```

Now, if you check to see what the *users* table definition is, you see that your changes have been made:

```
mysql> DESC users;
+----------+--------------+------+-----+---------+----------------+
| Field    | Type         | Null | Key | Default | Extra          |
+----------+--------------+------+-----+---------+----------------+
| uid      | int(3)       | NO   | PRI | NULL    | auto_increment |
| username | varchar(64)  | NO   | UNI |         |                |
| ranking  | decimal(5,2) | NO   | MUL | 0.00    |                |
| age      | int(3)       | NO   | MUL | 0       |                |
| state_id | int(5)       | NO   | MUL | 0       |                |
+----------+--------------+------+-----+---------+----------------+
```

For more information, the full syntax for ALTER TABLE can be found in two ways:

```
mysql> HELP ALTER TABLE;
```

... or MySQL's documentation at http://dev.mysql.com/doc/refman/5.1/en/alter-table.html.

Inserting Data

The next thing you probably want to do is to insert some data into the newly created tables. The SQL STATEMENT for insertion is INSERT. The INSERT statement's basic syntax is:

```
INSERT [LOW_PRIORITY | DELAYED | HIGH_PRIORITY] [IGNORE]
INTO table_name (col_name,...)
VALUES ({expr | DEFAULT}, ...), (...), ...
```

The syntax can be explained as:

❑   LOW_PRIORITY means that the data will not be inserted until there are no clients reading from the table. This option only works on tables that have table-level locking such as MyISAM, Memory, Merge, etc.

❑   DELAYED means that the data being inserted will be queued up and inserted into the table when the table is not being read from, allowing the client issuing the INSERT DELAYED to continue.

❑   HIGH_PRIORITY makes it so concurrent inserts are not utilized or overriding the low-priority-updates server setting.

❑   IGNORE makes it so errors with data insertion are treated as warnings. For instance, if there is an error inserting data that contains a duplicate value on a PRIMARY KEY or UNIQUE column, that row will not be inserted and a warning will be issued. If you are not using IGNORE, the INSERT statement will end when the first error is encountered.

Basic Insert

To begin inserting data into the *users* table, the two INSERT statements are issued:

```
mysql> INSERT INTO users (username, ranking, age, state_id)
    -> VALUES ('John Smith', 55.5, 33, 1);
Query OK, 1 row affected (0.00 sec)

mysql> INSERT INTO users (username, ranking, age, state_id)
    -> VALUES ('Amy Carr', 66.55, 25, 1);
Query OK, 1 row affected (0.00 sec)
```

It is recommended to always specify the column names into which you are inserting data within your application code. This will allow your application to continue working even if someone were to add extra columns to the table.

These two queries insert two rows into the *users* table. As you can see by the output 1 row affected, both INSERT statements succeeded. The first part of the query specifies what table to insert the data into, then provides a list of columns that data will be inserted into. The VALUES part of the statement is the list of the actual values you want to insert. These values have to match each column specified in the first half of the query. If you notice that the uid column was not specified, that is because it's not necessary to specify the uid column's value as the AUTO_INCREMENT attribute keyword was specified in the creation of the *users* table. The first row being inserted will result in the value of uid being 1, and the second row will result in item_id being 2. AUTO_INCREMENT will set the value of the uid column one more than the previous value for each subsequent row inserted.

You can also specify a MySQL parameter AUTO_INCREMENT_INCREMENT, *which sets the amount to increment by for each row insertion, making it possible to increment by a value other than 1.*

You can specify the value of an auto increment value if you choose to do so:

```
mysql> INSERT INTO users (uid, username, ranking, age, state_id)
    -> VALUES (4, 'Gertrude Asgaard', 44.33, 65, 1);
Query OK, 1 row affected (0.00 sec)
```

Notice, here, the query inserting a predetermined value for uid. When data is inserted this way, you must ensure that the values you are inserting match the columns of the table *as defined* when you created the table. Also, the uid column was specified by the input, not relying on AUTO_INCREMENT to supply this value. This is completely legitimate, but also requires that you ensure the value being inserted is unique because it is a PRIMARY KEY. If it was just a regular index, KEY, you could use any value even if not unique within the table. Also, the value inserted was 4 whereas if AUTO_INCREMENT had assigned the value it would have been 3. This means that the next value, if set using AUTO_INCREMENT, will be one more than the previous value, which means the value will be 5.

An alternate INSERT syntax is to set each column explicitly:

```
mysql> insert into users set uid = 4, username = 'Gertrude Asgaard',
    -> ranking = '44.33', age = 65, state_id = '65';
```

Bulk Insert

Bulk inserts can be a convenient way to insert multiple rows of data without having to issue multiple statements or connections to the database. In many cases, it's best to try to accomplish as much as possible within the database in as few statements as possible, and using bulk inserts is a way to do this. Another benefit of bulk inserts is that they are the fastest way to insert multiple rows of data into a table. The following example shows that four records are inserted.

You should try to use bulk inserts particularly when you find yourself using statements repeating the same insert statements with different data. One of the easiest ways to obtain more performance in an application is if you can cache your data in the client and then insert the cached data many rows at a time — this is what bulk inserts enable you to do.

An example of using a bulk INSERT statement is:

```
mysql> INSERT INTO users (username, ranking, age, state_id)
    -> VALUES ('Sunya Vadi', 88.1, 30, 2),
    -> ('Maya Vadi', 77.32, 31, 2),
    -> ('Haranya Kashipu', 1.2, 99, 3),
    -> ('Pralad Maharaj', 99.99, 8, 3);
Query OK, 4 rows affected (0.00 sec)
Records: 4  Duplicates: 0  Warnings: 0
```

A detriment of bulk inserts is that if there is a problem with any of the data being inserted the entire statement fails. For example, if you specified a value that violated a unique index in the statement in only one of the rows being inserted in a statement inserting 100 records, all 100 of those records would fail to be inserted even though 99 of them were bona fide statements that would otherwise successfully be inserted.

```
mysql> INSERT INTO users VALUES
    -> (1, 'Jake Smith', 11.12, 40, 4),
    -> (9, 'Franklin Pierce', 88.3, 60, 4),
    -> (10,'Daniel Webster', 87.33, 62, 4);
ERROR 1062 (23000): Duplicate entry '1' for key 1
```

As you can see, the first set of values specified in the bulk insert violated the integrity of the primary key on uid by trying to assign the value of 1 where there is already a record with that value. This causes the whole statement to fail. The other two sets of data would have otherwise been successfully inserted.

INSERT IGNORE

There are two ways to get around the problem of having multiple records fail in a bulk insert due to PRIMARY or UNIQUE key violations. You can either fix the data you're trying to insert, or employ the use of INSERT IGNORE. INSERT IGNORE inserts the values that wouldn't cause errors, while ignoring the ones that do:

```
mysql> INSERT IGNORE INTO users VALUES
    -> (1, 'Jake Smith', 11.12, 40, 4),

    -> (9, 'Franklin Pierce', 88.3, 60, 4),
    -> (10,'Daniel Webster', 87.33, 62, 4);
Query OK, 2 rows affected (0.01 sec)
Records: 3  Duplicates: 1  Warnings: 0
```

In this statement, INSERT IGNORE was used. As a result, the values that would have otherwise caused the whole statement to fail are ignored and the two valid sets of data are inserted.

The *states* table also will need to be populated with data:

```
mysql> INSERT INTO states VALUES
    -> (1, 'Alaska'),
    -> (2, 'Alabama'),
    -> (3, 'New York'),
    -> (4, 'New Hampshire'),
    -> (5, 'Hawaii');
```

This table is a lookup table that will be used for the discussion of the examples in the following sections.

Delayed and Low Priority INSERTs

In some cases, you have data that you don't need to be readily available and are more interested in inserting for purposes such as logging and statistics gathering. You do need to save this data, but to be able to save it "lazily" would be sufficient for your application's purposes. MySQL has just the means for accomplishing this using a *delayed insert*. An example of using delayed inserts to insert data into an application log is as follows:

```
mysql> INSERT DELAYED INTO weblog (ip_address, username, request_type, uri)
    -> VALUES ('192.168.1.133', 'GnaeusPompey', 'POST',
    -> 'http://triumvirate.com/legion?ruler=pompey');
```

Delayed inserts cache the rows being inserted into a buffer, which are written to the table when the table is not being used by any other thread. This can help overall performance because it batches writes.

Delayed inserts are only available for tables using the MyISAM storage engine.

Optionally, you could also use:

```
mysql> INSERT LOW_PRIORITY INTO weblog (ip_address, username,
request_type, uri)
    -> VALUES ('192.168.1.133', 'GnaeusPompey', 'POST',
    -> 'http://triumvirate.com/legion?ruler=pompey');
```

Using LOW_PRIORITY is different than DELAYED in that LOW_PRIORITY causes the client to wait until no other clients are reading from the table before it attempts insertion, whereas with DELAYED, the rows being inserted are queued in a buffer while the client is freed up to run other statements. What you will use depends on your application and what sort of behavior you require.

It should be noted that normally, you shouldn't use DELAYED or LOW_PRIORITY. You would utilize these if you using MyISAM tables and you desperately need some extra performance when all other options have failed.

For more information on how to use INSERT, use:

```
mysql> HELP INSERT;
```

... or the MySQL online manual at the URL: http://dev.mysql.com/doc/refman/5.1/en/insert.html.

Querying Data

The way to retrieve data from a table in a database is to use the SELECT statement. The basic syntax of a SELECT statement is:

```
SELECT select_expr FROM table_references
WHERE where_condition [GROUPING AND ORDERING]
[LIMIT {[offset,], row_count]
```

❑   select_expr indicates the column(s) you want to select.

❑   table_references indicates a list of one or more tables.

❑   where_condition indicates a condition that must be satisfied to return rows of columns indicated in select_expr.

❑   GROUPING AND ORDERING indicates you can specify what column you want to order the results by as well as what column you want to group by.

❑   LIMIT is a way of limiting the result by a given number offset (optional), meaning what row to begin from and row_count how many records in the result set to display (not optional).

Basic Queries

Using the SELECT statement, different queries can be performed against *users* and *states* to retrieve various data.

To see all the records in users:

```
mysql> SELECT * FROM users;
+-----+------------------+---------+-----+----------+
| uid | username         | ranking | age | state_id |
+-----+------------------+---------+-----+----------+
|   1 | John Smith       |   55.50 |  33 |        1 |
|   2 | Amy Carr         |   66.55 |  25 |        1 |
|   4 | Gertrude Asgaard |   44.33 |  65 |        1 |
|   5 | Sunya Vadi       |   88.10 |  30 |        2 |
|   6 | Maya Vadi        |   77.32 |  31 |        2 |
|   7 | Haranya Kashipu  |    1.20 |  99 |        3 |
|   8 | Pralad Maharaj   |   99.99 |   8 |        3 |
|   9 | Franklin Pierce  |   88.30 |  60 |        4 |
|  10 | Daniel Webster   |   87.33 |  62 |        4 |
+-----+------------------+---------+-----+----------+
```

As you can see, all the data you inserted is now stored in users. In this example, '*' is a special marker that stands for all columns, in this case meaning that all columns should be included in the rows returned (result set) from the query. No WHERE clause was applied to the query, so all rows are returned. You could also specify specific columns:

```
mysql> SELECT uid, username FROM users;
+-----+------------------+
| uid | username         |
+-----+------------------+
|   1 | John Smith       |
|   2 | Amy Carr         |
|   4 | Gertrude Asgaard |
|   5 | Sunya Vadi       |
|   6 | Maya Vadi        |
|   7 | Haranya Kashipu  |
|   8 | Pralad Maharaj   |
|   9 | Franklin Pierce  |
|  10 | Daniel Webster   |
+-----+------------------+
```

Aliasing

Another convenient feature of SQL is that you can alias (i.e., temporarily rename) result columns and table names. In the previous example, uid, username, and the table *users* all could be aliased:

```
mysql> SELECT uid AS `User Identification Number`,
    -> username `User Name`
    -> FROM users U WHERE U.uid <= 9;
+----------------------------+------------------+
| User Identification Number | User Name        |
+----------------------------+------------------+
|                          1 | John Smith       |
|                          2 | Amy Carr         |
|                          4 | Gertrude Asgaard |
```

```
    |     5 | Sunya Vadi         |
    |     6 | Maya Vadi          |
    |     7 | Haranya Kashipu    |
    |     8 | Pralad Maharaj     |
    |     9 | Franklin Pierce    |
    +---------------------------+-------------------+
```

If you notice, the first alias for uid, User Identification Number, was alias by the following uid with AS , and the second column *username* was followed by User Name, without the use of AS. Either of these is valid. The table name *users* is followed by U. Aliases are a convenient way to either have a more canonical column name on the output, or they can be used to shorten table or column names throughout the statement so the statement is easier to read. Also, the backtick character, known as the identifier quote character, was used to quote the column aliases in this example. This allows the alias to contain spaces or other character sets to be used. Other characters can also be used, such as single and double quotes, but the backtick is MySQL's default identifier quote character for quoting table names and columns. Although you can also use double quotes if you do the following:

```
mysql> SET sql_mode='ANSI_QUOTES';
mysql> CREATE TABLE t4 ("some column" int(8));
mysql> SELECT "some column" FROM t4;
```

The output of database dumps from MySQL's backup program mysqldump includes the use of the backtick character as the identifier quote character by default.

Also, aliases are required for joining a table to itself (a *self join*) to ensure that the table name used in the query is unique. For an example of this, see the later section "JOIN."

Limiting Results

If you want to return only the first two rows in a result, you can use LIMIT in the query:

```
mysql> SELECT * FROM users LIMIT 2;
+-----+------------+---------+-----+----------+
| uid | username   | ranking | age | state_id |
+-----+------------+---------+-----+----------+
|   1 | John Smith |   55.50 |  33 |        1 |
|   2 | Amy Carr   |   66.55 |  25 |        1 |
+-----+------------+---------+-----+----------+
```

... or if you want to return record number 5, use:

```
mysql> SELECT * FROM users LIMIT 5, 1;
+-----+------------------+---------+-----+----------+
| uid | username         | ranking | age | state_id |
+-----+------------------+---------+-----+----------+
|   5 | Sunya Vadi       |   88.10 |  30 |        2 |
+-----+------------------+---------+-----+----------+
```

WHERE Clause

The WHERE clause is used to select which rows you want to return from the result set. What if you want return a particular user's uid? Say, for instance, you have a function in your web application code to retrieve just a user's `uid` based on supplying the user's `username`. Just specify that in another `WHERE` clause:

```
mysql> SELECT uid FROM users WHERE username = 'Pralad Maharaj';
+-----+
| uid |
+-----+
|   8 |
+-----+
```

In the `WHERE` clause, you can use a lot of different operators to select which data you are interested in obtaining. This is described in the next several sections.

Operators

Numerous operators can be specified in a query:

```
mysql> SELECT uid, username FROM users WHERE age < 40 AND state_id = 3;
+-----+---------------+
| uid | username      |
+-----+---------------+
|   8 | Pralad Maharaj |
+-----+---------------+
```

The less-than operator < is used to restrict the rows found to any `age` less than 40 as well as `AND`, which includes the restriction that the `state_id` be limited to 3.

The operator `LIKE` allows for specification of word patterns. The percentage character (`%`) is a wildcard character in SQL, much like the asterisk (`*`) character is for file and directory names. You use this to allow the word "Jack" immediately followed by zero or more characters to be what is searched for:

```
mysql> SELECT uid, username FROM users WHERE username LIKE 'Jack%';
+-----+--------------+
| uid | username     |
+-----+--------------+
|  11 | Jack Kerouac |
+-----+--------------+
```

Ranges

You can specify ranges with the operators <, <=, =, <> , >, >= or BETWEEN.

```
mysql> SELECT uid, username FROM users WHERE uid >= 6 AND uid <= 7;
+-----+-----------------+
| uid | username        |
+-----+-----------------+
|   6 | Maya Vadi       |
|   7 | Haranya Kashipu |
+-----+-----------------+
```

Or, the previous statement can also use the `BETWEEN` operator to obtain the same results:

```
mysql> SELECT uid, username FROM users WHERE uid BETWEEN 6 AND 7;
```

```
+-----+-----------------+
| uid | username        |
+-----+-----------------+
|   6 | Maya Vadi       |
|   7 | Haranya Kashipu |
+-----+-----------------+
```

Ordering

Ordering, which is done using the ORDER BY clause, allows you to be able to sort the result of a query in a number of ways. The following examples show how you can use ORDER BY.

For instance, if you want to order your results with the youngest age first (ASC means "ascending"):

```
mysql> SELECT * FROM users ORDER BY age ASC;
+-----+-----------------+---------+-----+----------+
| uid | username        | ranking | age | state_id |
+-----+-----------------+---------+-----+----------+
|   8 | Pralad Maharaj  |   99.99 |   8 |        3 |
|   2 | Amy Carr        |   66.55 |  25 |        1 |
|   5 | Sunya Vadi      |   88.10 |  30 |        2 |
|   6 | Maya Vadi       |   77.32 |  31 |        2 |
|   1 | John Smith      |   55.50 |  33 |        1 |
|   9 | Franklin Pierce |   88.30 |  60 |        4 |
|  10 | Daniel Webster  |   87.33 |  62 |        4 |
|   4 | Gertrude Asgaard|   44.33 |  65 |        1 |
|   7 | Haranya Kashipu |    1.20 |  99 |        3 |
+-----+-----------------+---------+-----+----------+
```

... or with the oldest age first (DESC means "descending"):

```
mysql> SELECT * FROM users ORDER BY age DESC LIMIT 3;
+-----+-----------------+---------+-----+----------+
| uid | username        | ranking | age | state_id |
+-----+-----------------+---------+-----+----------+
|   4 | Gertrude Asgaard|   44.33 |  65 |        1 |
|  10 | Daniel Webster  |   87.33 |  62 |        4 |
|   9 | Franklin Pierce |   88.30 |  60 |        4 |
+-----+-----------------+---------+-----+----------+
```

You can also order by multiple columns:

```
mysql> SELECT * FROM users ORDER BY age DESC,state_id ASC LIMIT 3;
+-----+-----------------+---------+-----+----------+
| uid | username        | ranking | age | state_id |
+-----+-----------------+---------+-----+----------+
|   4 | Gertrude Asgaard|   44.33 |  65 |        1 |
|  10 | Daniel Webster  |   87.33 |  62 |        4 |
|   9 | Franklin Pierce |   88.30 |  60 |        4 |
+-----+-----------------+---------+-----+----------+
```

This would mean that the age is the first column that the ordering would use (descending), and then of that result, state_id would be used to sort in ascending order.

Grouping

Grouping is yet another operation in retrieving data that is very useful. GROUP BY is the SQL clause that provides grouping. With GROUP BY, the result of a query is grouped by one or more columns.

For instance, if you would like to have a count of users per state, this can be achieved by using COUNT() and GROUP BY, and is a very common query you will use in variations during the course of developing web applications and producing reports of your site's data.

```
mysql> SELECT COUNT(uid) AS `num users`,state_id,state_name
    -> FROM users JOIN states USING (state_id) GROUP BY state_id;
+-----------+----------+---------------+
| num users | state_id | state_name    |
+-----------+----------+---------------+
|         3 |        1 | Alaska        |
|         2 |        2 | Alabama       |
|         2 |        3 | NY            |
|         3 |        4 | New Hampshire |
+-----------+----------+---------------+
```

With GROUP BY, the data is grouped (or you could say "lumped" together) using the column or columns you specify. By using the aggregate function COUNT, it counts how many are in each grouping — for each grouping, which is then aliased to a column name such as num users in this example, then displayed in state_id and state_name, giving you a simple output of users per state.

There are numerous grouping functions that you will find of great use when grouping data, which will be shown in the later section on "Aggregate Functions."

JOIN

In the previous query, one of the columns in the result set is state_id. What would be more useful is to also have the state name included. In the examples, data was inserted into the states table for both state_id and state_name.

The states table contains:

```
mysql> SELECT * FROM states;
+----------+---------------+
| state_id | state_name    |
+----------+---------------+
|        1 | Alaska        |
|        2 | Alabama       |
|        3 | New York      |
|        4 | New Hampshire |
|        5 | Hawaii        |
+----------+---------------+
```

The *users* table, as seen in previous SELECTS, contains users who have state_id values corresponding to most of the values in *states*. To be able to include the state_name column with the result set from *users*, a join will have to be employed.

An SQL join works by conceptually creating a result set that contains all row combinations from all tables and then selecting, with the WHERE clause, which row combinations you are interested in. Normally, you want to see the rows that have the same value in two columns.

There are several types of joins: CROSS, INNER, OUTER, LEFT, and RIGHT. Each join type will be discussion in a later section. Also, a join can be used not just in SELECT statements but also in UPDATE and DELETE statements (which will be discussed in the next section).

For instance, if you want to include state_name as one of the columns in the result set from the previous query that sorted the results on the age, an *inner join* will accomplish this:

```
mysql> SELECT users.*,states.state_name
    -> FROM users,states
    -> WHERE users.state_id = states.state_id
    -> ORDER BY age ASC;
+-----+------------------+---------+-----+----------+---------------+
| uid | username         | ranking | age | state_id | state_name    |
+-----+------------------+---------+-----+----------+---------------+
|   8 | Pralad Maharaj   |   99.99 |   8 |        3 | New York      |
|   2 | Amy Carr         |   66.55 |  25 |        1 | Alaska        |
|   5 | Sunya Vadi       |   88.10 |  30 |        2 | Alabama       |
|   6 | Maya Vadi        |   77.32 |  31 |        2 | Alabama       |
|   1 | John Smith       |   55.50 |  33 |        1 | Alaska        |
|   9 | Franklin Pierce  |   88.30 |  60 |        4 | New Hampshire |
|  10 | Daniel Webster   |   87.33 |  62 |        4 | New Hampshire |
|   4 | Gertrude Asgaard |   44.33 |  65 |        1 | Alaska        |
|   7 | Haranya Kashipu  |    1.20 |  99 |        3 | New York      |
+-----+------------------+---------+-----+----------+---------------+
```

This type of join is known as an *implicit inner join* — implicit because the term INNER JOIN isn't explicitly listed in the query. The part of the query that defines what columns must be equal to, users.state_id = states.state_id, is known as a *join predicate*. In this example, the columns list is specified as users.*, states.state_name. The first users.* specifies all columns of the *users* table and states.state_name specifies only the state_name column from *states*. With a JOIN, if only a * had been used, all columns from both tables would have been returned.

This same JOIN query could have been written in several ways. An *explicit inner join*:

```
SELECT users.*,states.state_name FROM users INNER JOIN states
ON (users.state_id = states.state_id)  ORDER BY age ASC;
```

When you are doing a join between two tables only based on equality comparisons, called an *equi-join*, you can use the following shorter:

```
SELECT users.*,states.state_name
FROM users JOIN states using (state_id)
ORDER BY age ASC;
```

A *natural join*:

```
mysql> SELECT * FROM states NATURAL JOIN users ORDER BY age ASC;
+----------+---------------+-----+------------------+---------+-----+
| state_id | state_name    | uid | username         | ranking | age |
+----------+---------------+-----+------------------+---------+-----+
|        3 | New York      |   8 | Pralad Maharaj   |   99.99 |   8 |
|        1 | Alaska        |   2 | Amy Carr         |   66.55 |  25 |
|        2 | Alabama       |   5 | Sunya Vadi       |   88.10 |  30 |
```

```
|         | 2 | Alabama       |  6 | Maya Vadi        | 77.32 | 31 |
|         | 1 | Alaska        |  1 | John Smith       | 55.50 | 33 |
|         | 4 | New Hampshire |  9 | Franklin Pierce  | 88.30 | 60 |
|         | 4 | New Hampshire | 10 | Daniel Webster   | 87.33 | 62 |
|         | 1 | Alaska        |  4 | Gertrude Asgaard | 44.33 | 65 |
|         | 3 | New York      |  7 | Haranya Kashipu  |  1.20 | 99 |
+---------+---------------+----+------------------+-------+-----+
```

You'll notice that in this example, no specific columns were specified in the column list or in the join predicate. This is because a *natural join* implicitly joins the tables based on any columns that are named the same, and only prints once columns are named the same. This query may look cleaner and easier to read, but it is somewhat ambiguous. If a query like this was used in application code, and there were changes to the schema, things might break. That might make for one of those bugs that take a long time to find!

The other types of joins mentioned previously were LEFT and RIGHT joins. For instance, A LEFT join for *states* and *users* will always contain records of *states* (the "left" table), even if there aren't matching records from *users* (the "right" table). To see the meaning of this:

```
mysql> SELECT username, states.state_id, state_name
    -> FROM states LEFT JOIN users
    -> ON (users.state_id = states.state_id);
+------------------+----------+---------------+
| username         | state_id | state_name    |
+------------------+----------+---------------+
| John Smith       |        1 | Alaska        |
| Amy Carr         |        1 | Alaska        |
| Gertrude Asgaard |        1 | Alaska        |
| Sunya Vadi       |        2 | Alabama       |
| Maya Vadi        |        2 | Alabama       |
| Haranya Kashipu  |        3 | New York      |
| Pralad Maharaj   |        3 | New York      |
| Franklin Pierce  |        4 | New Hampshire |
| Daniel Webster   |        4 | New Hampshire |
| NULL             |        5 | Hawaii        |
+------------------+----------+---------------+
```

Because there are no users in the table *users* with a state_id of 5, which is the state_id of Hawaii, there is no match from *users*, so NULL is displayed. If the LEFT keyword had been omitted, the row containing the NULL would not have been displayed. LEFT and RIGHT joins are thus useful to find things that don't match!

A RIGHT join works the same way as a LEFT join, except the table on the right is the table that all records will be returned for, and the table on the left, *states*, will only contain records that match with *users*.

Because every user has a state_id value that exists in *states*, all records are returned and no NULLs present in the result set. To see how a RIGHT JOIN works, a user is inserted into *users* that contain a state_id that doesn't exist in *states*.

```
mysql> INSERT INTO users (username, ranking, age, state_id)
    -> VALUES ('Jack Kerouac', 87.88, 40, 6);
```

45

Then you perform the RIGHT JOIN query:

```
mysql> SELECT username, states.state_id, state_name
FROM states RIGHT JOIN users
ON (users.state_id = states.state_id);
+------------------+----------+---------------+
| username         | state_id | state_name    |
+------------------+----------+---------------+
| John Smith       |        1 | Alaska        |
| Amy Carr         |        1 | Alaska        |
| Gertrude Asgaard |        1 | Alaska        |
| Sunya Vadi       |        2 | Alabama       |
| Maya Vadi        |        2 | Alabama       |
| Haranya Kashipu  |        3 | New York      |
| Pralad Maharaj   |        3 | New York      |
| Franklin Pierce  |        4 | New Hampshire |
| Daniel Webster   |        4 | New Hampshire |
| Jack Kerouac     |     NULL | NULL          |
+------------------+----------+---------------+
```

And as you can see, then NULLs are displayed in the result set for the new entry in users that does not yet have a state that exists. Adding another record with a state_id for a state not contained in *states* helps to illustrate the concept of how, with RIGHT and LEFT joins, there won't necessarily be a 1:1 match in the result set.

This brings up another important point in schema design and how you tailor the queries you use in your application. If you have a parent to child relationship in your schema, when retrieving the results of a query to return a list of parents and their children, you need to use the correct query to give you the desired result.

Consider the two simple tables, *parent* and *children*:

```
mysql> SELECT * FROM parent;
+-----------+--------------+
| parent_id | name         |
+-----------+--------------+
|         1 | has kids     |
|         2 | empty nester |
+-----------+--------------+
2 rows in set (0.00 sec)

mysql> SELECT * FROM children;
+----------+-----------+--------+
| child_id | parent_id | name   |
+----------+-----------+--------+
|        1 |         1 | kid #1 |
|        2 |         1 | kid #2 |
+----------+-----------+--------+
```

If you use an INNER JOIN, the result set omits the record "empty nester" from *users*, because it doesn't have corresponding records in *children*:

```
mysql> SELECT * FROM parent p JOIN children c ON
(p.parent_id = c.parent_id);
```

```
+-----------+-----------+-----------+-----------+--------+
| parent_id | name      | child_id  | parent_id | name   |
+-----------+-----------+-----------+-----------+--------+
|         1 | has kids  |         2 |         1 | kid #2 |
|         1 | has kids  |         1 |         1 | kid #1 |
+-----------+-----------+-----------+-----------+--------+
```

This could be a problem if you intend to display all parents, even those without child records. The way to solve this issue is to use a LEFT JOIN. The *parent* table, the table for which you want the result to contain every record, is the "left" table. So you would need to specify this *parent* table first in the query:

```
mysql> SELECT * FROM parent p LEFT JOIN children c ON
(p.parent_id = c.parent_id);
+-----------+---------------+-----------+-----------+--------+
| parent_id | name          | child_id  | parent_id | name   |
+-----------+---------------+-----------+-----------+--------+
|         1 | has kids      |         2 |         1 | kid #2 |
|         1 | has kids      |         1 |         1 | kid #1 |
|         2 | empty nester  |      NULL |      NULL | NULL   |
+-----------+---------------+-----------+-----------+--------+
```

It all depends on what the relational organization of your data is and what data you want your application to retrieve. For instance, say you had a database of XML feeds, each of these feeds has items, and some of those items may or may not contain enclosures (enclosures are for media). If you wanted to display all the items of a feed and used an INNER JOIN between feeds and items, and an INNER JOIN between items and enclosures, the result would only contain the items with enclosures. To be able to display all the items for a feed you would need an INNER JOIN between feeds and items and a LEFT JOIN between items and enclosures.

Another type of INNER join is a table joined with itself, known as a *self-join*. The example that follows shows the table officials list of entries:

```
mysql> SELECT * from officials;
+-------------+-----------------+---------+
| official_id | name            | boss_id |
+-------------+-----------------+---------+
|           1 | American People |       0 |
|           2 | Barack Obama    |       1 |
|           3 | Joseph Biden    |       2 |
|           4 | Rahm Emanuel    |       2 |
|           5 | Ron Klain       |       3 |
|           6 | Robert Gates    |       2 |
|           7 | Jim Messina     |       4 |
+-------------+-----------------+---------+
```

As you can see, this is data that shows an organizational hierarchy of the President and some of his staff. If you wanted to see a better view of who works for each other, you can use the following INNER JOIN syntax:

```
mysql> SELECT o1.name AS name, o2.name AS boss
    -> FROM officials AS o1
    -> INNER JOIN officials AS o2
    -> ON o1.boss_id = o2.official_id;
```

```
+---------------+------------------+
| name          | boss             |
+---------------+------------------+
| Barack Obama  | American People  |
| Joseph Biden  | Barack Obama     |
| Rahm Emanuel  | Barack Obama     |
| Ron Klain     | Joseph Biden     |
| Robert Gates  | Barack Obama     |
| Jim Messina   | Rahm Emanuel     |
+---------------+------------------+
```

You'll notice this required the use of aliased table and column names. This is an extremely useful query for presenting a flattened view of a normalized table.

This type of join only joins tables based on equality comparisons. The syntax is specific to MySQL, Oracle and PostgreSQL.

UNION

The SQL statement UNION is another means of combining rows. UNION combines the result sets of multiple queries. Every result set must have the same number of columns in order for a UNION to be used:

```
mysql> SELECT uid, state_id, username FROM users
    -> UNION
    -> SELECT null, state_id, state_name FROM states;
+------+----------+------------------+
| uid  | state_id | username         |
+------+----------+------------------+
|    1 |        1 | John Smith       |
|    2 |        1 | Amy Carr         |
|    4 |        1 | Gertrude Asgaard |
|    5 |        2 | Sunya Vadi       |
|    6 |        2 | Maya Vadi        |
|    7 |        3 | Haranya Kashipu  |
|    8 |        3 | Pralad Maharaj   |
|    9 |        4 | Franklin Pierce  |
|   10 |        4 | Daniel Webster   |
|   11 |        6 | Jack Kerouac     |
|   12 |        4 | Jake B. Smith    |
| NULL |        1 | Alaska           |
| NULL |        2 | Alabama          |
| NULL |        3 | NY               |
| NULL |        4 | New Hampshire    |
| NULL |        5 | Hawaii           |
+------+----------+------------------+
```

UNION in conjunction with JOIN can be very useful for producing various result sets.

Take, for instance, a table of employees that has a parent-child relationship, an emp_id and a boss_id. Viewed in its flat form, you have to mentally piece together the hierarchy of the org chart.

```
+---------+---------+--------------------+
| emp_id  | boss_id | name               |
+---------+---------+--------------------+
|       1 |       0 | Boss Hog           |
|       2 |       1 | Rosco P. Coaltrain |
|       3 |       2 | Cleetus            |
|       4 |       0 | Uncle Jesse        |
|       5 |       4 | Daisy Duke         |
|       6 |       4 | Bo Duke            |
+---------+---------+--------------------+
```

With the right query using UNIONs and JOINs, it's possible to have MySQL produce a result set that makes it a lot more obvious what the org chart is, all without having to write Perl *glue hash trickery* — where you use Perl hashes to map the results of children to the results of the parent. The example that follows shows how a query utilizing JOIN and UNION can display a hierarchical relationship:

```
mysql> SELECT org_chart FROM
    ->      (SELECT name AS org_chart FROM employees WHERE boss_id = 0
    ->      UNION
    ->      SELECT CONCAT(a.name, ' - ', b.name) FROM employees a
    ->          JOIN employees b ON (a.emp_id = b.boss_id)
    ->              WHERE a.boss_id = 0
    ->      UNION
    ->      SELECT CONCAT(a.name, ' - ', b.name, ' - ', c.name)
    ->          FROM employees a
    ->          JOIN employees b ON (a.emp_id = b.boss_id)
    ->          LEFT JOIN employees c ON (b.emp_id=c.boss_id)) foo
    -> WHERE org_chart IS NOT NULL ORDER BY 1.

+------------------------------------------+
| org_chart                                |
+------------------------------------------+
| Boss Hog                                 |
| Boss Hog - Rosco P. Coaltrain            |
| Boss Hog - Rosco P. Coaltrain - Cleetus  |
| Uncle Jesse                              |
| Uncle Jesse - Bo Duke                    |
| Uncle Jesse - Daisy Duke                 |
+------------------------------------------+
```

This query essentially combines the results of three *self* joins — where a join is performed within the same table — eliminating the NULL results, ordering by the first column, which is the only column. The result is a hierarchical display, showing the top-level bosses with their subordinates and subordinates' subordinates.

One other thing about UNION is worth mentioning: A UNION can deliver more information in a single query since it is combining result sets, thus resulting in fewer database calls.

Ultimately, a good principle to keep in mind is simply to let the database do what it's good at. So many developers who still aren't familiar with JOIN or UNION end up using Perl code to do what is simple using a JOIN statement.

The MySQL client protocol supports sending multiple queries in one request, which can also help you to avoid unnecessary database calls. More about this in Chapter 6, which discusses the DBD::mysql option `mysql_multi_statements`.

INSERT . . . SELECT

The `INSERT ... SELECT` SQL statement combines `INSERT` and `SELECT`, using the result set of a `SELECT` statement to provide data to insert for the `INSERT` statement. It has the same basic syntax as `INSERT` does, except it uses a `SELECT` SQL statement to provide the values to be inserted. So, for instance, say you have a table with the same schema definition as *users* called `users_copy`:

```
mysql> INSERT INTO users_copy SELECT * FROM users;
Query OK, 10 rows affected (0.00 sec)
Records: 10  Duplicates: 0  Warnings: 0
```

This is a very fast way of copying data from within the database. You can modify the `SELECT` statement to provide any number or specific rows to be used in the `INSERT` as well.

Updating Data

In addition to inserting data and querying data, you'll also have to update data. The `UPDATE` SQL statement is what is used to do this. The `UPDATE` statement can update one or more tables, unlike `INSERT`s which are only one table at a time. The syntax for `UPDATE` is:

```
UPDATE [LOW_PRIORITY] [IGNORE] tbl_name(s)
    SET col_name1=expr1 [, col_name2=expr2] ...
    [WHERE where_condition]
    [ORDER BY ...]
    [LIMIT row_count]
```

An example of an `UPDATE` against the *users* table can be shown in the example of where the ranking of a user with the `uid` of 9 needs to be changed:

```
mysql> UPDATE users SET ranking = 95.5 WHERE uid = 9;
Query OK, 1 row affected (0.00 sec)
Rows matched: 1  Changed: 1  Warnings: 0
```

You will notice, as with `INSERT`, the client reports information on what actions on the table were performed. In this instance, one row was matched and one row was changed. Note that MySQL only counts rows that were actually changed. If the intent was to change all the score values, simply omitting the `WHERE` clause accomplishes this:

```
mysql> UPDATE users SET ranking = 96.5;
Query OK, 10 rows affected (0.00 sec)
Rows matched: 10  Changed: 10  Warnings: 0
```

In this case, 10 rows matched, 10 rows were changed. If you take this same query and apply a `LIMIT` as well as an `ORDER BY`, it's possible to update only the first two rows:

```
mysql> UPDATE users SET ranking = 97.5 ORDER BY uid LIMIT 2;
Query OK, 2 rows affected (0.00 sec)
Rows matched: 2  Changed: 2  Warnings: 0
```

In this example, the query is using the result set limit as well as an ORDER BY to guarantee that the first two rows are changed. This example is used to show that this can be done, but it is not necessarily the best way to limit the result set that will be used by the INSERT statement. Also, this is not recommended because there is no guaranteed order for rows in a database. The main reason you would use this is when you have many identical rows in a database and you only want to update one of them, and in this case using LIMIT 1 will allow you to do this!

An update of a particular range of rows can better be accomplished by using an index range:

```
mysql> UPDATE users SET ranking = 95.5 WHERE uid <= 2;
Query OK, 2 rows affected (0.00 sec)
Rows matched: 2  Changed: 2  Warnings: 0
```

This is much more efficient since this query is using an index to determine which rows to update.

MySQL in this case knows exactly what rows to update and is not using a result set to determine this.

You can also update multiple tables using a JOIN. The tables before the update:

```
mysql> select * from users;
+-----+------------------+---------+-----+----------+
| uid | username         | ranking | age | state_id |
+-----+------------------+---------+-----+----------+
|   1 | John Smith       |   95.50 |  33 |        1 |
|   2 | Amy Carr         |   95.50 |  25 |        1 |
|   4 | Gertrude Asgaard |   96.50 |  65 |        1 |
|   5 | Sunya Vadi       |   96.50 |  30 |        2 |
|   6 | Maya Vadi        |   96.50 |  31 |        2 |
|   7 | Haranya Kashipu  |   96.50 |  99 |        3 |
|   8 | Pralad Maharaj   |   96.50 |   8 |        3 |
|   9 | Franklin Pierce  |   96.50 |  60 |        4 |
|  10 | Daniel Webster   |   96.50 |  62 |        4 |
|  11 | Jack Kerouac     |   96.50 |  40 |        6 |
+-----+------------------+---------+-----+----------+

mysql> select * from states;
+----------+---------------+
| state_id | state_name    |
+----------+---------------+
|        1 | Alaska        |
|        2 | Alabama       |
|        3 | New York      |
|        4 | New Hampshire |
|        5 | Hawaii        |
+----------+---------------+
```

Now an UPDATE is executed against both *users* and *states*, being joined by the column state_id to update any user to have an age of 20 (I wish I could do this for myself so easily!) who have state_id matching "New York" in the *states* table as well as updating the values of state_name for the state with a state_name of "New York" to "NY:"

```
mysql> UPDATE users JOIN states USING (state_id)
    ->SET age = 20, state_name = 'NY'
```

```
    ->WHERE state_name = 'New York';
Query OK, 3 rows affected (0.00 sec)
Rows matched: 3  Changed: 3  Warnings: 0
```

And, of course, the client reports the number of rows updated in both tables as three. The tables after the UPDATE:

```
mysql> select * from users;
+-----+-----------------+---------+-----+----------+
| uid | username        | ranking | age | state_id |
+-----+-----------------+---------+-----+----------+
|   1 | John Smith      |   95.50 |  33 |        1 |
|   2 | Amy Carr        |   95.50 |  25 |        1 |
|   4 | Gertrude Asgaard|   96.50 |  65 |        1 |
|   5 | Sunya Vadi      |   96.50 |  30 |        2 |
|   6 | Maya Vadi       |   96.50 |  31 |        2 |
|   7 | Haranya Kashipu |   96.50 |  20 |        3 |
|   8 | Pralad Maharaj  |   96.50 |  20 |        3 |
|   9 | Franklin Pierce |   96.50 |  60 |        4 |
|  10 | Daniel Webster  |   96.50 |  62 |        4 |
|  11 | Jack Kerouac    |   96.50 |  40 |        6 |
+-----+-----------------+---------+-----+----------+

mysql> select * from states;
+----------+---------------+
| state_id | state_name    |
+----------+---------------+
|        1 | Alaska        |
|        2 | Alabama       |
|        3 | NY            |
|        4 | New Hampshire |
|        5 | Hawaii        |
+----------+---------------+
```

Both users with the uid of 3 now have age set to 20, and state_name for "New York" is now "NY."

Deleting Data

Deleting data from a table or tables is performed using the DELETE SQL statement. Its syntax for single-table deletions is:

```
DELETE [LOW_PRIORITY] [QUICK] [IGNORE] FROM tbl_name
    [WHERE where_condition]
    [ORDER BY ...]
    [LIMIT row_count]
```

... or for multiple-table deletions:

```
DELETE [LOW_PRIORITY] [QUICK] [IGNORE]
    tbl_name[.*] [, tbl_name[.*]] ...
```

```
          FROM table_references
          [WHERE where_condition]
```

... or:

```
    DELETE [LOW_PRIORITY] [QUICK] [IGNORE]
        FROM tbl_name[.*] [, tbl_name[.*]] ...
        USING table_references
        [WHERE where_condition]
```

To delete a specific record for a given uid from the table *users*, you would execute the SQL statement:

```
    mysql> DELETE FROM users WHERE username = 'Amy Carr';
    Query OK, 1 row affected (0.00 sec)
```

As with UPDATE, you can also apply a LIMIT to your statement:

```
    mysql> DELETE FROM users LIMIT 1 WHERE username = 'Amy Carr';
    Query OK, 1 row affected (0.00 sec)
```

This is particularly useful when you have identical rows in the table and only want to delete one of them.

Just as with UPDATE, you can also apply ranges:

```
    mysql> DELETE FROM users WHERE uid > 4;
    Query OK, 7 rows affected (0.00 sec)
```

Of course, without any WHERE clause, all rows of the entire table are deleted:

```
    mysql> DELETE FROM users;
    Query OK, 10 rows affected (0.00 sec)
```

The client reports 10 rows affected; all rows in this table are deleted. (This is a query that can often cause you great grief!)

> *On way to avoid accidental deletion or updates to a table is to start the client with the* --safe-updates *option. If you use this option, you are prevented from incurring these blunders and receive an error if you try to run either an* UPDATE *or* DELETE *statement without either a* LIMIT *or* WHERE *clause.*

This brings up a point worth discussing — that is, the question of what is the fastest way to delete all rows from a table. In the previous query, DELETE FROM users, the same thing could have been achieved with truncate users:

```
    mysql> truncate users;
    Query OK, 0 rows affected (0.00 sec)
```

In this SQL statement, the client reports zero rows as having been affected. If this deletes all the rows of a table, why does it report zero rows? That's because TRUNCATE essentially drops and recreates the table rather than deleting the data by rows. Thus, TRUNCATE is a much faster way to delete all data from a table (as well as an even more efficient way to shoot yourself in the foot!).

Another point to consider when comparing DELETE FROM table versus TRUNCATE table is whether the table has an auto_increment column. Consider the following table *t1* with a column id, which is an AUTO_INCREMENT column. It has three rows:

```
mysql> select * from t1;
+----+
| id |
+----+
|  1 |
|  2 |
|  3 |
+----+
```

If the data in the table is deleted, and then reinserted:

```
mysql> DELETE FROM t1;
Query OK, 3 rows affected (0.00 sec)

mysql> INSERT INTO t1 VALUES (),(),();
Query OK, 3 rows affected (0.00 sec)
Records: 3  Duplicates: 0  Warnings: 0

mysql> select * from t1;
+----+
| id |
+----+
|  4 |
|  5 |
|  6 |
+----+
```

If you don't specify a value upon inserting into an AUTO_INCREMENT *column, the value is assigned by* AUTO_INCREMENT.

As you can see, whatever the maximum value of the column with AUTO_INCREMENT prior to the deletion of all rows was, the next row inserted will result in that column being assigned the value succeeding that previous maximum value.

TRUNCATE is one way to avoid this:

```
mysql> TRUNCATE t1;
Query OK, 0 rows affected (0.00 sec)

mysql> INSERT INTO t1 VALUES (),(),();
Query OK, 3 rows affected (0.00 sec)
Records: 3  Duplicates: 0  Warnings: 0

mysql> SELECT * FROM t1;
+----+
| id |
+----+
|  1 |
|  2 |
|  3 |
+----+
```

Another way to solve this issue is to ALTER the table to set the initial value to start from 1.

```
ALTER TABLE t1 AUTO_INCREMENT=1;
```

As with UPDATE, you can modify (delete) multiple tables in one query. Consider the following tables:

```
mysql> SELECT * FROM parent;
+-----------+--------------+
| parent_id | name         |
+-----------+--------------+
|         1 | has kids     |
|         2 | empty nester |
+-----------+--------------+

mysql> SELECT * FROM children;
+----------+-----------+--------+
| child_id | parent_id | name   |
+----------+-----------+--------+
|        1 |         1 | kid #1 |
|        2 |         1 | kid #2 |
+----------+-----------+--------+

mysql> SELECT * FROM children_of_children;
+----------+-----------+------------------+
| child_id | parent_id | name             |
+----------+-----------+------------------+
|        1 |         1 | kid #1 of kid #1 |
|        2 |         1 | kid #2 of kid #1 |
|        3 |         2 | kid #1 of kid #2 |
+----------+-----------+------------------+
```

It is possible to delete a given record from a parent so that it "cascade" deletes — meaning that when a particular row is deleted on the *parent* table for a given unique key value, the rows on the *children* tables that refer to that row (having the same value as the parent's UNIQUE key on the column with the foreign key constraint) are deleted as well. Using a DELETE statement joining each table with a column (*parent_id*) to ensure the proper relational hierarchy, you can delete an entire "family" from three tables:

```
mysql> DELETE FROM parent, children, children_of_children
    -> USING parent, children, children_of_children
    -> WHERE parent.parent_id = children.parent_id
    -> AND children.child_id = children_of_children.parent_id
    -> AND parent.parent_id = 1;
Query OK, 6 rows affected (0.00 sec)
```

After which, it can be observed that the record in the *parent* table and all its child records have been deleted:

```
mysql> SELECT * FROM parent;
+-----------+--------------+
| parent_id | name         |
+-----------+--------------+
|         2 | empty nester |
+-----------+--------------+
```

```
mysql> SELECT * FROM children;
Empty set (0.00 sec)

mysql> SELECT * FROM children_of_children;
Empty set (0.00 sec)
```

Replacing Data

MySQL also supports REPLACE, a MySQL extension to the SQL standard. REPLACE performs either an insert or an insert and delete, depending on whether the record being replaced already exists or not. If it exists, it deletes that record and then reinserts it. If it doesn't exist, it simply inserts that record.

The syntax for REPLACE is like INSERT:

```
REPLACE [LOW_PRIORITY | DELAYED]
    [INTO] tbl_name [(col_name,...)]
    {VALUES | VALUE} ({expr | DEFAULT},...),(...),...
```

Or UPDATE:

```
REPLACE [LOW_PRIORITY | DELAYED]
    [INTO] tbl_name
    SET col_name={expr | DEFAULT}, ...
```

To see the full syntax of REPLACE:

```
mysql> help REPLACE INTO;
```

To demonstrate how REPLACE works, a new user record is inserted with REPLACE because this record does not yet exist:

```
mysql> REPLACE INTO users VALUES (12, 'Jake Smith', 78, 50, 4);
Query OK, 1 row affected (0.00 sec)
```

Note in this example, MySQL indicates one row was affected. That is a good indicator that the row was only inserted.

The same REPLACE statement is executed again:

```
mysql> REPLACE INTO users VALUES (12, 'Jake Smith', 78, 50, 4);
Query OK, 2 rows affected (0.00 sec)
```

In this example, MySQL indicates two rows were affected. This is because the row was first deleted (one row effected) and then reinserted (one more row affected) for a total of two rows affected. Also notice that despite this being the same data, it is still replaced. This is something to consider when developing applications. REPLACE may be convenient, but it's not the most efficient method.

The next example shows an alternate syntax used for REPLACE that resembles UPDATE, except you cannot specify a WHERE clause to update the record only if the data being replaced is different than what is already existing.

```
mysql> REPLACE INTO users
    -> SET age = 50, uid = 12, ranking = 77, state_id = 5, username = 'Jake Smith';
Query OK, 2 rows affected (0.00 sec)
```

Another caveat with REPLACE can be seen in the following statement:

```
mysql> REPLACE INTO users SET age = 50, uid = 12;
Query OK, 2 rows affected (0.00 sec)
```

```
mysql> SELECT * FROM users WHERE uid = 12;
+-----+----------+---------+-----+----------+
| uid | username | ranking | age | state_id |
+-----+----------+---------+-----+----------+
|  12 |          |    0.00 |  50 |        0 |
+-----+----------+---------+-----+----------+
```

With this example, only age and uid were specified, and REPLACE promptly deleted the existing row and then reinserted the row — but only with the value for uid and age. This is something to keep in mind when using REPLACE. Also notice that username and state_id are set to their respective default values of an empty string and zero.

As you can see, REPLACE is convenient in simple statements, but if efficiency is needed, REPLACE may not be the best solution — particularly if you intend to replace many rows of data. The next statement, INSERT . . . ON DUPLICATE KEY UPDATE is better suited to update only if the row (or rows) has changed.

INSERT ... ON DUPLICATE KEY UPDATE

The previous section showed REPLACE, which inserts a row of data if the row doesn't yet exist, or deletes and then reinserts that row if it does exist. Instead of deleting and then reinserting the data, there is another way of "replacing" a row of data that will instead insert the data if it is a new row or update if it is already existing.

If, in the previous example, you used INSERT . . . ON DUPLICATE KEY UPDATE instead of REPLACE, the results would be different.

If the row doesn't yet exist, it is inserted:

```
mysql> INSERT INTO users VALUES (12, 'Jake Smith', 78, 50, 4)
    -> ON DUPLICATE KEY UPDATE uid=12, username='Jake Smith', ranking=78,
age=50, state_id =4 ;
Query OK, 1 row affected (0.00 sec)
```

As you can see, only one row is affected because the data with uid of 12 doesn't yet exist.

If the row already exists, but the data is not different, no update occurs, as follows:

```
mysql> INSERT INTO users VALUES (12, 'Jake Smith', 78, 50, 4)
    -> ON DUPLICATE KEY UPDATE uid=12, username='Jake Smith', ranking=78,
age=50, state_id =4 ;
Query OK, 0 rows effected (0.00 sec)
```

It then reports that zero rows have been affected.

If the data is different, then whatever column is different is modified:

```
mysql> INSERT INTO users VALUES (12, 'Jake Smith', 78, 50, 4)
    -> ON DUPLICATE KEY UPDATE uid=12, username='Jake Smith', ranking=78,
age=49, state_id =4 ;
Query OK, 2 rows affected (0.00 sec)
```

This shows two rows have been affected.

Also, another benefit of INSERT . . . ON DUPLICATE KEY UPDATE is that if not every column is listed, in this case only uid and username, only the column that has a different value is updated.

```
mysql> INSERT INTO users VALUES (12, 'Jake Smith', 78, 50, 4)
    -> ON DUPLICATE KEY UPDATE uid=12, username='Jake B. Smith';
Query OK, 2 rows affected (0.00 sec)

mysql> SELECT * FROM users WHERE uid = 12;
+-----+---------------+---------+-----+----------+
| uid | username      | ranking | age | state_id |
+-----+---------------+---------+-----+----------+
|  12 | Jake B. Smith |   78.00 | 49  |        4 |
+-----+---------------+---------+-----+----------+
```

In this case, only the username column was modified, leaving all the others alone. This example shows that the problem illustrated earlier with REPLACE isn't a problem using INSERT . . . ON DUPLICATE KEY UPDATE.

It all depends on what you need in terms of behavior. REPLACE might work fine if you don't care whether the existing row is deleted or not, and is simple enough. However, if you want the statement to exhibit more discrimination in whether it updates or inserts if it needs to, then INSERT . . . ON DUPLICATE KEY UPDATE is preferred.

Operators

MySQL supports the standard SQL operators you would expect in a database. Some examples of mathematical operations you can use with MySQL are shown in the following table:

Operation	Sample Query	Result
Basic math	SELECT ((234 * 34567) / 32) + 1;	252772.1875
Modulus	SELECT 9 % 2;	1
Boolean	SELECT !0;	1
Bit operators | (or), & and	SELECT 1 | 0; SELECT 1 & 0	1 0
Right shift	select 8 << 1;	16
Left shift	select 8 >> 1;	4

For a complete listing of all operators and their usage, run the following from the MySQL command-line client:

```
mysql> help Comparison operators;
mysql> help Logical operators;
```

See the section "Using Help" for more information on how to use MySQL's help facility.

Functions

MySQL has numerous functions to take advantage of and give the developer yet more tools and tricks to use in development. The various functions perform a variety of purposes and act on various types of data including numeric, string, date, informational, binary data, as well as provide control flow functionality.

For a complete listing of the numerous MySQL functions, you can run the following from the MySQL command-line client:

```
mysql> help Numeric Functions;
mysql> help Bit Functions;
mysql> help Date and Time Functions;
mysql> help Encryption Functions;
mysql> help Information Functions;
mysql> help Miscellaneous Functions;
mysql> help String Functions;
mysql> help Functions and Modifiers for Use with GROUP BY;
```

Also, the MySQL online manual has a comprehensive listing at http://dev.mysql.com/doc/refman/5.1/en/functions.html.

This section explains several of these functions and provides some examples to help you understand just how useful these functions can be. MySQL offers a wide variety of functions, depending on your application requirements. Here we show you some of the more common ones. The MySQL user's manual covers all of them in much more detail than we can within the scope of this book.

When you are designing and coding your application, you often try to determine whether it's better to process something in the application code or in the database. The question comes down to this: What it is that you need to do? How much complexity do you want to allow in your application code on the one hand, and do you want the database to take care of storing and retrieving data so that the application is primarily displaying that data? The answer to the second question comes down to personal preference. With MySQL functions, you are given even more ways to solve the usual problems that arise when developing web applications.

Informational Functions

Informational functions are handy tools to provide you with information about the database as well as the interaction between tables and the data you are modifying them with, as shown in the following table:

Function	Description	Example

DATABASE(), SCHEMA()	This function provides you with the name of the schema you are connected to. This is very convenient if you are like the author of this book and sometimes forget what schema you've connected to!	```mysql> SELECT DATABASE();```
		 ``` +-----------+```
		 ``
			DATABASE() |```
			 ``` +-----------+```
			 ``
				webapps |```
				 ``` +-----------+```

CURRENT_USER(), CURRENT_USER	If you've forgotten what user you are currently connected to (again, like the author is known to do), this MySQL command will tell you what user and host you are connected to.	```mysql> SELECT CURRENT_USER();```
		 ``` +-------------------+```
		 ``
			CURRENT_USER() |```
			 ``` +-------------------+```
			 ``
				webuser@localhost |```
				 ``` +-------------------+```

LAST_INSERT_ID(), LAST_INSERT_ID	This function returns the last value automatically generated and assigned to a column defined with the AUTO_INCREMENT attribute.	```mysql> INSERT INTO users (username, ranking, age, state_id) -> VALUES ('Arthur Fiedler', 99.99, 84, 9);```
		
		 ```mysql> select LAST_INSERT_ID();```
		 ``` +------------------+```
		 ``
			LAST_INSERT_ID() |```
			 ``` +------------------+```
			 ``
				12 |```
				 ``` +------------------+```

For more information on informational functions, simply run:

```
mysql> help Information Functions;
```

Aggregate Functions

There are aggregate functions in MySQL that you can use to print out common statistics about data.

Aggregate Function	Description
MIN()	Returns the minimum value of a column in a result set or expression
MAX()	Returns the maximum value of a column in a result set or expression
AVG()	Returns the average value of a column in a result set or expression
SUM()	Returns the sum of all values of a column in a result set or expression
COUNT()	Returns the count of rows of a column or columns in a result set

Aggregate Function	Description
COUNT DISTINCT	Returns a count of the number of different non-NULL values
GROUP_CONCAT()	Returns a comma-separated string of the concatenated non-NULL values from a group or NULL if there are no non-NULL values
STDDEV() or STDDEV_POP()	Returns the population standard deviation of a column in a result set or expression
VARIANCE()	Returns the population standard variance of a column in a result set or expression

For example, if you wanted to see the minimum, average, maximum, sum, and standard deviation and variable for the ages of all users:

```
mysql> SELECT MIN(age), AVG(age), MAX(age), SUM(age), STDDEV(age),
    -> VARIANCE(age) FROM users\G
*********************** 1. row ***********************
      MIN(age): 20
      AVG(age): 40.5000
      MAX(age): 65
      SUM(age): 486
   STDDEV(age): 15.6605
VARIANCE(age): 245.2500
```

Or, if you wanted to count the number of users with the age greater than 40:

```
mysql> SELECT COUNT(*) FROM users WHERE age > 40;
+----------+
| COUNT(*) |
+----------+
|        3 |
+----------+
```

You have a very useful modifier for GROUP BY, ROLLUP, which in addition to the grouping and summation of ages per state, also shows you the total sum of ages for all states!

```
mysql> SELECT SUM(age) AS age_total, state_name
    -> FROM users
    -> JOIN states
    -> USING (state_id)
    -> GROUP BY state_name WITH ROLLUP;
+-----------+---------------+
| age_total | state_name    |
+-----------+---------------+
|        61 | Alabama       |
|       123 | Alaska        |
|       122 | New Hampshire |
|        40 | NY            |
|       346 | NULL          |
+-----------+---------------+
```

For more information on aggregate functions, simply run:

```
mysql> help Functions and Modifiers for Use with GROUP BY;
```

Numeric Functions

MySQL also has many numeric functions for various mathematical operations. A full listing of these functions can be found on MySQL's web site http://dev.mysql.com/doc/refman/5.1/en/numeric-functions.html. Some of these functions include geometrical conversions, numbering system conversions, logarithmic functions, as well as square root and raising a number to a power.

Here are examples of geometrical functions for sine, cosine tangent, cotangent:

```
mysql> SELECT COS(90), SIN(90), TAN(90), COT(90);
+-------------------+-------------------+-------------------+-------------------+
| COS(90)           | SIN(90)           | TAN(90)           | COT(90)           |
+-------------------+-------------------+-------------------+-------------------+
| -0.44807361612917 | 0.89399666360056  | -1.9952004122082  | -0.50120278338015 |
+-------------------+-------------------+-------------------+-------------------+
```

The function PI() generates an approximation to the number π that you can then convert from radians to degrees with the DEGREES() function.

```
mysql> SELECT DEGREES(PI()*1.5), DEGREES(PI()),
    -> DEGREES(PI()/2), DEGREES(PI()/4);
+-------------------+---------------+-----------------+-----------------+
| DEGREES(PI()*1.5) | DEGREES(PI()) | DEGREES(PI()/2) | DEGREES(PI()/4) |
+-------------------+---------------+-----------------+-----------------+
|               270 |           180 |              90 |              45 |
+-------------------+---------------+-----------------+-----------------+
```

This example shows raising a number to a power, and getting the square root of a number:

```
mysql> SELECT SQRT(4096), POWER(2,8);
+------------+------------+
| SQRT(4096) | POWER(2,8) |
+------------+------------+
|         64 |        256 |
+------------+------------+
```

And here are conversions to and from different numbering systems:

```
mysql> SELECT BIN(17), OCT(64), HEX(257), CONV('ABCDEF', 16, 10);
+---------+---------+----------+------------------------+
| BIN(17) | OCT(64) | HEX(257) | CONV('ABCDEF', 16, 10) |
+---------+---------+----------+------------------------+
| 10001   | 100     | 101      | 11259375               |
+---------+---------+----------+------------------------+
```

String Functions

MySQL has various string functions that can be found in detail in MySQL's online manual. Some of the common ones that you'll end up using are functions that you would often use in web site development, such as those that find patterns, concatenate strings, replace strings, etc.

The following example shows the use of CONCAT() and REPLACE() to achieve concatenation of three strings: username, a spacer string, and the result of replacing any occurrence of state_name having the value of "New Hampshire" with "NH."

```
mysql> SELECT CONCAT(username, ' : ', REPLACE(state_name, 'New
Hampshire', 'NH'))
    -> FROM users JOIN states USING (state_id)
    -> WHERE state_id = 4;
+------------------------------------------------------------------+
| concat(username, ' : ', replace(state_name, 'New Hampshire', 'NH')) |
+------------------------------------------------------------------+
| Franklin Pierce : NH                                             |
| Daniel Webster : NH                                              |
+------------------------------------------------------------------+
```

LENGTH() is also a very convenient function for web developers:

```
mysql> select username, length(username) from users where
length(username) > 10;
+------------------+------------------+
| username         | length(username) |
+------------------+------------------+
| Daniel Webster   |               14 |
| Franklin Pierce  |               15 |
| Gertrude Asgaard |               16 |
| Haranya Kashipu  |               15 |
| Jack Kerouac     |               12 |
| Jake B. Smith    |               13 |
| Pralad Maharaj   |               14 |
+------------------+------------------+
```

You can also use functions in INSERT and UPDATE statements, where you would normally have an actual value being changed. For instance, if you had a table called *lengths*, you could simply use the function call in the previous SELECT statement:

```
mysql> INSERT INTO lengths SELECT uid, LENGTH(username) FROM users;
```

There are also string comparison functions: LIKE, NOT LIKE, SOUNDS LIKE (SOUNDEX()), STRCMP(), and REGEXP.

The function LIKE is a simple SQL regular expression pattern-matching function.

```
mysql> SELECT username FROM users WHERE username like 'Am%';
+----------+
| username |
+----------+
| Amy Carr |
+----------+

mysql> SELECT 'Amy' LIKE '%my';
+------------------+
| 'Amy' LIKE '%my' |
+------------------+
|                1 |
```

```
+------------------+
mysql> SELECT count(*) FROM states WHERE state_name NOT LIKE '%shire%';
+----------+
| count(*) |
+----------+
|        4 |
+----------+
```

Note for this code:

❑   1 (TRUE): Means that you have a match.

❑   0 (NULL): Means that there are no matches.

❑   LIKE: Will return NULL if either argument is NULL.

It should be noted that SQL uses the % (percent) sign for wildcard matching of one or more. For single wildcard, _ (underscore) is used.

SOUNDS LIKE is also a useful function for words that *sound* alike. This performs the same query as SOUNDEX(string1) = SOUNDEX(string2). *Soundex* is a phonetic algorithm for indexing names by sound, as pronounced in English, so these functions primarily work with English words. For a complete description of soundex, see the wiki page at http://en.wikipedia.org.wiki/Soundex.

```
mysql> select 'aimee' sounds like 'amy';
+-------------------------+
| 'aimee' sounds like 'amy' |
+-------------------------+
|                       1 |
+-------------------------+

mysql> select soundex('Jennifer') = soundex('amy');
+--------------------------------------+
| soundex('Jennifer') = soundex('amy') |
+--------------------------------------+
|                                    0 |
+--------------------------------------+
```

Another example for using soundex is to compare two words or names pronounced the same but with different spellings. In this example, the return value of sound is the same for both "Patrick" and "Patrik" since when spoken, they are pronounced the same.

```
mysql> select soundex('Patrik'), soundex("Patrick");
+-------------------+--------------------+
| soundex('Patrik') | soundex("Patrick") |
+-------------------+--------------------+
| P362              | P362               |
+-------------------+--------------------+
```

Another way of comparing string values is to use regular expressions — a major part of life for a Perl programmer. They are available to use in MySQL as well. Pattern matching, which you are familiar with as a Perl programmer, works the pretty much same as the REGEXP function.

```
amysql> SELECT 'A road less traveled' REGEXP '.[var]ele.\s?';
+------------------------------------------------+
| 'A road less traveled' REGEXP '.[var]ele.\s?'  |
+------------------------------------------------+
|                                             1  |
+------------------------------------------------+

mysql> SELECT 'banana' REGEXP '(an){1,2}';
+----------------------------+
| 'banana' REGEXP '(an){1,2}' |
+----------------------------+
|                          1 |
+----------------------------+
```

The functions SUBSTR() — also named SUBSTRING() and STRCMP() — perform the same functionality as their C and Perl counterparts. If the two strings are the same, the value returned is 0. The return values is non-zero:

If the first string is smaller, then the result is 1; if the second string is smaller the result is -1.

```
mysql> SELECT strcmp('same', 'same');
+-----------------------+
| strcmp('same', 'same') |
+-----------------------+
|                     0 |
+-----------------------+

mysql> SELECT strcmp('same', 'different');
+----------------------------+
| strcmp('same', 'different') |
+----------------------------+
|                          1 |
+----------------------------+
```

SUBSTRING() works as you'd expect, but can take a variety of arguments:

```
mysql> SELECT SUBSTRING('foxtrot', 4);
+-----------------------+
| SUBSTRING('foxtrot', 4) |
+-----------------------+
| trot                  |
+-----------------------+

mysql> SELECT SUBSTRING('foxtrot', 2, 2);
+--------------------------+
| SUBSTRING('foxtrot', 2, 2) |
+--------------------------+
| ox                       |
+--------------------------+

mysql> SELECT SUBSTRING('foxtrot' from 3);
+----------------------------+
| SUBSTRING('foxtrot' from 3) |
```

```
+-----------------------------+
| xtrot                       |
+-----------------------------+
```

For more information on string functions, run the following:

```
mysql> help string functions;
```

Date Functions

For web developers, date functions are probably some of the most often-used database functions. Often you have to produce data from a table sorted or grouped by date, limited to a time frame, and then produce a date format that is more web-server friendly or compatible with the operating system time format. Whatever type of date operation you need, MySQL has a date function that most likely fulfills that requirement.

For the full listing of date functions, run the following:

```
mysql> help date and time functions;
```

You can also find documentation covering date and time functions on MySQL's developer web site at `http://dev.mysql.com/doc/refman/5.1/en/date-and-time-functions.html`.

This section covers the ones that we find useful in web development.

The function `NOW()` is probably one of the most-used functions. The convenient thing about it is that you can, in turn, pass it to other functions, as shown in this example:

```
mysql> SELECT NOW(), DAY(NOW()), WEEK(NOW()), MONTH(NOW()),
QUARTER(NOW()),
    -> YEAR(NOW()), DATE(NOW()), TIME(NOW()), TO_DAYS(NOW()),
WEEKOFYEAR(NOW())\G
*************************** 1. row ***************************
             NOW(): 2008-07-08 21:28:22
        DAY(NOW()): 8
       WEEK(NOW()): 27
      MONTH(NOW()): 7
    QUARTER(NOW()): 3
       YEAR(NOW()): 2008
       DATE(NOW()): 2008-07-08
       TIME(NOW()): 21:28:22
    TO_DAYS(NOW()): 733596
 WEEKOFYEAR(NOW()): 28
```

`NOW()` provides the current time and date of the database. To make it so you have one source of determining what time it is on your server and to ensure you don't have to worry if there's a time zone difference between your database and operating system, use `NOW()`. Also, you'll see that `NOW()` is the argument to various date functions in this SQL statement. Each one of these functions converts the value of now into a different representation of the current time. You can begin to imagine what applications could use this type of data!

UNIX_TIMESTAMP() is also another useful function that is often used as such:

```
mysql> SELECT UNIX_TIMESTAMP();
+------------------+
| UNIX_TIMESTAMP() |
+------------------+
|       1215567280 |
+------------------+
```

For example, UNIX_TIMESTAMP() returns the number of seconds since "Bridge Over Troubled Water" was song of the year and you drove your VW Bus to Half Moon Bay (1970 January 01).

You can also convert back from UNIX_TIMESTAMP:

```
mysql> SELECT FROM_UNIXTIME(UNIX_TIMESTAMP());
+---------------------------------+
| FROM_UNIXTIME(UNIX_TIMESTAMP()) |
+---------------------------------+
| 2008-07-08 21:47:58             |
+---------------------------------+
```

And thus produce the same value that NOW() would provide.

There are also data arithmetic functions such as DATE_ADD() and DATE_SUB():

```
mysql> SELECT NOW(), DATE_ADD(NOW(), INTERVAL 2 DAY),
    -> DATE_ADD('2007-07-01 12:00:00' ,
INTERVAL 1 WEEK),DATE_SUB(NOW(), INTERVAL 38 YEAR)\G
*************************** 1. row ***************************
                                        NOW(): 2008-07-08 21:58:25
              DATE_ADD(NOW(), INTERVAL 2 DAY): 2008-07-10 21:58:25
DATE_ADD('2007-07-01 12:00:00' , INTERVAL 1 WEEK): 2007-07-08 12:00:00
             DATE_SUB(NOW(), INTERVAL 38 YEAR): 1970-07-08 21:58:25
```

In this example, you can see how you can obtain the time and date of the some interval specified added to or subtracted from a date time value provided either explicitly or from the output of NOW().

You could also use functions like DATE_ADD() and DATE_SUB() to obtain records from a table within or before a given period of time. In this example, there is a table *items* which stores items of an XML feed, each having its own created date. This query is run in order to obtain a count of items that are older than four weeks:

```
mysql> SELECT COUNT(*) FROM items WHERE created < DATE_SUB(NOW(),
INTERVAL 4 WEEK);
+----------+
| count(*) |
+----------+
|   322180 |
+----------+
```

You might also want to use date functions to insert data that is older than a certain date from a source table to either a queue for deletions or even a historical table. In this example, items older than four weeks are inserted into a table that stores ids of the items that will later be deleted.

```
mysql> INSERT INTO items_to_delete
    -> SELECT item_id FROM items
    -> WHERE created < DATE_SUB(NOW(), INTERVAL 4 WEEK);
Query OK, 322180 rows affected (3.94 sec)
Records: 322180  Duplicates: 0  Warnings: 0
```

Another commonly used date function is DATE_FORMAT(). This is a formatting function that allows you to specify exactly how you want a date printed out. Its usage is:

```
DATE_FORMAT(date, format)
```

Depending on the formatting characters you choose as well as any other text in the format string, you can have the date printed any way you want:

```
mysql> select date_format(now(), '%Y, %M the %D');
+-----------------------------------+
| date_format(now(), '%Y, %M the %D') |
+-----------------------------------+
| 2008, July the 8th                |
+-----------------------------------+
```

For a more complete listing on how to use DATE_FORMAT, you can run the following:

```
mysql> help date_format;
```

... or visit the MySQL user manual page: http://dev.mysql.com/doc/refman/5.1/en /date-and-time-functions.html#function_date-format.

For a listing of all date functions, run:

```
mysql> help
```

Date and Time Functions; Control Flow Functions

Control flow functions allow you to write conditional SQL statements and the building blocks for writing useful triggers, functions, and stored procedures. The control flow functions are CASE, IF, IFNULL() and NULLIF().

Values in MySQL conditional expressions are interpreted the following way:

❑   0 is false.

❑   NULL is NULL (but in most cases can be regarded as false).

❑   1 (or any integer value <> 0) is regarded as TRUE.

The function CASE works just like the *case operator*, just as you have in other programming languages. The syntax for using CASE is essentially:

```
CASE value WHEN [compare_value] THEN result [WHEN [compare_value] THEN
result ...] [ELSE result] END

or

CASE WHEN [condition] THEN result [WHEN [condition] THEN result ...]
[ELSE result] END
```

A usage example is as follows:

```
mysql> SELECT CASE WHEN NOW() > DATE_ADD(NOW(), INTERVAL 1 DAY)
    -> THEN 'Later' ELSE 'Earlier' END;
+---------------------------------------------------------------------------+
| CASE WHEN NOW()> DATE_ADD(NOW(),INTERVAL 1 DAY) THEN 'Later' ELSE 'Earlier' END |
+---------------------------------------------------------------------------+
| Earlier                                                                   |
+---------------------------------------------------------------------------+

mysql> SELECT CASE WHEN NOW()> DATE_SUB(NOW(),INTERVAL 1 DAY)
    -> THEN 'Later' ELSE 'Earlier' END;
+---------------------------------------------------------------------------+
| CASE WHEN NOW()> DATE_SUB(NOW(),INTERVAL 1 DAY) THEN 'Later' ELSE 'Earlier' END |
+---------------------------------------------------------------------------+
| Later                                                                     |
+---------------------------------------------------------------------------+
```

This next example shows using CASE on a query against the *states* table from earlier examples. In this example, state_name is checked for specific values and if there is a match, the value following THEN is printed. Everything between CASE and END can then be treated as a return value in a result set and in this case is aliased with a column name of *slogan*.

```
mysql> SELECT state_name,
    ->    CASE WHEN state_name = 'Hawaii' THEN 'Aloha'
    ->         WHEN state_name = 'Alaska' THEN 'Denali'
    ->         WHEN state_name = 'Alabama' THEN 'Sweet Home'
    ->         WHEN state_name = 'New Hampshire' THEN 'Live Free or Die'
    ->         ELSE state_name END
    -> AS slogan FROM states;
+---------------+------------------+
| state_name    | slogan           |
+---------------+------------------+
| Alaska        | Denali           |
| Alabama       | Sweet Home       |
| NY            | NY               |
| New Hampshire | Live Free or Die |
| Hawaii        | Aloha            |
+---------------+------------------+
```

In this example, every state except *NY* is given a logo, *NY* defaulting to the state_name value. This example could also have been written as:

```
mysql> SELECT state_name,
    ->    CASE state_name WHEN 'Hawaii' THEN 'Aloha'
```

```
->              WHEN 'Alaska' THEN 'Denali'
->              WHEN 'Alabama' THEN 'Sweet Home'
->              WHEN 'New Hampshire' THEN 'Live Free or Die'
->              ELSE state_name END
-> AS slogan FROM states;
```

IF() is another conditional function that can be used to test a value and toggle to two possible outputs. The syntax of the IF conditional function is:

```
IF(condition, expr1, expr2)
```

As in:

```
mysql> SELECT IF(1, 'value1', 'value2');
+---------------------------+
| IF(1, 'value1', 'value2') |
+---------------------------+
| value1                    |
+---------------------------+

mysql> SELECT IF(0, 'value1', 'value2');
+---------------------------+
| IF(0, 'value1', 'value2') |
+---------------------------+
| value2                    |
+---------------------------+
```

Using IF() with other functions, you can come up with all manner of convenient statements.

```
mysql> SELECT TO_DAYS(NOW()), IF(TO_DAYS(NOW()) % 2, 'odd day',
'even day')
    -> AS `Type of Day`;
+----------------+-------------+
| TO_DAYS(NOW()) | Type of Day |
+----------------+-------------+
|         733600 | even day    |
+----------------+-------------+
```

Using Help

The section covered a portion of the total number of operators and functions available for MySQL. For a complete listing of all the various operators and functions available, in addition to MySQL's online documentation at http://dev.mysql.com/doc/, you can also use MySQL's help facility.

For a top-level listing of all the help categories available, run the following:

```
mysql> help contents;
You asked for help about help category: "Contents"
For more information, type 'help <item>', where <item>
is one of the following
categories:
    Account Management
```

```
    Administration
    Data Definition
    Data Manipulation
    Data Types
    Functions
    Functions and Modifiers for Use with GROUP BY
    Geographic Features
    Language Structure
    Storage Engines
    Stored Routines
    Table Maintenance
    Transactions
    Triggers
```

To see a listing of the top-level function and operator categories into which you can drill down deeper for more detailed information, run the following:

```
mysql> help functions;
You asked for help about help category: "Functions"
For more information, type 'help <item>', where <item>
is one of the following
topics:
    CREATE FUNCTION
    DROP FUNCTION
    PROCEDURE ANALYSE
categories:
    Bit Functions
    Comparison operators
    Control flow functions
    Date and Time Functions
    Encryption Functions
    Information Functions
    Logical operators
    Miscellaneous Functions
    Numeric Functions
    String Functions
```

To see a list of the various comparison operators that each have their own help pages:

```
mysql> help Comparison operators;
You asked for help about help category: "Comparison operators"
For more information, type 'help <item>', where <item>
is one of the following
topics:
    !=
    <
    <=
    <=>
    =
    >
    >=
    BETWEEN AND
    COALESCE
    GREATEST
```

```
IN
INTERVAL
IS
IS NULL
ISNULL
LEAST
NOT BETWEEN
NOT IN
```

The help information for the operator >= (greater than or equal) in particular is displayed by running the following:

```
mysql> help >=;
Name: '>='
Description:
Syntax:
>=

Greater than or equal:

URL: http://dev.mysql.com/doc/refman/5.0/en/comparison-operators.html

Examples:
mysql> SELECT 2 >= 2;
        -> 1
```

This is an extremely useful feature that is often overlooked but can work even when you are on a long plane trip with no Internet connectivity!

User-Defined Variables in MySQL

Just as with Perl, MySQL/SQL gives you the ability to define variables. These variables are durable during the particular connection being used. This means you can set them within a connection and refer to them in subsequent statements while using that same connection, and are freed when the connection is closed.

Using user-defined variables in MySQL is very simple. Variables are referenced as @variable, and are set in the following two ways:

```
mysql> SET @myvar = 'someval', @myothervar= 'someother val';
```

Or

```
mysql> SELECT @myvar, @myothervar;
+---------+---------------+
| @myvar  | @myothervar   |
+---------+---------------+
| someval | someother val |
+---------+---------------+
```

The = or := assignment operators can be used in SET. You can set one or more variables in one statement.

The other method to assign a variable is within any other statement not using SET, where only the :=
operator can be used, because within any other statement than SET, the = operator is treated as a comparison operator.

```
mysql> SELECT @othervar := 'otherval';
+-------------------------+
| @othervar := 'otherval' |
+-------------------------+
| otherval                |
+-------------------------+

mysql> SELECT @othervar;
+-----------+
| @othervar |
+-----------+
| otherval  |
+-----------+
```

As you can see, assignment and display happen in the first statement, and the value is verified as still
being set in the second statement.

```
mysql> SELECT @myvar := 'some new val', @myothervar := 'some other val';
+-------------------------+-------------------------------+
| @myvar := 'some new val' | @myothervar := 'some other val' |
+-------------------------+-------------------------------+
| some new val            | some other val                |
+-------------------------+-------------------------------+

mysql> SELECT @myvar, @myothervar;
+--------------+----------------+
| @myvar       | @myothervar    |
+--------------+----------------+
| some new val | some other val |
+--------------+----------------+
```

You can also set variables within data modification statements such as INSERT and UPDATE.

```
mysql> UPDATE t1 SET name = @name := 'first' WHERE id = 1;

mysql> INSERT INTO t1 (name) VALUES (@newname := 'Jim Beam');

mysql> select @name, @newname;
+-------+----------+
| @name | @newname |
+-------+----------+
| first | Jim Beam |
+-------+----------+

mysql> select * from t1;
+----+----------+
| id | name     |
+----+----------+
|  1 | first    |
```

```
|    2 | NULL      |
|    3 | third     |
|    4 | Jim Beam  |
+----+----------+
```

This makes a very convenient way of both modifying data and accessing the values you updated or inserted. You can also use variables with functions:

```
mysql> SET @a= 'Ab', @b= 'stract';

mysql> SELECT concat(@a,@b);
+---------------+
| concat(@a,@b) |
+---------------+
| Abstract      |
+---------------+
```

Another nifty usage example with user-defined variables is to use the result sets of a query to increment or sum its value:

```
mysql> select @a := @a * 33 from t1;
+---------------+
| @a := @a * 33 |
+---------------+
|            66 |
|          2178 |
|         71874 |
|       2371842 |
|      78270786 |
|    2582935938 |
|   85236885954 |
| 2812817236482 |
+---------------+
```

With user-defined variables, as with functions, you have another choice to make: whether to use your application code or database to store certain values between statements. It all depends on your development style and preference. In some cases, using user-defined variables means you can avoid a call to the database to retrieve a value that you then use in a subsequent statement, and therefore be more efficient.

MySQL Privileges

The MySQL privilege system is something that a web applications developer or database administrator should be familiar with. In the course of managing a database for web applications, you will have to be able to create and delete users as well as limit what resources the users have access to. The MySQL privilege system offers a lot of control over what database objects a user has access to and what SQL statements can be run against those objects, such as SELECT, INSERT, UPDATE, and DELETE, as well as control over creating functions, procedures, triggers, accessing system status, and administrative functions.

A MySQL user account is made up of a username and host from which that user can connect, and has a password. A MySQL account has no connection to any operating system user account. For instance,

MySQL comes installed with a *root* user as the default administrative user of the database, but the only connection between MySQL's *root* user and the operating system's *root* user is the name itself.

MySQL Access Control Privilege System

There are two stages to MySQL access control:

1. The server verifies if the given user can connect to the server.

2. If the user can connect, any statement issued by the user is checked by the server to determine if the user has privileges to execute that statement.

To connect to MySQL as a specific user with the MySQL client program *mysql*, the usage, as has been shown in previous sections, is:

```
mysql --user=username --password schemaname
```

Also, you do not have to specify a password on the command line:

```
mysql --user=username --password schemaname
```

With this last usage example, the *mysql* client program will prompt you for a password.

```
patg@hanuman:~$ mysql --user=webuser --password webapps
Enter password:
```

MySQL Global System User

The *root* user, which is the default administrative user for MySQL, has global privileges, meaning that this user has all privileges to all schemas and tables within those schemas, as well as the ability to create other users and grant those users privileges for the entire database server. By default (unless you later change permissions for this user), the *root* user, as installed, can only connect from the same host the database server has been installed on and requires no password (this can later be set to require one as well). To connect as the root user, simply specify *root* on the command line:

```
mysql -u root
```

Once connected, you can connect to any schema you need to by using the client command connect or use (both accomplish the same thing):

```
patg@hanuman:~$ mysql -u root
Welcome to the MySQL monitor.  Commands end with ; or \g.
Your MySQL connection id is 1852
Server version: 5.0.45

Type 'help;' or '\h' for help. Type '\c' to clear the buffer.

mysql> connect mysql
Reading table information for completion of table and column names
You can turn off this feature to get a quicker startup with -A
```

```
Connection id:    1853
Current database: mysql

mysql>
```

MySQL System Schema Grant Tables

The *mysql* schema is the schema in which MySQL stores its system table, and in particular those pertaining to the accounts system. The tables that exist in this schema can be displayed with the SHOW TABLES command:

```
mysql> show tables;
+---------------------------+
| Tables_in_mysql           |
+---------------------------+
| columns_priv              |
| db                        |
| func                      |
| help_category             |
| help_keyword              |
| help_relation             |
| help_topic                |
| host                      |
| proc                      |
| procs_priv                |
| tables_priv               |
| time_zone                 |
| time_zone_leap_second     |
| time_zone_name            |
| time_zone_transition      |
| time_zone_transition_type |
| user                      |
+---------------------------+
```

The various tables in the *mysql* schema can be seen in the output above.

Of these tables, *user*, *db*, *host*, *tables_priv*, *columns_priv* and *procs_priv* are the grant tables, which pertain to user privileges. These tables can be directly modified by normal SQL statements, but for the scope of this book, it is recommended that you use the GRANT and REVOKE statements to control user privileges.

If you ever want to see all the available privileges in MySQL, the statement SHOW PRIVILEGES will display all of them.

There is a certain hierarchy of scope of permission of these tables. The *user* table is the top-most grant table and is the first table checked to determine whether the user can connect to the MySQL instance (the first stage of authentication), and is essentially the global table for privileges. If you look at this table you will see entries for the default admin *root* system user as well as the user *webuser* that has been created for demonstrating examples in this book:

```
mysql> SELECT * FROM user where host='localhost' and (user='root' or
```

```
user="webuser")\G
*************************** 1. row ***************************
                    Host: localhost
                    User: root
                Password: *81F5E21E35407D884A6CD4A731AEBFB6AF209E1B
             Select_priv: Y
             Insert_priv: Y
             Update_priv: Y
             Delete_priv: Y
             Create_priv: Y
               Drop_priv: Y
             Reload_priv: Y
           Shutdown_priv: Y
            Process_priv: Y
               File_priv: Y
              Grant_priv: Y
         References_priv: Y
              Index_priv: Y
              Alter_priv: Y
            Show_db_priv: Y
              Super_priv: Y
  Create_tmp_table_priv: Y
        Lock_tables_priv: Y
            Execute_priv: Y
         Repl_slave_priv: Y
        Repl_client_priv: Y
        Create_view_priv: Y
          Show_view_priv: Y
     Create_routine_priv: Y
      Alter_routine_priv: Y
        Create_user_priv: Y
              Event_priv: Y
            Trigger_priv: Y
                ssl_type:
              ssl_cipher:
             x509_issuer:
            x509_subject:
           max_questions: 0
             max_updates: 0
         max_connections: 0
    max_user_connections: 0
*************************** 2. row ***************************
                    Host: localhost
                    User: webuser
                Password: *E8FF493478066901F07DC13F7E659283EFA30AB3
             Select_priv: N
             Insert_priv: N
             Update_priv: N
             Delete_priv: N
             Create_priv: N
               Drop_priv: N
             Reload_priv: N
           Shutdown_priv: N
            Process_priv: N
               File_priv: N
```

```
                   Grant_priv: N
              References_priv: N
                   Index_priv: N
                   Alter_priv: N
                 Show_db_priv: N
                   Super_priv: N
        Create_tmp_table_priv: N
             Lock_tables_priv: N
                 Execute_priv: N
              Repl_slave_priv: N
             Repl_client_priv: N
             Create_view_priv: N
               Show_view_priv: N
          Create_routine_priv: N
           Alter_routine_priv: N
             Create_user_priv: N
                   Event_priv: N
                 Trigger_priv: N
                     ssl_type:
                   ssl_cipher:
                  x509_issuer:
                 x509_subject:
                max_questions: 0
                  max_updates: 0
              max_connections: 0
         max_user_connections: 0

mysql> SELECT host, user FROM user WHERE user = 'webapp' OR
user = 'root';
+-------------+------+
| host        | user |
+-------------+------+
| 127.0.0.1   | root |
| localhost   | root |
| radha.local | root |
+-------------+------+
```

Each of the grant tables contains both scope and privilege columns. As shown in the output of the *user* table in the previous code, the columns *User*, *Host* and *Password* are the scope columns. The combination of User and Host is the unique combination used to determine if the given user at a specific host is allowed to connect. The password column contains the scrambled password of a given user. When authenticating, the server scrambles the password that the user has entered using the same scrambled algorithm in which the original password was stored, and compares it to the stored encrypted password in the password column. Depending on whether there is a match, the user connects. *Scrambled* here means that you cannot recover this password and that the original password cannot be deduced from the scrambled string.

The various privilege columns in *user* are the privilege names that the user is granted, each a specific database request he or she is allowed to perform. These privileges are granted or not granted depending on the value of Y or N respectively. Each of these privileges is described in more detail in the MySQL reference manual.

As you can see from the example, the global admin user *root* has three entries, each allowing root to connect from *localhost*, 127.0.0.1 and the hostname of the machine, in this case *haunuman*. These are all to allow *root* to connect from the same host the database server is running on. Notice, too, that *root* initially has an empty password, making it so a password doesn't need to be specified when connecting. Also, *root* is granted every privilege as indicated with all privilege columns being set to 'Y.' Since this entry is in *users*, which is the global privilege table, this means *root* has these privileges on all schemas and tables.

When the *webuser* user was created in Appendix A, the command issued was:

```
GRANT ALL PRIVILEGES ON webapps.* TO 'webuser'@'localhost'
IDENTIFIED BY 'mypass';
```

For the *user* table, this means that the user *webuser* was given an entry to connect and a password, but since *webuser* is not a global admin user, no other privileges at the global level were given. Because *webuser* is granted privileges to a specific schema, *webapps*, the privileges for *webuser* are granted in the table *db*, where schema-specific privileges are granted to regular users.

The table *db* controls what schemas a regular non-global user has access to. The output of the *db* table for the user *webuser* gives an idea of what exactly is meant by schema-level privileges:

```
mysql> SELECT *  FROM db WHERE user = 'webuser'\G
*************************** 1. row ***************************
                  Host: localhost
                    Db: webapps
                  User: webuser
           Select_priv: Y
           Insert_priv: Y
           Update_priv: Y
           Delete_priv: Y
           Create_priv: Y
             Drop_priv: Y
            Grant_priv: N
       References_priv: Y
            Index_priv: Y
            Alter_priv: Y
  Create_tmp_table_priv: Y
       Lock_tables_priv: Y
       Create_view_priv: Y
         Show_view_priv: Y
    Create_routine_priv: Y
     Alter_routine_priv: Y
          Execute_priv: Y
```

For the table *db*, the role columns are User, Host and DB; the various other *"priv"* columns are the privileges. These columns of course mean what username and from which host a user can connect, and to which schema that user can connect.

In the grant statement where *webuser* was created, shown previously, *webuser* was granted every privilege on the *webapps* schema, which can be seen by this output showing 'Y' as the value for all privileges, with the exclusion of the Grant_priv column. The Grant_priv column indicates the grant privilege, which merely gives the user the ability to also grant privileges to other users, and could have been given to the *webuser* user by appending to the original statement

```
WITH GRANT OPTION
```

For this book, it's not necessary for the *webuser* to have the grant privilege, but it was worth mentioning why the Grant_priv column was the only column with an N value.

The *host* table is not used in most MySQL installations. It is used to give access to the user to connect from multiple hosts and works when the value of the column Host for a given user in the *db* table is left blank. Also, this table is not modified by the GRANT or REVOKE statements.

The tables_priv table provides table-level privileges, and controls a user's privileges to a specific table. And columns_priv controls a user's privileges to specific columns of a table. The *procs_priv* table controls privilege access to stored procedures and functions.

Account Management

As stated, the tables in the last section can be modified directly or by using specific account management SQL statements. One of the purposes of this book is to give the web application developer a better understanding of how to properly manage his or her database server. Using these account management statements is preferable to direct modification of the system tables, and helps avoid shooting oneself in the foot!

CREATE USER

The statement CREATE USER is used to create a user. This creates a user with no privileges, which you can then assign to the user using the GRANT statement discussed next. CREATE USER results in the creation of a new record in the *user* system privilege table with a password and no permissions assigned. The syntax for CREATE USER is:

```
CREATE USER user [IDENTIFIED BY [PASSWORD] 'password']
```

For instance, to create a new user *webuser*, the following would be used:

```
CREATE USER webuser IDENTIFIED BY 's3kr1t';
```

DROP USER

The statement DROP USER is used to delete a user. This results in the user being deleted from the *user* system privilege table. The syntax for DROP USER is:

```
DROP USER user
```

In an example of deleting the user *webuser*, the statement would be:

```
DROP USER 'webuser'@'localhost';
```

Starting from MySQL version 5.0.2, DROP USER *drops both the user and all the user's privileges.*

SET PASSWORD

The SET PASSWORD statement is used to set a password for an existing user. As a web developer you will sometimes need to change the password of a user, and SET PASSWORD is a simple statement you use to do that. The syntax is:

```
SET PASSWORD FOR user = PASSWORD('value')
```

For example, to change the password for the *webuser* account, you would use the following statement:

```
SET PASSWORD FOR 'webuser'@'localhost' = PASSWORD('newpass');
```

GRANT

To be able to grant and revoke privileges to a user, as well as create users, the GRANT and REVOKE statements can be used.

The GRANT statement is used to grant privileges. It has a number of options to control what user and which host is allowed to connect, to which object and which privilege is being granted, connection number and frequency, as well as assigning a password to the user. GRANT also has options for SSL connections, which can be explained in more detail on MySQL's documentation web site. As seen you have seen, there are various privilege columns in each of the grant tables that correspond to each type of privilege a user is allowed or prohibited from running, either set to 'Y' or 'N' respectively. The GRANT statement is what sets each of these privileges, and the scope of that permission determines into which grant table a record specifying those privileges for that user is created. The syntax for the statement is:

```
GRANT privilege type [(column list)], ...
ON object name
TO user [IDENTIFIED BY [PASSWORD] 'password'], ...
[WITH with_option [with_option] ...]
```

The privilege type is one or more (comma separated) valid privileges as defined in the MySQL Reference Manual.

The object name could be a schema name like *webapps*, all schemas as *.*, a specific table within *webapps* listed as webapps.users, all tables in *webapps* as webapps.* or even just a table name which would give access to the table in your current active database.

WITH option can be any of the items in the following table:

Option	Description
GRANT OPTION	Gives the user the privilege to create or delete users, grant or revoke privileges
MAX_QUERIES_PER_HOUR count	Maximum number of queries per hour a user is allowed to perform
MAX_UPDATES_PER_HOUR count	Maximum number of INSERT, UPDATE, and DELETE statements a user can execute in an hour

Continued

(continued)

Option	Description
MAX_CONNECTIONS_PER_HOUR count	Maximum number of logins a user is allowed per hour
MAX_USER_CONNECTIONS count	Maximum number of simultaneous connections a user is allowed

The next example shows giving the user *fred* the permissions to connect from 192.168.1.100 to the *accounts* schema, using the password *s3kr1t*, and to perform any statement on any object in that schema.

```
GRANT ALL on accounts.* to 'fred'@'192.168.1.100' IDENTIFIED BY 's3kr1t';
```

The previous statement could have also used a netmask *to give the user* fred *the ability to connect other hosts on the 192.168.1.0 network. For instance,* 'fred'@'192.168.1.100/24' *would have made it so* fred *could connect from any host on the 192.168.1.0 network.*

The second GRANT example shows giving the user *sally* the permissions to connect to the *accounts* schema using the password *hidden* and being able to perform any statement only on the table *users* if connecting from any host from the *xyz* domain. Also worth mentioning, the user *sally* will in fact only be able to see the table *user* when issuing SHOW TABLES and only the database accounts when issuing SHOW DATABASES.

```
GRANT ALL PRIVILEGES on accounts.users to 'sally'@'%.example.com'
IDENTIFIED BY 'hidden';
```

The GRANT statement that follows granting the user *guest* the privilege to connect to the schema webapps but only to perform a select against the table *urls*. The user *guest* will only be able to see the table *urls* displayed when issuing SHOW TABLES:

```
GRANT SELECT on webapps.urls to 'guest'@'localhost'
identified by 'guest' ;
```

The final example shows granting the user *webuser* privileges to run the statements SELECT, UPDATE, DELETE, and INSERT to any table in the schema *webapps* when connecting from www1.mysite.com:

```
GRANT SELECT, UPDATE, DELETE, INSERT on webapps.* to
'webuser'@'www1.mysite.com' IDENTIFIED BY 's3kr1t';
```

The REVOKE statement does the opposite of the GRANT statement and is for removing the privileges of a user. The revoke syntax is similar to GRANT:

```
REVOKE privilege type [(column_list)], ... ON object
name FROM user [,user]...
REVOKE ALL PRIVILEGES, GRANT OPTION FROM user [, user] ...
```

privilege type is the type of privilege, such as SELECT, UPDATE, INSERT, etc. The object name can be the same as it was in GRANT — a schema name, a specific table of a schema, or just a table.

For instance, you could revoke the ability for the `webuser@www1.mysite.com` account to not be able to insert, update, or delete from any of the tables in the *webapps* schema:

```
REVOKE UPDATE, DELETE, INSERT FROM 'webuser'@'www1.mysite.com';
```

Or, if you want to have a more sweeping revocation for the user *webuser*:

```
REVOKE ALL PRIVILEGES, GRANT OPTION FROM 'webuser'@'www1.mysite.com';
```

SHOW GRANTS

It's also possible to view a user's privileges. The statement for this is SHOW GRANTS. The syntax is:

```
SHOW GRANTS [FOR user]
```

An example of the output of this statement for the *webuser* would be:

```
mysql> show grants for 'webuser'@'localhost'\G
*************************** 1. row ***************************
Grants for webuser@localhost: GRANT USAGE ON *.* TO 'webuser'@'localhost'
IDENTIFIED BY PASSWORD '*6C8989366EAF75BB670AD8EA7A7FC1176A95CEF4'
*************************** 2. row ***************************
Grants for webuser@localhost: GRANT ALL PRIVILEGES ON `webapps`.* TO
'webuser'@'localhost'
```

INFORMATION SCHEMA

You can also refer to information schema, which is chock-full of information about your MySQL instance to learn about your user privileges. You can get a list of all tables within the information schema by running the following:

```
mysql> SHOW TABLES FROM INFORMATION_SCHEMA;
```

The information schema tables (views) you would refer to are:

❑   COLUMN_PRIVILEGES: Privileges for users to given columns

❑   SCHEMA_PRIVILEGES: Privileges for users to a given schema or database

❑   TABLE_PRIVILEGES: Privileges for users to given tables

❑   USER_PRIVILEGES: Global privileges for users

The following example shows what the global privileges are for the user *webuser*:

```
mysql> connect INFORMATION_SCHEMA;
mysql> SELECT * FROM USER_PRIVILEGES WHERE GRANTEE LIKE '\'webuser\'@%';
+-----------------------+---------------+----------------+--------------+
| GRANTEE               | TABLE_CATALOG | PRIVILEGE_TYPE | IS_GRANTABLE |
+-----------------------+---------------+----------------+--------------+
| 'webuser'@'localhost' | NULL          | USAGE          | NO           |
+-----------------------+---------------+----------------+--------------+
```

The next example shows what schema tables the user *webuser* has access to for the schema *webapp*:

```
mysql> SELECT * FROM SCHEMA_PRIVILEGES
    -> WHERE GRANTEE LIKE '\'webuser\'@%' AND TABLE_SCHEMA= 'webapp';
+-----------------------+---------------+---------------+-----------------+----------------+
| GRANTEE               | TABLE_CATALOG | TABLE_SCHEMA  | PRIVILEGE_TYPE  | IS_GRANTABLE   |
+-----------------------+---------------+---------------+-----------------+----------------+
| 'webuser'@'localhost' | NULL          | webapp        | SELECT          | NO             |
| 'webuser'@'localhost' | NULL          | webapp        | INSERT          | NO             |
| 'webuser'@'localhost' | NULL          | webapp        | UPDATE          | NO             |
| 'webuser'@'localhost' | NULL          | webapp        | DELETE          | NO             |
| 'webuser'@'localhost' | NULL          | webapp        | CREATE          | NO             |
| 'webuser'@'localhost' | NULL          | webapp        | DROP            | NO             |
| 'webuser'@'localhost' | NULL          | webapp        | REFERENCES      | NO             |
| 'webuser'@'localhost' | NULL          | webapp        | INDEX           | NO             |
| 'webuser'@'localhost' | NULL          | webapp        | ALTER           | NO             |
| 'webuser'@'localhost' | NULL          | webapp        | CREATE          |                |
TEMPORARY TABLES | NO               |
| 'webuser'@'localhost' | NULL          | webapp        | LOCK TABLES     | NO             |
| 'webuser'@'localhost' | NULL          | webapp        | EXECUTE         | NO             |
| 'webuser'@'localhost' | NULL          | webapp        | CREATE VIEW     | NO             |
| 'webuser'@'localhost' | NULL          | webapp        | SHOW VIEW       | NO             |
| 'webuser'@'localhost' | NULL          | webapp        | CREATE ROUTINE  | NO             |
| 'webuser'@'localhost' | NULL          | webapp        | ALTER ROUTINE   | NO             |
+-----------------------+---------------+---------------+-----------------+----------------+
```

Summary

You should now have a good sense of what MySQL is and what its capabilities are, and how to feel comfortable interacting with a database. If you have used databases before and are familiar with MySQL and fluent with SQL, then perhaps this chapter has served as a good refresher of MySQL, covering some features and functionality you weren't aware of or might not use every day. This chapter covered the following:

❑ A basic explanation of what MySQL is including the section on how to use MySQL. You learned about the various client and utility programs that come with MySQL, what they do, and some basic usage examples of these programs.

❑ How to work with data within MySQL — schema and table creation and modification, inserting, querying, updating, and deleting data

❑ How to use SQL joins including examples (to spark your interest and creativity) and various functions in MySQL — informational, aggregate, numeric, string, date and control flow functions.

❑ A discussion about user-defined variables and how you can use them to store temporary variables in between SQL statements on the database.

❑ The MySQL access control and privilege system. You learned what the various system grant tables are, the scope they cover, and the granularity of access control that is set through numerous privilege columns. Numerous examples demonstrated how to create, drop, and modify database users.

3

Advanced MySQL

Now that you have had the basics of MySQL explained in Chapter 2, it's time to explore some of MySQL's more advanced features. There is so much more to MySQL than just having a database you store data in and retrieve data from for your web application.

In the term *Relational Database Management System*, the words *Management* and *System* really do mean something. It's an entire system that goes beyond the simple purpose of a data store. Rather, you have a system that actually has features to manage your data, and contains the functionality that can be implemented in the database that you might otherwise have to develop into your application. The purpose of this chapter is to explore the following functions:

❑   First, we will cover the more advanced SQL features, including triggers, functions and stored procedures, views, and User Defined Functions (UDF). This section gives you an idea of how you might be able to use some of these features when developing web applications.

❑   Next, the various storage engines will be discussed. These include MyISAM, InnoDB, Archive, Federated, Tina, MySQL's internal new storage engines Maria and Falcon, as well as PBXT, a storage engine written by Primebase. Each of these storage engines has different capabilities and performance features. You'll learn when you would use each, depending on your needs.

❑   The section following storage engines covers replication, including a functional overview of replication, a description of different replication schemes, details of replication settings, and detailed instructions on how to set up replication.

SQL Features

You have seen that beyond simple SELECT, INSERT, UPDATE, and DELETE, there are also functions and user defined variables that can be used from within MySQL. There are yet more features within SQL that MySQL supports, which allow even more functionality.

This section covers these particular additional features:

❑ **Triggers:** As the name implies, these are used to write events on a table to fire into action (or trigger) other SQL statements or processes.

❑ **Functions and procedures:** These give you the ability to create reusable code defined in the database to perform often-needed tasks.

❑ **Views:** These are queries stored in a database with a given name that are accessed just like a table. You can use these to give the ability to query a single table that may in fact be made up of a join of other tables.

❑ **User-Defined Functions (UDF):** Not specifically SQL, this MySQL feature allows you to write your own functions that can do pretty much anything you need. This section will show you how to write a simple UDF.

Stored Procedures and Functions

MySQL supports stored procedures and stored functions.

A *stored procedure* is a subroutine that is stored in the database server that can be executed by client applications. Stored procedures and *functions* provide a means of having functionality that would otherwise be implemented in application code and is instead implemented at the database level. One benefit of stored procedures is that business logic can be "hidden" in the database from regular application developers that might provide access to sensitive data or algorithms; a second benefit is being able to simplify application code.

Another advantage of using stored procedures is that clients, written in different programming languages or running on different platforms that need to perform the same operations, can each use stored routines instead of having the same SQL statements repeated in their code. This also makes it easier to make modifications to those SQL statements.

Stored procedures can return a single value on one or more result sets, just like a SELECT statement would return, and are evoked using CALL. On the other hand, a function returns a single value and can be used in regular SQL statements just like any other standard function.

Why Would You (Not) Want to Use Stored Procedures or Functions?

The question then arises: Why would you want to use stored procedures or functions? Depending on your organization and application, you may wish to have the database assume handling business logic functionality instead of the web application code. This could be desirable for security purposes or to make your web applications do less, therefore requiring fewer resources on the servers where the web applications run. Again, this depends on not only your application, but also the type of hardware you have.

Another benefit is to make it so your web applications are simply calling stored procedures, thereby reducing the complexity of SQL statements in your application code to a minimum. If you design your application correctly, ensuring that your stored procedures always take the same arguments, you could make it feasible to change core functionality with your application without requiring many changes to application code. Also, since stored procedures are stored in the database, the database also ends up storing some of the business logic.

Lastly, one more benefit to using stored procedures is that if you have to execute several statements at a time, a stored procedure is a lot faster than executing the statements separately from the client as you don't have any round trips on the wire for the data.

If you have developers who are not proficient with relational databases, or don't have a database expert available, that might be one primary reason to not use stored procedures. Also, if you have a busy database, you may want to push off the business logic into your application.

Syntax

The syntax for creating a stored procedure is as follows. (Note: the square brackets [and] indicate that what is contained within is optional.)

```
CREATE
    [DEFINER = { user | CURRENT_USER }]
    PROCEDURE <name> ([parameter(s)...])
    [characteristic(s) ...] routine_body
The syntax for creating a function is:
CREATE
    [DEFINER = { user | CURRENT_USER }]
    FUNCTION sp_name ([parameter(s)...])
    RETURNS type
    [characteristic(s) ...] routine_body
```

CREATE is the first word, followed by the optional DEFINER or owner of the stored procedure or function. If DEFINER is omitted, the default is used, in this case, the current user. Again, this is how access to the stored procedure can be controlled.

Next comes PROCEDURE or FUNCTION <name>, which states that a procedure or function is being created as well as what name that procedure will have. The parameters have the format of:

```
[IN | OUT | INOUT ] <parameter name> type
```

Where:

❑   IN means that the parameter is an input argument only supplying a value to the procedure.

❑   OUT means that the parameter is only used to store the return value.

❑   INOUT means that the parameter is used for both an input argument and a return value.

❑   Parameter name is the name of the Type, which is any valid MySQL data type.

For functions, there is also the RETURNS keyword, which simply states the type of data returned.

The characteristic part of the create statement is a non-mandatory, or advisory, listing about the data the routine utilizes. These characteristics, being advisory, mean that MySQL does not enforce what statements can be defined in the routine. These characteristics are listed as:

❑   LANGUAGE SQL: SQL is the language used in the routine body. More about this is discussed in the section on external language stored procedures.

❑   DETERMINISTIC/NOT DETERMINISTIC: If deterministic, the stored procedure or function always produces the same result based on a specific set of input values and database state when called, whereas NONDETERMINISTIC will return different result sets regardless of inputs and database state when called. The default characteristic is NOT DETERMINISTIC.

One of the following characteristics can be listed:

❑   CONTAINS SQL: The default characteristic if none is defined. This simply means that the routine body does not contain any statements that read or write data. These would be statements such as SET @myval= 'foo';

❑   NO SQL: This means that there are no SQL statements in the routine body.

❑   READS SQL DATA: This means that the routine body contains SQL statements that read but do not write data (for example SELECT).

❑   MODIFIES SQL DATA: This means that the routine body contains SQL statements that could write data (for example, INSERT or DELETE).

❑   The SECURITY characteristic: SQL SECURITY {DEFINER | INVOKER}: This determines what user the stored procedure or function is executed as, whether it is the user who created the stored procedure/function or the user who is executing the stored procedure/function.

❑   COMMENT: The comment is text that can be used to write information about the stored procedure or function and display it upon running SHOW CREATE PROCEDURE or SHOW CREATE FUNCTION.

❑   Lastly, the routine body. This is a listing of SQL procedural code. Just as was shown in the section on triggers, this begins with a BEGIN statement and ends with an END statement and has one or more SQL statements in between. A really simple example would be:

```
BEGIN
  SELECT 'my first routine body';
END
```

To help you get past the syntax concepts and gain a better idea of how to actually use stored procedures and functions, as always, we find examples are the best way to illustrate ideas.

Example 1

The first example is a simple procedure that performs the same functionality as an SQL statement shown earlier in this book — one that returns the average age of users stored in the table *users*:

```
mysql> DELIMITER |

mysql> CREATE PROCEDURE user_avg(OUT average NUMERIC(5,2))
    -> BEGIN
    ->   SELECT AVG(age) INTO average FROM users;
    -> END ;
    -> |
```

As with triggers, you want to use a delimiter character other than the semicolons (;) that the routine body contains, which you want to be ignored and not interpreted in creating the stored procedure. This stored procedure has one parameter defined, OUT only, of the same data type as the age column of *users*. The routine body has the BEGIN and END keywords, with the single query to obtain the average age in the *users* table, into the parameter *average*. Also, notice in this example that none of the optional stored procedure keywords were used because they aren't needed.

To execute this stored procedure, the CALL statement is used:

```
Mysql> DELIMITER ;

mysql> CALL user_avg(@a);

mysql> SELECT @a;
+-------+
| @a    |
+-------+
| 38.70 |
+-------+
```

The user-defined variable @a is used as the OUT parameter when calling user_avg (as defined above) to assume the value that user_avg obtains from the single statement is executed.

Example 2

The first example was a good start to see how a stored procedure is created and how it can return a value when called. This same result could also have been implemented with a function. The next example shows how a function can be used for simple tasks, particularly those that return single values. The following function, is_young(), returns a simple Boolean value of 1 or 0, depending on whether the supplied user's name is a user with an age less than 40.

```
CREATE FUNCTION is_young(uname varchar(64))
  RETURNS BOOLEAN
  DETERMINISTIC
BEGIN
  DECLARE age_check DECIMAL(5,2);
  DECLARE is_young BOOLEAN;
  SELECT age INTO age_check FROM users WHERE username = uname;

  IF (age_check < 40) THEN
    SET is_young = 1;
  ELSE
    SET is_young = 0;
  END IF;

  RETURN(is_young);
END;
```

A function is much the same as a procedure, except in a function one must state what type it will return, in this example a BOOLEAN. Again, a function can only return a single value, whereas a procedure can return result sets. A single argument of uname supplies the value of the user's name as would be found in the *username* column of *users*.

Two variables are declared, age_check, which is the same type as the age column in *users*, and is_young, a BOOLEAN. This function will use age_check to store the value returned from the subsequent query that selects the value of *age* into age_check for the given user supplied by uname. The variable is_young is assigned a Boolean 1 or 0, depending on whether the value of age_check is less than 40 or not, then returned.

Executing this function is the same as any other function. In this example, SELECT is used:

```
mysql> SELECT is_young('Amy Carr');
+----------------------+
| is_young('Amy Carr') |
+----------------------+
|                    1 |
+----------------------+

mysql> SELECT is_young('Jack Kerouac');
+-------------------------+
| is_young('Jack Kerouac') |
+-------------------------+
|                       0 |
+-------------------------+
```

Example 3

The next example shows how it's possible with stored procedures to hide table details from the application or user. It's quite common in a web application to want to obtain a user's user id when given a username. This is normally done with an application function or method that calls an SQL query on the database server, taking as its argument the user's username and returning the user's user id value from the database. This can also be done using a stored procedure, hiding the details of the SELECT statement to *users*. The following stored procedure demonstrates how this can be accomplished:

```
mysql> CREATE PROCEDURE get_user_id(IN uname VARCHAR(64), OUT userid INT)
    -> BEGIN
    ->   SELECT uid INTO userid FROM users WHERE username = uname;
    -> END;
    -> |
```

In this example of get_user_id(), two parameters are defined on an input-only variable uname and an output-only variable userid. The routine body simply selects the uid for the given username supplied by uname into the variable userid. To execute get_user_id(), the CALL statement is used, passing the username in the first argument and a variable @uid as the second argument. @uid is read with a SELECT statement:

```
mysql> CALL get_user_id('Haranya Kashipu', @uid);

mysql> SELECT @uid;
+------+
| @uid |
+------+
| 7    |
+------+
```

Example 4

The next example shows how application logic can be pushed down into the database. One of the most important functionalities in a web application is to log a user into the database and create a session. This usually involves some means of checking the password — comparing what has been input into an HTML form, using the sha1() cryptographic hash function to convert it to the value that the stored password uses, and then comparing that to the stored password. If they match, that means that the login was correct, in which case a session is generated. The id is commonly returned to the browser and stored in a cookie. This can easily be done in the web application, but alternatively, this functionality can also be implemented in the database using a stored procedure.

For this next example, a *password* column of type CHAR(40) (since the value from the sha1() function will always be 40) is added to the table *users* that was used in previous examples in this book:

```
mysql> ALTER TABLE users ADD COLUMN password CHAR(40) NOT NULL DEFAULT '';
```

Also, we will create a table named *sessions* with four columns: session_id to store the integer value session id, uid to indicate the user id of the user the session belongs to, date_created to store the value of when the session was created, and session_ref, a text/blob to store anything associated with the session, including a serialized Perl object (which will be discussed later in this book).

```
CREATE TABLE sessions (
    session_id bigint(20) unsigned NOT NULL,
    uid int(3) NOT NULL default '0',
    date_created datetime default NULL,
    session_ref text,
    PRIMARY KEY  (`session_id`),
    INDEX uid (uid)
)
```

The following stored procedure shows how this can be accomplished:

```
CREATE PROCEDURE login_user(uname VARCHAR(64),pass CHAR(32))

BEGIN

    DECLARE user_exists INT(3) DEFAULT 0;
    DECLARE password_equal BOOLEAN;
    DECLARE sessionid bigint(20) DEFAULT 0;

    SELECT uid INTO user_exists FROM users WHERE username = uname;

    IF (user_exists != 0) THEN
        SELECT password = sha1(pass) INTO password_equal
          FROM users
          WHERE username = uname AND password = sha1(pass);

        IF (password_equal = 1) THEN
            SET sessionid = CONV(SUBSTRING(MD5(RAND()) FROM 1 FOR 16), 16,10);
            INSERT INTO sessions (session_id, uid, date_created)
              VALUES ( sessionid, user_exists, now());
        ELSE
            SET sessionid = 0;
        END IF;
    END IF;
    SELECT user_exists, sessionid;
END
```

This stored procedure, login_user, takes two arguments: uname and pass. These two arguments will be used to find out if a user uname exists in the *users* table (which now has a password column) and if the value of the output of the sha1() function with *pass* as its argument matches the stored password, which is already in the form sha1() converted it to when the user was created.

Three variables are declared. Just as with table definitions, variables can be defined in the same tables columns would be defined. In this case, defaults for these variables are set. The variables declared are an unsigned bigint session_id, an integer user_exists, and Boolean password_equal. The session_id will store the session id that is created if both the user exists, and if the password that is supplied matches that stored in the database. The user_exist variable is an integer that stores the uid of the user uname if that user exists, or remains 0 if not. The password_equal is another Boolean variable used to indicate if the password in pass matches the stored password for that user.

After variable declaration, the first statement sets the value of user_exists. This is to know whether the user exists in the first place. If the user_exists is not equal to 0, this indicates that the user does exist and the next statement to execute is to query if the value of pass returned from sha1() equals the value of the user's password as stored. The part of the query password = sha1(pass) evaluates to 1 or 0, which is stored in password_equal.

Next, if password_equal is 1, true, the session_id is set to the output of the statement:

```
SET sessionid = CONV(SUBSTRING(MD5(RAND()) FROM 1 FOR 16), 16, 10);
```

This statement can be broken down thus:

Generate a random number with RAND(). The output of that would be something like:

```
+-------------------+
| rand()            |
+-------------------+
| 0.13037938171102  |
+-------------------+
```

Take the output of the MD() function with this random number as the argument. The output of this would be:

```
+----------------------------------+
| md5(0.13037938171102)            |
+----------------------------------+
| 306e74fa57cc23a101cdca830ddc8186 |
+----------------------------------+
```

Take the value of the characters from 1 through 16 of this md5 string, using SUBSTR(). The output of this would be:

```
+-----------------------------------------------------+
| substr('306e74fa57cc23a101cdca830ddc8186', 1, 16)   |
+-----------------------------------------------------+
| 306e74fa57cc23a1                                    |
+-----------------------------------------------------+
```

Convert this 16-character hex md5 string to decimal using CONV(). The output is:

```
+-------------------------------+
| conv('306e74fa57cc23a1', 16, 10) |
+-------------------------------+
| 3489855379822355361           |
+-------------------------------+
```

This final integer value is the session id. The md5 could easily be used as a session id, but since there is an index on the session_id column of the table *sessions*, using an integer requires less storage and makes for a faster index. If you end up exceeding this number and having a collision, you either have a really busy web site with an amazing amount of data, or you have other problems! Also, with sessions, you don't need to keep them stored in the *sessions* table for an amount of time longer than you set the user's session cookie for, which depending on the application could be a couple months at most, and certainly won't be like saving historical user data. You could have easily used something such as uuid_short() or even uuid(), because these have their own issues such as possibly being guessable — not something you want for a session id (see http://www.ietf.org/rfc/rfc4122.txt).

Once this session id value is assigned, the next SQL statement is an INSERT statement to insert the session id for the user into the *sessions* table.

Finally, the values for session_id and user_exists are issued via a SELECT statement. The various outputs of CALL login_user() shows just how this will work.

If the user doesn't exist or the password supplied doesn't match, a 0 for user_exists and sessionid is returned. This would mean that there is no user and they entered an invalid password. The web application would have informed the non-user that their entry was invalid and they need to possibly register on the site to obtain an account and password, or that they could enter their username to have their account information emailed to them.

```
mysql> CALL login_user('Tom Jones', 'xyz');
+-------------+-----------+
| user_exists | sessionid |
+-------------+-----------+
|           0 |         0 |
+-------------+-----------+
```

If the user does exist, but they entered an invalid password, the value for user_exists is that user's uid. But the value for sessionid is NULL. This would mean that web application would have to inform the user that they entered the incorrect password and then give them the necessary interface to either reenter their password or have their account information emailed to them.

```
mysql> call login_user('Sunya Vadi', 'xyz');
+-------------+-----------+
| user_exists | sessionid |
+-------------+-----------+
|           5 |      NULL |
+-------------+-----------+
```

Finally, if the user enters the correct credentials — both a username uname that exists in the *users* table and password pass that matches their stored password, then both the user_exists and sessionid values contain the user's uid and newly created session id.

```
mysql> call login_user('Amy Carr', 's3kr1t');
+-------------+---------------------+
| user_exists | sessionid           |
+-------------+---------------------+
|           2 | 2497663145359116726 |
+-------------+---------------------+
```

Also, an entry is inserted into the *sessions* table for this user's session:

```
mysql> select * from sessions;
+---------------------+---------------------+-------------+-----+
| session_id          | date_created        | session_ref | uid |
+---------------------+---------------------+-------------+-----+
| 2497663145359116726 | 2008-07-24 22:44:36 | NULL        |   2 |
+---------------------+---------------------+-------------+-----+
```

At this point, the web application would perform tasks such as issuing a cookie to the user's browser and displaying a message or page that indicates the user successfully logged in.

Example Summary

These examples have given you a basic idea of how to write stored procedures and functions and have shown some of the basic functionality they can facilitate. In more complex stored procedures, other functions or procedures can be called. For instance, the SQL statement to check if a user exists could have been implemented as a function named get_userid, and used to assign the value user_exists.

The stored procedure statement:

```
SELECT uid INTO user_exists FROM users WHERE username = uname;
```

... could instead have been written as the following function:

```
user_exists = get_userid(uname);
```

As you can see, functions and procedures can be extremely useful for performing common tasks, hiding database schema details from application developers with an added layer of security, and making it possible to implement business logic within the database. The several examples provided serve as a brief demonstration of implementing some common tasks that just about every web application developer will have to implement at one time or another. We hope this will give you one more box of tools to consider in your development process.

Triggers

A *trigger* is a database object consisting of procedural code that is defined to activate upon an event against a row in a MySQL table. Triggers can be defined to execute upon INSERT, UPDATE, or DELETE events, either before or after the actual data of the row in the table is added, modified, or deleted.

Triggers are used to add even-driven functionality to a database, making it so that the application using the database doesn't have to implement functionality that would otherwise add complexity to the application, thereby hiding the gory details of what the database does simply on an event against the table.

Triggers can do two things: First, they can run any valid statement that could be normally run on a database, such as a query to obtain a value that, in turn, could be stored in a user-defined variable and then acted upon in yet another statement. Second, triggers can call a function, stored procedure, or even a UDF. It's entirely possible to set up a trigger that also calls external programs, using a UDF, whenever a row in a table is modified.

Creating a Trigger

The syntax for creating a trigger is quite simple:

```
CREATE
    [DEFINER = { user | CURRENT_USER }]
    TRIGGER <trigger name> <BEFORE|AFTER> <trigger event>
    ON <table name> FOR EACH ROW <statement(s)>
```

Just as with any other create statement, a trigger begins with CREATE. The value DEFINER clause determines who the trigger is created by and can be used to control whether the trigger is executed, depending on what user is issuing an SQL statement that results in a change to the table that the trigger is associated with.

Following the DEFINER clause is the trigger name, followed by a trigger time BEFORE or AFTER. This means that the trigger is executed before or after the row of data in the table that is actually acted upon. This can be very important, especially if your trigger is dependent upon the data being modified (or not) by the statement that results in the trigger being run. For instance, say you have a trigger that contains a statement when executed that depends on that data not yet being deleted. If the value of the trigger time is AFTER, your trigger most likely won't work, or will at least give interesting results!

Next, a trigger event is either DELETE, INSERT, UPDATE or REPLACE, meaning that for whatever trigger event is defined for that trigger, the execution of that type of statement on the table the trigger is associated with will result in that trigger being executed for each row affected.

ON <table name> is the next part of the statement, which is the table the trigger is associated with. FOR EACH ROW <statement(s)> is the meat of the trigger, meaning that for each row affected by whatever type of event — DELETE, UPDATE, INSERT, REPLACE, it executes that trigger statement or statements. The statements, of course, can be any valid SQL statement or function call.

First Trigger Example

To get a better idea of how idea of how a trigger works, consider the example we saw in the previous chapter: the table *users*:

```
+----------+-------------+------+-----+---------+----------------+
| Field    | Type        | Null | Key | Default | Extra          |
+----------+-------------+------+-----+---------+----------------+
| uid      | int(3)      | NO   | PRI | NULL    | auto_increment |
| username | varchar(64) | NO   | UNI |         |                |
```

```
| ranking  | decimal(5,2) | NO   | MUL | 0.00    |              |
| age      | int(3)       | NO   | MUL | 0       |              |
| state_id | int(5)       | NO   | MUL | 0       |              |
+----------+--------------+------+-----+---------+--------------+
```

What if there was another table that stored statistics, the average age and score of users, and you needed it to have an up-to-date value for these statistics? A trigger would be just the thing to use to ensure the stats table is automatically updated when there is a change to *users*.

The *stats* table would be defined as:

```
+------------+--------------+------+-----+---------+-------+
| Field      | Type         | Null | Key | Default | Extra |
+------------+--------------+------+-----+---------+-------+
| stat_name  | varchar(32)  | NO   | PRI |         |       |
| stat_value | int(5)       | NO   |     | 0       |       |
+------------+--------------+------+-----+---------+-------+
```

Also, you would want to pre-populate it with placeholder rows where the averages will be stored. The two statistics that are needed are the average age of users and the average ranking of these users. Since a value for these stats is as yet unknown, stat_value isn't specified in the field list.

```
INSERT INTO stats (stat_name) VALUES ('average age'), ('average ranking');
```

Now, the fun part is to finally create the trigger. Since this trigger executes upon an UPDATE to a row in *users*, an appropriate name might be one that includes the table name that the trigger is associated with, *users*, as well as the other table that the trigger then updates, *stats*, as well as the type of statement that causes the trigger to execute, UPDATE. So, the name chosen in this example is users_stats_update. Because this trigger will execute whenever there is a change to a column in the *users* table, in this case an update, the statements the trigger executes won't depend on data being in any state either prior to or after the table modification. So, for this example the timing will be AFTER the update.

```
mysql> delimiter |
mysql> CREATE TRIGGER users_stats_update
    -> AFTER UPDATE ON users
    -> FOR EACH ROW BEGIN
    -> UPDATE stats SET stat_value = (SELECT AVG(age) FROM users)
    -> WHERE stat_name = 'average age';
    -> UPDATE stats SET stat_value = (SELECT AVG(ranking) FROM users)
    -> WHERE stat_name = 'average ranking';
    -> END |
Query OK, 0 rows affected (0.00 sec)
```

In this example, the command was issued to change the delimiter to a bar '|' (from the default semi-colon ';'). The delimiter is the character that indicates the end of the statement in the command-line client, *mysql*, and whatever precedes the semicolon is executed. If one creates the trigger from an application or a graphical client, you don't need to set the delimiter or end the trigger with '|'.

Since this particular trigger definition contains SQL statements (UPDATE) ending with semicolons, which are required for each statement to properly run when the trigger executes but not at the time this trigger is created, we set the delimiter to a '|'. You can use anything other than the semicolon, to ensure these semicolons at the end of these statements are ignored when creating the trigger. Also, since the delimiter is set to a bar '|', the trigger creation itself requires a bar '|' to terminate the statement defining the trigger creation.

Now that the trigger has been created, any update to records in *users* will result in this trigger being executed. The *stats* table starts out with the values shown here:

```
+------------------+------------+
| stat_name        | stat_value |
+------------------+------------+
| average age      |          0 |
| average ranking  |          0 |
+------------------+------------+
```

The *users* table contains:

```
+-----+------------------+---------+-----+----------+
| uid | username         | ranking | age | state_id |
+-----+------------------+---------+-----+----------+
|   1 | John Smith       |   55.50 |  33 |        1 |
|   2 | Amy Carr         |   95.50 |  25 |        1 |
|   3 | Gertrude Asgaard |   44.33 |  65 |        1 |
|   4 | Sunya Vadi       |   88.10 |  30 |        2 |
|   5 | Maya Vadi        |   77.32 |  31 |        2 |
|   6 | Haranya Kashipu  |    1.20 |  20 |        3 |
|   7 | Pralad Maharaj   |   96.50 |  20 |        3 |
|   8 | Franklin Pierce  |   88.30 |  60 |        4 |
|   9 | Daniel Webster   |   87.33 |  62 |        4 |
|  10 | Brahmagupta      |    0.00 |  70 |        0 |
+-----+------------------+---------+-----+----------+
```

If *users* is updated, then the trigger should be executed:

```
mysql> UPDATE users SET age = 41 WHERE UID = 11;
```

Just to verify:

```
mysql> select * from stats;
```

```
+------------------+------------+
| stat_name        | stat_value |
+------------------+------------+
| average age      |         39 |
| average ranking  |         63 |
+------------------+------------+
```

And it worked! As is shown, the values for average age and average ranking now reflect the averages of those values in the *users* table.

Because you would want to have any change on *users* recalculate these statistics, you would also need to have a trigger executed on a DELETE as well as an INSERT to *users*. The timing of both INSERT and DELETE is also very important. For INSERT, you would want the average to be calculated to include the new row being inserted, so the trigger would have to run *after* the data is inserted into *users*. The first part of trigger definition for the INSERT trigger would then read as this:

```
CREATE TRIGGER users_stats_insert AFTER UPDATE ON users
```

Also notice that the name users_stats_insert is used as a trigger name to reflect the statement that causes the trigger to execute. For DELETE, you would also want the trigger to execute *after* the row being deleted is actually deleted from *users*. The first part of the trigger definition for the DELETE trigger would then read as this:

```
CREATE TRIGGER users_stats_delete AFTER DELETE ON users
```

Second Trigger Example

As a variation on the idea shown in the previous example, another way to implement summation and averaging of values using a separate *stats* table is demonstrated in the following example, though without using the functions AVG() and SUM().

In this example, only the age column of the *users* table will be of interest for the sake of the point being made — not relying on SUM() and AVG(). The *stats* table is different for this example:

```
CREATE TABLE 'stats' (
   age_sum int(8) NOT NULL default 0,
   age_avg int(8) NOT NULL default 0,
   records  int(8) NOT NULL default 0,
   primary key (age_sum)
   );
```

The idea of this table is to keep track of both the sum of all ages in *users*, age_sum, the average of those ages, age_avg, and the number of records in *users*, records, which is used to obtain the average age, age_avg, by dividing age_sum by records.

The *stats* table initially has no data, so you need one single record in the table for this example to work. You can use the following INSERT statement to populate *stats* :

```
mysql> INSERT INTO stats (age_sum, age_avg, records)
    -> SELECT SUM(age), AVG(age), COUNT(*) FROM users;
```

Verify the *stats* table:

```
mysql> select * from stats;
+---------+---------+---------+
| age_sum | age_avg | records |
+---------+---------+---------+
|     416 |      42 |      10 |
+---------+---------+---------+
```

Now you need to create the triggers. In this example, all the triggers — UPDATE, INSERT and DELETE — will be shown below. First is the UPDATE trigger: users_stats_update. It will set age_sum equal to age_sum - OLD.age + NEW.age. Then age_avg will be assigned the average age value obtained from dividing the sum of ages, age_sum, by the number of records in *users*, records.

```
DELIMITER |
CREATE TRIGGER 'users_stats_update' BEFORE  UPDATE on users
FOR EACH ROW BEGIN
  UPDATE stats SET age_sum = age_sum - OLD.age + NEW.age;
  UPDATE stats SET age_avg = age_sum / records;
END |
```

The INSERT trigger, *users_stats_insert*, will set age_sum to the current value of age_sum added to the value of the age column of the new row being inserted, NEW.age, into *users* and increment records by 1. The average age is recalculated.

```
CREATE TRIGGER 'users_stats_insert' BEFORE INSERT on users
FOR EACH ROW BEGIN
  UPDATE stats SET age_sum = age_sum + NEW.age, records = records + 1;
  UPDATE stats SET age_avg = age_sum / records;
END |
```

The DELETE trigger, *users_stats_delete*, will subtract from the current value of age_sum the value of the age column of the row being deleted from *users*, OLD.age, and decrement records by 1. The average age is recalculated.

```
CREATE TRIGGER 'users_stats_delete' BEFORE DELETE on users
FOR EACH ROW BEGIN
  UPDATE stats SET age_sum = age_sum - OLD.age, records = records - 1;
  UPDATE stats SET age_avg = age_sum / records;
END |
```

Now to verify that these new triggers work! First, delete an existing record from users. You'll notice that all the values are correctly set — the value of age_sum decreases as do the number of records, records, and if you break out a calculator you will see also the value of age_avg is correct!

```
mysql> DELETE FROM users WHERE uid = 11;

mysql> SELECT * FROM stats;
+---------+---------+---------+
| age_sum | age_avg | records |
+---------+---------+---------+
|     346 |      38 |       9 |
+---------+---------+---------+
```

Then a new user is inserted into *users*. You will see that this trigger works as well. The number for records increases by one, the value of age_sum is increased by 88 and age_avg is correctly recalculated.

```
mysql> INSERT INTO users (username, age) VALUES ('Narada Muni', '88');
mysql> SELECT * FROM stats;
+---------+---------+---------+
| age_sum | age_avg | records |
+---------+---------+---------+
|     434 |      43 |      10 |
+---------+---------+---------+
```

Also, verify the update trigger. The value being assigned this time to `age` is set to a really high value, 1,000 (Narada Muni needs a lot of time to travel through the universe! see `http://en.wikipedia.org/wiki/Narada`). You will also see that with this particular update, the value of `age_avg` changes quite a bit because of the large value for age being used. This really affects the overall average.

```
mysql> UPDATE users SET age = 1000 WHERE username = 'Narada Muni';

mysql> SELECT * FROM stats;
+---------+---------+---------+
| age_sum | age_avg | records |
+---------+---------+---------+
|    1346 |     135 |      10 |
+---------+---------+---------+
```

Third Trigger Example

There are other aspects of creating triggers that can be illustrated with another example, namely, that you have access to the values being modified when a trigger is executed. For INSERT obviously, there are only new values. For DELETE and UPDATE, there are both the previous, or old, values as well as the new values that the row's columns will assume.

Using `OLD.<column name>`, the previous value of the named column of the row that's being updated or deleted can be read. For obvious reasons this value is read-only. Using `NEW.<column name>`, the new value of the named column, as set by the query that initiated the trigger, can be read as well as written.

The following trigger shows just how you can use the NEW and OLD keywords. Suppose you want a trigger that records an action on one table. This trigger will update a logging table every time there is a change on a table that contains user comments — for instance, when the user edits their comment. You also would like to have a way to back up the user's previous comment if they decide they would like to revert their changes. Consider the *comments* table, with an entry:

```
mysql> SELECT * FROM comments\G
*************************** 1. row ***************************
             id: 1
            uid: 9
current_comment: The weather today is hot and humid
    old_comment:
```

And a logging table, `comment_log`:

```
+------------+-------------+------+-----+---------+-------+
| Field      | Type        | Null | Key | Default | Extra |
+------------+-------------+------+-----+---------+-------+
| id         | int(3)      | NO   | MUL |         |       |
| uid        | int(3)      | NO   | MUL |         |       |
| action     | varchar(10) | NO   | MUL |         |       |
| entry_time | datetime    | YES  |     | NULL    |       |
+------------+-------------+------+-----+---------+-------+
```

A trigger that would perform the function of inserting an entry into `comment_log` and saving the previous value of the `current_comment` into `old_comment` would be defined like this:

```
mysql> DELIMITER |
mysql> CREATE TRIGGER comments_update BEFORE UPDATE ON comments
    -> FOR EACH ROW BEGIN
    -> SET NEW.old_comment = OLD.current_comment;
    -> INSERT INTO comment_log VALUES (OLD.id, OLD.uid, 'update', now());
    -> END |
```

This trigger, `comments_update`, is created to be executed before the table itself is updated. The first action it will perform is to set `NEW.old_comment`, which is the value to be inserted into `old_comment`, to the value of `OLD.current_comment`, which is the value of `current_comment`, before it is updated. Then, a record is inserted into `comment_log` with the current value of the `id` column of comments, which is not being changed, so `OLD.id` or `NEW.id` are both the same value and either could have been used.

Now, if there is an update to the existing comment with a new comment, you hope that your trigger will perform the appropriate actions:

```
mysql> UPDATE comments
    -> SET current_comment = 'The weather today was hot, now it has cooled'
    -> WHERE id = 1 AND uid = 9;

mysql> SELECT * FROM comments\G
*************************** 1. row ***************************
             id: 1
            uid: 9
current_comment: The weather today was hot, now it has cooled
    old_comment: The weather today is hot and humid

mysql> SELECT * from comment_log;
+----+-----+--------+---------------------+
| id | uid | action | entry_time          |
+----+-----+--------+---------------------+
|  1 |   9 | update | 2008-07-20 11:25:12 |
+----+-----+--------+---------------------+
```

As we can see, this worked as advertised! This is just a simple example, but shows that using the NEW and OLD keywords can give you a lot of flexibility in what you can have a trigger do. This example could have even used some logic in the trigger definition to test the values being updated:

```
IF NEW.current_comment != OLD.current_comment THEN
    SET NEW.old_comment = OLD.current_comment;
    INSERT INTO comment_log VALUES (OLD.id, OLD.uid, 'update', now());
END IF ;
```

In this example, the value of `current_comment` is checked to see if it has changed, and if so, then two statements to back up the previous value of the `current_comment` into `old_comment` and inserting into the `comment_log` table are performed.

Another example of how this trigger can be extended would be a system where you only back up the user's current comment into `old_comment` if they haven't updated this comment more than ten times:

```
SET @max_comments = (SELECT COUNT(*) FROM comment_log
WHERE id = OLD.id
```

```
  AND uid = OLD.uid AND ACTION = 'update')  ;
  IF @max_comments <= 10 THEN
    SET NEW.old_comment = OLD.current_comment;
    INSERT INTO comment_log VALUES (OLD.id, OLD.uid, 'update', now());
  END IF ;
```

Trigger Limitations in MySQL

There are a few limitations of triggers, as implemented in MySQL, worth mentioning.

MySQL doesn't have triggers on statements yet

MySQL can only have one trigger of each type (INSERT, UPDATE, DELETE) for a table

Views

Another useful feature that MySQL supports is a view. A view is a query stored in a database with a given name that is accessed just like a table. It acts likes like a table, smells like a table, and displays like a table, but is not a real table. It can be thought of as a *virtual* table, and behind the scenes it uses a temporary table for its results. Unlike a table, however, it doesn't permanently contain the data it accesses.

The query by which the view is defined can reference one or more tables, or can contain a subset or aggregate data of the entire data set of the table or tables it references. A view, just as a procedure or function, can also be used to hide details of the underlying schema, thereby providing a layer of security, depending on how permissions of the view and its underlying tables are arranged.

For instance, you can create a view that displays *users* joined with *states:*

```
mysql> CREATE VIEW v_users AS
    -> SELECT uid, username, ranking, age, states.state_id,
    -> states.state_name FROM users JOIN states USING (state_id);
```

If this view is described, the result appears as a single table with the rows specified in the view definition:

```
mysql> DESC v_users;
```

Field	Type	Null	Key	Default	Extra
uid	int(3)	NO		0	
username	varchar(64)	NO			
ranking	decimal(5,2)	NO		0.00	
age	int(3)	NO		0	
state_id	int(3)	NO		0	
state_name	varchar(25)	NO			

And it is accessed as if it were a table:

```
mysql> SELECT * FROM v_users WHERE uid < 5;
```

uid	username	ranking	age	state_id	state_name

```
|    1 | John Smith        |   95.50 | 33 |        1 | Alaska      |
|    2 | Amy Carr          |   95.50 | 25 |        1 | Alaska      |
|    3 | Gertrude Asgaard  |   96.50 | 65 |        1 | Alaska      |
+------+-------------------+---------+----+----------+-------------+
```

As you can see, this is a convenient means of having what is essentially a single table to access data of a join of two tables. This simple example shows how a view hides the details of the SQL join statement and of the underlying tables.

Views can also be created to display summary or aggregate information as if it, too, were a table. Consider a table of XML feed items, each having a date column. The web application process feeds via feed URL constantly, parsing items from the XML of the feed and storing those tables into a table called (interestingly enough) *items*. What would be convenient to know is how many items were processed every day over the last month. If, for instance, you needed a summary page to display this information, you could rely on a view to produce this information.

```
mysql> CREATE VIEW v_items_per_day
    -> AS SELECT DISTINCT DATE(items.created) AS 'creation date`,
    -> COUNT(*) AS 'items per day'
    -> FROM items
    -> GROUP BY 'creation date' ORDER BY 'creation date`;
```

Note in the above trigger example, the GROUP BY 'creation date' ORDER BY 'creation date' *is a MySQL feature that allows you to both* SORT *and* GROUP BY *on the name of an output column.*

This view could then be queried as if it were an actual database table:

```
mysql> SELECT * FROM v_items_per_day
    -> WHERE 'creation date' > date_sub(now(), INTERVAL 1 WEEK);
+---------------+---------------+
| creation date | items per day |
+---------------+---------------+
| 2008-07-21    |         56577 |
| 2008-07-22    |         55239 |
| 2008-07-23    |         53612 |
| 2008-07-24    |         58178 |
| 2008-07-25    |        165746 |
| 2008-07-26    |         42269 |
| 2008-07-27    |         49175 |
+---------------+---------------+
```

What this gives you is the ability to have convenient tables for summary information as shown in this example. Also, if you are like the author of this book, you sometimes forget the specific syntax of SQL queries from time to time — views take care of remembering for you! As you can see, if you run the SHOW CREATE TABLE on a view, you get the view definition, which includes the query that the view is defined by:

```
mysql> show create table v_items_per_day\G
*************************** 1. row ***************************
       View: v_items_per_day
Create View: CREATE ALGORITHM=UNDEFINED DEFINER=`webapps`@`localhost`
             SQL SECURITY DEFINER VIEW 'v_items_per_day' AS select distinct
```

```
cast(`items`.`created' as date) AS 'creation date`,count(0) AS 'items per
day' from 'items' group by cast(`items`.`created' as date) order by
cast(`items`.`created' as date)
```

You will also notice that MySQL has changed the original query defining this view. This is to allow the trigger to work in future MySQL versions with more reserved words.

The other benefit of views that has been mentioned is that they provide a layer of security. A view can be used to provide a limited view of data, limiting by table, columns, etc. A good example of this is to create a view of users with limitations — such as excluding the password and age columns (yes, hide users' ages, too!) from the SQL query. The view can be of users, or for this example can in fact be run against another view: v_users:

```
mysql> CREATE VIEW v_protected_users AS
    -> SELECT uid, username, ranking, state_name FROM v_users;
```

Also, as root, create a user that has only SELECT privileges (read-only) of this view, v_protected_users:

```
mysql> grant select on webapps.v_protected_users to 'webpub'@'localhost'
    -> IDENTIFIED BY 'mypass';
```

To demonstrate how useful this is, reconnect to the database as this user, to the schema webapps. You will see that this user can only see and has access to only one object, v_protected_users.

```
mysql> SHOW TABLES;
+-------------------+
| Tables_in_webapps |
+-------------------+
| v_protected_users |
+-------------------+

mysql> select * from v_protected_users;
+-----+------------------+---------+---------------+
| uid | username         | ranking | state_name    |
+-----+------------------+---------+---------------+
|   1 | John Smith       |   95.50 | Alaska        |
|   2 | Amy Carr         |   95.50 | Alaska        |
|   3 | Gertrude Asgaard |   96.50 | Alaska        |
|   4 | Sunya Vadi       |   96.50 | Alabama       |
|   5 | Maya Vadi        |   96.50 | Alabama       |
|   6 | Haranya Kashipu  |   96.50 | NY            |
|   7 | Pralad Maharaj   |   96.50 | NY            |
|   8 | Franklin Pierce  |   96.50 | New Hampshire |
|   9 | Daniel Webster   |   96.50 | New Hampshire |
+-----+------------------+---------+---------------+
```

Even if this user knows that the other database objects exist, they cannot access them. Any SQL statements referencing anything other than v_protected_users will not be permitted.

```
mysql> SELECT * FROM users;
ERROR 1142 (42000): SELECT command denied to user 'webpub'@'localhost' for
```

```
        table 'users'
mysql> select * from v_users;
ERROR 1142 (42000): SELECT command denied to user 'webpub'@'localhost' for
        table 'v_users'
mysql> SELECT * FROM v_protected_users;
```

User Defined Functions

MySQL also has available an API for writing user-defined functions, otherwise known as a user-defined function (UDF). A UDF is a function that is written in C or C++ that can do whatever the user needs it to do. Because a UDF is written in C or C++ and uses MySQL's UDF API, it runs within the server. Therefore, it has to be designed within the confines of the MySQL server.

Like any other function, a UDF returns a single value, either a string or numeric, and is also executed the same way as other functions. With UDFs, there are many possibilities for database functionality that a web developer who feels able to work with C and C++ and become familiar with the UDF API can implement. Some UDFs, such as the memcached Functions for MySQL, as you will see later in this book, are useful enough to developers in general and are used by many people.

The first thing that you would do to develop a UDF is to decide what sort of functionality you would like to be able to use from within MySQL. It could be something as simple as a conversion function, which translates a string or number to some desired output, or something more complex that initiates some external process when run.

For instance, the author of this book wrote a UDF that took as an argument an id of a column of a queuing table, which in turn was written to a socket that a simple server read. It retrieved the row of that id and then ran external perl processes with that id. Using triggers on the queuing table that called that UDF on an INSERT event, any time a row was inserted, it resulted in a perl process handling the row just inserted. This made it possible to implement an event-driven model of acting on the queue with perl programs, as opposed to a constantly polling cron script. The benefit of this method is that the process ran only when there was an insert to the queuing table. When the web site was experiencing little activity, the perl script was not being called unnecessarily.

Writing a UDF

If you have experience writing C or C++ programs, you can write a UDF. You should become familiar with the UDF API. There are examples in the MySQL source code that show five functions. These code examples are a good way to get started. (You can find them in the directory sql/udf_example.c.) If you have a great idea that you want to implement, just cut and paste from those examples, rename, and then you should be set! Seriously, though, there is a little more to learn before you write a UDF.

Things to know about writing a UDF:

❑   It must be run on an operating system that supports dynamic loading of libraries.

❑   It must be written in C or C++.

❑   Functions return and accept a string, integer, and real values.

❑   There are simple, single-row functions as well as multiple-row aggregate functions.

105

❑   You can have MySQL coerce arguments to a specific type. For instance, you may want to always use a string as an argument, when internally the function expects an integer. You can force it to accept a string, but internally convert it to an integer (atoi).

❑   There is a standard functionality in the API that allows checking of argument types, number, as well as argument names.

UDF Required Functions

To create a UDF, some standard, basic functions must be implemented. These standard functions correspond to the name of the function as they are called in SQL. For the sake of illustration, let's assume the function name my_func. The three basic functions (the first of which, my_func(), is mandatory; the last two, optional) that would be implemented are:

❑   my_func(): This is the main function where all the real work happens. Whatever output or action your function performs — be that calculations, connections to sockets, conversions, etc. — this is where you implement it.

❑   my_func_init(): This is the first function called, and is a setup function. This is where basic structures are initialized. Anything that is used throughout the UDF that requires allocation is allocated, and checking the correctness of number and type of arguments passed and/or coercing one type to another happens here.

❑   my_func_deinit(): This function is a cleanup function. This is where you would free any memory you allocated in my_func_init().

Simple User-Defined Function Example

A practical example of a UDF is one way to see how a user-defined function works. For this example, we will look at a simple function to retrieve a web page using libcurl, a multiprotocol file transfer library. Since curl is a popular, highly portable library that can be used to write handy programs to transfer files, it makes an excellent choice for showcasing the MySQL UDF API.

Here is a simple function that retrieves a web page using the HTTP protocol. This function will be named http_get().

As mentioned before, there are three primary functions that are defined for each UDF, as well as two other functions — a callback function and a function for allocating memory. For this example, the functions are as follows:

❑   http_get_init(): This is used for pre-allocating a structure for storing the results of a web page fetch as well as for checking input arguments for type.

❑   http_get_deinit() : This is used for freeing any data allocated in either http_get_init() or http_get().

❑   http_get() : This is the actual function that performs the main operation of the UDF — to obtain a web page.

❑   my_realloc(): This is for allocating a character array for the results http_get() obtains.

❑   result_cb() : This is a callback function required for specifying a character array where the results will be stored.

When writing a UDF, it's good to set up a basic package to contain source and header files, documentation, as well as autoconf files for making the build process easy:

```
radha:curludfs patg$ ls
AUTHORS         Makefile.am    aclocal.m4    docs       utils
COPYING         Makefile.in    config        sql
ChangeLog       NEWS           configure     src
INSTALL         README         configure.ac tests
```

Even if at first not everything is fully completed or fleshed out, it's a good practice to have this structure in place to facilitate the start of a good project. The src directory contains source and header files. For this project, one header file, common.h, is created. It contains the data types, constants, etc., needed for the one or more UDF source files. This file can be included and will make it convenient for having all data types available defined. Shown below is what is included in common.h, which defines several UDF constants as well as a container structure for the results of a web page access.

```
#include <curl/curl.h>
/* Common definitions for all functions */
#define CURL_UDF_MAX_SIZE 256*256

#define VERSION_STRING "0.1\n"
#define VERSION_STRING_LENGTH 4

typedef struct st_curl_results st_curl_results;
struct st_curl_results {
  char *result;
  size_t size;
};
```

curl_udf.c is the next source file that is created. It contains all the functions for this example. When creating other UDFs, they, too, can be included in this file. It is possible to create other UDFs in separate source files, however, they require modifications to the autoconf configuration files (Makefile.am).

❑ The first function in curl_udf.c is myrealloc(). This function is for correctly allocating or reallocating a pointer to a character array (where the results of the web page access are stored).

```
static void *myrealloc(void *ptr, size_t size)
{
  /* There might be a realloc() out there that doesn't like reallocating
     NULL pointers, so we take care of it here */
  if (ptr)
    return realloc(ptr, size);
  else
    return malloc(size);
}
```

❑ Next, a callback function result_cb() is defined. This is a required function for the libcurl API to handle the results from a web page access.

```
static size_t
result_cb(void *ptr, size_t size, size_t nmemb, void *data)
{
```

```
                    size_t realsize= size * nmemb;
                    struct st_curl_results *res= (struct st_curl_results *)data;

                    res->result= (char *)myrealloc(res->result, res->size + realsize + 1);
                    if (res->result)
                    {
                      memcpy(&(res->result[res->size]), ptr, realsize);
                      res->size += realsize;
                      res->result[res->size]= 0;
                    }
                    return realsize;
                  }
```

In this particular case, result_cb() sets up a st_curl_results structure pointer to properly be allocated to the returned data from a web page access, using the previous function my_realloc.

❏   The first UDF function shown is http_get_init().

```
                  my_bool http_get_init(UDF_INIT *initid, UDF_ARGS *args, char *message)
                  {
                    st_curl_results *container;

                    if (args->arg_count != 1)
                    {
                      strncpy(message,
                              "one argument must be supplied: http_get('<url>').",
                              MYSQL_ERRMSG_SIZE);
                      return 1;
                    }

                    args->arg_type[0]= STRING_RESULT;

                    initid->max_length= CURL_UDF_MAX_SIZE;
                    container= calloc(1, sizeof(st_curl_results));

                    initid->ptr= (char *)container;

                    return 0;
                  }
```

The first thing http_get_init() does is to set up a results structure pointer. Then it checks how many arguments were passed into the UDF, which in this case must be exactly one. Also, http_get_init() hard-sets the argument type passed into the UDF to be a string type. Next, it sets the maximum length CURL_UDF_MAX_SIZE, allocates a results structure, and then sets the UDF_INIT pointer to point to this newly allocated structure, thus making it available throughout all stages of the UDF.

❏   Next comes http_get(), the primary function that performs the main task of obtaining a web page.

```
                  char *http_get(UDF_INIT *initid, UDF_ARGS *args,
                                 __attribute__ ((unused)) char *result,
                                 unsigned long *length,
                                 __attribute__ ((unused)) char *is_null,
                                 __attribute__ ((unused)) char *error)
```

```
{
  CURLcode retref;
  CURL *curl;
  st_curl_results *res= (st_curl_results *)initid->ptr;

  curl_global_init(CURL_GLOBAL_ALL);
  curl= curl_easy_init();

  res->result= NULL;
  res->size= 0;

  if (curl)
  {
    curl_easy_setopt(curl, CURLOPT_URL, args->args[0]);
    curl_easy_setopt(curl, CURLOPT_WRITEFUNCTION, result_cb);
    curl_easy_setopt(curl, CURLOPT_WRITEDATA, (void *)res);
    curl_easy_setopt(curl, CURLOPT_USERAGENT, "libcurl-agent/1.0");
    retref= curl_easy_perform(curl);
    if (retref) {
        strcpy(res->result,"");
      *length= 0;
    }
  }
  else
  {
    res->result[0]= 0;
    *length= 0;
  }
  curl_easy_cleanup(curl);
  *length= res->size;
  return ((char *) res->result);
}
```

❏   `http_get()` first defines a curl connection, then obtains the `curl_results_st` previously stored in `http_get_init()` from `initid->ptr`. Next it performs curl initialization as well as curl connection allocation. It then sets the `curl_result_st` pointer `res` members to initial values. Then it sets various options for the curl connection handle, including the argument supplied to the UDF (the URL) as the URL to access, and sets the callback function `result_cb()` as the callback function to be used and sets the `curl_results_st` structure pointer `res` as the place where the results will be stored by the callback function. Also, a user agent string identifier is set.

❏   Finally, `curl_easy_perform()` is called, which accesses the web page supplied by `args->args[0]`. If there is a result of success, `res->result` contains the web page desired. If there is a failure of any sort, either here or during the original check to see if the `curl` handle was allocated, an empty string is copied to `res->result`. Then `curl_easy_cleanup()` frees up the curl handle. The next step (very important for any UDF you write!) is to set the `length` pointer. This ensures the UDF has the proper length, matching the length of what was returned. Finally, the string in `res->result` is returned, which inevitably displays back to the user.

❏   `http_get_deinit()` is the final function for the `http_get()` UDF.

```
void http_get_deinit(UDF_INIT *initid)
{
  /* if we allocated initid->ptr, free it here */
  st_curl_results *res= (st_curl_results *)initid->ptr;
```

```
        if (res->result)
            free(res->result);
        free(res);
        return;
    }
```

The whole purpose of `http_get_deinit()` is to free any remaining allocations or perform other "cleanups" that were allocated during `http_get_init()` or `http_get()`. In `http_get_init()` a `curl_st_results` structure was allocated and the address of which was pointed to by `initid->ptr`, which is then dereferenced to a local `st_curl_results` pointer variable `res`. Also, the character array (string) member of the `curl_st_results` structure pointer `res`, `res->result` was allocated in `result_cb()` using `mymalloc()`. First `res->result` is freed, and finally `res` itself is freed, making it so all memory allocated in the other functions is freed.

To build the UDF, if using autoconf/automake configuration, the configuration step from within the top-level directory of the UDF package is:

```
./configure --with-mysql --libdir=/usr/local/mysql/lib/mysql
```

Followed by:

```
make
sudo make install
```

These steps perform what would otherwise have to be done manually, that is, first to determine what compile flags are needed, particularly for libcurl:

```
patg@dharma:~$ curl-config --cflags --libs

-lcurl -lgssapi_krb5
```

And also obtain any other flags needed to compile the UDFs. The end results are dynamically loadable libraries, which make install places in the directory specified with `-libdir`, in this case: `/usr/local/mysql/lib/mysql`. This is a directory that MySQL will be able to load the dynamic library from. To then create the function, all that needs to be run is:

```
mysql> CREATE FUNCTION http_get RETURNS STRING SONAME "curl_functions_mysql.so";
```

This makes it so MySQL is able to call this function and know where the dynamic library for this function can be found. If ever you need to see what functions are installed on MySQL, you can view the contents of the `func` table by running this query:

```
mysql> SELECT * FROM mysql.func;
+----------+-----+-------------------------+----------+
| name     | ret | dl                      | type     |
+----------+-----+-------------------------+----------+
| http_get |   0 | curl_functions_mysql.so | function |
+----------+-----+-------------------------+----------+
```

As you can see, in this instance the query shows that only one function is installed.

While writing your UDF you release a new version and you compile and run `make install` for your new function, as long as the shared library file is named the same and the function is named the same, you don't have to perform the above CREATE FUNCTION statement.

The next thing to do is to run the new UDF.

```
mysql> SELECT http_get('http://patg.net/hello.html')\G
*************************** 1. row ***************************
http_get('http://patg.net/hello.html'): <html>
  <head><title>Test Hello Page!</title></head>
  <body>
  This is a test to verify that the UDF written for MySQL, http_get(),
  works.
  </body>
</html>

1 row in set (0.03 sec)
```

It works! This test was run against a simple test page, and shows that the UDF fetches the full page. Some other sites will give this output:

```
mysql> SELECT http_get('http://www.wiley.com')\G
*************************** 1. row ***************************
http_get('http://www.wiley.com'):
<!DOCTYPE HTML PUBLIC "-//IETF//DTD HTML 2.0//EN">
<html><head>
<title>302 Found</title>
</head><body>
<h1>Found</h1>
<p>The document has moved <a href="http://www.wiley.com/WileyCDA/">here</a>.</p>
</body></html>
```

This looks as if there is some sort of failure, but this is because the UDF performs a bare-bones page access. There needs to be more functionality built into the UDF to handle redirects, and/or anything else the web server requires to display the page requested. The main idea here is to show that this can be done in the first place!

As you can see, UDFs are a great way to extend MySQL and create functionality at the database level.

Storage Engines

One of the most useful features of MySQL is that it supports several storage engines. With MySQL 5.1, we saw the emergence of a pluggable storage engine interface, which allows not only the ability to have multiple storage engines (as was the case with earlier versions), but also to develop a storage engine outside the MySQL server and be able to dynamically load that storage engine.

A storage engine is a low-level interface to the actual data storage, whether that resides on disk, in memory, or is accessed via a network connection. Because MySQL has a layer above the storage engine — the handler level, which is very generic — it is possible to easily implement storage engines. So you have a good variety of storage engines to choose from.

Commonly Used Storage Engines

There are several different storage engines commonly in use. Some are internally developed at MySQL AB. Others are developed by different vendors. This section covers the well-known storage engines.

The various internal storage engines are:

Internal Storage Engine	Description
MyISAM	MySQL's standard non-transactional storage engine. This is the default storage engine in most MySQL installations unless otherwise specified during installation or configuration. Known for being fast for reads.
InnoDB	InnoBase/Oracle's standard transactional storage engine for MySQL. This is the most commonly used storage engine for those wanting transactional support with MySQL.
Maria	Maria is a new transactional storage engine for the MySQL relational database management system. Its goal is to first make a crash-safe alternative to MyISAM (now in beta) and then a full transactional storage engine.
Falcon	Falcon is another new transactional storage engine being developed internally.
Memory/Heap	A Memory storage engine; the data for the table exists in memory. These are good for running queries on large data sets and getting good performance since the data is in memory as opposed to disk. Data for Memory tables is lost if the server restarts, though the table remains.
Merge	Merge is made of several identical (same columns and column order) MyISAM (only) tables. Useful if you have multiple tables, for instance, logging tables for a small time period. This allows you to access all of them as one table.
Federated	A Network storage engine. A table is created that references a remote table on another MySQL instance. Data resides at the remote location, and this engine produces SQL that is used to either fetch that data source or update it.
Archive	Stores data in compact (gzip) format, being very well suited for storing and retrieving large amounts of data that may not need to be accessed often.
NDB	The NDB Cluster storage engine is for supporting data clustering and high performance, high availability.
CSV	Data stored in the comma-separated value format. Excellent for being able to exchange data between MySQL and applications that use CSV, such as spreadsheets.
Blackhole	No actual data is stored. The Blackhole storage engine is used in replication setups where what's desired is not to physically store data but rather to have a means to replicate the queries against the table, so the only thing being written are the replication binary logs, reducing disk I/O.

There are also some externally developed storage engines:

External Storage Engine	Description
Primebase XT (PBXT)	Developed by Primebase, this external storage engine is ACID compliant, supporting transactions, MVCC (multi-version concurrency control), enabling reads without locking, offers row-level locking for updates, uses a log-based architecture to avoid double-writes (write-once) and supports BLOB streaming.
RitmarkFS	This storage engine allows access and manipulation of filesystem using SQL queries. RitmarkFS also supports filesystem replication and directory change tracking.
FederatedX	This is a fork of the Federated network storage engine allowing more rapid development of the Federated engine, which includes fixing bugs and adding enhancements.

Storage Engine Abilities

It's important to know in advance what each storage engine supports, depending on your database needs both for the entire schema, and each individual table, since you can use different storage engines for each table. For instance, you may have user data that you need transactional support for. In this case, you would use InnoDB as the storage engine. However, if you have a logging table that you don't need to access often, the Archive storage engine would be useful.

Using Storage Engines

Using a particular storage engine for a table is quite simple. You simply specify ENGINE=<storage engine> in the create table statement. For instance, if you wanted to create a log table called site_log that you wanted to use for logging web site actions that you decided the Archive storage engine would be suitable for, you would issue a create table specifying the engine:

```
mysql> CREATE TABLE site_log (
    -> id INT(4) NOT NULL auto_increment,
    -> ts TIMESTAMP,
    -> action VARCHAR(32) NOT NULL DEFAULT '',
    -> PRIMARY KEY (id)
    -> ) ENGINE=ARCHIVE;
```

Another important thing you need to consider first is which storage engines are available on your MySQL server. The command for this is SHOW ENGINES.

```
mysql> SHOW ENGINES\G
*************************** 1. row ***************************
      Engine: InnoDB
     Support: YES
     Comment: Supports transactions, row-level locking, and foreign keys
```

```
Transactions: YES
          XA: YES
  Savepoints: YES
*************************** 2. row ***************************
      Engine: MRG_MYISAM
     Support: YES
     Comment: Collection of identical MyISAM tables
Transactions: NO
          XA: NO
  Savepoints: NO
*************************** 3. row ***************************
      Engine: BLACKHOLE
     Support: YES
     Comment: /dev/null storage engine (anything you write to it disappears)
Transactions: NO
          XA: NO
  Savepoints: NO
*************************** 4. row ***************************
      Engine: CSV
     Support: YES
     Comment: CSV storage engine
Transactions: NO
          XA: NO
  Savepoints: NO
*************************** 5. row ***************************
      Engine: FEDERATED_ODBC
     Support: YES
     Comment: Federated ODBC MySQL storage engine
Transactions: YES
          XA: NO
  Savepoints: NO
*************************** 6. row ***************************
      Engine: FEDERATED
     Support: YES
     Comment: Federated MySQL storage engine
Transactions: NO
          XA: NO
  Savepoints: NO
*************************** 7. row ***************************
      Engine: ARCHIVE
     Support: YES
     Comment: Archive storage engine
Transactions: NO
          XA: NO
  Savepoints: NO
*************************** 8. row ***************************
      Engine: MEMORY
     Support: YES
     Comment: Hash based, stored in memory, useful for temporary tables
Transactions: NO
          XA: NO
  Savepoints: NO
*************************** 9. row ***************************
      Engine: MyISAM
     Support: DEFAULT
```

```
     Comment: Default engine as of MySQL 3.23 with great performance
Transactions: NO
          XA: NO
  Savepoints: NO
```

The output of SHOW ENGINES lists all storage engines that were either compiled into the MySQL server or were installed as a plug-in. Each row for each storage engine lists the engine name, Support, which means it's enabled (YES), not enabled (NO), or the default storage engine (DEFAULT). Of course, in order to use a storage engine it must be enabled. If you create a table using a storage engine that is not enabled, the table will be created using the default storage engine. Other fields listed are comments on what the engine is (added by the developer of the engine), whether it supports transactions, the X/Open XA standard for distributed transaction processing, and savepoints.

Once you know what storage engines are available and the *Support* column is YES for that engine, you can create a table of that type. The following subsections will describe more details about each storage engine.

MyISAM

The first storage engine that MySQL released with was ISAM, which stands for *Indexed Sequential Access Method*, a method developed by IBM and originally used in mainframes for indexing data for fast retrieval, which is what MySQL, and MyISAM have been known and valued for. MyISAM became the default storage engine for MySQL from 3.32 onward. Some features MyISAM is known for are the following:

❑ Three files on disk per each table: <tablename>.MYD data file, <tablename>.MYI index file, and the <tablename>.frm, which is the table definition file. Data files and index files usually exist in the same schema directory they are created in, but can also exist separately in different directories, apart from one another.

❑ Maximum number of indexes per table is 64; can be changed in the source and recompiled.

❑ Maximum number of columns per index is 16.

❑ Maximum index length is 1,000 bytes; can be changed in source and recompiled

❑ NULL values are allowed in indexed columns.

❑ Arbitrary length UNIQUE constraints/indexes.

❑ Supports one AUTO_INCREMENT column per table.

❑ VARCHAR data type is supported, either fixed or dynamic row length.

❑ Sum of VARCHAR and CHAR columns may be up to 64KB.

❑ Supports BLOBS and TEXT.

❑ BLOB/TEXT columns can be indexed.

❑ Columns can have different character sets.

❑ Uses underlying operating system for caching reads and writes.

❑ Supports concurrent inserts, meaning that data can be inserted into a table while the table is also being read from. Concurrent insert support reduces contention between readers and writers to a table.

❑ All data values are stored low byte first, allowing for machine and operating system independence.

❑ Numeric index values are stored high byte first for better index compression.

❑ Supports large files (63-bit length).

Creating a MyISAM Table

The following example shows how to create a MyISAM table:

```
mysql> USE webapps;

mysql> CREATE TABLE t1 (
    -> id INT(3) NOT NULL AUTO_INCREMENT,
    -> name VARCHAR(32) NOT NULL DEFAULT '',
    -> PRIMARY KEY (id)) ENGINE=MyISAM;
```

For most installations of MySQL, MyISAM is the default storage engine and you don't even have to specify the engine type. As Appendix A shows you, the Windows installation wizard even gives the choice of MyISAM or InnoDB as the default storage engine. Of course, from the previous example showing SHOW STORAGE ENGINES, whatever engine has the value of DEFAULT for the column Supported is the default engine. Not specifying the engine type will result in the creation of a table with that type.

MyISAM Under the Hood

If you look in the data directory, where MySQL stores its various data files (specified in my.cnf), you will see directories for each schema.

```
root@hanuman:/var/lib/mysql# ls -l
total 12
drwxr-xr-x 2 mysql root  4096 2008-02-18 12:15 mysql
drwx------ 2 mysql mysql 4096 2008-08-01 15:29 test
drwx------ 2 mysql mysql 4096 2008-08-08 08:49 webapps
```

If you enter the directory for the webapps schema, you will see the newly created table's files:

```
root@hanuman:/var/lib/foo# cd webapps/

root@hanuman:/var/lib/foo/webapps# ls -l t1*
-rw-rw---- 1 mysql mysql 8586 2008-08-08 08:49 t1.frm
-rw-rw---- 1 mysql mysql    0 2008-08-08 08:49 t1.MYD
-rw-rw---- 1 mysql mysql 1024 2008-08-08 08:49 t1.MYI
```

As previously mentioned, there are three different files for each MyISAM table:

❑ t1.frm is the definition file.

❑ t1.MYD is where the data is stored.

❑ t1.MYI is the index file.

If you were to insert some data into t1:

```
mysql> INSERT INTO t1 (name) VALUES ('first'), ('second');
```

If you run the command strings against the data file, you'll see it actually has the values just inserted.

```
root@hanuman:/var/lib/mysql/webapps# strings t1.MYD
first
second
```

Only the name column's values are printed because the *id* column is an indexed column and its values, as well as a pointer to the data in the data file, are stored in t1.MYI. They are not readable since they are binary.

Reading directly from the MYD file of a MySQL database table is not something you would normally do and is only shown to give you an idea of how data is stored with the MyISAM storage engine.

MyISAM Table Maintenance

Sometimes a table can become corrupted. For observing the condition of a MyISAM table, there is the tool myisamchk, a command line tool, or from within MySQL, you can use CHECK TABLE.

myisamchk works from the command line and can be run using the table name or the specific data file or index file. As with any MySQL client program, to obtain the list of options for myisamchk, just run it with the -help option. Most often, you'll just run it with no options on the table name, and then subsequently you'll run it with the -r option to repair any errors you find. The following shows an example of finding an error on a table and repairing it.

```
root@hanuman:/var/lib/mysql/webapps# myisamchk t1
Checking MyISAM file: t1
Data records:        2    Deleted blocks:         0
myisamchk: warning: Table is marked as crashed
- check file-size
myisamchk: warning: Size of datafile is: 49             Should be: 40
- check record delete-chain
- check key delete-chain
- check index reference
- check data record references index: 1
- check record links
myisamchk: error: Wrong bytesec: 97-108-107 at linkstart: 40
MyISAM-table 't1' is corrupted
Fix it using switch "-r" or "-o"
```

With no options, myisamchk reports errors, and it even suggests two options that can be used with myisamchk to repair the table:

```
root@hanuman:/var/lib/mysql/webapps# myisamchk -r t1
- recovering (with sort) MyISAM-table 't1'
Data records: 2
```

```
- Fixing index 1
Wrong bytesec:  97-108-107 at           40; Skipped
```

After the repair, running `myisamchk` with no options shows the table no longer has errors:

```
root@hanuman:/var/lib/mysql/webapps# myisamchk t1
Checking MyISAM file: t1
Data records:        2   Deleted blocks:        0
- check file-size
- check record delete-chain
- check key delete-chain
- check index reference
- check data record references index: 1
- check record links
```

Another option for checking a table for corruption is CHECK TABLE, and REPAIR TABLE for repairing any errors encountered. CHECK TABLE works not only for MyISAM tables, but also InnoDB, Archive, and CSV tables.

```
mysql> CHECK TABLE t1\G
*************************** 1. row ***************************
    Table: webapps.t1
       Op: check
 Msg_type: error
 Msg_text: Table './webapps/t1' is marked as crashed and should be repaired
```

If a table is found to be corrupted upon running CHECK TABLE on a MyISAM table, REPAIR TABLE should then be run. This performs identically to `myisamchk -r`:

```
mysql> REPAIR TABLE t1;
+------------+--------+----------+----------+
| Table      | Op     | Msg_type | Msg_text |
+------------+--------+----------+----------+
| webapps.t1 | repair | status   | OK       |
+------------+--------+----------+----------+
```

InnoDB

InnoDB is a storage engine developed by InnoBase Oy, a Finnish subsidiary of Oracle. It provides MySQL ACID-compliant transactions and crash recovery as well as support for foreign keys, and is the most popular transactional storage engine for use with MySQL.

InnoDB differs from MyISAM and other storage engines in several ways:

❑ It uses logs for recovery and doesn't require full rebuilds of indexes or tables if there is a crash — it simply replays its logs to recover to a point in time.

❑ Whereas other engines use separate data files and indexes, InnoDB stores data and indexes in a single tablespace file (by default, but can be configured to use separate files).

❑ It physically stores data in primary key order, supporting what is known as *clustered indexes*.

❑ It implements its own functionality for caching of reads and writes instead of relying on the operating system.

❑   It supports raw disk partitions. This means that you can have a disk partition formatted to InnoDB's internal format as opposed to the operating system's; the disk partition functions as a tablespace itself.

Some other characteristic of InnoDB are:

❑   It supports ACID-compliant transactions (See Chapter 2 for details on ACID compliance).

❑   It has row-level locking, which means that the whole table isn't locked while a write to that table is being performed, as well as a non-locking read in SELECT statements.

❑   It supports foreign keys. A *foreign key* is an index on a table (referencing table) that references a primary or unique key on another table (referenced table) and is used to ensure the data being inserted into the referencing table refers to an index that exists on the referenced table.

InnoDB Configuration

Because InnoDB has functionality to support crash recovery, transactions, etc, it has some specific configuration parameters that are set in my.cnf/my.ini, such as for specifying the tablespace directory, size, and organization, logging, memory usage, buffering, etc. For the scope of this book, some of the more common options are mentioned.

As mentioned before, InnoDB uses tablespaces for storing both its data and indexes, as shown in the following table. These are some of the more common InnoDB server parameters. There are several others that haven't been mentioned here but can be found in the MySQL reference manual at http://dev.mysql.com/doc/refman/5.1/en/innodb.html.

Tablespace	Description
innodb_data_home_dir = path	This parameter simply specifies where InnoDB tablespace files will be created, much like the previously mentioned datadir parameter. If not specified, the location defaults to the value of datadir.
innodb_data_file_path = datafile_spec1[;datafile_spec2]...	This parameter specifies one or more tablespace files — what name and size, and whether they are autoextendable (meaning they can grow as needed). The format of the data file specification can be seen in the example that follows this table.
innodb_data_file_path=tablespace1:10G;tablespace2:10G:autoextend:max:50G	In this parameter example, the first time MySQL is started, two files (each 10 gigabytes) will be created named *tablespace1* and *tablespace2*. Only one file, the last file listed, can be specified as an *autoextend* tablespace file, in this example *tablespace2*. Also, the max option enforces a maximum size limit to tablespace2 of 50 gigabytes. This is optional, of course, and simply omitting it would allow tablespace2 to grow uninhibited.

Continued

(continued)

Tablespace	Description
innodb_log_group_home = path	This parameter specifies the directory log files are found.
innodb_log_file_size = size	This parameter specifies the maximum size (for instance 10M for 10 megabytes) a log can be.
innodb_log_buffer_size = size	This parameter specifies the size of log buffers before writing to a log. For this is a setting you will need to consider whether you might be inserting large bulk inserts on a regular basis or not for performance.
innodb_flush_log_at_trx_commit = 1 or 0 innodb_lock_wait_timeout = seconds	This parameter specifies the number of seconds a transaction will wait for a row lock.
innodb_buffer_pool_size = size	This parameter specifies the data and cache size in bytes for InnoDB tables.
innodb_additional_mem_pool_size	This parameter specifies size in bytes of a buffer used to cache internal data structures and data dictionary information in memory.

Creating An InnoDB Table

Creating an InnoDB table simply requires specifying InnoDB as the engine type in when creating a table:

```
mysql> CREATE TABLE 't1' (
    ->    'id' int(3) NOT NULL auto_increment,
    ->    'name' varchar(32) NOT NULL default '',
    ->    PRIMARY KEY  (`id`)
    -> ) ENGINE=InnoDB;
```

Alternatively, you can alter a table from one table type to another in this manner:

```
mysql> ALTER TABLE users ENGINE=InnoDB;
```

The altered table will retain all of the table's data and be henceforth an InnoDB table.

InnoDB Under the Hood

If you look in the directory you specified in innodb_data_home_dir or, if not defined, datadir, you will see both the InnoDB tablespace file (or files) and the log files.

```
root@hanuman:/var/lib/mysql# ls -l ib*
-rw-rw---- 1 mysql mysql 10485760 2008-08-12 08:06 ibdata1
-rw-rw---- 1 mysql mysql  5242880 2008-08-12 08:06 ib_logfile0
-rw-rw---- 1 mysql mysql  5242880 2008-02-18 12:15 ib_logfile1
```

The first file, ibdata, is the tablespace file where any InnoDB table defined is stored. The files ib_logfile0 and ib_logfile1 are the transaction logs.

Also worth noting is that InnoDB tables, as with any other table type in MySQL, still have .frm files, found in the schema directory where they are created:

```
root@hanuman:/var/lib/mysql/webapps# ls -l users.*
-rw-rw---- 1 mysql mysql 8698 2008-08-12 07:14 users.frm
```

The Beauty of Transactions

One of the key features of InnoDB is transactions. InnoDB supports ACID-compliance transactions. Recall that *ACID* stands for *Atomicity, Consistency, Isolation, Durability*. You can develop applications that in particular have atomic operations. These types of actions would certainly include anything where money is exchanged, user information is saved, or any functionality where you want several SQL statements to happen as one operation. In short, transactions.

To use a transaction, the process is quite simple:

```
mysql> BEGIN WORK;

mysql> ... various  data modification SQL statements as well as queries

mysql> COMMIT;
```

BEGIN WORK guarantees that AUTOCOMMIT is off for this transaction, telling MySQL that any following SQL statement is part of this transaction. COMMIT says to make permanent *(Durability)* whatever statements were executed after BEGIN WORK. Alternatively, if there was a problem or some statements weren't intended to be run, ROLLBACK reverts all statements that were executed after BEGIN WORK. This brings to mind another benefit of transactions — the ability to ROLLBACK "oopses."

```
mysql> BEGIN WORK;
Query OK, 0 rows affected (0.00 sec)

mysql> SELECT COUNT(*) FROM users;
+----------+
| COUNT(*) |
+----------+
|       11 |
+----------+
1 row in set (0.00 sec)

mysql> DELETE FROM users;
Query OK, 11 rows affected (0.00 sec)
```

OK, not good. You forgot the WHERE clause. Ack! Any minute now the boss will be calling in a state of panic. (Well, he'd call about other things in a state of panic anyway.)

The next DELETE statement shows an error being produced because you added the flag --safe-updates to your my.cnf file, and instead of a frantic call from your boss, you get an error message!

```
mysql> DELETE FROM users;
ERROR 1175 (HY000): You are using safe update mode and you tried to update a
Table without a WHERE that uses a KEY column
mysql> SELECT COUNT(*) FROM users;
```

```
+----------+
| COUNT(*) |
+----------+
|        0 |
+----------+
```

You can avoid this sort of problem by using the flag --safe-updates *in the* [mysql] *client section of either your global* my.cnf/my.ini *or your own private* .my.cnf. *This wonderful option prevents you from committing "oopses" by not allowing you to perform queries like this without a* WHERE *clause.*

This verifies the direness of the situation and you might be beginning to feel a sense of despondence settling in. But wait! This was done from within a transaction, so you can roll it back!

```
mysql> ROLLBACK;
Query OK, 0 rows affected (0.03 sec)

mysql> SELECT COUNT(*) FROM users;
+----------+
| COUNT(*) |
+----------+
|       11 |
+----------+
```

You breathe a sigh of relief and then feel jubilation. Then your boss calls you panicking about the search engine returning results he doesn't agree with.

From this example, you can see that within the "oops" transaction, after all rows were deleted, a query showed that they were in fact gone. Within the transaction they were gone, but not committed, luckily. This is the *Isolation* part of ACID compliance: Everything you do within a transaction doesn't have any effect until the transaction has been committed.

Consistency means that a transaction can't violate a database's consistency rules. If a transaction does violate a rule, it's rolled back, and the database stays consistent.

The *Atomicity* aspect of ACID is merely the fact that every action that occurs within BEGIN and COMMIT happens, or else none at all happen.

Another feature of transactions is SAVEPOINT and ROLLBACK TO SAVEPOINT. This allows you to name a transaction with an identifier. This means you can have different statement sets for each SAVEPOINT, and it is possible to be roll back to any SAVEPOINT along the way. The idea is shown here:

```
mysql> SELECT * FROM t1;
+----+--------+
| id | name   |
+----+--------+
|  1 | first  |
|  2 | second |
|  3 | three  |
|  4 | four   |
+----+--------+

mysql> BEGIN WORK;
```

```
mysql> SAVEPOINT a;

mysql> UPDATE t1 SET name = 'FIRST' WHERE id = 1;

mysql> SAVEPOINT b;

mysql> UPDATE t1 SET name = 'SECOND' WHERE id = 2;

mysql> SAVEPOINT c;

mysql> UPDATE t1 SET name = 'THIRD' WHERE id = 3;

mysql> SELECT * FROM t1;
+----+--------+
| id | name   |
+----+--------+
|  1 | FIRST  |
|  2 | SECOND |
|  3 | THIRD  |
|  4 | four   |
+----+--------+

mysql> ROLLBACK TO SAVEPOINT b;

mysql> SELECT * FROM t1;
+----+--------+
| id | name   |
+----+--------+
|  1 | FIRST  |
|  2 | second |
|  3 | third  |
|  4 | four   |
+----+--------+
```

As you can see, ROLLBACK TO SAVEPOINT reverts back to the state of t1 when SAVEPOINT b was issued, after the first update statement. Issuing a ROLLBACK would revert all of the transactions.

Archive

As a web applications developer, you might need to be able to store data such as logs or historical information that you might not need often but still must store in your database and be able to run summary queries on. The Archive storage engine is ideal for this. The Archive storage engine is an engine specifically created for organizations to have a means to store large amounts of data that they don't need to access often, while still being able to access this data occasionally. The benefit is that storing this data requires less disk space.

Some characteristics of the Archive storage engine are the following:

- ❑ It uses zlib (gzip) compression format for data storage, requiring less space.
- ❑ It does not support indexes.
- ❑ It supports INSERT and SELECT, but not UPDATE, REPLACE, or DELETE.

❑   It supports ORDER BY.

❑   It supports BLOBS and TEXT types and all other column types except spatial data types.

❑   If a SELECT statement is made on a table with BLOB or TEXT columns, if none of the BLOB columns are specified, it scans past that BLOB for increased performance.

❑   It creates an Archive table.

To create an archive table, you simply specify the engine type:

```
mysql> CREATE TABLE comment_log (
    -> id INT(3) NOT NULL,
    -> uid INT(3) NOT NULL,
    -> action VARCHAR(10) NOT NULL DEFAULT '',
    -> entry_time DATETIME DEFAULT NULL
    -> ) ENGINE=ARCHIVE;
```

Alternatively, if you have a large table you want to convert to an Archive table, you can simply ALTER that table:

```
mysql> ALTER TABLE comment_log ENGINE=ARCHIVE;
```

In some instances, an error such as this will be encountered:

```
ERROR 1069 (42000): Too many keys specified; max 0 keys allowed
```

This is because you cannot convert from a table with an engine that does support indexes to Archive, which does not support indexes. Before you could change the ENGINE type with an ALTER statement, it would be necessary to drop the indexes:

```
mysql> DROP INDEX id ON comment_log;
```

Or,

```
mysql> ALTER TABLE comment_log DROP PRIMARY KEY ;
```

Archive under the Hood

The Archive storage engine, like other engine types, has its own set of files that you can see from within the schema directory for the schema that the table was created in:

```
root@hanuman:/var/lib/mysql/webapps# ls -l comment_log*
-rw-rw---- 1 mysql mysql   19 2008-08-13 08:56 comment_log.ARM
-rw-rw---- 1 mysql mysql   86 2008-08-13 08:56 comment_log.ARZ
-rw-rw---- 1 mysql mysql 8660 2008-08-13 08:56 comment_log.frm
```

comment_log.ARM is the meta-data file used. comment_log.ARZ is the actual data file for *comment_log*, and is a gzip file containing the compressed data of the table in MySQL's internal binary storage format. Lastly, as with every table, there is a data definition file, comment_log.frm.

Interestingly, you can verify that comment_log.ARZ is indeed a gzip file:

```
root@hanuman:/var/lib/mysql/webapps# file comment_log.ARZ
comment_log.ARZ: gzip compressed data, from Unix
```

Archive Table Maintenance

Just as with MyISAM, there may be the rare occasion that an Archive table is corrupted.

```
mysql> CHECK TABLE comment_log;
+---------------------+-------+----------+----------+
| Table               | Op    | Msg_type | Msg_text |
+---------------------+-------+----------+----------+
| webapps.comment_log | check | error    | Corrupt  |
+---------------------+-------+----------+----------+
```

REPAIR TABLE can be used to fix the problem:

```
mysql> REPAIR TABLE comment_log;
```

The Federated Storage Engine

The Federated Storage Engine is a storage engine that instead of accessing data from a local file or tablespace, accesses data from a remote MySQL table through the MySQL client API. It essentially builds SQL statements internally, based on what the query was against the Federated table, and runs those statements on the remote MySQL table.

If the query against the Federated table is a write statement such as INSERT or UPDATE, the Federated storage engine builds a query, deriving the column names and values from internal data structures that are dependent on the fields and values of the original query. Then it executes the SQL to perform that write operation on the remote table, reporting back to the storage engine the number of rows affected.

If it's a read operation, it constructs a SELECT statement also built using internal data structures for column names, as well as WHERE clauses for ranges and indexes, and then executes that statement. After the statement is executed, the Federated storage engine retrieves the result set from the remote table and iterates over that result, converting it into the same internal format that all other storage engines use and, in turn, returning the data to the user.

A DELETE statement is similar to a SELECT statement in how the column names are built into the constructed SQL statement, as well as in building the WHERE clause. The main difference is that the operation is DELETE FROM versus SELECT, resulting in the rows specified in the SQL statement being deleted and the count of the rows affected being returned to the storage engine, which in turn decrements its total row count.

Characteristics of the Federated Storage Engine

The Federated storage engine was developed with some principles that IBM defines for their own Federated functionality, which is more or less its own standard. These basic principles are as follows:

❑ **Transparency:** The remote data sources and details thereof are not necessarily known by the user, such as how the data is stored, what the underlying schema is, and what dialect of SQL is used to retrieve information from that data source.

❑ **High degree of function:** To be able to have, as much as possible, the same functionality that is had with regular tables.

❑ **Extensibility and openness:** To adhere to a standard as defined in the ANSI SQL/MED (Management of External Data).

❑ **Autonomy of data sources:** Not affecting the remote data source, not interfering with its normal operation. This also means that the Federated storage engine cannot modify the definition of the remote data source, as in the case of statements such as ALTER and DROP TABLE not being sent to the remote data source.

❑ **Optimized performance:** Utilizing the optimizer to create the most efficient statements to run on the remote data source. Also, the long-term goal would be to have a means of delegating operations to the local server and remote server according to which is best suited for each operation.

Of course, not all of these guiding principles have been achieved, but these are certainly goals for development of the Federated storage engine that provide a roadmap of the long-term direction of Federated development.

Some of the basic characteristics of the Federated storage engine are these:

❑ When creating a Federated table, the table must have the same named columns as the remote table, and no more columns than the remote table. The remote table can have more columns than the Federated table.

❑ A query on a Federated table internally produces an entire result set from a table on a remote server, and as such, if that table contains a lot of data, all of that data will be retrieved. One way to deal with huge result sets is to define an index on a column of the Federated table, even if that column is not indexed on the remote table, and try to use any means to limit the result set. However, note that LIMIT *does not* affect the size of the result set from the remote table.

❑ The remote table must be in existence prior to creating the Federated table that references it.

❑ The Federated storage engine supports indexes insofar as the column that is defined as an index is specified in a WHERE clause in the SQL query the table generates, and that the column it specifies is an index on the remote table. This means that you could have a Federated table with an index on a column that is not an index on the remote table, which is not a problem, and in fact can be used to reduce result set size.

❑ The manual states a Federated table can reference a Federated table. This is a bad idea. Don't do it.

❑ Transactions aren't supported.

❑ Federated supports SELECT, INSERT, UPDATE, DELETE. However, ALTER TABLE cannot be used to change the remote table's definition (this would violate the very definition of a Federated table), but it can be used to modify the local Federated table's definition.

❑ DROP TABLE only drops the local Federated table.

It's worthwhile to mention that although the Federated storage engine may not support some features such as transactions as well as other enhancements, there is a fork of Federated called FederatedX, which is a more active development branch of Federated.

Creating a Federated Table

As with other storage engines, creating a Federated table involves setting ENGINE=FEDERATED. Also necessary with Federated is specifying a connection string of either a connection URL or a server name (more about Federated servers is covered in the next subsection):

```
CONNECTION=scheme://user:password@host/schema/table
```

```
CONNECTION=server

CONNECTION=server/tablename.
```

The following shows the creation of a non-Federated table on a remote data source, and then the creation of a Federated table.

The remote server is 192.168.1.118, and the schema is named *remote*:

```
mysql> CREATE TABLE 't1' (
    ->    'id' int(3) NOT NULL auto_increment,
    ->    'name' varchar(32) NOT NULL default '',
    ->    PRIMARY KEY  (`id`)
    -> );

mysql> INSERT INTO t1 (name) VALUES ('first'), ('second'), ('hello world');
```

Then on a local server, 192.168.1.100, in a schema named *federated*:

```
mysql> CREATE TABLE 't1' (
    ->    'id' int(3) NOT NULL auto_increment,
    ->    'name' varchar(32) NOT NULL default '',
    ->    PRIMARY KEY  (`id`)
    -> ) ENGINE=FEDERATED
    -> CONNECTION='mysql://feduser:feduser@192.168.1.118/remote/t1';
Query OK, 0 rows affected (0.07 sec)

mysql> SELECT * FROM t1;
+----+-------------+
| id | name        |
+----+-------------+
|  1 | first       |
|  2 | second      |
|  3 | hello world |
+----+-------------+

mysql> INSERT INTO t1 (name) VALUES ('hello federated');

mysql> SELECT * FROM t1;
+----+-----------------+
| id | name            |
+----+-----------------+
|  1 | first           |
|  2 | second          |
|  3 | hello world     |
|  4 | hello federated |
+----+-----------------+
```

Then back on the remote server:

```
mysql> SELECT * FROM t1;
+----+-----------------+
| id | name            |
```

```
+----+-----------------+
|  1 | first           |
|  2 | second          |
|  3 | hello world     |
|  4 | hello federated |
+----+-----------------+
```

This means there has been a successful Federated table creation.

Federated Servers

As you've seen in the example above, a URL-like string was specified to give the necessary information for the Federated table to be able to connect to the remote data source. In cases where there is a large number of Federated tables, changing these tables' connection information can be cumbersome and requires altering all of the tables with a modified connection string. For instance, if there was the need to change what server 1,000 Federated tables connect to, you would have to alter each one of those tables to have a new server in its connection string.

To devise a better solution, in MySQL 5.1, the idea of a *Federated Server* was developed. This concept was part of the SQL/MED specification. It essentially lets you create a named database object called a SERVER that is associated with various connection meta-data information. The other half of this functionality is that the Federated storage engine can merely specify the server name (as well as a table if it is desired to name the table differently than the Federated table). This means you can change the connection information of the table one or more Federated tables uses to connect to their remote data source with a single SQL statement against the SERVER. So, in the 1,000 table scenario, not a single table would have to be changed!

The syntax for a *Federated Server* is straightforward:

```
CREATE SERVER
server_name
FOREIGN DATA WRAPPER wrapper_name
OPTIONS (option [, option] ...)
```

In the previous example, to use a Federated server, you would create it as:

```
mysql> CREATE SERVER
    -> 'servera' FOREIGN DATA WRAPPER 'mysql'
    -> OPTIONS
    ->   (HOST '192.168.1.118',
    ->    DATABASE 'remote',
    ->    USER 'feduser',
    ->    PASSWORD 'feduser',
    ->    PORT 3306,
    ->    SOCKET '',
    ->    OWNER 'root' );
```

Then, to use this server with the previously created table, you would have to drop the table first (this the Federated standard method; the engine does not support ALTER on the remote table) and then recreate it, using the server name that was just created instead of a URL connection string:

```
mysql> DROP TABLE t1 ;
Query OK, 0 rows affected, 1 warning (0.00 sec)
```

```
mysql> CREATE TABLE 't1' (
    ->    'id' int(3) NOT NULL AUTO_INCREMENT,
    ->    'name' varchar(32) NOT NULL DEFAULT '',
    ->    PRIMARY KEY (`id`)
    -> ) ENGINE=FEDERATED DEFAULT CHARSET=latin1 CONNECTION='servera';

mysql> SELECT * FROM t1;
+----+----------------+
| id | name           |
+----+----------------+
|  1 | first          |
|  2 | second         |
|  3 | hello world    |
|  4 | hello federated|
+----+----------------+
```

A table name could have been specified in this example and would be separated from the server name with a forward slash '/'.

```
CONNECTION= 'servera/t1'
```

This would be useful if the remote table name and Federated table name differed.

Federated under the Hood

To gain a little insight to how Federated works, there are several things that can be observed. First, as mentioned before, Federated accesses its data not from a local file, but from a remote data source through the MySQL client library. This means there will only be one file created for a Federated table, the .frm file, which is the table definition file. For Federated, this file merely contains the connection information for the Federated table:

```
ishvara:/home/mysql/var/federated # ls
db.opt   t1.frm
```

The other revealing thing to look at is the SQL log, if it is turned on, on the remote server. On the server with the Federated table, you issue:

```
mysql> SELECT * FROM t1;
```

The query log on the remote sever shows:

```
080823 11:17:56          181 Connect      feduser@arjuna on remote

    181 Query      SET NAMES latin1

    181 Query      SHOW TABLE STATUS LIKE 't1'

    181 Query      SELECT 'id`, 'name' FROM 't1`
```

As you can see:

❑ The first command the server with the Federated table sends is SET NAMES <character set>. This is to ensure that the character set of the Federated table is set on the remote server.

❑ The second command sent is SHOW TABLE STATUS. This is to obtain information on the remote table, which Federated then uses to set values for the local Federated table, such as the number of records in the table.

❑ Finally, the Federated storage engine sends the query to obtain the data that was specified in the original query. The difference between the original query on the Federated table and the query that Federated constructs to be run against the remote table is that Federated specifies each column. It does this internally by looping over each field (column) in a data structure representing the structure of the table and appending each to the complete statement.

If data is inserted into the Federated table, such as with this query:

```
mysql> INSERT INTO t1 (name) VALUES ('one more value');
```

Then the statement as found in the log on the remote server is:

```
080823 11:29:06   181 Query   INSERT INTO 't1' (`id`, 'name`)
VALUES  (0, 'one more value')
```

Just as with the SELECT statement, the INSERT statement is built by the Federated storage engine, additionally appending into the VALUES half of the INSERT statement the values being inserted.

Viewing the SQL log on a remote server that a Federated table utilizes can be a very useful means of seeing how the Federated storage engine works, as well as a good debugging tool.

Tina/CSV Storage Engine

The CSV storage engine uses a CSV (comma-separated value) file as its underlying data store. This is a novel way of easily importing or exporting data between MySQL and various applications such as spreadsheets. Another benefit of the CSV storage engine is its ability to instantaneously load large amounts of data when you merely create a CSV table, and place data in CSV format named with the same table name into the schema directory in which the table is created.

Some characteristic of the CSV storage engine are:

❑ Uses CSV — comma-separated values — as its data format.

❑ Does not support indexes.

❑ Does not support AUTO_INCREMENT.

Creating a CSV Table

To create a CSV table, just specify the ENGINE value as CSV:

```
mysql> CREATE TABLE contacts (
    -> contact_id INT(8) NOT NULL,
    -> first varchar(32) NOT NULL DEFAULT '',
    -> last varchar(32) NOT NULL DEFAULT '',
    -> street varchar(64) NOT NULL DEFAULT '',
    -> town varchar(32) NOT NULL DEFAULT '',
```

```
    -> state varchar(16) NOT NULL DEFAULT '') ENGINE=CSV;
```

```
mysql> INSERT INTO contacts VALUES
    -> (1, 'John', 'Smith', '133 Elm St', 'Madison', 'WI'),
    -> (2, 'Alan', 'Johnson', '4455 Cherry Ave', 'Fitchburg', 'MA'),
    -> (3, 'Sri', 'Narayana', '1 Govardhana Way', 'Vrndavana', 'UP');
```

CSV under the Hood

Looking in the data directory, you see three files:

```
radha:test root# ls -l
total 40
-rw-rw----  1 _mysql  _mysql    35 Aug 24 13:04 contacts.CSM
-rw-rw----  1 _mysql  _mysql   154 Aug 24 13:04 contacts.CSV
-rw-rw----  1 _mysql  _mysql  8730 Aug 23 19:15 contacts.frm
```

The contacts.CSM file is a meta-data file containing information such as a total row count of *contacts* as well as the state of the table. contacts.CSV is the actual data file containing the records that were inserted above, and .frm file is of course the table definition file that every table in MySQL has, regardless of the storage engine employed.

If you view the contents of contacts.CSV, you'll see:

```
radha:test root# cat contacts.CSV
1,"John","Smith","133 Elm St","Madison","WI"
2,"Alan","Johnson","4455 Cherry Ave","Fitchburg","MA"
3,"Sri","Narayana","1 Govardhana Way","Vrndavana","UP"
```

You can edit this file directly, save it back to the data directory, and then use it. This gives you the ability to work with this data either through MySQL using SQL or any tool that works with CSV:

1. The code below shows copying the CSV data file to a user's document directory. Don't worry about the meta-data file. This will be updated to reflect the changes you made using the FLUSH TABLES statement from MySQL.

    ```
    radha:test root# cp contacts.CSV /Users/patg/Documents/
    ```

2. Then this CSV file can be edited by simply loading contacts.CSV into a spreadsheet, as shown in Figure 3-1.

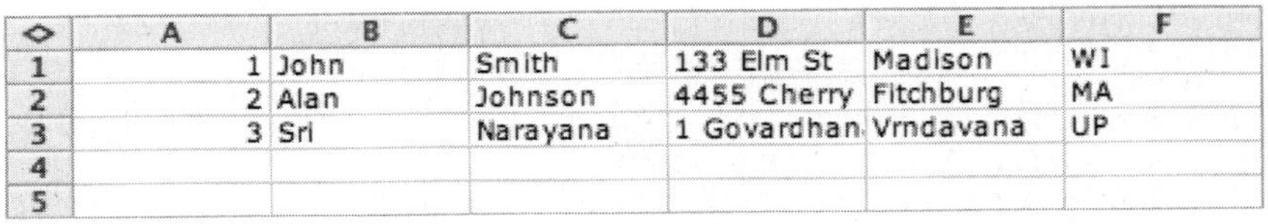

◇	A	B	C	D	E	F
1	1	John	Smith	133 Elm St	Madison	WI
2	2	Alan	Johnson	4455 Cherry	Fitchburg	MA
3	3	Sri	Narayana	1 Govardhan	Vrndavana	UP
4						
5						

Figure 3-1

3. You can then add a record in the spreadsheet, shown in Figure 3-2.

◇	A	B	C	D	E	F
1	1	John	Smith	133 Elm St	Madison	WI
2	2	Alan	Johnson	4455 Cherry	Fitchburg	MA
3	3	Sri	Narayana	1 Govardhan	Vrndavana	UP
4	4	Sarah	Shedrick	9988 51st St	Seattle	WA
5						
6						

Figure 3-2

4. Copy the CSV file back to the data directory:

    ```
    radha:test root# cp /home/patg/Documents/contacts.CSV
    ```

5. From within MySQL, issue a FLUSH TABLES command, which updates the meta-information. Then the newly added record is displayed:

    ```
    mysql> FLUSH TABLES;

    mysql> SELECT * FROM contacts;
    +------------+-------+----------+------------------+-----------+-------+
    | contact_id | first | last     | street           | town      | state |
    +------------+-------+----------+------------------+-----------+-------+
    |          1 | John  | Smith    | 133 Elm St       | Madison   | WI    |
    |          2 | Alan  | Johnson  | 4455 Cherry Ave  | Fitchburg | MA    |
    |          3 | Sri   | Narayana | 1 Govardhana Way | Vrndavana | UP    |
    |          4 | Sarah | Shedrick | 9988 51st St. NE | Seattle   | WA    |
    +------------+-------+----------+------------------+-----------+-------+
    ```

And now, handily, the records added from an external application are available from within MySQL with minimal effort.

Blackhole Storage Engine

Last, but not least, there is the Blackhole storage engine. This storage engine is a bit like the roach motel — data goes in, but doesn't ever get out! Seriously, the question you might be asking as you read this is, "Why would there be an engine like this?" The main reason the Blackhole storage engine was written is to provide a means for running data modification statements on a table without actual data storage, yet retain the benefit of those statements being logged to a binary log, which is at the core of how replication works.

Other benefits of the Blackhole storage engine include being able to vary SQL statement syntax, particularly the syntax contained in a dump created with mysqldump. Also, the Blackhole storage engine can be used to measure performance excluding the actual storage engine performance, as well as the effects of binary logging.

To create a table using the Blackhole storage engine:

```
mysql> CREATE TABLE deadend (
    ->   id int(8) NOT NULL auto_increment,
```

```
        ->    name varchar(32) NOT NULL DEFAULT '',
        ->    PRIMARY KEY (id)
        -> ) ENGINE=BLACKHOLE;
```

And have fun trying to insert actual data into the newly created table, deadend!

```
mysql> INSERT INTO deadend (name) VALUES ('not'), ('here'), ('at'), ('all');
Query OK, 4 rows affected (0.00 sec)
Records: 4  Duplicates: 0  Warnings: 0

mysql> SELECT * FROM deadend;
Empty set (0.00 sec)
```

As you can see, data is not stored in this table. Also, note that creating this table allowed indexes and auto_increment to be used. The indexes themselves don't physically exist, but their definitions do. This facilitates the ability to use the same table definitions the MyISAM or InnoDB uses, without any changes. This makes it simple to import a schema creation file that was dumped from another database (mysqldump -d), regardless of the storage engine for the tables dumped. All this requires is for the setting default-storage-engine=BLACKHOLE to be specified in the my.cnf/my.ini. When the schema dump is imported to the database with Blackhole set as the default, the tables will automatically be correctly defined.

> If you alter a real table with data to become a Blackhole table, all the data will be lost.

Replication

Replication is the means of copying data from a MySQL master database instance to one or more slave database instances. MySQL replication is asynchronous, meaning that data replication is not instantaneous and, as such, the slave doesn't have to be connected continuously to the master; this also allows the slaves to replicate from the master over a long-distance connection.

Replication can be used for many purposes such as scaling out read-intensive applications by having multiple read slaves to reduce the reads on the master. Another application for replication is a backup slave that allows for data backups without affecting any of the database servers being used by live applications. Also, you can use replication to replicate to tables that use different storage engines than on the master. One example would be using the Blackhole storage engine for a logging table on a master database that replicates to an archive logging table on the slave.

MySQL replication supports either statement-based or row-based replication (in MySQL 5.1 and higher), or mixed (both statement and row-based replication, MySQL 5.1 and higher). Statement-based replication uses SQL statements from the master run on the slaves to replicate data, whereas row-based replication duplicates the actual binary-level changes on the table from the master to the slave.

Replication Overview

Figure 3-3 shows the basic concept of how MySQL replication works.

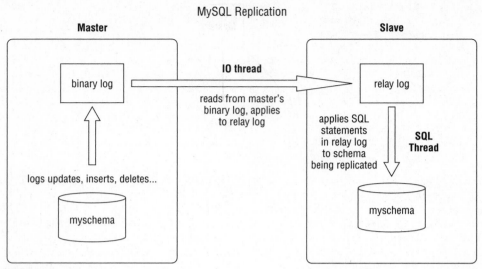

Figure 3-3

The first part of replication is the binary log, which resides on the master. When binary logging is turned on, the master records changes (events) to the binary log. These changes are any data modification statement, such as UPDATE, INSERT, DELETE, TRUNCATE, etc. Also, these events correspond to a position in the binary log. Moreover, this log rotates over time, and each new log has a new log name sequence.

The other half of replication is the slave. There are two threads (processes) that run on a slave — the I/O thread, and the SQL thread. The I/O thread reads the master's binary log changes (events, SQL statements) and stores them in relay logs. The SQL thread reads the SQL statements from relay logs and applies them to the local database instance to whatever schema or table that should be replicated. Like the binary log, the relay log also rotates, in numeric sequence. The slave always maintains the mapping of SQL statements (events) it has to perform to the original binary log position (and binary log name) of the master where it read that statement from. This makes it possible to know how far behind the slave is from the master.

The reason for having two threads for replication is simple. The I/O thread "collects" the statements from the master, and the SQL thread runs those commands. This allows for the reading of events from the master without waiting for those events to be executed on the slave — hence the "asynchronous" nature of MySQL replication.

Replication schemes

MySQL allows for various replication schemes. There is the simple single master with one or more slaves (see Figure 3-4) attached.

Another replication scheme is a dual master with each master having one or more slaves attached, as Figure 3-5 shows.

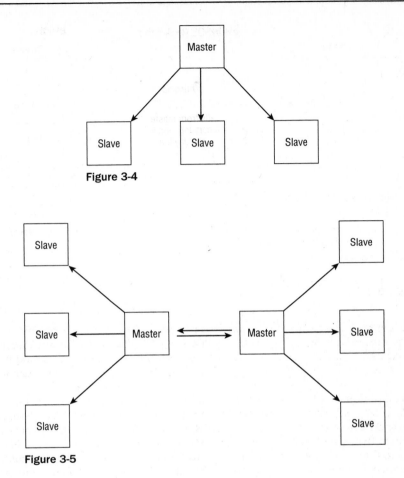

Figure 3-4

Figure 3-5

The dual master configuration is possible because a slave can also be a master as well. Each master is also a slave of the other. Writes occurring on each master are replicated to each other, which, in turn, are replicated to the slaves of each dual master. A dual master can be a particularly useful scheme, as it allows you to have two masters available, like having a pair of kidneys! The benefit of this is that should one of those masters fail, you would simply point its slaves to the other master.

With this in mind, another replication scheme, as shown below in Figure 3-6, is known as the ring configuration.

This configuration can be useful in that it creates multiple masters, allowing you to split up writes, which although not shown in Figure 3-6, can also have slaves attached to each. It does present a requirement: Each master/slave must be able to automatically switch over to a new master should its master fail. With this ring scheme, if any master/slave's replication is broken or down, it breaks the overall replication of the entire ring. Just think about how Christmas tree lights break!

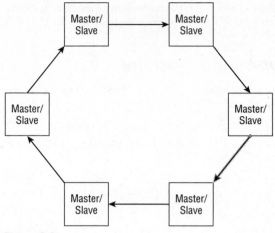

Figure 3-6

One other replication scheme worth mentioning, shown below in Figure 3-7, is the previously mentioned benefit of the Blackhole storage engine — using a master/slave MySQL instance to act as a filter
or dummy logging server, which has slaves attached. The filter logging server is a MySQL instance that
is a slave of the main master, which, in turn, is a master of other slaves, either on a separate machine or
running on the same server as the main master that has the Blackhole storage engine as its default storage
engine (--default-storage-engine=BLACKHOLE in my.cnf/my.ini). Using replication filtering rules set
to filter (a) particular schema(s) specified results in a much smaller binary log, and therefore less network traffic to the slaves connected to this filter logging server. Also with this setup, because the tables
are using the Blackhole storage engine, the disk I/O for this MySQL instance is low. This is because the
actual table data isn't written to disk — only SQL statements being logged to the binary log are written.
These in turn are read by the slaves connected to it that do have actual data.

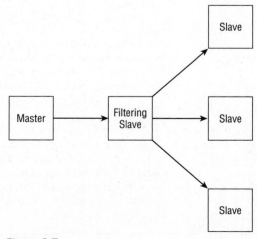

Figure 3-7

MySQL replication is very flexible, and there are many other schemes that can be used beyond these basic four. It depends on your application, ratio of reads to writes, hardware allotment, data center locations, and most importantly, budget.

Replication Command Options

MySQL replication command options, like other MySQL command options, are set in MySQL's configuration file my.cnf or my.ini respectively.

The command options listed here have two dashes (--) in front of the name of the option as if they were specified in the command line for mysqld. *In the my.cnf/my.ini file, they are listed without the two dashes.*

Also, for the items --report-host = <canonical name of host> *and* --report-port = <numeric port *in the following table, the output for* SHOW SLAVE HOSTS *is as follows:*

```
mysql> show slave hosts;
+-----------+---------+------+-------------------+-----------+
| Server_id | Host    | Port | Rpl_recovery_rank | Master_id |
+-----------+---------+------+-------------------+-----------+
|         3 | slave-b | 3308 |                 0 |         1 |
|         2 | slave-a | 3307 |                 0 |         1 |
+-----------+---------+------+-------------------+-----------+
```

The replication command options are as follows:

Command Option	Description
--log-bin [= <binary log name>] or: --log-bin --logbin = <binary log name>	Turns on the binary log for a master and optionally sets the name of the binary log. The name is the base name of the file, where each log file will have this name as well as the numeric value that increments each time a log file is rotated to a new log file.
--binlog-do-db = <schema name> --binlog-ignore-db = <schema name>	Used to control if data modification statements (UPDATE, INSERT, DELETE, etc.) are logged or not logged to the binary log per the schema listed.
--log-slave-updates	Turns on logging of data modification statements that occurred via replication, which is explained later on. This is used for the dual master or ring replication scheme, as well as if you want a backup slave and want to use the binary log for incremental backups.
--log-bin-index = <filename>	Name of file containing inventory of binary logs that exist.
--expire-logs-days = <number>	The maximum age, in days, that binary logs are allowed to remain on the master. Make sure not to set this to a value that ends up causing logs to be deleted that slaves might not have read yet, particularly if you have a situation where slaves might not regularly connect to the master to update.

Continued

(continued)

Command Option	Description
`--server-id = <number>`	This is a unique number (unique among all servers in a given replication paradigm). The only requirement is that every server has a different value. It's quite common to give the first id, 1, to the main master, and increment from there. For instance, in a dual master scheme, one master would be 1, the other master 2, the slaves with 1 as their master would be numbered odd and the slaves with 2 as their master would be even.
`--report-host = <canonical name of host>` `--report-port = <numeric port>`	This is a feature available in 5.1 that is the preferred hostname, port of the slave as reported to the master, and displayed in the output of SHOW SLAVE HOSTS.
`--master-host = <hostname, ip address>`	This is the hostname or IP address of the master the slave connects to.
`--master-user = <slave user name>`	This is the username the slave uses to connect to the master. This user requires REPLICATION SLAVE privileges in order to connect to the master and read its binary logs.
`--master-password = <slave user's password>`	Password of the slave user required to connect to the master.
`--master-port = <numeric port>`	The port that the master is running on, default 3306. In the case of a MySQL master instance being run on a different port, you would explicitly set this.
`--relay-log = <relay log>`	The base name of the relay log to be used. If no path is specified, the value of datadir is used as the location of the relay log.
`--relay-log-info-file = <log file name>`	The name of the file that stores the current name and position of the relay log being processed.
`--relay-log-index = <log file name>`	The name of the file that stores an inventory of the relay logs existing on the slave.
`--master-ssl` `--master-ssl-ca=file_name` `--master-ssl-capath=directory_name` `--master-ssl-cert=file_name` `--master-ssl-cipher=cipher_list` `--master-ssl-key=file_name`	These command options are for replication over SSL (Secure Sockets Layer). More detail on these can be found in the MySQL user's manual.
`--replicate-do-db = <schemaname>` `--replicate-ignore-db = <schemaname>`	Filter rule specifying the schema to be replicated or ignored (do-db means to replicate, ignore-db means ignore, do not replicate). For statement-based replication, only SQL statements that contain the schema name of the default database, as specified in USE schemaname, are replicated. For row-based replication, it's any change to any table in schemaname, regardless of default database.

Command Option	Description

`--replicate-do-table =`
`schemaname.tablename`
`/ --replicate-ignore-table =`
`schemaname.tablename`
	Filter rule specifying the table from a specific schema to replicate or not replicate.

`--replicate-do-wild-table =`
`schemaname.tablename%`
`--replicate-ignore-wild-table=`
`schemaname.tablename%`
	Filter rules giving even more granularity over what is replicated or ignored. This option allows you to use wildcards — SQL wildcards `%` for multiple characters, and `_` for a single character. Whatever syntax works with LIKE works with this rule.

`replicate-do-wild-table = webap%.%`	Replicate any schema starting with the name webap, any table. This would be `webapps.t1`, `webapps2.t3`, `webappbak.t3` — all would be replicated.
`replicate-ignore-wild-table =` `webapps.t%`	Do not replicate any table in `webapps` schema that begins with *t* followed by any one or more characters.
`--replicate-rewrite-db=from_name->` `to_name`	This allows you to replicate a schema on a master to a differently named schema on the slave. For instance, if you wanted to replicate a schema called `myschema` on the master to `yourschema` on the slave's configuration file, you would have `— replicate-rewrite-db=myschema->yourschema`.

Setting Up Replication

Setting up replication is a fairly straightforward task. It mainly consists of ensuring that binary logging is enabled on a master, that privileges are in place for slaves to connect to the master, and that the slaves know what binary log name and position to start reading from. Other considerations are that you have already ensured that the data on the slave is at a state where replicated statements will result in the slave being equal, in terms of data, to the master, which is usually accomplished by loading a data dump from the master on the slave.

The following section will show in detail how to set up replication. In this case, we show a dual master replication setup using two instances of MySQL running on the same machine on separate ports. Also, this replication setup will only be using statement-based replication.

Running Multiple Instances of MySQL with mysqld_multi

`mysqld_multi` is a utility script that comes bundled in the MySQL distribution. It allows you to run multiple instances of MySQL on the same server. Whether you need to use it for one or multiple servers, it is a very useful script. Its usage is simple. For example, if you had two MySQL instances set up, identified in the my.cnf as `mysqld1` and `mysqld2`, the way to start both servers would be:

```
mysql_multi start 1,2
```

And to stop both servers you would use this:

```
mysqld_multi stop 1,2
```

You can also specify an action for each individual server, such as:

```
mysqld_multi start 2
```

To be able to use `mysqld_multi`, you must have separate sections in your my.cnf/my.ini for each server. Instead of the normal:

```
[mysqld]
...options...
```

You would use this:

```
[mysqld1]
... options for mysql instance 1 ...

[mysqld2]
... options for mysql instance 2 ...
```

Also, each instance should have its own data directory. For example, in a source install, a single instance of MySQL, you would have `/usr/local/mysql/var` be the data directory. For the example in this book, each server will have its own data directory in `/usr/local/mysql/var/dataN`, with `N` corresponding to the number of the server. To set this up, you would simply:

1. Copy what is in `/usr/local/mysql/var` to `/usr/local/mysql/var/dataN`, as well as make sure the permissions of `/usr/local/mysql/var/dataN` are owned by both the `mysql` user and `mysql` group. You would also make sure the current MySQL instance is not running.

   ```
   mkdir /usr/local/mysql/var/data1

   cp -r /usr/local/mysql/var/* /usr/local/mysql/var/data1

   chown -R mysql:mysql /usr/local/mysql/var/data1
   ```

2. You do the same for the second instance, except the data directory is `data2`.

3. Set up my.cnf to allow for two servers to run. The first thing is that `mysqld_multi` requires its own section in my.cnf.

   ```
   [mysqld_multi]
   mysqld      = /usr/local/mysql/bin/mysqld_safe
   mysqladmin  = /usr/local/mysql/bin/mysqladmin
   user        = root
   ```

   `mysqld_multi` needs to know which programs to run as the `mysqld` daemon as well as `mysqladmin` (for stopping the servers), and runs as root to be able to run these processes (`mysqld_safe` runs as the `mysql` user).

4. Next, each server has its own section:

   ```
   [mysqld1]
   mysqld                = /usr/local/mysql/bin/mysqld_safe
   mysqladmin            = /usr/local/mysql/bin/mysqladmin
   user                  = mysql
   ```

```
port                = 3306
socket              = /tmp/mysql.sock
datadir             = /usr/local/mysql/var/data1
```

Shown above are the basic command options for the first server. The command options for the second server would be as follows:

```
[mysqld2]
mysqld              = /usr/local/mysql/bin/mysqld_safe
mysqladmin          = /usr/local/mysql/bin/mysqladmin
user                = mysql
port                = 3307
socket              = /tmp/mysql2.sock
datadir             = /usr/local/mysql/var/data2
```

5. With these in place, it should be possible to start the servers.

    ```
    radha:~ root# mysqld_multi start 1,2
    ```

6. And checking with ps, it's possible to see that both are now running (this output is cleaned up/reduced from the original!).

    ```
    radha:~ root# ps auxww|grep mysqld|grep -v mysqld_safe

    mysql    7936    0.0   0.6    134988  12720 s000  S    Tue11PM   0:52.05
    /usr/local/mysql/libexec/mysqld --datadir=/usr/local/mysql/var/data1
    --user=mysql --socket=/tmp/mysql.sock -
    -port=3306

    mysql    33148   0.0   0.1    135020  2200   ??   S    22Aug08   1:40.33
    /usr/local/mysql/libexec/mysqld --datadir=/usr/local/mysql/var/data2
    --user=mysql --socket=/tmp/mysql2.sock --port=3307
    ```

Now that you have two MySQL instances running, you can set up replication!

Adding Replication Command Options

This section details how to add replication with a dual master setup using the two separate instances of MySQL that were shown in the previous section. Listed below are the steps required to set up the my.cnf/my.ini for both servers for replication to run. When it's mentioned that each setting is made for both servers, this means that the command options are made below each server section, as indicated by [mysqld1] and [mysqld2]. The configuration file of this example can be seen in its entirety in Appendix B.

To turn on binary logging on both servers, follow these steps:

1. Add the log-bin to my.cnf or my.ini respectively for Windows, for both servers (under [mysqld1], [mysqld2]).

    ```
    [mysqld1]

    log-bin             = /usr/local/mysql/var/data1/bin.log
    ```

```
[mysqld2]

log-bin              = /usr/local/mysql/var/data2/bin.log
```

2. To turn on log-slave-updates, just specify in `my.cnf`/`my.ini` for both servers:

    ```
    log-slave-updates
    ```

3. You want to set `-master-host`, `--master-user`, `--master-password` slave command options for both servers. For this example, the user `repl` and password of `repl` will be used. (Don't do this in a production environment! `repl` is not a secure password, and you should never use the same value for a password that you have as the username.) The port value will be 3307 because the second master/slave `[mysqd2]` will be running on port 3307.

    ```
    master-host     = localhost
    master-user     = repl
    master-password = repl
    master-port     = 3307
    ```

    This is for the first master/slave.

4. For the second master/slave, you would use

    ```
    master-port       = 3306
    ```

    . . . because the first master/slave is running on the default port of 3306.

5. Set relay logs for both servers. These logs reside in the `datadir` for that server. For the first master/slave, this is `/usr/local/var/data1`, and for the second master/slave it is `/usr/local/mysql/var/data2`.

    ```
    relay-log               = /usr/local/mysql/var/data1/relay.log
    relay-log-info-file     = /usr/local/mysql/var/data1/relay-log.info
    relay-log-index         = /usr/local/mysql/var/data1/relay-log.index
    ```

6. Specify schema(s) to be replicated for both servers. In this example, `webapps` schema and all tables will be replicated. For both master/slave servers, the setting is:

    ```
    replicate-wild-do-table = webapps.%
    ```

7. Next you want to set `-auto-increment-increment` and `-auto-increment-offset` to ensure you have no conflicts of auto-increment values between the dual masters. Without specifying this, you would have each master/slave incrementing in the same sequence, one at a time, and starting at 1, resulting in a conflict. To avoid this, `-auto-increment-increment` overrides the default increment of one greater than previous to a value that must be at minimum equal to the number of masters. For a dual master setup, the value of 2 must be used. If, for instance, you have five master/slaves in a ring replication setup, this value must be at

least 5. This number can be set to a larger number than the total number of master/slaves to allow for growth. The other piece of this is -auto-increment-offset, a point from which the server starts counting. To explain this better, the first master/slave needs to start at 1, increment by 2, so that the sequence is 1,3,5 . . . , and the second master/slave needs to start at 2, increment by 2, so that the sequence is 2,4,6 . . . , thus preventing collisions between both servers. The values in my.cnf/my.ini would appear as:

```
auto-increment-increment = 2
auto-increment-offset    = 1
```

for the first master/slave, and

```
auto-increment-increment = 2
auto-increment-offset    = 2
```

for the second master/slave.

8. You want to set up permissions for both servers to be able to connect to their respective masters. The permissions required for replication are REPLICATION SLAVE, and can be granted on the first master/slave with the command:

```
radha:~ root# mysql -u root -P 3306 -h hostname

mysql> GRANT REPLICATION SLAVE ON *.* TO 'repl'@'localhost' IDENTIFIED BY
'repl';
```

Then grant permissions on the second master/slave by connecting to the specific socket (mysql -S).

```
radha:~ root# mysql -u root -S 3307 -h hostname

mysql> GRANT REPLICATION SLAVE ON *.* TO 'repl'@'localhost' IDENTIFIED BY
'repl';
```

If the *webapps* schema already exists, dump that schema from the first master/slave, and then load it on the second master/slave, thus:

```
radha:~ patg$ mysqldump -u root -S /tmp/mysql.sock webapps >webapps.sql
radha:~ patg$ mysql -u root -S /tmp/mysql2.sock webapps < webapps.sql
```

9. If the *webapps* schema doesn't already exist, when both servers are restarted with the new settings, creating the schema on one master/slave will result in it being created on the other master/slave, due, of course, to replication.

10. Finally, restart both servers:

```
radha:~ root# mysqld_multi stop 1,2
radha:~ root# mysqld_multi start 1,2
```

Verify the Replication is Running

Now replication should be running! To verify that replication is running, the first thing is to run SHOW MASTER STATUS and SHOW SLAVE STATUS on both servers:

1. Enter the first master/slave as follows:

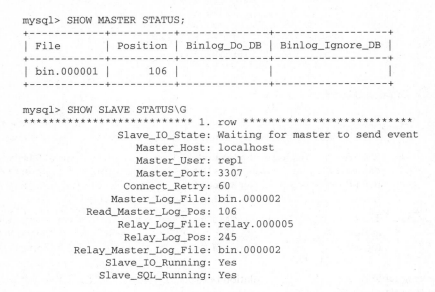

```
mysql> SHOW MASTER STATUS;
+------------+----------+--------------+------------------+
| File       | Position | Binlog_Do_DB | Binlog_Ignore_DB |
+------------+----------+--------------+------------------+
| bin.000001 |      106 |              |                  |
+------------+----------+--------------+------------------+

mysql> SHOW SLAVE STATUS\G
*************************** 1. row ***************************
               Slave_IO_State: Waiting for master to send event
                  Master_Host: localhost
                  Master_User: repl
                  Master_Port: 3307
                Connect_Retry: 60
              Master_Log_File: bin.000002
          Read_Master_Log_Pos: 106
               Relay_Log_File: relay.000005
                Relay_Log_Pos: 245
        Relay_Master_Log_File: bin.000002
             Slave_IO_Running: Yes
            Slave_SQL_Running: Yes
```

There are more output parameters reported by SHOW SLAVE STATUS, but they have been omitted here for brevity. The values of interest in this output are:

❑   Slave_IO_Running and Slave_SQL_Running, which are in this case both "Yes," which is an indication that replication is running.

❑   Master_Log_File, which is bin.000002 and Read_Master_Log_Pos, which is 106. This is the master log file name and position of the binary log on the second master/slave.

❑   The binary log name and position from SHOW MASTER STATUS which is named bin.000001, and position 106. When SHOW SLAVE STATUS is executed on the second master/slave, Master_Log_File and Read_Master_Log_Pos should be bin.000001 and 106, respectively.

2. Enter the second master/slave as follows:

```
mysql> SHOW MASTER STATUS;
+------------+----------+--------------+------------------+
| File       | Position | Binlog_Do_DB | Binlog_Ignore_DB |
+------------+----------+--------------+------------------+
| bin.000002 |      106 |              |                  |
+------------+----------+--------------+------------------+

mysql> SHOW SLAVE STATUS\G
*************************** 1. row ***************************
```

```
        Slave_IO_State: Waiting for master to send event
           Master_Host: localhost
           Master_User: repl
           Master_Port: 3306
         Connect_Retry: 60
       Master_Log_File: bin.000001
   Read_Master_Log_Pos: 106
        Relay_Log_File: relay.000002
         Relay_Log_Pos: 245
 Relay_Master_Log_File: bin.000001
      Slave_IO_Running: Yes
     Slave_SQL_Running: Yes
```

Of interest are the following:

❑ Slave_IO_Running and Slave_SQL_Running on the second master/slave both show
   "Yes," verifying that replication is running on the second master/slave.

❑ SHOW MASTER STATUS on the second master/slave shows that the master binary log
   name and position corresponds to the binary log name and position that was noted
   from the first master/slave values for Master_Log_File and Read_Master_Log_Pos
   from SHOW SLAVE STATUS — that is, bin.000001 and 106.

❑ The output of SHOW SLAVE STATUS on the second master/slave shows Master_Log_File
   as bin.000001 and Read_Master_Log_Pos as 106 — which was the value of the binary
   log as shown from the output of SHOW MASTER STATUS on the first master/slave.

The following table summarizes the correlation between log positions of the binary master log on a
master to the relay log of a slave and vice versa for both dual slave/masters.

First Master/Slave	Second Master/Slave
Values from SHOW MASTER STATUS	Values from SHOW SLAVE STATUS
Binary log name: bin.000001	Master_Log_File: bin.000001
Binary log position: 106	Read_Master_Log_Pos: 106
Values from SHOW SLAVE STATUS	Values from SHOW MASTER STATUS
Master_Log_File: bin.000002	Binary log name: bin.000002
Master_Log_Pos: 106	Binary log position: 106

The next way of proving that replication is working is to modify a table on either server and verify that
the change occurs on the other server.

1.   Enter the first master/slave. (SHOW VARIABLES is used to demonstrate the first master/slave
         is being used in this client session.)

```
mysql> SHOW VARIABLES LIKE 'port';
```

```
+---------------+-------+
| Variable_name | Value |
+---------------+-------+
| port          | 3306  |
+---------------+-------+

mysql> SELECT * FROM t1;
+----+--------+
| id | name   |
+----+--------+
|  1 | first  |
|  2 | second |
|  3 | third  |
|  4 | four   |
+----+--------+

mysql> INSERT INTO t1 (name) VALUES ('fifth value');

mysql> SELECT * FROM t1;
+----+-------------+
| id | name        |
+----+-------------+
|  1 | first       |
|  2 | second      |
|  3 | third       |
|  4 | four        |
|  5 | fifth value |
+----+-------------+
```

2. Enter the second master/slave as follows:

```
mysql> SHOW VARIABLES LIKE 'port';
+---------------+-------+
| Variable_name | Value |
+---------------+-------+
| port          | 3307  |
+---------------+-------+

mysql> SELECT * FROM t1;
+----+-------------+
| id | name        |
+----+-------------+
|  1 | first       |
|  2 | second      |
|  3 | third       |
|  4 | four        |
|  5 | fifth value |
+----+-------------+
```

The values inserted on the first master/slave were replicated to the second!

3. Now insert some values from the second master/slave:

```
mysql> INSERT INTO t1 (name) VALUES ('sixth value');

mysql> SELECT * FROM t1;
```

```
+----+------------+
| id | name       |
+----+------------+
|  1 | first      |
|  2 | second     |
|  3 | third      |
|  4 | four       |
|  5 | fifth value |
|  6 | sixth value |
+----+------------+
```

4. Now verify that these were replicated from the second master/slave to the first master/slave:

```
mysql> SHOW VARIABLES LIKE 'port';
+---------------+-------+
| Variable_name | Value |
+---------------+-------+
| port          | 3306  |
+---------------+-------+

mysql> SELECT * FROM t1;
+----+------------+
| id | name       |
+----+------------+
|  1 | first      |
|  2 | second     |
|  3 | third      |
|  4 | four       |
|  5 | fifth value |
|  6 | sixth value |
+----+------------+
```

Which it did!

Manually Setting the Master

Another demonstration worth showing is how to manually set the master. In the previous demonstration, it wasn't necessary to manually set the master with CHANGE MASTER, but often you will be required to run this statement in order to connect to the master. To illustrate this, the master on the first master/slave will be reset. This causes the master to delete all of its binary logs and start from scratch — which would break replication on the second master/slave because it would still be pointing to the binary log file before the reset.

```
mysql> RESET MASTER;

mysql> SHOW MASTER STATUS;
+------------+----------+--------------+------------------+
| File       | Position | Binlog_Do_DB | Binlog_Ignore_DB |
+------------+----------+--------------+------------------+
| bin.000001 |      106 |              |                  |
+------------+----------+--------------+------------------+
```

On the second master/slave:

```
mysql> SHOW SLAVE STATUS\G
*************************** 1. row ***************************
               Slave_IO_State:
                  Master_Host: localhost
                  Master_User: pythian
                  Master_Port: 3306
                Connect_Retry: 60
              Master_Log_File: bin.000001
          Read_Master_Log_Pos: 586
```

As you can see, the second master/slave is pointing to the wrong binary log position. This can be fixed by using the CHANGE MASTER statement.

```
mysql> STOP SLAVE;

mysql> CHANGE MASTER TO master_user='repl',
master_password='repl', master_host='localhost', master_port=3306,
master_log_file='bin.000001', master_log_pos=106;

mysql> START SLAVE;
Query OK, 0 rows affected (0.00 sec)

mysql> SHOW SLAVE STATUS\G
*************************** 1. row ***************************
               Slave_IO_State: Waiting for master to send event
                  Master_Host: localhost
                  Master_User: repl
                  Master_Port: 3306
                Connect_Retry: 60
              Master_Log_File: bin.000001
          Read_Master_Log_Pos: 106
```

This shows that replication has been restored.

CHANGE MASTER can be used anytime to set a slave to read from the correct master or change to a different master for whatever reason — a failure of the current master, or even during maintenance, when a backup master is used.

Searching Text

Searching text is one of the most common functions of a web site and a must-have for RDBMSs. Sometimes, developers will search text in the database using the LIKE operator, but this is very inefficient, especially if there is a large data set involved. This is where Full-text search engines become a necessity.

There are two means of supporting Full-text search functionality using MySQL, that this book will cover: Full-text indexes, which are part of the functionality of MySQL, and Sphinx Full-Text Search Engine, an open-source project that is designed to work well with MySQL.

MySQL FULLTEXT Indexes

MySQL supports full-text indexes, which are b-tree indexes that are created against columns containing text and built by indexing words found in the text fields with a pointer to the word in the actual location where it exists, eliminating stopwords such as *the, and*, etc. For a complete list of default stopwords, see `http://dev.mysql.com/doc/refman/5.0/en/fulltext-stopwords.html`.

When the index is used in a search, the term being searched is matched against the index. The location is known because the index provides a pointer to the text where the term is physically located.

Creating a full-text index is as easy as creating a regular index. It can be specified when creating a table or on an existing table:

FULLTEXT *indexes are only supported with tables created using either the MyISAM or Maria storage engines.*

```
mysql> CREATE TABLE books_text (
    -> book_id int(8) NOT NULL DEFAULT 0,
    -> title varchar(64) DEFAULT '',
    -> content text,
    -> PRIMARY KEY (book_id),
    -> FULLTEXT INDEX title (title),
    -> FULLTEXT INDEX content (content)) ENGINE=MyISAM;
```

Or, alternatively:

```
mysql> CREATE FULLTEXT INDEX title ON books_text (title);
 mysql> CREATE FULLTEXT INDEX content ON books_text (content);
```

Once these indexes are created, they are ready for use.

To use full-text indexes, there is the full-text search function MATCH() ... AGAINST. Its syntax usage is:

```
MATCH (col1,col2,...) AGAINST (expr  [search_modifier])

search_modifier:
  {
      IN BOOLEAN MODE
    | IN NATURAL LANGUAGE MODE
    | IN NATURAL LANGUAGE MODE WITH QUERY EXPANSION
    | WITH QUERY EXPANSION
  }
```

The search modifier values can be explained as such:

❑   BOOLEAN MODE: Uses a search string that has its own syntax containing the terms to be searched for. This syntax allows word weighting, negation, and/or, etc., omitting stopwords.

❑   NATURAL LANGUAGE MODE: Uses a string as is, without special syntax, and searches for the string specified. Words that are present in more than 50 percent of the rows are not matched.

❏ NATURAL LANGUAGE MODE WITH QUERY EXPANSION: Basically the same as NATURAL LANGUAGE MODE except the results from the search of the initial search terms aren't returned to the user, but are added to the original search terms, which are then searched again. These results are then returned to the user. This is also known as "bling query expansion." An example of this would be if the initial search term was *database*, which returned results with *MySQL* and *Oracle*, which then were searched to return results containing *database*, *Oracle*, or *MySQL*.

Using MySQL Full-text Indexes

MySQL provides a sample database that you can load into any schema on your instance of MySQL you like. It's called *sakila*, and can be found on MySQL's developer web site at the URL `http://dev.mysql.com/doc/sakila/en/sakila.html`.

This database contains a table, complete with data, called `films_text`, that has full-text indexes, which will be used for demonstration of full-text indexes in this book.

The best way to see how to use FULLTEXT is to provide several examples:

❏ Natural language mode:

```
mysql> SELECT film_id, title FROM film_text
    -> WHERE MATCH(title,description)
    -> AGAINST('Frisbee' IN NATURAL LANGUAGE MODE) LIMIT 5;
+---------+---------------+
| film_id | title         |
+---------+---------------+
|     308 | FERRIS MOTHER |
|     326 | FLYING HOOK   |
|     585 | MOB DUFFEL    |
|     714 | RANDOM GO     |
|     210 | DARKO DORADO  |
+---------+---------------+
```

❏ Boolean mode — matched term must have *technical* and *writer*:

```
mysql> SELECT film_id, title, description FROM film_text
    -> WHERE MATCH(title,description)
    -> AGAINST('technical +writer' IN BOOLEAN MODE) LIMIT 5\G
*************************** 1. row ***************************
    film_id: 19
      title: AMADEUS HOLY
description: A Emotional Display of a Pioneer And a Technical Writer who must
Battle a Man in A Balloon
*************************** 2. row ***************************
    film_id: 43
      title: ATLANTIS CAUSE
description: A Thrilling Yarn of a Feminist And a Hunter who must Fight a
Technical Writer in A Shark Tank
*************************** 3. row ***************************
    film_id: 44
      title: ATTACKS HATE
description: A Fast-Paced Panorama of a Technical Writer And a Mad Scientist
who must Find a Feminist in An Abandoned Mine Shaft
```

```
*************************** 4. row ***************************
    film_id: 67
      title: BERETS AGENT
description: A Taut Saga of a Crocodile And a Boy who must Overcome a Technical
Writer in Ancient China
*************************** 5. row ***************************
    film_id: 86
      title: BOOGIE AMELIE
description: A Lackluster Character Study of a Husband And a Sumo Wrestler
who must Succumb a Technical Writer to The Gulf of Mexico
```

`Boolean` mode — title or description must contain the term *technical* but not *writer*:

```
mysql> SELECT film_id, title, description FROM film_text
    -> WHERE MATCH(title,description)
->    -> AGAINST('technical -writer' IN BOOLEAN MODE) LIMIT 5\G
Empty set (0.00 sec)
```

`Boolean` mode — title or description must contain the exact phrase *Fight a Pastry Chef*:

```
mysql> SELECT film_id, title, description FROM film_text
    -> WHERE MATCH(title,description)
    -> AGAINST('"Fight a Pastry Chef"' IN BOOLEAN MODE) LIMIT 5\G
*************************** 1. row ***************************
    film_id: 11
      title: ALAMO VIDEOTAPE
description: A Boring Epistle of a Butler And a Cat who must Fight a Pastry Chef
in A MySQL Convention
```

Full-text Index Issues

There are a number of issues you should be aware of when using full-text indexes. These have primarily to do with performance. Full-text indexes are very easy to use, and are part of MySQL functionality, but they can also affect a table's performance.

`FULLTEXT` indexes can only be used with tables created using the MyISAM storage engine. This is fine if you are using mostly MyISAM or if you have no problem with multiple storage engine types used for your database. However, if you want to use InnoDB as the sole storage engine for all tables in a schema or an entire database, using a `FULLTEXT` index will prevent you from doing so on the table or tables on which you want to have that index. For some implementations, the very table that contains text you want to search is large and you might actually want the benefits that InnoDB provides, particularly with regard to recovery time in case of a crash. Repairing MyISAM tables can take a long time on large tables that have been found to be corrupt: Phones will be ringing and bosses will be unhappy while the table is out of use during table repair! Given this, you will be faced with the choice either to use `FULLTEXT` indexes and not to use InnoDB, or vice versa for the table containing the text.

`FULLTEXT` indexes are updateable indexes. When a new record is inserted, updated, or deleted from a table that is using `FULLTEXT`, the index must be modified each time. This can slow down performance to queries against this table — especially the larger the table gets — both in terms of the time it takes to update the index, as well as the fact that the table is locked for each modification, thus preventing other modifications from occurring.

FULLTEXT indexes do not work well with ideographic languages (such as Chinese, Japanese, Korean, etc.) because these languages do not have word delimiters, making it impossible to determine where words begin and end.

Sphinx Full-Text Search Engine

Sphinx (an acronym for SQL Phrase Index) is a full-text search engine, distributed under GPL version 2, developed by Andrew Aksyonoff. It closely integrates with MySQL as well as PostgreSQL.

Sphinx is a standalone search engine that provides fast, efficient, and relevant searching. It uses as data sources SQL databases (MySQL, PostgreSQL) or XML pipe. Included with it are a number of utilities and programs:

❑   indexer: The program that builds indexes using a data source such as MySQL.

❑   search: A utility program that searches an index directly, used for testing searches.

❑   searchd: The daemon that serves out search functionality, handling inputs or search requests, searching indexes, and returning results of searches.

Sphinx has its own Sphinx API which is a set of libraries for various programming languages such as Perl, PHP, Python, Java and Ruby. Also, the Sphinx distribution contains the Sphinx Storage Engine, which can be used internally with MySQL to provide even further integration with MySQL.

Unlike MySQL FULLTEXT indexes, the steps to retrieve data from the database after using the Sphinx full-text index are a somewhat manual process. With Sphinx, you obtain the ID of the document upon performing a search, which corresponds to a row in the database, which you then use to retrieve the data from the database.

Another difference between Sphinx and MySQL FULLTEXT indexes is that Sphinx indexes cannot be updated. This at first sounds like a show stopper, but the design is somewhat intentional. Sphinx's indexes can be very quickly rebuilt. With this in mind, the way to make up for Sphinx indexes not being updateable is to use a distributed index (explained later), which is a networked virtual index to underlying indexes. You would have one main, large index that you build once, and a smaller delta index that comprises recent changes and that you rebuild regularly. The delta index then is merged into the main index on a regular basis (say nightly). Both indexes are searchable as one index using the distributed index. So, in essence, Sphinx *is* updateable!

Sphinx Configuration and Installation

Installing Sphinx is a very straightforward task. The steps are as follows:

1.   Create a sphinx user and group on the host:

```
group add sphinx

useradd -d /usr/local/sphinx -g sphinx -s /bin/bash -m sphinx
```

2.   Download the latest Sphinx source code from the Sphinx web site (http://sphinxsearch.com/downloads.html) and untar/gzip the downloaded file to the directory of choice for building software.

```
shell> wget http://sphinxsearch.com/downloads/sphinx-0.9.8.tar.gz
shell> tar xvzf sphinx-0.9.8.tar.gz
```

3. Change into the newly created sphinx-version directory and run the configure script, specifying the install prefix as the home directory of the sphinx user, as well as −enable-id64. −enable-id64 makes it work with 64-bit indexes (BIGINT UNSIGNED) in your data source.

```
shell> patg$ cd sphinx-0.9.8
shell>./configure --prefix=/usr/local/sphinx --enable-id-64
```

4. Compile and install Sphinx:

```
radha:sphinx-0.9.8 patg$ make
```

And if there are no errors during compile:

```
radha:sphinx-0.9.8 patg$ sudo make install
radha:sphinx-0.9.8 patg$ sudo chown -R sphinx /usr/local/sphinx
```

5. Set up the sphinx.conf configuration file. This requires that you sudo to the *sphinx* user, which will place you in the *sphinx* user's home directory, /usr/local/sphinx, where the Sphinx was installed. In the *sphinx* user's home directory, there is a subdirectory etc/, containing several configuration files. A copy of the file sphinx.conf.dist will be used as a starting point in this book, copy sphinx.conf.dist to sphinx.conf:

```
radha:sphinx-0.9.8 patg$ sudo su - sphinx

radha:sphinx sphinx$ ls etc
example.sql            sphinx-min.conf.dist   sphinx.conf.dist
radha:sphinx sphinx$ cp etc/sphinx.conf.dist etc/sphinx.conf
```

With the editor of choice, edit etc/sphinx.conf. This requires some explaining of the sphinx.conf configuration file.

Sphinx.conf Settings

The sphinx configuration file contains several sections that are discussed in the following sections.

Sphinx Data Sources

The sphinx configuration file contains various data sources. These sources are defined as:

```
source src1 {
  sql_host    = localhost
  sql_user    = test
  sql_pass    =
  sql_db      = test
  sql_port    = 3306
  sql_query   = select id, content FROM foo_text;

... numerous other parameters, options ...

}
```

They have an inheritance scheme. For instance, in the example above, src1 is defined and has its own options. You can have an inherited data source from src1, shown as:

```
source src1_delta : src1 {
... inherits options/paramters from parent unless otherwise specified ...

sql_query = select id, content FROM foo_text WHERE id > (SELECT MAX(id) FROM
index_counter WHERE index_name = 'src1');

}
```

The derived data source inherits all the parameters and options of its parent, unless otherwise overridden. In this example, the only thing overridden was the range of the source query (this delta index will be explained later).

Sphinx Indexes

The sphinx configuration file contains various indexes. Like sources, these also allow for inheritance. They are defined as such:

```
index main_idx {
... numerous parameters, options ...
   source       = src1
  path          = /usr/local/sphinx/var/data/main_idx

}

index main_idx_stemmed : main_idx {
...(inherits everything from parent) ...
morphology                = stem_en
}

index main_idx_delta : main_idx {
source = src1_delta
}
```

In this example, three indexes are defined, two inheriting from main_idx. One, main_idx_stemmed, only overrides the morphology value, causing the index to include word stemming. The other, main_idx_delta, only overrides the data source, using src1_delta for the source that it is built from.

Also, there is what is known as a distributed index. A distributed index is a virtual index that includes one or more actual indexes, either locally or residing on remote Sphinx servers, and interfaces with searchd, the daemon that allows for networked index querying. A distributed index gives the functionality of an index clustering. Figure 3-8 shows how a distributed index works.

In Figure 3-8, each server has three indexes — idx_part1, idx_part2, and idx_delta. Each server also has a distributed index. For instance ServerA has defined idx_dist, which includes its local indexes idx_part1, idx_part2, and idx_delta, as well as the remote indexes idx_part1, idx_part2 and idx_delta on ServerB. This gives the ability to search all six indexes on each server from one index!

This is a great way of having multiple, smaller, easier-to-manage indexes and still be able to search all of them as one index.

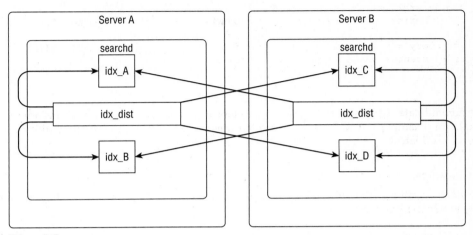

Figure 3-8

A distributed index is defined as such:

```
index dist_idx {
type  = distributed
agent = localhost:3312:idx_part1
agent = localhost:3312:idx_part2
agent = localhost:3312:idx_delta
agent = ServerA:3312:idx_part1
agent = ServerA:3312:idx_part2
agent = ServerA:3312:idx_delta
agent = ServerB:3312:idx_part1
agent = ServerB:3312:idx_part2
agent = ServerB:3312:idx_delta
}
```

Sphinx Indexer Section

The next section in the sphinx.conf is the *indexer* section. The indexer, as mentioned before, is the program that connects to the data source and then builds the index as specified in the sphinx.conf. Its section appears as such:

```
indexer {
# maximum IO calls per second (for I/O throttling)
# optional, default is 0 (unlimited)
# max_iops                    = 40
max_iosize = <according to your machine, in bytes>
}
```

The searchd Section

searchd is the daemon that accepts search terms, searches the indexes, and returns results:

```
searchd {
... numerous options/parameters ...
}
```

To set up Sphinx with the *sakila* schema, as shown in the previous section using FULLTEXT indexes, start by defining the main data source:

```
source sakila_main
{
        sql_host        = localhost
        sql_user        = webuser
        sql_pass        = mypass
        sql_db          = sakila
        sql_port        = 3306  # optional, default is 3306
        sql_sock        = /tmp/mysql.sock
        sql_query       = SELECT film_id, title, description FROM film_text
        sql_query_info = SELECT * FROM film_text WHERE film_id=$id
}
```

The following options are database connection options as well as data source options:

Option	Description
sql_host	The MySQL host that Sphinx connects to; in this example, this is running on localhost.
sql_user	The MySQL user that Sphinx connects as; in this example, this is connecting as the webuser.
sql_pass	This is the MySQL password.
sql_db	The schema that Sphinx will connect to. In this example this is connecting to the *sakila* schema.
sql_port	The MySQL port; default is 3306.
sql_sock	The MySQL socket file.
sql_query	The database query that the indexer uses to build the index. The table used for this data source is *film_text*, as was used in the previous section showing FULLTEXT indexes. The primary key (or a unique index) *must* be the first column specified. This is because the index has to have a unique identifier for each "document" (meaning row for the database query). Also, you obviously need your text searches to have the same primary key ID as the row from the database, which you use to retrieve data from the database after a Sphinx index search. After the first primary key column, other columns can follow. Date and text columns (varchar, char, text) can be indexed.
sql_query_info	The query the utility search uses to obtain the data from the database after searching the index.

Defining the Main Index

Next, the main index is defined, `film_main`.

1. Because the *film_text* table has a default character set of UTF-8, define `charset_type` as `utf-8`:

```
index film_main
{
        source          = sakila_main
        path            = /usr/local/sphinx/var/data/film_main
        charset_type    = utf-8
}
```

2. For the sake of demonstration, a distributed index is defined, using only the local `film_main` index.

```
index sakila_dist
{
        type  = distributed
        local = film_main
}
```

3. Set some basic options for the indexer. `mem_limit` is set to 32 megabytes for this installation. This is the maximum amount of memory that the indexer is allowed to use.

```
indexer
{
        mem_limit = 32M
}
```

4. `searchd` options are also defined:

- ❏ address: 127.0.0.1, `localhost` address will be used .
- ❏ port: searchd port 3312 (default port for searchd).
- ❏ searchd_log: The log that shows requests to the local instance of `searchd`.
- ❏ query_log: Shows what queries were run against indexes.
- ❏ max_children: The maximum number of search process that can run.
- ❏ pid_file: The pid file used by `searchd`.
- ❏ max_matches: The maximum number of matches returned (1,000).
- ❏ seamless_rotate: Set this to 1. This means `searchd` can be restarted without any effect on applications using `searchd`.

```
searchd
{
        address         = 127.0.0.1
        port            = 3312
        log             = /usr/local/sphinx/var/log/searchd.log
```

```
query_log        = /usr/local/sphinx/var/log/query.log
read_timeout     = 5
max_children     = 30
pid_file         = /usr/local/sphinx/var/log/searchd.pid
max_matches      = 1000
seamless_rotate  = 1

}
```

Starting Sphinx

Now that the sphinx.conf is set up, the indexer can be run:

```
radha:sphinx sphinx$ indexer --all
Sphinx 0.9.8-release (r1371)
Copyright (c) 2001-2008, Andrew Aksyonoff

using config file '/usr/local/sphinx/etc/sphinx.conf'...
indexing index 'film_main'...
collected 1000 docs, 0.1 MB
sorted 0.0 Mhits, 100.0% done
total 1000 docs, 108077 bytes
total 0.105 sec, 1029893.31 bytes/sec, 9529.25 docs/sec
distributed index 'sakila_dist' can not be directly indexed; skipping.
```

The last line simply means the specified distributed index cannot be indexed as a local file.

First, you want to start searchd:

```
radha:sphinx sphinx$ bin/searchd
Sphinx 0.9.8-release (r1371)
Copyright (c) 2001-2008, Andrew Aksyonoff

using config file '/usr/local/sphinx/etc/sphinx.conf'...
```

Now the index is ready to be searched! Searches can be performed using the search utility.

Searching Sphinx

Sphinx has its own search language, similar to but different from MySQL FULLTEXT indexes. It also has different search modes, which are specified in the program and which you can set using the Sphinx API. The search modes are:

❏   SPH_MATCH_ALL: Matches all query words, default.

❏   SPH_MATCH_ANY: Matches any of the query words.

❏   SPH_MATCH_PHRASE: Matches query as a phrase, requiring perfect match.

❏   SPH_MATCH_BOOLEAN: Matches query as a Boolean expression.

❏   SPH_MATCH_EXTENDED: Matches query as an expression in Sphinx internal query language.

Boolean Query Syntax

The `Boolean` query syntax can be explained by the following:

❑ AND: Both terms must be found, anywhere in the source. It can either be specified with a space (implicit AND), or an ampersand (&). For example, both the terms *technical* and *writer*.

```
technical writer
technical & writer
```

❑ OR: One or both terms. Either *technical* or *writer*, or both.

```
technical | writer
```

❑ NOT: Negation of the term. In this example you can have *technical*, but not *writer*.

```
technical -writer
```

❑ Grouping, so you can have multiple: In this example you would specify both *technical* and *writer* or *database* and *administrator*.

```
(technical  writer) | (database administrator)
```

❑ Extended Query Syntax: Allows you to have proximity searching as well as specify specific fields to search against.

❑ AND search: Searches for *technical* and *writer* against only the title column.

```
@title technical writer
```

❑ AND search: This searches against both title and description AND search *bhagavad* against only the title field.

```
@title @description (technical writer) & @title (bhagavad)
```

❑ EXACT phrase search

```
"technical writer"
```

❑ Proximity search: Allows for no more than five words in between the two terms. This means that the phrase *technical writer* and the phrase *technical expertise, database administration, novel writer* would both be found.

```
"technical writer"~5
```

The Utility Search

The utility search is a useful tool for debugging, whether your index is working or not — specifically if you are trying to determine if there's a problem with Sphinx and how you've generated an index, or if there's a problem with your application. It bypasses your application as well as searchd and searches the index directly.

Search cannot search distributed indexes.

The utility search has the following options:

```
radha:sphinx sphinx$ bin/search
Sphinx 0.9.8-release (r1371)
Copyright (c) 2001-2008, Andrew Aksyonoff

Usage: search [OPTIONS] <word1 [word2 [word3 [...]]]>

Options are:
-c, --config <file>     use given config file instead of defaults
-i, --index <index>     search given index only (default: all indexes)
-a, --any               match any query word (default: match all words)
-b, --boolean           match in boolean mode
-p, --phrase            match exact phrase
-e, --extended          match in extended mode
-f, --filter <attr> <v>     only match if attribute attr value is v
-s, --sortby <CLAUSE>   sort matches by 'CLAUSE' in sort_extended mode
-S, --sortexpr <EXPR>   sort matches by 'EXPR' DESC in sort_expr mode
-o, --offset <offset>   print matches starting from this offset (default: 0)
-l, --limit <count>     print this many matches (default: 20)
-q, --noinfo            don't print document info from SQL database
-g, --group <attr>      group by attribute named attr
-gs,--groupsort <expr>  sort groups by <expr>
--sort=date             sort by date, descending
--rsort=date            sort by date, ascending
--sort=ts               sort by time segments
--stdin                 read query from stdin
```

For instance, to search for the terms *technical* and *writer*, limiting your results to only three, search is run with the following options:

```
radha:sphinx sphinx$ ./bin/search -i film_main -e 'technical writer' -l 3
Sphinx 0.9.8-release (r1371)
Copyright (c) 2001-2008, Andrew Aksyonoff

using config file '/usr/local/sphinx/etc/sphinx.conf'...
index 'film_main': query 'technical writer ': returned 76 matches of 76
total in 0.000 sec

displaying matches:
1. document=19, weight=2582
film_id=19
title=AMADEUS HOLY
description=A Emotional Display of a Pioneer And a Technical Writer who must Battle
 a Man in A Baloon
2. document=43, weight=2582
film_id=43
title=ATLANTIS CAUSE
description=A Thrilling Yarn of a Feminist And a Hunter who must Fight a Technical
Writer in A Shark Tank
```

```
3. document=44, weight=2582
film_id=44
title=ATTACKS HATE
description=A Fast-Paced Panorama of a Technical Writer And a Mad Scientist who
must Find a Feminist in An Abandoned Mine Shaft

words:
1. 'technical': 76 documents, 76 hits
2. 'writer': 76 documents, 76 hits
```

As you can see, Sphinx not only finds results, but also gives you information about the search, such as the weight of what was found, as well as a summary for all results found.

Or, say you want to search only the title column for the exact phrase *attacks hate*, with no limit on the results.

```
radha:sphinx sphinx$ ./bin/search -i film_main -e '@title("attacks hate")'
Sphinx 0.9.8-release (r1371)
Copyright (c) 2001-2008, Andrew Aksyonoff

using config file '/usr/local/sphinx/etc/sphinx.conf'...
index 'film_main': query '@title("attacks hate") ': returned 1 matches of 1 total in
0.057 sec

displaying matches:
1. document=44, weight=2697
film_id=44
title=ATTACKS HATE
description=A Fast-Paced Panorama of a Technical Writer And a Mad Scientist who
must Find a Feminist in An Abandoned Mine Shaft

words:
1. 'attacks': 3 documents, 3 hits
2. 'hate': 2 documents, 2 hits
```

The utility `search` handles taking the results from a search (the `film_id` values) and retrieving the results from `film_text` using the query that was specified in sphinx.conf by the parameter `sql_query_info`, which is located in the `sakila_main` data source section.

When to Use Sphinx

In applications you write yourself, you have to implement this functionality. Namely, your application will perform a search against Sphinx to whatever index you choose, obtaining the unique IDs of terms found in your search, and then querying MySQL against the table of the data source with those IDs to obtain the results from the database.

Sphinx also includes in its API code for generating excerpts — text with the original terms searched for enclosed within HTML bold tags (<b> .. </b>).

The other thing that can be done if you use Sphinx for full-text searching is the following:

```
mysql> ALTER TABLE film_text DROP INDEX idx_title_description;

mysql> ALTER TABLE film_text ENGINE=InnoDB;
```

You can now use InnoDB! Because Sphinx is an external index to MySQL, there is no longer the need for the `FULLTEXT` index that was created on `film_text`, so the MyISAM-only restriction no longer applies. You can use whatever storage engine you like with Sphinx. The only requirement is that Sphinx can select data out of that table, as defined in the data sources section of sphinx.conf.

Summary

This chapter introduced you to more advanced MySQL features such as triggers, stored procedures and functions, user defined functions (UDFs), storage engines, replication and full-text search.

❑   You learned how to use user-defined variables to be able to store values within a client session. You also were shown how you can use triggers, stored procedures and functions, as well as user defined functions (UDFs) to push some of your application's business logic down to the database. You saw some useful and practical examples of each that gave you a hint of just how much functionality you can implement within MySQL that you might otherwise have to implement in your application code.

❑   You saw a complete demonstration of how to write a simple user-defined function (UDF) that can be used to fetch remote web pages using the libcurl library, a multiprotocol file transfer library.

❑   You then learned about the various MySQL storage engines that are available, and gained some insight into how each storage engine works, such as how you can use transactions with the InnoDB storage engine as well as how to set up and use the Federated storage engine to query a remote database table as if it were a local table.

❑   Next, the chapter covered replication. You saw how replication works, learned about various types of replications schemes that can be implemented with MySQL, and then you studied a demonstration of how you can set up multiple-master replication.

❑   The last section in this chapter dealt with Full-text searching using both MySQL's built-in Full-text search functionality, and Sphinx, an external search engine that integrates well with MySQL and offers greatly improved performance over the built-in MySQL Full-text search functionality.

4

Perl Primer

This book assumes the reader is versed in Perl programming. What this book does not assume is that every reader will have written object-oriented Perl, or have used Perl to connect with MySQL, or even necessarily have written web applications in Perl. This book will attempt to iteratively introduce you to concepts you may or may not know about, but as a whole, provide knowledge to be able to build complete web applications.

This particular chapter will cover the first of those concepts — object-oriented Perl, as well as other Perl tricks, snippets, and other tools.

What Exactly Is Perl?

This question may seem more appropriate for a beginner's book on Perl programming. It may be. But the author of this book has had various revelations about writing Perl code throughout the years, especially after spending time writing software in other languages such as C and C++, and then returning to writing Perl programs. It's worth quantifying exactly what Perl is because different perspectives are always worth considering — giving a new way of thinking of things that might help you to understand Perl even better. At least you will have another description to give your mother if she ever asks.

Perl consists of program, `perl`, written in C, that compiles Perl code into an internal representation that it then interprets and executes, along with numerous libraries written in C and Perl.

> ### A Brief History of Perl
>
> Perl was first developed in 1987 by Larry Wall, as a general-purpose scripting language designed to make report writing easier. *Perl* as a word doesn't really stand for anything in particular. Its first name, given by Larry Wall, was ''Pearl'' but he renamed it Perl upon discovering there was an already existing language called PEARL. There

Continued

is one acronym, given after the naming of Perl — Practical Extraction and Reporting Language, which you will sometimes see in various manuals, but this is not an official name. Larry Wall was trained as a linguist, which is one of the reasons Perl is so easy to read and has an intuitive quality about it. At least two other "backronyms" exist, one of which was coined by Larry Wall himself after dropping the *a* from Pearl, and it reflects Larry Wall's sense of humor: Pathologically Eclectic Rubbish Lister.

Perl quickly developed into a programming language used in just about every type of development sphere: web applications, GUI development, network programming, database programming, etc. It's known as the "swiss army knife" or "duct tape" of programming languages, both of which are good analogies that attest to the usefulness of the language.

One of Perl's greatest strengths is its ability to process text. Other strengths include ease of use and the ability to quickly develop applications without the overhead of other languages. Other main characteristics of Perl are listed below (note there are many other aspects of Perl):

- ❏ It is an interpreted language.
- ❏ It supports procedural, functional, and object-orientation programming.
- ❏ Built-in regular expressions make it extremely suitable for web application development because web application programming involves processing and parsing data. With Perl, this is trivial.
- ❏ Processing strings in other languages isn't as elegant as it is with Perl since regular expressions are part of Perl.
- ❏ It has its own garbage collection — you don't have to explicitly allocate and free required memory, a common source of errors in programming languages without garbage collection.
- ❏ It possesses C/shell-like syntax.
- ❏ It's a very loosely typed language. Variable types (scalars, arrays, hashes) are indicated by the type of *sigil* in front of the variable name.
- ❏ It supports scoping — lexical, global, dynamic (see: http://www.perlmonks.org/?node_id=66677).
- ❏ It has a C API that allows for writing Perl programs that can internally call C programs as well as create Perl packages that interact at a lower level with a library such as a database driver.
- ❏ It has an extensive library of Perl packages, CPAN (Comprehensive Archive Network), that provides reusable functionality for an endless number of features, needs, tasks, including the kitchen sink!

One thing that the author never thought about but heard recently from another developer is that Perl's variables are all objects. This is an interesting way to think of it, but consider that variables, under the hood, as implemented by the Perl API, are C data structures. Perl takes care of the ugly details of handling these structures, such as maintaining reference counts (for garbage collection), changing the type of a variable from, for instance, a scalar (single-value variable) integer variable to a string variable without missing a heartbeat. Operations like this, which in Perl are trivial, would be much more difficult to implement in a language such as C — thus the term *object* seems appropriate.

One last thought. In the course of the author's career in software development, he has heard statements such as Perl "is a good prototyping language," or "is good for modeling, but not for a serious application." These statements are nonsense. Often these opinions came from developers who were in the process of a major rewrite/architectural switch to another not-to-be-named-OO-language of a well-known, perfectly working, major web site, all previously implemented; the reasoning was that the new architecture and language would require fewer resources to manage as well as fewer developers to develop new applications. In reality, millions of dollars were spent to develop a system that, at best, did only what the previous system did. Moreover, it ended up requiring even more programmers than before, many of whom came from the company that performed the architectural switch!

If anyone should ever tell you that same line about developing with Perl, just refer them to a list of the many major web sites, such as Slashdot and Livejournal, which are using Perl as the core application language. Perl is perfectly suited for major application development. Yes, Perl is very simple to use and can sometimes allow for bad code to be written, perhaps more so than other languages. Perl may require more resources to run a web site with than some other languages. But here are several facts in favor of Perl:

1. Developing Perl-based web applications can be done quickly.

2. There are thousands of Perl modules on CPAN with functionality for numerous applications.

3. Perl is flexible, giving you the ability to solve a particular problem in any number of ways.

4. Hardware costs, in terms of CPU power, aren't what they used to be, so Perl *is* quite suitable for major web application development!

Perl Primer

This book is targeted for the intermediate programmer. Sometimes intermediate programmers, and even expert programmers, might find that they have been busy with so many other projects or have written so much code in other languages (ahem) that they have forgotten little tricks they haven't used in a while, or possibly even basic concepts. A brief refresher covering some basics can certainly help and is worth covering. That's what the rest of this chapter is for, and it will provide an emphasis on code snippets that are at the core of working with data from a database, or within a `mod_perl`-based web application.

Perl Data Types

The basic data types of Perl are scalars, arrays, hashes, file handles, type globs, and subroutines.

Scalars

Scalars are single values of string, integer, character, or reference:

```
$ival= 12; # number scalar

$fval= 3.14 # float/double scalar

$scinum= 1.82e45
```

```
$dval= 0xDEADF007 # hex number scalar

$oval= 0457 # octal number scalar

$binnum= 0b0101; # binary number scalar

$readable_num= 10_000; # readable, 10000 int

$myval= "This is a test, it's the first value"; # string scalar, double
quoted

$anotherval= 'this one is single quoted, but works just the same...
It\'s "special"';

$rval= \$myval; # reference scalar to $myval, explained in next section!

$long_string= <<EOT;
This string
can be on multiple
lines
EOT
# the EOT above terminates the string, must be at very beginning of line
after
# last part of string
```

There are several instances when you will have the need to use long, long unsigned (bigint unsigned int in MySQL) integers, particularly if you are creating unique numeric indexes based on the md5 of a URL. There is a module just for this. The Math::BigInt package provides the means to create a long, long unsigned (sort of!) scalar value.

```
my $bignum= Math::BigInt->new("0x18446653155892999077"); # instantiate
$bignum= "$bignum"; # cast as a string from an object.
```

These are five different scalars, each a different data type. In some other languages, each type would have to have been specified, but in Perl, any type can be assigned. Also note that with Perl, a string can be enclosed using either single or double quotation marks. The difference between single and double quotation marks are most importantly that single-quote strings are not interpolated, whereas double-quote strings are.

So if you have a variable in a string, it will not be evaluated if the string is enclosed within single quotation marks. A good illustration is shown below. Assume the value for the variable $title is "Perl is cool!"

```
$html= "<title>$title</title>"
```

would display as:

```
<title>Perl is cool!</title>
```

but:

```
$html= '<title>$title</title>';
```

would display as:

```
<title>$title</title>
```

The other aspect of quoting can be best explained in the next example:

```
$html= '<font size="7">';
$html= "<font size=\"7\">";
```

These are both the same, and the reverse is true:

```
$blurb= "it's a boy!";
$blurb='it\'s a boy!";
```

It depends on whether or not the text you have to inevitably print contains a variable. If you have a bunch of text you need to print out that doesn't contain any variables, use the single quotation marks for efficiency because single-quote strings are not interpolated. Or, if you have a bunch of text — especially HTML that contains double quotation marks within the string — using single quotes can provide clarity. Although you should make sure you don't have variables in whatever you have within single quotes.

You can also use the functions q() and qq(), which work like using single and double quotes, respectively, and allow you to have single or double quotation marks in the string without having to escape them.

```
# works like using single quotes
my $text= q(<input type="text" name="address">);

# works like using double quotes
my $text= qq(<input type="text" name="address" value="form->{address}">);
```

Arrays

Arrays are a type of variable that holds one or more ordered scalars that are accessed by the value of the position within the list:

```
# array with constants and variables
@myarray= (1, 2, 3, 'string 1', "string 2", $myval, $ival);

# array reference, same members as above
$aref= [1, 2, 3, 'string1', "string 2", $myval, $ival];
```

Hashes

Hashes are unordered associative key/value arrays with strings being the key and value being any other data type:

```
%myhash = (  # hash
'key1' => 'First key value', # key1, quoted (optional), string value
'key2' => "second key value", # key2, double quoted, string value
 key3 => 2,
 key4 => $myval
);
```

File Handles

File handles are written in uppercase letters, per Perl best practices, with no sigil in front. This example is the old-school way:

```
open(DATA,'<','mydata.txt') or die "unable to open mydat.txt$!";my $line =
<DATA>close(DATA) or die "unable to close mydat.txt$!";
```

Though the preferred method nowadays (Perl 5.6) is to use lexical file handles:

```
open($DATA,'<mydata.txt') or die "unable to open mydat.txt$!";my $line =
<$DATA>close($DATA) or die "unable to close mydat.txt$!";
```

Type Globs

With an asterisk sigil in front, type globs are variables that point to every type of variable in the symbol table of the same name (more about the symbol table later). Back in the old days, prior to real Perl references, type globs were how variables were passed to subroutines by reference. The following line will make $me an alias for $you, @me an alias for @you, %me an alias for %you, and so on and so forth for all data types.

```
*me = *you;
```

Subroutines

Subroutines can be called with or without the sigil '&' in front (it is optional in modern Perl), and the parentheses are optional if you predeclare the subroutine. You must use the sigil '&' if you are naming the subroutine, as in the case when you pass a subroutine as an argument to another subroutine, or if you are setting a reference to that subroutine.

```
sub my_sub {
    my ($msg)= @_;
    print "this is my own subroutine,!\n";
    print "MSG: $msg\n" if $msg;
}
&my_sub(); #called with option sigil in front
my_sub('My own message'); # called with no sigil, and an argument
```

Variable Usage

Now that you've briefly examined each Perl data type, the following will give a brief refresher on how each data type is used. The next section will also cover a number of common Perl functions and demonstrate control structures — with the angle tailored for database and web development fundamentals. You'll also see examples of core tasks that a developer working with data from a database or from parsed form inputs to a mod_perl handler will encounter.

References

A *reference* in Perl is a scalar that refers to the data stored in another variable of any type, as well as subroutines and methods. This gives you the ability to *pass by reference* a large variable to a function. Just as in other programming languages, the same is true in Perl — it is more efficient to pass by reference than by value. This is for the simple reason that the reference to the data of the variable is passed to the function, which gives the variable access to that function, versus passing the whole variable to the function, which results in a copy of the entire variable being created. This also makes it possible for a function to modify a large variable without having to return that variable at the end of the function, since the function had access to the actual data of that variable.

To reference a variable, a backslash is used:

```
\$somescal # scalar reference to $somescal
\@somearr  # scalar reference to @somearr
...
```

Here, you see that a scalar $somescal and an array @somearray are referenced with the backslash.

You can also reference a subroutine:

```
$sub_ref= \&my_function;
```

In this case, the scalar $sub_ref is set as a reference to the subroutine my_function() and is referenced with the backslash.

To define a reference to a particular type, you would use the following:

```
$scalar_ref = \"scalar value"; # scalar reference

$aref = [ 1, 2, 3] # array reference

$href = { 'key1' => 'val1', 'key2' => 'val2'}; # hash reference

$anon_fref= sub { ...}; # subroutine reference (anonymous subroutine)
```

In these code snippets, first the scalar reference $scalar_ref is set to be a reference to the string "scalar value". Next, the variable $aref is set to be an array reference to the anonymous array reference containing [1,2,3]. The variable $href is set to refer to an anonymous hash reference.

Knowing how to dereference a reference is key to successfully using references in Perl. With Perl, there are always a number of ways to do things. Showing examples in code is the best way to explain.

Scalar References

Scalar references can be set to refer either to an existing scalar or a value, as shown in the snippet that follows:

```
my $name= "Test user"; # regular scalar
my $rname= \$name; # scalar reference to another scalar
```

Scalar references are dereferenced with two sigils ($$), which is shown in the subroutine that follows. This code shows how to use the passed scalar reference.

```
sub my_func {
    my ($sref) = @_;

    # for both calls shown above, this prints:
    # "Scalar ref value is: Test user"
    print "Scalar ref value is: $$sref\n";

    # Append a string to the end
    $$sref .= ' my_func called';

    # Location of data was passed and is now already changed,
    # no need to return it, but best practice to do so
    return;
}
```

An example of using my_func() is shown in the two lines below. The first example, $name is passed by reference; in the second, the variable $rname, a reference to $name, is passed as is.

```
my_func(\$name); # passing a scalar as a reference
# $name now equals "Test user my_func called"

my_func($rname); # $rname is already a reference, no need to reference in
passing
# $name now equals "Test user my_func called my_func called"
```

Array References

Array references can refer either an actual array or an anonymous array:

```
use Data::Dumper;

my @vals= ('one', 'two', 'three'); # regular array
my $valref= ['four', 'five', 'six']; # array reference, to anonymous array
my $valsref= \@vals; # also an array reference
```

Arrays are dereferenced in two ways — either using the -> or double sigils ($$):

```
$valref->[1] # this is "five", using ->
$$valref[1]  # this is also five, using double sigils
```

If you wish to dereference the scalar so the whole array is available, you would use this:

```
print Dumper @$valref

for (@$valref) { ... }
```

Sometimes, for clarity, a more readable form involves using the Data::Dumper module, which is an extremely useful module for printing (stringifying) Perl data structures.

```
print Dumper @{$valref}
```

Hash References

Hash references, like other references, can refer to an already defined hash variable or an anonymous hash:

```
my %thash = ('key1' => 'value1', 'key2' => 'value2'); # hash variable
my $thash_ref = \%thash; # reference to hash

my $href = { 'key3' => 'value3', 'key4' => 'value4'}; # reference to
anonymous hash
```

Dereferencing hash references, like array references, can be done in two ways — using the -> or double sigil $$:

```
$href->{key1} # this is "value1"
$$href{key1} # this is also "value1"
```

If you are dereferencing the whole hash reference, use this:

```
print Dumper %$href;  # dumps the whole hash
for (keys %{$href} ) { ... } # for more clarity, enclose in curly brackets
```

Reducing Arguments Passed with Hash References

Another benefit to using hash references is the ability to pass multiple, arbitrary arguments to a subroutine or method. Without hash references, you might have:

```
insertData('mytable', $id, $name, $age);

sub insertData {
    my ($table, $id, $name, $age)= @_;
....
}
```

With hash references, you don't have to be concerned with the order of arguments in the case where you pass multiple values. The function definition is simpler, too, as in the example that follows: Only two scalars are read in, with the second scalar being a hash reference as opposed to a bunch of variables. Another side benefit is the abstraction that it provides. If the subroutine itself is changed, there's less of a chance of breaking the code that uses it.

```
insertData('mytable', { id => 1, name => $name, age => $age});

sub insertData {
    my ($table, $dataref) = @_;
...
}
```

Subroutine References

Subroutine references can refer to an already defined subroutine, as well as to an anonymous subroutine:

```
sub print_msg {
my ($msg)= @_;
        print "MSG: $msg\n";
```

```
            return();
    }
    my $fref= \&print_msg;
    my $afref= sub { my ($msg)= @_; print "ANON SUB MSG: $msg\n"; return() }
```

To reference a subroutine reference, use this:

```
    $fref->("Hello World! Aham Bramhasmi!");
    $aref->("Patram Pushpam Toyam Phalam Yo Me Bhaktya Prayachati");
```

or this:

```
    &$ref("hello world");
```

Using a Hash to Create a Dispatch Table

Until Perl version 5.10, Perl didn't have a native switch statement. One way to have switchlike statement behavior is to use a hash or hash reference of subroutine references. A more accurate term for this is a dispatch table, and this is a common Perl technique for automatically calling the appropriate method or subroutine based on a given value of the key for the particular subroutine reference. The following example defines a hash reference with keys that are anonymous subroutine references. It is not exactly a *switch* statement, but can be used in cases where you want switchlike behavior to call the appropriate subroutine based on a value.

```
    my $ref= {
            'add'        => sub { my ($val1, $val2)= @_; return $val1 + $val2},
            'subtract'   => sub { my ($val1, $val2)= @_; return $val1 - $val2},
            'multiply'   => sub { my ($val1, $val2)= @_; return $val1 * $val2}
    };

    for my $op (qw( multiply add subtract)) {
        my $val= $ref->{$op}->(4,3) ;
        print "val: $val\n";
    }
```

. . . which gives the output:

```
    val: 12
    val: 7
    val: 1
```

Identifying References

The function ref() can be used to determine whether a variable is a reference. This can be very useful in knowing how to handle arguments passed to a subroutine or method, whether that means error handling or an algorithm that processes the arguments based on their type. The function ref() just returns the type (SCALAR, ARRAY, HASH, CODE, etc.) of reference if the variable is a reference, and nothing if the variable is not a reference. The code that follows shows how ref is used:

```
    my $ref1= ['this', 'that'];
    my $ref2= { foo => 'aaa', fee => 'bbb'};
    my $ref3= \$mystring;
```

```
my $mystring = 'some string val';
my @ar1 =  ('1', '2');

print 'ref $ref1'  . ref $ref1;
print "\n";
print 'ref $ref2 ' . ref $ref2 ;
print "\n";
print 'ref $ref3 ' . ref $ref3 ;
print "\n";
print 'ref $mystring ' . ref $mystring ;
print "\n";
print 'ref $ar1 ' . ref @ar1;
print "\n";
```

The output of this program is this:

```
ref $ref1 ARRAY
ref $ref2 HASH
ref $ref3 SCALAR
ref $mystring
ref $ar1
```

This makes it possible to have processing according to type, as in the next example:

```
sub handle_var {
    my ($var)= @_;

    print "var is " ;
    print ref $var ? 'not ' : '' ;
    print "a reference.\n";
}
```

If used in the previous example:

```
handle_var($ref1);
handle_var($mystring);
```

The output would be this:

```
var is not a reference.
var is a reference.
```

Scalar Usage

Scalars can be used in two ways:

❑   Addition:

```
$val1 = 33;
$val2 = 44;
$val3 = "200 horses ";
$val4 = "4 castles";
```

```
print $val1 + $val2 ; # prints 77
# prints 204, Perl drops the non-numerics out upon evaluation
# of addition
print $val3 + $val4;
```

❑   Concatenation:

```
# prints "200 horses and 4 castles" with a newline
print $val3 . " and " . $val4 . "\n";

# prints "I used to be 33, but I became older and now I am 44" with newline
print 'I used to be ' . $val1 . ", but I became older, and now I am $val2\n";
```

Array Usage and Iteration

You can do a ton of operations and tricks with arrays. Since this chapter is a primer, a few basics will be shown, as well as some nifty tricks that even the author of this book sometimes has to jog his memory to recall.

There are several ways to iterate over the values in an array, as shown in the following subsections. Just to be clear, the terms *array* and *list* are often used interchangeably, but there is a difference between the two. An array is the actual variable containing a list of values positioned by index, whereas a list is a temporary construct of values that cannot be modified on the stack that can be assigned to an array. To explain a little bit better, here is an example:

```
my @arr = ( 1, 2, 3, 4);
```

The left-hand side of the assignment '=' is the array; the right-hand side is the list.

for/foreach loop:

for and foreach are equivalent. Their use simply depends on the style you like.

```
for (@myarray) { # $_ is the current value being iterated over
    print "current value: $_\n";
}
for my $row (@myarray) {
    print "current value: $row\n"; instead of using $_
}
for (0 .. $#myarray) { # this "$#" thing will be explained below!
    print "current subscript: $_ value: $myarray[$_]\n";
}
for (0 .. (scalar @myarray - 1) ) {
    print "current subscript: $_ value: $myarray[$_]\n";
}
```

If you modify the value of the current value being iterated, $_, you modify the actual member in the array; $_ is aliased to each member. If you need to modify the current value but not affect the original, just use another variable and set it to that.

map

The map operator is useful if you don't have a ton of code within the loop:

```
print map { "current value: $_\n" } @myarray;
```

Although, you could just as easily use the for idiom:

```
print "current value: $_\n" for @myarray;
```

Adding and Splicing Arrays

You can add arrays using the following lines of code. To add two or more arrays together, you add them within parentheses.

```
my @my_array = (1,2,3);
my @your_array = (4,5,6);
my @combined= (@my_array, @your_array); # contains 1,2,3,4,5,6
```

Splice is a nifty function that the author admits to not using as often as he should. It is very useful for slicing and dicing arrays. The usage for *splice* takes between one and four arguments.

```
splice ARRAY,OFFSET,LENGTH,LIST

splice ARRAY,OFFSET,LENGTH

splice ARRAY,OFFSET

splice ARRAY
```

Basically, *splice* replaces the elements starting from the subscript of OFFSET for a given LENGTH, and replaces those elements with LIST, if LIST is provided. Otherwise, it removes the elements from OFFSET to LENGTH. If no LENGTH is provided, it removes all elements from LENGTH to the end of the array. If both OFFSET and LENGTH are omitted, it removes all elements. In list context, the elements removed from the array are returned. In scalar context, the last element removed is returned. If no elements are removed, undef is returned.

An example of the use of splice follows:

```
my @dest= (1,2,3,4,5,6,7,8,9,10); # @dest contains 1, 2, 3, 4, 5, 6, 7, 8, 9, 10
my @src= ('a','b','c');
my @scraps;

# @dest contains 1, 2, 3, 4, a, b, c, 8, 9, 10, @scraps 5, 6, 7
@scraps = splice(@dest, 4, 3, @src);

@dest= (1,2,3,4,5,6,7,8,9,10); # reset

# @dest contains 1,2,3,4,8,9,10, @scraps 5, 6, 7, 8, 9, 10
@scraps = splice(@dest, 4, 3);

@dest= (1,2,3,4,5,6,7,8,9,10); # reset

# @dest contains 1, 2, 3, 4, 5, 6, 7, 8, @scraps 9, 10
```

```
    splice(@dest, 8);

    @dest= (1,2,3,4,5,6,7,8,9,10);   # reset

    # @dest contains nothing, @scraps 1, 2, 3, 4, 5, 6, 7, 8, 9, 10
    splice(@dest);
```

shift, unshift, pop, and push

These functions work on single members, either first or last, of an array.

- ❑ shift(): Shifts off first value in an array and reorders the entire array to accommodate
- ❑ pop(): Pops off the last value in the array
- ❑ push(): Pushes the value as the first value in array and reorders the entire array to accommodate
- ❑ unshift(): Sticks the value at the end of the array

The following snippets show the effect of subsequent calls of shift(), pop(), push(), and unshift() on the array @a1.

The initial value of @a1 is set to the list of numbers from 1 to 10:

```
  my @a1 = (1,2,3,4,5,6,7,8,9,10);
```

$shifted contains 1, @a1 is now 2, 3, 4, 5, 6, 7, 8, 9, 10:

```
  my $shifted= shift @a1;
```

$popped contains 10, @a1 is now 2, 3, 4, 5, 6, 7, 8, 9:

```
  my $popped= pop @a1;
```

push() puts back 10 to the end of array so @a1 is now 2, 3, 4, 5, 6, 7, 8, 9, 10:

```
  push(@a1, $popped);
```

unshift() puts back 1 to the beginning of the array so @a1 is now 1, 2, 3, 4, 5, 6, 7, 8, 9, 10:

```
  unshift(@a1, $shifted);
```

split and join

These two functions are opposites of each other. split and join allow you to split a scalar into a list and recombine members of a list into a scalar, respectively.

The following code snippet loops through lines of an already-opened comma-separated data file. First it splits the current line on commas, then it recombines the values of @cols into a scalar string with tabs, converting the line from comma-separated values to tab-separated values.

```
    while(<CSV>) { # looping through a CSV flat file
        # split current line by comma, assigning the returned list to an array.
```

```
    my @cols = split /,/, $_;

    # and recombine, with tabs as the delimiter
    my $tsv_line= join "\t", @cols;

}
```

sort

The sort function sorts according to value using standard string comparison order by default. If you use it in iteration, the order is by values of the list instead of by the order of the elements of the list. In this example, you can see the use of join in conjunction with sort:

```
my @a1= ('x', 'd', 'h', 'z', 'a', 'm', 'g' ); # unordered array
my $ordered= join ", ",sort @a1; # ordered = "1, 2, 3, 4, 5, 6, 10"
print "ordered $ordered\n";
ordered a, d, g, h, m, x, z
```

However, if you have a list of numbers assigned to the array and you perform the same type of sort, you would get this:

```
@a1= ( 4,5,1,3,6,2,10); # unordered array
$ordered= join ", ",sort @a1; # ordered = "1, 2, 3, 4, 5, 6, 10"
print "ordered $ordered\n";
ordered 1, 10, 2, 3, 4, 5, 6
```

You can clearly see it didn't perform a numeric sort. It sorted the values by ordinal/ASCII order. To sort numerically, use the following:

```
ordered= join ", ",sort {$a <=> $b} @a1; # ordered = "1, 2, 3, 4, 5, 6, 10"
print "ordered $ordered\n";
ordered 1, 2, 3, 4, 5, 6, 10
```

The $a <=> $b forces a numeric sort. This is one of those Perl tidbits you want to email yourself for when you forget!

reverse

reverse() reverses the order of the elements in list context. In scalar context, the elements of the list are concatenated and a string value is returned with all the characters appearing in the opposite order.

```
my @values= (1,2,3,4);
my @seulav= @values; # contains 4,3,2,1
```

scalar

This returns a scalar value, numeric, of the total number of members in a list:

```
my $num_values= scalar @values; # should be 4, using array from last
example
```

Last Subscript Value of Array

The $# sigil combination means "subscript of last array member." This is something you will most likely use in the course of development.

```
for my $iterator (0 .. $#values ) { ... # this would loop from 0 to 3 .. }
my $last_member_index = $#values; # this would equal 3
```

Array Slices

Quite often, you will be presented with the task of writing a program that takes an array and splits it up. Say for instance that you have a large array of feed URLs obtained from a database that you need to divide into specified "slices" and hand each "slice" to a forked child process, in effect processing in parallel the entire array. Perl makes this easy.

The basic concept is this:

```
@a1= (1,2,3,4,5,6,7,8,9,10);
@a2= @a1[5 .. 10]; # this would contain 5, 6, 7, 8, 9, 10
```

The example mentioned would be implemented as such:

```
my $concurrency= 8; # number of children
my $start= 0; # starting point of range
my $end= 0; # end point of range
my $slice_size= int scalar @big_list/ $concurrency; # size of each slice
my $remainder= scalar @big_list % $concurrency; # this will be added to
last slice
for my $iter (1 .. $concurrency) {
    $end += $slice_size; # each iteration, this increments
    $end += $remainder if $iter == $concurrency; # add if last range

    my $pid= fork(); # fork

    if ($pid) {
      # ... parent
    }

    elsif ($pid == 0) { # this is the child

        for (@big_list[$start .. $end]) { # slice from $start to $end
          # processing for each "slice"
        }
    }

    # must add one more to $end for $start to assume correct
    # value on next iteration
    $start= $end + 1;
}
```

Printing an Array

Another handy trick is printing an array, so that its contents will be printed separated by spaces through interpolation, which causes the Perl special variable '$"', the single-space variable, to be inserted between each of the array elements:

```
my @a1= (1,2,3,4,5, "fun"); print "@a1\n" # prints 1 2 3 4 5 fun
```

Working with Hashes

Working with hashes is similar in many ways to working with arrays, since hashes are in essence associative arrays. An array contains a list of values positioned by an index, whereas a hash is an unordered list positioned by key values.

Where the similarities to arrays end is that there are some specific functions for iterating over hashes.

Looping: keys and values

The two primary functions for hash iteration are keys and values. Each produces either a list (array) of keys or values of the hash, respectively. keys returns keys in the same order that values are returned by values. In other words, the output of each corresponds to and is in the same order as the other.

```
for (keys %myhash) {
    print "current key is $_, value $myhash{$_}\n";
}
```

Or:

```
print map { "current value $_\n" } values %myhash;
```

Make a Hash Out of Two Arrays

One thing you might run across while developing web applications is the need to take two arrays and make a hash out of them. Your first impulse might be to iterate over one array, and assign a key from the current iterated value of the first array, and a value of the current iterated value of the second array. But really, it's much simpler than that and requires no explicit iteration — this is the beauty of Perl! Note also the use of sort listed prior to keys for ordering:

```
my %h1;
my @a1 = ('a','b','c');
my @a2 = ('x','y','z');
@h1{@a1} = @a2;
print "key $_ value $h1{$_}\n" for sort keys %h1;
```

The output would be:

```
key a value x
key b value y
key c value z
```

Hashes as Arrays

You can always assign the key-value pairs of a hash to an array as follows:

```
@a1 = %h1 # @a1 will contain key, value, key, value ... of %h1
```

You can also create an array out of keys and values:

```
@a1 = sort keys %h1; # a, b, c
@a1 = sort keys %h1, values %h1 # this would give a, b, c, x, y, z
```

Many other things that can be done with hashes are beyond the scope of this book. However, you can learn more about them by typing:

```
man perldsc
```

This is the Perl manpage for Perl data structures, titled "Perl Data Structures Cookbook." It provides documentation about working with complex Perl data structures.

Later chapters in this book will provide you with many opportunities to practice using hashes and hash references. The preceding information presented just the basics and core concepts that are useful when working with data to jog the memory.

Complex Perl Data Structures

With Perl programming using databases, you often deal with result sets of database queries. These result sets can be more complex than a single-dimension hash reference or array reference, and can contain both references to arrays of hashes or references to hashes of arrays, and multidimensional array references. You can see how much depth is possible, although the basic principles of arrays and hash references still apply.

Knowing how to navigate these multidimensional data structures using references is key to being able to work with databases and web application programming in Perl.

For instance, the following reference refers to a data structure that has references to various types: scalars, arrays, and hashes. One way to be able to process such a structure is to use recursion. The following example shows a data structure that has varying depth and type:

```perl
my $ref1= [
    {
        '22' => [ 'John Smith', 33, 'Cincinati'],
        '27' => [ 'Laxmi Narayan', 24, 'Cochin'],
        '34' => [ 'Lars Jensen', 42, 'Stockholm']
    },
    {
        'CA' => {
            'San Diego'     => [32.4, 117.1, 'Coronado Bay Bridge'],
            'Los Angeles'   => [33.4, 118.1, 'Vincent Thomas Bridge'],
            'San Francisco' => [37.4, 122.2, 'Golden Gate Bridge'],
        },
        'NH' => {
            'Concord'     => [43.3, 71.2, 'I93'],
            'Manchester'  => [42.5, 71.8, 'Queen Street Bridge'],
            'Cornish'     => [43.3, 72.2, 'Cornish Windsor Covered
Bridge']
        },
    },
    {
        'scalar_key' => "I'm a string!"
    }

];
```

To properly process each type of reference, you must know its type — hash, array, or scalar — to know how to iterate through it. The next example shows a simple subroutine `ref_iterate()` that accomplishes this. It takes three arguments:

- The reference being passed in.

- A flag that signifies the very first call or top-level of the reference that is being processed.

- A tab string that contains the number of tabs to print according to depth, which through recursion is properly incremented, as well as being lexical and incrementing only within scope.

`ref_iterate()` uses the `ref()` function to check the type of variable passed, and assumes only scalar, array, and hash references will be passed. For each type of reference a different means of iteration is applied, and is printed accordingly.

```
sub ref_iterate {
my ($ref1,$top_flag,$tabcount) = @_;
    my $tabchar= '    ';

    if (ref($testref) eq 'HASH') {
        $tabcount++;
        for (keys %$testref) {
            print $tabchar x $tabcount . "$_ => ";
            print "\n" unless $top_flag; # no need for newline if first
time
            print "\n" if ref($testref->{$_}); # newline if a reference
            ref_iterate($testref->{$_}, 0, $tabcount);
        }
    }
    elsif (ref($ref1) eq 'ARRAY') {
        $tabcount++;
        print $tabchar x $tabcount;
        print "[ " unless $top_flag;
        for my $i (0 .. $#{$ref1}) {
            ref_iterate($ref1->[$i],0, $tabcount);
            print ', ' unless $i == $#{$ref1}
        }
        print " ],\n" unless $top_flag;
    }
    else {
        print "\"$ref1\"";
    }
    return;

}
```

The output of this program resembles a pseudo-Data::Dumper. The purpose here is to show a possible algorithm for handling a reference of variable type and depth.

```
radha:perl patg$ ./struct.pl
            27 =>
            [ "Laxmi Narayan", "24", "Cochin" ],
        22 =>
            [ "John Smith", "33", "Cincinati" ],
```

```
        34 =>
          [ "Lars Jensen", "42", "Stockholm" ],
        NH =>
          Concord =>
             [ "43.3", "71.2", "I93" ],
          Cornish =>
             [ "43.3", "72.2", "Cornish Windsor Covered Bridge" ],
          Manchester =>
             [ "42.5", "71.8", "Queen Street Bridge" ],
    CA =>
        San Francisco =>
             [ "37.4", "122.2", "Golden Gate Bridge" ],
        Los Angeles =>
             [ "33.4", "118.1", "Vincent Thomas Bridge" ],
        San Diego =>
             [ "32.4", "117.1", "Coronado Bay Bridge" ],
      scalar_key => "I'm a scalar!"
```

File Handles

File handles are yet another Perl variable type. A file handle is essentially a label given to a connection to a file on disk, directory, or open a pipe to a process. By convention, file handles are usually named with capital letters, and are the only Perl variable type that doesn't use a sigil. A file handle can be named any name except the following:

❑ STDIN

❑ STDOUT

❑ STDERR

❑ ARGV

❑ ARGVOUT

❑ DATA

File Functions

Many Perl functions work with file handles.

The simplest example of opening a file using a file handle, which opens the file in input mode, is:

```
my $filename = 'my.txt';
open(my $fh, $filename) or die "Unable to open $filename $!";
```

There are other IO modes of opening a file that can be specified upon opening:

❑ Read-only: For reading contents of a file:

```
open my $fh, '<', $filename or die "Unable to open $filename $!";
```

❑ Write: For writing to a file. This will clear the existing contents of the file:

```
open my $fh, '>', $filename or die "Unable to open $filename $!";
```

❑   Append: For appending to the file. This appends to end of existing contents of the file:

```
open my $fh, '>>', $filename or die "Unable to open $filename $!";
```

Reading Files

The following shows how a file is used in read-only mode:

```
my $filename = 'my.txt';
open my $fh, '<', $filename
  or die "Unable to open '$filename' for reading: $!\n";
for my $filerow (<$fh>){
  print "$filerow\n";
}

close($fh) or die "unable to close $filename $!\n";
```

You can also read the entire file into an array. Each array member will be a line in the file:

```
my @file_array= <$fh>;
```

Normally, if you use a scalar to read from the file handle, it reads only one line of that file at a time. If you want the whole file into a scalar, you have to undefine the output record separator (See Appendix C):

```
{
    # this allows you to undefine the output record separator
    # just for this code closure

  local($/);
    my $file_contents= <$fh>;
}
```

In this example, an enclosure is used to localize the output separator so that it is undefined only within the enclosure instead of being program-wide. You can also use the Perl module File::Slurp:

```
use File::Slurp;
my $file_contents = read_file($filename);
```

Any time you read from a file handle, the position is modified to the last line read. If you read the entire file into a scalar or array as in the previous examples, the file handle will point to the end of the file. You can return to the beginning of the file using the seek function. Its usage is this:

```
seek FILEHANDLE, OFFSET, WHENCE
```

OFFSET is where in the position is the file relative to WHENCE. These positions are in bytes, not line numbers. Position 0 is the beginning of the file. So, to "rewind" to the beginning of the file, you would use the following example:

```
seek(MYFILE, 0 , 0) or die "Seek to start of '$filename' failed: $!"
```

A more portable way to do this is:

```
use Fcntl;
open my $fh, $filename or die "Unable to open $filename $!\n";
seek $fh, 0, SEEK_SET ;
close($fh);
```

Here are two more useful things to know about reading files: If you need to know the line number while reading through a file, you can utilize the `$.` special Perl variable. It gives the current line or record number, without having an increment variable! If you need the actual byte position, you can use the `tell` function:

```
while (<MYFILE>) {
    print "current line is: $. current byte position is " . tell . "\n";
}
```

Writing to Files

As shown earlier, a file can also be opened in write or append modes:

```
my $filename = '/tmp/somefile.txt';
open my $fh, '>', $filename
    or die "Can't open '$filename' for writing: $!\n";

( print $fh "print text to file\n" )
    or die "Writing text to '$filename' failed: $!\n";
```

In the previous example, `print` specified the specific file handle. Using the function `select`, you can make it so any subsequent `print` statements automatically print to this file.

```
select $fh;
print "This will be printed to somefile.txt";

close $fh
    or die "Can't close '$fh' after writing: $!\n";
```

STDOUT and STDERR

As was mentioned earlier, there are some reserved system file handles that you can't use when naming your own file handle. These two file handles, STDOUT and STDERR, can be convenient for you. Here is how. As a web developer, you will most likely have to write Perl utility scripts that you might need to run as cron jobs. You will need these files to be able to print to a log any errors or other output they encounter. The trick to achieve this is to open these handles, using *globbing* to other files. Here is an example:

```
my $log = '/tmp/myutil.log';
open *STDERR, '>>', $log or die "unable to open (STDERR) $log $!\n";

open *STDERR, '>>', $log
    or die "Unable to open '$log' for appending (STDERR): $!\n";
```

```
open *STDOUT, '>>', $log or die "unable to open (STDOUT) $log $!\n";
... < program contents > ...
print localtime() .  " processed such and such.\n";
```

File Handles to Processes

File handles can also be used to open processes to write to or read from. In addition to files, you can open pipes to programs to read the output of the program.

Reading from Process File Handles

Reading from a process file handle is done by specifying a command, along with any arguments it takes, with a pipe symbol at the end denoting that the process is being opened for reading:

```
my $ls = 'ls -l';
open($fh, "$ls|") or die "unable to open $ls $!\n";
my @dir_contents = <$fh>;
close $fh or die "unable to close $ls $!\n";
print "$_" for @dir_contents;

close($ls);
```

Writing to Process File Handles

Writing to a process file handle is similar to reading from a process file handle, except the pipe symbol is at the beginning of the program, denoting that the program will be opened to take input:

```
my $log= '/tmp/mysql.out';
open(*STDERR, ">>$log");
open(*STDOUT, ">>$log");
my $mysql_client = 'mysql -u root information_schema';
open(my $fh, "|$mysql_client") or die "Unable to open '$mysql_client'
$!\n";
select $fh;
print 'show tables;';
close($fh) or die "unable to close '$mysql_client'\n";
```

Directory Handles

Another type of file handle is a directory handle. A directory handle allows work within the contents of a directory. Directory handles also have their own functions:

- ❑   opendir(): Creates a file handle, opening the directory

- ❑   readdir(): Reads the contents of a directory

- ❑   telldir(): Gives the current byte position of the directory handle

- ❑   seekdir(): Moves to position of handle within directory

- ❑   rewinddir(): Sets position of handle back at the beginning of the directory

- ❑   closedir(): Closes the directory handle

Just What Is a Directory?

Have you ever edited a directory on UNIX by accident? With the vim editor, you can view a directory as a file. A directory is essentially a file, except it provides a structure to organize filenames, having pointers to actual files on disk. So, opening a directory is more like opening a file than it first appears.

```perl
#!/usr/bin/perl


use strict;
use warnings;

my $homedir='/home/perluser';
my $dh;
opendir($dh, $homedir) or die "unable to open $homedir: $!\n";
while(my $curfile= readdir($dh)) {
    my $pos= telldir $dh;
    my $type= -d "$homedir/$curfile" ? 'directory' : 'file';
    print "$type : $curfile pos $pos\n";
}
closedir($dh);

opendir($dh, $homedir) || die "can't opendir $homedir: $!";
my @images= grep { /\.jpg|\.gif|\.png|\.tiff?$/i && -f "$homedir/$_" }
readdir($dh);
closedir($dh);
print "image: $_\n" for @images;
closedir($dh);
```

Subroutines

Subroutines and functions are the same thing in Perl and the names can be used interchangeably. There are numerous ways to declare and define subroutines.

Declaring subroutines in Perl is optional; defining them is sufficient. The basic form of declaring a subroutine in Perl is this:

```perl
sub mysub;
```

Or, you can use:

```perl
sub mysub(prototype);
```

The basic form of defining a subroutine in Perl is this:

```perl
sub mysub { block };
```

... or:

```perl
sub mysub(prototype) { block};
```

The *prototype* is an optional list of variable types passed to the subroutine. If not specified, the subroutine takes any number of arguments.

> *Using prototypes is not considered a* best practice; *however you will probably run across them in your adventures as a Perl code wrangler, so understanding how they work can help you to either deal with them or else modify the code you inherited to not use them.*

An example of using a prototype is:

```
sub mysub($$@);
```

This would mean that the function `mysub()` takes three arguments: two scalars and one an array. An important note: Since the third argument is an array, which is a list of scalars, this would make it so `mysub()` requires at least three arguments, but could take more since the last argument is an array.

For instance, if `mysub()` can be correctly called with any of the variables:

```
# just as it's defined
mysub($val1, $val2, @ar1);

# $val3 is a single scalar, just like an array with only one member
mysub($val1, $val2, $val3);

# $val3 and $val4 treated like two member array
mysub($val1, $val2, $val3, $val4);

# $val3, %hval1, @ar1 all treated as a single array
mysub($val1, $val2, $val3, %hval1, @ar1);
```

... then the following would cause an error because there aren't enough values:

```
mysub($val1, $val2);
```

The error printed:

```
Not enough arguments for main::mysub...
```

If `mysub()` is defined as this:

```
mysub($$$);
```

... then `mysub()` will have to be called with exactly three arguments.

In this book, subroutine calls have been shown with closing parentheses for the variables being passed. This is optional and a style preference of the author, but subroutines can be called without parentheses. The following two calls to `mysub()` are equivalent:

```
mysub($var1, $var2, $var3);

mysub $var1, $var2, $var3;
```

shift Versus Using @_

There are several ways to read in the variables passed to a subroutine. The two most common ways are either to use `shift()` or to directly assign values from the @_ array.

```
sub mysub {
    my $var1 = shift;
}
```

Or:

```
sub mysub {
    my ($var1)= @_;
}
```

Are these equivalent? The one thing to consider is that `shift()` is a call, and is yet one more operation, as opposed to simply assuming the values of the @_ array. If only a few values are being shifted, this is negligible. However, if you are passing multiple variables to a subroutine, you would have to call `shift()` to set each of those variables. Using the @_ can all be done on one line with no calls required. So, it really depends on what you need to do with the variables that are being passed to a subroutine. You may, in fact, want to use `shift()` to shift in some variables and then use the remaining members of @_:

```
sub mysub {
        my $bar = shift;
        my $baz = shift;
        # use $bar and $baz here
        old_mysub( @_ );

    }
```

Who Called?

You can identify what the caller of a subroutine is with the `caller()` function. This function returns the name of the package from which it was called:

```
sub mysub {
    print "caller " . caller() . "\n";
}
```

In the case of a Perl script, the package name would be main, and, as shown in the code below:

```
sub main {
    mysub();
}
```

The output is:

```
caller main
```

The benefit of this may not be apparent in this example, but in later discussions on packages and object-oriented programming, you will see that `caller()` can be extremely useful.

Variable Scope

One thing that is worth reviewing is variable scope. This is something that the author of this book often has to review from time to time.

Symbol Table

Perl has what is known as a symbol table, which is a hash where Perl keeps all the global variables, Perl special variables, and subroutine names for a given package. (More about packages will be presented in the next section, "Perl OO Primer.") The keys of this hash are the symbol names. The values are typeglob values of the current package. The default package of any Perl program is `%main::`, or just `%::` if a package name is not specified.

Looking under the hood always helps to make certain concepts more understandable, so the following simple code example, along with its output, is presented to show you just what a symbol table contains:

```perl
our $var1= "var1 value";
our $var2= "var2 value";
my $var3= "var3 value";
sub sub1 { print "sub1\n"};
printf("%-20s => %25s,\n", $_, $main::{$_}) for keys %main::;
```

Here is the output:

```
/                    =>                      *main::/,
stderr               =>                 *main::stderr,
utf8::               =>                 *main::utf8::,
"                    =>                      *main::",
CORE::               =>                 *main::CORE::,
DynaLoader::         =>           *main::DynaLoader::,
stdout               =>                 *main::stdout,
attributes::         =>           *main::attributes::,
                     =>                      *main::,
stdin                =>                  *main::stdin,
ARGV                 =>                   *main::ARGV,
INC                  =>                    *main::INC,
ENV                  =>                    *main::ENV,
Regexp::             =>                *main::Regexp::,
UNIVERSAL::          =>            *main::UNIVERSAL::,
$                    =>                      *main::$,
_<perlio.c           =>             *main::_<perlio.c,
main::               =>                  *main::main::,
var2                 =>                   *main::var2,
-                    =>                      *main::-,
_<perlmain.c         =>           *main::_<perlmain.c,
sub1                 =>                   *main::sub1,
perlIO::             =>                *main::perlIO::,
_<universal.c        =>          *main::_<universal.c,
0                    =>                      *main::0,
                     =>                       *main:,
@                    =>                      *main::@,
_<xsutils.c          =>           *main::_<xsutils.c,
var1                 =>                   *main::var1,
```

```
STDOUT             =>            *main::STDOUT,
IO::               =>           *main::IO::,
                   =>          *main::,
_                  =>          *main::_,
+                  =>          *main::+,
STDERR             =>          *main::STDERR,
Internals::        =>        *main::Internals::,
STDIN              =>         *main::STDIN,
DB::               =>          *main::DB::,
<none>::           =>        *main::<none>::,
```

As you can see, the variables defined as global with our, var1 and var2, as well as the subroutine sub1, are pointing to typeglobs main::var1, main::var2, main::sub1. So, really, there is *no such thing* as a global in Perl! A *global* is really a package variable of main. (Again, you will explore more about packages in the next section.)

The point here is to explain scoping of variables in Perl. The Perl scoping mechanisms are:

❑   my: This is *lexical scoping*, meaning that the variable is only visible within the block of code it is declared in, including functions called within that block. For instance, in the following code, even though the variable $val assumes a value of the current value being iterated over, since it is declared as my, aka *lexical*, within that for loop (in a block, within brackets). It is not the same variable as the variable $val declared at the beginning of mysub(). The variable $val, is returned at the end of mysub(), which returns a reference to this lexical variable, giving it life beyond mysub(). This means the variable $val itself is no longer in scope, but rather a reference to it. It is returned, gives access to it, and it "survives." Internally, Perl keeps a reference count of variables that is a count of any reference created for this variable. When the reference count reaches zero, the variable is destroyed.

```
sub mysub {
    my $val= 'x';
    for (0 .. 1) {
        my $val= $_;
     }
    return $val;
}
```

❑   local: This is *dynamic scoping*, meaning dynamic variables are visible to functions called within a block where those variables are declared. In other words, if you declare a global (*package*) variable and in another block declare that same variable as *local*, the value it previously had is temporarily stashed, and the new value assigned. Once the block containing the variable scoped as *local* is exited, the previous original value (prior to the local assignment) is assumed. This gives *local* the effect of being able to temporarily override a global variable with a different value without losing the original value, hence the name *dynamic* scoping.

❑   our: This is *package scoping*, meaning all subroutines have access to this variable. In previous versions of Perl, this was done by the following:

```
use vars qw(var1 var2);
$var1= 'some value';
$var2= 33;
```

It is now done with:

```
our ($var1, $var2);
```

Scope Example

Working code is always a good way to see a concept in action. The following example shows how scoping works:

```
our $foo= "our foo";

sub main {
    print "main: $foo\n";
    my_foo('main');
    local_foo('main');
}
sub my_foo {
    my ($caller)= @_;
    my $foo= "my foo";
    print "my_foo foo: $foo, caller $caller\n";
    inner_foo('my_foo');
}
sub local_foo {
    my ($caller)= @_;
    local $foo= "local foo";
    print "local_foo foo: $foo, caller $caller\n";
    inner_foo('local_foo');
}
sub inner_foo {
    my ($caller)= @_;
    print "1: inner_foo foo $foo, caller $caller\n";
    my $foo= "my foo";
    print "2: inner_foo foo $foo, caller $caller\n";
}
main();
```

Notice the following about the previous example:

❑ The global/package variable `$foo` is declared at the top level of the code, outside any subroutines. This makes this variable visible in all subroutines.

❑ The `main()` subroutine just prints out `$foo` without making any changes.

❑ `my_foo()` declares a lexical `$foo`, which is not the global `$foo`, that will have its own value that is only scoped within `my_foo()` and not available to `inner_foo()`, which it then calls.

❑ `local_foo()` scopes `$foo` as local, which will temporarily set the global `$foo` to `"local foo"`. This should be visible to `inner_foo()`, which it calls, until the end of `local_foo()`.

❑ `inner_foo()` first prints out whatever the current value of `$foo` is, then declares its own lexical `$foo`, just to drive home the idea of lexical variables. Regardless of whatever value that `$foo` was, whether scoped via `our` or `local`, the lexical variable will be `"inner foo"` until the end of `inner_foo()`.

The program's output confirms the expected functionality:

```
main: our foo

my_foo foo: my foo, caller main

1: inner_foo foo our foo, caller my_foo

2: inner_foo foo my foo, caller my_foo

local_foo foo: local foo, caller main

1: inner_foo foo local foo, caller local_foo

2: inner_foo foo my foo, caller local_foo
```

Forcing Scope Adherence

One way to ensure that your code is using scoped variables (and also a good Perl programming practice generally), is to use the *strict pragmatic* module. A *pragmatic* module works somewhat like compiler directives (pragmata) in that they tend to affect the compilation of your Perl program by Perl. The *strict* pragmatic module prohibits the use of unsafe constructs. When you use it, it causes your code to fail to compile should you not have variables scoped properly, or have other violations of stricture, such as improper use of variables, symbolic references, or are using bareword identifiers that are not subroutine names.

To use it:

```
use strict;
```

Another pragmatic module you will want to use is the *warnings pragmatic* module. To use it:

```
use warnings;
```

Packages

Having discussed variable scope, subroutine calls, `caller()`, the symbol table, and having mentioned packages, this chapter now turns to a discussion of packages. As mentioned before, a Perl program is by default within the *main* namespace. A *namespace* is the name of the compilation unit, or anything from the beginning of the program (or from where the namespace is defined with the *package* declaration) to the end of the enclosing block or program. This allows variables to exist independently from other packages' variables.

A Perl package is a way to explicitly specify the namespace of a Perl program. As discussed and shown in the previous example in which the symbol table was printed out, a program without a package declaration assumes the package name of *main*. An explicitly named package has its own symbol table, which defines the namespace in which variables and subroutines (or methods) exist. This provides the independence from other packages or the program using the package, and protects both the package's variables from being modified by other packages and vice versa.

To create a package, simply begin the code block with the *package* declaration, as the example shows:

```
package MyPackage;
```

With this declaration, any code after it exists within the MyPackage namespace. A more complete example shows how this package would be used:

```
#!/usr/bin/perl

my $val= 'this is a test';

MyPackage::printThis($val);

print "$MyPackage::val2\n";


package MyPackage;

our $val2; # package variable, package scope

sub printThis {
    print "MyPackage::printThis: $_[0]\n";
    $val2= $_[0]; # sets the package variable
}

package MyPackage::OtherPackage;

our $val1;
sub printThis {
    print "MyPackage::OtherPackage::printThis: $_[0]\n";
}
```

Notice the following concerning the previous example:

❑   Everything prior to package MyPackage is within the *main* namespace.

❑   Everything after package MyPackage and before package MyPackage::OtherPackage, is within the MyPackage namespace, which in this example, is the variable $val2 and the subroutine printThis().

❑   Everything from package MyPackage::OtherPackage to the end of the file is within the MyPackage::OtherPackage namespace, which in this example, is the variable $val1 and the other printThis() subroutine.

In the previous section, it was mentioned that there is no *real* global variable scoping, but there is package scoping. In this case, $var2 is a *package* variable of MyPackage. In the example above, the code above the package declaration shows how to access MyPackage's variable $var2 and how to call its subroutine printThis() by prefixing both with the MyPackage name. Also shown is how the package variable $var2 is set within printThis() and is accessible outside of the package.

Perl Modules

The previous example is very simple, and shows both the code using the package as well as the package within the same file. More commonly, the code for a package is stored within its own file, with the filename convention being the name of the package with a .pm extension. This is what is known as a Perl module. In other words, a Perl module is a file with a .pm extension containing Perl code for one or more package definitions.

Perl modules enable you to reuse code, having functionality that you often use in a library of its own. Modules are written to abstract the details of code so the program using the module need only use these subroutines. This is conceptually similar to using dynamic libraries in C, allowing the main C program to not have to implement these library functions. In the course of development, you may have code déjà vu — code that you find yourself often reimplementing that performs common tasks. This is when you should consider making that code a module — write once, reuse often! An example of this is code that you write into a script or application, or at least use require to include a Perl file that contains functions such as storing a user's information. This would be a prime candidate for turning into a module.

Writing a Perl Module

With Perl modules, the :: (double colon) is the package delimiter that can signify the directory a package is found in, just as a '.' delimiter in java signifies a directory for its classes. It is important to note however, that a single Perl file can contain multiple packages.

Either use or require translates the "::" in the expression or module name into a directory delimiter character "/" and assumes a ".pm" extension of the expression or specified module name. This assumes that, for require, the expression is a bareword (doesn't have any quotes around it), and for use, the module name is a bareword.

In the previous example showing the MyPackage and MyPackage::OtherPackage packages:

❑   The code from the package declaration to the end of the example would be stored in a file, MyPackage.pm.

❑   MyPackage::OtherPackage module would exist in a subdirectory with the MyPackage module MyPackage/, stored as OtherPackage.pm.

To explain this better, the layout would be this:

```
./MyPackage.pm
./MyPackage
./MyPackage/OtherPackage.pm

...

1;
```

The use statement expects to find <modulename>.pm either in the current directory or within the path where Perl finds its modules, known as the *include path*. You can find out what your include path is by running the tiny Perl expression at the command line:

```
radha:perl patg$ perl -e 'print join "\n", @INC'
/System/Library/perl/5.8.8/darwin-thread-multi-2level
/System/Library/perl/5.8.8
/Library/perl/5.8.8/darwin-thread-multi-2level
```

```
/Library/perl/5.8.8
/Library/perl
/Network/Library/perl/5.8.8/darwin-thread-multi-2level
/Network/Library/perl/5.8.8
/Network/Library/perl
/System/Library/perl/Extras/5.8.8/darwin-thread-multi-2level
/System/Library/perl/Extras/5.8.8
/Library/perl/5.8.6
/Library/perl/5.8.1/darwin-thread-multi-2level
/Library/perl/5.8.1
```

This example in particular shows the Perl include path on an Apple OS X computer. This path varies according to OS, distribution, etc. The variable @INC is a special Perl variable that stores the include path.

You can add your own directory to the Perl include path using this:

```
use lib '/home/patg/perllib';
```

This simply adds /home/patg/perllib to the start of @INC, the array of paths that Perl searches to find any module that has been specified with the use statement. This gives you the means to use any module you write from whatever directory you choose to locate your modules, if it is not a standard Perl library path.

The use statement is similar to the require statement. The difference is that require happens at compile time, while use happens at run time. Also, use imports any exportable variables or subroutines from the module, inserting an entry into the program's symbol table, while require does not. So this:

```
# imports printThis of subroutine
BEGIN { require MyPackage; import MyPackage qw(printThis) };
```

. . . is the same as this:

```
# imports printThis subroutine
use MyPackage qw(printThis);
```

and this:

```
BEGIN { require MyPackage; } # imports no subroutines
```

. . . is the same as this:

```
use MyPackage ()   # imports no subroutines
```

Often, you may not want to import every subroutine or method from a module. In this case you would use:

```
use MyPackage qw(printThis);
```

. . . which would just import the printThis subroutine.

By importing package subroutines and variables into your program and having an entry for them made in the program's symbol table, you can use them in your program without a full package qualifier. To show the full concept of this, let's suppose you were to create a module with MyPackage from the previous example. You would create MyPackage.pm with the code from the package block stored in this file. Additionally, if you want to allow the printThis subroutine to be imported into our program, it would now have the code:

```
package MyPackage;

use strict;

use Exporter qw(import);

our @EXPORT = qw(&printThis $val2);

our $val2; # package variable, package scope

sub printThis ($) {
    print "MyPackage::printThis: $_[0]\n";
    $val2= $_[0]; # sets the package variable
}

1;
```

In this example, two new lines are added to use the Exporter Perl module and import is its import method. This provides a means for any module to export subroutines and variables to any program's namespace using the module. In this example, MyPackage is able to export the subroutine printThis and the scalar variable var2 by setting the @EXPORT array, which is an array Exporter uses to export symbols.

The program that uses this module now need only specify the full module name in calling the printThis subroutine or the $val2 scalar:

```
#!/usr/bin/perl

use strict;
use warnings;
use MyPackage;

printf("%-18s => %20s,\n", $_, $::{$_}) for keys %::;

printThis("test");
print "\$val2 $val2\n"; # printThis sets this
$val2= 'my val'; # now set here
print "\$val2 $val2\n"; # should be 'my val'
```

The output of this program is this:

```
MyPackage::printThis: test
$val2 test
$val2 my val
```

To see the effect of importing a module's symbols on a program's symbol table, the previous code to print out the symbol table (excluding all other entries) shows there are new entries for the module itself, as well as the module's variable and subroutine that were imported:

```
printThis        =>      *main::printThis,
MyPackage::      =>    *main::MyPackage::,
val2             =>          *main::val2,
```

What this shows you is that indeed, the imported symbols are part of the main package now, as if they were defined in the program. In essence, importing subroutines from a module makes it as if the code from the module has been copied and pasted into the program. The convenience you enjoy is that they are contained in a module that can be reused, making your program easier to read and contain less code.

One thing to keep in mind is that if you are writing a method in a class module (object-oriented, which will be covered in Chapter 5), as opposed to a subroutine in a non-object-oriented module, you want to avoid exporting methods because they will be accessed via an object.

@ISA array

In the previous example, using Exporter, like so:

```
use Exporter qw(import);
```

. . . could have also been accomplished using this:

```
require Exporter;
@ISA = qw(Exporter);
```

. . . with the require not importing Exporter into MyPackage's namespace. This can, however, be accomplished used the @ISA array. The @ISA array is where the interpreter searches for symbols it cannot find in the current package, and also handles inheritance (hence the "is-a" name). More about this will be discussed in Chapter 5, which covers object-oriented Perl.

Documenting Your Module

Perl is easy enough to read, and you can often ascertain what the original intent of code is. However, having more documentation is better than having less. Even more so, having a concise way to display that documentation is even better. Perl gives you a great way to do this with POD, *Plain Old Documentation*. POD is a markup language you use in your Perl code that allows you to write documentation that is viewable using another Perl utility, perldoc. For instance, the module used in previous examples has its own documentation, as do the large collection of CPAN modules that are available.

To use perldoc to read Exporter's documentation, you simply run:

```
perldoc Exporter
```

It will display the documentation in the same manner as UNIX manpages are displayed.

POD removes any excuses you may have to not document your code because it's so easy to use! POD can even be used for non-Perl projects using yet another Perl tool, pod2man. For instance, projects such as libmemcached and Memcached Functions for MySQL (both C projects), use POD and run through pod2man to produce manpages.

The next example shows MyPackage with POD documentation added:

```
package MyPackage;

use strict;

use Exporter qw(import);

our @EXPORT = qw(&printThis $val2);
our $VERSION = '0.0.1';


our $val2; # package variable, package scope

sub printThis ($) {
print "MyPackage::printThis: $_[0]\n";
    $val2= $_[0]; # sets the package variable
}

=head1 NAME

MyPackage - Simple Perl module example for showing how to write Perl
modules

=head1 SYNOPSIS

    use MyPackage;

    my $text= 'test';

    printThis($text);

    MyPackage::printThis($text);

    print "val2 $val2\n";

    print "val2 $MyPackage::val2\n";

=head1 DESCRIPTION

This module is written to show how to write the most I<simple> Perl module,
as well as how to document that module using POD, and how B<easy> it is!

=head2 Subroutines
=over 4

=item C<printThis($text)>
```

```
    Prints the $text scalar passed to it, then sets the package variable $var2
    to $text

    =back

    =head2 Package variables

    =over 4

    =item C<$var2>

    Scalar variable

    =back

    =head1 AUTHORS

    Patrick Galbraith

    =head1 COPYRIGHT

    Patrick Galbraith (c) 2008

    =cut


    1;
```

As you can see in the previous example, the documentation begins with =head1 and ends with =cut commands and the Perl interpreter ignores everything in between. This is a top-level heading, out of 4 levels 1-4, which you would use for sections such as the NAME, SYNOPSIS, DESCRIPTION, AUTHORS, COPYRIGHT — anything that you might feel is a top-level section header. The convention is that such headers appear in all caps. The next heading level shown here is =head2. You would usually use this level for listing subroutines or methods in a module, showing what arguments the method takes, what it does, and what it returns.

Each subroutine would be listed, starting with a =over 4 command and ending with a =cut command. The number after =over is the indent level, and each subroutine =item command. This documentation uses POD markup for code. The markup for POD is:

❏   C<code>
❏   I<italic>
❏   B<bold>
❏   U<underlined>

To view the output of this documentation, you would type the command:

```
    perldoc MyPackage
```

... if `MyPackage` is in your module path, or if not:

```
perldoc /Users/patg/perl/modules/MyPackage.pm
```

It should be apparent that POD is not limited to modules. You can document regular scripts this way as well. The output of the above POD documentation displays as:

```
MyPackage(3)          User Contributed perl Documentation       MyPackage(3)
```

NAME

        MyPackage - Simple Perl module example for showing how to write Perl
        modules

SYNOPSIS

        use MyPackage;

        my $text= 'test';

        printThis($text);

        MyPackage::printThis($text);

        print "val2 $val2\n";

        print "val2 $MyPackage::val2\n";

        This module is written to show how to write the most simple Perl
        module, as well as how to document that module using POD, and how **easy**
        it is!

        Subroutines

        "printThis($text)"
            Prints the $text scalar passed to it, then sets the package
            variable $var2 to $text

        Package variables

        $var2
            Scalar variable

AUTHORS

        Patrick Galbraith

COPYRIGHT

        Patrick Galbraith (c) 2008


```
perl v5.8.8              2008-10-05                MyPackage(3)
```

This displays a really nice looking page of documentation. It is well worth the effort and allows others who use your code to understand it. This was a simple example. If you need to learn more about POD syntax, just type:

```
perldoc perlpod
```

Making Your Module Installable

In some instances, you may want to have your module installed into the Perl system library so you don't have to specify a library path with use lib to run your code. For this, you can use a file that you create with your module, Makefile.PL, which for the previous example would contain the following code:

```
use ExtUtils::MakeMaker;
# See lib/ExtUtils/MakeMaker.pm for details of how to influence
# the contents of the Makefile that is written.
print "\nIMPORTANT!\nTo install this module you will need ....";
WriteMakefile(
    'NAME'         => 'MyPackage',
    'VERSION_FROM' => 'MyPackage.pm', # finds $VERSION
        # 0 could be used, but is printed (which is confusing)
        # so use '' instead
    'PREREQ_PM' => {
      'Data::Dumper'      => '',
      },
    'PREREQ_PRINT'     => 1,
    'PM'           => {
    'MyPackage.pm' => '$(INST_LIBDIR)/MyPackage.pm' ,
    'MyPackage/SubPackage.pm' => '$(INST_LIBDIR)/MyPackage
/SubPackage.pm',
      }
);
```

This file makes it easy to install your module system-wide. It also takes care of any prerequisites that are required for your module to run. It also handles what directories to install your module into.

To make use of it, you simply run:

```
perl Makefile.PL
make
sudo make install
```

Then you can run your code without specifying where the module is located. It all depends on whether you want to keep your own modules separate from the system-wide modules. There are varying opinions on this matter. It's Perl, so it's your choice!

Testing

You can easily add tests to your module. You should accustom yourself to this good practice whenever you add a new feature. To add tests, you first create a 't' directory in your package directory. For this example, three new subroutines will be added to MyPackage.pm:

```
sub addNumbers {
    my ($num1, $num2) = @_;
```

```
    return $num1 + $num2;
}

sub subtractNumbers {
    my ($num1, $num2) = @_;
    return $num1 - $num2;
}

sub doubleString {
    my ($string) = @_;
    return "$string$string";
}
```

These subroutines are very simple and not all that exciting, but they serve to show you how you can add tests to your module!

In the 't' directory, create test files. These are named with numeric file names, which determine the order in which the tests are run, like so:

```
ls -1 t/
00basic.t
01add.t
02subtract.t
03string.t
```

Each test will test a specific feature of MyPackage. The Perl module Test::More is the module you use for testing. It provides a clean, easy-to-follow API for creating tests. (Run perldoc Test::More to see the full usage.) Essentially, you list how many tests are going run with the value specified in tests => N. You can use various Test::More methods such as is, ok, and cmp_ok to test the return values of a test. The tests are:

❑   t/00basic.t: This tests if the various modules can simply be loaded:

```
        use strict;
        use warnings;

        use Test::More tests => 3;
        BEGIN {
            use_ok('Data::Dumper') or BAIL_OUT "Unable to load Data::Dumper";
            use_ok('MyPackage') or BAIL_OUT "Unable to load MyPackage";
            use_ok('MyPackage::SubPackage') or
        BAIL_OUT "Unable to load MyPackage::SubPackage";
        }
```

❑   t/01add.t: This specifically tests addNumbers():, testing both if the value of $retval is set using the method ok, as well as if $retval is the correct value using the method is:

```
        use Test::More tests => 6;
        use MyPackage;

        ok my $retval = MyPackage::addNumbers(3,3);
```

```
is $retval, 6, "Should be 6";

ok $retval = MyPackage::addNumbers(16,16);

is $retval, 32, "Should be 32";

ok $retval = MyPackage::addNumbers(32,-16);

is $retval, 16, "Should be 16";
```

❑ t/02subtract.t: This tests subtractNumbers():

```
use strict;
use warnings;

use Test::More tests => 6;
use MyPackage;

ok my $retval = MyPackage::subtractNumbers(6,3);

is $retval, 3, "Should be 3";

ok $retval = MyPackage::subtractNumbers(64,32);

is $retval, 32, "Should be 32";

ok $retval = MyPackage::subtractNumbers(32,-16);

is $retval, 48, "Should be 48";
```

❑ t/03string.t: This tests if the value of $retval matches the expected text value with the method cmp_ok:

```
use strict;
use warnings;

use Test::More tests => 4;
use MyPackage;

ok my $retval = MyPackage::doubleString('this');

cmp_ok $retval, 'eq', 'thisthis';

ok $retval = MyPackage::doubleString('them');

cmp_ok $retval, 'eq', 'themthem';
```

Then if you rebuild MyPackage, you can run make test:

```
radha:modules pgalbraith$ perl Makefile.PL

IMPORTANT!
```

```
To install this module you will need ....Writing Makefile for MyPackage
radha:modules pgalbraith$ make
Skip blib/lib/MyPackage.pm (unchanged)
Skip blib/lib/MyPackage/SubPackage.pm (unchanged)
Manifying blib/man3/MyPackage.3pm
radha:modules pgalbraith$ make test
PERL_DL_NONLAZY=1 /usr/bin/perl "-MExtUtils::Command::MM" "-e"\
    "test_harness(0, 'blib/lib', 'blib/arch')" t/*.t
t/00basic.......ok
t/01add.........ok
t/02subtract....ok
t/03string......ok
All tests successful.
Files=4, Tests=19,  0 wallclock secs ( 0.08 cusr +  0.04 csys =  0.12 CPU)
```

And now your module has the beginnings of a test suite!

Adding a MANIFEST file

Adding a file named MANIFEST to your module's directory, containing all the files you want to put into a distribution, allows you to run make dist, which creates a tar.gz file of your package for distribution.

Just run this:

```
find . > MANIFEST
```

... from within the directory of your module. Also, remove any lines that are directory-only — those that only specify a directory — so that the only things listed in MANIFEST are files:

```
foo.pl
Makefile.PL
MANIFEST
MyPackage/SubPackage.pm
MyPackage.pm
t/00basic.t
t/01add.t
t/02subtract.t
t/03string.t
```

Then, when you run make dist, you will see it make a package file:

```
make dist
rm -rf MyPackage-0.0.1
/usr/bin/perl "-MExtUtils::Manifest=manicopy,maniread" \
                -e "manicopy(maniread(),'MyPackage-0.0.1', 'best');"
mkdir MyPackage-0.0.1
mkdir MyPackage-0.0.1/t
mkdir MyPackage-0.0.1/MyPackage
Generating META.yml
tar cvf MyPackage-0.0.1.tar MyPackage-0.0.1
MyPackage-0.0.1/
MyPackage-0.0.1/foo.pl
```

```
MyPackage-0.0.1/Makefile.PL
MyPackage-0.0.1/MANIFEST
MyPackage-0.0.1/META.yml
MyPackage-0.0.1/MyPackage/
MyPackage-0.0.1/MyPackage/SubPackage.pm
MyPackage-0.0.1/MyPackage.pm
MyPackage-0.0.1/t/
MyPackage-0.0.1/t/00basic.t
MyPackage-0.0.1/t/01add.t
MyPackage-0.0.1/t/02subtract.t
MyPackage-0.0.1/t/03string.t
rm -rf MyPackage-0.0.1
gzip --best MyPackage-0.0.1.tar
```

And now you have a distribution file that you can make available to others — or even put on CPAN if it's something you want to share with the world!

CPAN

Most often, you can find an existing Perl module to do something you need on CPAN (Comprehensive Perl Archive Network). This can save you countless hours of work since modules that other people have already written can do just about everything you'd ever need. Some common Perl modules you'll use from CPAN (and these are usually already installed on most operating systems, particularly Linux) for web application development are the following:

❑ DBI: Database access methods.

❑ DBD::mysql: Low-level Perl driver for MySQL, used by DBI, automatically loaded by DBI.

❑ Apache:DBI: Apache web server/mod_perl-specific database layer to handle DBI calls.

❑ Cache::Memcached: memcached data access methods.

❑ Apache2::Const: Provides return codes for mod_perl handlers.

❑ LWP: Provides web client functionality.

❑ HTML::Mason: Perl web application templating.

❑ Template: Another Perl web application template solution.

❑ Date::Manip: Date handling methods.

❑ Getopt: Standard, convenient, and simple methods for processing program flags and arguments.

So, before you start hacking together a Perl module to run your house's heat exchange system or to display seismometer readings into a report, first find out if there is a module for your needs by accessing the CPAN search page at http://search.cpan.org/.

Installing a CPAN module, once you know its name, is done with the cpan program. You can run it by command line or with an interactive shell. To install a module with a single command line, as the root user, use this:

```
radha:~root# cpan -i Date::Manip
```

Or, to install it via the shell, use this:

```
radha:~ root# cpan

cpan shell -- CPAN exploration and modules installation (v1.7602)
ReadLine support enabled

cpan> install Date::Manip
```

This handy program will download the module from the CPAN site, compile it (some Perl modules have C code for core functionality), run tests, and install it if all the tests pass.

> **Check your operating system's packaging system first to see if there is already a package for a given Perl module you might otherwise try to install with CPAN.**

Before this chapter comes to a close, it's worthwhile to revisit regular expressions. Regular expressions in Perl are one of the key features that make Perl suitable for database and web application development. Being able to parse strings and pattern-match, as well as perform substitutions on regular expressions easily is one of the core functionalities of Perl that facilitates rapid development. Other languages require more work — requiring more coding — to do what is trivial in Perl. Regular expressions in Perl use the same basic syntax as other tools, such as grep, sed, awk, so the knowledge is transferable.

Regular expressions are a complex enough topic to justify an entire book, and there are many good books and web site pages on the topic. For the sake of saving many trees, this book won't attempt to be comprehensive! However, let's cover some information on the subject.

Regex One-Liners

You may find yourself searching for various quick and convenient one-liner regular expressions that you have forgotten.

For example, to obtain a value from regex grouping when you try to parse a value from your *my.cnf*, you would apply a regular expression to the string that contains it. Then, if you want to obtain the value from the grouping, you would use $1.

```
my $var1= "innodb_buffer_pool_size = 64M";
$var1=~ /pool_size\s+=\s+(\d+\w)\b/;
my $innodb_bsize= $1;
```

If you wish, the last two lines could instead be done in one step:

```
my ($innodb_bsize) = $var1=~ /pool_size\s+=\s+(\d+\w)\b/;
```

So the previous code would give you:

```
64M
```

Similarly, if you are using a regex with a global modifier, you can store every grouping match in an array (the author really loves this trick):

```
var1= "This is a test. So many things to test. I have 2 cats and one dog";
@var2 = $var1 =~ /([^\s\d]{3,})/g;
```

This array contains (using `Data::Dumper`) the following:

```
$VAR1 = [
          'This',
          'test.',
          'many',
          'things',
          'test.',
          'have',
          'cats',
          'and',
          'one',
          'dog'
        ];
```

The same holds true for replacement. A convenient one-liner for testing if a replacement actually took place is this:

```
$stuff= "cat and dog";
for (1 .. 2 ) {
    my $replaced = $stuff =~ s/dog/mice/;
    print "$_: was" . $replaced ? '' : "n't" . " replaced\n";
}
```

Some extra-tricky conditional-string appending was added to this example, the point being that `$replaced` can be used to determine if the string was affected by the substitution. In the first iteration of the `for` loop, the output of this snippet is:

```
1: was replaced
2: wasn't replaced
```

Storing Regular Expressions in Variables

Storing regular expressions in variables is another useful feature. This can be done with the `qr//` regexp quote-like operator.

```
$regex= qr/PATTERN/imosx;  # the trailing characters are various regex
  options
$val =~ /$regex/;
```

For instance, you might have an admin interface in your web application that gives admin users the ability to enter regular expressions that filter whatever the site administrator wants filtered — perhaps submitted comments for certain patterns you may want to block. Slashcode, for example, the source code that runs Slashdot.org, has this feature. An arbitrary list of these regular expressions would be stored in the database and retrieved when the web server starts. The following example shows how this works:

```perl
my $stuff= "1st, second and 3rd, but not fourth, but maybe 5th, or even
sixth";

for my $rawpat ('(\d\w\w)\b', '([a-zA-Z]+th)\b') {
    $pat= qr/$rawpat/;
    my (@matched)= ($stuff =~ /$rawpat/g);
    print Dumper \@matched;
}
```

You can see how two strings that contain regex patterns can in turn be interpolated as regexes is applied within a loop. In a real-world situation, the regex strings in an array would be retrieved from the database and applied in the same way.

Regex Optimizations

There are some basic optimizations you can apply to your regular expressions. These optimizations can save a CPU cycle here and there, which can add up in the end!

Regex Compilation

Using the /o "once-only" modifier at the end of a regular expression causes it to be compiled and cached only once. One thing to keep in mind: When using this modifier, you cannot change the regular expression after compiling it once (for example if you use interpolation to create a regular expression). In the previous example, using a variable as a pattern would not have worked with this once-only modifier because its value varied within the iterative for loop, so Perl would not have heeded the change!

```perl
$var1 =~ /pattern/o
```

Grouping Optimization

By not storing grouped patterns, in other words the $1, $2, $N ... variables, you can make your regular expressions more efficient. This, of course, is if you don't need to store the value and want to use the grouping only for matching instead of capturing. To prevent capturing, you would use this:

```perl
$var1 =~ /(?:pattern)/;
```

Perl 6 Tidbits

Perl 6.0 is slated to be the next major revision of Perl and promises many new and exciting features. Although Perl 6 has not yet been released, some of its syntactic features have been back-ported to Perl 5.10.

To use these new syntactic features, you use the *feature* pragma:

```perl
use feature ':5.10'; # enables all features

use feature qw(switch say); # loads only switch and say
```

Some of the new syntactic features are:

❑ say(): This is a new printing function that automatically includes a new line in what it prints out:

```perl
my $you = "you";
my $me = "me";
my @always = ('say', 'it', 'together', 'naturally');

say "say";
say $you;
say $me;
say $_ for @always;
```

Also new is the defined "or" // operator, which allows you to write the following code:

```perl
my $val1 = 'val1';
my $val2 = undef;

my $val3 = defined ($val2) ? $val2 : $val1;
```

... to instead be written as:

```perl
my $val3 = $val2 // $val1 ;
```

❑ switch(): Native switch() has arrived for Perl! With the given/when construct, you can now enact switch() within your code. It can work on numeric values like so:

```perl
my $someval = 33;
given ($someval) {
    when (31) { say "31 is the value"}
    when (32) { say "32 is the value"}
    when (33) { say "33 is the value"}
    default { say "none of the above"}
};
```

... and also on strings — using equality or regex:

```perl
print "enter a value:";
$someval = <STDIN>;
chomp($someval);
given ($someval) {
    when ("this")    { say "You entered 'this'"}
    when (/that/)    { say "You entered 'that'"}
    when (/^z/)      { say "You entered a word begging with 'z'"}
    default { say "You entered $someval"}
}
```

There are several other new features available for use with Perl 5.10, which you can read more about by running perldoc feature.

Summary

This chapter serves as a Perl refresher for several categories of developers: (1) those who perhaps aren't familiar with Perl but who have programmed using other languages and now wish to learn about Perl, (2) former Perl programmers who have more recently been busy working with other languages and now need to review various Perl concepts, and (3) even avid Perl programmers who want to revisit some of the basics. The following topics were discussed in this chapter:

❑   The various Perl data types, usage, and scope, as well as references, subroutines, file and directory handles, and Perl modules.

❑   How to code a simple Perl module.

❑   How to use POD for documenting the module.

❑   How to create tests and use a MANIFEST file for creating a distribution file of a module.

You were also shown some new Perl 6.0 syntactic features that are available with Perl 5.10.

5

Object-Oriented Perl

Perl is a procedural language by nature. Many of the early programs written in Perl that you occasionally stumble upon on the Internet attest to this. With the advent of Perl 5.0, syntax and semantics were added to Perl to facilitate its use as an object-oriented language. As with many other aspects of Perl, Perl's implementation of object orientation is not "strict," and is not an inherent attribute of the language. This in no way diminishes its use as an object-oriented language, though it may incur the scorn of some object-oriented language purists. This has been the topic of many heated debates. Just buy your Java programmer friends lunch, and everything will be OK!

Chapter 4 covered references and packages/modules, both of which are key to understanding how to work with object-oriented Perl. With packages, you can have reusable code within a file that has variables and subroutines that are pertinent to a given functionality, as well as their own namespace. The subroutines and variables are accessed by specifying the package name. You saw how you could set a reference to a subroutine. These two things combined, along with the magical Perl function `bless` (which will be discussed in this chapter), essentially give you what you need for object-oriented programming in Perl!

This chapter gives an overview of object-oriented Perl. Much of the code you will write for `mod_perl` database-driven web applications takes advantage of the benefits of object orientation — whether you write your own classes or use the multitude of Perl modules available that have object-oriented interfaces. This makes your application a lot easier and faster to develop, modify, fix bugs for, and add enhancements to, because with object orientation, your code will innately have structure and organization. Also with object-oriented programming, you can have convenient objects providing APIs that you can use in programs, such as `mod_perl` handlers. These APIs could include object methods that handle user sessions, obtaining user information from the database, or methods that perform operations such as displaying page content.

This chapter will cover the basic concepts and terminology of object orientation. It starts with a bare-bones class, presenting code examples using that class, and then gradually fleshes them out. In the opinion of the author, this is one of the best ways to explain a concept and is also a good way to develop classes and the applications that use them.

About Object Orientation

What exactly is object orientation? This might be clearer if we start with some definitions:

Term	Definition
Class	Object orientation starts with grouping code with similar functionality and attributes into a *class*. This is the blueprint of a given type of object.
Object	A specific instance of a particular class. Objects provide access to data.
Method	A subroutine or function of a class is a *method*, providing access to a given object of the particular class. A method is the thing an object can do — for instance, an object that is of the Lion class would have a roar() method.
Attribute	The container for data belonging to an object.
Abstraction	The simplification of complexity. An object is a particular type of "thing" that hides the gory details of how the functionality is implemented — this is *abstraction*.
Interface	The overall set of methods or functionality that provides access to a given class. This provides the definition for how the class is actually used.
Implementation	The actual implementation details of the object's functionality which are abstracted from the user through the means of the members of the class being encapsulated. The class's *implementation* can internally change, but not the interface.
Encapsulation	How access to a particular class's member (attribute or method) is concealed within a given class, preventing direct access to that member. It is the class's interface that provides access to encapsulated class members.

With object-oriented programming, the user's focus is on writing an application or other program that uses the object, without being too concerned with how that object works under the hood. Object orientation makes writing applications easier and faster to implement since you have reusable code that provides functionality you don't have to implement in your program. It also makes the program aesthetically pleasing to read and easier to follow.

With this said, objects support *inheritance*, either inheriting from a parent object or derived objects. Inheritance might be best explained in Figure 5-1, which uses the species *Felidae* — the cat.

The top-level class in Figure 5-1 is the main species of cats, *Felidae*, which has two subclasses, otherwise known as *derived classes:* the families *Pantherinea* and *Felinea*. The derived classes inherit from *Felidae*, and in turn, each derived class has its own derived classes. So a tiger is a Pantherinea, and it inherits attributes and other distinct qualities of that family, while the family Pantherinea inherits its qualities from the top species, Felidae. The major qualities and attributes that a Felidea has are also possessed by a tiger and by a domestic cat, but with some variance. For example, all cats — tigers, lynx, housecats, and lions — have coats of fur (even those odd-looking hairless cats). But fur differs among them. A tiger's fur has stripes; a lion's does not. Male lions have a mane; male tigers do not. A lynx has long fur, particularly on its feet, and domestic cats have all types of fur. This *fur attribute*, which in the top-level class is generic, is *overridden* in each subclass and implemented in its own way. This ability for a derived class (child class) to override a behavior or attribute of the class from which it is derived (from parent or ancestor class) is known as *polymorphism*.

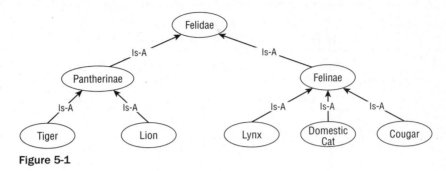

Figure 5-1

Object Orientation in Perl

Perl object orientation is just as full-featured as any other object-oriented programming language. Here are some things about Perl object orientation you should know:

- ❑ It supports classes, class attributes, and methods
- ❑ It provides a means of instantiation
- ❑ It supports inheritance
- ❑ It supports polymorphism
- ❑ It supports using objects (instantiated classes)
- ❑ Public/private is not enforced by design, only encouraged through implementation

To better understand just what Perl object-oriented programming is and what it means, this section will show you how to write a simple class, slowly fleshing out its details, adding members and the methods for accessing these members to this class. It also will show you how to use inheritance to create derived classes, as well as how Perl programs can instantiate and use this class.

Writing a Perl Class

How does Perl implement and provide object-orientation functionality? Packages and references are two of the key components to how Perl provides object orientation. Plus, as others have stated before: syntactic sugar.

The object-oriented programming terms were described in the table in the previous section. Building on these terms and on what you covered in Chapter 4, you should know the following about Perl object-oriented programming:

- ❑ *Classes* are defined using packages. With Perl, a class is nothing more than a package with a *constructor* subroutine.
- ❑ A *constructor* is the subroutine that instantiates or creates the object in the first place, returning a reference to the instantiated class.

213

❏ *Methods* are simply a class's subroutines. There are two types of methods in Perl: static methods, in which the first argument passed to the method is the class name; and instance or object methods, in which the first argument passed to the method is an object reference to itself.

❏ An *object* is simply an instantiated class, accessible via a reference. This reference "knows" what type of object it is because of the Perl bless() function, which will be discussed in the "Constructors" section.

Writing a class in Perl is quite simple and involves:

❏ Creating a package that can contain package variables such as those for version and other attributes

❏ Creating a constructor method (static method) that will be used to instantiate the class

❏ Adding instance methods

Creating a Package

The following code shows the beginning of writing a Perl class. The first thing that must be done is to create a package.

```
package Felidea;

1;
```

This, of course, sets what namespace this class will be using — what type of class an object belonging to this will be.

The next thing to add is the $VERSION package variable and then set a version. $VERSION is another special variable name, just like @EXPORT, @EXPORT_OK, etc. You can use any value for $VERSION, depending on which version format you choose. In this case, it'll be <main version>.<minor version>:

```
our $VERSION = 0.001;
```

Using a package $VERSION variable also provides an easy way to find out what version of a module or class you're using:

```
perl -MFelidea -e 'print "$Felidea::VERSION\n";'
0.001
```

Constructors

Now, you create a constructor method to Felidea.pm. The purpose of a constructor method is to instantiate a class as an object, returning a variable that is a reference to that object. This reference is used to interact with the object.

```
sub new {
    my ($class, $opts)= @_;

    # some common attributes
```

```
        my $self= {
            '_fur'              => '',
            '_weight'           => 50,
            '_claws'            => 1,
            '_fur_color'        => '',
            '_fur_length'       => '',
            '_tail'             => 1,
            '_fangs'            => 1,
        };

        # other options that can be passed
        $self->{$_} = $opts->{$_} for keys %$opts;

        # this makes it so $self belongs to the class Felidea
        bless $self, $class;

        # return the object handle
        return $self;

    }
```

The new() subroutine or method is the constructor for *Felidea*. Its purpose is to instantiate a Felidea object. With Perl, an object is a reference to any data type that "knows" to what class — or namespace — it belongs. The Perl function bless() is the key to this. It makes object orientation possible. The function bless() tells the *thingy* (yes, this is terminology!), which in this case is a variable called $self, that it belongs to a class — in this case whatever the value of $class is. Now, $self, the class's object reference to itself, is what other programming languages call "*this*," however, the variable name "self" is only a common convention in Perl and could be called anything you want it to be.

The new() method is a *static* method (class method) since it takes as its first argument the name of the class, as well as a hash reference that contains various options that may be set upon instantiation. An anonymous hash, referred to by $self, is set with some attributes — key names beginning with underscores to denote privacy. Privacy in Perl object orientation is not enforced by design, although can it be enforced in a number of ways, like using closures or even Perl modules such as Moose.

Next, any values in $options are keyed into $self. These are what are known as *instance* variables — variables that are set upon instantiation. As already stated, the bless() function is the key to instantiation and Perl's object orientation. The bless() function makes it so $self belongs to the class specified in $class. In this case, $self now is a reference to a Felidea object. Finally, $self is returned, the caller now having a reference to the Felidea object.

The constructor method name "*new*" is a convention, but is not a reserved word in Perl as it is in other programming languages and does not have to be used as the name of the constructor. In other languages, the name of the class is the name of the constructor; the constructor in this example could have just as easily have been named Felidea instead of new.

To begin using this object, as with a module, your program will use the Felidea module in your program or script:

```
    use Felidea;
```

Different from using a regular module (non-object-oriented) is the use of the new method of the `Felidea` class to obtain an instantiated (with `bless`) Felidea object reference, which it can now call `Felidea` methods through:

```
my $fel= new Felidea();
```

The call to new in the first line is not the same as it is in C++ and other object-oriented languages. As mentioned before, new is not a reserved word — you're actually calling the new() constructor method listed in the Felidea class, not allocating memory for an object as you would in a programming language such as C++. Another way of writing the above call to the constructor is this:

```
my $fel= Felidea->new();
```

In this example, you can see how it is a call to Felidea's new subroutine/method. Also, notice the use of:

```
Felidea->new
```

. . . as opposed to:

```
Felidea::new
```

. . . which was used in the last chapter for package subroutine calls. As you saw previously in the implementation of the constructor, the constructor takes as its first argument the name of the class that it is going to instantiate.

To accomplish this using the `::` notation, you would have had to write:

```
my $fel= Felidea::new('Felidea');
```

It would be tedious and redundant to have to construct all of your methods this way. The arrow method call takes care of this for you. So in object orientation, you will be using:

```
$object_handle->method_name
```

Remember, you don't have to use new as the constructor name. If you had used the convention of naming the constructor the same name as the class, the line above would be written like so:

```
my $fel= Felidea Felidea();
```

. . . or like so:

```
my $fel= Felidea->Felidea();
```

Now that the constructor has been called, you have an object reference that will be used for all subsequent uses of the object. This is why it's important to understand that references are one of the key concepts of object-oriented programming. This object reference is similar to the reference to a subroutine shown in Chapter 4, except that an object reference knows what type of class it is (which was accomplished by using the function `bless()`), and can call all the methods in the class that it refers to.

Both object references are to different instantiated objects for the same class. Also, because instance variables are allowed, it is also possible to instantiate `Felidea` with arguments:

```
my $fel= Felidea->new({
    DEBUG       => 1,
    fur_color   => 'pink',
    fur_length  => 'long'}
    );
```

Adding Methods

Next, you want to add methods to `Felidea.pm`. These methods can be a variety of functionalities, either setting object attributes or retrieving attributes. This next section will show you how this is done.

Accessors

The first method that will be added is a simple method to provide encapsulation — accessing a "private" class/object attribute by way of a method:

```
sub hasFur {
    my ($self)= @_;
    return $self->{_fur};
}
```

You'll notice that the method above, hasFur(), is different than the subroutines of regular Perl modules shown in the previous chapter. hasFur() is an object or instance method, as opposed to a regular package subroutine. For those readers who are familiar with object-oriented programming in other languages, hasFur() could also be considered a *virtual* method in that it can be overridden, though the term *virtual method* is not often used in Perl object-oriented programming. hasFur() takes as its first argument an object reference, $self, to the instantiated class, as opposed to *class* methods, such as new(), which take the name of the object.

> One thing to keep in mind: The constructor method's first argument was the *name* of the class, so it is a *static* method. In an instance method, the first argument is a *reference* to the object, so the rest of the methods shown in the Felidea class are instance methods.

In the new method, the class attribute $self->{_fur} was defined and set to a default of 1, using an underscore key name to denote privacy. This method simply provides proper access to that private attribute. To use this method in your program, you would call it:

```
print "has fur\n" if $fel->hasFur();
```

Since Perl doesn't enforce privacy, you could have called it like so:

```
print "has fur\n" if $fel->{_fur};
```

But this would be rude! Seriously, you are welcome to do whatever you like in terms of using the nomenclature of *public* versus *private*. Perl doesn't enforce it by name alone, so you can do whatever you like. That is Perl's nature. However, it might be good to follow some sort of naming convention and to use underscores as a standard naming convention, as this is often used for naming private methods and attributes in Perl programming.

Setting Methods

As well as retrieving attributes, you also want to set attributes. Again, you set an attribute that is intended to be private from within Felidea.pm:

```
sub furColor {
    my ($self, $fur_color)= @_;
    $self->{_fur_color}= $fur_color if defined $fur_color;
    return $self->{_fur_color};
}
```

The method furColor() simply takes as an argument the fur color that program wishes to pass and sets its private attribute _fur_color to that passed argument. To use this method in your program, it is called just like any other method is called, except you can either specify a value or not as an argument:

```
$fel->setFurColor('tan');
```

This sets the private attribute _fur_color to 'tan'. To access the fur color:

```
print "fur color " . $fel->furColor() . "\n";
```

This returns the _fur_color attribute. You could also call it this way:

```
print "fur color" . $fel->furColor('tan') . "\n";
```

The previous snippet both sets and accesses _fur_color. So, the complete Felidea class as defined in Felidea.pm is now:

```
package Felidea;

use strict;
use warnings;

our $VERSION = 0.001;

{ # this is a closure

# The subroutines in this enclosure are here to give
# access to lexical variables which are not visible outside
# the closure, aka encapsulation

    # this is a listing of permitted instance variables
    # are permitted
    my $OPTIONS= {
        '_DEBUG'        => 1,
        '_fur'          => 1,
```

```perl
                '_weight'          => 1,
                '_fur_color'       => 1,
                '_fur_length'      => 1
        };

        # this gives a true or false of whether an option is permitted
        sub _permitted_option {
                # if 2 args, called as method, if only 1, subroutine
                my $key= scalar @_ == 2 ? $_[1] : $_[0];
                $key= '_'. $key;
                return exists $OPTIONS->{$key};
        }

}
sub new {
        my ($caller, $opts)= @_;

        # this allows an already instantiated object to be able to
        # be used to instantiate another object- to behave as either
        # a static or dynamic method
        my $class= ref($caller) || $caller;

        # some common attributes
        my $self= {
                '_name'            => '',
                '_fur'             => 1,
                '_weight'          => 50,
                '_claws'           => 1,
                '_fur_color'       => '',
                '_fur_length'      => '',
                '_tail'            => 1,
                '_fangs'           => 1,
        };


        # instance variables passed via $opts hashref
        for (%$opts) {
                # Only if _permitted_option returns a true value
                $self->{$_} =
                        $opts->{$_} if _permitted_option($_);

        # this makes it so $self belongs to the class Felidea
        bless $self, $class;

        # return the object handle
        return $self;

}

sub name {
        my ($self, $name)= @_;
        $self->{_name}= $name if defined $name;
        return $self->{_name};
}
```

```perl
sub fur {
    my ($self, $fur)= @_;
    $self->{_fur}= $fur if defined $fur;
    return $self->{_fur};
}
sub weight {
    my ($self, $weight)= @_;
    $self->{_weight}= $weight if defined $weight;
    return $self->{_weight};
}

sub claws {
    my ($self, $claws)= @_;
    $self->{_claws}= $claws if defined $claws;
    return $self->{_claws};
}

sub furColor {
    my ($self, $fur_color)= @_;
    $self->{_fur_color}= $fur_color if defined $fur_color;
    return $self->{_fur_color};
}

sub furLength {
    my ($self, $fur_length)= @_;
    $self->{_fur_length}= $fur_length if defined $fur_length;
    return $self->{_fur_length};
}

sub tail {
    my ($self, $tail)= @_;
    $self->{_tail}= $tail if defined $tail;
    return $self->{_tail};
}
sub fangs {
    my ($self, $fangs)= @_;
    $self->{_fangs}= $tail if defined $fangs;
    return $self->{_fangs};
}
sub solitary {
    my ($self, $solitary)= @_;
    $self->{_solitary}= $tail if defined $solitary;
    return $self->{_solitary};
}

1;
```

Each attribute now has its own accessor method. You'll notice the naming convention follows these rules:

❑ If the attribute is a single word with no underscores, the method name is the same.

❑ If the attribute value contains underscores, the underscore is omitted and the first character following the underscore is capitalized in the method name.

This style is known as *CamelCase*, and is often used in object-oriented languages. However, this is just a style preference and not a requirement. Use whatever naming convention you prefer.

Also added is an $OPTIONS hash reference, scoped lexically, inside an enclosure. This reference makes it possible for $OPTIONS or any of its members to be accessed directly. An accompanying _permitted_option() method is used to obtain a true or false value, telling you whether the instance variables exist in $OPTIONS or not. This controls which instance variables can be set at the time of instantiation. Also note that this can be called as either a subroutine or a method, since it checks the number of arguments that are passed. If there are two arguments, this means it was called as a method and you should use the second argument. If there is only one argument, it was called as a subroutine and you should use the one and only argument.

The other thing you'll notice or realize is that it seems a bit redundant to have to list all the methods for each attribute. Your developer's brain is probably screaming, "I see duplication!" For each attribute you might add to the Felidea class, you would also have to code a method to match it. Fear not, there is a way to make this more compact!

On-Demand Method Manifestation Using AUTOLOAD

In Perl, autoloading — using the subroutine AUTOLOAD() — is one way to create subroutines (or, in the case of object-orientation, methods) that are not defined and have them handled without an error. It allows a method to function upon its invocation without having to have the method defined in your class. It can be used in the case of the Felidea class to dynamically create accessor methods for each of its attributes.

> *It should be noted that using AUTOLOAD() is the traditional or "old school" way of autogenerating methods and is now not considered to be a Perl "best practice," although you are free to use it if you want. The Perl cops won't come and arrest you if you do. Life can be made easier for you because there are now a number of philosophies and ways to autogenerate methods, by using various Perl modules such as Class::Std, Class::InsideOut, Object::InsideOut, Class::Accessor and Moose. These can a bit more straightforward than AUTOLOAD().*

> *However, because you will still find many articles online and books in print that still show AUTOLOAD() as the mechanism used in Perl for creating accessor get/set methods, it is good to understand how it works. Seeing this done with AUTOLOAD() will also give you appreciation for some of the newer methods, which is the reason for this section. After this chapter covers AUTOLOAD(), you will then see an easier way of doing this with Moose in the next section!*

How does AUTOLOAD() work? When a subroutine in a package — or a method in a class in object orientation — is called, if it doesn't exist in the class, and is not found by looking recursively through @ISA, Perl next checks to see if there is a subroutine called AUTOLOAD() and calls it if it exists. AUTOLOAD() is called in the same exact way that the intended method was called, with the same number and order of arguments. Next, the package variable $AUTOLOAD (which has already been declared a package-scoped variable with our) assumes the fully qualified name of the called method. Subsequent calls to this method are handled by whatever code is defined in the AUTOLOAD method.

The Felidea class is then changed to the following:

```
package Felidea;
```

```perl
use strict;
use warnings;

# this is so we can use croak - which gives more info
# than "die"
use Carp qw(croak);

our $VERSION = 0.001;

{ # this is a closure.

# The subroutines in this enclosure are here to give
# access to lexical variables which are not visible outside
# the closure, aka encapsulation

    # this is a listing of permitted instance variables
    # are permitted
    my $OPTIONS= {
        '_DEBUG'        => 1,
        '_fur'          => 1,
        '_weight'       => 1,
        '_fur_color'    => 1,
        '_fur_length'   => 1
    };

    # this gives a true or false of whether an option is permitted
    sub _permitted_option {
        # if 2 args, called as method, if only 1, subroutine
        my $key= scalar @_ == 2 ? $_[1] : $_[0];
        $key= '_'. $key;
        return exists $OPTIONS->{$key};
    }

    # this can be used both in supplying a list of attributes that are
    # members in the class, as well as in the constructor
    my $ATTRIBS= {
        '_name'         => 'felidea',
        '_fur'          => 1,
        '_weight'       => 50,
        '_claws'        => 1,
        '_fur_color'    => '',
        '_fur_length'   => 'unset',
        '_tail'         => 1,
        '_fangs'        => 1,
        '_solitary'     => 1,
    };

    # returns default of attribute
    sub _attrib_default {
        # if 2 args, called as method, if only 1, subroutine
        my $arg= scalar @_ == 2 ? $_[1] : $_[0];
        return $ATTRIBS->{$arg}
    }

    # returns true/false of whether attribute exists or not
```

```perl
    sub _attrib_exists {
        # if 2 args, called as method, if only 1, subroutine
        my $arg= scalar @_ == 2 ? $_[1] : $_[0];
        return exists $ATTRIBS->{$arg}
    }

    # returns a list of class attributes
    sub _attrib_keys {
        return keys %$ATTRIBS
    }
} # end of closure

# Creates methods if existing in $ATTRIBS
sub AUTOLOAD {
    my ($self, $value) = @_;

    # only want the attribute value, not the full package name
    my ($attrib) = (our $AUTOLOAD) =~ /^.*::(\w+)$/ or die "Error:
$AUTOLOAD";

    # again, converting from Capital studly caps
    $attrib=~ s/([A-Z])/_\l$1/g;

    # leading underscore
    $attrib = '_' . $attrib;

    # only if the attribute is a member, do you create it
    if (_attrib_exists($attrib)) {
        $self->{$attrib}= $value if $value;
        return $self->{$attrib};
    }

    # this handles if the attribute, and therefor the method,
    # does not exist - except for DESTROY, which is automatically called
    # when done with an object
    croak "Method $AUTOLOAD is not a valid method!\n"
        unless $AUTOLOAD =~ /DESTROY/;
}

sub new {
    my ($class, $opts) = @_;

    # some common attributes
    my $self;
    $self->{$_} = _attrib_default($_) for _attrib_keys();

    # instance variables passed via $opts hashref
    for (keys %$opts){
        # Only if _permitted_option returns a true value
        $self->{$_} =
            $opts->{$_} if _permitted_option($_);
    }

    # this makes it so $self belongs to the class Felidea
    bless $self, $class;
```

```
        # return the object handle
        return $self;

}

1;
```

The changes made to the `Felidea` class are summarized here:

❑ A lexically scoped `$ATTRIBS` hash reference: This is added in the enclosure that already contains `$OPTIONS`. This `$ATTRIBS` hash reference has keys, which are the attributes the class will use. This is where you would add new attributes, resulting in new class accessor/modifier methods for those attributes.

❑ Encapsulated hash reference accessor subroutines: These are added to prevent direct access to `$ATTRIBS`.

❑ `_attrib_default()`: Returns the default of the attribute. It can be called as either a method or subroutine since it has logic to check the number of arguments just as `_permitted_options()` does.

❑ `_attrib_keys()`: Returns a list of the keys, or attributes. Can be called as either a method or subroutine.

❑ `_attrib_exists()`: True/false of whether the attribute exists or not, whether it should have a method AUTOLOADed for it. Can be called as either a method or subroutine.

❑ Adding the use of `Carp` This has subroutines to act as `warn()` or `die()` but with useful information. For `Felidea`, `croak()` functions like `die()`, and is used when an attribute is not existing.

❑ AUTOLOAD: The AUTOLOAD subroutine/method is added. This contains the functionality to dynamically generate methods based on the attribute name. Because the method naming style used here is `studly-caps`, the attribute supplied needs to be converted from word fragments (if it exists) separated by capitalization, to word fragments separated by underscores, giving the correct attribute name. Furthermore, a check to ensure that the attribute exists using `_attribute_exists()` is made. If it does exist, the same code as used before in each individual method is called. Finally, if the attribute did not exist, the `croak()` function handles the error with a message printing out `$AUTOLOAD`, which will call the full method name, unless the method is DESTROY, which is automatically called when the program exits.

❑ The constructor `new()`: This now uses `_attribute_keys()` to obtain an attribute list, mapping each by key for populating attributes to `$self`.

Notice now that this class no longer has the various accessor methods! AUTOLOAD takes care of this for you. If you want to add attributes and associated methods for each, just add to `$ATTRIBS`.

The following code block shows the program used to test this. It uses all the different methods to give you an idea how this program is used, and also shows that AUTOLOAD does its trick:

```
#!/usr/bin/perl

use strict;
use warnings;
```

```
use Felidea;
my $fel= new Felidea();
print "has fur\n" if $fel->fur();
print "Setting fur color to tan.\n";
$fel->furColor('tan');
print "fur color " . $fel->furColor() . "\n";
$fel->furLength('short');
print "fur length" . $fel->furLength() . "\n";
$fel->weight(30);
print "weight " . $fel->weight() . "\n";

print "Has a tail.\n" if $fel->tail();
print "Has fangs.\n" if $fel->fangs();
print "Has claws.\n"  if $fel->claws();
$fel->claws(0);
print "But, declawed now.\n" unless $fel->claws();
```

The output of this program verifies that AUTOLOAD works as advertised:

```
has fur
Setting fur color to tan.
fur color tan
fur lengthshort
weight 30
Has a tail.
Has fangs.
Has claws.
But, declawed now.
```

What about calling a method that doesn't exist? This is easy enough to check:

```
print "This Fildea is going to moo: " . $fel->moo(); "\n";
```

This results in the Felidea object letting you know that you called an invalid method:

```
Method Felidea::moo is an invalid method!
 at ./feline_app.pl line 21
```

You can now also see the benefit of using the carp() error handling.

Although autoloading is useful, there are some issues that need to be brought up:

❑ As stated before, AUTOLOAD() is not considered to be a Perl "best practice," particularly when you have a derived class that has its own AUTOLOAD() subroutine, yet you end up with the hierarchical search using the top-level class's AUTOLOAD() instead. There are ways to get around this issue, though you end up having to add more code, which makes your AUTOLOAD() methods more complex and slower, and thus more difficult for you to maintain.

❑ There is some overhead with this method generation every time the method is called, as opposed to having the method already defined in the class. This can result in slower overall execution of the code. (There is a way around this that will be discussed later.)

❏ As a developer, you have to ensure you have a mechanism to handle methods that don't exist (as already shown). Nothing in life is *free*!

❏ The other question is: How could you have read-only methods, as well as methods that have a different naming convention than you've already been shown? The answer lies in what you want to implement. With AUTOLOAD, you have to provide the functionality to make sure it creates the methods you want, handles errors for missing arguments or methods that are called for attributes that don't exist, and controls access to those methods. You have more work up front, but of course it saves you from having duplicate code and having to write the same method functionality over and over again.

As an example, some developers want to have their methods named get_<attribute>, and set_<attribute>. They also want it so that certain attributes cannot be written. The following modification to the Felidea class shows how this can be done:

```perl
package Felidea;

use strict;
use warnings;

use Carp qw(croak carp);

our $VERSION = 0.001;

our $AUTOLOAD;

{ # enclosure
    # this is a listing of permitted instance variables
    # are permitted
    my $OPTIONS= {
        '_DEBUG'        => 1,
        '_fur'          => 1,
        '_weight'       => 1,
        '_fur_color'    => 1,
        '_fur_length'   => 1
    };

    # this gives a true or false of whether an option is permitted
    sub _permitted_option {
        my $key= '_'. $_[0];
        return exists $OPTIONS->{$key};
    }

    # these are the class's attributes, value a hashref of
    # the default, and rw (read-write) flag
    my $ATTRIBS= {
        '_name'         => { default => 'felidea', rw => 0 },
        '_fur'          => { default => 1,         rw => 1},
        '_weight'       => { default => 50,        rw => 1},
        '_claws'        => { default => 1,         rw => 1},
        '_fur_color'    => { default => 'grey',    rw => 1},
        '_fur_length'   => { default => 'unset',   rw => 1},
        '_tail'         => { default => 1,         rw => 0},
        '_fangs'        => { default => 1,         rw => 0},
```

```perl
    '_solitary'    => { default => 1,           rw => 0},
};

# true/false if an attribute is writeable
sub _attrib_canwrite { return $ATTRIBS->{$_[0]}{rw} }

# returns default of attribute
sub _attrib_default { return $ATTRIBS->{$_[0]}{default}}

# returns true/false of whether attribute exists or not
sub _attrib_exists { return exists $ATTRIBS->{$_[0]}}

# returns a list of class attributes
sub _attrib_keys {return keys %$ATTRIBS}

} # end enclosure

sub AUTOLOAD {
    my ($self, $value) = @_;
    return if $AUTOLOAD =~ /::DESTROY/;

    my ($action, $attrib)=
        ($AUTOLOAD) =~ /^.*::(get|set)([A-Z]\w+)$/
        or croak "Invalid method $AUTOLOAD\n";
    $attrib=~ s/([A-Z])/_\l$1/g;

    if ($action && $attrib && _attrib_exists($attrib)) {
        if ($action eq 'set' && attrib_canwrite($attrib) ) {
            carp "No value to $AUTOLOAD supplied!" unless defined $value;
            $self->{$attrib}= $value if defined $value;
        }
        return $self->{$attrib};
    }
    croak "Method $AUTOLOAD is an invalid method!\n";
}


sub new {
    my ($class, $opts)= @_;

    # some common attributes
    my $self;
    $self->{$_}= _attrib_default($_) for _attrib_keys();


    # instance variables passed via $opts hashref
    for (keys %$opts) {
        # Only if _permitted_option returns a true value
        my $priv_attrib= '_' . $_;
        $self->{$priv_attrib} =
            $opts->{$_} if _permitted_option($_);
    }

    # this makes it so $self belongs to the class Felidea
    bless $self, $class;
```

```
        # return the object handle
        return $self;

    }

    1;
```

All the dual-purpose accessor methods are now replaced with get<Attrib> and set<Attrib> methods. The changes made to the Felidea class were the following:

❑ A modified $ATTRIBS hash ref: Instead of the attribute value being a scalar (which is the default value), its value is now a hash reference with two members: one default, which is the default value of the attribute; the other rw, which is a simple flag the code will now use to determine if the attribute is writeable. The default key will be used in the constructor method new() and the rw key will be used in AUTOLOAD to control access to the attribute.

❑ The addition of _attrib_canwrite(): This subroutine returns true or false based on whether the rw value for the attribute is 1 or 0.

❑ The _attrib_default() was modified to return the default key value for the attribute.

❑ The package-scoped variable $AUTOLOAD is defined prior to use in AUTOLOAD() subroutine: This is because the previous code defined and used $AUTOLOAD at the same time. Now it's required to check the value of $AUTOLOAD for the method DESTROY, which would result in an error of $AUTOLOAD not being defined the way it was coded before.

❑ The check for the DESTROY() method moved to the top of the AUTOLOAD() subroutine. This is because the subsequent lines that use regular expressions to extract both the $action and $attrib from the value of $AUTOLOAD will not parse DESTROY() correctly. Also, this is more efficient to immediately return if DESTROY() is the method being called.

❑ The value of $action is checked for *set*. This determines if the method is a set method as well as if the attribute is writeable. If it is writeable, then writes to the class attribute will be permitted. In this example, there could be a message returned to the user using either croak() or carp() in the event the attribute is not permitted to be written to, but instead silent failure is what is used. This is where documentation would be useful. Also, there is a warning message using carp() if there is not value passed into the *set* method. Finally, the attribute is set if $value is defined.

❑ The constructor method is modified: Instead of using the previous scalar value of the keyed $ATTRIB hash reference, you're using the value of the *default* hashref that results from the keying of the $ATTRIB hashref.

The program using the Felidea object is also changed to utilize the new read-write checking functionality:

```perl
#!/usr/bin/perl -w

use Felidea;

my $fel = Felidea->new();
print "has fur\n" if $fel->getFur();
print "Setting fur color to tan.\n";
$fel->setFurColor('tan');
print "fur color " . $fel->getFurColor() . "\n";
```

```
$fel->setFurLength('short');
print "fur length" . $fel->getFurLength() . "\n";
$fel->setWeight(30);
print "weight " . $fel->getWeight() . "\n";
$fel->setWeight();

print "Has a tail.\n" if $fel->getTail();
$fel->setTail(0);
print "Still has a tail.\n" if $fel->getTail();
print "Has a fangs.\n" if $fel->getFangs();
print "Has claws.\n"  if $fel->getClaws();
$fel->setClaws(0);
print "But, declawed now.\n" unless $fel->getClaws();
```

The main changes to the program are to change any method calls that were previously reading values from <attribute>() to get<Attribute>(), and to change any that modified attributes from <attribute>(somevalue) to set<Attribute>. A line calling setWeight() with no argument is added. This attempt will fail with a warning message. Also, an attempt is made to cut off the tail of this Felid. Depending on the type of cat, this could result in anything from a scratch to the arm to getting your head clawed or bitten off! Luckily, here it just results in a warning message. $fel->setTail(0) will fail because the attribute _tail in $ATTRIBS has a rw value of 0. The output verifies that the changes are working, including both error handing and access control to attributes:

```
has fur
Setting fur color to tan.
fur color tan
fur lengthshort
weight 30
No value supplied! at ./feline_app.pl line 14
No value supplied to Felidea::setWeight ! at ./feline_app.pl line 14
Has a tail.
Still has a tail.
Has fangs.
Has claws.
But, declawed now.
```

As previously mentioned, one shortcoming of AUTOLOAD() is that every time the method is created with AUTOLOAD(), it has to first try to locate a method for the method called in the calling program and when it doesn't find one, it has to use AUTOLOAD(). This certainly adds some overhead. This happens yet again when the method is called. What would be useful is if when AUTOLOAD() is called, the implementation details of the method called are stashed and used as if they were actually hard-coded in the class. There is a way to do this and gain the benefits.

This is accomplished using the package's symbol table. As you recall, the symbol table is particular to a package and contains all symbol names for that package. A way to get your AUTOLOAD-created methods to behave as if they were hard-coded is to get the Felidea package to have entries for these subroutines/methods. This can be accomplished within AUTOLOAD(); before you had code to handle what the method should do. Now, the first time AUTOLOAD() is called for a particular method, you have that same code in an anonymous subroutine. You then must ensure that an entry in the symbol table for Felidea with the symbol name of the method being called is set to this anonymous routine.

```
sub AUTOLOAD {
```

```
    my ($self, $value) = @_;
    return if $AUTOLOAD =~ /::DESTROY/;

    # parse get or set, and rest of the name of the method
    my ($action, $attrib)=
        ($AUTOLOAD) =~ /^.*::(get|set)([A-Z]\w+)$/
        or croak "Invalid method $AUTOLOAD\n";

    # convert from attributeName to attribute_name
    $attrib=~ s/([A-Z])/_\l$1/g;

    if ($action && $attrib && _attrib_exists($attrib)) {
        # $method is used to properly handle the method the first time
        # it's handled by AUTOLOAD. Subsequent calls will be handled by
        # code stored in symbol table
        my $method;
        if ($action eq 'set' && _attrib_canwrite($attrib)) {
            # set symbol table entry to anon sub
            *{$AUTOLOAD}= $method= sub {
                print "DEBUG: $AUTOLOAD called.\n" if $_[0]->{_DEBUG};
                carp "No value supplied to $AUTOLOAD !" unless defined $_[1];
                $_[0]->{$attrib}= $_[1];
                return $_[0]->{$attrib};
            };
        }
        else {
            # set symbol table entry to anon sub
            *{$AUTOLOAD}= $method= sub {
                print "DEBUG: $AUTOLOAD called.\n" if $_[0]->{_DEBUG};
                return $_[0]->{$attrib};
            };
        }
        # return using anon sub ref, next time done via symbol table
        return $method->($self, $value);

    }
    else { croak "Invalid method $AUTOLOAD\n"; }

}
```

You also need to add one important line to `Felidea.pm`:

```
package Felidea;

use strict;
use warnings;
no strict 'refs';
```

The changes to the Felidea class are shown. This time, only the AUTOLOAD method was changed. The changes can be explained as such:

❑ Declare a variable called $method. Even though the goal is to have the code inserted into the symbol table for a given method, the code still has to be able to handle the method call the first time AUTOLOAD handles it. This variable will be set to the same subroutine that the typeglob is set to — just so it can be called this first time around. All subsequent calls will be handled by code in the symbol table for this package/class.

❑ The $AUTOLOAD variable has the value Felidea::methodname. Using a typeglob *{$AUTOLOAD} translates to *Felidea::methodname, which is in turn set to the anonymous subroutine that will handle subsequent calls of this method. Also, $method is also set to the same value, this anonymous subroutine.

With the symbol table ready for subsequent calls to this method, it still has to be handled this first time around. So, since $method is set to the proper subroutine, just call it by dereferencing it with the proper arguments.

The addition of no strict 'refs' at the top of Felidea.pm is required for setting *{$AUTOLOAD} to the anonymous subroutines. Otherwise you will encounter this error:

```
Can't use string ("Felidea::getFur") as a symbol ref while "strict
refs" in use at
Felidea.pm line 89.
```

Other Methods

Now that the Felidea class has its various accessor methods, you can also add other methods to it. So far, the methods shown have been attribute accessor methods. Other types of methods can be added to the Felidea class as well. For the sake of discussion, as well as to explain inheritance concepts later in this chapter, two methods will be added:

```
sub makeSound {
    my ($self) = @_;
    print "Generic Felidea vocalization\n";
    return;
}

sub attackPrey {
    my ($self, $preyType) = @_;
    if ($preyType eq 'fast') {
        print "sprint after prey\n";
    }
    elsif ($preyType eq 'big') {
        print "Jump and chew on neck\n";
    }
    else {
        print "Pounce\n";
    }
    return;
}
```

Debug

Throughout these examples, you have seen that the constructor method has the ability to pass in $options, which are checked to make sure they are valid options in the $OPTIONS hash reference. One of these keys is _DEBUG. This can be used to set a debug flag, which throughout the class can be used to perform useful actions such as printing various information, particularly during the development phase or when researching a bug.

To use this option, develop a method that allows you to set the debug value either during instantiation or after instantiation. The simple method to do this is called debug():

```
sub debug {
    my ($self, $debug)= @_;
    $self->{_DEBUG}= $debug;
    return $self->{_DEBUG};
}
```

In AUTOLOAD(), simple modifications are made to take advantage of debug():

```
if ($action eq 'set' && $ATTRIBS->{$attrib}{rw}) {
        # set symbol table entry to anon sub
        *{$AUTOLOAD}= $method= sub {
            print "DEBUG: $AUTOLOAD called.\n" if $_[0]->{_DEBUG};
            carp "No value supplied to $AUTOLOAD !" unless defined $_[1];
            $_[0]->{$attrib}= $_[1];
            return $_[0]->{$attrib};
        };
    }
    else {
        # set symbol table entry to anon sub
        *{$AUTOLOAD}= $method= sub {
            print "DEBUG: $AUTOLOAD called.\n" if $_[0]->{_DEBUG};
            return $_[0]->{$attrib};
        };
    }
```

Anything could have been done based on whether or not the class attribute _DEBUG is set. In this example, the code prints out the fully qualified package name.

To turn debug on or off, the application code is changed to either set debug on instantiation, like so:

```
my $fel= Felidea->new({_DEBUG => 1});
```

... or after instantiation, in this way:

```
$fel->debug(0);
```

The output of some of the methods if debug is on appears as such:

```
DEBUG: Felidea::getFur called.
has fur
Setting fur color to tan.
DEBUG: Felidea::setFurColor called.
DEBUG: Felidea::getFurColor called.
```

You can add whatever functionality to your debug mechanism that you like. In later chapters, you'll see how to create debug routines that print out nicely formatted debug information.

Documentation

Certainly, you want your class to be documented. As shown in the previous chapter, POD is a simple way to add documentation to your Perl code. In the case of this class, you will have to remember that despite using AUTOLOAD(), you will still need to add documentation for the methods that you use AUTOLOAD() to dynamically generate.

Add to the end of Felidea.pm:

```
# ... rest of code ...
1;

__END__
=pod

=head1 NAME

Felidea - A class representing the the biological family of cats, Felidea

=head1 SYNOPSIS

    use Felidea;

    my $fel= Felidea->new({<OPTIONS>});

    $fel->fur_color('green');
    print "Fur color " . $fel->getFurColor() . "\n";
    $fel->fur_length('long');
    print "Fur color " . $fel->getFurLength() . "\n";


=head1 DESCRIPTION

A class representing a Felidea. Felidea is the name for the
biological family of cats, each member called a felid. Felids
are the most strictly carnivorous of all families in the order
of Carnivora.


=head2 METHODS

=over 4

=item C<makeSound()>

Produces the sound the particular Felid makes ie "Roar", "meow", "growl"

=item C<attackPrey()>

Prey attacking method, prints out steps the Felid attacks its prey

=item C<debug(1|0)>

Sets the debug to true or false
```

```
=item C<getFur()>

Retrieves the fur color of the Felid

=item C<setFur('value')>

Sets the fur color of the Felid

=back

=head2 OPTIONS/CLASS ATTRIBUTES

These can be set at instantiation

my $fel= Felidea->new({
    DEBUG       => 1,
    fur_color   => 'brown',
    fur_length  => 'short',
    ...
});


Felid fur length, ie 'long', 'short', 'fuzzy'

=item fangs

True/False of whether the felid has fangs or not. Cannot be set.

=item solitary

True/False of whether the felid is a solitary animal or not

=item ... all other options ...


=back

=head1 AUTHORS

Patrick Galbraith

=head1 COPYRIGHT

Patrick Galbraith (c) 2008

=cut
```

Inheritance and Felidea Subclassing

Perl implements inheritance simply with the use of a package variable aptly named @ISA — as in the phrase "is a." In the case of Pantherinea, which needs to inherit from Felidea, this would be accomplished simply with:

```
@ISA = qw(Felidea);
```

Pantherinea *"is a"* Felidea, so this mechanism is very intuitive and simple to use. @ISA is another one of the reserved package variable names like @EXPORT, @EXPORT_OK, $VERSION, etc.

Also, the package of the class specifies the namespace the class takes on, and naturally you will want this to reflect the inheritance hierarchy. This can be demonstrated using our example by showing how to subclass the Felidea class.

From Figure 5-1, you saw how *Felidea* was the top-level family, or object. The next level down were the Pantherinea and Felinea families, and below that were the species — tiger, lions, domestic cats, lynx and cougar. The first step in creating these derived classes is to create the package files with the proper class definitions, starting out with the first descendant, then on to the species classes. The examples shown here provide the same concept and techniques that can be used for any type of object.

The Perl classes (package names) to match the object hierarchy shown in Figure 5-1 would need to be named as such:

- ❏ Felidea
- ❏ Felidea::Pantherinea
- ❏ Felidea::Pantherinea::Tiger
- ❏ Felidea::Pantherinea::Lion
- ❏ Felidea::Felinea
- ❏ Felidea::Felinea::Cougar
- ❏ Felidea::Felinea::DomesticCat
- ❏ Felidea::Felinea::Lynx

As already mentioned, the :: class delimiter can signify a directory structure in Perl where each subclass has its own package file. This means that there will need to be a directory structure to contain these classes. The directory structure will look like this:

```
Felidea/
Felidea/Pantherinea/

Felidea/Felinea
```

Each directory will contain the derived classes and be at the same level as the class being derived from. In other words:

```
Felidea.pm

Felidea/

Felidea/Pantherinea.pm

Felidea/Pantherinea/

Felidea/Pantherinea/Tiger.pm

Felidea/Pantherinea/Lion.pm
```

```
Felidea/Felinea/

Felidea/Felinea/Cougar.pm

Felidea/Felinea/DomesticCat.pm

Felidea/Felinea/Lynx.pm
```

The first step is to create the `Felidea` directory, and then create a `Pantherinea.pm` and `Felinea.pm`. `Pantherinea.pm` is shown in the following code:

```perl
package Felidea::Pantherinea;

use strict;
use warnings;
no strict 'refs';

use base qw(Felidea);

use Carp qw(croak carp);


{ # enclosure
    my $ATTRIBS= {
        '_name'  => { default => 'pantherinea',    rw => 0 },
    };
    # returns default of attribute
    sub _attrib_default {
        # if 2 args, called as method, if only 1, subroutine
        my $arg= scalar @_ == 2 ? $_[1] : $_[0];
        return $ATTRIBS->{$arg}{default};
    }

    # returns a list of class attributes
    sub _attrib_keys {
        return keys %$ATTRIBS
    }
} # end enclosure

sub new {
    my ($class, $opts)= @_;

    # some common attributes
    my $self = $class->SUPER::new($opts);
    $self->{$_}= _attrib_default($_) for _attrib_keys();

    # this makes it so $self belongs to the class Felidea
    bless $self, $class;

    # return the object handle
    return $self;
}

1;
```

The differences in this derived class from its parent class you already saw implemented can be explained thus:

❑   The package name changes to `Felidea::Pantherinea`

❑   The next line, `use base qw(Felidea)`, sets the base class that `Felidea::Pantherinea` inherits from. It is the equivalent to the two lines below, which first would use the top level class `Felidea`, as well as set the `@ISA` array to contain the class name that says what class `Pantherinea` inherits from:

```
use Felidea::Pantherinea;

@ISA= qw(Felidea);
```

❑   `Felidea::Pantherinea` class has its own `$ATTRIBS` hash reference in an enclosure, which in this case has only the `_name` attribute set. This overrides the `_name` attribute `Pantherinea` would have inherited from the class it descends from, the parent, Felidea. Also, `_attrib_keys()` and `_attrib_default()` are implemented. It would have been possible to use `$self->SUPER::_attrib_<xxx>`, but because this code uses encapsulation for the class attributes in `$ATTRIBS`, that would result in the `$ATTRIBS` of Felidea being read.

❑   The call of `my $self = $class->SUPER::new($opts)` SUPER is a pseudo-package that refers to the parent package of the current package, in this case Felidea. The end result here is that Felidea's `new()` method is called, which instantiates a Felidea object. All the option checking and setting up of package variables, as well as creating an object variable to Felidea, is accomplished because of this. This makes it so you don't have to reimplement a constructor for `Pantherinea`. Anything other than what `SUPER::new` accomplishes construes overriding Felidea.

❑   The `_name` class attribute is overridden, which the line `$self->{$_} = _attrib_default($_)` for `_attrib_keys();` does. As stated before, `_attrib_keys()` is reimplemented since it needs to return the default value for the attribute from the lexical `$OPTIONS` hashref in `Pantherinea`, which in this case contains only the `_name` attribute.

❑   Finally, `$self` is blessed as a `Felidea::Pantherinea` object.

`Felidea::Pantherinea` is a class that represents a family of Felidea. It really won't be used that much, and the only specific attributes that discern it for this example at least (of course, there are DNA differences that aren't within the scope of this book) from the other family, Felinea, is the `_name` attribute. If there were other attributes and more complexity in the top-level class — for instance DNA markers — those also would be overridden.

The `Felinea` class would be implemented the same way `Pantherea` was, except of course with a different package name and `_name` attribute. The main purpose here is to show how to create classes representing the inheritance hierarchy of Figure 5-1, starting from the `Felidea` class on down. Of real interest are the species classes which will be subclasses of `Pantherinea` and `Felinea`.

Now that the `Pantherinea` and `Felinea` family classes have been created, to create their subclasses, two subdirectories named `Pantherinea` and `Felinea` must be created. Each of these directories will contain their subclasses. For discussion, the lion species class will be created. To make it easy, just use the `Pantherinea.pm`, since it is pretty minimal, as a template:

```
cp Pantherinea.pm Pantherinea/Lion.pm
```

Then you would create Lion.pm:

```perl
package Felidea::Pantherinea::Lion;

use strict;
no strict 'refs';
use base qw(Felidea::Pantherinea);
use Carp qw(croak carp);


{ # closure
    my $ATTRIBS= {
        '_name'       => { default => 'lion',         rw => 0 },
        '_latin_name' => { default => 'panthera leo', rw => 0 },
        '_family'     => { default => 'pantherinea',  rw => 0 },
        '_solitary'   => { default => 0,              rw => 0 },
        '_fur_color'  => { default => 'light tan',    rw => 1 },
        '_weight'     => { default => 250,            rw => 1 },
    };
    # returns default of attribute
    sub _attrib_default {
        # if 2 args, called as method, if only 1, subroutine
        my $arg= scalar @_ == 2 ? $_[1] : $_[0];
        return $ATTRIBS->{$arg}{default};
    }

    # returns a list of class attributes
    sub _attrib_keys {
        return keys %$ATTRIBS
    }
} # end closure

sub new {
    my ($class, $opts)= @_;

    # some common attributes
    my $self = $class->SUPER::new($opts);
    $self->{$_}= _attrib_default($_) for _attrib_keys();

    # this makes it so $self belongs to the class Filidea
    bless $self, $class;

    # return the object handle
    return $self;
}

sub fightOffHyenas {
    my ($self)= @_;
}

sub shareKillWithPride {
    my ($self)= @_;
}
```

```perl
sub makeSound {
    my ($self)= @_;
    print "ROAR!\n";
}

sub attackPrey {
    my ($self, $preyType)= @_;
    $self->fightOffHyenas();
    $self->SUPER::attackPrey($preyType);
    $self->shareKillWithPride();

}

1;
```

The Lion class implementation shown above can be explained like so:

❏ Package name is declared as Felidea::Pantherinea::Lion; the @ISA array is set with the class Felidea::Pantherinea with the line use base qw(Felidea::Pantherinea).

❏ The attributes _name, _latin_name, _family, _solitary (lions are one type of cat that are actually social creatures, living in the constructs of pride), _fur_color, _fur_length are set, overriding the values inherited from Felidea and from Felidea::Pantherinea.

❏ The methods fightOffHyenas() and shareKillWithPride() are added. These are methods specific to just the Lion class and aren't overriding any methods inherited.

❏ makeSound() is overridden with the lion's trademark sound of a "ROAR."

❏ attackPrey() is overridden, but extended using the parent class's attackPrey(), plus its own particular functionality.

This is script to exhibit how the Lion class works:

```perl
use Felidea::Pantherinea::Lion;

my $fel = Felidea::Pantherinea::Lion->new();
print "Name: " . $fel->getName() . "\n";
print "Latin Name: " . $fel->getLatinName() . "\n";
print "Is not a solitary cat\n" unless $fel->getSolitary();
print "Weight: " . $fel->getWeight() . "\n";
$fel->attackPrey('wilderbeast');
$fel->makeSound();
```

It produces the output:

```
Name: lion
Latin Name: panthera leo
Is not a solitary cat
Weight: 250
Fight off hyenas
Pounce
Share kill with pride
ROAR!
```

So, you probably see that that extending the `Felidea` class through inheritance is relatively easy, and didn't require a lot of coding because so much of the needed functionality was in the parent class. Once you have the top-level class's functionality nailed down, you should only have to add overridden functionality to the inherited classes. This is what they mean when they say "reusable" code!

Every species class can be implemented much in the same way as `Lion` was. Each species has its own particular attributes, which make it distinct from its general parent classes and from the other species. You simply code the species class, or any class in object-orientated programming according to those particular attributes.

Making Life Easier: Moose

You saw in the previous sections how to create classes and derived classes, as well as how to use `AUTOLOAD()` to automatically generate methods that aren't implemented based on the attributes of the class. There are more current ways to do this that involve using a number of Perl modules, such as Class::Std, Class::InsideOut, Object::InsideOut, Class::Accessor, and Moose. Of these, Moose, a more recent object-oriented system for Perl, looks very promising. This section will show you how to use Moose to easily implement the classes shown in the previous section.

Moose is described on the project web site `http://www.iinteractive.com/moose/` as ...

> "a postmodern object system for Perl 5 that takes the tedium out of writing object-oriented Perl. It borrows all the best features from Perl 6, CLOS (LISP), Smalltalk, Java, BETA, OCaml, Ruby and more, while still keeping true to its Perl 5 roots."

Moose is an entire system with a ton of functionality — so much so that the discussion here only touches the tip of the iceberg. Moose really does take out the tedium of writing object-oriented Perl, and will save your tired hands and wrists many keystrokes!

Showing you the reimplementation of the `Felidea` class using Moose in the code that follows is the best way for you to get an idea of just how much easier it is to use Moose, and how much simpler you code will become:

```
package Felidea;

use strict;
use warnings;

use Moose;
use Carp qw(croak carp);

our $VERSION= 0.001;

has '_name' => (
    default => 'felidea',
    reader  => 'getName',
    writer  => 'setName',
    is      => 'rw' );
has '_latin_name' => (
    default => 'felidea',
    reader  => 'getLatinName',
```

```perl
    is      => 'ro');
has '_family' => (
    default => 'felidea',
    reader  => 'getFamily',
    is      => 'ro');
has '_fur'   => (
    default => 1,
    reader  => 'getFur',
    writer  => 'setFur',
    is      => 'rw' );
has '_weight' => (
    default => 50,
    reader  => 'getWeight',
    writer  => 'setWeight',
    is      => 'rw',
    isa     => 'Int');
has '_claws'     => (
    default => 1,
    reader  => 'getClaws',
    writer  => 'setClaws',
    is      => 'rw',
    isa     => 'Int');
has '_fur_color' => (
    default => 'grey',
    reader  => 'getFurColor',
    writer  => 'setFurColor',
    is      => 'rw');
has '_fur_length' => (
    default => 'unset',
    reader  => 'getFurLength',
    writer  => 'setFurLength',
    is      => 'rw');
has '_tail' => (
    default => 1,
    reader => 'getTail',
    is      => 'ro',
    isa     => 'Int');
has '_fangs' => (
    default => 1,
    reader => 'getFangs',
    is      => 'ro',
    isa     => 'Int');
has '_solitary'=> (
    default => 1,
    reader  => 'getSolitary',
    is      => 'ro',
    isa     => 'Int');

sub makeSound {
    my ($self)= @_;
    print "Generic Felidea vocalization\n";
}

sub attackPrey {
    my ($self, $preyType)= @_;
```

```
            $preyType ||= '';
            if ($preyType eq 'fast') {
                print "sprint after prey\n";
            }
            elsif ($preyType eq 'big') {
                print "Jump and chew on neck\n";
            }
            else {
                print "Pounce\n";
            }
    }
    sub debug {
        my ($self, $debug)= @_;
        $self->{_DEBUG}= $debug;
        return $self->{_DEBUG};
    }

    1;
```

What you see in the code can be described as follows:

❑ Notice, there is no constructor method such as new() listed. Moose takes care of this for you by way of inheriting from Moose::Object.

❑ You only need to import Moose to get started. No need for strict 'refs' as with AUTOLOAD().

❑ Less code altogether!

❑ Instead of a hash reference (see the previous sections) containing all the class attributes along with their default values and whether they are read or write, there is a standard means of defining and installing class attributes using has. There are numerous options available; some of the ones shown in the previous code example are the following:

> ❑ The option is has the value of 'ro' (read-only) or 'rw' (read-write) for creating read-only or read-write accessors.

> ❑ The default option specifies the default value of the attribute.

> ❑ The options reader and writer can be used to specify the method names for accessing or writing to the attribute. If not specified, then the accessor has the same name as the attribute.

> ❑ The isa option enforces a constraint on the attribute and forces run-time checking to ensure that the attribute is of the specified type, as specified in Moose::Util::TypeConstraints.

Also, setting up inheritance for the derived classes Pantherinea and Lion are much simpler:

```
package Felidea::Pantherinea;

use strict;
use warnings;
use Moose;

extends 'Felidea';
```

```perl
has '+_name'       => ( default => 'pantherinea');
has '+_latin_name' => ( default => 'pantherinea');

1;
```

That was easy! To override the _name and _latin_name attributes, the "+" character is prefixed with the attribute name, which allows you to clone and extend the attribute of the parent class. In this case, it overrides the default option with a new value. The same things are done with the Lion class:

```perl
package Felidea::Pantherinea::Lion;

use strict;
use warnings;

use Moose;

extends 'Felidea::Pantherinea';

has '+_name'       => (default => 'lion');
has '+_latin_name' => (default => 'panthera leo');
has '+_family'     => (default => 'pantherinea');
has '+_solitary'   => (default => 0);
has '+_fur_color'  => (default => 'light tan');
has '+_weight'     => (default => 250);

sub fightOffHyenas {
    my ($self)= @_;
    print "Fight off hyenas\n";
}

sub shareKillWithPride {
    my ($self)= @_;
    print "Share kill with pride\n";
}

sub makeSound {
    my ($self)= @_;
    print "ROAR!\n";
}
sub attackPrey {
    my ($self, $preyType)= @_;
    $self->fightOffHyenas();
    $self->SUPER::attackPrey($preyType);
    $self->shareKillWithPride();

}

1;
```

As you see, using Moose makes object-oriented programming in Perl even easier than it normally is. There is so much more to Moose than what this brief section can cover. It is worthy of an entire section or even book of its own. Again, the web site http://www.iinteractive.com/moose is an excellent resource, where you can continue to learn about Moose and build on what you learned in this section.

Summary

Although it is not what Perl was originally designed for, object-oriented programming is very much supported and, as with everything else with Perl, very easy to use. From this chapter, you learned the following:

❑ Perl implements objects using packages, which differ from regular modules in that they have a constructor class that takes as its first argument a class name. The class name then uses the Perl command `bless` to create a reference that knows to which class it belongs and returns that reference. That returned reference from the constructor is the object reference that an application uses to interact with the object.

❑ `AUTOLOAD()` is a special method in a Perl class that is used to dynamically generate attribute accessor class methods based on the list of those attributes. This saves explicitly writing these methods as well as development time. Also, using typeglobs, these dynamically generated methods can be stored in the package symbol table, making it so that subsequent calls to these methods don't have to rely on `AUTOLOAD` regenerating the methods each time they are called.

❑ Inheritance in Perl is implemented using package naming as well as the `@ISA` array. The `@ISA` array stores the name of the class's parent, providing the mechanism of Perl's inheritance. Using the pragmatic module base, as in 'use base', is an easy way to establish an *is-a* relation instead of working directly with the `@ISA` array.

❑ How a top-level class, `Felidea`, was created. This was extended with the `Felidea::Pantherinea` class, which was in turn extended with the `Felidea::Pantherinea::Lion` class. All of these inherited from the parent class from which they were derived.

❑ The Moose postmodern object system for Perl 5 was briefly covered, showing you how easy it is to implement the chapter's examples (the `Felidea` class and its derived classes), and particularly how you can use Moose to implement dynamic generation of accessor methods without having to use `AUTOLOAD()`.

By now, you should have a good understanding about object-oriented Perl. It is the author's hope that you at least have reviewed some concepts in such a way as to refresh your understanding of Perl object-oriented programming.

6

MySQL and Perl

The first several chapters of this book have covered both MySQL and Perl, showing you how both are very powerful and easy-to-use tools: one a powerful, open-source database that you can use as your backend data store, the other a flexible, rapid-development, great-at-parsing text, and even an object-oriented programming language. This chapter shows how both can be used together.

Ever since the advent of MySQL, Perl has been a natural choice for many programmers to work with MySQL. With so much data to process within a database, having an easy programming language to build applications that access and modify that data makes for a potent combination — one that has resulted in the development of many great applications, particularly web applications that major sites run.

This chapter gives you an overview of the Perl module, Database Independent Interface (DBI) and the API calls it provides, as well as how to start writing applications with MySQL in Perl. It will primarily focus on MySQL and Perl alone. The web applications that use both will be discussed in later chapters.

In addition, this chapter explains DBI, which is a standard set of database calls that work on a variety of databases. It also discusses the lower-level driver, DBD::mysql (*DBD* stands for database driver), which is MySQL-specific. This chapter gives an overview of various DBI methods, attributes, API method descriptions as well as some examples, and gives you a good start on how to write programs using DBI.

After covering DBI, this chapter next shows you how to write a DBI wrapper API and how it can make writing programs even more simplified.

Perl DBI

The MySQL RDBMS (Relational Database Management System) comprises both a server and client. The client is where you have all your interactions with the database server. This client is manifested in the various client drivers, in various languages, available to MySQL. The MySQL server's client library, libmysql, is written in C and is what programs such as the `mysql` client command shell, `mysqldump`, `mysqladmin`, as well as other programs use to connect to the MySQL server. Libmysql is a straightforward API that makes it fairly simple to write C programs that connect to MySQL.

A Little More about Perl

Perl was one of the first languages to have a driver for MySQL. Originally, there was a Perl driver specific to MySQL that supported both MySQL and mSQL. It was written on top of libmysql using XS as the "glue" code to interface with the underlying C functions. Then around 1998, DBI became the standard for Perl-based database applications.

DBI and DBD

DBI is the Database Independent Interface for Perl — independent in that it was created to allow developers to write applications using standard API methods, variables, and conventions that will work regardless of the RDBMS. DBI doesn't know or care about the underlying data source being used. Prior to DBI, various databases had to implement their own Perl drivers with their own API calls. DBI simplified life for anyone wishing to interact with RDBMSs using Perl. It is a standard that makes it much easier to quickly write applications. It also lends itself to portable applications. For instance, if you had written an application using Oracle, and wanted to allow the application to use MySQL, the code using DBI would need very few changes, and most likely only the SQL statements would need to be changed to the dialect of SQL being used for MySQL versus Oracle, which has some of its own specific syntax.

DBI is the interface between application code and the underlying driver, which in this case is `DBD::mysql`. The driver interface, DBD, is driver specific. There is a vast array of DBD modules for various RDBMSs as well as other client methodologies such as ODBC, or even pure-Perl language drivers.

`DBD::mysql` is written using XS glue to use libmysql for its underlying database calls. Using the C client library as the underlying mechanism makes for a fast and efficient driver.

Figure 6-1 shows the basic idea of how DBI and `DBD::mysql` work. The Perl application code utilizes DBI API calls, which in turn are dispatched by DBI to the driver, `DBD::mysql`, which uses libmysql, which then executes the actual database statements against MySQL. These statements can either be write statements that return the number of database rows affected, or query result sets or cursors to those query results sets that the driver must return in a usable form the database to the DBI handle. The DBI API provides methods for processing these result sets, as well as ensuring that the database operation — write or read statement — ran successfully.

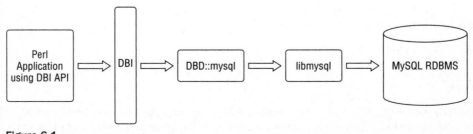

Figure 6-1

Installation

You need to install both DBI and DBD::mysql to be able to write programs to access MySQL. Linux distributions often already have both installed, particularly if you selected MySQL to be installed during the installation. Even if they weren't installed, they are very easy to install after the fact, as is illustrated in the following sections.

Ubuntu

To install on Ubuntu, just use apt-cache to find both DBI and DBD::mysql:

```
root@hanuman:~# apt-cache search DBI
```

This provides a large list of various debian packages; the two you want are:

```
libdbd-mysql-perl - A Perl5 database interface to the MySQL database

libdbi-perl - Perl5 database interface by Tim Bunce
```

Then, you would install them.

```
root@hanuman:~# apt-get install libdbi-perl libdbd-mysql-perl
```

If you install each separately, DBI has to be installed first.

Redhat, CentOS

With Redhat variants, you use yum to find the package name to install:

```
[root@localhost ~]# yum search DBI
```

This provides a large list of various RPM packages. These are the two you want from the list (versions may vary):

```
libdbi.x86_64 : Database Independent Abstraction Layer for C

perl-DBD-MySQL.x86_64 : A MySQL interface for perl
```

CPAN

You may just want to use CPAN, particularly if the vendor for your OS provides packages that are out of date. CPAN installations are really simple:

```
cpan -i DBI

cpan -I DBD::mysql
```

DBI API

The DBI is a very straightforward and intuitive API for writing applications that access MySQL. There are methods for connecting to the database, preparing SQL statements, executing prepared statements, retrieving results in numerous formats, and many others.

Loading DBI

To write a program using DBI, the first thing to do is to load the DBI module. The use statement, as shown previously in other chapters, is used for this: `use DBI;`

Driver Methods

DBI provides a means to see what drivers are available. This is done with the `available_drivers()` method:

```
use DBI;

my @driver_names= DBI->available_drivers;

for my $driver_name(@driver_names) {
    print "available: $driver_name\n";
}
```

... which produces the output (this varies according to your server installation and configuration):

```
available: DBM
available: ExampleP
available: File
available: Proxy
available: SQLite
available: Sponge
available: mysql
```

To find out what data sources are available with your MySQL instance, you can use the `data_sources()` method:

```
my @data_sources=DBI->data_sources('mysql', {
                    host        => 'localhost',
                    port        => 3306,
                    user        => 'root',
                    password    => 's3kr1t'
                    });
```

This produces an output like this one (depending on what schemas your MySQL installation has):

```
data source: DBI:mysql:information_schema
data source: DBI:mysql:admin
data source: DBI:mysql:contacts_db
data source: DBI:mysql:mysql
data source: DBI:mysql:sakila
data source: DBI:mysql:test
data source: DBI:mysql:webapps
```

... which displays the various schemas within your MySQL installation in a DSN (Data Source Name) format. DSN will be explained in Chapter 7.

Another driver method is:

```
my $drh= DBI->install_driver('mysql');
```

This method obtains a driver handle, which can be used for administrative functions that will be shown later in the "Server Admin" section of this chapter.

The following code returns a list of name and driver handle pairs suitable for assignment to a hash.

```
my %drivers= DBI->installed_drivers;
```

In most applications, you won't be using these much, but they are useful for database administration and for knowing what drivers and data sources you have available on your system.

Connect

The next thing to do is to connect to the database and obtain a database handle, and this is done using the DBI::connect() method:

```
my $dsn= 'DBI:mysql:test;host=localhost';

my $username= 'username';

my $password= 'mypassword';

my $attributes= {    RaiseError => 1,
                     AutoCommit => 1,
              };

my $dbh= DBI->connect($dsn, $username, $password, $attributes);
```

The DBI::connect() method returns a database handle, a reference to an instantiated DBI object. This database handle is what you will use to interact with the database in the course of your program that uses MySQL.

DBI::connect takes four arguments, discussed in the following sections.

$dsn

This is the DSN, or data source name value. If you are familiar with ODBC, you may already be aware that it has a data source name, which is a way of naming a connection and having meta-data information about that connection associated with a canonical name. The canonical name is used to connect without requiring all the various connection parameters listed. The $dsn variable is a similar concept to this ODBC DSN.

The format of the DSN string always begins with the scheme part of the string, DBI (can be upper or lower case), followed by the driver, in this case mysql. You might have been wondering why it wasn't required to use DBD::mysql because DBD::mysql is the required driver Perl module. It's the very specification of mysql in the DSN that causes DBI to automagically use DBD::mysql as the underlying database client driver.

The next parameter in the DSN string is the schema name. Other parameters following can be host, port, and socket. The format can also vary from what is listed in this example. Also, the value would be:

```
DBI:mysql:test
```

```
DBI:mysql:test@localhost:3306

DBI:mysql:database=test;host=localhost;port=3306
```

The last format is preferred over the previous one because it adheres to the ODBC style. You will notice, the primary components — scheme, driver, and database (schema) — of this DSN are delimited by a single colon. There are other options that can be used in the DSN string, such as host, port, etc., that are delimited by a semicolon.

Additionally, there are other options that can be used in the DSN that are MySQL-specific, which you can specify in the DSN string, or, of course, delimit with a semicolon:

```
mysql_server_prepare=1|0
```

This turns on server-side prepared statements. A prepared statement is a way of caching the execution plan of a query on the MySQL server. An execution plan is how the optimizer decides to retrieve data from the database. This makes it so if you use server-side prepared statements, the server stores the execution plan for the SQL statement, using the SQL statement itself as the key for that execution plan. This is particularly useful when inserting a bunch of rows; you would prepare the INSERT statement, and then simply insert the data on the prepared statement handle. The database does not having to parse that statement over again. By default, DBD::mysql emulates a prepared statement by doing all the grunt work of parsing the statement for placeholders and replacing placeholders with actual values. More on prepared statements will be covered later, in the section "Writing Data." This option can also be set with the environment variable MYSQL_SERVER_PREPARE:

```
export MYSQL_SERVER_PREPARE=1
```

This option can be set during the execution of the program by changing the attribute in the database handle $dbh:

```
$dbh->{mysql_server_prepare} = 1;

$dbh->{mysql_server_prepare} = 0;
```

You can also set this option in the statement handle, which will be discussed more later.

```
mysql_auto_reconnect
```

mysql_auto_reconnect causes DBD::mysql to reconnect to MySQL in the event that the connection is lost. This is off by default *except* in the case of either CGI or mod_perl since they depend on this driver behavior, in which case, the driver detects the environment variables GATEWAY_INTERFACE or MOD_PERL and sets mysql_auto_reconnect to on (1). If AutoCommit is turned off, mysql_auto_reconnect will be ignored regardless of value:

```
mysql_use_result
```

By default, the driver uses the mysql_store_result() C API call after executing a query that causes a result set to be stored in local buffers or temporary tables. Using mysql_use_result driver option causes the client driver to use the `mysql_use_result()` C API call. `mysql_use_result()` initiates result set retrieval, but doesn't read the result set into the client, requiring each row of the result set be read individually. `mysql_use_result()` uses less memory and can be faster than using `mysql_store_result()`, but the downside is that because it ties up the server while each row is being fetched, it prevents updates from other threads to tables from which the data is being fetched. This can be a problem particularly if you are doing a lot of processing for each row. The default is off, meaning `mysql_store_result()` is used.

```
mysql_client_found_rows=1|0
```

`mysql_client_found_rows` enables Q16 (1) or disable (0) the MySQL client flag CLIENT_FOUND_ROWS while connecting to the MySQL server. This has a somewhat funny effect: Without `mysql_client_found_rows`, if you perform a query like:

```
UPDATE $table SET id = 1 WHERE id = 1
```

the MySQL engine will always return 0, because no rows have changed. With `mysql_client_found_rows`, however, it will return the number of rows that have an id of 1, as some people are expecting. (At least for compatibility to other engines.)

Other things of note:

❑ `mysql_compression` turns on/off compression between the client and server:

```
mysql_compression=1|0
```

❑ `mysql_connect_timeout` sets the time, given in seconds, that a request to connect to the server will timeout:

```
mysql_connect_timeout=<numeric value>
```

❑ `mysql_read_default_group` allows you to specify a `mysql` configuration file where client settings are set. You could, for instance, have it set as:

```
mysql_read_default_file=<file location>

mysql_read_default_group=<my.cnf file location>
```

❑ `/home/jimbob/my.cnf` would need the following sections:

```
$dsn= 'DBI:mysql:test:host=
somehost;mysql_read_default_file=/home/jimbob/my.cnf'
```

❑ In the following example, you would by default be connected to `localhost`:

```
[client]
host=localhost
port=3306
```

❑ If you added to `/home/jimbob/my.cnf` the following code:

```
[perl]
host=dbfoo.myhost.com
port=3306
```

... you would by default be connected to *dbfoo.myhost.com*. Also, the previous `[client]` section example must come before the current `[perl]` section example.

❑ In the following code, `mysql_socket` lets you specify the socket file:

```
mysql_socket=<socket file>
```

Normally, you don't have to concern yourself with this, although there are occasions where `libmysql` was built with a different default socket than what the server is using:

```
mysql_ssl=1|0
```

❑ `mysql_ssl` turns on encryption (`CLIENT_SSL` libmysql flag) when connecting to MySQL. Other options for using `ssl` are:

```
mysql_ssl_client_key
mysql_ssl_client_cert
mysql_ssl_ca_file
mysql_ssl_ca_path
mysql_ssl_cipher

mysql_local_infile=1|0
```

❑ `mysql_local_infile` enables/disables the ability to execute the command LOAD DATA in libmysql, which the server by default may have disabled.

```
mysql_multi_statements=1|0
```

❑ `mysql_multi_statements` enables/disables the ability to run multiple SQL statements in one execution, such as

```
INSERT INTO t1 VALUES (1); SELECT * FROM t1;
```

The previous example of running two queries may cause problems if you have server-side prepare statements enabled with `mysql_server_prepare=1`

❑ The option `mysql_embedded_options` can be used to pass "command-line" options to the embedded server.

```
mysql_embedded_options
```

❑ The following example causes the command-line help to the embedded MySQL server library to be printed:

```
 use DBI;
$testdsn="DBI:mysqlEmb:database=test;mysql_embedded_options=
--help,--verbose";
$dbh = DBI->connect($testdsn,"a","b");
```

❑ The option `mysql_embedded_groups` can be used to specify the groups in the config file (my.cnf) which will be used to get options for the embedded server.

```
mysql_embedded_groups
```

❑ If not specified, the settings of the sections `[server]` and `[embedded]` groups will be used. An example of using `mysql_embedded_groups` in the DSN string would be:

```
$testdsn="DBI:mysqlEmb:database=test;mysql_embedded_groups=
embedded_server,common";
```

❑ The option `mysql_enable_utf8` will result in the driver assuming that strings as well as data are stored in UTF-8. Default is off.

```
mysql_enable_utf8
```

$username and $password

The next two arguments to `DBI::connect` are $username and $password, which are pretty straightforward:

```
my $username = 'webuser';
my $password = 's3kr1t';
my $dbh= DBI->connect($DSN, $username, $password);
```

The above example shows a simple connection for the user webuser using the password s3kr1t.

$attributes

The final argument is a hash reference containing various attributes. These attributes are set to 1 or 0, such as:

```
{ ..., Attribute => 0 }
```

These attributes can also be set after the connection is created with:

```
$dbh->{Attribute}= <value>;
```

The various attributes are presented in the following table:

Attribute	Description
AutoReconnect	Sets the driver to reconnect automatically if the connection to the database is lost.
AutoCommit	Sets the driver so that any transactional statement is automatically committed.
RaiseError	Turns on the behavior in DBD::mysql which causes a die() upon an error: "$class $method failed: $DBI::errstr" Where $class is the driver class and $method is the name of the method that failed, for instance: DBD::mysql::prepare failed: error text
PrintError	Similar to RaiseError, except the error is only printed; a die() is not issued.
PrintWarn	Prints warnings if they are encountered.

HandleError	Allows you to specify your own error handler. For instance:
	
	``perl
	my $attr= {
	        RaiseError => 1,
	        HandleError => sub { my ($err)= @_;
	    print "Argh! Problems: $err\n"; }
	        };
	    my $dbh= DBI->connect($dsn, $username,
	$password, $attr);
	``
	
	Used in conjunction with RaiseError, this will result in your error handler being called and a subsequent die().

ErrCount	Contains the number of errors encountered.
TraceLevel	Allows you to turn on debug tracing in the driver to a specific numeric value. Depending on what value is coded in the source code of DBD::mysql, having that level set will result in that debug message to be printed.

connect_cached

This method works the same as connect(), except that it stores the connection handle in a hash based on the parameters that it connected with.

```perl
$dbh = DBI->connect_cached($data_source, $username, $password,
\%attributes);
```

Any subsequent connections that use `connect_cached()` to connect will return this cached handle if the parameters are the same. If somehow the cached handle was disconnected, the connection will be reestablished and then returned.

The cached handle is global, but can be made private by enforcing privacy through the `$attributes` hash reference. Using a key prefixed with `private_<keyname>` can accomplish this, as you can see in the following example:

```
my $dbh= DBI->connect_cached('DBI:mysql:test',
                             'username',
                             's3kr1t',
                             { private_connection_key1 => 'connX'})
```

The previous example will make it so unless you connect using that same attribute key and value, even if the rest of the other values such as username, password and DSN are the same, you will still not obtain that cached connection.

Statement Handles

Once you have a database handle, you can start interacting with the database. You will issue SQL statements against the database. To do so, you will prepare a statement with the DBI `prepare()` method. The usage for prepare is:

```
$sth= $dbh->prepare($sql_statement);
```

```
$sth= $dbh->prepare_cached($sql_statement);
```

Both return a prepared statement handle, `prepare_cached()`, returning an already cached statement handle for the SQL statement in question. Also of note, several of the options for the database handle `$dbh` can also be set in the statement handle, and in a number of ways. For instance, `mysql_server_prepare` turns on server-side prepared statements:

```
$sth= $dbh->prepare("insert into t1 values (?, ?)",
{ mysql_server_prepare => 1});
```

... for this `prepare()` call as well as any subsequent `prepare()` calls.

A statement handle is a Perl reference that you will use to call DBI methods that execute and fetch data from MySQL. Once you have a statement handle, you will call `execute()`:

```
$sth->execute(...);
```

This returns the number of rows affected by an UPDATE, INSERT, DELETE, or other data modification statements, or, if a SELECT query has been executed, the result set will be retrieved through the statement handle:

```
while (my $ref= $sth->fetch()) { ...}
```

That's the basic idea, anyhow. Some code examples will help explain statement handles in more detail.

Writing Data

The most simple example can be shown with an INSERT statement:

```
my $sth= $dbh->prepare("insert into t1 values (1, 'first')")
        or die "ERROR in prepare: " . $dbh->errstr . "\n";

my $rv= $sth->execute();

print "rows affected $rv\n";
```

In the previous example, a simple SQL INSERT statement is prepared. If the statement is successfully prepared, a statement handle reference $sth is returned. If it fails to prepare, die() exits printing the value in $dbh->errstr, which will show why prepare() failed.

Also, an SQL statement can contain what are called *placeholders*, which are question mark characters in an SQL query. They are essentially markers that indicate where the actual values will be transliterated to in the SQL statement when it is inevitably executed. The values for these columns are supplied in execute(), the process of which is called *binding*. Using placeholders and bind values is a good way to avoid SQL injection attacks because it forces proper value checking through the prepare-execution process, as opposed to just executing a string to which you have manually appended the values. The previous example can also be written as:

```
$sth= $dbh->prepare("insert into t1 values (?, ?)")
        or die "ERROR in prepare: " . $dbh->errstr . "\n";

my $rv= $sth->execute(1, 'first');

print "rows affected $rv\n";
```

For the previous code, note the following:

- ❑ First, the statement is prepared, then executed.
- ❑ If you are using server-side prepared statements, prepare() checks the syntax of the SQL statement, parsing the placeholders. Prepare will fail if the statement has a syntax error in the SQL statement, using the error handling that prints out the value of $dbh->errstr. This is because with server-side prepared statements, the database server parses the SQL statement, checking syntax, and then devises an execution plan. When execute() is called, that execution plan is used with any values provided to execute.
- ❑ If you are not using the server-side prepared statements, DBD::mysql emulates prepared statements by parsing the SQL statement itself, looking for placeholders, which, if found, interpolate the values each time execute() is called. If there is a syntax error, prepare() will not catch it. execute() will fail when subsequently called.

You may ask: why not use server-side prepared statements all the time? The problem is that the server-side prepared statements in libmysql have issues that have never been completely resolved. In 2006, it was decided within MySQL that drivers should by default emulate prepared statements, while in some cases leaving the option to the user to use server-side prepared statements. DBD::mysql gives this option with mysql_server_prepare.

Server-side prepared statements can give a performance boost and reduce the necessity of having the database re-parse the SQL statement, as well as reduce network traffic. The benefit of using server-side prepared statements is especially pertinent with data modification statements — UPDATE, DELETE, INSERT. For instance, you could have an application that inserts thousands of records into a table using a single SQL INSERT statement. In the case of server-side prepared statements, you would only prepare the one statement, then call execute() for each row of data that needs to be inserted. This would be much faster than executing the same statement over and over again. Also, as previously stated, server-side prepared statements also parse the original SQL query for correctness; emulated prepared statements do not.

With read statements — in other words, regular queries — it may not make much sense to use server-side prepared statements. Earlier chapters have mentioned MySQL's query cache. This is a no-brainer in that the query cache contains the results of SQL queries. For instance, if you run the same query against a table thousands of times, if the query cache is turned on (by default), the MySQL server would only parse that query and come up with an execution plan once as well as produce result sets for that query. The MySQL server would then cache the results (not the execution plan itself). All subsequent queries against that table would obtain the result set from the query cache — as long as the data in that table doesn't change.

In this case of development, there is no *right* way. It all depends on the application and what table a query is running against, and whether it changes a lot or not. The one good practice to adhere to is to use prepared statements in general, whether server-side or emulated, to avoid SQL injection attacks. Even if you are using emulated prepared statements, the driver is very efficient at parsing placeholders and transliterating them with values.

Here is an example showing how server-side prepared statements can be beneficial in the case of inserting multiple values into a table:

```
$dbh->{server_side_prepare} = 1;

$sth= $dbh->prepare("insert into t1 values (?, ?)")
        or die "ERROR in prepare: " . $dbh->errstr . "\n";

my $charcol;
my @chars = grep !/[001Iil]/, 0..9, 'A'..'Z', 'a'..'z';
for my $iter (1 .. 1000) {
        $charcol= join '', map { $chars[rand @chars] } 0 .. 7;
    $sth->execute($iter, $charcol);
}

$dbh->{server_side_prepare} = 0; # turn it off if we want
```

In the previous example, server-side prepared statements are turned on just for this data insertion block. The initial INSERT statement is prepared with two placeholders, then in an iterative loop the data is inserted into the table using execute() with the two values as arguments, which are transliterated to values in the insert operation on the database in the subsequent loop. A random character generator is used to create the data to be inserted into the varchar column, the iteration number for the integer value. This all happens within the iterative loop, which runs 1,000 times, inserting 1,000 rows of data, which, since the database has already created an execution plan with the one and only prepare() call, it knows exactly how to insert this data. This is much faster than if each INSERT statement were run without using placeholders.

Reading Data

You can also use prepare to execute read statements. The process is similar to write statements, except after calling execute(), you need to fetch the resultant data set:

```perl
$sth= $dbh->prepare("select * from t1");

$sth->execute();

print "Number of rows in result set: " . $sth->rows . "\n";

my $names= $sth->{NAME};
for (@$names) {
    printf("%-15s",$_);
}
print "\n";

while (my $row_ref= $sth->fetch()) {
    for (@$row_ref) {
        printf("%-15s",$_);
    }
    print "\n";
}
```

In the previous example is a simple SELECT statement, which is prepared, returning a statement handle. The statement handle is then executed, at which point the statement handle then can be used to retrieve results. The number of rows is reported using the statement handle method rows(). This is a very useful method in that you can find out in advance how large the data set is for the data you are about to retrieve. Also, the statement handle attribute NAME contains an array reference to the column names of the result set, which is used to print out a formatted string for the header. Finally, each row is fetched from the statement handle using fetch(), which returns an array reference of each row. The while() loop runs until every row is fetched.

Fetch Methods, One Row at a Time

The above example is not the only way to fetch data after executing a SELECT query. There two other fetching methods for a statement handle, both are the same, with fetch() being an alias.

❑   fetch, fetchrow_arrayref

  ❑   The following returns a reference to an array holding the field values:

```perl
$row_ref= $sth->fetchrow_arrayref() or $row_ref= $sth->fetch()
```

  ❑   The following fetches the current row as a list containing the field values, as opposed to array reference:

```perl
@row= $sth->fetchrow_array()
```

❑   fetchrow_hashref. Here is an example:

```perl
$row_hashref= $sth->fetchrow_hashref()
```

The previous line of code fetches the current row as a hash reference keyed by column names. For instance, the previous example would have not needed to use $sth->{NAME} to obtain the column names and could have been coded as:

```
my $row_num= 0;
while (my $row_href= $sth->fetchrow_hashref()) {
    if ($row_num == 0) {
        printf("%-15s",$_) for keys %$row_href;
        print "\n";
    }
    printf("%-15s",$row_href->{$_}) for keys %$row_href;;
    print "\n";
    $row_num++;
}
```

Fetch Methods — the Whole Shebang

You can also fetch all the rows, the entire result set, at once if you like. The methods for this are as follows:

fetchall_arrayref

This returns a result set as an `arrayref`; all arguments, $slice and $max_rows, are optional:

```
$resultset_aref= $sth->fetchall_arrayref($slice, $max_rows);
```

The return array reference, $resulset_ref, is a reference of arrays — an array reference of rows that are references to an array of each row's columns such that:

```
$resultref_aref= [
    [ col1val, cal2val, col3val, colNval, ...], # first row
    [ col1val, cal2val, col3val, colNval, ...], # second row
    [ col1val, cal2val, col3val, colNval, ...], # third row
    # ... Nth row ...
];
```

An example of using `fetchall_arrayref()` with no arguments could be applied to a previous code example, in which 1000 newly inserted rows were subsequently retrieved would be coded as:

```
my $names= $sth->{NAME};
for (@$names) {
    printf("%-15s",$_);
}
print "\n";

my $resultset_ref= $sth->fetchall_arrayref();

for my $row_ref(@$resultset_ref) {
    for (@$row_ref) {
        printf("%-15s",$_);
    }
    print "\n";
}
```

The $slice argument is a convenient way to specify what parts of the result set you want. The $slice argument allows you to specify how you want each row served up:

```
# each row is an array ref with only the first column
$resultset_ref = $sth->fetchall_arrayref([0]);

# each row is an array ref with the first and second column
$resultset_ref = $sth->fetchall_arrayref([0,1]);

# each row an array ref, 2nd to last and last columns
$resultset_ref = $sth->fetchall_arrayref([-2, -1]);

# each row in the array is a hash reference
$resultset_ref = $sth->fetchall_arrayref({});

# each row is a hash reference of the columns name
# and someothercol
$resultset_ref =
$sth->fetchall_arrayref({ name => 1, someothercol => 1});
```

For instance, in the previous example, you could have it so that each row (array member) in the result set array reference is a hash reference (the entire data structure is an array reference of array members that are hash references to each column):

```
my $resultset_ref= $sth->fetchall_arrayref({});

# only attempt if results
if (defined $resultset_ref) {
   # since we have the whole result set, we can print the header
   # column names from the first row
   printf("%-15s",$_) for keys %{$resultset_ref->[0]};
   print "\n";

   for my $row_href(@$resultset_ref) {
      printf("%-15s",$row_href->{$_}) for keys %$row_href;;
      print "\n";
   }
}
```

The last argument is $max_rows, which simply limits the result set to that number.

fetchall_hashref

The following code returns a result set of hash references, each member a hash reference corresponding to a row, which must be keyed by a unique column specified. This must be a column that is either the primary key or a unique index for the result set that will be produced.

```
$result_ref= $sth->fetchall_hashref( $unique_column)
```

The result hash reference would be:

```
$result_ref= {
 unique_column_id1 =>
```

```
        { col1 => col1val, col2 => col2val, col3 => col3val, ...}, # 1st row
    unique_column_id2 =>
        { col1 => col1val, col2 => col2val, col3 => col3val, ...}, # 2nd row
    unique_column_id3 =>
        { col1 => col1val, col2 => col2val, col3 => col3val, ...}, # 3rd row
    unique_column_idN =>
        { col1 => col1val, col2 => col2val, col3 => col3val, ...}, # Nth row
};
```

For instance, the previous example would be written as:

```
my $resultset_href= $sth->fetchall_hashref('id');

my $row_num = 0;

for my $id (sort keys %$resultset_href) {
    my $row_ref= $resultset_href->{$id};

    # print a header
    if ($row_num == 0) {
        printf("%-15s",$_) for keys %$row_ref;
        print "\n";
    }
    printf("%-15s",$row_ref->{$_}) for keys %$row_ref;
    print "\n";
    $row_num++;
}
```

You can also specify column number:

```
$resultset_href= $sth->fetchall_hashref(0);
```

... which would key the results by the first column, id, as in the previous example.

Finish

This method tells the statement handle that it will no longer fetch any rows.

```
$return_code= $sth->finish() ;
```

This method is seldom required usually automatically called unless you manually fetch data and stop prior to fetching all rows. Even if you need a single row, using the selectall, selectrow methods, which will be discussed later, will automatically call finish().

Binding Methods

Sometimes, you may want to "bind," or associate explicitly, a value with a placeholder in an SQL statement, or even specify the SQL data type that you want to bind the value as. For this, DBI has various binding methods. Here, we will discuss bind_param().

The MySQL driver does not support the DBI bind_param_inout() method.

Binding Input Parameters

You can also explicitly bind input parameters using the DBI method `bind_param()`. This method is called prior to `execute()`.

```
$return_code= $sth->bind_param($param_number, $value, $bind_type);
```

The first two arguments `$param_number` and `$value` are required. `$param_number` is the position of the placeholder in the SQL statement, starting from 1. `$value` is the value you are binding to that placeholder. An example of this would be:

```
$sth->prepare('INSERT INTO t1 (id,name) VALUES (?, ?)');

    ...

$sth->bind_param(1, 22);

...

$sth->execute();
```

This achieves binding the number 22 to the first placeholder for the `id` column, resulting in the call to `execute()` inserting 22 into the id column. Notice that since `bind_param()` is being used, there is no need to supply the values to `execute()`.

The third argument shown, `$bind_type`, can either be a hash reference or scalar, and is optional. This allows you to specify what data type you are binding `$value` as. An example of using a hash reference would be:

```
$sth->bind_param(1, 22, { TYPE => SQL_INTEGER });
```

Passing `$bind_type` as a scalar, you would supply the integer value of the SQL data type. An example of this would be:

```
$sth->bind_param(1, 22, SQL_INTEGER);
```

In this example, the constant `SQL_INTEGER` was used. To be able to use SQL constants, you must import them:

```
use DBI qw(:sql_types);
```

The following example modifies a previous code example to use `bind_param()` to bind two placeholders to two values in a loop that incremented an integer value and generated a random string for the varchar value:

```
$sth= $dbh->prepare("insert into t1 values (?, ?)") ||
        die "ERROR in prepare: " . $dbh->errstr . "\n";

my @chars = grep !/[001Iil]/, 0..9, 'A'..'Z', 'a'..'z';
for my $iter (1 .. 1000) {
   my $charcol= join '', map { $chars[rand @chars] } 0 .. 7;
        $sth->bind_param(1, $iter);
```

```
$sth->bind_param(2, $charcol);
$sth->execute();
}
```

Binding Output Parameters

You can also bind output parameters. This means you can associate a variable or multiple variables to particular columns in a result set from a SELECT statement.

```
$return_code= $sth->bind_col($column_number, \$var_to_bind, $bind_type);
```

The method bind_col() binds a single variable to a given column indicated by a position number, starting from 1. This method is called *after* execute().

The first argument, shown as $column_number, is a column number, starting from 0 and corresponding to the position of the column in the result set from a SELECT statement. Of course, this makes it necessary for you to know what the order of the columns will be if you use SELECT * in your statement. The second argument, which is a scalar reference shown as a, is the output variable you wish the result set to associate with the column specified in $column_number, resulting in $var_to_bind, assuming the value of that column upon fetching the result set.

An example of using bind_col() would be:

```
my $sth= prepare('SELECT id, name FROM t1');
...
$sth->execute()
...
my ($id, $name);
$sth->bind_col(1, \$id);
$sth->bind_col(2, \$name);
```

The third argument, $bind_type, is optional. It can be either a hash reference with TYPE as a key and the value of the SQL data type of the column being bound, or the shortcut, which is simply a scalar of the type.

Usage examples would be as follows:

❏ Using a hash reference:

```
$sth->bind_col(1, \$id, { TYPE => SQL_INTEGER});
$sth->bind_col(2, \$name, { TYPE => SQL_VARCHAR});
```

❏ Using a scalar:

```
$sth->bind_col(1, \$id, SQL_INTEGER);
$sth->bind_col(2, \$name, SQL_VARCHAR);
```

An example of using bind_col() to bind to output variables in the previous example demonstrating the fetching the 1000 values just inserted is as follows:

```
$sth= $dbh->prepare("select * from t1");
```

```
$sth->execute();

my ($id, $name);
$sth->bind_col(1, \$id);
$sth->bind_col(2, \$name);

my $col_names= $sth->{NAME};
for (@$col_names) {
    printf("%-15s",$_);
}
print "\n";

while ($sth->fetch()) {
    printf("%-15d %-15s\n",$id, $name);
}
```

There is also a way to bind multiple columns to multiple variables in one call using the `bind_columns()` method:

```
$return_code= $sth->bind_columns(\$col1, \$col2, \$colN, ...);
```

`bind_columns()` requires a list of scalar references having the same number of columns as the SELECT statement would produce.

The previous example showing `bind_col()` could be implemented as:

```
$sth->bind_columns(\$id, \$name)
```

or,

```
$sth->bind_columns(\($id, $name));
```

Then, of course:

```
while ($sth->fetch()) {
    printf("%-15d %-15s\n",$id, $name);
}
```

Other Statement Handle Methods

In addition to `prepare()`, `execute()`, and the various fetching methods, there are also some really useful statement handle methods.

rows

This returns the number of rows affected by the SQL statement executed — the same as the return value from `$sth->execute()`.

```
$sth->rows()
```

For instance, the following example runs against a table containing 1,000 rows of data:

```
my $return_value= $sth->execute();

my $rows= $sth->rows();

print "return value $return_value rows $rows\n";
```

Both `$return_value` and `$rows` will both be 1000:

```
return value 1000 rows 1000
```

dump_results

This method is useful for debugging or prototyping SQL statements. It simply dumps the result set from an executed statement handle:

```
$sth->dump_results($maxlen, $line_separator, $field_separator,
$file_handle);
```

The arguments are:

Argument	Status	Description
$maxlen	Optional	Maximum number of rows to dump. Default unlimited.
$line_separator	Optional	This specifies the line separator between rows. Default is newline.
$field_separator	Optional	This specifies the field/column separator. Default is a comma.
$file_handle	Optional	This specifies a file handle that you can pass where the results get dumped to. Default is STDOUT.

Statement Handle Attributes

Statement handles also have various attributes that can be very useful in applications, providing information about the underlying data structure of a result set or about the underlying columns. These attributes are worth reiterating, as even the most seasoned developers can forget about them (ahem)! These attributes can be accessed by specifying them as:

```
$sth->{attribute name}
```

Most of these attributes are read-only, so trying to set them would result in a warning. The previously listed attributes that can be used upon connecting to the database or in the database handle ($dbh) that can also be set in the statement handle and work the same way are RaiseError, PrintError, PrintWarn, HandleError, ErrCount, TraceLevel.

The attributes that are specific only to the statement handle are shown in the following table:

Attribute	Description
NUM_OF_FIELDS	The number of columns that a result set would return from a SELECT statement. If a write SQL statement such as DELETE, UPDATE, or INSERT, this number is 0. Read-only.
NUM_OF_PARAMS	The number of placeholders of the prepared statement. Read-only.
NAME	Returns an array of the column names. Read-only.
NAME_lc, NAME_uc	Same as NAME, except all lowercase uppercase respectively. Read-only.
NAME_hash, NAME_lc_hash, NAME_uc_hash	Similar to NAME, except a hashref of column names, the values the index of the column. Read-only.
TYPE	Returns an array reference of integer values representing the date type of the column in the order of the columns of the result set. These integer values correspond to the ODBC data type standard specified in the international standard specs ANSI X3.135 and ISO/IEC 9075. Read-only.
PRECISION	Returns an array reference of integer values for each column representing the maximum number of digits of the data type of the underlying columns. Read-only.
SCALE	Returns an array reference of integers representing the column scale in the result set. Read-only.
NULLABLE	Returns an array reference indicating if the column of the result set is nullable. Read-only.
CursorName	Returns the name of the cursor associated with the result statement, if available. This is not supported with DBD::mysql yet. Read-only.
Database	Returns the database handle $dbh of the statement. Read-only.
ParamValues	Returns a hash reference containing the values currently bound to the placeholders. Read-only.
ParamArrays	Returns a hash reference containing the values bound to placeholders using execute_array() or bind_param_array(). Read-only.
ParamTypes	Returns a hash reference of data types of the columns of the currently bound placeholders. Read-only.
Statement	Returns the SQL statement that the statement handle was prepared with Read-only.
RowsInCache	Returns the number of rows pre-cached upon execute().

MySQL-Specific Statement Handle Attributes

There are also some DBD::mysql-specific statement handle attributes that are very useful, convenient, and quite often overlooked (even by the author of this book!) for obtaining particular result set information. These are presented in the following table:

Attribute	Description
ChopBlanks=1|0	Causes leading and trailing blanks to be chopped off upon fetching data.
mysql_insertid	As shown in a previous example, this gives you the last insert id — PRIMARY KEY value assumed due to auto increment upon the insertion of a row, after $sth->execute().
mysql_is_blob	Provides an array reference of true/false Boolean values, each member corresponding to columns of a result set in the order found, of whether the column is a blob column or not, after execute().
mysql_is_autoincrement	Provides an array reference of Boolean values, each member corresponding to columns of a result set in the order found, true/false of whether the column is auto increment or not, after execute().
mysql_is_pri_key	Provides an array reference of Boolean values, each member corresponding to columns of a result set in the order found, true/false of whether the column is the primary key or not, after execute().
mysql_is_key	Provides an array reference of Boolean values, each member corresponding to columns of a result set in the order found, true/false of whether the column is indexed or not, after execute().
mysql_is_num	Provides an array reference of Boolean values, each member corresponding to columns of a result set in the order found, true/false of whether the column is a numeric column or not, after execute().
mysql_length	Provides an array reference, each member corresponding to columns of a result set in the order found, the values of each being the maximum length of the data type for the column, after execute().
mysql_type	Provides an array reference, each member corresponding to the columns of a result set in the order found, numeric value of the MySQL data type for the column, after execute(). These values of each being the MySQL data types found in include/mysql.com.h, enum enum_field_types.
mysql_type_name	Provides an array reference, each member corresponding to columns of a result set in the order found, the values of each being the data type name for the column, after execute().

You can see an example of the outputs of these handy attributes in the following code. It's a simple program where a statement selecting three columns from a table of four types — *id* an int, *name* a varchar, *age* an int and *info* a text/blob column — shows the use of these attributes and their output using Data::Dumper:

```
my $sth =
  $dbh->prepare('insert into t1 (name, age, info) values (?, ?, ?)',
       {mysql_server_prepare => 1});

$sth->execute('John', 33, 'some text here');
print "\$sth->{mysql_insertid} " . $sth->{mysql_insertid} . "\n";

$sth->execute('Jim', 40, 'more text here');
print "\$sth->{mysql_insertid} " . $sth->{mysql_insertid} . "\n";
$sth->execute('Sally', 20, 'text text text');
print "\$sth->{mysql_insertid} " . $sth->{mysql_insertid} . "\n";

$sth= $dbh->prepare('select * from t1');
$sth->execute();
for my $var(qw( mysql_table
                mysql_is_auto_increment
                mysql_is_blob
                mysql_is_pri_key
                mysql_is_key
                mysql_is_num
                mysql_length
                mysql_type
                mysql_type_name)) {
    print "\$sth->{$var}\n";
    print Dumper $sth->{$var};
  }
```

And the output is:

```
$sth->{mysql_insertid} 1
$sth->{mysql_insertid} 2
$sth->{mysql_insertid} 3
$sth->{mysql_table}
$VAR1 = [
          't1',
          't1',
          't1',
          't1'
        ];
$sth->{mysql_is_auto_increment}
$VAR1 = [
          1,
          '',
          ${\$VAR1->[1]},
          ${\$VAR1->[1]}
        ];
$sth->{mysql_is_blob}
$VAR1 = [
          '',
```

```
            ${\$VAR1->[0]},
            ${\$VAR1->[0]},
            1
        ];
$sth->{mysql_is_pri_key}
$VAR1 = [
            1,
            '',
            ${\$VAR1->[1]},
            ${\$VAR1->[1]}
        ];
$sth->{mysql_is_key}
$VAR1 = [
            1,
            ${\$VAR1->[0]},
            '',
            ${\$VAR1->[2]}
        ];
$sth->{mysql_is_num}
$VAR1 = [
            1,
            0,
            1,
            0
        ];
$sth->{mysql_length}
$VAR1 = [
            4,
            32,
            3,
            65535
        ];
$sth->{mysql_type}
$VAR1 = [
            3,
            253,
            3,
            252
        ];
$sth->{mysql_type_name}
$VAR1 = [
            'integer',
            'varchar',
            'integer',
            'blob'
        ];
```

Multistep Utility Methods

DBI also offers methods that automatically call, prepare, execute, and fetch. All of these methods take as their first argument either a scalar containing an SQL statement, or a prepared statement handle. If you use a prepared statement handle as the first argument, these methods will skip the prepare() step. If you pass a string value containing an SQL statement, as opposed to a statement handle, all three steps (prepare, execute, and fetch) will be run. So, you need to keep in mind that prepare() is only called once, which would making using these methods suitable for situations where you don't need to take advantage of single statements being prepared and executed multiple times. You'll notice with these methods, you call using a database handle as opposed to a statement handle.

do

do() prepares and executes a single statement and returns the rows affected. This is a convenient method if you only need to run a single write statement — a data modification statement such as UPDATE, DELETE, INSERT, as well as data definition statements such as ALTER, DROP, CREATE, TRUNCATE.

```
$rows= $dbh->do($statement, $attr_hashref, @bind_values)
```

The arguments for do() are presented in the following table:

Argument	Status	Description
$statement	Required	A scalar containing an SQL statement to be executed. This would be a statement not producing a result set, such as ALTER, DROP, DELETE, INSERT, TRUNCATE, etc.
$attr_hashref	Optional	A hash reference containing attributes.
@bind_values	Optional	An array of bind values that would be used if the $statement contained placeholders.

Some examples of using do() are as follows:

❑   The first example runs a query to alter a table. No return value is needed.

```
$dbh->do('ALTER TABLE t1 ADD COLUMN city VARCHAR(32)') or die $dbh-
>errstr;
```

❑   The second example is an INSERT statement with a single placeholder, then the value 'Narada Muni' supplied, and the number of rows this INSERT statement results in are returned from do():

```
my $insert= 'INSERT INTO t1 (name) VALUES (?)';

my $rows_inserted= $dbh->do($insert, undef, qw('Narada Muni'))
```

selectall_arrayref

selectall_arrayref() is similar to the previously discussed method, fetchall_arrayref. It, too, is used for returning data from a SELECT SQL statement (statements with result sets).

```
$resultref_arrayref= $dbh->selectall_arrayref(
                                        $statement,
```

```
                              $attrib_hashref,
                              @bind_values);
```

The return array reference has the same structural organization as the method `fetchall_arrayref()`:

```
$resultref_aref= [
      [ col1val, cal2val, col3val, colNval, ...], # first row
      [ col1val, cal2val, col3val, colNval, ...], # second row
      [ col1val, cal2val, col3val, colNval, ...], # third row
      # ... Nth row ...
   ];
```

The arguments are presented in the following table:

Argument	Status	Description
$statement	Required	This argument can be either a previously prepared statement handle, or a scalar containing an SQL statement. If this argument is a previously prepared statement handle, `selectall_arrayref()` skips the prepare stage it would normally run.
$attrib_hashref	Optional	The second argument usage example shows the second argument $attrib_hashref hash reference. This is used to set several attribute values that affect the result set. If $attrib_hashref is omitted, the result set includes the values for all columns as array references: `$attrib_hashref= { Attribute => value };`
@bind_values	Required if statement contains placeholders	The third argument is a list of values that are used to replace the value as indicated by a placeholder ? when the SQL statement is executed. This argument is required if you are using placeholders in your SQL statement.

The different attributes that can be set are `Slice`, `Columns`, and `MaxRows`. `Slice` and `Columns` can be used to modify result set output in terms of which columns to include and whether to use a hash reference for each row. The usage is:

Attribute Usage	Description
{ Slice => [0,1,2,N] }	Include values for the 1st, 2nd, 3rd, and Nth, starting from 0 in the result set.
{ Columns => [1,2,3,N] }	Include values for the 1st, 2nd, 3rd, and Nth, starting from 1 in the result set.
{ MaxRows => N }	Only fetch N number of rows.

For instance:

```
$resultset_arrayref= $dbh->selectall_arrayref('SELECT id, name FROM t1',
                                               { Slice => [0]});
```

... would make it so only the first column specified in the SELECT statement, id, has its column values included in the result set, such that:

```
$resultset_arrayref= [ [1], # row1
                       [2], # row2
                       [3], # row3
                       ... # row N...
];
```

Using the Columns attribute is the same as Slice except Columns starts from one. In other words, the id column would be referenced as index number 0 with Slice and 1 with Columns in the previous example:

```
{ Slice => {}}
or
{ Columns => [1,2,3,N...]}
```

The result set is an array reference of hash references (rows, each row having column name key, value the column value). The result set reference would be structured as:

```
$resultref_aref= [
     [ col1 => col1val, col2 => cal2val, col3 => col3val,
colN => colNval, ...],
     [ col1 => col1val, col2 => cal2val, col3 => col3val,
colN => colNval, ...],
     [ col1 => col1val, col2 => cal2val, col3 => col3val,
colN => colNval, ...],
];
```

The MaxRows attribute can be used to limit the number of rows retrieved in the result set to that value specified. Whatever value is specified with MaxRows, once that many rows have been retrieved, finish() will be called for that result set.

selectall_hashref

selectall_hashref() combines prepare(), execute() and fetchall_hashref() into one single method. selectall_hashref() returns a hash reference with the same structural organization as fetchall_hashref():

```
$hash_ref = $dbh->selectall_hashref($statement, $key_field);
```

The arguments for selectall_hashref() are:

Argument	Status	Description
`$statement`	Required	Scalar containing an SQL statement or a prepared statement handle. If the argument is a prepared statement handle, the `prepare()` stage is skipped.
`$key_field`	Required	Can be a single scalar containing the name of a column or an array reference of multiple columns that specify the hash keys that are used for each row in the returned result set hash reference. If you intend to have a hash for each row, you should ensure the column you use contains all unique values in the result set, otherwise rows will be replaced for each duplicate value.

selectcol_arrayref

`selectcol_arrayref()` is a method that combines `prepare()`, `execute()` and `fetch()`, returning by default an `arrayref` containing only the first column of the result set for a given query.

```
$ary_ref  = $dbh->selectcol_arrayref($statement, \%attributes);
```

The arguments are presented in the following table:

Argument	Status	Description
`$statement`	Required	Scalar containing the SQL `SELECT` statement or prepared statement handle. If `$statement` is a prepared statement handle, then the `prepare()` step is skipped.
`$attributes`	Optional	Hash reference containing the attributes `Columns`, `Slice` or `MaxRows`. Works the same as `selectall_arrayref`. This would override the default behavior of `selectcol_arrayref` (returning only one column, the first column).

selectrow_array

Combines `prepare()`, `execute()` and `fetchrow_array()` to retrieve a single row (the first row if multiple rows are returned) as an array, with each column an array member:

```
@row_ary  = $dbh->selectrow_array($statement, \%attributes,
@bind_values);
```

Returns an array containing the columns of a single row, such that:

```
@row_ary = (col1val, col2val, col3val, colNval, ...);
```

The arguments are presented in the following table:

Argument	Status	Description
$statement	Required	Scalar containing an SQL SELECT statement or prepared statement handle. If a prepared statement handle is provided, the prepare step is skipped.
\%attributes	Hash reference, optional	Used to specify the attributes Slice, Columns or MaxRows, working as other similar methods
@bind_values	Required if the statement contains placeholders	Array containing scalars to pass to a statement containing placeholders

A usage example of this method would be:

```
my @resultset_array=
        $dbh->selectrow_array("select * from t1 where id = ?", undef, (33));

print "returned: " . join("\t", @resultset_array) . "\n";
```

selectrow_arrayref

Combines prepare(), execute(), and fetchrow_arrayref(). This works the same way as selectrow_array except that it returns an array reference of the single row, with each column an array member.

```
$ary_ref  = $dbh->selectrow_arrayref(
                    $statement, \%attributes, @bind_values);
```

selectrow_hashref

This combines prepare(), execute(), and fetchrow_hashref(). This works the same way as selectrow_array and selectrow_arrayref except that it returns a hash reference with each member a column keyed by column name.

```
$hash_ref = $dbh->selectrow_hashref(
                            $statement,
                            \%attributes, @bind_values);
```

Other Database Handle Methods

In addition to methods that deal with executing SQL statements, there are also several useful methods that can be called from a database handle.

last_insert_id

If you are inserting data into a table with an auto-increment primary key value, you often want to know what value the auto-increment column assumed due to insertion. There are two ways to do this:

```
$dbh->insert_id($database, $schema, $table, $field, \%attributes) ;
```

or,

```
$sbh->{mysql_insertid}
```

For the first option, some databases require the $database and $schema arguments. For MySQL, you should only need the $table argument. The use of these two means of obtaining the last inserted value of an auto-increment table can be shown in the following example:

```
my $create= <<EOC;
create table t1
    (id int(4) auto_increment,
    name varchar(32) not null default '',
    primary key (id))
EOC

my $return_value= $dbh->do($create);

...

$sth= $dbh->prepare("insert into t1 (name) values (?)");

$sth->execute($charcol);

# the values of both of these should be the same
print "last insert id: (dbh) " .
            $dbh->last_insert_id(undef, undef, 't1', undef,undef) .
            "mysql_insert_id " . $sth->{mysql_insertid} . "\n";
```

ping

The simplest way to test if the database handle is still connected to the database is as follows:

```
$dbh->ping();
```

If that database handle AutoReconnect attribute is not set, you can implement your own reconnect:

```
my $connected= $dbh->ping();

if ($connected) {
    print "connected\n";
        }
else {
    $dbh= DBI->connect($dsn, $username, $password, $attr);
}
```

clone

The following clones a database handle:

```
$cloned_dbh= $dbh->clone(\%attributes);
```

The $attributes hash reference is optional and, if supplied, overrides and is merged with the database handle's options it is being cloned from.

Transactional Methods — begin_work, commit, rollback

If you are using InnoDB tables you can, of course, use transactions. There are three methods for running transactions in your code, as shown in the following table:

Method	Description
$dbh->begin_work();	This results in BEGIN WORK being issued on the database server by turning off AutoCommit. This initiates the beginning of a unit of work. It marks the beginning of the issuance of one or more SQL statements that will not be committed (made permanent) until COMMIT is called. If AutoCommit is off, an error will be returned.
$dbh->rollback();	This rolls back any uncommitted SQL statements. If AutoCommit is off, the statements made since the last commit, or since the beginning of the current session, are rolled back. If AutoCommit is on, the statements that are rolled back are any statements issued after BEGIN WORK (DBI call $dbh->begin_work()). If BEGIN WORK was not called and AutoCommit is on, rollback() has no effect except for causing a warning to be issued.
$dbh->commit();	This commits database changes. If AutoCommit is off, this means database changes since the last commit, or since the beginning of the current session. If AutoCommit is on, this means any SQL statements issued after BEGIN WORK ($dbh->begin_work()) are those that are committed. If BEGIN WORK was not issued and AutoCommit is on, this has no effect.

Here is a simple example of how to use these three methods:

```
$dbh->begin_work();

eval {
    $sth1= $dbh->prepare("insert into t1 (name) values (?)");

    $sth2= $dbh->prepare("insert into t2 (city,state) values (?, ?)");
};

# if any of the statement failed to prepare, roll back
if ($@) {

    $dbh->rollback();
    die "prepare ERROR: " . $dbh->errstr . "\n";
```

```
    }

    eval {
        # execute first statement
        $sth1->execute('Jim Bob');

        # execute second statement
        $sth2->execute('Peterborough', 'New Hampshire'); };
    };

    # if any of the executions failed, roll back
    if ($@) {

        $dbh->rollback();
        die "execute ERROR: " . $sth->errstr . "\n";
    }

    # if everything went ok, commit
    $dbh->commit;
```

In this example, the first thing that is called is begin_work() to issue BEGIN WORK on the database server to begin the transaction. All statements issued thereafter will not be made permanent until COMMIT is issued. Within the first eval block, two statements are prepared, and two statements are executed in the second one. If any errors are encountered by way of $@ being set, rollback() is called, resulting in ROLLBACK being issued and a return to the state prior to begin_work() being called. This is the essence of using transactions in Perl.

Stored Procedures

Working with stored procedures using DBI is pretty simple. When you use stored procedures, it's quite common to have a procedure that calls multiple SQL queries, therefore producing multiple result sets. With this in mind, there needs to be a way to retrieve numerous result sets. As described earlier in this chapter, when you fetch all the rows of a query, the statement handle has the method finish() applied. There is no way to retrieve any more data from that statement handle. The method more_results() solves this problem.

The usage for more_results() is basically:

```
$sth= $dbh->prepare('call stored_proc()');

$sth->execute();

$resultset_ref= $sth->fetchall_arrayref();

$sth->more_results();

$resultset_ref= $sth->fetchall_arrayref();

$sth->more_results();
```

... for each result set produced.

To see a practical working example, the following code demonstrates how to work with stored procedures. This example creates a stored procedure that queries two tables, producing two result sets. The first table is a two-column table (state_id, state) containing the states of India (two records in this case). The second table is a three column table (city_id, state_id, city) containing cities, in this case, cities in India with a relationship to the states table via the column state_id.

Follow these steps:

1. First, create the stored procedure — do this in Perl of course!

```
$dbh->do('drop procedure if exists india_cities');

my $proc = <<EOP;
  CREATE PROCEDURE india_cities ()
  BEGIN
    SELECT state_id, state FROM states;
    SELECT state_id, city_id, city FROM cities order by state_id;
  END;
EOP

$dbh->do($proc);
```

2. Once the procedure is created, it can be utilized. One thing you can do to avoid code duplication when working with and displaying multiple result sets is to create a subroutine to print out these results, which is shown in the example below:

```
sub print_results {
    my ($sth)= @_;
    my $resultset_ref= $sth->fetchall_arrayref();

    my $col_names= $sth->{NAME};

    print "\n";
    map { printf("%-10s", $_)} @$col_names;
    print "\n";

    for my $row (@$resultset_ref) {
        printf("%-10s", $_) for @$row;
        print "\n";
    }
}
```

This subroutine takes a statement handle that has already been executed, with a result set to be retrieved.

3. Finally, the process to work with multiple result sets is this:

```
$sth= $dbh->prepare('call india_cities()')
        or die "prepare error: " . $dbh->errstr . "\n";

$sth->execute() or die "execute error: " . $sth->errstr . "\n";
```

```
        print_results($sth);

        $sth->more_results();

        print_results($sth);
```

The single call to the stored procedure india_cities() is made by a prepare() and execution of the statement. Then the first result set is retrieved and printed. Then with more_results(), the next result set is retrieved and can then be printed out. This is how you write Perl programs that use stored procedures. This is a very simple example, but the idea can be built upon.

Error Handling

Previous examples in this chapter showed variations in how to handle errors, mostly by using manual error handling. This was to make you familiar with the fact that each DBI call can fail and needs to be handled. As you have seen, you can set the database handle attributes at the time of connection or afterward, particularly with RaiseError, PrintError, and PrintWarning, which cause errors to be handled automatically.

Manual error handling:

```
my $dbh= DBI->connect('DBI:mysql:test', 'username', 's3kr1t')

                    or  die "Problem connecting: $DBI::errstr\n";


my $sth= $dbh->prepare('insert into t1 values (?, ?)')
      or die "Unable to prepare: " . $dbh->errstr . "\n";

$sth->execute(1, 'somevalue')
      or die "Unable to execute " . $sth->errstr . "\n";

    . . .
```

This type of error handling is explicit in that every DBI method call requires its own error handling using the method errstr(). This is one of three error handling methods that can be used with either a database handle or statement handle (see the following table):

Method	Description
$h->errstr	Returns the error text reported from MySQL when an error is encountered. This can also be accessed via $dbh->{mysql_error}.
$h->err	Returns the error code from MySQL when an error is encountered. This can also be accessed via $dbh->{mysql_errno}.
$h->state	Returns a five-character code corresponding to the error.

Furthermore, another way to explicitly print out the error from the last handle used is to use these functions via the DBI class level variable, as was shown in the very first line in the example above. The example becomes:

```
my $dbh= DBI->connect('DBI:mysql:test', 'username', 's3kr1t') or
            die "Problem connecting: $DBI::errstr\n";

my $sth= $dbh->prepare('insert into t1 values (?, ?)') or
            die "Unable to prepare: $DBI::errstr\n";

$sth->execute(1, 'somevalue') or die "Unable to execute $DBI::errstr\n";

...
```

You'll also notice that since this is a variable, its value can be assigned to the error message.

Automatic error handling can be achieved using:

Error Handler	Description
$h->{RaiseError}	RaiseError causes the error to be printed out via die()
$h->{PrintError}	PrintError causes the error to be print out via warn()

The handle attributes can be set either on connection via attributes, or after connection with whatever handle you need to set either database connection or prepared statement handles.

Without automatic error handles, the previous example now becomes much less verbose:

```
my $dbh = DBI->connect('DBI:mysql:test', 'username', 's3kr1t',
    { RaiseError => 1} );

my $sth = $dbh->prepare('insert into t1 values (?, ?)');
$sth->execute(1, 'somevalue');
```

Any errors will be automatically handled and cause the program to die.

You may not always want to have automatic error handling, at least for the whole program.

```
use Carp qw(croak);

my $dbh= DBI->connect('DBI:mysql:test', 'username', 's3kr1t')
or croak "Unable to connect Error: $DBI::errstr\n";

$dbh->{RaiseError}= 1;

eval {
    $sth= $dbh->prepare('insert into t1 values (?, ?)');
};
if ($@) { croak "There was an error calling prepare: $DBI::errstr\n";
```

In this example, automatic error handling was not turned on for connecting to the database, and manual error handling was used to print a custom message using `croak()` from the Carp module. After connecting, `RaiseError` was turned on, though the next call and prepare were run in an eval block, after which the `$@` variable was checked to see if there was an error. If an error was found, a specific error message for the failed prepare printed out via `croak()`.

As always with Perl, there are numerous ways to solve a problem, and with error handling, that maxim holds true.

Server Admin

Driver-level administrative functions are also available. At the beginning of this chapter, you saw how you obtained a driver handle. This is one way you can perform these administrative functions using the `func()` method. The other means is via a database handle.

Database handles are convenient methods if you intend to write any administrative code. Hey, anyone up for writing a Perl version of PHPMyAdmin called PerlMyAdmin?!

As previously shown, to install a driver handle, you use the `install_driver()` DBI method:

```
use DBI;
use strict;
use warnings;

my $drh= DBI->install_driver('mysql');
```

The functions are:

❑   createdb: Creates a schema; performs the equivalent of CREATE DATABASE. With a driver handle, call the `func()` method with administrative login credentials.

```
$drh->func('createdb', $schema_name, $hostname, $admin_user_name,
    $password)
```

With a database handle, the handle has to be one created with sufficient privileges to run CREATE DATABASE.

```
$dbh->('createdb', $schema_name, 'admin');
```

❑   dropdb: Drops a schema; performs the equivalent of DROP DATABASE. With a driver handle:

```
$drh->func('dropdb', $schema_name, $hostname, $admin_user_name,
    $password)
```

With a database handle:

```
$dbh->func('dropdb', $schema_name, 'admin');
```

❑ `shutdown`: Shuts down the MySQL instance. Of course, no subsequent calls will work after calling this until you restart MySQL. This functions the same as `'mysqladmin shutdown'`.

```
$drh->func('shutdown', 'localhost', $admin_user_name, $password)
```

❑ `reload`: Reloads the MySQL instance, causing MySQL to reread its configuration files.

```
$drh->func('reload', 'localhost', $admin_user_name, $password)
```

The following example provides some context for how to use these functions. This simple script could be used to create, or drop and recreate, a schema.

```perl
#!/usr/bin/perl

use strict;
use warnings;

use DBI;
use Data::Dumper;
use Getopt::Long;

our $opt_schema;
our $opt_user= 'adminuser';
our $opt_host= 'localhost';
our $opt_password= '';
our $opt_port= 3306;

GetOptions (
    'h|host=s'      => \$opt_host,
    'p|password=s'  => \$opt_password,
    'port=s'        => \$opt_port,
    's|schema=s'    => \$opt_schema,
    'u|user=s'      => \$opt_user,
);

$opt_schema or usage("You need to provide a schema name!");

my $drh= DBI->install_driver('mysql');

my @data_sources=$drh->data_sources({
                        host        => $opt_host,
                        port        => 3306,
                        user        => $opt_user,
                        password    => $opt_password
                        });

my $schemas;
for (@data_sources) { /:(\w+)$/; $schemas->{$1}= 1;}


print Dumper $schemas;
if ($schemas->{$opt_schema}) {
    # schema exists, must drop it first
```

```
            print "dropping $opt_schema\n";
            $drh->func('dropdb',
                    $opt_schema,
                    $opt_host,
                    $opt_user,
                    $opt_password, 'admin'

            ) or die $DBI::errstr;
    }

    print "creating $opt_schema\n";

    $drh->func('createdb',
                $opt_schema,
                $opt_host,
                $opt_user,
                $opt_password, 'admin'

    ) or die $DBI::errstr;
```

Notice in this example that the method `data_sources()` is used to provide a list of all schemas for this MySQL instance, which then in a loop uses a regular expression to obtain the actual schema name (stripping off `DBI:mysql:`), which is then used in a hash reference to test if the schema exists or not. If the schema exists, it is first dropped and then recreated. If it doesn't exist, it is just created.

Summary

This chapter introduced you to writing MySQL database-driven perl applications using the Perl DBI module. You learned that DBI is the database-independent layer and `DBD::mysql` is the database-specific driver, and that both work together to provide an API as well as database connectivity.

The numerous DBI methods were explained in detail, and examples were provided to demonstrate how you can take advantage of the DBI API. You learned the concepts of database and statement handles and looked at how you connect to the database to obtain a database connection handle, with which you then prepare an SQL statement, which then returns a statement handle. The statement handle is then what you use to execute the statement. Next, you either retrieve the number of rows affected if the statement was an `INSERT`, `UPDATE`, `DELETE`, etc., or else retrieve result sets with a `SELECT` statement. The chapter also explained the methods that allow you to accomplish all steps without having to use a statement handle through the database connection handle.

As stated in earlier chapters and underscored in this one, Perl references are key to working with data and writing database-driven applications. A good number of the DBI methods return data from `SELECT` statements in the form of either hash or array references, and being able to iterate or navigate through these references to access the data they've returned.

You should now be ready to tackle writing Perl database applications.

7

Simple Database Application

Now that the DBI API has been discussed in detail, you probably would like to see a practical example using what you've learned and see a database-driven Perl program in action. The purpose of this chapter is to give you a simple example of using Perl to write a MySQL database-driven application using the DBI Perl module and its API, without web functionality so the focus is solely on Perl and MySQL. The application will be a simple command-line interface contact list. This will be a fully functional Perl program with a simple menu for selecting different operations, which prompts the user for various decision making as well as data inputs.

Planning Application Functionality

The first thing to do in writing any application is to think about what functionality you want it to have — inputs and expected outputs. What primary operations does it need to be able to do?

With a contacts application, you would probably want to do the following operations:

- ❑ Add contacts (INSERT)

- ❑ Update contacts (UPDATE)

- ❑ Delete contacts (DELETE)

- ❑ Edit a contact (calls UPDATE or INSERT)

- ❑ List contacts (SELECT)

- ❑ Display menu of choices

- ❑ Allow lookup of contacts (selective list)

Schema Design

For a program to store contacts and support all of these operations, you will want a simple table containing various contact attributes:

```
CREATE TABLE $table (
    contact_id  int(4) not null auto_increment,
    first_name  varchar(32) not null default '',
    last_name   varchar(32) not null default '',
    age         int(4) not null default 0,
    address     varchar(128) not null default '',
    city        varchar(64) not null default '',
    state       varchar(16) not null default '',
    country     varchar(24) not null default '',
    primary key (contact_id),
    index first_name (first_name),
    index last_name (last_name),
    index age (age),
    index state (state),
    index country (country)
    );
```

As this table creation shows, there are nine different columns. The contact_id column is the primary key and is an auto increment field.

Writing Up a Wire-Frame

All these operations can be implemented with a relatively simple Perl script. Indexes, created on any column, are used to look up a contact. In this case, every column except address can be used to look up a contact.

The first thing to do, then, is to code a wire-frame with simple print statements and comments to help you think about what each subroutine will do as well as give you something you could actually run from the start and incrementally add functionality. One thing you want to strive for is abstracting the database calls into short subroutines, and, if possible, avoid mixing code that directly interacts with the database from the user interface code.

```
sub insert_contact {
    my ($contact)= @_;
     # insert contact using $contact reference
    print "insert_contact() called\n";
}
delete_contact {
    my ($contact_id)= @_;
     # delete contact with id $contact_id
    print "delete_contact($contact_id) called\n";
}
update_contact {
    my ($contact)= @_;
     # update a given contact with $contact reference
    print "update_contact() called\n";
}
```

```
list_contacts { # displays the contacts
      my ($contact_ids) = @_; # take one or more ids
      # obtain contacts from the db

      # obtain a result set of contacts from the db
      my $contacts = get_contacts($contact_ids);
      print "listing of contacts here...\n";
}
get_contacts {  # obtains the data to display
      my ($contact_ids) = @_; # take one or more ids
      # select contacts from db table IN (... id list ... )

      # return the result set
}
find_contact {
      # prompt user to enter search parameters
      # get ids from database given those search parameters
      # call list function for those list of ids
      print "find contact called\n";
}
display_menu {
   # display choices. Use single letters to represent operations
   print "Add Menu Here.\n"
}
dispatch {
      # prompt user to make a choice (from menu choices)
      # process choice
      display_menu();
      my $choice= <STDIN>;
      chomp($choice); # get rid of newline
      print "calling other subroutines here using selected value: $choice\n";
}
initialize {
      # connect to db
      # set up any variables
}
main {
      # this is the entry point of the program
      initialize();
      dispatch();
}
```

As you can see, this doesn't do much other than simple printing. It is a very simple stubbing of the functionality needed for this application. There are many details that still must be provided, but at least this wire-frame gives you a skeleton onto which you'll hang the flesh — inevitably giving your program full functionality.

Declarations, Initializations

Now that you have a wire-frame, you want to flesh out functionality, starting from the top level, with prerequisites that are required for this program to work. The first thing that comes to mind is a database connection! Also, package scoped variables need to be declared and you need to determine if values need to be set prior to use. If so, you need to define/set them. The declarations can be done at the top of the program and the database connection and variable definitions can be done in a subroutine, which, as shown in the wire-frame, is called `initialize()`.

```perl
#!/usr/bin/perl


use strict;
use warnings;

use Getopt::Long;
use DBI;
use Carp qw(croak carp);
use IO::Prompt;

# declare database handle variable
my $dbh;

# declare $fields array ref, will be populated with initialize()
my $fields= [];

our $opt_debug;
our $opt_reset;

# defaults, GetOptions can over-ride
our $opt_schema= 'contacts_db';
our $opt_hostname= 'localhost';

our $opt_username= 'contacts';
our $opt_password= 's3kr1t';

GetOptions (
    'debug'         => \$opt_debug,
    'reset|r'       => \$opt_create,
    'schema|s=s'    => \$opt_schema,
    'username|u=s'  => \$opt_username,
) or usage();

my $dsn = "DBI:mysql:$opt_schema;host=$opt_hostname";

my $table= 'contacts';

# the subscript of the position of fields that are searchable
my $search_fields= [1,2,3,5,6,7];

# fields that are required when creating a new contact
my $required=   {
    'first_name' => 1,
    'last_name'  => 1
};

# the brain/nerve-center
my $ops = {
    'c' => \&create_contacts_db,
    'd' => \&delete_contact,
```

```
        'e' => \&edit_contact,
        'f' => \&find_contact,
        'l' => \&list_contacts,
        'm' => \&display_menu,
};
```

For this code, you have the top part of the program where required modules are imported, and variables used throughout the program are declared and/or defined. Of interest, IO::Prompt is a useful Perl module for processing user input and will be used wherever a message and expected input will be required throughout the program.

The database connection $dbh database handle variable is lexically scoped outside any subroutine, so that all subroutines have access to it. This will make it so that you don't have to pass the database handle around as a subroutine argument. In some cases, you might want the database handle variable lexically scoped within a subroutine, but for the purpose of this program and simplicity in demonstration, it'll be scoped at the top of the program.

Notice the $opt_xxx variables. These are package variables which GetOptions sets if provided on the command line. GetOptions is a handy way to process command arguments, both long style --option and short style -o (provided by Getopt::Long). As shown, these options can either be true/false (no argument), or accept a value (using =s), specified in each key which in turn points to a scalar reference to the $opt_<xxx> variable or even a subroutine.

If GetOptions returns false, that means incorrect options were used and the usage() subroutine is called. The usage subroutine simply prints out the program options.

Also shown is the hash reference variable $ops. From earlier chapters, you'll remember the discussion about using a hash reference as a method or subroutine dispatcher, which this example will do.

This functionality is just what is required for having a means to call lower-level subroutines based on a choice made by the user in a top-level user-interface subroutine. Not only that, you avoid if/else cruft entanglement. The menu subroutine displays the menu, and the dispatch subroutine will read user input, which in turn can use the input value with a hash reference, where each possible choice is a key and the value the subroutine you want calls for that choice. This is the nerve center of the program and provides a mechanism to connect all the various subroutines to the top level of the program.

The other variables shown are for other required parts of the program that will become apparent in the discussion of the various subroutines.

Now, for the database connection as well as for setting up the $fields array reference variable, you would call the subroutine initialize():

```
sub initialize {

    $dbh=
     DBI->connect($dsn, $opt_username, $opt_password)
                    or die "Unable to connect to the database $DBI::errstr\n";

    $dbh->{RaiseError}= 1; # enable internal error handling

    scalar @$fields && return;
```

```
    my $query= <<EOQ;
SELECT COLUMN_NAME FROM information_schema.COLUMNS
WHERE TABLE_NAME='contacts' AND  TABLE_SCHEMA='contacts_db';
EOQ
    print "fields query:\n$query\n" if $opt_debug;

    my $sth= $dbh->prepare($query);
    $sth->execute();
    my $ref= $sth->fetchall_arrayref();
    push(@$fields, $_->[0]) for @$ref;


    return;
}
```

initialize() simply connects to MySQL, with the handle to the database being $dbh. initialize() also ensures the array reference variable $fields is populated using a query of the *information_schema* table *COLUMNS* to provide the column names of the contacts, if not previously populated. The variable $fields provides all the field/column names in the same order a SELECT * FROM contacts would list them and is used throughout the program, particularly for displaying field names in contact listing. Once populated, it will contain:

```
$fields = [
    'contact_id',
    'first_name',
    'last_name',
    'age',
    'address',
    'city',
    'state',
    'country'
    ];
```

Program Entry Point

The entry point subroutine is called main(), which has been shown in the wire-frame. This is an arbitrary name and is only a style preference, despite its resembling other programming languages. For this example, it shall be the entry point into this program.

```
sub main {
    initialize();
    dispatch();
}
```

This is pretty simple, and is the same as what was shown in the wire-frame example. main() simply calls initialize() to set up $fields and the database connection $dbh, and then calls dispatch(), which provides top-level user interface functionality, particularly the user interface that in turn calls lower-level subroutines.

In order to explain dispatch(), some context is required. A menu display is required to provide the user with a list of choices that he or she will make that dispatch() will then act upon. display_menu() is the simple subroutine to print out this information.

```
sub display_menu {
    print <<MENU_END;

Menu: (enter one)

-----------------------------------

c        Create a new contacts table
d        Delete a contact
e        Edit a contact (add or update)
f        Find user
l        List all contacts
q        Quit


-----------------------------------

MENU_END

  return;
}
```

For the menu to be able to do more than just display, there also must be a way to process user input for the available menu choices. This is accomplished with the aforementioned dispatch() subroutine. You might think that this could be part of the menu subroutine, but it would be better to have this be separate from the menu so as to make each subroutine have a specific task, thus separating each functionality.

```
sub dispatch {
   display_menu();
   while (prompt "Enter choice: ") {
     my $choice = $_;
     exit if ($choice eq 'q');
     defined $choice or $choice = 'm';

     # this catches an option that doesn't exist which would result
     # in an error, with this it will silently fail and call dispatch()
     eval {$ops->{$choice}->()};
     display_menu();
   }
}
```

dispatch() will read the selection from the user using the IO::Prompt method prompt, and exit if the choice is 'q' for 'quit'. If a choice is not made, it will default the choice to 'm' to redisplay the menu. Next, the $ops hash reference will automatically call the appropriate subroutine through dereferencing whatever is keyed by the value chosen. The method dispatch() is wrapped in an eval block to make it silently fail should the choice be none of the keys defined. Whether the subroutine is called or silently fails, the while loop will result in the display of the menu and ask for a choice yet again, until of course the user enters '**q**', ending the while loop, or Ctrl+C's out of the program. With the display_menu() and dispatch() subroutines implemented, most of the functionality is now implemented for the top-level user interface.

At this point, you could begin testing whether the menu and program selection works. Since the wireframe has the not-yet-implemented subroutines stubbed out using print statements, you can just test the logic of `display_menu()`, along with `dispatch()`. Each selection made using options in `dispatch()` should result in the correct print statement being printed.

Table Creation Subroutine

The first subroutine that makes sense to implement is the one that creates the *contacts* table. As you can see, one of the choices from the menu is `'c'` for creating a new contacts table, otherwise called resetting. Whatever you want to call it, its job is to create the *contacts* table if it does not already exist and drop and re-create it if it does.

You might not necessarily have a subroutine to do this. Why would you have a subroutine that re-creates the table containing the data for contacts when this could be accomplished with an SQL script causing the table to be dropped and re-created? The answer is, for convenience. In this case, it's going to be in the program. It'll allow you to effectively delete all contacts, should you want to. `create_contacts_db()` is the top-level subroutine that does this. It will call three lower-level database access methods: `contacts_table_exists()` to perform the actual check to see if the table is there; `drop_contacts_table()` if the table exists and the user agrees to its deletion; and `create_contacts_table()` to create the actual *contacts* table.

```
sub create_contacts_db {
    initialize() unless $dbh;

    # if the table already exists, prompt user to make sure they want
    # to drop and re-create it
    if (contacts_table_exists()) {
        prompt "Do you wish to re-create the contacts table? [y|N] ";
        my $answer= $_;

        $answer eq 'y' or return;

        print "Recreating the contacts table.\n";
        drop_contacts_table();

    }
    else {
        print "Creating the contacts table.\n";
    }

    print "Created table contacts.\n";
}
```

`contacts_table_exists` uses information schema to determine if the *contacts* table exists:

```
# this subroutine performs a check using information_schema to see
# if the contacts table exists
sub contacts_table_exists {
    # check information schema to see if the table exists already
    my $contacts_exist = <<END_OF_QUERY;
select count(*) from information_schema.TABLES
  where TABLE_NAME = '$table'
```

```
        and TABLE_SCHEMA= '$opt_schema'
    END_OF_QUERY

        my $sth= $dbh->prepare($contacts_exist);
        $sth->execute();
        my $exists= $sth->fetchrow_arrayref();
        return $exists->[0];
    }
```

`drop_contacts_table()` simply deletes *contacts*:

```
    # this method simply drops the contacts table
    sub drop_contacts_table {
      $dbh->do("drop table if exists $table");
    }
```

```
    create_contacts_table() creates
    # this simple subroutine creates the contacts table
    sub create_contacts_table {
        # create statement
        $create= <<END_OF_TABLE;
    CREATE TABLE $table (
        contact_id  int(4) not null auto_increment,
        first_name  varchar(32) not null default '',
        last_name   varchar(32) not null default '',
        age         int(4) not null default 0,
        address     varchar(128) not null default '',
        city        varchar(64) not null default '',
        state       varchar(16) not null default '',
        country     varchar(24) not null default '',
        primary key (contact_id),
        index first_name (first_name),
        index last_name (last_name),
        index age (age),
        index city (city),
        index state (state),
        index country (country)
    );
    END_OF_TABLE

        $dbh->do($create);

    }
```

Using information_schema

This subroutine gives a good example of how to use the information_schema schema to check if a given table in a given schema exists. This is a schema that most RDBMSs implement and contains ANSI standard read-only views that provide information about tables, views, procedures, and columns in all schemas — the idea being that the database eats its own dog food and contains information about itself within itself! Earlier versions of MySQL didn't have an information_schema, but with the release of version 5, this became standard to MySQL.

Previously, you would have used SHOW TABLES to obtain this sort of information:

```
mysql> show tables from contacts_db;
+----------------------+
| Tables_in_contacts_db |
+----------------------+
| contacts             |
+----------------------+
```

SHOW TABLES is simple enough and certainly can be used. However, information_schema contains even more information and is a standard, making your application portable if you ever need it to work with another RDBMS. Notice how much more information is shown using the information_schema, which can also give you the functionality for checking whether the table exists in the first place:

```
mysql> select * from information_schema.TABLES
    -> where information_schema.TABLES.TABLE_NAME = 'contacts'
    -> and information_schema.TABLES.TABLE_SCHEMA= 'contacts_db'\G
*************************** 1. row ***************************
    TABLE_CATALOG: NULL
     TABLE_SCHEMA: contacts_db
       TABLE_NAME: contacts
       TABLE_TYPE: BASE TABLE
           ENGINE: MyISAM
          VERSION: 10
       ROW_FORMAT: Dynamic
       TABLE_ROWS: 4
  AVG_ROW_LENGTH: 58
      DATA_LENGTH: 232
 MAX_DATA_LENGTH: 281474976710655
     INDEX_LENGTH: 2048
        DATA_FREE: 0
  AUTO_INCREMENT: 5
      CREATE_TIME: 2008-11-07 18:55:43
      UPDATE_TIME: 2008-11-07 20:26:53
       CHECK_TIME: NULL
  TABLE_COLLATION: latin1_swedish_ci
         CHECKSUM: NULL
  CREATE_OPTIONS:
    TABLE_COMMENT:
```

So, create_contact_table() checks to see if the *contacts* table exists in the first place, and if it does, asks the user if he or she really wants to drop and re-create it. If the user chooses not to, create_contact_table() returns and the user is back in the main menu. If the user chooses to drop the table, the table is dropped and the subroutine continues.

Finally, the *contacts* table is created, a message is displayed, and the user is returned to the menu.

Listing Contacts

One of the other main functionalities you would want (which is also a menu choice) is listing one or more contacts using the subroutine list_contacts(). This would require this listing subroutine to accept a list of contact ids, if provided. `list_contacts()` first passes the values of `$contact_ids` to `get_contacts()` to obtain a result set of contacts.

```perl
sub list_contacts {
    my ($contact_ids)= @_;
    my $contacts = get_contacts($contact_ids);
    # if contact doesn't exist, notify user
    unless (scalar @$contacts) {
        # if contact id, the means a specific user didn't exist
        if ($contact_ids) {
            print "\nContact(s) not found.\n";
            return 0;
        }
        # otherwise, no users existing
        print "\nYou have no contacts in your database.\n";
        return 0;
    }

    for my $contact (@$contacts) {
        print '-' x 45 ,"\n";
        for my $field_num (0 .. $#{$contact}) {
            my $label= make_label($field_num);
            printf("%-15s %-30s\n", $label,$contact->[$field_num]);
        }
    }
    return 1;
}
```

The fetched array reference containing the result set from `get_contacts()` is printed out using an iterative loop with the array subscript variable starting from 0 to the last member (column) of the contact using `$#{$contact}`. The reason a subscript is used as opposed to just printing the value is that, in addition to the value, the program needs to print out what the column name is for that value. This is accomplished using the subroutine `make_label(<subscript>)`, which takes the lower-cased column name and which may also contain underscores. It returns a more human-friendly column name. `make_label()` requires a column subscript value in order to return the proper column name.

```perl
sub make_label {
    my ($field_num)= @_;
    my $label= "\u$fields->[$field_num]"; # uppercase first letter
    $label =~ s/_/ /g; # convert underscore to space
    return $label;
}
```

`make_label` utilizes the array reference `$fields`, which was populated with the correct field names in the proper order in the subroutine `initialize()` to provide a field name at the subscript `$field_num`. In turn, `$field_num` formats `$label`, uppercasing the first letters and removing underscores.

`list_contacts()` then prints out the label and field value using the line:

```perl
printf("%-15s %-30s\n", $label,$contact->[$field_num]);
```

This makes an easy-to-read, formatted line of text.

Based on whether or not a list (using an array reference) of contact ids is provided from the caller, in this case list_contacts(), then get_contacts() will build the appropriate SQL query. If a contact id list is provided by $contact_ids, the query is appended with a WHERE clause specifying placeholders for these contact ids. If no contact id list is provided, the SQL query will not have a WHERE clause appended and all contacts will be listed.

```perl
sub get_contacts {
   my ($contact_ids) = @_;
   # build select query
   my $query= "select * from $table" ;
   # append where clause if contact id supplied
   if ($contact_ids) {
      # the following join will join an array of placeholder
      # characters per number of $contact_ids with commas
      $query .= ' where contact_id in ('
          . join(',', ('?') x @$contact_ids)
          . ')';

   }
   $query .= ' order by contact_id';

   print "list query:\n$query\n" if $opt_debug;

   my $sth= $dbh->prepare_cached($query);

   # execute with contact_ids bind params if exists
   $sth->execute(defined @$contact_ids ? @$contact_ids : ());

   # fetch data
   my $contacts= $sth->fetchall_arrayref();

}
```

For the execution of the prepared statement, if a contact id list is provided, it is supplied to $sth->execute() since the query that had been built contained the number of placeholders to the number of contact ids. If no data is returned via fetching, that means either the specified contact doesn't exist or no contacts exist (depending on whether the contact id list was provided), in which case a 0 (false) is returned. This allows the calling function to know if finding a contact was successful.

At this point, if you were to insert a test user into the *contacts* table manually, you should be able to have it print properly.

```
mysql> insert into contacts
    -> (first_name, last_name, age, address, city, state, country)
    -> values ('Test', 'User', 30, '111 Test Ave.', 'Someville', 'XX', 'US');
```

Then run the program and use -d to see the SQL being printed:

```
Menu: (enter one)

----------------------------------

c      Create a new contacts table
```

```
d       Delete a contact
e       Edit a contact (add or update)
f       Find user
l       List all contacts
q       Quit


------------------------------------

Enter choice: l
list query:
select * from contacts
--------------------------------------------
make_label query:
SELECT COLUMN_NAME FROM information_schema.COLUMNS
WHERE TABLE_NAME='contacts' AND  TABLE_SCHEMA='contacts_db';

Contact id      1
First name      Test
Last name       User
Age             30
Address         111 Test Ave.
City            Someville
State           XX
Country         US
```

Excellent! The program prints out the test user you inserted, as well as the SQL statements that the debug option caused to print. Also notice the nice, lovely labels. Eye candy indeed! You now have the means to print the menu, receive input for a menu selection, and print contacts. That means you can continue to add functionality.

Editing a Contact

The next step would be to flesh out the edit_contact() subroutine. This is yet another user interface subroutine which is used to either add or edit (update) a contact. It will have to be able to take input from the user — both decision-making input (add or edit) and the actual contact data. So it would make sense to split the functionality up into two subroutines to handle both levels of input processing.

edit_contact() will be the top-level method that prompts the user for a decision about whether to add or update a contact. It will then call edit_contact_fields() to process the input for each contact field. Depending on the value of the decisions made, edit_contact() will then call the lower-level database subroutines that insert or update the contact record with the contact information that edit_contact_fields() processed.

```
sub edit_contact {
    my $new_values;
    my $contact_id = '';

    print "The current contacts are:\n";
    list_contacts(); # list all contacts, contact id listed
    while (not length($contact_id)) {
      prompt "\nEnter which contact id you would like to edit, or 'a' for add new: ";
      $contact_id = $_;
```

```
    unless (length($contact_id)) {
      print "You need to supply a contact id or add!\n";
    }
  }

  unless ($contact_id eq 'a') {
      # This will be used for update_contact() where clause
      $new_values->{contact_id}= $contact_id;

      # unless this is a new contact, list the specific user given
      # by the contact id
      list_contacts([$contact_id]) or return;
  }

  # this subroutine prompts the user for each value
  edit_contact_fields(\$new_values, $contact_id);


  if ($contact_id eq 'a') {
      my $contact_id= insert_contact($new_values);
      print "Added contact_id $contact_id\n";
      return;
  }
  update_contact($contact_id, $new_values);
  print "Updated contact_id $contact_id\n";
  return;
}
```

In the previous code, notice the following:

❑ First, a `$new_values` hash reference is declared. This will be used later to contain contact values either for a new or existing contact. `edit_contact()` then prints out all the current contacts using `list_contacts()` with no contact id specified.

❑ Next, the user is prompted for input to select what particular user to edit using the contact id value displayed from the contact listing above or to add a contact by means of 'a':

  ❑ If the user enters nothing, `edit_contact()` prints out a message telling the user that he or she didn't select a value and then recursively calls itself so as to prompt the user for input again. The user has to enter something, even if he or she becomes annoyed and enters Ctrl+C!

  ❑ If the user enters a contact id value, that value is passed to `list_contacts()` so that the specific contact the user wants to edit is displayed before prompting the user to enter new values. Notice that the value is passed as a single member of an array reference, as `list_contacts()` expects. If the contact is not found, meaning `list_contacts()` returns a false, then `edit_contact()` returns to its calling subroutine, `dispatch()`.

❑ `$new_values->{contact_id}` is set to the value of the `contact_id` selected if it is a contact id and not 'a' for creating a contact. This will be the primary key value used in the WHERE clause in the case of `update_contact()`.

❑ Next, `edit_contact_fields()` is called with `$new_values` passed by reference, which will be used to store user input for each contact field.

❑   Finally, the contact is either updated or inserted by passing $new_values to either $insert_contact or $update_contact and edit_contact() returns to the calling subroutine, dispatch().

The subroutine edit_contact_fields(), which you saw was called by edit_contact(), uses an iterative loop that starts from 1 through $#{$fields}, the last index value of $fields. This sets the subscript variable $field_num to the current index value to process user input for each contact field value. The reason the loop starts at 1 is because 0 is the first field/column, which is contact_id — the primary key value — and cannot be set by the user, so it is skipped. The user input is read into $value. The user can skip the column by entering nothing and hitting enter. If the user is adding a contact, he or she is required to enter **first_name** and **last_name** columns using a while loop to check if he or she entered something and using the $required hash reference to check if the current column name is a required one. As the user enters values, they are stored in the hash reference $new_values, keyed by column name.

```
sub edit_contact_fields {
  my ($new_values, $contact_id) = @_;
    # start from subscript #1 -- skipping the primary key column contact_id which
    # cannot be set by the user
    for my $field_num (1 .. $#{$fields}) {
        my $label = make_label($field_num);
        prompt "Enter new value for $label (empty string to not change
if update) :\n";
        my $value = $_;
        # for a new user, there has to be some required fields.
Do not allow the
        # user to enter empty values for these fields/columns.
A while loop is
        # just the tool for forcing the issue!
        while (! length($value) &&
            $contact_id eq 'a' &&
            $required->{$fields->[$field_num]}) {
            prompt "Adding a new contact requires a value for
$label :\n";
            $value = $_;
        }

        $$new_values->{$fields->[$field_num]}= $value if length($value);
    }
    return;
}
```

You can begin testing this contact edit functionality. Of course at this point, nothing will be saved because the lower-level database subroutines have yet to be implemented. However they are stubbed out with print statements. One way to debug the newly implemented edit and add functionality is to use Data::Dumper. Because both update_contact() and insert_contact() take as an argument, the $new_values hash reference, you can use Data::Dumper to print out $new_values to make sure that the values you've modified or created are. Or, you could also use a debugger!

If you want to use Data::Dumper to verify that the values set in $new_values are what you expect them to be, make sure to import Data::Dumper at the top of the program and add it to both insert_contact() and update_contact() with the following:

```
print Dumper $new_values;
```

Now let's test `edit_contact()`. First, edit an existing contact, the one already added by hand:

```
Menu: (enter one)

-----------------------------------

c       Create a new contacts table
d       Delete a contact
e       Edit a contact (add or update)
f       Find user
l       List all contacts
q       Quit


-----------------------------------

Enter choice: e
The current contacts are:
--------------------------------------------
Contact id      1
First name      Test
Last name       User
Age             30
Address         111 Test Ave.
City            Someville
State           XX
Country         US

Enter which contact id you would like to edit, or 'a' for add new: 1
Enter new value for First name (empty string to not change if update) :
Henry
Enter new value for Last name (empty string to not change if update) :
Thoreau
Enter new value for Age (empty string to not change if update) :
40
Enter new value for Address (empty string to not change if update) :
Walden Pond
Enter new value for City (empty string to not change if update) :
Concord
Enter new value for State (empty string to not change if update) :
MA
Enter new value for Country (empty string to not change if update) :
US
$VAR1 = {
          'country' => 'US',
          'city' => 'Concord',
          'contact_id' => '1',
          'address' => 'Walden Pond',
          'age' => '40',
          'state' => 'MA',
          'last_name' => 'Thoreau',
          'first_name' => 'Henry'
        };
insert_contact() called
```

Excellent! It seems to work. As you can see, the proper value for the `contact_id` is retained and the new values that you entered are found in the `$new_values` hash reference. Now let's test adding a new contact:

```
Enter which contact id you would like to edit, or 'a' for add new: a
Enter new value for First name (empty string to not change if update) :
John
Enter new value for Last name (empty string to not change if update) :
Smith
Enter new value for Age (empty string to not change if update) :
33
Enter new value for Address (empty string to not change if update) :
100 Main St.
Enter new value for City (empty string to not change if update) :
Peterborough
Enter new value for State (empty string to not change if update) :
NH
Enter new value for Country (empty string to not change if update) :
US
insert_contact() called
$VAR1 = {
          'country' => 'US',
          'city' => 'Peterborough',
          'address' => '100 Main St.',
          'age' => '33',
          'state' => 'NH',
          'last_name' => 'Smith',
          'first_name' => 'John'
        };
```

So, you see the logic for adding or editing an existing contact works and the hash reference that stores the new values properly does so. Now `insert_contact()` and `update_contact()` can be implemented.

Inserting a Contact

`insert_contact` takes as an argument a hash reference containing the keys corresponding to the columns of the database and the values that will be inserted for those columns. What you must do is to use that hash reference to build an SQL INSERT statement and prepare and execute that INSERT statement.

Since it's a good practice to use prepared statements, the SQL INSERT statement will contain as many placeholders as there are columns in `$new_values` that will be prepared with `prepare()` and to then in turn pass the proper values in the proper order to a subsequent `execute()` call.

```perl
sub insert_contact {
    my ($new_values)= @_;

    # append each field name separated by comma
    my $insert_statement_fields
      = join ',', keys %$new_values;
    # append placeholders for each column
```

```perl
      my $insert_statement_values
        = join ',', ( '?' ) x keys %$new_values;

      # glue the full insert statement together
      my $insert_statement = "insert into $table
($insert_statement_fields)"
                             . " values ($insert_statement_values)";

      print "insert statement: $insert_statement\n" if $opt_debug;
      my $sth= $dbh->prepare_cached($insert_statement);

      my $rows= $sth->execute(values %$new_values);
      return ($dbh->last_insert_id(undef, $opt_schema, $table, undef, undef));

}
```

The SQL INSERT statement that is used to insert the contact is built by first joining the keys of $new_values with commas to construct the columns specification string, $insert_statement_fields. Then the values specification string, $insert_statement_values, is built by joining placeholders by the number of columns being inserted with commas. Then the entire SQL statement is built using both $insert_statement_fields and $insert_statement_values transliterated in the main SQL string. The end result is a string that will have a column specification (col1, col2, col3...) as well as the values in VALUES (?, ?, ? ...).

The SQL INSERT statement is prepared with prepared_cached(), and then executed with the output of values %$new_values in the form of an array, as is required for execute().

To know whether insert_contact() successfully inserted the contact, last_insert_id() is returned along with its own return value to the calling subroutine, edit_contact(). If the insert statement was successful, a non-zero value (the value of the $contact_id for the inserted contact) is returned. If there was a failure, undef is returned.

Updating a Contact

update_contact(), like insert_contact(), also uses the key/value pairs of the $new_values hash reference to construct an SQL UPDATE statement. What needs to be appended is slightly different than with an INSERT.

```perl
sub update_contact {
    my ($new_values)= @_;

    # save the value of contact_id which we need for the where clause later
    # and delete the contact id from $new_values so @values won't obtain it
    my $contact_id = delete $new_values->{contact_id};

    # @values are the values for the bind array
    my @values= values %$new_values;

    # build up the update statement string
    my $update_statement = "update $table set "
                           . join( ',', map { "$_ = ? " } keys %$new_values )
                           . " where contact_id = ?";
```

```
        # tack on contact id to the end of the @values bind array since contact_id
        # is the the last placeholder value
        push(@values, $contact_id);

        print "update contact statement:\n$update_statement\n" if $opt_debug;
        my $sth= $dbh->prepare_cached($update_statement);

        $sth->execute(@values);

    }
```

The first thing is to take from $new_values the contact id and then delete it from $new_values, since $new_values will be used to build the UPDATE statement. You only need one join-map combination to build the part of the UPDATE statement specifying the new values as "col=val" for each column and value, and since column_id was deleted from $new_values, it will not be included.

$contact_id has the value saved from $new_values->{contact_id}, which has since been deleted. This is the primary key value that will be used for the WHERE clause of the UPDATE statement (and has a placeholder for it). It is simply "tacked on" to the end of @values. It is also important to make sure, as with insert_contact(), to pass the array of values in the same order of the columns in the statement that the placeholders will be transliterated with.

Deleting a Contact

One other low-level database write operation that will be needed is a subroutine to delete a contact. That's where delete_contact() comes in.

delete_contact() needs to prompt the user for decisions just as edit_contact() does. It's important to make sure in the interface that there is user verification to ensure that the user really wants to delete a contact. Such verification allows he or she to confirm that deleting a contact (or not) is what he or she wants to do. It's also helpful to print a list of the contacts to give the user the list of contacts that exist currently in order to help the user make a decision.

```
    sub delete_contact {
        list_contacts();
        prompt "\n\nEnter the contact id of the contact you wish to delete: ";
        my $contact_id=  $_;

        print "\ncontact id selected $contact_id:\n";

        list_contacts([$contact_id]) or return;

        prompt "Do you realy want to delete contact id $contact_id? [y|N] ";
        my $answer= $_;

        if ($answer eq 'y') {
            if (delete_contact_db($contact_id)) {
                print "\nDeleted contact $contact_id\n";
            }
            else {
                print "\nError deleting $contact_id\n";
            }
```

```
        }
        else {
            print "\nNot deleting contact id $contact_id\n";
        }

        return;
    }
```

The user is prompted with a 'y' or 'N' as to whether or not he or she wants to delete a contact. 'y' is the only character that will result in a contact being deleted. 'N' or any other value will cancel the deletion. This behavior is common for most command-line interfaces and is what is being coded into this application.

Since there is so much user interface logic in this subroutine, to keep the number of lines down and separate logic further, making the design more concise, the actual low-level subroutine that deletes the contact from the database is implemented in its own subroutine, delete_contact_db(). This is an extremely simple subroutine. All it has to do is prepare an SQL DELETE statement with a single placeholder for the contact_id column value:

```
sub delete_contact_db {
    my ($contact_id)= @_;

    return ($dbh->do("delete from $table where contact_id = ?", undef,
$contact_id));
}
```

Testing update_contact, insert_contact, and delete_contact

You now have a way to add, edit, and delete a contact. You can now test these three functionalities, as demonstrated in the next sections.

Editing a Contact

This time, editing a contact should result in the user being changed, as opposed to a simple printout as before.

```
Enter which contact id you would like to edit, or 'a' for add new: 1
---------------------------------------------
Contact id      1
First name      Test
Last name       User
Age             30
Address         111 Test Ave.
City            Someville
State           XX
Country         US
Enter new value for First name (empty string to not change if update) :
Henry
Enter new value for Last name (empty string to not change if update) :
```

```
Thoreau
Enter new value for Age (empty string to not change if update) :
40
Enter new value for Address (empty string to not change if update) :
Walden Pond
Enter new value for City (empty string to not change if update) :
Concord
Enter new value for State (empty string to not change if update) :
MA
Enter new value for Country (empty string to not change if update) :
US
Updated contact_id 1

Menu: (enter one)

-----------------------------------

c       Create a new contacts table
d       Delete a contact
e       Edit a contact (add or update)
f       Find user
l       List all contacts
q       Quit


-----------------------------------

Enter choice: l
---------------------------------------------
Contact id      1
First name      Henry
Last name       Thoreau
Age             40
Address         Walden Pond
City            Concord
State           MA
Country         US
```

Editing works! A contact with a contact_id of 1 was chosen, the values changed, and the listing of contacts shows that this user was indeed modified.

Adding a Contact

Testing the addition of a contact will determine if the entered contact is saved. A listing of contacts should display this new contact in addition to the previously modified contact.

```
Enter which contact id you would like to edit, or 'a' for add new: a
Enter new value for First name (empty string to not change if update) :
John
Enter new value for Last name (empty string to not change if update) :
Brown
Enter new value for Age (empty string to not change if update) :
30
Enter new value for Address (empty string to not change if update) :
```

```
111 Main St.
Enter new value for City (empty string to not change if update) :
Denver
Enter new value for State (empty string to not change if update) :
CO
Enter new value for Country (empty string to not change if update) :
US
Added contact_id 2

Menu: (enter one)

-----------------------------------

c       Create a new contacts table
d       Delete a contact
e       Edit a contact (add or update)
f       Find user
l       List all contacts
q       Quit


-----------------------------------

Enter choice: l
---------------------------------------------
Contact id      1
First name      Henry
Last name       Thoreau
Age             40
Address         Walden Pond
City            Concord
State           MA
Country         US
---------------------------------------------
Contact id      2
First name      John
Last name       Brown
Age             30
Address         111 Main St.
City            Denver
State           CO
Country         US
```

And this test is successful! Both the new contact and the previous contact are displayed with the values entered.

Deleting a Contact

Now we'll test the deletion of a contact. The way to test this functionality is to select a contact to delete, and cancel the deletion by not selecting 'y.' Then select another contact to delete and choose 'y.' Finally, verify that the selected contact was deleted.

Some of the output is deleted from brevity.

```
Enter choice: d
---------------------------------------------
Contact id        1
First name        Henry
Last name         Thoreau
Age               40
Address           Walden Pond
City              Concord
State             MA
Country           US
---------------------------------------------
Contact id        2
First name        John
Last name         Brown
Age               30
Address           111 Main St.
City              Denver
State             CO
Country           US


Enter the contact id of the contact you wish to delete: 2

contact id selected 2:
---------------------------------------------
Contact id        2
First name        John
Last name         Brown
Age               30
Address           111 Main St.
City              Denver
State             CO
Country           US
Do you realy want to delete contact id 2? [y|N] n

Not deleting contact id 2

Menu: (enter one)


------------------------------------

c       Create a new contacts table
d       Delete a contact
e       Edit a contact (add or update)
f       Find user
l       List all contacts
q       Quit


------------------------------------

Enter choice: d
---------------------------------------------
Contact id        1
First name        Henry
```

```
Last name          Thoreau
Age                40
Address            Walden Pond
City               Concord
State              MA
Country            US
----------------------------------------------
Contact id         2
First name         John
Last name          Brown
Age                30
Address            111 Main St.
City               Denver
State              CO
Country            US


Enter the contact id of the contact you wish to delete: 2

contact id selected 2:
----------------------------------------------
Contact id         2
First name         John
Last name          Brown
Age                30
Address            111 Main St.
City               Denver
State              CO
Country            US
Do you realy want to delete contact id 2? [y|N] y

Deleted contact 2

Menu: (enter one)

------------------------------------

c      Create a new contacts table
d      Delete a contact
e      Edit a contact (add or update)
f      Find user
l      List all contacts
q      Quit


------------------------------------

Enter choice: l
----------------------------------------------
Contact id         1
First name         Henry
Last name          Thoreau
Age                40
Address            Walden Pond
City               Concord
```

```
State          MA
Country        US
```

This shows that deletion works. The contact selected is properly deleted if the user confirms deletion by selecting 'y.'

Lookup of a Contact

The last bit of needed functionality is being able to perform a lookup of a contact. This means being able to specify values for any number of contact attributes — first name, last name, age, city, and country.

The subroutine find_contact() will be the subroutine to implement the user interface functionality. The user interface is fairly simple. It simply needs to prompt the user for each field/column in the *contacts* table, storing the values in a hash reference with key/value pairs corresponding to each column.

```perl
sub find_contact {
    print "Lookup user(s)\n";
    my $lookup;

    print "Enter any of the following, return to ignore.\n";

    for (@$search_fields) {
        my $label= make_label($_);
        print "Enter $label: ";
        my $val= <STDIN>;
        chomp($val);
        $lookup->{$fields->[$_]}= $val if length($val);
    }

    my $contact_ids = get_contact_id($lookup);

    unless ($contact_ids) {
        print "No contacts could be found.\n";
        return ;
    }
    list_contacts($contact_ids);
    return;
}
```

An iterative loop is used looping through the values of the $fields array reference. If the user enters a value, that value is stored. If he or she enters nothing and hits return, it is ignored. Once all fields have been iterated through, get_contact_id() is called with the $lookup hash reference. This returns a list of one or more contact ids as the results. These contact ids are then passed as arguments to list_contacts(), which will list the results of the lookup.

The subroutine get_contact_id() performs the actual lookup in the *contacts* table for whatever is specified in the hash reference $contact.

```perl
sub get_contact_id {
    my ($contact)= @_;
```

```
# build up the query
my $query = "select contact_id from $table where "
  . join( ' AND ', map { "$_ = ? " } keys %$contact );

my $sth= $dbh->prepare($query);
$sth->execute(values %$contact);
my $id_ref= $sth->fetchall_arrayref();

# return a simple array reference, not result set
my $result_ref;
push @$result_ref, $_->[0] for @$id_ref;
return $result_ref;

}
```

Just as was done in `insert_contact()` and `update_contact()`, the SQL query WHERE clause is built by appending a column name and a placeholder for the number of keys in $contact. The full query is then glued together, prepared, and executed with the values of $contact, which are in the order of the columns in the executed statement. The results of the query are fetched with `fetchall_arrayref()`. This is an array reference of arrays that must be converted to a simple array reference of contact ids, so a mapping loops through the result set, and then the array reference is returned.

Testing Lookup of a Contact

Now that both `find_contact()` and `get_contact_id()` are implemented, you can test the lookup of a contact.

For testing, let's assume more data has been added:

```
------------------------------------------
Contact id       1
First name       Henry
Last name        Thoreau
Age              40
Address          Walden Pond
City             Concord
State            MA
Country          US
------------------------------------------
Contact id       3
First name       Ralph
Last name        Emerson
Age              50
Address          Old Manse
City             Concord
State            MA
Country          US
------------------------------------------
Contact id       4
First name       Walt
Last name        Whitman
Age              30
```

```
Address            33 Fulton St.
City               Brooklyn
State              NY
Country            US
---------------------------------------------
Contact id         5
First name         William
Last name          Wordsworth
Age                65
Address            Scafell Pike
City               Lake District
State              Lakeland
Country            UK
```

For a successful testing, supplying a specific value for any of the contact attributes should return the appropriate contact.

The following test searches just on a supplied country value:

```
Enter choice: f
Lookup user(s)
Enter any of the following, return to ignore.
Enter First name:
Enter Last name:
Enter Age:
Enter City:
Enter State:
Enter Country: UK
---------------------------------------------
Contact id         5
First name         William
Last name          Wordsworth
Age                65
Address            Scafell Pike
City               Lake District
State              Lakeland
Country            UK
```

Excellent! That worked. Now let's try a lookup by first name:

```
Enter choice: f
Lookup user(s)
Enter any of the following, return to ignore.
Enter First name: Henry
Enter Last name:
Enter Age:
Enter City:
Enter State:
Enter Country:
---------------------------------------------
Contact id         1
First name         Henry
Last name          Thoreau
Age                40
```

```
Address        Walden Pond
City           Concord
State          MA
Country        US
```

That worked, too!

Now, to make sure search functionality doesn't return false searches, perform the previous search again with UK for the country value:

```
Enter choice: f
Lookup user(s)
Enter any of the following, return to ignore.
Enter First name: Henry
Enter Last name:
Enter Age:
Enter City:
Enter State:
Enter Country: UK
No contacts could be found.
```

Great! Lookup functionality is now implemented, completing the contacts application.

Summary

Building on what you learned in Chapter 6, this chapter has shown you the implementation of a simple Perl database application using the DBI module to retrieve and modify data with MySQL. This was a great start to understanding how easy it is to write Perl database applications. Web applications have even more complexity, so this chapter's demonstration was a good foundational exercise because it focused only on using Perl and MySQL together.

Now you should have a good fund of knowledge to build upon and add other concepts to. As you continue reading through this book and come to the end of each chapter, you will repeatedly realize what you have in this chapter: that using Perl to program your applications is great and easy to work with.

The full program listing for this contacts application can be seen in the download file "Chapter 7: Simple command-line contact list application." Visit www.wrox.com to download this code.

8

memcached

Web applications are all about data. Being able to process data, both storing data that a user submits, as well as retrieving data to display, is the primary function of a web application. How fast and efficiently the application obtains that data is the most important issue pertaining to scalability. You have learned in this book that MySQL is a relational database system where data is organized and stored, and is the primary data source for web applications. Certainly, the database is the durable data store where all your data will be stored and available for the web application to use, however, having to retrieve data from a database does have a cost, depending on the type of database query executed and the subsequent result set that is retrieved.

Various types of data are frequently retrieved from the database for the application to function properly, including data that frequently changes, such as user or session data, as well as data that doesn't change as often, such as actual page content. Having to access the database for this data can affect performance significantly, and is a major scaling consideration.

This is where it would be useful *not* to have to always access the database to obtain this data — to have a *cache*. This is the problem that memcached solves.

What Is memcached?

memcached is a high-performance, distributed memory object caching system. It is essentially a simple memory server that provides a caching layer for applications to store data to alleviate database load, as well as a dictionary, or hash lookup table — something that you as a Perl programmer can certainly understand. The data stored in memcached is not durable — meaning it's gone when the memcached server is shut down or restarted — and it has no failover or authentication, so it is up to the application using memcached to implement how data is managed and kept up to date.

memcached has a structure that is known as an *LRU* (*Least Recently Used*) cache, so that stored data that is the oldest and least accessed will be replaced with newer items when memcached's memory capacity is reached. Also, memcached provides expiration timeouts for stored data, so you can set data you are storing to expire some time in the future, or not at all. memcached will replace data that has expired first, then replace the least recently used data, when its memory capacity has been reached.

memcached can run in any type of configuration: either on one or more servers, or even in multiple instances on the same server. The memcached server simply provides a storage structure where the data is stored by key value and a hash lookup table that is used for retrieval. The intelligence that really glues it all together is implemented in the memcached client, which takes a hash value of the key to reference what is being stored or retrieved. It uses a particular hashing algorithm that determines which servers the request for one or more keys should be sent to. Once the client knows which servers to request for a given item, it sends the requests in parallel to the appropriate servers. Each server then uses its hash key lookup table to retrieve the stored item and sends the results to the client. The client then aggregates the results for the application to use them.

Figure 8-1 shows how a memcached cluster comprises multiple servers and the client library provides the functionality for all of them to work as a single source of storage via a single connection to the application utilizing memcached.

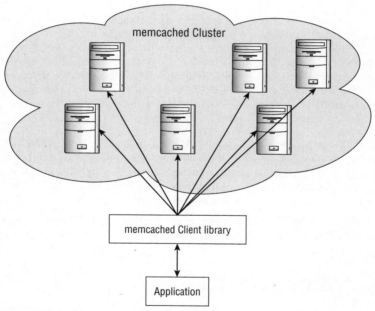

Figure 8-1

memcached is extremely fast for both storing and retrieving data since it uses memory instead of a disk to store data. It doesn't require much from the CPU, and can be run on the same server that the Apache web server is running on, or on any servers that have spare memory available.

With memcached, a common architecture setup is to have a number of servers that are simply configured for the sole purpose of providing memory. Because memcached needs memory more than it needs CPU power, in contrast to what a database would require, it's possible to use hardware that is much more affordable than that required for a database. This lets you use multiple lower-end servers to provide a distributed memory caching layer for your web application, and makes for easier and more affordable scaling.

Prior to the advent of memcached, developers used various schemes to cache data that they wanted to avoid having to access the database to obtain. One way was to cache data in the web process (since mod_perl is persistent). The problem with this is that each child ended up having a copy of the same data that other processes have already cached, resulting in duplicated data across threads/children. There were also some file-based caching systems (the various Perl Cache:: modules), but, of course, the best means of caching is to use memory, not disk. Another trick was to use IPC (IPC::Sharable in Perl), but this was tricky (speaking from experience) and only worked per machine.

Along came memcached, which was developed for the site Livejournal.com by Brad Fitzpatrick, who wanted a better caching solution than those that existed at the time. Livejournal is a social web site with millions of users and millions of dynamic page views per day. With memcached, the millions of page views that previously accessed the database for all this data could now use a lightweight cache to obtain data, thereby reducing the load on their database to almost nothing.

How memcached Is Used

Normally, when you either store or retrieve data in your application, your application runs a query if retrieving data, or an INSERT or UPDATE statement when storing data directly to the database. With a cache system like memcached, the design of your application changes to take advantage of the caching. There are two types of caching: read-through caching and write-through caching.

- ❑ **Read-through caching:** When data is retrieved, the application checks the cache first to see if the data being retrieved is already there. If the data is in the cache, it just returns that data without having to query the database. If it's not in the cache, the data is obtained from the database, then stored in the cache, and finally returned to the user. The idea is that a read operation not only obtains data, but also ensures that the cache has the required data for subsequent reads. Figure 8-2 shows a diagram of how a read-through cache works.

- ❑ **Write-through caching:** Data is written to memcached, and a separate process reads the stored data from memcached to the databases. The mechanism that initiates that separate process can be implemented in several ways:

  - ❑ When the data is written to memcached, a job is requested by a Gearman client; Gearman then assigns the job to a worker that then obtains the stored data from memcached and stores it in MySQL.

  - ❑ When the data is written to memcached, an entry is made to a simple catalogue table that contains the hash key value of the data stored to memcached.

  - ❑ A trigger exists on this table that, when executed (when data is inserted), sends a command to a server that in turn calls the process that pulls the data from memcached and then stores it in MySQL.

  - ❑ A cron job periodically runs and reads the stored keys from this catalogue table, retrieves the stored data for those keys from memcached, and then stores that data in MySQL. This is known as "lazy" processing/caching.

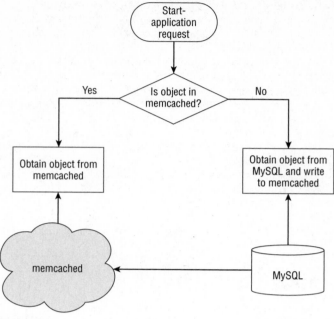

Figure 8-2

Figure 8-3 shows write-through caching with three possible mechanisms, as just described, of getting data that is stored in memcached stored into MySQL.

Caching also gives you liberty to use all sorts of useful tricks. You can use the cache to perform "lazy" processing. For instance, imagine an application that processes RSS feeds and needs to both store the components of the feed into the database as well as provide a JSON cache of the feed for an AJAX client application to display.

One part of the application, run via a web request, requests an RSS feed from the Internet. It obtains the RSS feed, which is an XML file. The application then parses this XML file into a DOM Perl object and also converts the XML into JSON. The JSON is then stored in memcached, available for being served by the application to the AJAX client, and the XML DOM object is stored as a separate object in memcached and an entry is made in a queue table containing the key of the DOM object. By some mechanism, either cron job or trigger to a UDF on the queue table, the queue table is read from by yet another process (non-web) that obtains all keys stored in this queue table, retrieving the DOM objects that have been stored in memcached with these key values. This process then loops through each DOM object, storing each feed item in the database. This process also deletes the entries in the queue table and deletes the DOM objects from memcached that it has processed.

What memcached allows for is that an application that would normally have to perform all of these actions within the web application layer can now be split into two processes: The first is a web application, which mainly has to take care of fetching and caching. The second is a non-web application that can run asynchronously apart from the web request, which takes care of the heavier database processing at whatever frequency is desired.

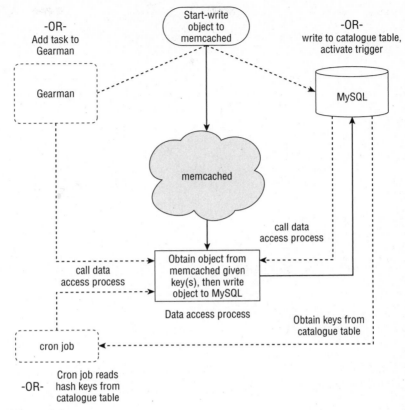

Figure 8-3

What Is Gearman?

Gearman is yet another useful project from the same people who created memcached and Danga — Brian Fitzpatrick, et al. It is a server that is used for dispatching assign, or to "farm out" jobs to machines that are better suited to run these tasks than the machine that made the call. Thus tasks can be run in parallel, allowing for load balancing and better scaling, and even being able to call functions that are not written in the same programming language as the application code.

Gearman consists of a server called, interestingly enough, gearmand and clients: caller clients that make requests to the server, and workers that can perform the work requested by the clients. There are client APIs for Perl, PHP, Ruby, Python and others.

You can use Gearman to handle things like processing items stored in memcached (write-through caching) as well as for any processing you want to distribute so as to relieve the load on your main server.

In Chapter 18, you will see just how useful Gearman is. This chapter provides a search engine application as a practical example of how you can use Gearman.

Caching Strategies

There are different types of caching strategies you can employ for different types of data, depending on how often that data changes and what type of data is being stored:

❏ **Deterministic cache:** This is the caching described in the read-through cache example. Data is requested. If it is in memcached, it simply returns that data. If it is not in memcached, data is obtained from MySQL and then written to memcached and returned to the requester.

❏ **Nondeterministic cache:** This is data that you would assume to always be in memcached. This would be particularly useful for more static data. This would also require the promise that the data is always loaded into memcached, for example when a web server is started. Also, if possible, you would want to try to keep this cache on its own server, where it would have other types of objects stored that might cause the more static data to be replaced through the mechanism of LRU.

❏ **Session or state cached:** This is cache that you would use for storing using data such as user session data — something that could be particularly useful for applications such as shopping carts.

❏ **Proactive caching:** Similar to nondeterministic caching, proactive caching is where data is automatically updated in cache on a database write. This could be done using triggers and the Memcached Functions for MySQL, which will be covered in Chapter 10.

❏ **File system or page caching:** This is where you would cache templates or HTML code that makes up the design of your web site. This would allow you to avoid having to use the file system to obtain your site content.

❏ **Partial page caching:** This is where you would have page components stored. You could avoid having to use expensive queries that provide calculations, such as comment or story popularity, to display a page every time. You could instead build these components on a regular basis and then store them in memcached. When the page is displayed, it just obtains these pre-built components from memcached and displays them!

❏ **Cache replication:** You can build the functionality into your application so that it writes data to multiple memcached servers for each item stored to ensure that you have redundancy.

Installing memcached

Installing memcached is very simple. You can either use a package installer for most Linux distributions or else compile the source. There is only one prerequisite package that memcached requires — libevent. Libevent is an API that memcached uses to scale any number of open connections. You can install this on most Linux distributions with package management or by source.

CentOS

To install memcached on a CentOS Linux server, follow these steps:

1. Start out by running:

```
[root@testbox ~]# yum search memcached
```

This produces various results, the two most important of which are: (This is on a 64-bit CPU. On a 32-bit it may be i386.)

```
memcached.x86_64 : High Performance, Distributed Memory Object Cache
memcached-selinux.x86_64 : SELinux policy module supporting memcached
```

The SELinux package is to ensure that memcached has the correct firewall settings to be allowed to be run. Memcached runs by default on port 11211. You could just as easily set the firewall to allow 11211 through.

2.　Next you run the install:

```
[root@testbox ~]# yum install memcached.x86_64
....
Dependencies Resolved

===================================================================
 Package              Arch       Version         Repository     Size
===================================================================
Installing:
 memcached            x86_64     1.2.5-2.el5     epel           59 k
Installing for dependencies:
 libevent             x86_64     1.1a-3.2.1      base           21 k

Transaction Summary
===================================================================
Install       2 Package(s)
Update        0 Package(s)
Remove        0 Package(s)

Total download size: 80 k
Is this ok [y/N]:
```

As you can see, libevent is automatically included as a dependency, so there is no need to specifically install it.

3.　Select **y** to complete the installation. The installer will also set up the init scripts that start memcached when the operating system is booted.

Ubuntu

With Ubuntu, use apt-cache search:

```
root@hanuman:~# apt-cache search memcached
libcache-memcached-perl - Cache::Memcached - client library for memcached
libmemcache-dev - development headers for libmemcache C client API
libmemcache0 - C client API for memcached memory object caching system
memcached - A high-performance memory object caching system
```

All of these packages are ones that you might as well install. The *libmemcached* packages are for the high-performance client library libmemcached, which will be explained later in this chapter. The package libcached-memcached-perl is the one that supplies the Perl client libraries needed for writing programs in Perl using memcached; you'll need this also. Use apt-get install to install these packages:

```
apt-get install memcached libcache-memcached-perl libmemcache-dev
libmemcache0
Reading package lists... Done
```

```
Building dependency tree
Reading state information... Done
The following extra packages will be installed:
  libevent1 libstring-crc32-perl
The following NEW packages will be installed:
  libcache-memcached-perl libevent1 libmemcache-dev libmemcache0
 libstring-crc32-perl memcached
0 upgraded, 6 newly installed, 0 to remove and 96 not upgraded.
Need to get 227kB/278kB of archives.
After unpacking 946kB of additional disk space will be used.
Do you want to continue [Y/n]? Y
```

As with yum, apt-get will ensure that libevent is installed, taking care of any dependencies.

Installing memcached from Source

You can also install memcached by source. This may be your preferred option, especially if you want the latest and greatest release. The web page for memcached is found at Danga.com (http://www.danga.com/memcached/). From there you will find a link to the latest source, or repository in either git or subversion. If you are not using a packaged version of libevent, you'll need to obtain that, too, from http://monkey.org/~provos/libevent/.

Now, follow these steps:

1. Download libevent:

   ```
   wget http://monkey.org/~provos/libevent-1.4.8-stable.tar.gz
   ```

2. Compile and install libevent:

   ```
   tar xvzf libevent-1.4.8-stable.tar.gz

   cd libevent-1.4.8-stable

   ./configure

   make

   make install
   ```

3. Download memcached:

   ```
   [root@testbox src]# wget http://www.danga.com/memcached/dist/
   memcached-1.2.6.tar.gz
   ```

4. Compile and install memcached:

   ```
   tar xvzf memcached-1.2.6.tar.gz

   cd memcached-1.2.6

   ./configure
   ```

```
                     make

                     make install
```

Starting memcached

Depending on where memcached is installed, you will need to start it from that location. You can start memcached by hand. To see all options available to memcached, use the -h switch:

```
[root@testbox memcached-1.2.6]# /usr/local/bin/memcached -h
memcached 1.2.6
-p <num>      TCP port number to listen on (default: 11211)
-U <num>      UDP port number to listen on (default: 0, off)
-s <file>     unix socket path to listen on (disables network support)
-a <mask>     access mask for unix socket, in octal (default 0700)
-l <ip_addr>  interface to listen on, default is INDRR_ANY
-d            run as a daemon
-r            maximize core file limit
-u <username> assume identity of <username> (only when run as root)
-m <num>      max memory to use for items in megabytes, default is 64 MB
-M            return error on memory exhausted (rather than removing
              items)
-c <num>      max simultaneous connections, default is 1024
-k            lock down all paged memory.  Note that there is a
              limit on how much memory you may lock.  Trying to
              allocate more than that would fail, so be sure you
              set the limit correctly for the user you started
              the daemon with (not for -u <username> user;
              under sh this is done with 'ulimit -S -l NUM_KB').
-v            verbose (print errors/warnings while in event loop)
-vv           very verbose (also print client commands/reponses)
-h            print this help and exit
-i            print memcached and libevent license
-b            run a managed instanced (mnemonic: buckets)
-P <file>     save PID in <file>, only used with -d option
-f <factor>   chunk size growth factor, default 1.25
-n <bytes>    minimum space allocated for key+value+flags, default 48
```

The most common options you will use are -u and -m. The first option, -u specifies the user, defaults to the current user, and won't let you run memcached as root, so if you start memcached as root, you will have to specify a non-root user. The second option, -m, is the size in megabytes of the block of memory that will be slated for memcached. The default is 64 megabytes.

If you are logged in as yourself and just want to run memcached with defaults, you can certainly just start it, backgrounded:

```
/usr/local/bin/memcached &
```

If you want to run memcached in super-mega-umlaut verbose mode to a log file:

```
/usr/local/bin/memcached -u username -vv >>/tmp/memcached.log 2>&1 &
```

The -vv flag causes memcached to print out any request to the server. You can see exactly what memcached is doing if you run it with -vv.

Startup Scripts

Alternatively, there are startup scripts that come with memcached found in the scripts directory of the source package, if you are running a UNIX variant that uses SYSV startup scripts. Some of these scripts are a bit dated and you will most likely have to edit them for the particular setup of your system.

```
[root@testbox scripts]# ls
memcached-init  memcached.sysv  memcached-tool  start-memcached
```

The scripts of interest depend on what UNIX variant or Linux distribution you're running. If you are running Debian-based Linux, you will need to edit memcached-init and start-memcached to have the correct path information. For Redhat-based systems (Redhat, CentOS, Fedora), you will only edit memcached.sysv.

Debian-Based Startup Scripts

memcached-init relies on start-memcached, which also needs to be edited and placed in a directory specified in memcached-init.

Once you have memcached-init edited, copy it as /etc/init.d/memcached. Make sure to set the correct permissions.

```
chmod 755 /etc/init.d/memcached
```

Then set up the run-level permissions for this script to be automatically started (linked to their appropriate run-levels), ensuring that memcached will start up upon system boot:

```
root@testbox:~# update-rc.d memcached-init defaults
 Adding system startup for /etc/init.d/memcached-init ...
   /etc/rc0.d/K20memcached-init -> ../init.d/memcached-init
   /etc/rc1.d/K20memcached-init -> ../init.d/memcached-init
   /etc/rc6.d/K20memcached-init -> ../init.d/memcached-init
   /etc/rc2.d/S20memcached-init -> ../init.d/memcached-init
   /etc/rc3.d/S20memcached-init -> ../init.d/memcached-init
   /etc/rc4.d/S20memcached-init -> ../init.d/memcached-init
   /etc/rc5.d/S20memcached-init -> ../init.d/memcached-init
```

Redhat-based Startup Scripts

You will have to edit scripts/memcached.sysv. You must ensure the correct paths, port, and the user that memcached runs as:

```
PORT=11211
USER=nobody
MAXCONN=1024
CACHESIZE=64
OPTIONS=""
```

One other change you might have to make to ensure the path to memcached is known to the startup script is to add the variable prog_path right after prog:

```
prog="memcached"
prog_path="/usr/local/bin/memcached"
```

Then you would change:

```
daemon memcached -d -p $PORT -u $USER  -m $CACHESIZE -c $MAXCONN...
```

to:

```
daemon $prog_path -d -p $PORT -u $USER  -m $CACHESIZE -c $MAXCONN...
```

Once the script is ready, it can be copied as /etc/init.d/memcached. To set up the script to be started upon system reset, first add it:

```
[root@testbox memcached-1.2.6]# chkconfig --add memcached
```

Verify that it will still need to have its levels set up:

```
[root@testbox memcached-1.2.6]# chkconfig --list memcached
memcached               0:off   1:off   2:off   3:off   4:off   5:off   6:off
```

Then set memcached to run in the proper levels (2, 3, 4, 5):

```
[root@testbox memcached-1.2.6]# chkconfig --level 2345 memcached on
```

Then verify that the changes were made:

```
[root@testbox memcached-1.2.6]# chkconfig --list memcached
memcached               0:off   1:off   2:on    3:on    4:on    5:on    6:off
```

Installing the Cache::Memcached Perl Module

In addition to memcached, you will also want to install the Perl module, *Cache::Memcached*, which you will use for writing Perl programs that connect to memcached. As stated before, the client for memcached is where most of the real functionality that allows caching of data amongst multiple memcached servers is implemented.

Cache::Memcached can be installed (as shown in previous install procedures) through operating system packages or via CPAN:

Using Cache::Memcached

Using memcached is extremely easy. The first thing you do in your program is to open a connection to your memcached cluster — meaning one or more instances of memcached running on one or more servers. This is accomplished by instantiating a Cache::Memcached object. The constructor is called in the example below:

Connecting, Instantiation

The first thing you will want to do in order to interact with a memcached server using Perl is to instantiate the Cache::Memcached module.

```
use Cache::Memcached;
my $memc = new Cache::Memcached({
    'servers' => [
        "172.16.221.128:11212",
        "172.16.221.128:221122"],
    'debug' => 0,
    'compress_threshold' => 10_000});
```

The constructor takes a hash reference of various options. First and foremost is `servers`. The value of this key is an array reference of servers. The *servers* array reference values are IP:port, in this case there are three different memcached servers that this client will refer to as one memcached object (one on the local server and the other two both on the same remote server, but running on different ports). The standard port that memcached servers default to using is 11211, but other ports can also be used. Either way, you must provide this port. The servers you use can also be set with the method `set_servers()`:

```
$memc->set_servers(['127.0.0.1:11211', ...]);
```

The *debug* option determines whether Cache::Memcached will be instantiated in debug mode or not. If *debug* is 1 (true), debug messages of what the client is setting or fetching from the memcached server will be printed to STDERR. You can also set this value with the method `set_debug()`

```
$memc->set_debug(1|0);
```

The other option, `compress_threshold`, is the value in bytes that, if exceeded by the object being stored, will result in compression being applied to that store operation of that object. You can change this value after instantiation with the method `set_compress_threshold()`:

```
$memc->set_compress_threshold(10_000);
```

You can also turn on or off compression altogether with `enable_compression()`:

```
$memc->enable_compression(1|0);
```

Other options used for instantiation are:

- ❑ no_rehash: If set to true, this disables finding a new memcached server when one goes down. You can set this value after instantiation with `set_norehash()`:

    ```
    $memc->set_no_rehash(1|0);
    ```

- ❑ readonly: If set to true, this makes it so you can only read from the memcached servers the client object references. It is useful for debugging. You can set this after instantiation with the method `set_read_only()`:

    ```
    $memc->set_readonly(1|0);
    ```

❏   namespace: This causes a value to automatically be prepended to any key you set. For instance, if you have *namespace* set to myapp:, and you subsequently set the key t1, the actual key being set on the server will be myapp:t1.

Memcached Operations

The next thing you probably want to see is an example of how to use memcached for caching! The basic operations in memcached are quite a bit simpler than with a database and are worth reviewing:

❏   **Set:** Sets a value given by key, regardless of whether it is there already. If it's not there, a completely new object is set. If an existing object is there, it will replace that object. You can also set this value to expire upon setting it.

❏   **Get:** Fetches a value, by key.

❏   **Add:** Adds a value by the given key, if it doesn't yet exist.

❏   **Replace:** Replaces a value by the given key, if that key exists.

❏   **Delete:** Deletes a value stored by the given key.

❏   **Increment:** Increments a value of the given key. You can use this as a sequence or central counter.

❏   **Decrement:** Decrements a value of the given key. You can use this as a sequence or central counter.

❏   **Stats:** Returns statistics of the memcached servers.

Cache::Memcached API

This section explains the various Cache::Memcached methods and gives examples for each. The methods that Cache::Memcached provides for these basic operations are as follows:

❏   set: Sets the value $value specified by the key $key, regardless of whether it was already existing. $value can be a scalar value or any Perl data type. $expiration, in seconds, is optional. The default is 0, which means no expiration. Returns true if the value was stored successfully.

```
$was_set= $memc->set($key, $value[, $expiration]);
```

❏   get: Retrieves the value $value specified by $key.

```
$value= $memc->get($key);
```

❏   get_multi: Retrieves a hash reference of the values specified by the array @keys, with each value referenced by the key value that was specified in @keys.

```
$hashref= $memc->get_multi(@keys);
```

❏   add: Adds a value $value specified by the key $key if that value hasn't yet been stored. Optional $expiry sets the value of when $value will expire. The default for $expiry is 0, which means no expiration. Returns true if that value was stored.

```
$was_added= $memc->add($key, $value[, $expiry]);
```

❑ replace: Replaces the value $value specified by the key $key if that value exists. Optional $expiry sets the value of when $value will expire.

```
$was_replaced= $memc->replace($key, $value[, $expiry]);
```

❑ delete/remove (either works): Deletes the value from the memcached cluster referred to by $key. The optional value $time will block writes to that object, in seconds. This is a hack to prevent race conditions.

```
$was_deleted= $memc->delete($key[, $time]);
```

❑ incr: Increments a numeric value specified by $key by 1 or by optional $value. Returns the newly incremented value.

```
$increment_value= $memc->incr($key[, $value])
```

❑ decr: Decrements a numeric value specified by $key by 1 or by optional $value. Returns the newly decremented value.

```
$decrement_value= $memc->decr($key[, $value]);
```

❑ stats: Returns a hash reference of memcached statistics, either all statistics, or those specified by $keys.

```
$stats_hashref= $memc->stats([$keys]);
```

The statistics keys available are:

❑ misc: The statistics that running a stats command on the memcached server would return: pid, uptime, version, get_bytes, etc.

❑ malloc: The statistics that running a 'stats malloc' command on the memcached server would return: total_alloc, arena_size, etc.

❑ sizes: The statistics that are returned from running a 'stats sizes' on a memcached server.

❑ self: The statistics for the memcached object itself, a copy of $memc.

❑ maps: The statistics returned by running 'stats maps' on a memcached server.

❑ cache_dump: The statistics returned by running 'stats cachedump' on a memcached server.

❑ slabs: The statistics returned by running 'stats slabs' on a memcached server.

❑ items: The statistics returned by running 'stats items' on a memcached server.

To better understand what these stats look like and see just how much useful information they provide, a dump of these stats is shown here.

The code:

```perl
my $memc = new Cache::Memcached({
    'servers' => [
        "127.0.0.1:11211"],
        'debug' => 0,
        'compress_threshold' => 10_000});

my $stats_hashref= $memc->stats();

print Dumper $stats_hashref;
```

... produces the output:

```perl
$VAR1 = {
        'hosts' => {
                    '127.0.0.1:11211' => {
                                    'misc' => {
                                            'bytes' => '0',
                                            'curr_connections' => '3',
                                            'connection_structures' => '4',
                                            'pointer_size' => '32',
                                            'time' => '1228227275',
                                            'total_items' => '0',
                                            'cmd_set' => '0',
                                            'bytes_written' => '0',
                                            'evictions' => '0',
                                            'curr_items' => '0',
                                            'pid' => '1093',
                                            'limit_maxbytes' => '67108864',
                                            'uptime' => '5',
                                            'rusage_user' => '0.001329',
                                            'cmd_get' => '0',
                                            'rusage_system' => '0.004006',
                                            'version' => '1.2.6',
                                            'get_hits' => '0',
                                            'bytes_read' => '7',
                                            'threads' => '1',
                                            'total_connections' => '4',
                                            'get_misses' => '0'
                                            }
                                    }
                    },
            'self' => {},
            'total' => {
                        'cmd_get' => 0,
                        'bytes' => 0,
                        'get_hits' => 0,
                        'connection_structures' => 4,
                        'bytes_read' => 7,
                        'total_items' => 0,
                        'total_connections' => 4,
```

```
                          'cmd_set' => 0,
                          'bytes_written' => 0,
                          'curr_items' => 0,
                          'get_misses' => 0
                      }
          };
```

As you can see, stats provides every tidbit of information you would ever want to know about your memcached cluster. In this example, only one host was used (for brevity, so this book doesn't become an encyclopedia of Data::Dumper!). You can see that in the statistics hash reference, each server is keyed.

Other methods include the following:

❑   `disconnect_all`: The name speaks for itself. Disconnect and close all cached sockets from all memcached connections. You must use this if you are using forking in your program and the parent the child spawned from used `Cache::Memcached`.

```
$memc->disconnect_all();
```

❑   `flush_all`: This method also speaks for itself. It flushes all cached items from all memcached servers the connection references. Only use this if you really mean to!

```
$memc->flush_all();
```

Simple Examples

To help you get started with Perl programs that take advantage of memcached, the following sections show simple examples of using memcached to perform the basic functions described above — set, get, delete, add, replace, increment, decrement, etc.

Storing a Scalar

The first example shows setting, retrieving, and then deleting a simple scalar:

```
use Cache::Memcached;

my $memc = new Cache::Memcached({
    'servers' => [ "127.0.0.1:11211"],
    'compress_threshold' => 10_000});

# use the return value of set() to check if the value was actually set
if ($memc->set('key1', 'value1')) {
    my $val= $memc->get('key1');
    print "val $val\n";
    $memc->delete('key1');
}
else {
    print "unable to set 'key1'\n";
}
```

If you are curious, you can see what the memcached server is doing if you run memcached with the –vv flag (make sure to shut it down first if it's already running):

```
radha:memc patg$ /usr/local/bin/memcached -vv >>
/tmp/memcached.log 2>&1 &
```

And the log shows the output from running the previous script:

```
...
slab class  38: chunk size 391224 perslab      2
slab class  39: chunk size 489032 perslab      2
<4 server listening
<5 server listening
<6 send buffer was 9216, now 7456540
<6 server listening (udp)
<7 new client connection
<7 set key1 0 0 6
>7 STORED
<7 get key1
>7 sending key key1
>7 END
<7 delete key1
>7 DELETED
<7 connection closed.
```

This is a highly useful way to debug your programs. If you are working on a program and pulling your hair out trying to figure out if something was really stored or not, this is one way to know for certain what really happened on the memcached server. Of course, you do have to realize that if you are running multiple memcached servers and $memc was instantiated against those servers, you'll have to keep an eye on the output of each one of those servers.

Complex Data Types

The next example shows that you can store more complex Perl objects in memcached, in this case an array reference:

```
my $ar_ref= ['this', 'is', 'a', 'test'];

# store the array reference
if ($memc->set('key1', $ar_ref)) {
    my $val= $memc->get('key1');
    print "scalar key1: " . scalar @$ar_ref . "\n";
    $memc->delete('key1');
}
```

This is because Cache::Memcached uses Storable, which will serialize Perl objects, making it possible to store scalars, arrays, hashes, and references to scalars, arrays, and hashes. You cannot store glob references or subroutine references — Storable doesn't like that. The author of this book tested each type to ensure what he was writing was valid. (Reading the Storable documentation also would have revealed this!)

About expiration — this is another extremely useful feature you can take advantage of. You may have data to temporarily store that you want to be automatically deleted after a given amount of time. For instance, you may have session data or CAPTCHA strings that you need to make sure aren't used more than once, but over a short period of time, such as fifteen minutes. The following example shows expiration in action (the term *action* being used in an unexciting sense):

```
my $val= 'test';
# set a expiration of 10 seconds
if ($memc->set('test1', $val, 10)) {
    for (0 .. 15) {
        my $retval = $memc->get('test1');
        print "count: $_ ";
        if ($retval) {
            print "still there: $retval\n"
        }
        else {
            print "toasted.\n";
            exit;
        }
        sleep 2;
    }
}
```

The output shows the excitement:

```
radha:memc pgalbraith$ ./memc5.pl
count: 0 still there: test
count: 1 still there: test
count: 2 still there: test
count: 3 still there: test
count: 4 still there: test
count: 5 toasted.
```

Just think of how many times you have had to code something to go back into the database and delete data that you didn't need anymore. So, not only do you not have to store the data in the database in the first place, you also don't have to run a DELETE on the database to delete that data! You can imagine how quickly the savings adds up.

Add and Replace

Normally, you will most likely use set() to store values in memcached, whether they are there or not. There are times when you may want to have logic to only store something if it doesn't exist or replace it if it does. The following code snippet shows the implementation of its own handling of setting an object:

```
sub my_set {
    my ($key, $val, $exp)= @_;
    defined $exp or $exp = 0;

    my $retval= $memc->get($key);
    if ($retval) {
        print "$key exists ";
        if ($retval eq $val) {
```

```
            print "\n";
            return;
        }
        print "replacing ";
        if ($memc->replace($key, $val, $exp)) {
            print "replaced key $key";
        };
        print ".\n";
    }
    else {
        print "adding $key.\n";
        if ($memc->add($key, $val, $exp)) {
            print "added $key\n";
        }
    }
}
```

This can then be used just like the regular set() method:

```
my_set('key1', 'val1');
my_set('key1', 'val1');
my_set('key1', 'val2');
```

The output shows how it works:

```
adding key1.
added key1
key1 exists
key1 exists replacing replaced key key1.
```

A More Practical Example

So you have seen some simple examples of how to deal with storing data in memcached. Now you probably want to see how you can actually use memcached in a practical manner and reduce the load on your database.

User Application

Imagine an application for user data storage. The database schema this application will use has a table for users (users) that stores attributes such as the user's username, email, full name, address, city, state, account level, or any other information you might want in your application. Also, for good, normalized schema design, this database uses foreign keys on columns of the user table to ensure referential integrity to other tables such as states, cities, regions, account levels, and any other user attribute (column) that otherwise would be repeated, and also provides other data for each possible user attribute. This application provides an API for user data retrieval and modification, as well as retrieval of data from the other tables.

To show how memcached can be a benefit to this user application, it will be useful to show this application as it works with only the database first, without any caching. Then any part of the code that would benefit from using memcached will be modified, and the cases where reduced access to the database are achieved will be detailed.

The following application is a somewhat practical application library. It could be used in a web site application that stores user or customer data. It allows you to view, create, and change a user. Also, it has geographical information that can either be used for the user or stand alone. The main idea here is to show a subset of your common database application that can greatly benefit from caching.

Data Design

The first thing to conceptualize this application is to define the database tables that it will use. A real application would have a much more complex schema, but again, this is a subset of a full-fledged application. For the purposes of this discussion, a subset of a schema of an application like this will suffice. These are the tables that will be used:

❑   *users*: Contains user data with a foreign key each to *account_levels* and *cities*.

❑   *account_levels*: Various account levels, one of the attributes of a user.

❑   *cities*: Cities data, one of the attributes of a user, has a foreign key to *regions*.

❑   *states*: States data, one of the attributes of a user.

❑   *regions*: Regions data, such as a region name like "Pacific Northwest."

Here are the table definitions for *users*:

```
CREATE TABLE users (
    uid int(8) NOT NULL auto_increment,
    username varchar(32) NOT NULL default '',
    email varchar(32) NOT NULL default '',
    password char(16) NOT NULL default '',
    firstname varchar(32) NOT NULL default '',
    surname varchar(32) NOT NULL default '',
    address varchar(128) NOT NULL default '',
    city_id int(8) NOT NULL default 0,
    account_level int(3) NOT NULL default 0,
    PRIMARY KEY (uid),
    UNIQUE INDEX username (username),
    UNIQUE INDEX email (email),
    INDEX password (password),
    INDEX city_id (city_id),
    INDEX account_level (account_level),
    CONSTRAINT city_id FOREIGN KEY (city_id)
        REFERENCES cities (city_id)
        ON DELETE CASCADE ON UPDATE CASCADE,
    CONSTRAINT account_level FOREIGN KEY (account_level)
        REFERENCES account_levels (account_level)
        ON DELETE CASCADE ON UPDATE CASCADE
    ) ENGINE = InnoDB;
```

The *users* table is any user attribute you would want to store. This particular application example will be similar to many other web applications — uid (a user id), username (like a nickname), email, password, first name, surname (last name), address, city_id foreign key to *cities*, account_level foreign key to the *account_levels* table.

The next table is *cities*:

```
CREATE TABLE cities (
  city_id int(8) NOT NULL auto_increment,
  city_name varchar(32) NOT NULL default '',
  state_id int(4) NOT NULL default 0,
  region_id int(3) NOT NULL default 0,
  population int(3) NOT NULL default 0,
  PRIMARY KEY (city_id, state_id),
  INDEX state_id (state_id),
  INDEX region_id (region_id),
  INDEX city_name (city_name),
  CONSTRAINT region_id FOREIGN KEY (region_id) REFERENCES regions
(region_id)
      ON DELETE CASCADE ON UPDATE CASCADE
) ENGINE=InnoDB AUTO_INCREMENT=1;
```

The *cities* table provides not only a city name for a user, but also various attributes for this city. In addition to providing user attributes, the application can also provide geographical information about cities.

cities in turn has a foreign key to *states* on state_id. So, to know what state a user belongs to, you have to join *users* to *cities* on city_id and join *states* on state_id.

```
CREATE TABLE states (
  state_id int(4) NOT NULL auto_increment,
  state_abbr varchar(3) NOT NULL default '',
  state_name varchar(32) NOT NULL default '',
  state_bird varchar(32) NOT NULL default '',
  state_flower varchar(32) NOT NULL default '',
  PRIMARY KEY (state_id),
  INDEX state_name (state_name)
) ENGINE=InnoDB AUTO_INCREMENT=1;
```

cities has a foreign key to *regions* on region_id, so if you need to obtain the region of a user, you would have to join *users* with *cities* using city_id and join *cities* to *regions* on region_id.

```
CREATE TABLE regions (
  region_id int(3) NOT NULL,
  region_name varchar(16) NOT NULL default '',
  PRIMARY KEY (region_id)
) ENGINE=InnoDB;
```

Also, there is a table for account levels:

```
CREATE TABLE account_levels (
  account_level int(3) NOT NULL default 0,
  account_level_name varchar(16) NOT NULL default '',
  primary key (account_level)
) ENGINE= InnoDB;
```

UserApp Package

The application will be implemented using a class that will be called UserApp. All the usual setup will be required for creating a Perl class, which, since you've already read Chapter 3, you are well aware of!

```
package UserApp;

use strict;
use warnings;
use DBI;
# for MD5-hexing passwords
use Digest::MD5 qw(MD5_hex);
```

This application will, of course, use DBI, and *strict* and *warnings*. Another module this example will use is Digest::MD5 for the function MD5_hex() to calculate the MD5 digest of the password to avoid storing the password itself. When the password needs to be verified, the MD5 digest of the password is calculated and compared against the stored MD5 digest.

Instantiation

The first method this application will implement is instantiation via new().

```
sub new {
    my ($class) = @_;
    my $this= {};
    bless $this, $class;
    $this->connectDB();
    return $this;
}
```

Database Connector Method

If you'll notice, new() also calls a method called connectDB(), which does just what it says — connect to the database. A class attribute $this->{dbh} is assigned the database connection handle that will be available to all methods:

```
sub connectDB {
    my ($this)= @_;
    # wrap in eval to catch failure
    eval {
        $this->{dbh}= DBI->connect_cached('DBI:mysql:userdb;host=
localhost',
                                     'webuser',
                                     'webuser');
    };
    if ($@) {
        die "Unable to connect to database! $@\n";
    }
    # set RaiseError once successfully connected
    $this->{dbh}->{RaiseError}= 1;
}
```

Data Retrieval Methods

Next, the method getUser() obtains all the user attributes for a given username in a single query and returns a hash reference with these attributes. This might not seem to be the most object-oriented way of doing things, but it is extremely convenient. The $user can always be turned into an object easily enough — it helps you sleep at night. As you can see, the query below in getUser() uses a join to four tables to obtain canonical names of a state, region, and account level, since the *state_id*, *region_id*, and *account_level* columns are foreign key ids and would not necessarily be attributes you would use when displaying user information. This would probably be the first candidate for caching — anything that would reduce the need to perform this five-table join.

```
sub getUser {
    my ($this, $username)= @_;
    my $query= <<EOQ;

SELECT uid, username, email, firstname, surname, address, city_id,
password,
    cities.city_name as city_name,
    states.state_id AS state_id,
    states.state_name AS state_name,
    regions.region_id AS region_id,
    regions.region_name AS region_name,
    account_levels.account_level AS account_level,
    account_levels.account_level_name AS account_level_name
FROM users
JOIN cities USING (city_id)
JOIN states ON (cities.state_id = states.state_id)
JOIN regions ON (cities.region_id = regions.region_id)
JOIN account_levels USING (account_level)
WHERE username = ?
EOQ

    my $sth= $this->{dbh}->prepare($query);
    $sth->execute($username);
    my $user_ref= $sth->fetchrow_hashref();
    return $user_ref;
}
```

Also, there are generic methods for obtaining other data types, such as for *cities* and *states*. These can return a single record or all records, depending on arguments. All columns that could be requested are selected. Each one of these methods would greatly benefit from caching, especially since they retrieve data that doesn't change often.

```
# method to obtains one or more cities, depending on $cols reference
# which will result in a specific WHERE clause being set
sub getStatesFromDB {
    my ($this, $cols)= @_;
    my $states;

    my @bind_vals;

    # define the base query
    my $query=
```

```
        'SELECT state_id, state_abbr, state_name, state_bird, state_flower
        FROM states';

    # build a where clause using the hashref $cols
    $this->_makeWhereClause($cols,\$query,\@bind_vals);

    my $sth= $this->{dbh}->prepare($query);

    $sth->execute(@bind_vals);
    $states= $sth->fetchall_arrayref({});

    return $states;

}


# method to obtains one or more cities, depending on $cols reference
# which will result in a specific WHERE clause being set
sub getCities {
    my ($this, $cols)= @_;
    my $cities;

    my @bind_vals;

    # define the base query
    my $query=
        'SELECT city_id, city_name, cities.state_id as state_id,
        state_abbr, state_name, cities.region_id, region_name, population
            FROM cities
            JOIN regions USING (region_id)
            JOIN states USING (state_id) ';

    # build a where clause based off of hashref $cols
    $this->_makeWhereClause($cols, \$query, \@bind_vals);

    my $sth= $this->{dbh}->prepare($query);

    $sth->execute(@bind_vals);
    $cities= $sth->fetchall_arrayref({});

    return $cities;

}
```

Notice the handy private method _makeWhereClause(). This is an attempt to reduce redundancy in the code. While writing the code examples, the author noticed he was writing the same code over again, which is a blinking light notifying one of the need for cut-and-paste into a convenient, reusable method. This method, _makeWhereClause(), takes three arguments:

❑ $cols: A hash reference containing the column names as keys, the values of which are the actual values to use for the query being built.

❑ $query: A scalar reference to the string containing the full query that will inevitably be run. This string will be built (appended to) by the method _makeWhereClause()

❑ $bind_vals: An array reference where each value being plucked from $cols is pushed into for later use when the query is run.

You may be looking at this and thinking, "Well, it could be abstracted further." Yes, it can and will be in a later chapter. For now, it's as it is for the sake of discussion. _makeWhereClause builds a query, appending column names and placeholders according to what keys representing columns are in $cols, and pushing each value into the array reference $bind_values. This makes it so each method performing a query doesn't have to recode this dynamic query building.

Notice the overall picture is one of clean, short methods. This is a good practice to try to follow!

```perl
sub _makeWhereClause {
  my ($this, $cols, $query, $bind_vals)= @_;
  return unless keys %$cols;
  my $where;

# if column parameters were specified, build a where clause
 my $where = join( ' AND ', map { "$_ = ?" } keys %$cols );
 push @$bind_vals, values %$cols;

  # if a where clause was built, add to main query
  $where= " WHERE $where";
  # chop of trailing AND (including spaces)
  $where= substr($where, 0, -5);
  $$query .= $where;
  return;
}
```

For further abstraction, you could create simple one-record return methods to use the generic database methods explained above to obtain a single state or city. These can be as convenient as you want. getState() even lets you specify a state name or abbreviation for the lookup.

These methods are not where caching would be implemented, if caching is already implemented at a lower level.

```perl
# uses getCities, specifying a single city-state abbrev.
sub getCity {
  my ($this, $city_name, $state)= @_;
  return undef unless defined $city_name and defined $state;

  # need to specify the correct column name based off of what it sees
  my $state_key= length($state == 2) ? 'state_abbr' : 'state_name';
  my $city_ref= $this->getCities({
      city_name  => $city_name,
      $state_key => $state});

  # return single record
  return $city_ref->[0];
}

sub getState {
  my ($this, $name)= @_;
  return undef unless $name;
  # this allows you to use either a state name or abbreviation
  my $col= length($name) == 2 ? 'state_abbr' : 'state_name';
  my $state_ref= $this->getStatesFromDB({ $col => $name });
```

```
    # return single record
    return $state_ref->[0];
}
```

Simple Accessor Methods

The head bone is connected to the ... neck bone is connected to the ... shoulder bone. Even more abstract are accessor methods that use the above single-entity accessor methods. These accessor methods return various attributes of other data objects such as *states* and *cities*. These use the single-record accessor methods above, which select all columns that could be requested. You might think, "Why not select only the columns you need?" These could be implemented that way, but for this type of data, there's no real overhead for selecting all columns, and doing it this way reduces the number of methods that have to query the database in your library code. You could also use dynamic method loading, as shown in Chapter 3.

None of these methods really needs caching, if the caching is implemented at a lower level.

```
sub getStateID {
    my ($this, $name)= @_;
    my $state_ref= $this->getState($name);
    return $state_ref->{state_id};
}
sub getStateBird {
    my ($this, $name)= @_;
    my $state_ref= $this->getState($name);
    return $state_ref->{state_bird};
}
sub getStateFlower {
    my ($this, $name)= @_;
    my $state_ref= $this->getState($name);
    return $state_ref->{state_flower};
}
sub getCityID {
    my ($this, $city, $state)= @_;
    my $city_ref= $this->getCity($city, $state);
    return $city_ref->{city_id};
}
sub getCityRegion {
    my ($this, $city, $state)= @_;
    my $city_ref= $this->getCity($city, $state);
    return $city_ref->{region_name};
}
sub getCityPopulation {
    my ($this, $city, $state_abbr)= @_;

    my $city_ref= $this->getCity($city, $state_abbr);
    return ($city_ref->{population});
}

sub getStateBird {
    my ($this, $name)= @_;
    my $state_ref= $this->getState($name);
```

```
        return $state_ref->{state_bird};
    }
sub getStateFlower {
    my ($this, $name)= @_;
    my $state_ref= $this->getState($name);
    return $state_ref->{state_flower};
    }
```

Data Modification Methods

It's great to be able to access (read) data, but you also need to write data, too. This includes inserts, updates and deletion. For insert (creation) and updates, there is a setUser() method.

```
sub setUser {
  my ($this, $user_ref)= @_;

  unless (defined $user_ref->{username}) {
    warn "ERROR: No username specified!\n";
    return;
  }

 $user_ref->{account_level} = 0 unless defined $user_ref
->{account_level};


  my $user= $this->getUser($user_ref->{username});

  if ($user->{password} && length($user->{password})) {
    $user->{password}= MD5_hex($user->{password});
  }

  # the user exists, so update
  if ($user && $user->{uid}) {
    warn "user $user->{username} exists (uid $user->{uid}), updating.\n";
    $user_ref->{uid}= $user->{uid};
    unless ($this->updateUser($user_ref)) {
      return 0;
    }
  }
  else {
    # otherwise, create the new user
    $user_ref->{uid}= $this->createUser($user_ref);
  }
  return $user_ref->{uid};
}
```

So, setting can mean either create or update. setUser() uses getUser() to determine if the user exists, and if the user exists, calls update. If the user does not exist, it creates a new user and returns the user id of the newly created user.

The method createUser() calls the actual SQL INSERT statement. It performs the insert of the user and returns the uid value from the newly inserted row. Its job is to nail down all the values for a user prior to the insert, such as any foreign keys that must have valid values for the insert to succeed.

```perl
sub createUser {
  my ($this, $user_ref)= @_;
  my @bind_cols;
  my $insert= 'INSERT INTO users ';

  for my $field (keys %$user_required) {
    unless (defined $user_ref->{$field}) {
      warn "ERROR: you are missing the required field $field\n";
      return 0;
    }
  }

  unless ($this->setUserGeoParams($user_ref)) {
    warn "ERROR: unable to set state and city ids\n";
    return 0;
  }

  $this->_makeInsertStatement($user_ref, \$insert, \@bind_cols);
  my $sth= $this->{dbh}->prepare($insert);
  if ($sth->execute(@bind_cols)) {
    # returns UID for new user
    return $this->{dbh}->last_insert_id('', $database, 'users', 'uid');
  }
  # failed to insert
  return 0;
}
```

Since a user has parameters that are foreign keys to other tables — city_id, state_id — these foreign key ids will have to be obtained from the canonical state_name and city_name values of the yet-to-be-inserted user. To do this, there is a convenient method, setUserGeoParams(), which obtains both the city_id and state_id. These values have to be valid for the insert to succeed due to foreign key restraints. This, of course, requires a query of the *states* and *cities* tables to obtain these ids. This certainly would be another place where caching could prevent database accessing.

```perl
sub setUserGeoParams {
  my ($this, $user_ref)= @_;
  # these are all foreign keys that have to be set prior to insert
  $user_ref->{state_id} ||= $this->getStateID($user_ref->{state_name});
  unless ($user_ref->{state_id}) {
    warn "ERROR: unable to obtain state_id for $user_ref->{state_name}\n";
    return 0;
  }
  $user_ref->{city_id}||= $this->getCityID(
                                    $user_ref->{city_name},
                                    $user_ref->{state_name});
  # Unless there was a city_id
  unless ($user_ref->{city_id}) {
    warn "ERROR: unable to obtain city_id for $user_ref->{city_name}\n";
    return 0;
  }

  # we will not insert these columns
  delete $user_ref->{state_name};
```

```
        delete $user_ref->{city_name};
        return;
    }
```

To build the insert statement, use the method _makeInsertStatement(), which is basically the same concept as _buildWhereclause():

```perl
    sub _makeInsertStatement {
        my ($this, $user_ref, $insert, $bind_cols)= @_;
        my ($cols, $placeholders);

        for (keys %$user_ref) {
            $cols.= $_ . ',';
            $placeholders.= '?, ';
            push(@$bind_cols, $user_ref->{$_});
        }

        # remove trailing comma from each
        chop($cols);
        $placeholders= substr($placeholders, 0, -2);

        $$insert= "$$insert ($cols) VALUES ($placeholders)";
        return;
    }
```

_makeInsertStatement() uses the $user_ref hash reference to build both a list of the appropriate number of placeholders and columns from the keys of $user_ref. It also pushes into the $bind_cols array reference the values of $user_ref.

updateUser() updates an existing user:

```perl
    sub updateUser {
        my ($this, $user_ref)= @_;
        my $update= 'UPDATE users SET ';
        my @bind_cols;
        unless ($user_ref->{uid} || $user_ref->{username}) {
            warn "ERROR: you must have either a UID or username specified!\n";
            return 0;
        }
        unless ($this->setUserGeoParams($user_ref)) {
            warn "ERROR: unable to set state and city ids\n";
            return 0;
        }

        $this->_makeUpdateStatement($user_ref, \$update, \@bind_cols);
        my $sth= $this->{dbh}->prepare($update);
        return ($sth->execute(@bind_cols));
    }
```

_makeUpdateStatement works just like _makeInsertStatement, but is used for updates:

```perl
    sub _makeUpdateStatement {
        my ($this, $user_ref, $update, $bind_cols)= @_;
```

```
    for (keys %$user_ref) {
      # we don't want to update UID or username
      next if ($_ eq 'uid' || $_ eq 'username');
      $$update .= "$_ = ?, ";
      push(@$bind_cols, $user_ref->{$_});
    }
    # remove trailing comma and space
    $$update= substr($$update, 0, -2);

    my $pk= $user_ref->{uid} ? 'uid' : 'username';
    $$update .= " WHERE $pk = ?";
    push(@$bind_cols, $user_ref->{$pk});

  }
```

Finally, there is a method to delete a user:

```
sub deleteUser {
  my ($this, $user_ref)= @_;
  my $col= $user_ref->{uid} ? 'uid' : 'username';
  my @bind_vals;
  push (@bind_vals, $user_ref->{$col});

  # don't bother if the user doesn't even exist
  $this->getUser($user_ref->{$col}) or return;

  return($this->{dbh}->do("DELETE FROM users WHERE $col = ?", {}, @bind_vals));

}
```

deleteUser() allows the use of either uid or username as the unique identifier to obtain a user. You could abstract this even further by having a deleteUserByUsername(), which would take only a username. How much abstraction you use is up to you.

So, for writes, there are several places that caching could provide a means to reduce database accesses:

❑ Checking if the user exists to determine whether the user needs to be created, updated, or deleted.

❑ Obtaining both state and city foreign key values based off canonical values.

Using UserApp

To use this library, instantiate it and then simply use it.

```
use strict;
use warnings;
use Data::Dumper;
use UserApp;

my $uapp;
```

```
# instantiate the UserApp object
$uapp= new UserApp;

# obtain user reference
my $user= $uapp->getUser('capttofu');
print Dumper $user;
print "$user->{username}'s state is $user->{state_name}\n";
print "State flower for $user->{state_name} is " .
        $uapp->getStateFlower($user->{state_name}) . "\n";

print "Seattle's region is " . $uapp->getCityRegion('Seattle', 'WA') . "\n";

print "Tampa's region is " . $uapp->getCityRegion('Tampa', 'FL') . "\n";

print "Portland Oregon's region is " .
        $uapp->getCityRegion('Portland', 'OR') . "\n";

print "Portland Maine's region is " .
        $uapp->getCityRegion('Portland', 'ME') . "\n";

print "Wasilla Alaska's region is " .
        $uapp->getCityRegion('Wasilla', 'AK') . "\n";

print "Arizona state bird is: " . $uapp->getStateBird('AZ') . "\n";

print "Bakersfield, CA, population is: " .
        $uapp->getCityPopulation('Bakersfield', 'CA') . "\n";

print "Burlington, VT, population is: " .
        $uapp->getCityPopulation('Burlington', 'VT') . "\n";
```

The output shows:

```
$VAR1 = {
            'firstname' => 'Patrick',
            'city_id' => '47',
            'uid' => '1',
            'account_level_name' => 'Free',
            'state_id' => '30',
            'state_name' => 'New Hampshire',
            'region_name' => 'New England',
            'username' => 'capttofu',
            'surname' => 'Galbraith',
            'email' => 'capttofu@capttofu.org',
            'password' => '65a8f5ebd748ae11',
            'region_id' => '15',
            'account_level' => '0',
            'address' => '100 Main St.',
            'city_name' => 'Peterborough'
        };
capttofu's state is New Hampshire
State flower for New Hampshire is Purple lilac
Seattle's region is Pacific Northwest
Tampa's region is Gulf Coast
```

```
Portland Oregon's region is Pacific Northwest
Portland Maine's region is New England
Wasilla Alaska's region is Alaska
Arizona state bird is: Cactus Wren
Bakersfield, CA, population is: 315000
Burlington, VT, population is: 38889
```

Here is an example of creating, updating, and deleting a user:

```
# instantiate the UserApp object
    $uapp = new UserApp;

    my $new_user= {
       'username'   => 'jimbob',
       'firstname' => 'Jim',
       'surname'    => 'Bob',
       'email'      => 'jimbob@foo.com',
       'password'   => 'bleh',
       'account_level' => 0,
       'address'          => '',
       'city_name'      => 'Tampa',
       'state_name'     => 'Florida'
    };

    my $uid= $uapp->setUser($new_user);
    # UID of newly created user
    print "UID $uid\n";

    # set a different email address
    $new_user->{email}= 'james_robert@newsite.com';

    # this should update the user
    $uid= $uapp->setUser($new_user);

    # now delete the user
    $uapp->deleteUser({ username => 'jimbob'});
```

As you can see, all of these methods have to perform queries on one or more tables to obtain data, regardless of whether they are read-only methods or write methods. A lot of the data that is being accessed is data that doesn't change often, and is thus a prime candidate for caching.

Memcached Connector Method

To have any caching, the first thing required is a connection to memcached. Just as with the database, there can be a class attribute for this connection to memcached that will allow the connection to be used throughout the program. Just as with the database, a memcached connection method will be called upon instantiation. This will be similar to connectDB, except in how a memcached object is instantiated compared to connecting via DBD::mysql.

```
sub connectMemcached {
    my ($this)= @_;
    $this->{memc} = new Cache::Memcached({
        'servers'                 => [ "127.0.0.1:11211"],
        'compress_threshold' => 10_000});
```

```
    unless ($this->{memc}->set('testping', 1)) {
        die "Unable to connect to memcached!\n";
    }
    return;
}
```

With DBD::mysql, the connect is wrapped within an eval, and if it fails $@ contains an error. This method of failure trapping doesn't work with Cache::Memcached, so a good way of testing if a connection was made is to set something immediately after connecting, as shown with set(). You might think, "Why not use stats()?" The author of this book also thought of trying that, but instead of getting a nice true/false, even when wrapped in an eval, it just spews errors.

Caching Implementation Plan

The main idea to adding caching to the subroutines previously presented is to access the cache when obtaining data to avoid accessing the database. This requires:

❑ Checking first to see if the data exists in the cache, and if not, obtaining the data from the database and then writing that data to the cache (read-through caching), so that all subsequent calls will be able to obtain the data from the cache, and then finally returning the data to the calling subroutine.

❑ Listing all the places where caching could be implemented. Any data that seldom changes should simply be available. In this *case, states, cities,* and *regions* would fit into this category. This would automatically eliminate database accesses to these tables upon saving user data where the foreign key values have to be obtained. All the various methods such as getStatesFromDB(), getState(), getStatexx(), getCities(), getCity(), and getCityxxx().

❑ Pre-caching data in the cache. This pre-caching would occur when the program is first executed. In the case of a mod_perl application, this would mean when the web server is first started (more on this will be covered in later chapters).

❑ getUser(): Even though user data changes often, it still can be cached. The key is to make sure if any writes occur that they also are written to the cache to help avoid the thundering herd problem. This caching will eliminate the multi-table JOIN to obtain user data.

❑ setUser(): Since users do change often, setUser() would also have to ensure it writes to the cache when a user is created or updated. setUser() itself would also be able to use caching when it calls getUser() to determine if a user exists or not, as well as geographical data that can be precached.

❑ setUserGeoParams() can now obtain user geographical data from the various "get" methods that formerly required database queries.

Where to Add Caching?

The next question is how you want to store the data in the cache — what identifier you will use for the value of the lookup key to associate with the data you store in memcached, which you will also use when fetching that data from the memcached. You would want to use a unique identifier that makes for easy lookup of the data you need.

❑ *users:* The username column makes a good key for the user data since it's unique in the database as well as what is used in the SQL query to obtain the data from the database. This would be a *nondeterministic* cache because it can't necessarily depend on the user data being in the cache, and so it obtains the data from the database if not in memcached and then re-populates the data in memcached.

❑ *states*: The state abbreviation, `state_abbr` column, is an appropriate key since it's unique and is what the application uses in the SQL query to look up the state to obtain state data from the database. Since there aren't a huge number of states, you store two state objects, one using state name, and the other using state abbreviation. This would be a *deterministic* cache in that the application could assume that the data is in memcached and the cache is kept up to date periodically with a process such as a perl cron job.

❑ *cities*: As anyone from New England knows, every New England state has a Concord, Amherst, Groton, etc., so the city name alone is not a unique identifier! However, the city's name in combination with either a state name or state abbreviation will ensure uniqueness. This also could be a *deterministic* cache, because city data doesn't change.

❑ *regions*: The *regions* table is a simple lookup table while the `region_id` is the only column used to look up a region when joining with the table *cities*. It's never accessed by itself, so there's no need to cache regions. When caching a user as well as cities, the region name will be one of the city attributes that will be cached.

❑ *account_levels*: This, too, is a lookup table, and will only be used when caching other objects, so there is no need to precache or go to a lot of trouble to cache. This would be a *deterministic* cache.

Caching Key Scheme

In addition to the unique identifiers discussed above, you can also use a namespace to prefix the key for the type of object it is. For instance, if what you are caching is a user, you would most likely use the name of the table *users* as a namespace. Examples of this key scheme are:

❑ Caching of users: If user's username is *capttofu*, the full key value that you would use as a key would be `users:capttofu`. Also, since you may want to look up a user using the user id (UID), you can also use the key value `users:1` (if the `uid` were 1).

❑ Caching of cities: If the city being cached was Concord in the state of New Hampshire, the key value would be `cities:Concord-NH`.

❑ Caching of states: If the state being cached was California, you could use two key values such as `states:CA` and `states:California`.

With a plan in place for how caching will work (including what to store, when to store, and how to store), the caching code can be added to the different methods.

Precaching

The first area to look at for implementing caching will be the geographical data. To precache data that doesn't change (as already mentioned, states, cities, regions), you would implement a method that fetches every city and then caches each with two types of namespaces, `cities:<city_name>-<state abbreviation>` and `cities:<city_name>-<state name>`.

Precaching Cities

The method `cacheCities()` will utilize `getCities()` to obtain all the city data and then cache each entry with two different hashing keys in order to look up city data by city name along with either state name or state abbreviation.

```
sub cacheCities {
  my $this= $_[0];

  # a simple true/false to indicate that cities have been cached
  if ($this->{memc}->get('cities_cached')) {
    return;
  }
  my $cities= $this->getCities();
  for (@$cities) {
    my $state_name_safe= $_->{state_name};
    $state_name_safe =~ s/\s/_/g;
    my $city_name_safe= $_->{city_name};
    $city_name_safe =~ s/\s/_/g;
    # example - cities:San_Francisco-CA
    my $key1= 'cities:' . $city_name_safe . '-' . $_->{state_abbr};
    # example - cities:Santa_Fe-New_Mexico
    my $key2= 'cities:' . $city_name_safe . '-' . $state_name_safe;
    $this->{memc}->set($key1, $_);
    $this->{memc}->set($key2, $_);
  }

# indicate that cities have been cached
  unless ($this->{memc}->set('cities_cached', 1)) {
    warn "ERROR: setting 'cities_cached'\n";
  }
}
```

Please note several things about `cacheCities()`:

❑ The code will not cache the entire result set of `getCities()`. It's better to convert the result set into individual records so that what will be fetched from memcached won't be large.

❑ A simple cached object called `cites_cached` is used to set a true/false value indicating the cities have already been cached. This prevents having to recache all the cities if they have already been cached. Why access the database any more than you have to?

❑ The key cannot contain spaces. This is the reason for `$city_name_safe` and `$state_name_safe`.

Precaching States

`cacheStates()` will perform the same precaching as `cacheCities`, and the same concepts as `cacheCities()` are used.

```
sub cacheStates {
  my ($this)= @_;
```

```
# a simple true/false to indicate that cities have been cached
if ($this->{memc}->get('states_cached')) {
  return;
}
my $states= $this->getStatesFromDB();
for (@$states) {
  my $state_name_safe= $_->{state_name};
  $state_name_safe =~ s/\s/_/g;
  # example - states:NH
  my $key1= 'states:' . $_->{state_abbr};
  # example - states:New_Hampshire
  my $key2= 'states:' . $state_name_safe;
  unless ($this->{memc}->set($key1, $_)) {
    warn "ERROR: unable to set $key1";
  }
  unless ($this->{memc}->set($key2, $_)) {
    warn "ERROR: unable to set $key2"
  };
}

# indicate that cities have been cached
unless ($this->{memc}->set('states_cached', 1)) {
  warn "ERROR: unable to set 'states_cached'\n";
}

return;
}
```

Using Instantiation for Precaching Method Calls

Both cacheCities() and cacheStates() can automatically be called from the constructor.

```
sub new {
  my ($class) = @_;
  my $this= {};
  bless $this, $class;
  $this->connectDB();
  $this->connectMemcached();

  # cache all cities records
  $this->cacheCities();

 # cache all cities records
  $this->cacheStates();

  return $this;
}
```

Modifying Accessor Methods to Use Cache

Next, getCity() and getState() need to be modified to utilize the precached data. Why not getCities() and getStatesFromDB(), since those are where the database is accessed? Because city and state data was cached per-record, and getStatesFromDB() and getCities() can return one or more cities. It would be possible to code it so you could obtain multiple records from memcached, but in this application, having multiple records returned for cities and states is seldom required, except in the initial caching with cacheCities() and cacheStates() of cities and states, which was part of the reason for having a getCities() and getStatesFromDB()!

getCity()

In getCity(), $city_ref is scoped at the beginning of the program, as opposed to when it's retrieved from the database, because it could be retrieved from memcached first. A lookup key, $memc_key is first constructed, of course without allowing any spaces in the key. The key is the same as how each city was stored. The method get() looks up the object, and if found and actually set, $city_ref is simply returned and the database is never touched.

```
sub getCity {
    my ($this, $city_name, $state)= @_;
    my $city_ref;
    return undef unless $city_name && $state;

    # check memcached first
    my $memc_key = "$city_name-$state";

    # no spaces allowed
    $memc_key =~ s/ /_/g;
    $memc_key= "cities:$memc_key";
    $city_ref= $this->{memc}->get($memc_key);
    return $city_ref if $city_ref->{city_name};

    # need to specify the correct column name based off of what it sees
    my $state_key= length($state == 2) ? 'state_abbr' : 'state_name';
    $city_ref= $this->getCities({
        city_name    => $city_name,
        $state_key => $state});

# return single record
    return $city_ref->[0];
}
```

getState()

The same type of changes are made to getState()

```
sub getState {
    my ($this, $name)= @_;
    my $state_ref;
    return undef unless $name;

    # check memcached for state
    my $memc_key = $name;
    $memc_key =~ s/ /_/g;
    $memc_key= "states:$memc_key";
    $state_ref= $this->{memc}->get($memc_key);
    return $state_ref if $state_ref->{city_name};

    # this allows you to use either a state name or abbreviation
```

```
    my $col= length($name) == 2 ? 'state_abbr' : 'state_name';
    $state_ref= $this->getStatesFromDB({ $col => $name });

    # return single record
    return $state_ref->[0];
  }
```

No Change Needed for Accessor Methods

Now both getCity() and getState() check memcached for the requested object first before accessing the database. This also means that any other method that requires state information for a city or state now has the added benefit of caching:

❑ All the getStatexxx() and getCityxxx() accessor methods. Because these applications all use getState() and getCity(), they also get the benefit of caching. This means one less database operation any time these are called.

❑ setUserGeoParams(), which also uses getStateID() and getCityID(). Therefore, there are two fewer database operations in writing a user.

User Data Caching — Set Method Modifications

To implement user caching, the first place to add the caching is to setUser(). Of course, setUser() calls getUser() to determine if a user exists in the first place, so getUser() could have caching implemented first as well, but it makes no sense to check memcached for data that doesn't yet have a method implemented that stores the data in it in the first place!

Any time a user is written, the simplest thing to do would be to write it to the cache, regardless of whether it's a user creation or update. It can be assumed the setUser() is called for a good reason, that the user is changed or created one way or another. This also ensures the cached user object reference is always up to date. Also note that this is not write-through caching, which would only write to memcached and activate some process that would read from memcached to the database.

The Cache::Memcached method set(), as you will recall, will either update or create a memcached entry. You could alternatively call add() or replace(), depending on whether there is a create or update, but why not just use the simplicity of set()? For this example, set() will be used.

For the memcached key, this example will use both users:<username> and users:<user id> since you may want to look up the user based off of the user's username or UID, as is allowed in the database lookup code.

```
sub setUser {
  my ($this, $user_ref)= @_;
  my ($memc_key1, $memc_key2);

  unless ($user_ref->{username}) {
    print "ERROR: No username specified!\n";
    return;
  }
  $user_ref->{account_level}||= 0;

  my $user= $this->getUser($user_ref->{username});
```

```
  if ($user->{password} && length($user->{password})) {
    $user->{password}= MD5_hex($user->{password});
  }

  if ($user && $user->{uid}) {
    $user_ref->{uid}= $user->{uid};
    unless ($this->updateUser($user_ref)) {
      return 0;
    }
  }
  else {
    $user_ref->{uid}= $this->createUser($user_ref);
  }

  # cache the user both using uid and username
  $this->{memc}->set("users:$user_ref->{ $_ }", $user_ref )
    for qw( uid username );


  return $user_ref->{uid};
}
```

User Data Caching — Get Method Modifications

Now that setUser() has the code needed to cache a user, the next part of user caching would be to add caching functionality to getUser().

```
sub getUser {
  my ($this, $username)= @_;
  my $memc_key= 'users:' . $username;
  my $user_ref;

  # check memcached first
  $user_ref= $this->{memc}->get($memc_key);

  # simply return from memcached if already cached
  return $user_ref if $user_ref->{username};

  # obtain from db if not in memcached
  my $query= <<'EOQ';
SELECT uid, username, email, firstname, surname, address, city_id,
password,
  cities.city_name as city_name,
  states.state_id AS state_id,
  states.state_name AS state_name,
  regions.region_id AS region_id,
  regions.region_name AS region_name,
  account_levels.account_level AS account_level,
  account_levels.account_level_name AS account_level_name
FROM users
JOIN cities USING (city_id)
JOIN states ON (cities.state_id = states.state_id)
JOIN regions ON (cities.region_id = regions.region_id)
```

```
JOIN account_levels USING (account_level)
WHERE username = ?
EOQ

  my $sth= $this->{dbh}->prepare($query);
  $sth->execute($username);
  $user_ref= $sth->fetchrow_hashref();

  # store in memcached (Read-through caching!)
  return unless $user_ref;
  unless ($this->{memc}->set($user_key, $user_ref)) {
    warn "ERROR: unable to set user!\n";
  }

  # return user reference
  return $user_ref;
}
```

The changes made to getUser() shown in the code eliminate the need to always obtain the user from the database using the multi-table JOIN for every access. With the added caching, the code now first checks to see if it exists in memcached. If it does, the code simply returns it. If it doesn't, the code obtains the user from the database using the multi-table JOIN only one time, and then stores it in memcached for subsequent retrievals. It then returns the data that was just retrieved. This is a good example of read-through caching.

UserApp Now Has Caching!

Caching has been added to the UserApp class! The various benefits of not having to access the database for every data request are as follows:

❑   In obtaining a user (hash reference. This also means not having to perform a multi-table JOIN.

In writing a user: accessing *states* and *cities* tables for the foreign key values of these tables.

❑   In obtaining geographical information for states and cities.

This application was a very simple example of how memcached can add the benefit of caching to reduce database accesses. You can probably imagine how valuable memcached would be if you had a much more complex application with numerous data access needs that is running a huge, busy site. Using memcached for caching can add up to immense savings in resources, both on the database and the web server running the application.

Other Caching Issues

There are other caching issues that are worth discussing. The next section will help you to understand issues that you will encounter in the course of implementing caching using memcached.

Cache Stampede/Dog-Piling/Thundering Herd

In the previously shown examples, you saw a read-through, or deterministic, cache implemented. An object was requested that, if found in memcached, was returned. Or if it was a cache miss, it was obtained from MySQL and then written to memcached to replace what was initially missing and then returned to the requester. This works well most of the time, particularly if you ensure that what is in cache is updated whenever a write to that object occurs, writing to both MySQL and memcached.

However, there is a problem that can sometimes occur where a large number of requests simultaneously are requesting an item that is no longer in memcached — either it has since expired or is no longer there due to the LRU functionality. In such cases, these requests then go to MySQL, hammering the database all at once to obtain the item that was not in memcached. This is known by several terms, including *cache stampede*, *dog-piling*, and *thundering herd*. For this section, this phenomena will be referred to as *dog-piling*. Whatever it is called, it can be a problem and can cause a significant slowdown in your application.

There are several ways to address the problem of *dog-piling*:

❑ Limit the rate of requests on your web server, and set the wait timeout (`wait_timeout`) low and maximum clients (`max_clients`) on MySQL to a number less than the maximum number of concurrent connections MySQL can handle for your specific hardware.

❑ Use two keys — one for the actual data being stored, and one that is associated with the data being stored that has a value of an expiration time that is used to force that item to be refreshed.

❑ Again, make certain to always write the item to memcached whenever you store the item in MySQL.

❑ Regularly run cron jobs to update particular items.

❑ Use cache distribution, storing the item on multiple servers to ensure that the data has a higher chance of being found in the cache.

There is no right or wrong way, or one solution that fits all for dealing with this issue. It all depends on the type of data you have, how you are caching it, the traffic of your site, the capacity of your database, and how you have your architecture scaled.

Example of a Stale Key Used to Avoid Dog-Pile Effect

The following is an example of a cache fetching method you would use to fetch your data and help reduce the chance for the dog-piling issue. This example is a Perl adaptation of the one by Alexy Kovrin written in Ruby at `http://blog.kovyrin.net/2008/03/10/dog-pile-effect-and-how-to-avoid-it-with -ruby-on-rails-memcache-client-patch/`.

The idea of this method is to use both a *main* key to reference the actual stored data that expires at a later time than normal, and a *stale* key that will expire earlier. When a value is read from memcached, the stale key value is also read. If the stale key has expired, the expiration time is recalculated and the stale key is restored with that new value.

This method takes as one of its arguments a reference to the method or subroutine that obtains the data from the database as well as the arguments that this method requires, which are different from what the cache fetch method requires.

Variables this new method requires are:

```
my $STALE_REFRESH = 1;
my $STALE_CREATED = 2;
```

```
my $EXPIRY = 300;
my $GENERATION_TIME = 30;
```

The method for implementation is this:

```
sub memcGet {
  my ($this,
      $key,
      $db_get_method, $db_method_args,
      $expiry,
      $generation_time)= @_;

  $expiry = $EXPIRY unless defined $expiry;
  $generation_time = $GENERATION_TIME unless defined $GENERATION_TIME;

  # simply return if not using an expiration
  return $this->{memc}->get($key) unless $expiry;

  # create window for data refresh
  my $full_expiry = $expiry + $generation_time * 2;

  # set the stale key
  my $stale_key = "$key:stale";
  my $value = $this->{memc}->get($key);
  my $stale_value = $this->{memc}->get($stale_key);

  # if not defined, create and set
  unless( defined $stale_value)  {
    $this->{memc}->set($stale_key, $STALE_REFRESH, $generation_time) ;
    print "SETTING stale_value\n";
    $value= undef;
  }

  # if no value, then obtain using the db access method that was
  # passed
  unless (defined $value) {
    $value= $db_get_method->($this, $db_method_args);
# then set both keys
    $this->{memc}->set($key, $value, $full_expiry);
    $this->{memc}->get($stale_key, $STALE_CREATED, $expiry);
  }
  # return the value
  return $value;
}
```

To use this in the previous examples, you would have to recode wherever you set values in memcached from within various "get" methods to let this method handle obtaining and setting from the database the value being requested. In the example that follows, getUser() is modified into a more generic method that now uses two other methods: the new getMemc() method, and the actual code that retrieved the user from the database is moved to getUserFromDB().

```
sub getUserFromDB {
  my ($this, $username)= @_;
```

```
    # obtain from db if not in memcached
    my $query= <<EOQ
SELECT uid, username, email, firstname, surname, address, city_id,
password,
    cities.city_name as city_name,
    states.state_id AS state_id,
    states.state_name AS state_name,
    regions.region_id AS region_id,
    regions.region_name AS region_name,
    account_levels.account_level AS account_level,
    account_levels.account_level_name AS account_level_name
FROM users
JOIN cities USING (city_id)
JOIN states ON (cities.state_id = states.state_id)
JOIN regions ON (cities.region_id = regions.region_id)
JOIN account_levels USING (account_level)
WHERE username = ?
EOQ
;

    my $sth= $this->{dbh}->prepare($query);
    $sth->execute($username);
    my $user_ref= $sth->fetchrow_hashref();

    return unless $user_ref;

    # return user reference
    return ($user_ref);
}
```

The `getUserFromDB()` is the method that is passed by reference to `getMemc()`:

```
sub getUser {
    my ($this, $username)= @_;
    my $memc_key1= 'users:' . $username;
    my $user_ref;

    # check memcached first
    $user_ref= $this->memcGet($memc_key1, \&getUserFromDB,
$username, 300, 30);
    return;

}
```

You can use a method such as `getMemc()`, along with the other ideas mentioned above, to reduce the problem of dog-piling, or you can come up with your own ideas. Again, there is no correct way to deal with issues like this.

Replicating Data to Multiple Caches

Another issue in caching data involves losing a particular memcached server, and this can mean losing a significant part of your cached data on which your application relies. One way to get around this is to replicate your data to multiple memcached servers upon storing an item.

To do this, you can employ a simple array or hash reference that contains connections to each memcached server. Whenever you store an item, you loop through the servers, storing the item in each. For retrieval, you can just use a single memcached connection that is connected to all servers. You will get the data one way or another because they all have the item stored. The example that follows shows how this can be done.

First, five servers are connected to individually, each connection stored as a member in a hash reference of connections. Also, a single connection is created that specifies all memcached servers and is used for fetching data:

```perl
use Cache::Memcached;

my $con_href;

my $servers= [
    '127.0.0.1:11221',
    '127.0.0.1:11222',
    '127.0.0.1:11223',
    '127.0.0.1:11224',
    '127.0.0.1:11225' ];

for my $server (@$servers) {
  $con_href->{$server} = new Cache::Memcached({
                    servers            => [ $server ],
                    compress_threshold => 10_000 });
}
my $main_con= new Cache::Memcached({
                    servers            => $servers,
                    compress_threshold => 10_000});


my $value = "Test value";
my $key = "test:key1";

my $rc = multi_set($key, $value);

my $retval = $main_con->get($key);

print "retval: $retval\n";
```

Instead of using the regular "get" method, the subroutine `multi_set()` is used for storing data on all servers specified in `con_href`. This stores the item on all servers.

```perl
sub multi_set {
  my ($key, $value) = @_;
  my $all_set= 0;
  for my $server (@$servers) {
    my $rc = $con_href->{$server}->set($key, $value);
    unless ($rc) {
      print "ERROR: unable to set $key in server $server\n";
      $all_set--;
    }
    $all_set++;
```

```
        }
    return ($all_set == scalar @$servers);
}
```

Of course, there are other ways of implementing this. Numerous articles and information are available online.

Summary

Memcached is a high-performance, distributed memory object caching system that will give you the ability to cache data that you would otherwise have to obtain from the database. This can benefit your application in many ways, such as relieving the load on the database, reducing application calls to the database, and providing faster data access because obtaining data from memcached is extremely fast — faster than obtaining it from the database. This chapter showed you everything you would want to know about using memcached, including the following:

❑ Basic concept of memcached: How memcached is a simple memory server that allocates a block of memory for storing data that is accessible with key values. Also, the chapter covered how memcached can run on multiple servers so you can utilize less-powerful machines (than database or web server machines) that have ample memory and have all machines work collectively as a cluster.

❑ Read-through and write-through caches: A read-through cache is where there is a cache miss (the data being requested is not in the cache). The data that is obtained from the database for the read request is then written to the cache prior to returning to the requester. A write-through cache is written to. A separate process obtains data that is cached in memcached and stores it to the databases.

❑ The Perl client library for memcached: Cache::Memcached.

❑ A step-by-step demonstration for modifying a simple database user application to have caching functionality using memcached with the Perl module Cache::Memcached. This demonstration showed where the caching should be implemented in the code, how the application should be modified, and how and in what way the added caching benefited that application in terms of reduced database calls and overall increased efficiency of the application.

❑ How to deal with dog-piling, also known as cache stampede or thundering herd: This is where a requested cached item no longer exists and so a large number of requests then go to the database simultaneously to retrieve the data that was not in memcached.

❑ How to replicate data to multiple memcached servers.

You should now have a good understanding of how to use memcached. You should now be able to create new applications that implement caching using memcached as well as modify existing applications to use memcached.

libmemcached

The Perl module for memcached, Cache::memcached, is a client library for accessing memcached that is written entirely in Perl. This was the first client library for memcached and works just fine for most applications. Though, as any programmer knows, there is always room for more efficiency and speed, and sometimes you just have to implement code in C if you need speed. Brian Aker had a need for such a thing and started a new client library for memcached: libmemcached.

What Is libmemcached?

libmemcached is a memcached client library written in C. It is a faster, more efficient, thread-safe, full-featured C library that has a significant performance gain over existing client libraries. Not only that, you also have much more control to affect how the client functions because you can set the client behavior (memcached_behavior_set()) with numerous behavior settings, such as hashing algorithm or whether the client is blocking or nonblocking, CAS (Check and Set) support, server host sorting, etc.

Perl support for libmemcached comes in two approaches: a lower-level one-to-one C API mapping Memcached::libmemcached and Cache::memcached::libmemcached, which is a drop-in replacement for Cache::memcached. This chapter will explain both of these in greater detail.

Do you want to use libmemcached instead of Cache::memcached? It is much newer than Cache::memcached and some developers or administrators shy from using newly released software, but its performance benefits and added features, which will be shown, provide justification for using it over Cache::memcached for your applications that need to use memcached. Since it is a new client library, there may be kinks to work out, bugs that manifest themselves — as is the case with any project that is new. However, libmemcached is actively being developed and many people are now using it, exposing any issues rapidly. A changelog is always a good thing to examine with any open-source project and the changelog for libmemcached reveals that memcached is an ideal open-source project — it is released early and often, particularly when there are bugs that need to be fixed.

libmemcached Features

Some of the design notes for memcached are:

- ❑ Synchronous and asynchronous support
- ❑ Ability to set with high degree of control how the client behaves
- ❑ Ability to fetch and store data by a master key, which gives the ability to group values or objects to a specific server
- ❑ TCP and Unix Socket protocols
- ❑ Half a dozen or so different hash algorithms
- ❑ Implementations of the new CAS, replace, and append operators
- ❑ Extensive documentation covering in detail the entire API
- ❑ Implements both modulo and consistent hashing solutions, which have to do with how data is partitioned among servers within the cluster

Consistent hashing is a scheme where a hash table is employed for mapping keys to slots for each server. It provides a means of not having to significantly change the mapping of keys to slots when one slot is removed. Rather, it only requires the remapping of K/n keys (with K the number of keys and n the number of slots). Modulo hashing is another scheme where data is partitioned to nodes based on the division of the number of nodes within a network. With modulo hashing, additions or subtractions to nodes in the network result in high miss rates.

Libmemcache Utility Programs

libmemcached also includes several command-line tools (shown in the following table) that allow you to debug your memcached cluster and gauge its performance:

Command	Description
memcat	Copy the value of a key to standard output
memflush	Flush the contents of your servers
memrm	Remove a key(or keys) from the server
memcp	Copy files to a memcached server
memstat	Dump the stats of your servers to standard output
memslap	Generate testing loads on a memcached cluster

Also, of particular interest to readers of this book, libmemcached provides several client interfaces/libraries to other languages such as Ruby, Python, PHP, and Perl.

Installing libmemcached

libmemcached can be installed via the OS vendor's specific install utilities such as yum or apt-get. However, since libmemcached is a new project and changes often, it's preferable to compile libmemcached from source or use the latest RPM from the libmemcached project page if you're using a Linux distribution that uses RPM. The project page for libmemcached is found at: http://tangent.org/552/libmemcached.html

To install RPM:

```
rpm -ihv libmemcached-0.25-1.x86_64.rpm
```

Source install:

```
tar xvzf libmemcached-0.25.tar.gz
./configure
make
sudo make install
```

At this point, libmemcached will be installed. You can write programs that utilize the libmemcached library (including the Perl driver, which will soon be discussed) and use the utility programs.

libmemcached Utility Programs

As mentioned before, libmemcached includes useful utility programs that provide various functionalities for testing your memcached cluster. These utilities are simple to use and all specify a list of servers to use with the --servers option.

memcat

This utility displays the output of one or more cached values in memcached by key value. For instance, two values were stored using the code snippet:

```
my $memc = new Cache::memcached({ servers => ['localhost:11211',
'localhost:22122'],
                              compress_threshold => 10_000});

$memc->set('somekey', "This is a value in memcached");
$memc->set('anotherkey', 123456789);
```

You can view these stored values by using memcat:

```
patg@vidya libmemcached]$ memcat -servers=localhost:22122,localhost:
11211 somekey anotherkey
This is a value in memcached
123456789
```

This is a convenient means to quickly check what you have stored for a certain value, without having to write any code. Now, if you have stored a Perl data structure other than a simple scalar, it will probably not display correctly since it is stored serialized in memcached.

You can also use this to figure out what value is cached on what server:

```
[patg@vidya ~]$ memcat --servers=localhost:11211 somekey anotherkey
123456789
```

```
[patg@vidya ~]$ memcat --servers=localhost:22122 somekey anotherkey
This is a value in memcached
```

As you can see, in both cases, both keys were used and only one value was fetched. In the first case, you can see the value for anotherkey is obtained from the memcached server running on port 11211, whereas in the second case the value for some key is obtained from the memcached server running on port 22122.

memflush

This utility does what the name implies — it cleans house, flushing all servers listed in the argument to -servers. This code shows the usage and result (or lack thereof) after using memflush:

```
[patg@vidya ~]$ memflush --servers=127.0.0.1:22122,127.0.0.1:11211

[patg@vidya ~]$ memcat --servers=localhost:22122,localhost:11211
somekey anotherkey

[patg@vidya ~]$
```

memcp

This is a really nifty utility that allows you to copy a file to memcached. The file will be keyed with the name of the file sans directory path:

```
[patg@vidya ~]$ cat /etc/redhat-release
CentOS release 5.2 (Final)

[patg@vidya ~]$ memcp --servers=localhost:11211 /etc/redhat-release
[patg@vidya ~]$ memcat --servers=localhost:11211 redhat-release
CentOS release 5.2 (Final)
```

memstat

This utility lists the status of one or more memcached servers (just like the Cache::memcached method stats()):

```
[patg@vidya ~]$ memstat --servers=localhost:11211
Listing 1 Server

Server: localhost (11211)
 pid: 3055
 uptime: 1367933
 time: 1229221949
 version: 1.2.6
 pointer_size: 64
 rusage_user: 2.904558
 rusage_system: 2.159671
 curr_items: 3
```

```
total_items: 18
bytes: 323
curr_connections: 2
total_connections: 80
connection_structures: 3
cmd_get: 103
cmd_set: 18
get_hits: 78
get_misses: 25
evictions: 0
bytes_read: 323
bytes_written: 323
limit_maxbytes: 67108864
threads: 1
```

memrm

This utility removes a value from memcached:

```
[patg@vidya ~]$ memrm --servers=localhost:11211 redhat-release

[patg@vidya ~]$ memcat --servers=localhost:11211 redhat-release

[patg@vidya ~]$
```

memslap

This is a load generation simulation and benchmark tool for memcached servers. The options it takes can be displayed with --help:

```
 [patg@vidya ~]$ memslap --help
memslap v1.0

Generates a load against a memcached cluster of servers.

Current options. A '=' means the option takes a value.

 --concurrency=
Number of users to simulate with load.
 --debug
Provide output only useful for debugging.
 --execute-number=
Number of times to execute the given test.
 --flag
Provide flag information for storage operation.
 --flush
Flush servers before running tests.
 --help
Diplay this message and then exit.
 --initial-load=
```

```
Number of key pairs to load before executing tests.
 --non-blocking
Set TCP up to use non-blocking IO.
 --servers=
List which servers you wish to connect to.
 --tcp-nodelay
Set TCP socket up to use nodelay.
 --test=
Test to run (currently "get" or "set").
 --verbose
Give more details on the progression of the application.
 --version
Display the version of the application and then exit.
 --binary
forgot to document this function :)
```

An example of running memslap with a concurrency of 100 and 10 test runs would be:

```
[patg@vidya ~]$ memslap --servers=localhost:22122,localhost:11211
--concurrency=500
 --execute-number=20 --verbose

Threads connecting to servers 500
Took 1.020 seconds to load data
```

As you can see, this is much faster than such a test would be against a database server!

memerror

This prints the canonical error message for a given memcached server error code. In the example below, we see an error code of 13:

```
memerror 13

CONNECTION DATA DOES NOT EXIST
```

libmemcached Perl Driver

As mentioned, the libmemcached client API and library can be used with Perl in two forms:

❑   Memcached::libmemcached: A low-level Perl driver for libmemcached offering Perl equivalents to libmemcached C API functions.

❑   Cache::memcached::libmemcached: A higher-level interface that uses/inherits from Memcached::libmemcached. It is a drop-in replacement of Cache::memcached and can be used with very little modification.

Figure 9-1 gives a graphical representation to better explain the various modules discussed and the languages they are implemented in:

Installation

You can install both Memcached::libmemcached and Cache::memcached::libmemcached by installing Cache::memcached. Some Linux/Unix distributions come with both included, although since libmemcached changes often, these packaged versions may be stale and out of date. The best bet is to use CPAN to install:

```
cpan -i Cache::memcached::libmemcached
```

Memcached::libmemcached and libmemcached API using Memcached::libmemcached

The thin, low-level Perl driver for libmemcached is Memcached::libmemcached, written by Tim Bunce of DBI (and many other projects) fame, with some help from Daisuke Maki (who now is the current maintainer) and the author of this book. It offers a cent-per-cent, straight binding to libmemcached's C API, but for Perl. It has extensive documentation and is an extremely clean implementation. It's almost entirely written in C, so its performance should be on par with an application using the C library directory.

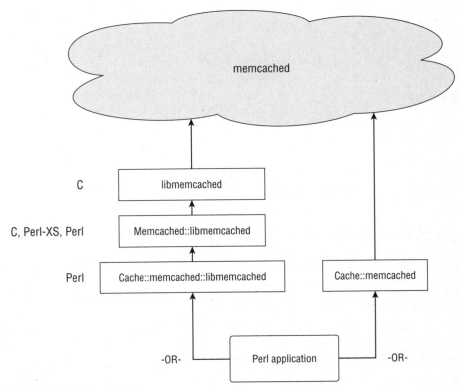

Figure 9-1

Because Memcached::libmemcached is a one-to-one binding to the C API, whatever functions the C API provides, you also have access to with this. The usage of each is the same. It's important to become familiar with the libmemcached C API if you wish to use Memcached::libmemcached. Fortunately, there is plenty of documentation with numerous manual pages for each libmemcached API function, as well as POD documentation for Memcached::libmemcached:

```
perldoc Memcached::libmemcached
```

Another thing to remember with Memcached::libmemcached is that it is a straight, no-frills Perl binding to libmemcached. There is no automatic serialization as with Cache::memcached, so you cannot simply store complex Perl data types — only scalars.

Connection Functions

These functions pertain to the connection, and are shown in various examples as $memc. They are for establishing a connection, setting the servers that $memc is associated with, counting the number of servers that $memc is associated with, and disconnecting from memcached.

❑ memcached_create(): Creates and returns a memcached connection handle that represents the state of communication with the cluster of memcached servers. The C equivalent of this $memc function is a connection structure. Think of this as a $dbh in DBI.

```
  my $memc = memcached_create();
```

❑ memcached_free(): Frees the memory associated with $memc, the underlying C structure that was allocated upon memcached_create(). After calling this, you can no longer use $memc.

```
  memcached_free($memc);
```

❑ memcached_server_count(): Returns a numeric value of the number of memcached servers within the cluster that $memc is associated with.

```
  $server_count = memcached_server_count($memc);
```

❑ memcached_server_add(): Adds a memcached server via TCP/IP, as defined in $hostname and $port, to the memcached cluster associated with $memc.

```
  memcached_server_add($memc, $hostname, $port);
```

❑ memcached_server_add_unix_socket(): Adds a memcached server via UNIX domain socket to the memcached cluster associated with $memc.

```
  memcached_server_add_unix_socket($memc, $socket_file);
```

libmemcached Behavioral Functions

libmemcached provides functionality that allows you to set and retrieve the behavior of the client itself and its functions. These affected client behaviors include object distribution amongst servers, hashing of keys, network parameters, etc.

The various libmemcached behaviors are as follows:

Behavior	Description
MEMCACHED_BEHAVIOR_NO_BLOCK	Causes libmemcached to use asynchronous IO. This is the fastest transport available for storage functions.
MEMCACHED_BEHAVIOR_SUPPORT_CAS	Turns on support CAS. Off by default since there is a very small performance penalty when it is on.
MEMCACHED_BEHAVIOR_BINARY _PROTOCOL	Enables binary protocol. This cannot be set on an open connection, only prior to a connection.
MEMCAHCED_BEHAVIOR_CONNECT _TIMEOUT	Sets the value of the timeout for nonblocking mode during socket connection.
MEMCACHED_BEHAVIOR_SERVER _FAILURE_LIMIT	Enables and sets the value that, when exceeded, results in the automatic removal of a server.
MEMCACHED_BEHAVIOR_DISTRIBUTION	Sets the type of object distribution to servers. Default is MEMCACHED_DISTRIBUTION_MODULA. To use consistent hashing, you would use MEMCACHED_DISTRIBUTION_CONSISTENT (alias to MEMCACHED_DISTRIBUTION_CONSISTENT_KETAMA), which provides better distribution and allows servers to be added to the overall cluster with minimal cache losses.
MEMCACHED_BEHAVIOR_KETAMA	Sets the default distribution to MEMCACHED_DISTRIBUTION_CONSISTENT_KETAMA and the hashing algorithm to MEMCACHED_HASH_MD5.
MEMCACHED_BEHAVIOR_KETAMA _WEIGHTED	Sets the default distribution to MEMCACHED_DISTRIBUTION_CONSISTENT_KETAMA with weighted support, and the hashing algorithm to MEMCACHED_HASH_MD5.
MEMCACHED_BEHAVIOR_SND_TIMEOUT	Sets microsecond behavior of the socket against the SO_SNDTIMEO flag. Will still allow you to have timeouts on the sending of data in cases where you can't utilize nonblocking I/O.
MEMCACHED_BEHAVIOR_RCV_TIMEOUT	Sets microsecond behavior of the socket against the SO_SNDTIMEO flag. Will still allow you to have timeouts on the reading of data in cases where you can't utilize nonblocking I/O.
MEMCACHED_BEHAVIOR_TCP_NODELAY	Turns on the no-delay feature for connecting sockets, which may be faster in some environments.

Continued

(continued)

Behavior	Description
MEMCACHED_BEHAVIOR_HASH	Sets the default hashing algorithm for keys. The values that can be set are: MEMCACHED_HASH_DEFAULT MEMCACHED_HASH_MD5 MEMCACHED_HASH_CRC MEMCACHED_HASH_FNV1_64 MEMCACHED_HASH_FNV1A_64 MEMCACHED_HASH_FNV1_32 MEMCACHED_HASH_FNV1A_32 MEMCACHED_HASH_JENKINS MEMCACHED_HASH_HSIEH MEMCACHED_HASH_MURMUR
MEMCACHED_BEHAVIOR_KETAMA_HASH	Sets the hashing algorithm for host mapping on continuum. The values can be: MEMCACHED_HASH_DEFAULT MEMCACHED_HASH_MD5 MEMCACHED_HASH_CRC MEMCACHED_HASH_FNV1_64 MEMCACHED_HASH_FNV1A_64 MEMCACHED_HASH_FNV1_32 MEMCACHED_HASH_FNV1A_32
MEMCACHED_BEHAVIOR_CACHE_LOOKUPS	Turns on named lookup caching to make it so DNS lookups only occur once.
MEMCACHED_BEHAVIOR_POLL_TIMEOUT	Sets timeout value used by poll(). Default is -1. Signed integer must be used to change this value.
MEMCACHED_BEHAVIOR_BUFFER_REQUESTS	Enables buffered I/O, which makes commands buffered instead of being sent immediately. A get operation, quitting, or closing down the connection will cause the buffer to be sent to the remote connection.
MEMCACHED_BEHAVIOR_VERIFY_KEY	Enables testing of the validity of all keys by libmemcached.
MEMCAHCED_BEHAVIOR_SORT_HOSTS	Enables host additions to be placed into the host list in sorted order. This will defeat consistent hashing.
MEMCACHED_BEHAVIOR_IO_MSG_WATERMARK	Sets the value to the number of messages that will be sent before libmemcached starts to automatically drain the input queue. Do not set this value too high because it could result in deadlocking.
MEMCACHED_BEHAVIOR_IO_BYTES_WATERMARK	Sets the number of bytes that will be sent before libmemcached starts to automatically drain the input queue. You will need at least 10 I/O requests without reading the input buffer. Do not set this value too high because it could result in deadlocking.

The behavioral functions that are applied to the connection $memc are described in this table:

Function	Description
memcached_behavior_set	Changes the value of various behaviors, as shown in the following code, for the connection, $memc: `memcached_behavior_set($memc, $behavior_name, $behavior_value);`
memcached_behavior_get	Obtains the value of a particular behavior for $memc: `memcached_behavior_get($memc, $behavior_name);`

Functions for Setting Values

The functions for setting values in memcached include set, replace, add, and delete. Additionally, libmemcached supports *CAS*, which is a check and set operation that sets the value only if the value has not been updated by anyone else since it was last fetched.

As previously mentioned, libmemcached also supports the ability for setting values for each server, a process known as key partitioning. This is done with a *master key*, and the functions for doing this key partitioning are named <function name>_by_key. For instance, the key partitioning variant of memcached_set is memcached_set_by_key. Key partitioning functionality is available for both set and get operations. Here is a list of the libmemcached methods used for setting values:

- ❏ memcached_set: Sets the value of $key to $value. $expiration, which is optional, is a numeric value that specifies how long the value stored as $key will exist within the memcached cluster. This defaults to 0. $flags is also optional and is used to set options for the value being stored; it also defaults to 0. If function memcached_set_by_key, the value of $master_key is used to map objects to particular servers.

    ```
    memcached_set($memc, $key, $value);

    memcached_set($memc, $key, $value, $expiration, $flags);

    memcached_set_by_key($memc, $master_key, $key, $value);

    memcached_set_by_key($memc, $master_key $key, $value, $expiration, $flags);
    ```

- ❏ memcached_add: Does the same thing as memcached_set, memcached_set_by_key, but only sets the value specified by $key to $value if it doesn't yet exist, and returns an error if it does exist.

    ```
    memcached_add($memc, $key, $value);

    memcached_add($memc, $key, $value, $expiration, $flags);

    memcached_add_by_key($memc, $master_key, $key, $value);

    memcached_add_by_key($memc, $master_key, $key, $value, $expiration, $flags);
    ```

- ❏ memcached_replace: Replaces the value specified by $key if $key exists in memcached; otherwise, an error is returned. $expiration and $flags are optional and work the same as in memcached_set(), memcached_set_by_key().

```
memcached_replace($memc, $key, $value);

memcached_replace($memc, $key, $value, $expiration, $flags);

memcached_replace_by_key($memc, $master_key, $key, $value);

memcached_replace_by_key($memc, $master_key, $key, $values, $expiration, $flags);
```

❑ memcached_prepend: Prepends $value to the existing value specified by $key, or returns an error if $key doesn't exist. $expiration and $flags are optional and work the same as in memcached_set(), memcached_set_by_key().

```
memcached_prepend($memc, $key, $value);

memcached_prepend($memc, $key, $value, $expiration, $flags);

memcached_prepend($memc, $master_key, $key, $value);

memcached_prepend($memc, $master_key, $key, $value, $expiration, $flags);
```

❑ memcached_append: Appends $value to the existing value specified by $key, or returns an error if $key doesn't exist. $expiration and $flags are optional and work the same as in memcached_set().

```
memcached_append($memc, $key, $value);

memcached_append($memc, $key, $value, $expiration, $flags);

memcached_append_by_key($memc, $master_key, $key, $value);

memcached_append_by_key($memc, $master_key, $key, $value, $expiration, $flags);
```

❑ memcached_cas: Overwrites the value specified by key with $value if $cas has the same value in the server. In order to use cas, you must have support for it turned on in libmemcached using memcached_behavior_set().

```
memcached_cas($memc, $key, $value, $expiration, $flags, $cas);

memcached_cas_by_key($memc, $master_key, $key, $value, $expiration, $flags, $cas);
```

Data Retrieval (get) Functions

The functions that fetch data come in two varieties: one simply fetches data with one or more keys (get and mget), and the other or those that get data.

❑ memcached_get(): Gets the value referred to by $key from memcached. Returns undef on error. $flags is optional and when used is updated to the value of $flags for the $value when it was set. $rc is optional and is the return code of the operation.

```
$value= memcached_get($memc, $key);

$value= memcached_get($memc, $key, $flags, $rc);

$value= memcached_get_by_key($memc, $key);
```

```
$value= memcached_get_by_key($memc, $master_key, $key, $flags, $rc);
```

❑ `memcached_mget()`: Fetches the values of multiple keys asynchronously, at once. This function is the fastest way to fetch data for multiple keys. It is the first of two steps for retrieval of multiple keys; the second step is to fetch the values that were retrieved from the server using `memcached_fetch()` or `memcached_fetch_result()`. No errors are given for keys that are not found.

To obtain multiple keys without having to explicitly fetch them **and/only** if you are using the object-oriented interface to Memcached::libmemcached (this will be explained later) you can use the `mget_info_hashref()` method.

```
memcached_mget($memc, \@keys);

memcached_mget($memc, \%keys);

memcached_mget_by_key($memc, $master_key, \@keys);

memcached_mget_by_key($memc, $master_key, \%keys);
```

❑ `memcached_fetch()`: Fetches the next `$key` and `$value` pair returned in the response to a `memcached_mget()` call. This is analogous to fetching data from a database result set after executing a database query. Returns undef when all values have been fetched. `$flag` is optional and when used assumes the value that `$flag` was set to for the value being fetched. `$rc` is also optional and is updated with the return code.

`memcached_fetch()` is similar to `memcached_get()` except that it is fetching results from a previous call of `memcached_mget()`. Instead of `$key` specifying a value to get, it is instead an output parameter that assumes the value of the key being fetched from the result set.

```
$value= memcached_fetch($memc, $key);

$value= memcached_fetch($memc, $key, $flag, $rc);
```

Increment, Decrement, and Delete

These functions are used to increment integer values stored in memcached. There are no *_by_key* variants of these functions.

❑ `memcached_increment()`: Works just like `memcached_decrement()` except it increments the value. The function increments the integer value referred to by `$key` by the amount specified in `$offset`, if `$offset` is specified; otherwise, it increments by 1. `$offset` is optional. `$new_value_out` is optional and assumes the newly incremented value.

```
memcached_increment($key, $offset, $new_value_out);
```

❑ `memcached_decrement()`: Decrements the integer value referred to by `$key` by the amount specified in `$offset`, if `$offset` is specified; otherwise, it decrements by 1. `$offset` is optional. `$new_value_out` is optional and assumes the newly decremented value.

```
memcached_decrement($key, $offset, $new_value_out);
```

❑   memcached_delete(): Deletes the value referred to by $key from memcached. $expiration is optional and specifies the number of seconds when the value will be expired from the cache. memcached_delete_by_key() has an additional $master_key for deleting objects that were set with server key distribution.

```
memcached_delete($memc, $key);

memcached_delete($memc, $key, $expiration);

memcached_delete_by_key($memc, $master_key, $key);

memcached_delete_by_key($memc, $master_key, $key, $expiration);
```

Informational and Utility Functions

In addition to functions that you use for working with items stored in memcached, libmemcached also provides informational and utility functions that you can use to determine the version of the memcached server or client library, error code translation, as well as to flush your server of all objects or disconnect from memcached servers.

❑   memcached_lib_version(): Returns a string containing the version of the libmemcached client library version.

```
$libmemcached_version= memcached_lib_version();
```

❑   memcached_version(): Depending on context, memcached_version() returns either a string value containing the server version, or, as in the code snippet that follows, a three-member list containing the three components of the version of the first memcached server in the memcached cluster specified by $memc.

```
$memcached_version= memcached_version($memc);

($major, $minor, $micro)= memcached_version($memc);
```

❑   memcached_verbosity(): Modifies the verbosity of the memcached servers specified by $memc.

```
memcached_verbosity($memc, $verbosity);
```

❑   memcached_flush(): Clears all memcached servers specified by $memc. This results in deleting all previously stored values.

```
memcached_flush($memc, $expiration);
```

❑   memcached_quit(): Disconnects from all currently connected memcached servers and resets the libmemcached state specified by $memc.

```
memcached_quit($memc);
```

❑   memcached_strerror(): Returns a descriptive string to describe a return code value specified by $rc.

```
$error_string= memcached_strerror($memc, $rc);
```

Object-Oriented Interface

The API calls for Memcached::libmemcached shown have used the procedural interface. Memcached::libmemcached also has an object-oriented interface. To use it, the first thing you would want to call is instantiation:

```
my $memc= Memcached::libmemcached->new; # same as memcached_created
```

This creates the object handle to a Memcached::libmemcached object, which you will use for all subsequent API calls. For instance, to use memcached_set, which would be written procedurally:

```
memcached_set($memc, $key, $value)
```

... the object-oriented interface usage would be:

```
$memc->memcached_set($key, $value)
```

So, the calls are all the same as any procedural call *except* you no longer explicitly pass in the connection handle as the first argument along with the other arguments (well, it is passed automatically to the method as the first argument according to the way OO works in Perl).

Also with the object-oriented interface, you can use the all-in-one multiple get and fetch method, mget_into_hashref:

```
$memc->mget_into_hashref(\@keys, \%results);
```

%results will be populated with the values fetched from memcached.

For errors, you can access via errstr:

```
my $errstr = $memc->errstr;
```

Procedure Memcached::libmemcached Program Example

The following example shows a simple program using Memcached::libmemcached. This example uses a procedural style of usage which requires you import Memcached::libmemcached *subroutines*. The exporter allows you to use patterns for the import list, as shown here:

```perl
use strict;
use warnings;

#import using pattern, all memcached_xxx subroutines
use Memcached::libmemcached qw(/^memcached/);

# allocation of $memc
my $memc = memcached_create();

# add both memcached servers
memcached_server_add($memc, 'localhost', 11211);
memcached_server_add($memc, 'localhost', 22122);
```

```
# set behavior to non-blocking
memcached_behavior_set($memc, MEMCACHED_BEHAVIOR_NO_BLOCK, 1);

# set a value with expiration of 60 seconds
memcached_set($memc, 'key1', 'this is a value', 60);

my $rc= memcached_replace($memc, 'key1', 'replaced value', 60);

memcached_set($memc, 'key2', 'bbbbb', 60);

memcached_set($memc, 'key3', 'ccccc', 60);

# fetch the value
my $retval= memcached_get($memc, 'key1', {}, $rc);

# mget and fetch
memcached_mget($memc, ['key1', 'key2', 'key3']);
# fetch, one at a time and must be in order
my $retval= memcached_fetch($memc, 'key1');
print "key1: $retval\n";

$retval= memcached_fetch($memc, 'key2');
print "key2: $retval\n";

$retval= memcached_fetch($memc, 'key3');
print "key3: $retval\n";

# disconnect from the memcached server(s)
memcached_quit($memc);

# free the memcached object
memcached_free($memc);
```

Notice in this example, memcached_free() is called. Yes, in Perl you don't have to worry about memory allocation, but this is a low-level Perl driver to libmemcached, and in the C equivalent you must free the $memc (connection structure in C). So you must also free it from Perl.

Object-Oriented Memcached::libmemcached Program Example

The next example shows that you can also use an object-oriented approach to this program. This doesn't require that you have to import the Memcached::libmemcached *methods*. Also in this example is mget_into_hashref, which the object-oriented interface provides.

```
use strict;
use warnings;

use Memcached::libmemcached;

# allocation of $memc
my $memc = Memcached::libmemcached->new;
```

```
# add both memcached servers
$memc->memcached_server_add('localhost', 11211);
$memc->memcached_server_add('localhost', 22122);

# set behavior to non-blocking
$memc->memcached_behavior_set(MEMCACHED_BEHAVIOR_NO_BLOCK, 1);

# set a value with expiration of 60 seconds
$memc->memcached_set('key1', 'aaaaa', 60);
$memc->memcached_set('key2', 'bbbbb', 60);
$memc->memcached_set('key3', 'ccccc', 60);

# get
my $key1val = $memc->memcached_get('key1');
print "key1val $key1val\n";

# mget
$memc->memcached_mget(['key1', 'key2', 'key3']);
# fetch, one at a time, and must be in order
my $retval = $memc->memcached_fetch('key1');
print "retval $retval\n";

$retval = $memc->memcached_fetch('key2');
print "retval $retval\n";

$retval = $memc->memcached_fetch('key2');
print "retval $retval\n";

# must set it as a hashref prior to using it
my $ret_ref= {};

# convenient way to mget
$memc->mget_into_hashref(['key1', 'key2', 'key3'], $ret_ref);
map { print "$_ => $ret_ref->{$_}\n"} sort keys %$ret_ref;

# disconnect from the memcached server(s)
$memc->memcached_quit();

# free the memcached object
$memc->memcached_free();
```

As you can see, you can take two approaches in programming philosophy with Memcached::libmemcached!

Cache::memcached::libmemcached

Cache::memcached::libmemcached is a Perl module written by Daisuke Maki. It uses (and inherits from) Memcached::libmemcached as its low-level interface to libmemcached. Whereas Memcached::libmemcached was meant to provide a Perl API to libmemcached, Cache::memcached::libmemcached is meant to provide API compatibility to Cache::memcached.

To use it, simply change instantiation from:

```
my $memc= Cache::memcached->new({
        servers             => $servers,
        compress_threshold  => 10_000});
```

... to:

```
my $memc= Cache::memcached::libmemcached->new({
        servers             => $servers,
        compress_threshold  => 10_000});
```

That's all! All the code you have that is currently using Cache::memcached should work as is.

Performance Comparisons

The real issue and reason for potentially using Cache::memcached::libmemcached is performance. To see what performance gains there are and to justify why you might want to use it, Cache::memcached::libmemcached has a utility script within the tools directory of the distribution. The author of this book modified this script to only compare Cache::memcached::libmemcached to Cache::memcached. Here are the numbers:

```
[root@vidya tools]# perl ./benchmark.pl
Module Information:
 + Cache::memcached => 1.24
 + Cache::memcached::libmemcached => 0.02008

Options:
 + Memcached server: localhost:11211
 + Include no block mode (where applicable)? :NO

Prepping clients...

==== Benchmark "Simple get() (scalar)" ====
                 Rate perl_memcached    libmemcached
perl_memcached   7092/s            --           -78%
libmemcached    32051/s          352%             --
==== Benchmark "Simple get_multi() (scalar)" ====
                 Rate perl_memcached    libmemcached
perl_memcached   1810/s            --           -85%
libmemcached    11848/s          555%             --
==== Benchmark "Serialization with get()" ====
                 Rate perl_memcached    libmemcached
perl_memcached   6394/s            --           -74%
libmemcached    24876/s          289%             --
==== Benchmark "Simple set() (scalar)" ====
                 Rate perl_memcached    libmemcached
perl_memcached  17544/s            --           -36%
libmemcached    27624/s           57%             --
Pretty compelling
```

The numbers are pretty compelling! Even the last test, with a gain of 57 percent over Cache::memcached. That's reason enough to use it.

Writing Your Own Comparison Script

Not content to just use the utility script that comes included with Cache::memcached::libmemcached? A separate test script/tool can be written to see if the type of performance gains displayed in the previous example of running benchmark.pl hold true for a different program. This also provides a good example of how you might benchmark memcached.

This test script is written using both Cache::memcached::libmemcached and Cache::memcached. It runs several operations — set, get, replace, increment, decrement, delete — each within a loop that iterates a given number of times, as chosen via a command-line option. This script will record the duration from the beginning of the loop to the end of the loop for each of these operations using Time::HiRes and store the results in a hash reference, which it will then print out at the end of all tests. It then compares the differences between the timings of the test using Cache::memcached versus using Cache::memcached::libmemcached:

```perl
use strict;
use warnings;

use Cache::memcached;
use Cache::memcached::libmemcached;
use Time::HiRes qw(tv_interval gettimeofday);

use Getopt::Long;

# global options
our $opt_num_loop;
our $opt_servers;

GetOptions(
  'loops|l=s'    => \$opt_num_loop,
  'servers|s=s'  => \$opt_servers,
) or usage();

# defaults
$opt_servers||= '127.0.0.1:11211';
$opt_num_loop||= 10;

sub main {

  # hashref containing key values
  my $scalars = {};
  my $servers;
  # results of tests
  my $results;
  # set up servers
  (@$servers)= split(',', $opt_servers);

  # build up hashref, outside of timing and before
  # any memcached access
  for (0 .. $opt_num_loop) {
    $scalars->{hashkey()} = hashkey();
  }

  for my $opt_libmemcached (0 .. 1) {
```

```perl
# toggle which library to use
my $memc= $opt_libmemcached ?
  Cache::memcached::libmemcached->new({
      servers            => $servers,
      compress_threshold => 10_000}) :
  Cache::memcached->new({
      servers            => $servers,
      compress_threshold => 10_000});

# clear all values
$memc->flush_all();

# obtain start time
my $start_time= my $t0 = [gettimeofday];

# loop through entire hashref
# set operation
for my $key (keys %$scalars) {
  # set, get, replace, incr, decr, delete...
  $memc->set($key, $scalars->{$key});
}
my $elapsed = tv_interval( $t0 );
push @{$results->{set}}, $elapsed ;

# get operation
$t0 = [gettimeofday];
for my $key(keys %$scalars) {
  my $var = $memc->get($key);
}
$elapsed = tv_interval ( $t0 );
push@{$results->{get}}, $elapsed;

# replace operation
$t0 = [gettimeofday];
for my $key (keys %$scalars) {
  $memc->replace($key, 1);
}
$elapsed = tv_interval( $t0 );
push @{$results->{replace}}, $elapsed ;

# increment operation
$t0 = [gettimeofday];
for my $key (keys %$scalars) {
  $memc->incr($key, 10);
}
$elapsed = tv_interval( $t0 );
push @{$results->{increment}}, $elapsed;

# decrement operation
$t0 = [gettimeofday];
for my $key (keys %$scalars) {
  $memc->decr($key, 5);
}
$elapsed = tv_interval( $t0 );
push @{$results->{decrement}}, $elapsed;
```

```
        # delete operation
        $t0 = [gettimeofday];
        for my $key (keys %$scalars) {
          $memc->delete($key);
        }
        $elapsed = tv_interval( $t0 );
        push @{$results->{'delete'}}, $elapsed;

        # obtain total time
        $elapsed = tv_interval( $start_time );
        push @{$results->{'total'}}, $elapsed;
    }
    printf("%-10s %-16s %-14s %-14s %-14s\n",
            'Operation',
            'Cache::memcached',
            'libmemcached',
            'libmem % faster',
            'C::M % slower');

    for my $op qw(set get replace increment decrement delete total) {
        # lexical variables to make easier to read
        my $cm_t= $results->{$op}[0];
        my $lm_t= $results->{$op}[1];
        printf("%-10s %-16s %-14s %-14.2f %-14.2f\n",
            $op,
            $cm_t,
            $lm_t,
            (($cm_t - $lm_t)/$lm_t) * 100,
            (($lm_t - $cm_t)/$cm_t) * 100);
    }
}

sub hashkey {
    my @chars = grep !/[0O1Iil]/, 0..9, 'A'..'Z', 'a'..'z';
    return join '', map { $chars[rand @chars] } 0 .. 7;

}
sub usage {
    print <<'EOM';
    loops|l        <number of loops>
    servers|s      <server1:port, server2:port, ...>

EOM

    exit();
}
main();
```

Simply running this test several times (with 1,000, 10,000, and 100,000 iterations) affirms the first test's optimism:

```
[patg@vidya perl]$ ./memtest.pl -l 1000
Operation  Cache::memcached libmemcached  libmem % faster C::M % slower
set        0.087627         0.079952      9.60            -8.76
```

get	0.169981	0.057917	193.49	-65.93
replace	0.082767	0.063166	31.03	-23.68
increment	0.087826	0.054967	59.78	-37.41
decrement	0.080666	0.055666	44.91	-30.99
delete	0.083432	0.060025	39.00	-28.06
total	0.592368	0.371783	59.33	-37.24

```
[patg@vidya perl]$ ./memtest.pl -l 10000
```

Operation	Cache::memcached	libmemcached	libmem % faster	C::M % slower
set	0.810394	0.66024	22.74	-18.53
get	1.62237	0.582148	178.69	-64.12
replace	0.834778	0.64598	29.23	-22.62
increment	0.864778	0.57	51.72	-34.09
decrement	0.807877	0.559809	44.31	-30.71
delete	0.770756	0.544149	41.64	-29.40
total	5.711064	3.562453	60.31	-37.62

```
[patg@vidya perl]$ ./memtest.pl -l 100000
```

Operation	Cache::memcached	libmemcached	libmem % faster	C::M % slower
set	8.537003	6.638635	28.60	-22.24
get	17.22665	5.921637	190.91	-65.63
replace	8.64765	6.8835	25.63	-20.40
increment	8.246872	5.765545	43.04	-30.09
decrement	8.294751	5.522195	50.21	-33.43
delete	7.84551	5.41309	44.94	-31.00
total	58.798621	36.144834	62.68	-38.53

Using Cache::memcached::libmemcached obviously is faster than Cache::memcached on every operation in every test, particularly get(), which is around 190 percent faster. get is an operation that you will be calling a lot! Overall, the various operations combined show a performance gain of around 60 percent. This was a very simple test in that it runs serially but backs up the generally increased performance from the first test, benchmark.pl.

Summary

libmemcached is a memcached client library written in C to have a faster, more efficient, thread-safe, full-featured C library with performance gain over existing client libraries. It also offers the ability to adjust and tune the behavior of the client. libmemcached, written in C, has two Perl interfaces: Memcached::libmemcached, which offers a direct interface to the C API, and Cache::memcached::libmemcached, which uses libmemcached as the underlying client to memcached and works as a drop-in replacement to Cache::memcached. With Cache::memcached::libmemcached, you can use all the code that you've written using Cache::memcached without making any modifications.

This chapter covered the following topics:

❑ How to install libmemcached, Memcached::libmemcached, and Cache::memcached::libmemcached.

❑ That Memcached::libmemcached is a thin, highly efficient wrapper around the libmemcached library. It offers a 1:1 binding to the libmemcached API.

❑ Cache::memcached::libmemcached is a drop-in replacement for Cache::memcached (covered in Chapter 8), and the API is exactly the same in terms of use.

❑ The libmemcached API using Memcached::libmemcached. We explained the various behaviors that you can tune with libmemcached. Also provided were some simple usage examples with Memcached::libmemcached.

❑ Code examples of usage and demonstrations showed Cache::memcached::libmemcached using two scripts, the results of which proved increased performance with Cache::memcached:: libmemcached. One example showed the Cache::memcached::libmemcached distribution, benchmark.pl. Another example was written solely for this book and showed how to write such an application for memcached. This example provided results that were in line with the first script, which gives you a good justification for using Cache::memcached::libmemcached over Cache::memcached.

You should now have a good understanding of what libmemcached is — how to install it, its numerous API calls, and client behaviors — as well as its performance benefits.

10

Memcached Functions for MySQL

You were introduced to memcached in Chapter 8, where you learned about Cache::Memcached and how to write programs to use memcached. In Chapter 9, you learned about libmemcached, a faster client library. So, you should now have a good idea how to use memcached with Perl.

What about memcached and MySQL? Is there any sort of interoperability between the two, since they are so commonly used together? It would be great if there was some sort of "glue" between the two, without having to write Perl code, to get data to and from MySQL and memcached.

Well there is. This is why the Memcached Functions for MySQL, aka memcached UDFs, were written.

What Are Memcached Functions for MySQL?

MySQL has an API for writing user-defined functions (otherwise known as UDFs), as you learned in Chapter 3. There, you saw the example of a UDF using libcurl. Because the UDF API is so flexible, it's possible to write many different functions to do a number of things. With the advent of libmemcached, it became obvious that there could be UDFs that interact with memcached through libmemcached and provide all the functionality that one would normally implement with an external language at the application layer.

The Memcached Functions for MySQL, written by Patrick Galbraith and Brian Aker, are a suite of functions available to use with MySQL that allow you to store, retrieve, and delete data, as well as perform most of the functions/operations that are available with libmemcached, such as server connectivity to the client, server status, client behaviors, and more.

Additionally, since these functions can be used from within MySQL, you have at your disposal the power of the SQL engine, which can be used to initiate caching or data retrieval using the result sets from query. You can combine the fetching of data from one or more tables with the fetching of data from memcached and be able to apply any SQL operations on that result set, such as LIMIT, sorting and other conditional operations.

Some features of the Memcached Functions for MySQL include the following:

❑ Written in C using libmemcached and the MySQL UDF API

❑ Provide get, set, delete, replace, add, flush, stats, behavior setting and retrieval, as well as other functionality

❑ Can be used in stored procedures and triggers

❑ Allow one to interact with memcached and MySQL independent of the language of the application using them, or for languages that don't have clients for memcached

❑ Open source

How Do the Memcached Functions for MySQL Work?

The user-defined functions utilize libmemcached. When a particular UDF is called, say for instance when the user types memc_get(`mykey´), the UDF processes the arguments, ensuring the proper number of arguments have been passed (in this case one argument, the key mykey) for the value that is desired to be retrieved. The UDF then passes this argument to the appropriate libmemcached API call, in this case memcached_mget(), memcached_fetch_result(), and then finally memcached_result_value(). So, what these UDFs provide are convenient functions that have the advantage of using the fast, light-weight libmemcached library, hiding the implementation details of the libmemcached calls much in the same way that the Cache::Memcached::libmemcached does for Perl.

Figure 10-1 illustrates the concept of how the Memcached Functions for MySQL give the user the ability to access data from MySQL and memcached, and how simple UDF functions are implemented with API functions of libmemcached. Also, the application using MySQL can be implemented in any programming language that has client support for connecting to MySQL. This isn't a problem for Perl, but there are some languages that don't have clients for memcached.

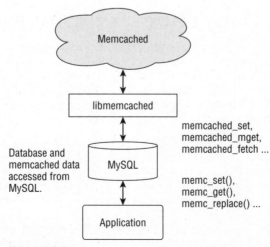

Figure 10-1

Install the Memcached Functions for MySQL

The MySQL plug-in interface allows for easy loading of UDFs. All that is involved with using a UDF is to compile, install, and then run the SQL command to load the UDF shared library. To obtain the source for the Memcached Functions for MySQL go to:

```
http://tangent.org/586/Memcached_Functions_for_MySQL.html.
```

This page provides links to the source code as a source archive file, or you can use the Mercurial revision control system repository to obtain the latest source.

Prerequisites

The prerequisites for building, installing, and using the Memcached Functions for MySQL are these:

- ❏ A MySQL database server
- ❏ libmemcached installed (see Chapter 9)
- ❏ One or more memcached servers
- ❏ A compiler

Configure the Source

To configure the source, follow these simple steps:

1. Untar/gzip the source package: `tar memcached_functions_mysql-0.7.tar.gz`
2. Enter the project directory: `cd memcached_functions_mysql`
3. Run the configure script:

```
./configure --with-mysql=/usr/local/mysql/bin/mysql_config
--libdir=/usr/local/mysql/lib/mysql/plugin/
```

The two arguments can be explained as follows:

- ❏ `--with-mysql`: This argument tells the configure program where to find the `mysql_config` program, which provides the necessary compiler flags for the specific system so the UDFs can be built properly.
- ❏ `--libdir`: This is the directory where the compiled shared library will be installed. On MySQL 5.0, this would be the directory where other libraries are found. With 5.1, the plug-in interface was changed for programs such as storage engines and UDFs so that shared libraries would reside in a directory on a level deeper within the normal library directory, called *plugin*.

Additionally, you may want to add an entry on your operating system to be able to load the shared library. Some operating systems might need this set because, by default, they don't load dynamic libraries in directories that are in their library path. For instance, if you needed to add an entry for

/usr/local/mysql/lib/mysql/plugin, you would add a mysql.conf file in /etc/ld.so.conf.d that might look like this:

```
/usr/local/mysql/lib/mysql
/usr/local/mysql/lib/mysql/plugin
/usr/lib64/mysql/
```

You would then run ldconfig to create the necessary links and cache to the most recent shared libraries found in the directories you specified in /etc/ld.so.conf.d/mysql.conf:

```
sudo ldconfig
```

Build the Source

The next thing you'll do is compile the source:

```
make
sudo make install
```

When you install the built source, the dynamic libraries created from the compilation are installed to the same directory specified in the directory you used in the --libdir argument.

Install the UDF

Now that the dynamic library is installed, you should be able to load the various UDFs. There are two ways to do this. The source package comes with several goodies (which will be explained in detail later in this chapter). There are two install methods — an SQL script that you can either run or cut and paste, or a Perl utility.

SQL Script Install

The SQL script that contains the SQL statements to install the UDFs can be found in the sql directory install_functions.sql of the source distribution. It contains statements for each function, such as this one for memc_get:

```
CREATE FUNCTION memc_get RETURNS STRING SONAME "libmemcached_functions_mysql.so";
```

You can simply run this script by loading with the MySQL command-line client, which you will need to run as the root user because creating functions in MySQL requires this privilege level:

```
mysql -u root -p < sql/install_functions.sql
```

Perl Install Utility

The utility install.pl is another way to install the UDFs. It can be run interactively or noninteractively. To see the available options for this program use this:

```
./utils/install.pl -h
```

When running it, you will have to specify a user and password to run it as — which must be a user that has system privileges. With only the `--user` and `--password` arguments, the program runs interactively:

```
[root@vidya memcached_functions_mysql]# ./utils/install.pl -u root -p root
function memc_cas_by_key doesn't exist. Create? [Y|n]
Y
Running: CREATE FUNCTION memc_cas_by_key
RETURNS INT SONAME 'libmemcached_functions_mysql.so'
function memc_cas doesn't exist. Create? [Y|n]
Y
Running: CREATE FUNCTION memc_cas
RETURNS INT SONAME 'libmemcached_functions_mysql.so'
function memc_servers_set doesn't exist. Create? [Y|n]
```

If you supply the argument `-s` or `-silent`, it will run without interaction:

```
./utils/install.pl -u root -p root -s
```

Checking Installation

After installing the functions, you can check the table in the `mysql` system schema, using `func` to verify that the UDFs were installed. You should see:

```
mysql> select * from mysql.func;
+---------------------------+-----+----------------------------------+----------+
| name                      | ret | dl                               | type     |
+---------------------------+-----+----------------------------------+----------+
| memc_add                  |   2 | libmemcached_functions_mysql.so  | function |
| memc_add_by_key           |   2 | libmemcached_functions_mysql.so  | function |
| memc_servers_set          |   2 | libmemcached_functions_mysql.so  | function |
| memc_server_count         |   2 | libmemcached_functions_mysql.so  | function |
| memc_set                  |   2 | libmemcached_functions_mysql.so  | function |
| memc_set_by_key           |   2 | libmemcached_functions_mysql.so  | function |
| memc_cas                  |   2 | libmemcached_functions_mysql.so  | function |
| memc_cas_by_key           |   2 | libmemcached_functions_mysql.so  | function |
| memc_get                  |   0 | libmemcached_functions_mysql.so  | function |
| memc_get_by_key           |   0 | libmemcached_functions_mysql.so  | function |
| memc_delete               |   2 | libmemcached_functions_mysql.so  | function |
| memc_delete_by_key        |   2 | libmemcached_functions_mysql.so  | function |
| memc_append               |   2 | libmemcached_functions_mysql.so  | function |
| memc_append_by_key        |   2 | libmemcached_functions_mysql.so  | function |
| memc_prepend              |   2 | libmemcached_functions_mysql.so  | function |
| memc_prepend_by_key       |   2 | libmemcached_functions_mysql.so  | function |
| memc_increment            |   2 | libmemcached_functions_mysql.so  | function |
| memc_decrement            |   2 | libmemcached_functions_mysql.so  | function |
| memc_replace              |   2 | libmemcached_functions_mysql.so  | function |
| memc_replace_by_key       |   2 | libmemcached_functions_mysql.so  | function |
| memc_servers_behavior_set |   2 | libmemcached_functions_mysql.so  | function |
| memc_udf_version          |   0 | libmemcached_functions_mysql.so  | function |
```

```
| memc_list_behaviors           |   0 | libmemcached_functions_mysql.so | function |
| memc_stats                    |   0 | libmemcached_functions_mysql.so | function |
| memc_stat_get_keys            |   0 | libmemcached_functions_mysql.so | function |
| memc_stat_get_value           |   0 | libmemcached_functions_mysql.so | function |
+-------------------------------+-----+---------------------------------+----------+
```

This means you have successfully installed the functions. Using the functions will verify that everything works.

Using the Memcached Functions for MySQL

The Memcached Functions for MySQL use libmemcached, and each function mirrors the API functions of libmemcached. As you may recall from Chapter 3, the way to call a UDF is to use a SELECT statement, like so:

```
mysql> select memc_get('abc');
+-----------------+
| memc_get('abc') |
+-----------------+
| this is a test  |
+-----------------+
```

Or, use a SET statement, assigning the variable to a user-defined variable:

```
mysql> set @test = memc_get('abc');

mysql> select @test;
+----------------+
| @test          |
+----------------+
| this is a test |
+----------------+
```

Depending on which of the memcached UDFs you run, some may return a value retrieved from memcached or set a value in memcached (retrieving a true/false indicating success or failure).

Establishing a Connection to the memcached Server

The first thing you need to do when using these UDFs is to establish a connection to the memcached servers being used.

memc_servers_set

memc_servers_set makes a connection to the memcached servers being used.

```
memc_servers_set(`server1:port, server2:port, serverN:port ...´);
```

You supply a list of servers with their port numbers, as many as you like, delimited by commas. Upon success, a 1 is returned; −1 means a failure has occurred.

```
mysql> SELECT memc_servers_set('127.0.0.1:11211, 127.0.0.1:22122');
+------------------------------------------------------+
```

```
| memc_servers_set('127.0.0.1:11211, 127.0.0.1:22122') |
+------------------------------------------------------+
|                                                    0 |
+------------------------------------------------------+
```

Once a connection is established, you can begin to use all the other functions to store and retrieve values.

memc_server_count

The function `memc_server_count()` takes no arguments and will return the number of memcached servers that you are connected to.

```
memc_server_count();
```

If for instance, you had connected to two servers as in the preceding example of `memc_servers_set()`, `memc_server_count()` will show:

```
mysql> select memc_server_count();
+---------------------+
| memc_server_count() |
+---------------------+
|                   2 |
+---------------------+
```

Setting Values

Just as with libmemcached, there are functions in the Memcached Functions for MySQL to store values in memcached servers.

memc_set

The function `memc_set()` allows you to store a value in memcached. It takes two required arguments — the key for what's being stored, and a value. The value being stored can be either a string or a numeric value. If it's a string, it of course must be quoted, if numeric, it doesn't need to be quoted. `memc_set()` can also take a third numeric optional expiration argument for the expiration time in seconds. `memc_set()` returns a zero upon success or a nonzero value upon failure. The syntax for `memc_set()` is:

```
memc_set(`key´, value, expiration);
memc_set(`key´, value);
```

This example below shows a value of xyz being stored with the key foo for 5 seconds:

```
mysql> select memc_set('foo', 'xyz', 5);
+---------------------------+
| memc_set('foo', 'xyz', 5) |
+---------------------------+
|                         0 |
+---------------------------+
```

The above `memc_set()` would set the value xyz keyed with foo to be stored for 5 seconds in the memcached server. If you run the following three statements on the same line (so they run all at once), you can see the effect of putting an expiration value on something being stored in memcached. (You'll also see the use of memc_get(), which will be explained in detail later.)

```
mysql> select memc_set('foo', 'xyz', 5); select memc_get('foo'); select sleep (6);
    ->  select memc_get ('foo');
+---------------------------+
| memc_set('foo', 'xyz', 5) |
+---------------------------+
|                         0 |
+---------------------------+
1 row in set (0.01 sec)

+-----------------+
| memc_get('foo') |
+-----------------+
| xyz             |
+-----------------+
1 row in set (0.00 sec)

+-----------+
| sleep (6) |
+-----------+
|         0 |
+-----------+
1 row in set (6.01 sec)

+------------------+
| memc_get ('foo') |
+------------------+
| NULL             |
+------------------+
1 row in set (0.01 sec)
```

As you see, after 6 seconds, foo is expired to the bit-bucket in the sky.

The following will of course set foo to the value of xyz without an expiration.

```
mysql> select memc_set('foo', 'xyz');
+------------------------+
| memc_set('foo', 'xyz') |
+------------------------+
|                      0 |
+------------------------+
```

memc_set_by_key

The function memc_set_by_key() functions the same way as memc_set(), except the first argument is a master server key that allows you to group stored values by server. The rest of the keys are the same as memc_set, except they are shifted by one. The second argument is the key for the object being stored, the third is the value being stored, and the optional fourth value is a numeric expiration in seconds. The syntax for memc_set_by_key() is:

```
memc_set_by_key(`master key´, `key´, value);
memc_set_by_key(`master key´, `key´, value, expiration);
```

The example below shows storing of a value by server key:

```
mysql> select memc_set_by_key('A', 'key1', 'test');
+--------------------------------------+
| memc_set_by_key('A', 'key1', 'test') |
+--------------------------------------+
|                                    0 |
+--------------------------------------+
```

memc_add

The function `memc_add()` takes two required arguments — a string key and a value, either numeric or string, that will be stored as a value in memcached specified by the `key` if not already set — as well as a third optional numeric argument for the number of seconds that the value will be stored before being expired. `memc_set()` returns a zero upon success or a nonzero value upon failure.

The function `memc_add_by_key()` works the same as `memc_add()`, except it has as its first argument a master server key that allows you to group stored values by server. The arguments following the master key argument are the same as those for `memc_add()`, just shifted in order.

Syntax of `memc_add()` and `memc_add_by_key()` is:

```
memc_add(`key`, value);
memc_add(`key`, value, expiration);
memc_add_by_key(`master key`, `key`, value);
memc_add_by_key(`master key` `key`, value, expiration);
```

The example shows a value being added that yet doesn't exist:

```
mysql> select memc_set('key1', 333);
+----------------------+
| memc_set('key1', 333) |
+----------------------+
|                    0 |
+----------------------+
```

memc_replace

The function `memc_replace` takes two required arguments: a string key and a value, either numeric or string, that will replace the existing value of the `key` already stored. `memc_replaced` returns a zero upon success or a nonzero value upon failure.

The function `memc_replace_by_key()` works the same as `memc_replace()`, except it has as its first argument a master server key, which allows you to group stored values by server. The arguments following the master key argument are the same as for `memc_replace()`, just shifted in order.

Syntax of `memc_replace()` and `memc_replace_by_key()` is:

```
memc_replace(`key`, value);
memc_replace(`key`, value, expiration);
memc_replace_by_key(`master key`, `key`, value);
memc_replace_by_key(`master key`, `key`, value, expiration);
```

This example shows the retrieval of a value previously stored and then replaced:

```
mysql> select memc_get('key2');
+------------------+
| memc_get('key2') |
+------------------+
| before value     |
+------------------+

mysql> select memc_replace('key2', 'replaced value');
+----------------------------------------+
| memc_replace('key2', 'replaced value') |
+----------------------------------------+
|                                      0 |
+----------------------------------------+
mysql> select memc_get('key2');
+------------------+
| memc_get('key2') |
+------------------+
| replaced value   |
+------------------+
```

The next example shows memcached trying to replace a value that yet doesn't exist and returning an error code of 14:

```
mysql> select memc_replace('doesntexist', 'abcdefg');
+----------------------------------------+
| memc_replace('doesntexist', 'abcdefg') |
+----------------------------------------+
|                                     14 |
+----------------------------------------+
```

memc_cas

The function memc_cas() sets a value if the cas value is the same as the cas value on the server itself.

Syntax for memc_cas() and memc_cas_by_key() is:

```
memc_cas(`key´, value, cas);
memc_cas(`key, value, cas, expiration);
memc_cas_by_key(`master_key´, `key´, value, cas, expiration);
```

This functionality is still experimental and you have to enable it by setting the behavior MEMCACHED _BEHAVIOR_SUPPORT_CAS

```
mysql> select memc_servers_behavior_set('MEMCACHED_BEHAVIOR_SUPPORT_CAS', 1);
+----------------------------------------------------------------+
| memc_servers_behavior_set('MEMCACHED_BEHAVIOR_SUPPORT_CAS', 1) |
+----------------------------------------------------------------+
|                                                              0 |
+----------------------------------------------------------------+
```

memc_prepend

The function `memc_prepend()` prepends `value` to the beginning of an existing stored value, stored by `key`. The value being prepended can be either numeric or a string, *if* the value already stored is a string. You *cannot* prepend anything to *an existing* stored numeric value or it will result in that value being set to a NULL value. The expiration argument is optional and sets the expiration time in seconds.

The function `memc_prepend_by_key()` works the same as `memc_prepend` except the first argument is a master server key to which the value is being prepended. All other values work the same.

Syntax for `memc_prepend()` and `memc_prepend_by_key()` is:

```
memc_prepend(`key´, value);
memc_prepend(`key´, value, expiration);
memc_prepend_by_key(`master key´, `key´, value);
memc_prepend_by_key(`master key´, `key´, value, `expiration´);
```

The example shows a value initially set to `this is some text` has prepended to it `this will be prepended...` by `memc_prepend()`:

```
mysql> select memc_set('abc', ' this is some text');
+-------------------------------------+
| memc_set('abc', ' this is some text') |
+-------------------------------------+
|                                   0 |
+-------------------------------------+

mysql> select memc_get('abc');
+-------------------+
| memc_get('abc')   |
+-------------------+
|  this is some text |
+-------------------+

mysql> select memc_prepend('abc', 'this will be prepended.. ');
+------------------------------------------------+
| memc_prepend('abc', 'this will be prepended... ') |
+------------------------------------------------+
|                                              0 |
+------------------------------------------------+

mysql> select memc_get('abc');
+------------------------------------------+
| memc_get('abc')                          |
+------------------------------------------+
| this will be prepended...  this is some text |
+------------------------------------------+
```

memc_append

The function `memc_append()` appends the argument *value* to the existing value stored as `key`. The value being appended can be either numeric or a string, *if* the value already stored is a string. You *cannot* append anything to an existing stored numeric value or it will result in that value being set to NULL. The argument expiration is optional and specifies the expiration time in number of seconds.

The function memc_append_by_key() works the same as memc_append() except the first argument is a master key value that the value stored was stored as.

Syntax for memc_append() and memc_append_by_key() is:

```
memc_append(`key´, value);
memc_append(`key´, value, expiration);
memc_append_by_key(`master key´, `key´, value):
memc_append_by_key(`master key´, `key´, value, expiration);
```

An example showing what memc_append() does is shown next. First an existing value has text appended to it, and a subsequent memc_get() retrieves the value, verifying that it had the text appended by memc_append():

```
mysql> select memc_append('abc', ' .. this will be appended to the end');
+-----------------------------------------------------------------+
| memc_append('abc', ' .. this will be appended to the end') |
+-----------------------------------------------------------------+
|                                                               0 |
+-----------------------------------------------------------------+

mysql> select memc_get('abc');
+-----------------------------------------------------------------------------------+
| memc_get('abc')                                                                   |
+-----------------------------------------------------------------------------------+
| this will be prepended.. this is some text ..this will be appended to the end |
+-----------------------------------------------------------------------------------+
```

memc_delete

The function memc_delete() deletes from memcached the value stored as key. Expiration is an optional numeric value in seconds. The return value is zero if the value is deleted and a nonzero value if it is not.

Just as with the other *_by_key() functions, memc_delete_by_key() works the same as memc_delete(), except it has as its first argument a master key that is the key representing the server that the object was stored with.

Syntax for memc_delete() and memc_delete_by_key() is:

```
memc_delete(`key´);
memc_delete(`key´, expiration);
memc_delete_by_key(`master key´, `key´);
memc_delete_by_key(`master key´, `key´, expiration);
mysql> select memc_delete('foo');
+------------------------+
| memc_delete('foo', 15) |
+------------------------+
|                      0 |
+------------------------+
```

Fetching, Incrementing, and Decrementing Functions

The Memcached Functions for MySQL have the means to fetch data, of course. These return the actual value stored, one value per function call. There aren't any functions at the present time to fetch multiple values at once because the UDF interface only allows for one row to be returned.

Also, there may be times when you want a centralized counter, without having to use a table. You can do this using the increment or decrement (if you want an *anti*counter!). The thing to remember is that that data is not durable.

memc_get

As you have seen in the examples showing the setting functions, memc_get() fetches a value stored in memcached. memc_get_by_key() additionally has as its first argument the server key which would be whatever the server key the value was stored with.

Syntax for memc_get() and memc_get_by_key() is:

```
memc_get(`key´);
memc_get_by_key(`master_key´, `key´);
```

This example shows how memc_get() is used:

```
mysql> select memc_get('abc');
+---------------------------+
| memc_get('abc')           |
+---------------------------+
| A value that was stored... |
+---------------------------+


mysql> set @a = memc_get('abc');

mysql> select @a;
+---------------------------+
| @a                        |
+---------------------------+
| A value that was stored... |
+---------------------------+
```

memc_increment

The function memc_increment() is used to increment an integer value stored in memcached by key. The value argument is optional and is the number by which the stored value will be incremented. If the value is not supplied, the value of 1 is the default assumed. The incremented value is returned upon a successful increment of the value. If you use an invalid value to increment by, memc_increment() will ignore it and return the existing value.

Syntax for memc_increment():

```
memc_increment(`key´);
memc_increment(`key´, value);
```

The example that follows shows how to use `memc_increment()` to increment a value counter by 1, which is the default increment value that is used when not supplying an increment value, as well as by explicitly supplying the increment value to increment the value `counter` by 12.

```
mysql> select memc_set('counter', 1);
+----------------------+
| memc_set('counter', 1) |
+----------------------+
|                    0 |
+----------------------+

mysql> select memc_get('counter');
+--------------------+
| memc_get('counter') |
+--------------------+
| 1                  |
+--------------------+

mysql> select memc_increment('counter');
+--------------------------+
| memc_increment('counter') |
+--------------------------+
|                        2 |
+--------------------------+

mysql> select memc_increment('counter', 10);
+------------------------------+
| memc_increment('counter', 10) |
+------------------------------+
|                           12 |
+------------------------------+
```

memc_decrement

The function `memc_decrement()` decrements an integer value stored in memcached as the first argument `key`. The optional `value` argument is the amount to decrease by, which defaults to 1 if not supplied. You cannot decrement a value below 0. The return value of `memc_decrement()` is the decremented value.

The syntax of `memc_decrement()` is:

```
memc_decrement(`key`);
memc_decrement(`key`, value);
```

The examples that follow show how to use `memc_decrement()` to decrement a value by 1 (the default) by not supplying a decrement value, and by 20, an explicitly supplied decrement value of 20.

```
mysql> select memc_decrement('counter');
+--------------------------+
| memc_decrement('counter') |
+--------------------------+
|                       21 |
+--------------------------+
```

```
mysql> select memc_decrement('counter',20);
+------------------------------+
| memc_decrement('counter',20) |
+------------------------------+
|                            1 |
+------------------------------+
```

Behavioral Functions

libmemcached gives you a lot of control over the behavior of the client as you saw in Chapter 9 and the Memcached Functions for MySQL have a means to extend this versatility.

memc_list_behaviors

The function memc_list_behaviors() displays a list of all the available behavior types that you can set for the client.

The syntax for memc_list_behaviors() is:

```
memc_list_behaviors()
```

The example below shows the output of memc_list_behaviors():

```
mysql> select memc_list_behaviors()\G
*************************** 1. row ***************************
memc_list_behaviors():
+-----------------------------------------+
| MEMCACHED SERVER BEHAVIORS              |
+-----------------------------------------+
| MEMCACHED_BEHAVIOR_SUPPORT_CAS          |
| MEMCACHED_BEHAVIOR_NO_BLOCK             |
| MEMCACHED_BEHAVIOR_TCP_NODELAY          |
| MEMCACHED_BEHAVIOR_HASH                 |
| MEMCACHED_BEHAVIOR_CACHE_LOOKUPS        |
| MEMCACHED_BEHAVIOR_SOCKET_SEND_SIZE     |
| MEMCACHED_BEHAVIOR_SOCKET_RECV_SIZE     |
| MEMCACHED_BEHAVIOR_BUFFER_REQUESTS      |
| MEMCACHED_BEHAVIOR_KETAMA               |
| MEMCACHED_BEHAVIOR_POLL_TIMEOUT         |
| MEMCACHED_BEHAVIOR_RETRY_TIMEOUT        |
| MEMCACHED_BEHAVIOR_DISTRIBUTION         |
| MEMCACHED_BEHAVIOR_BUFFER_REQUESTS      |
| MEMCACHED_BEHAVIOR_USER_DATA            |
| MEMCACHED_BEHAVIOR_SORT_HOSTS           |
| MEMCACHED_BEHAVIOR_VERIFY_KEY           |
| MEMCACHED_BEHAVIOR_CONNECT_TIMEOUT      |
| MEMCACHED_BEHAVIOR_KETAMA_WEIGHTED      |
| MEMCACHED_BEHAVIOR_KETAMA_HASH          |
| MEMCACHED_BEHAVIOR_BINARY_PROTOCOL      |
| MEMCACHED_BEHAVIOR_SND_TIMEOUT          |
| MEMCACHED_BEHAVIOR_RCV_TIMEOUT          |
| MEMCACHED_BEHAVIOR_SERVER_FAILURE_LIMIT |
+-----------------------------------------+
```

memc_behavior_get

The function `memc_behavior_get()` retrieves the current value of any of the behaviors that can be set in libmemcached, either numeric or a named value. If the value returned is one of the object distribution or hash algorithm behaviors, `memc_behaviors_get()` is versatile enough to convert it to the named canonical value instead of the numeric value.

The function `memc_servers_behavior_get()` is the same as `memc_behavior_get()` and exists for historical purposes.

You must call the function `memc_servers_set()` to connect to one or more memcached servers prior to calling `memc_behavior_get()`. In the example that follows, you can see that `memcached_behavior_get` obtains a named hash algorithm, a binary true or false value, as well as an integer value, depending on the behavior being obtained.

The syntax of `memc_behavior_get()` and `memc_servers_behavior_get()` is:

```
memc_behavior_get(`<behavior name>´);
memc_servers_behavior_get(`<behavior name>´);
```

Here is an example of using `memc_behavior_get()` to obtain the values of several behaviors:

```
mysql> select memc _behavior_get;('MEMCACHED_BEHAVIOR_HASH');
+-------------------------------------------------------+
| memc_servers_behavior_get('MEMCACHED_BEHAVIOR_HASH')  |
+-------------------------------------------------------+
| MEMCACHED_HASH_DEFAULT                                 |
+-------------------------------------------------------+

mysql> select memc_behavior_get('MEMCACHED_BEHAVIOR_SUPPORT_CAS');
+--------------------------------------------------------------+
| memc_servers_behavior_get('MEMCACHED_BEHAVIOR_SUPPORT_CAS')  |
+--------------------------------------------------------------+
| 1                                                            |
+--------------------------------------------------------------+

mysql> select memc_behavior_get('MEMCACHED_BEHAVIOR_POLL_TIMEOUT');
+---------------------------------------------------------------+
| memc_servers_behavior_get('MEMCACHED_BEHAVIOR_POLL_TIMEOUT')  |
+---------------------------------------------------------------+
| 1000                                                          |
+---------------------------------------------------------------+
```

memc_behavior_set

The function `memc_behavior_set()` allows you to set any one of the behaviors that libmemcached allows you to modify, as shown in `memc_behaviors_list()`. Some behaviors are Boolean 1 or 0, and some are canonical constant values that are internally converted to their actual numeric values. The numeric values can either be quoted or not, but the canonical values must be quoted.

You must call `memc_servers_set()` to connect to one or more memcached servers prior to setting a client behavior.

The syntax of `memc_behavior_set()` is:

```
memc_behavior_set(`<behavior name>´, value);
memc_servers_behavior_set(`<behavior name>´, value)
```

The following example shows the setting of a numeric and a canonical hash type value, and then the retrieval of those behaviors to verify that they were indeed set:

```
mysql> select memc_behavior_set('MEMCACHED_BEHAVIOR_POLL_TIMEOUT', 2000);
+----------------------------------------------------------+
| memc_behavior_set('MEMCACHED_BEHAVIOR_POLL_TIMEOUT', 2000) |
+----------------------------------------------------------+
|                                                        0 |
+----------------------------------------------------------+

mysql> select memc_behavior_set('MEMCACHED_BEHAVIOR_HASH', 'MEMCACHED_HASH_MD5');
+-----------------------------------------------------------------+
| memc_behavior_set('MEMCACHED_BEHAVIOR_HASH', 'MEMCACHED_HASH_MD5') |
+-----------------------------------------------------------------+
|                                                               0 |
+-----------------------------------------------------------------+

mysql> select memc_behavior_get('MEMCACHED_BEHAVIOR_POLL_TIMEOUT');
+-----------------------------------------------------+
| memc_behavior_get('MEMCACHED_BEHAVIOR_POLL_TIMEOUT') |
+-----------------------------------------------------+
| 2000                                                |
+-----------------------------------------------------+

mysql> select memc_behavior_get('MEMCACHED_BEHAVIOR_HASH');
+---------------------------------------------+
| memc_behavior_get('MEMCACHED_BEHAVIOR_HASH') |
+---------------------------------------------+
| MEMCACHED_HASH_MD5                           |
+---------------------------------------------+
```

memc_list_hash_types

The function `memc_list_hash_types()` lists the canonical hash value types that can be assigned using `memc_behavior_set()`, or are returned from using `memc_behavior_get()` for the behavior types `MEMCACHED_BEHAVIOR_HASH` or `MEMCACHED_BEHAVIOR_KETAMA_HASH`.

The syntax of `memc_list_hash_types()` is:

```
memc_list_hash_types();
```

The example shows the output of `memc_list_hash_types()`:

```
mysql> select memc_list_hash_types()\G
*************************** 1. row ***************************
memc_list_hash_types():
MEMCACHED_HASH_DEFAULT
MEMCACHED_HASH_MD5
```

```
MEMCACHED_HASH_CRC
MEMCACHED_HASH_FNV1_64
MEMCACHED_HASH_FNV1A_64
MEMCACHED_HASH_FNV1_32
MEMCACHED_HASH_FNV1A_32
MEMCACHED_HASH_JENKINS
MEMCACHED_HASH_HSIEH
```

To read more about these hash types, use the following:

```
man memcached_behavior_set
```

memc_list_distribution_types

The function `memc_list_distribution_types()` lists the canonical distribution types for values among servers that can be assigned using `memc_behavior_set()`, or are returned using `memc_behavior_get()` for the behavior type `MEMCACHED_BEHAVIOR_DISTRIBUTION`.

The syntax of `memc_list_distribution_types()` is:

```
memc_list_distribution_types()
mysql> select memc_list_distribution_types()\G
*************************** 1. row ***************************
memc_list_distribution_types():
MEMCACHED_DISTRIBUTION_MODULA
MEMCACHED_DISTRIBUTION_CONSISTENT
MEMCACHED_DISTRIBUTION_KETAMA
```

Statistical Functions

You can also obtain statistics about each memcached server with the various statistical functions. This can be extremely useful in obtaining information such as usage statistics, server version, process id, uptime, and many other details. This type of information could be used in managing connections to memcached, as well as if you were building an application that keeps and displays statistics on your overall system.

memc_stats

The function `memc_stat()` returns a list of the various statistics from one or more memcached servers specified in the single argument for servers, which is in the same format you would provide to the function `memc_server_add()`.

The syntax for `memc_stats()` is:

```
memc_stats(`server1:port, server2:port, ...´);
```

The output of `memc_stats()` is shown as follows:

```
mysql> select memc_stats('127.0.0.1:11211')\G
*************************** 1. row ***************************
memc_stats('127.0.0.1:11211'): Listing 1 Server

Server: 0.0.1 (26)
 pid: 32446
```

```
uptime: 89157
time: 1232245757
version: 1.2.6
pointer_size: 64
rusage_user: 1.344795
rusage_system: 0.916860
curr_items: 3
total_items: 7
bytes: 215
curr_connections: 2
total_connections: 53
connection_structures: 7
cmd_get: 8
cmd_set: 7
get_hits: 7
get_misses: 1
evictions: 0
bytes_read: 215
bytes_written: 215
limit_maxbytes: 67108864
threads: 1
```

memc_stat_get_value

The function `memc_stat_get_value()` can be used to retrieve a particular statistic from a memcached server. The first argument is a comma-separated list of one or more servers; the second argument is the statistic name.

The syntax for `memc_stat_get_value()` is:

```
memc_stat_get_value(`server1:port, server2:port, ...´, `stat name´);
```

The example that follows shows how this can be quite handy to retrieve a statistic, such as the memcached server version:

```
mysql> select memc_stat_get_value('127.0.0.1:11211', 'version');
+--------------------------------------------------+
| memc_stat_get_value('127.0.0.1:11211', 'version') |
+--------------------------------------------------+
| 1.2.6                                            |
+--------------------------------------------------+
```

memc_stat_get_keys

The function `memc_stat_get_keys()` takes no arguments and returns statistic keys available to be used with the function `memc_stat_get_value()`:

```
memc_stat_get_keys()
```

Version Functions

Also available are version functions that provide version information for both the UDF package themselves as well as the library that the Memcached Functions for MySQL were built against.

memc_libmemcached_version

The function `memc_libmemcached_version()` takes no arguments and returns the version of libmem-cached library that the Memcached Functions for MySQL were linked against.

The syntax for `memc_libmemcached_version()` is:

```
memc_libmemcached_version()
```

This example shows the output of `libmemcached_version()`:

```
mysql> select memc_libmemcached_version();
+----------------------------+
| memc_libmemcached_version() |
+----------------------------+
| 0.22                       |
+----------------------------+
```

memc_udf_version

The function `memc_udf_version()` takes no arguments and returns the version of the Memcached Functions for MySQL that are being used.

The syntax for `memc_udf_version()` is:

```
memc_udf_version()
```

The output of `memc_udf_version()` is shown here:

```
mysql> select memc_udf_version();
+--------------------+
| memc_udf_version() |
+--------------------+
| 0.8                |
+--------------------+
```

Using memcached UDFs

Now that you've read about all the functions, you are probably wondering how you can use them. In the previous chapters you saw how to write data to memcached using Perl. With these UDFs, you can do all of your interaction with memcached through MySQL, as opposed to Perl client libraries. This may provide some performance advantages, with MySQL retrieving or setting values directly in memcached with a fast C library instead of going back and forth from MySQL to your application and then back to memcached and vice versa. You already are connected to MySQL with DBI/DBD::mysql, which is sufficient for these UDFs, yet you won't need an additional handle to a memcached cluster. Also, you can move some of the caching logic from your application to the database.

The following sections will show you two practical usage examples:

❑ The first approach will show you how you would change the Perl application from a previous chapter, which handled caching data for MySQL using a database connection with DBD::mysql and a memcached connection with Cache::Memcached, to just a single database connection.

❑   The second approach details setting up triggers that automatically cache data to memcached when a table has data inserted or updated.

Single Database Handle Example

The following section will show you how you can use the Memcached Functions for MySQL without having to rely on Perl to connect to memcached using either Cache::Memcached or Cache::Memcached::libmemcached.

There are two things to consider:

❑   Cache::Memcached and Cache::Memcached::libmemcached automatically take care of serializing Perl data structures (particularly those other than simple scalars) stored in memcached for you. To do the same with the memcached UDFs, you will have to handle serialization and deserialization using the Perl module STORABLE.

❑   Cache::Memcached and Cached::Memcached::libmemcached have compression functionality with `compress_enable` and `compress_threshold`. This is done using the Compress::Zlib Perl module to compress or decompress a value being stored if it exceeds `compress_threshold`. This also can be added to your code easily enough. For the sake of brevity in this example, however, you won't be adding in this functionality. Also, none of what this example stores exceeds the size limits of what can be stored to memcached.

Changes to Connection

The first thing you would change in the code is to remove the import of `Cache::Memcached` and add the import of the STORABLE Perl module. For this example, we only need `nfreeze()` and `thaw()`:

```
use Storable qw(nfreeze thaw);

    my $memc_servers = ["127.0.0.1:11211"];
```

The use of `nfreeze()` here is significant. Use this instead of `freeze()` for portability, regardless of architecture. The author of this book once had to spend hours tracking down a bug that caused errors in reading session data on a 64-bit server that was stored from a 32-bit server!

The next thing to change would be the method that connected to memcached, `connectMemcached()`:

```
sub connectMemcached {
  my ($this)= @_;
  $this->{memc} = Cache::Memcached->new({
      'servers' => $memc_servers,
      'compress_threshold' => $memc_compress_threshold});
  unless ($this->{memc}->set('testping', 1)) {
    die "Unable to connect to memcached!\n";
  }
}
```

This is changed to:

```
sub connectMemcached {
  my ($this)= @_;
  # for memc_servers_set();
```

```perl
    my $memcached_servers= join(`,´, @$memc_servers);
    my $sth= $this->{dbh}->prepare("SELECT memc_stat_get_value(?, ?)");

    # with memc_stat_get_value, only one server can be checked at a time
    for my $server(@$memc_servers) {
      $sth->execute($server, `version´);
      my $ret_ref= $sth->fetchrow_arrayref();
      unless ($ret_ref->[0]) {
        $sth->finish;
        die "ERROR: Unable to connect to memcached server '$server'\n";
      }
    }
    $sth->finish;

    $sth= $this->{dbh}->prepare("SELECT memc_servers_set(?)");

    # here a string of comma-separated servers can be used
    $sth->execute($memcached_servers);
    my $ret_ref= $sth->fetchrow_arrayref();
    unless (defined $ret_ref->[0]) {
      die "ERROR: Unable to set servers for memcached\n";
    }
    $sth->finish;

  }
```

The method connectMemcached() performs the same essential function it did before: It connects to one or more memcached servers. The difference is that it now connects to memcached from within MySQL, as opposed to a handle in Perl that connects directly to memcached. All interactions with memcached will now be through the database handle.

Since the UDF memc_servers_set() takes a string of comma-separated servers, $memcached_servers is built using a join of the elements in the array referenced by $memc_servers, with commas.

Before an actual connection is made, an attempt using UDF memc_stat_get_value() is made to obtain the version to each of the servers in the $memc_servers array reference. If any of the servers don't provide a version, that means that server cannot be connected to. If all servers return a version, then a connection is made.

Another thing to make sure of is that connectMemcached() is called after a database connection is made. Previously, this was not a concern since memcached had its own handle independent of MySQL. If you will recall, the new() method was where a connection was established for the UserApp application for subsequent calls to memcached:

```perl
sub new {
  my ($class) = @_;
  my $this= {};
  bless $this, $class;
  $this->connectDB();
  $this->connectMemcached();
  # cache all cities records
  $this->cacheCities();
  # cache all states records
```

```
        $this->cacheStates();
        return $this;
    }
```

Changes to getUser()

To provide practical examples of how these UDFs can be used, there are several get/set calls in this library that retrieve and store different types of data — users, states, regions, cities, etc. The method that retrieves a user, getUser(), will be the one used here to show what changes need to be made because it has both the retrieval and storing of user data in memcached, and the types of changes you would make in this method you would also make to other methods.

As you recall from Chapter 8, getUser() had caching added to it that checked first to see if a user was already stored in memcached before it attempted to read the user from MySQL. The keys for storing the user were the name of the table, *users*, a colon, and the username and UID. The sole argument to getUser, the variable $username, is the value used to construct on the memcached keys that check if the user is stored in memcached. If the user is in memcached, the variable $user, which is a hash reference of a user, is returned. If not, a query to retrieve the $user hash reference is issued against MySQL. Once retrieved from the database, it's also stored in memcached (a read-through cache). The memcached-specific code is in boldface type in this example for easier reading:

```
    sub getUser {
        my ($this, $username)= @_;
        my $memc_key1= "users:$username";
        my $user_ref;

        # check memcached first
        $user_ref= $this->{memc}->get($memc_key);

        # simply return from memcached if already cached
        return $user_ref if $user_ref->{username};

        # obtain from db if not in memcached
        my $query= <<EOQ
    SELECT uid, username, email, firstname, surname, address, city_id, password,
        cities.city_name as city_name,
        states.state_id AS state_id,
        states.state_name AS state_name,
        regions.region_id AS region_id,
        regions.region_name AS region_name,
        account_levels.account_level AS account_level,
        account_levels.account_level_name AS account_level_name
    FROM users
    JOIN cities USING (city_id)
    JOIN states ON (cities.state_id = states.state_id)
    JOIN regions ON (cities.region_id = regions.region_id)
    JOIN account_levels USING (account_level)
    WHERE username = ?
    EOQ
    ;

        my $sth= $this->{dbh}->prepare($query);
        $sth->execute($username);
```

```
    $user_ref= $sth->fetchrow_hashref();

    # now that we have UID from DB
    my $memc_key2= 'users:' . $user_ref->{uid};

    # store in memcached (Read-through caching!)
    return unless $user_ref;

    unless ($this->{memc}->set($memc_key1, $user_ref)) {
      print "ERROR: unable to set user!\n";
    }
    unless ($this->{memc}->set($memc_key2, $user_ref)) {
      print "ERROR: unable to set user!\n";
    }

    # return user reference
    return ($user_ref);
  }
```

What would need to be changed in this method is to remove the get() and set() calls to memcached through the class member memc (to Cache::Memcached) and replace them with calls to the appropriate UDFs via MySQL.

These lines ...

```
    # check memcached first
    $user_ref= $this->{memc}->get($memc_key);

    # simply return from memcached if already cached
    return $user_ref if $user_ref->{username};
```

are replaced with these:

```
# obtain from MySQL
my $user_serial= $this->{dbh}->selectrow_arrayref("SELECT memc_get(?)", {}, ($memc_key1));

# de-serialize
$user_ref= thaw($user_serial->[0]) if defined $user_serial->[0];

# simply return from memcached if already cached
return $user_ref if $user_ref->{uid};
```

... and also result in the storing of the user when the user has been read from the database. Replace these lines ...

```
    # now that we have UID from DB
    my $memc_key2= 'users:' . $user_ref->{uid};

    # store in memcached (Read-through caching!)
    return unless $user_ref;

    unless ($this->{memc}->set($memc_key1, $user_ref)) {
      print "ERROR: unable to set user!\n";
```

```
        }
        unless ($this->{memc}->set($memc_key2, $user_ref)) {
          print "ERROR: unable to set user!\n";
        }
```

with these lines:

```
    # 2nd key with UID
    my $memc_key2= 'users:' . $user_ref->{uid};

    # serialize $user_ref
    my $user_serial= nfreeze($user_ref);

    # prepare query
    my $sth= $this->{dbh}->prepare("select memc_set(?, ?)");

    # store both in memcached
    $sth->execute($memc_key1, $user_serial);
    $sth->execute($memc_key2, $user_serial);
```

As you can see, there are a few more lines of code, but now everything is happening through MySQL. Also, if you are like the author of this book and you see places where code becomes redundant, you realize there might be the need for a generic get and set method to take care of the details of storing, retrieving, serialization and deserialization of data.

Creating More Convenience with Generic Get and Set Methods

Whenever you see code that you know will be used in multiple places and multiple times, you should hear an alarm in your head telling you to create a convenient function or method containing that code. To change this UserApp application to use the Memcached Functions for MySQL (memcached UDFs), you create generic set and get methods.

An example of a generic store method would be:

```
    sub memc_set {
      my ($this, $key, $value)= @_;
      my $sth = $this->{dbh}->prepare_cached('SELECT memc_set(?, ?)');

      my $storable_value = ref $value ? nfreeze($value) : $value;
      $sth->execute($key, $storable_value);
      my $stored = $sth->fetchrow_arrayref();
      # returns 0 on success, greater than 0 error

      return $stored->[0];

    }
```

The method memc_set() provides a simple way to store data in memcached without having to consider any of the details of how to both serialize the data and prepare and execute the SQL statement calling the UDF. The method memc_set() takes two arguments: $key and $value. $key is the key that you want to associate with the $value you store.

Furthermore, $value is only serialized if it is a reference — for instance, if you were trying to store a hash reference such as the $user in previous examples. If $value is a simple scalar, it is stored as is. The value of calling memc_set(), which is 0 if successful and > 0 if a failure, is returned.

memc_set() is also the place where you would add in the compression functionality that is currently missing using the Perl module Compress::Zlib.

An example of a generic fetching method would be:

```
sub memc_get {
  my ($this, $key)= @_;
  my $de_serialized;
  my $sth= $this->{dbh}->prepare_cached('SELECT memc_get(?)');

  $sth->execute($key);
  my $stored= $sth->fetchrow_arrayref();
  # will be 1 or 0

  if (defined $stored->[0]) {
    eval { $de_serialized = thaw($stored->[0])};
    return $@ ? $stored->[0] : $de_serialized;
  }
  else {
    return undef;
  }
}
```

This method memc_get() provides a simple interface to fetching data using the memc_get() UDF, hiding all the details of deserialization and preparing, executing, and fetching the stored value. An eval block is used to attempt a call to thaw() for the retrieved value. Conveniently, thaw() will fail if the value is not a serialized object. The variable $@ indicates that eval failed, and if so, it will just return the value as is. Otherwise it will return the value that successfully was thawed. If no value was retrieved, then undef is returned.

With these two methods (memc_set() and memc_get()), the previous code of storing and retrieving the user reference becomes even simpler. The method getUser() checked if the user hash reference already existed in memcached to avoid a database lookup:

```
# check memcached first
$user_ref= $this->memc_get($memc_key1);

# simply return from memcached if already cached
return $user_ref if $user_ref->{username};
```

And getUser() stored the user hash reference if retrieved from the database:

```
# store both
if ($this->memc_set($memc_key1, $user_ref)) {;
  print "ERROR: unable to store $memc_key1\n";
  return;
}
if ($this->memc_set($memc_key2, $user_ref)) {;
```

```
    print "ERROR: unable to store $memc_key2\n";
    return;
  }
```

In fact, it is really simple now to replace the previous Cache::Memcached calls with this generic method, as illustrated here. Throughout the code, set ...

```
$this->{memc}->set($key, $val);
```

... can be replaced with:

```
$this->memc_set($key, $val);
```

And get ...

```
$return_val= $this->{memc}->get($key, $val);
```

... can be replaced with:

```
$return_val= $this->memc_get($key, $val);
```

Fun with Triggers (and UDFs)

You can get really creative with the use of triggers and the Memcached Functions for MySQL. As you will recall, triggers provide a means to have a given action take place upon a change to a row in a table — insert, update, and delete — either before or after the change is made. With memcached, you could hide a lot of the details of caching from the application code, at least the part of caching where data is written to the database and you want the data in memcached to mirror the changes made to the database.

In the distribution directory containing the source code to the Memcached Functions for MySQL, there is a file in the sql/ directory called trigger_fun.sql. This interesting file contains some practical examples of how you can employ triggers to use these UDFs to do things such as work as a sequence, as well as store data in memcached whenever there is a change to a row in a table.

The first thing this file creates is a simple table called urls that contains two columns: an id, which is the primary key, and url, which is a string which URL values will be stored.

```
drop table if exists urls;
create table urls (
  id int(3) not null,
  url varchar(64) not null default '',
  primary key (id)
  );
```

The next thing that is set up is the connection to memcached:

```
select memc_servers_set('localhost:11211');
```

And then a simple sequence object that will start at 0 is established:

```
select memc_set('urls:sequence', 0);
```

Then the INSERT trigger is created:

```
DELIMITER |

DROP TRIGGER IF EXISTS url_mem_insert |
CREATE TRIGGER url_mem_insert
BEFORE INSERT ON urls
FOR EACH ROW BEGIN
    SET NEW.id = memc_increment('urls:sequence');
    SET @mm = memc_set(concat('urls:',NEW.id), NEW.url);
END |
```

The trigger url_mem_insert does two things upon (before) the insertion of a row to *urls*:

❑   Increments the counter object, urls:sequence by 1.

❑   Sets the URL value keyed by concatenating the string users: with the new id value that was just incremented and then calls memc_set(). The SQL statement SET must be used because you cannot call SELECT from within a trigger.

For instance, the first record inserted will increment urls:sequence to 1, which the value of id will assume, hence the key created will be `users:1´, then whatever url value is being inserted into *urls* will also be inserted into memcached as users:1.

Next comes an update trigger:

```
DROP TRIGGER IF EXISTS url_mem_update |
CREATE TRIGGER url_mem_update
BEFORE UPDATE ON urls
FOR EACH ROW BEGIN
    SET @mm = memc_replace(concat('urls:',OLD.id), NEW.url);
END |
```

The trigger url_memc_update is executed any time a record in users is updated. It uses the same scheme to create a memcached key by concatenating *urls*: with the id of the record being updated. For example, if the first record is updated, its existing url value **`http://www.foo.com´ with `http://www.fee.com´, memc_replace(`urls:1´, `http://www.fee.com´);** will subsequently be called. The syntax SET is used because you cannot call SELECT from within a trigger.

Then finally, here is a DELETE trigger:

```
DROP TRIGGER IF EXISTS url_mem_delete |
CREATE TRIGGER url_mem_delete
BEFORE DELETE ON urls
FOR EACH ROW BEGIN
    SET @mm = memc_delete(concat('urls:',OLD.id));
END |
```

The trigger url_mem_delete is executed on the deletion of any row in *urls*. It also uses the scheme to build a memcached key that the other two triggers use. For example, upon the deletion of a record that contains 'http://www.fee.com', which has the id value of 1, the UDF memc_delete(`users:1´) is called.

`trigger_fun.sql` also has some use case SQL statements to show the triggers in action:

1. First, the data is inserted:

```
insert into urls (url) values ('http://google.com');
insert into urls (url) values ('http://lycos.com/');
insert into urls (url) values ('http://tripod.com/');
insert into urls (url) values ('http://microsoft.com/');
insert into urls (url) values ('http://slashdot.org');
insert into urls (url) values ('http://mysql.com');
```

2. An SQL statement to verify that the data exists in the table is issued:

```
select * from urls;
```

3. Each value that should be stored as a result of the previous inserts is retrieved and should match the output of the previous `select` statement:

```
select memc_get('urls:1');
select memc_get('urls:2');
select memc_get('urls:3');
select memc_get('urls:4');
select memc_get('urls:5');
select memc_get('urls:6');
```

4. One of the records is updated and immediately the key for this record is selected from the table as well as fetched from memcached. It should have the updated value — the same value as the `select` statement following the `update`:

```
update urls set url= 'http://mysql.com/sun' where url = 'http://mysql.com';
select url from urls where url = 'http://mysql.com/sun';
select memc_get('urls:6');
```

5. The same type of test is performed, except this time a record is deleted:

```
delete from urls where url = 'http://microsoft.com/';
select * from urls where url = 'http://microsoft.com/';
select memc_get('urls:4');
```

6. You can run `trigger_fun.sql` by command line to verify that these triggers work as advertised:

```
mysql -u root -p test < trigger_fun.sql

memc_servers_set('localhost:11211')
0
memc_set('urls:sequence', 0)
0
```

This is the output of selecting all records after inserting the six records:

```
id      url
1       http://google.com
2       http://lycos.com/
```

```
3        http://tripod.com/
4        http://microsoft.com/
5        http://slashdot.org
6        http://mysql.com
```

The following code is the output of fetching the same records from memcached. You'll see that all of the values were in fact stored via the trigger:

```
memc_get('urls:1')
http://google.com
memc_get('urls:2')
http://lycos.com/
memc_get('urls:3')
http://tripod.com/
memc_get('urls:4')
http://microsoft.com/
memc_get('urls:5')
http://slashdot.org
memc_get('urls:6')
```

The following code is the output after the update statement, first from the *urls* table, then from memcached. And yes, they match!

```
http://mysql.com
url
http://mysql.com/sun
memc_get('urls:6')
http://mysql.com/sun
```

Then the result of memc_delete(), which of course, the select from *urls* for the URL 'http://microsoft.com' yields nothing, but for memcached NULL is returned (correct).

```
memc_get('urls:4')
NULL
```

So, you can see all the triggers work as advertised.

Using triggers can hide all of these details from the application. Values are automatically cached upon writing to the database. This is very convenient and powerful in that it offers an integration of durable data store (MySQL) and lightweight, fast caching (memcached)!

Read-Through Caching with Simple Select Statements

One last part of this chapter is to show how you can use these UDFs to cache data in a single select.

As you saw earlier in this chapter, a user would be fetched from the database and memcached in separate SQL statements. You can combine obtaining data and caching in one step.

For instance, you can cache a single user, in this case the user with the username of capttofu.

```
mysql> SELECT uid, username, email, firstname, surname,
    -> memc_set(concat('users:uid:',username), uid),
    -> memc_set(concat('users:username:',uid), username),
```

```
    -> memc_set(concat('users:email:', username), email),
    -> memc_set(concat('users:firstname:', username), firstname),
    -> memc_set(concat('users:surname:', username), surname)
    -> from users where uid = 1\G
*************************** 1. row ***************************
                                    uid: 1
                               username: capttofu
                                  email: capttofu@capttofu.org
                              firstname: Patrick
                                surname: Galbraith
            memc_set(concat('users:uid:',username), uid): 0
        memc_set(concat('users:username:',uid), username): 0
        memc_set(concat('users:email:', username), email): 0
memc_set(concat('users:firstname:', username), firstname): 0
    memc_set(concat('users:surname:', username), surname): 0
```

In this example, the key used is `tablename:column:unique_identifier`. Also, since both `uid` and `username` are unique, you can create a key using both, particularly storing so you can look up each using the other. For instance, you cache `user:uid:capttofu` to have the value of 1 and `user:username:1` to have the value of `capttofu` — you can look up either given either key.

To see that these values were stored, you can select them all out on one line:

```
mysql> select memc_get('users:uid:capttofu') as uid,
    -> memc_get('users:username:1') as username,
    -> memc_get('users:email:capttofu') as email,
    -> memc_get('users:firstname:capttofu') as firstname,
    -> memc_get('users:surname:capttofu') as surname;
+-----+----------+-----------------------+-----------+-----------+
| uid | username | email                 | firstname | surname   |
+-----+----------+-----------------------+-----------+-----------+
| 1   | capttofu | capttofu@capttofu.org | Patrick   | Galbraith |
+-----+----------+-----------------------+-----------+-----------+
```

. . . which is how you can cache without using serialization. You just have to keep your keys in order!

Also, you can use the Power of the SELECT™ to cache multiple records in one fell swoop!

If you will recall, some things, such as geographical data like states, can be precached at the beginning of a program's execution, and the UserApp example did this very thing. This can be done with one simple SQL statement.

```
mysql> select state_abbr, state_name,
    -> memc_set(concat('states:state_abbr:',state_name), state_abbr),
    -> memc_set(concat('states:state_name:', state_abbr), state_name),
    -> memc_set(concat('states:state_flower:',state_abbr), state_flower)
    -> from states\G
*************************** 1. row ***************************
                                              state_abbr: AL
                                              state_name: Alabama
    memc_set(concat('states:state_abbr:',state_name), state_abbr): 0
    memc_set(concat('states:state_name:', state_abbr), state_name): 0
memc_set(concat('states:state_flower:',state_abbr), state_flower): 0
*************************** 2. row ***************************
                                              state_abbr: AK
```

```
                                                     state_name: Alaska
       memc_set(concat('states:state_abbr:',state_name), state_abbr): 0
       memc_set(concat('states:state_name:', state_abbr), state_name): 0
   memc_set(concat('states:state_flower:',state_abbr), state_flower): 0
*************************** 3. row ***************************
                                                       state_abbr: AR
                                                     state_name: Arkansas
       memc_set(concat('states:state_abbr:',state_name), state_abbr): 0
       memc_set(concat('states:state_name:', state_abbr), state_name): 0
   memc_set(concat('states:state_flower:',state_abbr), state_flower): 0
  ...
  ...
*************************** 49. row ***************************
                                                       state_abbr: WI
                                                     state_name: Wisconsin
       memc_set(concat('states:state_abbr:',state_name), state_abbr): 0
       memc_set(concat('states:state_name:', state_abbr), state_name): 0
   memc_set(concat('states:state_flower:',state_abbr), state_flower): 0
*************************** 50. row ***************************
                                                       state_abbr: WY
                                                     state_name: Wyoming
       memc_set(concat('states:state_abbr:',state_name), state_abbr): 0
       memc_set(concat('states:state_name:', state_abbr), state_name): 0
   memc_set(concat('states:state_flower:',state_abbr), state_flower): 0
*************************** 51. row ***************************
                                                       state_abbr: DC
                                              state_name: District of Columbia
       memc_set(concat('states:state_abbr:',state_name), state_abbr): 8
       memc_set(concat('states:state_name:', state_abbr), state_name): 0
   memc_set(concat('states:state_flower:',state_abbr), state_flower): 0
```

This query will cache all the states for the columns specified in memc_set using concatenation to create the key, just like the previous example, except with this there are 51 records in the result set, all of which are now cached!

To select the data:

```
mysql> select memc_get(concat('states:state_abbr:',state_name)) as state_abbr,
memc_get(concat('states:state_name:',state_abbr)) as state_name,
memc_get(concat('states:state_flower:',state_abbr)) from states limit 20;
+------------+------------+----------------------------------------------------+
| state_abbr | state_name | memc_get(concat('states:state_flower:',state_abbr)) |
+------------+------------+----------------------------------------------------+
| AL         | Alabama    | Camellia                                           |
| AK         | Alaska     | Forget Me Not                                      |
| AR         | Arkansas   | Apple Blossom                                      |
| AZ         | Arizona    | Saguaro Cactus Blossom                             |
| CA         | California | California Poppy                                   |
| CO         | Colorado   | Rocky Mountain Columbine                           |
| CT         | Connecticut| Mountain Laurel                                    |
| DE         | Delaware   | Peach Blossom                                      |
| FL         | Florida    | Orange Blossom                                     |
| GA         | Georgia    | Cherokee Rose                                      |
| HI         | Hawaii     | Pua Aloalo                                         |
```

```
| ID        | Idaho       | Syringa - Mock Orange           |
| IA        | Iowa        | Wild Prairie Rose               |
| IN        | Indiana     | Peony                           |
| IL        | Illinois    | Purple Violet                   |
| KS        | Kansas      | Sunflower                       |
| KY        | Kentucky    | Goldenrod                       |
| LA        | Louisianna  | Manolia                         |
| ME        | Maine       | White pine cone and tassel      |
| MD        | Maryland    | Black-eyed susan                |
+-----------+-------------+---------------------------------------------------------+
```

Fantastic! You now have a multiple-key data fetch from memcached. The table *states* essentially provides the list of keys. Notice also that any SQL statement condition can be used, in this case a LIMIT clause.

OK, so you may think this chapter is now done and you can go to sleep (if you haven't already). Well, there's one more trick to show you!

Updates, Too!

Consider a simple table *foo*; it has one column 'a,' which is an int. Not important other than for showing this example. Follow these steps:

1. Insert four values into this table, then set a value in memcached using a key that maps to the table:

    ```
    mysql> insert into foo values (1), (2), (3), (4);
    Query OK, 4 rows affected (0.00 sec)
    Records: 4  Duplicates: 0  Warnings: 0

    mysql> select memc_set('foo:3', 3);
    +----------------------+
    | memc_set('foo:3', 3) |
    +----------------------+
    |                    0 |
    +----------------------+
    ```

2. Fetch the value to verify it was set:

    ```
    mysql> select memc_get('foo:3');
    +-------------------+
    | memc_get('foo:3') |
    +-------------------+
    | 3                 |
    +-------------------+
    ```

3. Now update the table *and* memcached!

    ```
    mysql> update foo set a = 33 where a = 3 and not memc_replace('foo:3', 33);
    Query OK, 1 row affected (0.00 sec)
    Rows matched: 1  Changed: 1  Warnings: 0
    ```

4. Verify it was replaced:

```
mysql> select memc_get('foo:3');
+-------------------+
| memc_get('foo:3') |
+-------------------+
| 33                |
+-------------------+
```

Which it was!

The trick here is that you can use a conjunction in an `update` statement — so long as the condition evaluates to `true`. Recall that `memc_set()`, and `memc_replace()` return `false` (a zero) upon a successful data store. So, for the condition to be evaluated as `true` and then make the `update` statement occur, you would negate the return value of `memc_replace()`.

Summary

The Memcached Functions for MySQL are a suite of user-defined functions (UDFs) available to use with MySQL that allow you to store, retrieve, and delete data. With these functions, you can manage your data in MySQL and the data you cached from MySQL alone.

This chapter explained or contained the following:

❑   What exactly the Memcached Functions for MySQL are and the basic concept of how they work — using the MySQL UDF API and the libmemcached C library. A detailed explanation of syntax and examples were provided to teach you how to use each of these UDFs.

❑   A demonstration using the Perl user application from Chapter 8 showed how to modify this application from using the Perl library, Cache::Memcached, to using these UDFs. This gave a good example of how an application can use these UDFs to make MySQL the source for both durable data in the database, as well as volatile/mortal data in memcached. Also shown was how to make a generic store and retrieval method that can hide the specific UDF calls to MySQL and provide a means of serializing complex Perl data types that need to be stored in memcached.

❑   Finally, the chapter closed with a discussion showing how to employ the use of triggers to automatically keep memcached objects in sync with data changes to the source table for insert, update, and delete.

You should now have a good understanding of how you can utilize the Memcached Functions for MySQL in application development.

11

Apache

From 1996 until the present time, the Apache HTTP Server has the most popular web server. Maintained by the Apache Software Foundation, an open community of developers, it is an open-source HTTP (Hypertext Transfer Protocol) server that runs on numerous UNIX variants as well as Microsoft Windows platforms. It includes a programming interface (API) that can extend Apache using numerous programming languages, including C, Perl (with CGI and mod_perl, which we will discuss later), PHP, Java, Python, Ruby, and Tcl. Apache also includes functionality for SSL (Secure Sockets Layer) and TLS (Transport Layer Security) for running secure web sites.

Apache is one of the core technologies of this book, and as such this chapter will discuss in detail how Apache is installed and configured, as well as how it works.

Understanding Apache: An Overview

As an HTTP server, Apache is an agreed-upon standard client/server communications application-level protocol as defined by the Internet Engineering Task Force in RFC 2616. HTTP is a generic, stateless protocol, meaning that when connections are made between the client and server, no client information is maintained between requests. HTTP provides the mechanism for a server (the web server) to respond to a request from a client (a web browser or other client program requesting content). The basic function of HTTP follows this pattern:

❑   The server waits for a request.

❑   A client connects to the server, sending a request header that contains several lines: a particular method (HEAD, GET, POST, PUT, etc.) followed by a URI/URL (Uniform Resource Identifier/Locator) for a particular document or other data source such as an image, video, sound file, etc., various headers, and an optional message body.

❑   The server:

  ❑   Reads the request, specifically what URI is being requested.

❏ Through a configuration file, figures out what file or resource on disk to serve based on the relative path.

❏ Responds to the client with a response header containing several lines — a numeric status code and a textual reason phrase (a canonical term such as OK, Not Found, Moved, etc.) indicating success or failure in returning the resource to the client, content length indicating the size of what is being returned, the type of content, character set, etc., and then finally the response body, which contains the contents of the file.

Figure 11-1 illustrates a client request and server response that is the result of an access of a web browser to the Wiley web page (publishers of this book). As you can see, both the request and response contain information about both the client making the request and the server giving the response. (In fact, both the request and response in this example were reduced to fit into the illustration — there is usually much more data in both.)

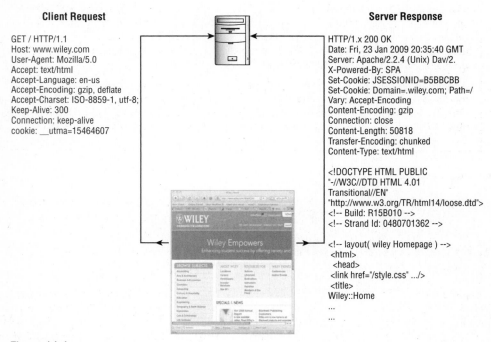

Client Request

```
GET / HTTP/1.1
Host: www.wiley.com
User-Agent: Mozilla/5.0
Accept: text/html
Accept-Language: en-us
Accept-Encoding: gzip, deflate
Accept-Charset: ISO-8859-1, utf-8;
Keep-Alive: 300
Connection: keep-alive
cookie: __utma=15464607
```

Server Response

```
HTTP/1.x 200 OK
Date: Fri, 23 Jan 2009 20:35:40 GMT
Server: Apache/2.2.4 (Unix) Dav/2.
X-Powered-By: SPA
Set-Cookie: JSESSIONID=B5BBCBB
Set-Cookie: Domain=.wiley.com; Path=/
Vary: Accept-Encoding
Content-Encoding: gzip
Connection: close
Content-Length: 50818
Transfer-Encoding: chunked
Content-Type: text/html

<!DOCTYPE HTML PUBLIC
"-//W3C//DTD HTML 4.01
Transitional//EN"
"http://www.w3.org/TR/html14/loose.dtd">
<!-- Build: R15B010 -->
<!-- Strand Id: 0480701362 -->

<!-- layout( wiley Homepage ) -->
 <html>
  <head>
  <link href="/style.css" .../>
  <title>
Wiley::Home
  ...
  ...
```

Figure 11-1

Brief History of Apache

Due to the efforts of Rob McCool and other developers, Apache was first released in 1994. Previously, Rob had been involved in the development of Apache's predecessor, NCSA (National Center for Supercomputing Applications) HTTP web server, which stalled when Rob left NCSA. As a result, various patches started circulating via email, and the Apache Group formed to address how to integrate these patches into a new web server. With all the patches, this new server was considered "a patchy" server — Apache.

The new Apache project became increasingly popular due to the features it offered, including running CGI (Common Gateway Interface) programs written in shell, C or Perl, and PHP. In addition, Apache became the standard web server preinstalled on another popular open-source operating project, Linux. Both Linux and Apache grew together, resulting in Apache becoming the most popular web server in 1996.

With the coming of Apache, setting up a web server was not only free, it was also simple! All you had to do was install Linux, opt to install Apache, configure networking, and edit the stock HTML pages that came bundled with Apache — then you had a running web server. It was also extremely easy to produce CGI programs — simply write them and put them in a cgi-bin directory. You could have a web server with dynamic content — applications — with minimal configuration.

mod_perl, developed by Lincoln Stein, was also developed around this time and was a tremendous advancement over running CGI Perl scripts because it presented a new approach — it embedded a Perl interpreter into Apache (versus CGIs), which ran as forked executions of Perl. Now you could write Perl handlers (more about this later) that had access to the Apache API, which meant persistence within Perl-based applications and which saved on the overhead of forking.

Apache 2.0, a substantial rewrite of Apache 1.x, generally became available in 2002 and included further development of APR (Apache Portable Runtime), a portability layer. Other developments included threading on UNIX, better non-UNIX support, and a new API. With Apache 2.0, and now 2.2, mod_perl 2.0 followed.

Other functions of the HTTP server are these:

- ❏ To manage child processes of the server. Generally, a main process launches initially and starts other child processes or threads, depending on whether Apache uses the pre-fork or worker model to handle requests.

- ❏ To kill those child processes that the main process started after they have served out their maximum number of requests, as defined in the Apache configuration.

Understanding HTTP and how the web server works, particularly that it is a stateless protocol, helps you understand the limitations and parameters of developing web applications. HTTP is all about connecting, requesting info, and getting info from the server in single shots. To maintain some sort of semblance of persistence, tricks like cookies (the ultimate hack!), state encoded in URLs, and state encoded in hidden form fields, are employed. In fact, you should think of duct tape when you think of web programming; many technologies were developed to make a stateless protocol have the *illusion* of state.

This is the *world* of web programming and developers must be aware of the confinements within which they work.

Understanding the Apache Modules API

One of Apache's best features is that it has an API that allows for the extension of the web server using loadable modules. These are extensions of Apache — much like Linux plug-ins are DSOs (Dynamically Shared Object files) — which the Apache server loads. In essence, the module code becomes part of the

Apache server process when the web server process, `httpd`, is started. This allows the site administrator to have the web server include only the functionality he or she wants.

Originally, much of what is now modular functionality was compiled into the Apache web server binary, `httpd`, such as mod_perl. Then many of these features, such as mod_perl, PHP, and mod_layout, were made into loadable modules. Now, in addition to external features, even the core functionalities are made into modules. This makes it possible for module developers to alter Apache's basic functionality. With modularization, you can choose only what you want to be linked into the server, making for a smaller, more efficient Apache process.

Apache 2.2 Changes Since Apache 1.3

Many existing books available for Perl web development, CGI, and mod_perl are based on Apache 1.3, and in fact, many web sites still use Apache 1.3 because it works well. This book is specifically for Apache 2.2. The following is a list of the new Apache 2.2 features:

❏ **Modularization of the server:** Whereas Apache 1.3 used modules for various external features, now even what used to be part of the Apache server is modularized, allowing module developers to modify even the basic functionality of Apache.

❏ **Simplified, modular configuration file:** The confusion as to what was considered an Apache configuration file (the author can attest to this!) has been cleared up. The configuration files have been cleaned, cruft stripped, with confusing directives jettisoned and trashed. For instance, `Port` and `BindAddress` are gone; greater clarity is possible through the use of directives `Listen` (IP address binding) and `ServerName` (server name and port number, used for virtual host recognition and redirection). The common setup is to have a main configuration file with other parts of the configuration including security and virtual hosts. A new virtual host often means merely creating a virtual host configuration file in the proper directory, which automatically loads the next time Apache restarts.

❏ **New Apache API:** It is now much easier to load Apache modules than back in the old days!

❏ **Apache Model:** Apache now has four execution/MPM (Multiprocessing Modules) models:

  ❏ **MPM Worker:** UNIX threading through a hybrid of multiprocess and multi-threaded server. This model uses multiple servers to provide stability, with each server having its own threads to answer requests and thus saving resources since multiple processes for each request aren't required.

  ❏ **MPM Prefork:** This is similar to how Apache 1.3 works. The parent process forks children to serve requests, with each child remaining until MAX_REQUESTS is served.

  ❏ **MPM NT:** Windows threading, using Windows native networking features. Consists of a single control process that launches a single child process, which creates threads to handle requests.

  ❏ **MPM Event:** Here is a caveat: this is experimental, based on MPM Worker. This model passes subsequent requests from main threads to supporting threads in order for the main threads to serve out new/initial requests.

❏ **Filtering:** Apache modules can be written as filters that enable applications to act upon content going both to and from the server. This uses mod_filter, dynamic configuration of the filter chain, as well as conditional insertion of a filter based on a request or response header.

❑ **Large file support:** With web sites that serve videos, audio, and other large files, Apache 2.2 now supports files greater than 2 gigabytes. Let the floodgates open!

❑ **Better regular expression support:** As a Perl developer, you use regular expressions. In fact, they are one of the key reasons you love Perl! Apache uses a library called PCRE (Perl Compatible Regular Expressions), which provides Apache regular expressions for redirect rules, parsing configuration files, etc. Other projects, such as Drizzle, use PCRE as well.

❑ **Authentication code refactoring:** Along with the new module mod_authn_alias to simplify authentication, the authentication code itself has been refactored.

Apache 2.2 Request Phases

The Apache 2.2 request phases have changed somewhat from Apache 1.3. Whereas Apache 1.3 had 11 request phases, Apache 2.2 now has four primary request phases (see http://httpd.apache.org/docs/2.2/developer/request.html), as shown in Figure 11-2. The following sections further discuss each phase.

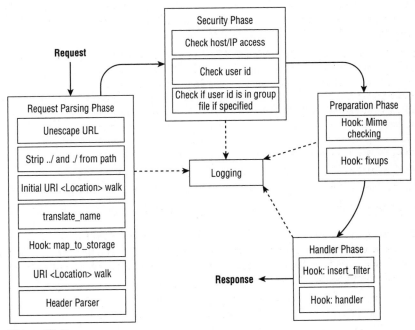

Figure 11-2

Request Parsing Phase

This phase is where the initial client request is parsed and the incoming URI is doctored into a form that can be used to compare against configuration directives, particularly <Location>, <Directory>, <Files>, and <Proxy>. The following are steps that occur within the request parsing phase:

1. Un-escape the request URI, unless proxy.

2. Strip away the ../ and ./ from the request URI.

3. Initial URI <Location> walk: This ensures that <Location> sections are enforced.

4. translate_name: Where directives such as <Alias> or <VirtualHost> are used to modify the file or directory name.

5. map_to_storage hook: This is the phase where the actual resource, be it a file on the server or a proxy URL, is mapped to the request. Per-directory sections such as <Directory>, <Files>, and <Proxy> (if mod_proxy) are merged together. This is a *hook* that, at this stage, allows for modules to implement their own processing, if desired.

6. URI Location walk (second): Another location walk to test the translated request URI against <Location> sections. Unless the URI has been changed from the previous location walk due to processing, previous processing from the previous step is utilized for efficiency.

7. Header parser hook: This step parses the client headers and provides a hook, allowing for module developers to implement additional functionality at this phase, if desired.

Security Phase

In this phase, the server checks if the request URI specified in a <Directory> section requires an access control check, authentication and authorization. Depending on whether the directive Satisfy is the value Any or All, any or all of the following checks will give the request access to the resource:

❏ If the directive Order is specified, ap_run_access_checker determines if the host or IP of the client request is given access.

❏ If the directive Require is specified, the credentials of the user for the request are checked against the user file specified with the directive AuthUserFile, and a group file, if it is specified with AuthGroupFile, exists.

Preparation Phase

This phase provides two hook opportunities:

❏ MIME checking hook: Checks the resource being requested for the MIME type and responds accordingly by setting the MIME information of the request. This hook also allows modules an opportunity to perform their own processing or filtering.

❏ Fixups hook: Previous phases and steps may have modified the state of what certain modules require of the request object. This hook allows modules an opportunity to reestablish the state and ownership of the request object and its fields.

Handler Phase

This phase is not officially part of the processing function that handles the previous three phases, ap_process_request_internal. This phase provides two hook opportunities:

❏ insert_filter hook: This is the last opportunity for a module to modify the content that will be returned in the response.

❏ Handler hook: This provides the content serving opportunity for modules. This is where the content is dished out!

If you are feeling adventurous and want to explore the Apache 2.2 source code, you can view the request phases, as well as where you can use hooks, by pursuing the source files in the server/ *subdirectory of the Apache source code, particularly the files* request.c *and* exports.c.

Understanding Hooks and Filters

Apache 2.2 supports what are called *hooks*, which are essentially locations in the code that implement the Apache request phase cycle. Hooks allow Apache module developers to "hook in" and take advantage of particular points in the Apache request phase cycle. The developer can choose to skip the remaining phases or even specific phases, thus modifying the default server request behavior.

Filters, or the Filter Chain, is a new functionality in Apache 2.0 and above. Application developers can now write filters that process both input (on either the request body or the connection itself) and output data (on either the response body or the connection) independent of the request phases. Filters allow you to modify either the data the server is reading from the client or the data that the server is returning to the client.

New and Modified Modules

As stated before, Apache has a modular design, allowing developers to write functionality that can be used to alter Apache's behavior. Apache 2.2 has a plethora of new, modified, renamed, and refactored modules compared to what was available with Apache 1.3.

The following table lists new modules for Apache 2.2.

Module	Description
mod_ssl	Supports Open SSL protocols SSL (Secure Sockets Layer)/TLS (Transport Layer Security).
mod_dav	Supports web development using HTTP DAV (Distributed Authoring and Versioning)
mod_deflate	Allows for page compression upon a request from browsers that support and request compression.
mod_version	Provides the ability to have configuration blocks enabled, depending on version of the server
mod_proxy_load_balancer	Provides load balancing services for mod_proxy.

The following lists the modules that are complete rewrites or are renamed:

Module	How Changed	Description of Rewrite/Rename
mod_proxy	Rewrite	Divided into specific support of FTP and HTTP with support modules proxy_connect, proxy_ftp and proxy_http. Is now HTTP/1.1 compliant. Now takes advantage of the filter infrastructure. New <Proxy> sections for better readability, control, and performance of proxied sites. Overloaded <Directory proxy:... > no longer supported.
mod_imap	Renamed	Renamed to mod_imagema.

The following table lists the various changes made to modules:

Module	Change
mod_headers	Allows for more flexibility such as conditionally setting response headers and setting mod_proxy request headers.
mod_include:	Uses Perl-compatible regular expressions, utilizing results from grouping with $0 .. $9 variables. New directives for SSI for more flexibility.
mod_autoindex	Allows directory index listing to be displayed using HTML tables.
mod_info	Passes config to return Apache configuration directives, much like you see when running httpd -V at the command line.

The following table list changes to the Authentication modules:

Module	Description of Change
mod_auth	Split into mod_auth_basic and mod_authn_file.
mod_auth_dbm	Renamed to mod_authn_dbm.
mod_access	Is now mod_authz_host.
mod_authn_alias	New module.
mod_authnz_ldap	New module. Allows for basic authentication credentials to be stored in an LDAP database.
mod_authz	New module. Uses user permissions on files to determine whether they can be accessed. This would be good for hosting companies.

Installing Apache

Installing Apache is quite simple, and in most UNIX/Linux distributions, it often occurs by default as part of the operating system installation process when you select general installation types, such as an Internet server.

The three main components you want, whether you install from source or use a package, are provided in the following list. The order of the list corresponds to the order in which you will need to install them.

❑ **Apache web server:** Known as Apache HTTP Server, which has already been described.

❑ **mod_perl:** One of the most important components in this book. This module provides a Perl interpreter that is built into the Apache web server so you don't have to run Perl separately as CGI does.

❑ **Apache Request library, libapreq/libapreq2:** This is a C library with Perl bindings that gives you the functionality to parse HTTP headers, particularly cookies, POST, and GET. You may have used the Perl module CGI in your programs.

The last two of these components are covered in more detail later in this chapter. The point here is to let you know that you do want to install them! The rest of the subsections cover how you will install them.

Installing Apache on Windows

For Windows platforms, you'll want to access `http://apache.org` and search for **HTTP Server project** (`Apache.org` hosts many other projects other than the HTTP server). The download page for the most recent version of Apache HTTP server appears as shown in Figure 11-3:

- Unix Source: httpd-2.2.9.tar.gz [PGP] [MD5]
- Unix Source: httpd-2.2.9.tar.bz2 [PGP] [MD5]
- Win32 Source: httpd-2.2.9-win32-src.zip [PGP] [MD5]
- Win32 Binary without crypto (no mod_ssl) (MSI Installer): apache_2.2.9-win32-x86-no_ssl-r2.msi [PGP] [MD5]
- Win32 Binary including OpenSSL 0.9.8h (MSI Installer): apache_2.2.9-win32-x86-openssl-0.9.8h-r2.msi [PGP] [MD5]
- Other files

Figure 11-3

Depending on whether you intend to run a web server with support for HTTPS using OpenSSL, select either one of the MSI installers. Once it is downloaded, execute the downloaded file. Upon executing the MSI file, the installation wizard presents you with a number of prompts for you to supply various values (Figure 11-4).

1. The first prompt, shown in Figure 11-4, asks you to supply the following:

❏ **Network Domain:** Type the base domain for your site, in this example **patg.net**.

❏ **Server Name:** This is the actual web site name. Type the domain plus a hostname such as **www** or in this example, **virtual**.

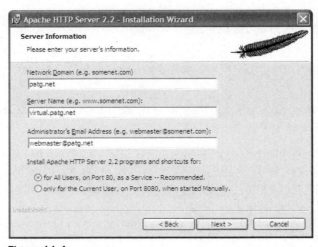

Figure 11-4

❑ **Administrator Email Address:** Provide the email address where you want administrator email to go to.

2. Click Next. The next several prompts are self-explanatory.

3. You most likely want the Typical install. Click Next.

4. Select the default path provided by the installer for Apache to be installed. This should suffice. This is the base directory of your web server where you will place all of your documents pertaining to your web server. Click Next.

5. Click Finish.

Installation of mod_perl

This assumes you've installed Perl already on your Windows system, in particular ActiveState Perl, found at http://www.activestate.com/. The following simple steps will install mod_perl on your system:

1. Bring up a command prompt and run the following:

```
ppm install http://cpan.uwinnipeg.ca/PPMPacka ges/10xx/mod_perl.ppd
```

You will be asked where to install the dynamic library file for mod_perl, as shown in the screen shot in Figure 11-5.

```
C:\DOCUME~1\PGALBR~1>ppm install http://cpan.uwinnipeg.ca/PPMPackages/10xx/mod_p
erl.ppd
Downloading mod_perl-2.000004...done
Unpacking mod_perl-2.000004...done
Generating HTML for mod_perl-2.000004...done
Updating files in site area...done
Downloading mod_perl-2.000004 install script...done
Running mod_perl-2.000004 install script...
The Apache2 module mod_perl.so is needed to complete the installation,
and should be placed in your Apache2 modules directory. I will
now fetch and install this for you.

Fetching http://cpan.uwinnipeg.ca/PPMPackages/10xx/x86/mod_perl.so ... done!
Where should mod_perl.so be placed? [D:/Apache2.2/modules] C:\Program Files\Apac
he Software Foundation\Apache2.2\modules
mod_perl.so has been successfully installed to C:/PROGRA~1/APACHE~1/Apache2.2/mo
dules.
To enable mod_perl, put in the directives
    LoadFile "C:/Path/to/Perl/bin/perl510.dll"
    LoadModule perl_module modules/mod_perl.so
in httpd.conf. For more information, visit
    http://perl.apache.org/
and especially see
    http://perl.apache.org/docs/2.0/rename.html

done
  470 files unchanged
    4 files updated
```

Figure 11-5

2. Then from your start menu, select from the "Start" button, select from the menu "All Programs" -> "Apache HTTP Server 2.2" -> "Configure Apache Server" -> "Edit the Apache httpd.conf Configuration File." This brings you into Notepad, where you can edit your Apache configuration file. Add to your Apache configuration file the following:

```
LoadFile "C:/Perl/bin/perl510.dll"
LoadModule perl_module modules/mod_perl.so
```

3. Depending on where you will have your Perl scripts and programs running, you can add the following:

```
Alias /perl/ "C:/Documents and Settings/username/web/Perl/"
<Location /perl/>
    SetHandler perl-script
    PerlResponseHandler ModPerl::Registry
    PerlOptions +ParseHeaders
    Options +ExecCGI
    Order allow,deny
    Allow from all
</Location>
```

4. Restart Apache by selecting from the Start button "Apache HTTP Server 2.2" -> "Control Apache Server" -> "restart." You now have the ability to write mod_perl programs on your Windows box!

Installing Apache and mod_perl on a Working UNIX System

For cases where Apache was not installed by default for whatever reason, it's simple enough to install using the operating system's software package management system. The following will show you how to install Apache for a number of Linux distributions as well as Apple OS X.

Ubuntu/Debian-based Linux

1. Run the following:

```
sudo apt-cache search
```

This gives you a big list of various packages that have something to do with Apache, including the server itself. Particularly:

```
apache2
apache2-mpm-prefork
apache2-mpm-worker
```

The *apache2* package installs a threaded Apache by default, libapreq (required), and a PostgreSQL library.

Considering this book is about developing applications using MySQL as the back-end database, a discussion of the PostgreSQL library is not needed for the scope of this book. Also the apache2 package defaults to a threaded Apache, which if you want a forked Apache, will not work. Instead, use one of the other listed packages: apache2-mpm-worker or apache2-mpm-prefork, depending on whether you want to use a threaded Apache or the traditional forking model. Select the mpm-worker for threaded or mpm-prefork for forked.

2. These packages can be installed by running:

```
sudo apt-get install <package, ...>
```

You can install one or more packages at a time.

3. Other required modules (for the scope of this book) are:

```
libapache2-mod-perl2 - Mod_perl
libapache2-mod-apreq2 -- Apache request library
libapache-dbi-perl - Apache::DBI
```

You will also see numerous libapache-"mod" packages. These are optional and offer various extensions to Apache functionality, some of which are mentioned later in this chapter. You can refer to Ubuntu documentation for more information on each. As well, there are the "dev" packages that match the name of the base packages. These are also optional and can be installed if needed. Again, refer to Ubuntu documentation.

4. To enable mod_perl and Apache request/libapreq2, you will have to run the command:

```
sudo a2enmod perl
```

```
sudo a2enmod apreq
```

This ensures that the Apache modules for mod_perl and Apache request/libapreq2 are loaded when Apache is started.

You have two ways to start Apache. This:

```
sudo /etc/init.d/apache2 <start|stop|restart>
```

... or this:

```
sudo /usr/sbin/apache2ctl <start|stop|restart>
```

Redhat-Based Systems (Centos, Fedora, Redhat Enterprise, etc.)

Yum is the tool for finding RPM packages to install, and it takes care of satisfying dependencies such as prerequisite RPMs.

1. To use, find a listing of Apache and related packages:

```
yum-search apache
```

2. This gives a large list of Apache and Apache-related packages (just as the apt-cache search did for Ubuntu). The ones that you would want to install in this case are:

```
httpd.x86_64 : Apache HTTP Server
httpd-devel.i386 : Development tools for the Apache HTTP server.
mod_ssl.x86_64 : SSL/TLS module for the Apache HTTP server
libapreq2.i386 : Apache HTTP request library
mod_perl.x86_64 : An embedded Perl interpreter for the Apache Web server
mod_perl-devel.x86_64 : Files needed for building XS modules that use
mod_perl
perl-Apache-DBI.noarch : Persistent database connections with
```

```
Apache/mod_perl
apr-util.x86_64 : Apache Portable Runtime Utility library
```

The dev packages are optional, but depending on how much you intend to tinker, you may want to install these as well. Also, mod_ssl.x86_64 is an optional install, but if you intend to have a secure web server, then it will be required. Also note that "x86_64" is for the 64-bit architecture. For the 32-bit architecture, the name would be "i386."

3. To install these, run the Yum install command:

```
yum-install <package, ...>
```

You can install one or more packages at a time.

Installing Apache on Apple OS X (10.5)

Installing the Xcode developer CD that comes with either your new Mac or with OS X, if you bought OS X separately, will automatically install Apache 2.2. It's that simple!

Apache Source Install on UNIX

A great Jedi once said to his disciple "Use the Source, Luke!" Seriously, you often want to build a software package from source to get the latest and greatest version. You also want to have the source around for development using Apache (for instance if you want to write your own Apache modules). In fact, this method is a good way to learn more about Apache. Many Linux distributions or other operating systems have done such a great job packaging Apache, with everything working perfectly out of the box, that you rarely get a chance to really get your hands dirty, like in the old days. This is the perfect opportunity to explain to you how to set up Apache because a source install starts from scratch. Not to mention, with a source install you can specify that Apache is installed in its own directory, which keeps it all in one place. This can be convenient, especially for learning purposes.

To install Apache from source, including how to get the server up and running as quickly as possible, follow these steps.

1. First and foremost, log in or sudo as root and create the apache group and user both:

```
sudo groupadd apache

sudo useradd -d /usr/local/apache/htdocs -g apache -s /sbin/nologin
```

2. Obtain the Apache source code. From Apache's web site, obtain the UNIX source distribution for the Apache HTTP Server, download the source to a directory such as /usr/local/src

```
tar xvzf httpd-2.2.xx.tar.gz

cd httpd-2.2.xx
```

3. Read the file INSTALL. It will provide you with instructions on building Apache, as well as mention you can run:

```
./configure -help
```

This lists all the options that you can supply the auto configure — what directory to install Apache into, what modules to build, suexec settings, etc.

4. For this building of Apache demonstration, the command line that follows will suffice. The option to -enable-mods-shared=all commands the compiler to build all the modules that come with Apache (this doesn't include mod_perl), and build them shared so they can be dynamically loaded.

```
./configure --prefix=/usr/local/apache2 --enable-mods-shared=all
make
```

5. After all the source has been built, install Apache, which will require root privileges:

```
sudo make install
```

At this point, the build source has now been installed to /usr/local/apache2 and the server is ready for configuration! This section won't delve into a full-fledged configuration, but will provide the steps necessary for getting a web server up and running.

6. Go ahead and enter the directory containing the newly installed Apache.

```
cd /usr/local/apache2/
```

7. Now examine the contents that were installed:

```
root@ispconfig apache2]# ls -l
total 112
drwxr-xr-x  2 root root  4096 Jan 24 09:45 bin
drwxr-xr-x  2 root root  4096 Jan 24 09:45 build
drwxr-xr-x  2 root root  4096 Jan 24 10:28 cgi-bin
drwxr-xr-x  4 root root  4096 Jan 24 10:16 conf
drwxr-xr-x  3 root root  4096 Jan 24 09:58 error
drwxr-xr-x  2 root root  4096 Dec  6 07:16 htdocs
drwxr-xr-x  3 root root  4096 Jan 24 09:45 icons
drwxr-xr-x  2 root root  4096 Jan 24 09:45 include
drwxr-xr-x  4 root root  4096 Jan 24 09:45 lib
drwxr-xr-x  2 root root  4096 Jan 24 10:16 logs
drwxr-xr-x  4 root root  4096 Jan 24 09:45 man
drwxr-xr-x 14 root root 12288 Dec  6 07:18 manual
drwxr-xr-x  2 root root  4096 Jan 24 09:45 modules
```

The directories in /usr/local/apache2 contain different components of the entire server package. Of importance for this section are the ones listed in the following table:

Directory	Description
Bin	Where Apache binaries are found. These binaries include the server binary httpd, benchmarking, daemon start utility, and other programs for managing the server.
Conf	Where the configuration files are found.
Htdocs	Where the actual web site documents are found.
Icons	Where the icons the server uses for things like directory listings are found.
Logs	Where the access and error logs are found.
Modules	Where the loadable Apache modules are found.

8. As you will notice from the previous output, these are all owned by the root user when first installed. For all of these directories, go ahead and change their ownership permissions to apache:apache:

```
chown -R apache:apache <directory>
```

9. Additionally, the directory cgi-bin contains CGI scripts that will need to be executable:

```
chmod 755 cgi-bin/*
```

10. Make some small changes to the main Apache configuration file. Edit the file conf/httpd.conf. In this file you will find the lines for which user Apache will run as. Since you created an apache user and group, use these. Change the lines from the value that is in this stock httpd.conf from:

```
User daemon
Group daemon
```

to

```
User apache
Group apache
```

11. You should now be able to start Apache. Run the program:

```
/usr/local/apach/bin/apachectl start
```

This is a shell script that starts the actual Apache server (httpd).

If you check with the command ps, you should see Apache running now:

```
ps auxwww|grep apache
root      21955  0.0  0.1 27412  1956 ?        Ss   10:16   0:00
 /usr/local/apache2/bin/httpd -k start
```

```
apache   21956  0.0  0.1  27544  1992 ?        S    10:16   0:00
 /usr/local/apache2/bin/httpd -k start
apache   21957  0.0  0.1  27544  2024 ?        S    10:16   0:00
 /usr/local/apache2/bin/httpd -k start
apache   21958  0.0  0.1  27544  2016 ?        S    10:16   0:00
 /usr/local/apache2/bin/httpd -k start
apache   21959  0.0  0.1  27544  2024 ?        S    10:16   0:00
 /usr/local/apache2/bin/httpd -k start
apache   21960  0.0  0.1  27544  2000 ?        S    10:16   0:00
 /usr/local/apache2/bin/httpd -k start
apache   21997  0.0  0.1  27544  1996 ?        S    10:17   0:00
 /usr/local/apache2/bin/httpd -k start
```

Notice in the previous listing that there is one Apache process running as root. This is the main Apache process, which was started and then spawned child processes running as the user specified in the Apache configuration file.

You should be able to access your site now. The stock Apache 2.2 comes with a very simple front page. If you access your site, you should see the message "It works!" You can even use the telnet program, telneting your server's IP address at port 80 to get the server to give you a page :

```
telnet 127.16.221.130 80
Trying 127.16.221.130...
Connected to 127.16.221.130 (127.16.221.130).
Escape character is '^]'.
GET / HTTP/1.1
Host: localhost
User-Agent: telnet/100.1
Accept: text/html

HTTP/1.1 200 OK
Date: Sat, 24 Jan 2009 19:12:55 GMT
Server: Apache/2.2.11 (Unix) DAV/2
Last-Modified: Sat, 20 Nov 2004 20:16:24 GMT
ETag: "8f38c-2c-3e9564c23b600"
Accept-Ranges: bytes
Content-Length: 44
Content-Type: text/html

<html><body><h1>It works!</h1></body></html>
```

The IP address in this example would be whatever is the IP address of your own server you installed Apache on. For this example, it was on a virtual machine, which seems to be assigned 172.xx addresses. You need to enter everything up to and including `Accept: text/html`, then hit Enter twice. The web server will then print out the output of the web page to your terminal screen as shown above.

You now have a working, albeit very basically configured, Apache 2.2! This chapter will cover configuration in more detail in later sections. This installation demo was provided just to show you how easy it is to set up Apache, even from source.

Installing mod_perl from Source

Now that you have freshly built from source and installed the Apache 2.2 server, you can build and install mod_perl. Just like installing Apache, this also is a fairly simple procedure, much more so now than previously with Apache 1.3. Now there are more enhancements and improvements to the Apache module API.

Follow these steps:

1. Visit the main site for mod_perl at `http://perl.apache.org/`. This is where you can find the source for mod_perl which you will build, as well as a documentation, mailing list subscription information, bug reporting, and many other useful resources. The download URL for the current mod_perl source distribution is conveniently the same, regardless of release. From `/usr/local/src` you can use `wget` to obtain it: `wget http://perl.apache.org/dist/mod_perl-2.0-current.tar.gz`

2. Once the download is complete, you can untar it, then enter the directory:

    ```
    tar xvzf mod_perl-2.0-current.tar.gz

    cd mod_perl-2.0.4
    ```

3. Just as with so many open source packages, there is a file called INSTALL which contains the installation instructions for mod_perl. This file you will find is pretty much verbatim an Apache source installation.

4. The first command you'll run, like with so many other Perl module compilations, is this:

    ```
    perl Makefile.PL MP_APXS=/usr/local/apache2/bin/apxs
    ```

    The one argument shown here, `MP_APXS`, tells the compilation where to find the program `apxs`.

What is `apxs`?

It's a program that comes with the Apache source distribution that is used for building and installing Apache modules. As previously mentioned, these modules that are built are DSOs, *Dynamically Shared Object* files, which Apache loads when starting up. So, in building any Apache module, the directory path for this program is crucial.

---

5. Build and install mod_perl (for the `make install`, either run as root or using `sudo`):

    ```
    make
    make install
    ```

At this point, mod_perl is installed. The dynamic library module file has been compiled and installed into the modules directory for the installed Apache (in this example `/usr/local/apache/modules`).

6. Ensure that mod_perl is loaded by Apache. In `/usr/local/apach/conf/httpd.conf`, you'll see multiple lines containing:

    ```
    LoadModule userdir_module modules/mod_userdir.so
    LoadModule alias_module modules/mod_alias.so
    LoadModule rewrite_module modules/mod_rewrite.so
    ```

    Add to this the line:

    ```
    LoadModule perl_module modules/mod_perl.so
    ```

7. Restart Apache. Then you can verify that mod_perl is loaded with the argument to `httpd -D DUMP_MODULES`, which will show which modules have been loaded:

    ```
    /usr/local/apache2/bin/httpd -t -D DUMP_MODULES
    ```

In the output, along with all the other modules listed, you should see the line:

```
perl_module (shared)
```

You now have a mod_perl-enabled Apache!

Installing libapreq2 from Source

Installing the Apache request library, libapreq2, is not as straightforward as the Apache install was. What is convenient, however, is that you can use CPAN to fetch the source. Notice that the word *fetch* was used, as opposed to *install*. The reason is because when you use CPAN to install a module, it automatically compiles and installs the modules, and in some cases the proper compile flags aren't provided to `perl Makefile.PL` in order for the package to successfully be built. Particularly with a Perl module that has an underlying C library, you want to make sure that the build configuration has the correct compile flags. Apache request /libapreq2 is very much in the category of those modules needing the proper build flags, particularly the path to `apxs`, which it needs to properly build.

You may have to install the library expat (dev) prior to building libapreq2, an XML parsing library. Use whatever package tool is required according to your operating system documentation.

Follow these steps.

1. With CPAN, fetch the source (note emphasis on *Apache2* — not just *Apache*)

    ```
    perl -MCPAN -e "get Apache2::Request"
    ```

2. Go to your CPAN build directory:

   ```
   cd ~/.cpan/build

   cd libapreq2-2.xx
   ```

3. Build the package:

   ```
   perl Makefile.PL --with-apache2-apxs=/usr/local/apache2/bin/apxs
   ```

4. Install (either as root or using `sudo`):

   ```
   make install
   ```

   Apache request is installed, and the dynamically shared object module libapreq2.so is installed into `/usr/local/apache/modules`.

5. The only thing remaining to do is to add it to `httpd.conf` to be loaded:

   ```
   LoadModule apreq_module modules/mod_apreq2.so
   ```

6. Restart Apache. Then you can verify, just as you did with mod_perl, that libapreq2 is loaded:

   ```
   /usr/local/apache2/bin/httpd -t -D DUMP_MODULES
   ...
   apreq_module (shared)
   ```

You now have Apache request loaded with Apache!

Apache Configuration

Now that all the pieces are installed, whether from source or packages, you can configure Apache to your own settings. There are numerous configuration parameters found in the Apache configuration file, for the source installation, `httpd.conf`. This setup does vary depending upon whether you installed Apache from source or used a binary distribution.

Understanding the Apache configuration file is a good way to understand your overall Apache configuration. This section covers the basic settings you'll find in most Apache configuration files for both source Apache installations and packaged Apache installations of various operating system distributions.

Because of the encyclopedic amount of information on Apache configuration, a full discussion is far beyond the scope of this book. You can find all the information you need at: `http://httpd.apache.org/docs/2.2/configuring.html`.

You should understand that an Apache configuration file is constructed in SGML (Standard Generalized Markup Language), of which XML and HTML are a type, so it's pretty easy to read. Apache configurations have numerous directives, some of which are the SGML tags in this file, known as Configuration Section Containers, both with an open tag and a close tag. Directives are either outside or within these configuration sections. This is how you scope directives and can sectionalize your configuration file. If a particular directive is outside the configuration section, it applies for the whole server; if inside the configuration section tag, that directive is scoped for whatever constraint that tag applies. For instance, there is a `<Directory>` configuration section, and say you had `<Directory /www/mypages>`. Any directive listed between `<Directory /www/mypages>` and `</Directory>` would scope in such a way to apply only within the path `/www/mypages`.

With Apache 2.2, you are not confined to having only one configuration file. You can modularize your Apache configuration to whatever scheme you want, separating out sections into other "sub" configuration files that that you include in your main Apache configuration file with the directive `Include`. An example of a virtual host's configuration parameters kept in a separate file is:

```
Include   /etc/apache2/conf.d/mysite.conf
```

Configuration Section Container Directives

To become familiar with the directives to use in your Apache configuration, here is a listing of the Configuration Section Container directives. Note that all of these, as mentioned above, have a begin `<tag>` and end `</tag>`.

<Directory> and <DirectoryMatch>

Usage: `<Directory /path/to/dir>`, `<DirectoryMath path-pattern>`

`<Directory>` is used to sectionalize directives by a directory path on disk. Any directive defined in this section is applied to the directory and its subdirectories.

The directory path can use wildcards such as:

```
<Directory /www/sites/*>
```

... as well as regular expressions with the use of the tilde character (~)

```
<Directory ~ "/www/site_[\d]+">
```

`<DirectoryMatch>` allows the use of regular expressions without having to specify the ~ character. The last example would appear as:

```
<DirectoryMatch /www/site_[\d]+>
```

Another good example is the stock Apache configuration file that is included with the monitoring tool Nagios :

```
<DirectoryMatch (/usr/share/nagios2/htdocs|/usr/lib/cgi-bin/nagios2)>
```

<Files> and <FilesMatch>

Usage: `<Files filename>, <FilesMatch filename-pattern>`

You use this to sectionalize directives based on a filename. The example:

```
<Files ~ "^\.ht">
```

... would scope directives for `.htaccess` files.

`<FilesMatch>` lets you use regular expressions without specifying the ~ character:

```
<FilesMatch "\.(htm[l]?|php|xml)$">
```

... would scope directives for files ending with `.htm`, `.html`, `.php`, `.xml`

<Location>

Usage: `<Location URL or URL path>`

As a Perl/mod_perl web developer, this is one of the most common tags you use. `<Location>` is used to sectionalize based on a URL path, per the web server. This is similar to `<Directory>` except that `<Location>` deals with the URL that you access via the web server, as it serves it, as opposed to the path on disk that you have with `<Directory>`. You would most often use `<Location>` for setting up your mod_perl handlers, and for limiting access to server URLs such as server-status.

For URLs that are origin, not proxy, requests, only the URL path can be used — no scheme, port, or query string such as `http://xyz.com/foo.pl?this=them&that=those` may be used. For URLs that are for proxy requests, you can use a full-fledged URL with scheme and all.

As with the other directives, you can use wildcards and regular expressions:

```
<Location /webapp/*>
```

```
<Location ~  "/user_data/[a-m].*$">
```

<LocationMatch>

Usage: `<LocationMatch regex>`

This does the same thing as `<Location>` except it takes as an argument a regular expression. This makes it so you don't have to specify a tilde (~) character to indicate regular expression. These two lines are the same:

```
<Location ~ "/foo/app[_].*$">
```

```
<LocationMatch "/foo/app[_].*$">
```

<IfDefine>

Usage: `<IfDefine parameter or ! parameter>`

This makes it so directives are conditional based on the parameter set upon whether Apache was started with the -D parameter. For instance, if you started Apache with this:

```
httpd -D capttofu
```

... in the configuration file, then you would use:

```
<IfDefine capttofu> ... </IfDefine>
```

<IfModule>

Usage: `<IfModule modulename>`

Conditional directives are based upon whether a specific module has been included. For instance, for mod_perl, you might have this:

```
<IfModule mod_perl.c>
<Location /somedir>
    SetHandler perl-script
    PerlModule MyModule
    ....
</Location>
</IfModule>
```

This would only specify the directives within the `<IfModule>` tags if mod_perl was installed and loaded.

<IfVersion>

Usage: `<IfVersion operator version>`

Conditional directives are based upon the version of Apache, the various operator being ==, =, <, >, <=, >=, ! An example would be:

```
<IfVersion > 1.3>
  # various directives.... Apache 2.0 and above
</IfVersion>
```

<Limit>

Usage: `<Limit method [method] ...>`

The `<Limit>` directive limits access controls to the methods specified. For instance, this example:

```
<Directory /var/www/publishing>
  <Limit GET POST OPTIONS PROPFIND>
```

```
        Order allow,deny
        Allow from all
    </Limit>
</Directory>
```

... would enforce the policy of allowing from all addresses the use of the HTTP methods GET and POST (web apps, forms) as well as OPTIONS, for requesting information about communications available on a request/response. It would allow the use of PROPFIND to request information about a resource for Distributed Authoring and Versioning (DAV), within the directory /var/www/publishing.

<LimitExcept>

Usage: <LimitExcept method [method] ...>

Works just like <Limit> except ... except! <LimitExcept> means every method *but* the listed methods. This is a better choice if you want to avoid forgetting about all the various HTTP methods to apply a policy.

<Proxy>

Usage: <Proxy URL>

This applies directives only to the URL as specified via a proxy server. This can be a means of enforcing the access to content via a proxy server, as in this example:

```
<Proxy *>
    Order Deny, Allow
    Deny from All
    Allow from proxy.candycoated.com
</Proxy>
```

This would enforce the use of a proxy server to access content on your server for the hostname proxy.candycoated.com.

You can also use tricks such as this example:

```
PerlModule ModPerl::Registry
Alias /perl /usr/local/perl
<Location /perl>
  SetHandler perl-script
  PerlHandler ModPerl::Registry
  PerlSendHeader On
  PerlOptions +ParseHeaders
  Options +ExecCGI
</Location>
```

This would result in any proxy request for files with a .pl extension within the URL http://nomodperl .com/perl to have mod_perl turned on, and would make it possible to run CGI scripts through mod- _perl. More about ModPerl::Registry and mod_perl will be presented in Chapter 13 "mod_perl."

<ProxyMatch>

Usage: `<ProxyMatch regex>`

This works just like `<Proxy>` except that it allows the use of regular expressions.

<VirtualHost>

Usage: `<VirtualHost address[:port] [address[:port] ...>`

The `VirtualHost` tag is one of the most common sectionalized directives you'll be using. `<VirtualHost>` encloses directives for a virtual host as listed in one or more addresses, port if specified. Here are examples of the types of addresses that can be used:

```
<VirtualHost 192.168.1.33>
    ServerName privatebox.com
    DocumentRoot /var/www/privatebox
    ErrorLog /var/log/apache2/privatebox-error.log
    TransferLog /var/log/apache2/privatebox-access.log
</VirtualHost>
```

And here is a named virtual host:

```
NameVirtualHost *
<VirtualHost *>
ServerName patrampushpamtoyam.com
DocumentRoot /var/www/patrampushpamtoyam.com
<VirtualHost>
```

Basic Directives

The following directives are the more basic directives in an Apache configuration file that control fundamental settings for your web server.

ServerName

Usage: `ServerName [schema://]fully-qualified-domainname[:port]`

The scheme (optional), hostname, and port (optional) that you wish the web server to respond to. For instance, the full name of the machine of patg.net might be chakra.patg.net, but the name it should respond to is either patg.net or www.patg.net. An example would be as follows:

```
ServerName patg.net:80
```

`ServerName` becomes especially important when using name-based virtual hosts. You must have `ServerName` set within a `<VirtualHost>` directive if you wish for that host to respond by that name.

ServerRoot

Usage: `ServerRoot directory`

This is the directory in which Apache lives and which most often contains configuration and log directories. Different OS distributions, however, spread Apache components into other directories within the operating system than what a source installation would default to: A source installation will install Apache into its own directory, usually `/usr/local/apache` or `/usr/local/apache2`, and that directory will contain every component of Apache.

DocumentRoot

Usage: `DocumentRoot directory`

This is the base directory from which Apache will serve content. Any path within a URL for the server is relative to `DocumentRoot`. For instance, if the `DocumentRoot` is `/usr/local/apache/htdocs`, and the client requests the URL `http://somesite.com/pictures`, the actual directory on disk would be `/usr/local/apache/htdocs/pictures`.

Include

Usage: `Include path`

This allows you to include a separate configuration file. This gives the ability to modularize and separate out different parts of your configuration into files of their own. Various operating system distributions take advantage of this, as you will see in a later section.

Paths can be absolute or relative to the directory specified in the ServerRoot directive.

An example of including all configuration files in `/etc/apache2/mods-enabled` with the extension of `.conf` would be:

```
Include /etc/apache2/mods-enabled/*.conf
```

Listen

Usage: `Listen [IP]port [protocol]`

This tells Apache to which IP address (optional), port (required), and protocol (optional) it needs to respond. By default, if you don't specify an IP address, Apache will respond to all IP addresses on the machine that it is running on. An example would be:

```
Listen 192.168.1.33:80
```

You can also specify Apache to listen to multiple ports by having multiple Listen directives, like so:

```
Listen 192.168.1.33:80
Listen 192.168.1.33:81
```

You only need to specify protocol if you want to explicitly tell Apache to respond with a particular protocol such as HTTPS on a nonstandard port. The last example with port 81, for instance, could be forced to responds with HTTPS:

```
Listen 192.168.1.33:81 https
```

This directive is mandatory; the server will not start without it.

LoadModule

Usage: `LoadModule modulename filename`

Loads a module, a library, or an object file, linking it into the list of active modules and enabling it for the Apache server process. An example of loading mod_perl would be:

```
LoadModule perl_module /usr/lib/apache2/modules/mod_perl.so
```

Options

Usage: `Options [ + | − ] option [[ + | − ] option]...`

This controls which features are set within a `<Directory>`. Values other than `All` or `None` can have a plus (+) or minus (−) sign in front of them for true or false (enabled or disabled, specifically). For instance, the default is `All`, and you could specify `−Includes`, which would mean everything *but* `Includes` (`SSI`, server-side includes).

The following table provides a list of options that can be set within a `<Directory>` sectional directive:

Value	Description
`All`	(Default) All options.
`None`	No options.
`ExecCGI`	Ability to run CGI scripts.
`FollowSymLinks`	Whether or not to allow Apache to serve pages from links to real directories outside the directory specified. Ignored inside <Location> directive.
`Includes`	Allow server-side includes. The Apache module that provides this is `mod_include`.
`IncludesNOExec`	Allow server-side includes, but without `#exec cmd` and `#exec cgi`.
`MultiViews`	Allow for content negotiation. This lets you deliver content based on client specifics, such as language and browser type. It also lets you deal with incomplete negotiation information. The Apache module that provides this is mod_negotiation.
`Indexes`	Allow automatic directory listing when a page is not specified in the URL being requested on a directory without an index file as specified in DirectoryIndex (for instance index.html, index.php, ...). This functionality is provided by mod autoindex.

Value	Description
SymLinksIfOwnerMatch	Allows for symbolic links to be used if the target file is owned by the same user as the symbolic link pointing to the file.
IncludesNoExec	Server-side includes are permitted, but with #exec cmd and #exec cgi disabled.

Redirect

Usage: `Redirect [status] local-URL URL`

With this, you can set a URL on your site so that it redirects elsewhere. The status is optional and is either an HTTP code or a named status of that redirect, such as `permanent`, `temp`, `seeother`, or `gone`. If omitted, the default is `temporary`.

An example of this where a local URL named google redirects to `http://google.com` is as follows:

```
Redirect permanent /google http://google.com
```

You could also redirect a URL where you're doing work that's not yet complete:

```
Redirect /new_application http://workingsite.com
```

User

Usage: `User <#UID | username>`

This specifies the UNIX user the process will run as. Of course, if running the web server on a port below 1024, you start the server as root, and the main Apache process runs as root and then all children spawned will run as the user specified with `User`.

AddType

Usage: `AddType type file-extension`

This is a common option you will often see that maps a filename extension to determine how the server will serve out the file — what type of header it emits in Content-type: `<type>`.

Here is an example of adding a type for files named `.tgz`, which is just a shortened way of writing `tar.gz` (from back in the old days when we used to download Slackware onto floppies, so the filenames would work with DOS!):

```
AddType application/x-tar .tgz
```

So, when serving up a file ending in `.tgz`, Apache will emit `"Content-type: application/x-tar\n\n"` in its header.

Standard types are usually kept in a file defined with the `TypesConfig` file, which points to a file, `/etc/mime.types`, that contains a huge list of mime types followed by the extension of the file for that type.

Server Tuning Directives

These are directives that control the performance of Apache, depending upon which MPM you are running. These include things like how many child processes or threads to initially start up, how many requests each thread or child process serves, the maximum number of children or threads, etc. With these directives, you have a lot of control over how Apache runs. However, you also have to be careful to think about the settings you are making to ensure that you're not setting values that will exceed your machine's capacity.

StartServers

Usage: `StartServers number`

This is the number of child processes to start when Apache starts up. It is used both for hybrid/threaded (worker) and forked (prefork) servers. During run-time, the number of processes is determined by load. The default for forked is 5, and for threaded, 3.

MaxClients

Usage: `MaxClients number`

This is the maximum number of connections that are allowed to be served simultaneously. Extra connections will be queued until a child process is freed up to service the awaiting request. The number of allowed queued connections is determined by the directive `ListenBacklog`.

`MaxClients` for forked servers (prefork) also mean the maximum number of child process that will be spawned to serve requests, should the number of requests require it. For threaded and hybrid/threaded servers (worker), this means the maximum total number of threads, regardless of the number of child processes, that will be allowed to serve requests. For hybrid/threaded servers, `MaxClients` is determined by the product of `ServerLimit` (total number of child processes for the lifetime of the Apache process) and `ThreadsPerChild` (the maximum number of threads for the lifetime of a given child). So break out your calculator if you want to determine what value each should be.

MaxSpareServers

Usage: `MaxSpareServers number`

This is a setting you don't want to use unless you have a really busy site. You will have to get out your calculator and scratch pad to carefully determine the value to use.

As the name implies, this is the maximum number of spare child processes, which means idle processes that aren't currently handling any requests and that the server should allow to remain running. The culling of child processes is performed by the main parent process. The default value is 10.

MinSpareServers

Usage: `MinSpareServers number`

This is the same concept as `MaxSpareServers`, except this equates to the minimum number of idle child processes that the main parent process will ensure are running. If the number of child processes drops below this number, the main parent process will spawn new child process, one per second, until the `MinSpareServers` number is achieved. The same caveat applies here as with `MaxSpareServers`: You don't want to modify this setting unless you have a busy site. The default is 5.

ServerLimit

Usage: `ServerLimit number`

This allows you to override the compiled-in limit of `MaxClients` for the life of the Apache process (default 256) for a prefork Apache, and a combination of `ServerLimit` and `ThreadLimit` for a threaded, worker Apache. Changing this setting won't have any affect with a restart. You have to completely stop and start the server for it to take effect, though you can change `MaxClients` up to the value of `ServerLimit` with a restart.

This is a setting you usually don't want to tinker with unless you really know what you're doing. You have to take special care to not set it to a value that exceeds your machine's capacity.

MaxRequestsPerChild

Usage: `MaxRequestsPerChild number`

This is the maximum number of client requests that a process will serve before the parent kills it off. The default is 10,000. If left to the value of 0, then there is no limit. There are many discussions about this setting, especially whether it's good to keep it at a lower number in the case that there are memory leaks either in the code (due to bugs) or operating system libraries. It all depends upon what works best for you. Also, the best policy is to fix bugs — fix them, don't just work around them! Like a manager once used to say "What's the first thing'a you do in the morning? You look at your a' bugs and you fix'a them."

ThreadLimit

Usage: `ThreadLimit number`

This allows you to override the compiled-in limit of `ThreadsPerChild` for the duration of the running Apache process. Changing this setting won't have any effect on a restart. You have to completely stop and start the server for it to take effect, though you can change `MaxRequestsPerChild` up to the value of `ThreadLimit` with a restart.

ThreadsPerChild

Usage: `ThreadsPerChild number`

This is the total number of threads that a child processes will create, no more, no less. Unlike the `prefork` MPM, a child creates all the threads it will ever use at startup. This is true for each child, so you have to consider what type of threaded MPM you are using. If you're using an MPM such as the `worker` MPM, which spawns a number of children that then spawn threads, you must figure out how many total threads you have based on the product of the number of children and `ThreadsPerChild`. If you're using a MPM that is purely threaded, such as MPM `winnt`, which spawns only one child process that subsequently spawns threads, you must ensure you have enough threads to serve out the traffic of your web server.

KeepAlive

Usage: `KeepAlive On | Off`

This allows multiple requests to be served from the same connection, making for a persistent connection. The number of requests served out within a single connection, with `KeepAlive` turned on, is not counted toward `MaxRequestsPerChild`. The default is 'on.'

MaxKeepAliveRequests

Usage: `MaxKeepAliveRequests number`

This refers to the total number of requests a connection, with `KeepAlive` turned on, will serve out.

KeepAliveTimeout

Usage: `KeepAliveTimeout seconds`

This is the time in seconds that a process, `KeepAlive` enabled, waits after serving a request for a subsequent request before disconnecting.

Timeout

Usage: `Timeout seconds`

This is the number of seconds the server will wait, depending on event. The types of events are: the duration of a `GET` request, the duration of receiving data from a `POST` or `PUT`, and the duration of time between ACKs on transmissions of packages in responses. The default is 300.

Logging Directives

Apache has various options for logging. You can control what the format of log entries, the level of logging, as well as whether to log to a file or a process.

CustomLog

Usage: `CustomLog file|pipe format|nickname [env=[!]environment-variable]`

This defines the file that Apache requests are logged to, as well as the format to use. The file is either an absolute path or relative to `ServerRoot`.

The format can be either an explicit format string or a name of a format. You can also define new format string names.

An example of logging to a regular file with an explicit format string is as follows:

```
CustomLog logs/access_log "%h %l %u %t \"%r\" %>s %b"
```

Then you can define format nicknames with the LogFormat directive:

```
LogFormat "%h %l %u %t \"%r\" %>s %b"      common
LogFormat "%v %h %l %u %t \"%r\" %>s %b"     vhost_common
```

Then use the aliases with a log:

```
CustomLog logs/mysite_acces_log vhost_common
```

Here is an example of using a pipe to send the output of the logs to a process that creates a new log every time with the date stamp as the file name, archiving old logs:

```
CustomLog "|/usr/sbin/rotatelogs -l /var/log/apache/access_log.%Y-%m-%d 86400"
```

You have all manner of logs using CustomLog. For instance, you may want to just have a log that logs cookies along with your main Apache log:

```
CustomLog /var/log/apache2/access.log combined
CustomLog /var/log/apache2/cookie.log cookielog
```

TransferLog

> Usage: TransferLog file-path|log_processor

The same as CustomLog except you cannot specify a log format.

ErrorLog

> Usage: ErrorLog file-path|log_proccessor

This sets the file errors are logged to. The file path is either absolute or relative to ServerRoot.

LogFormat

> Usage: LogFormat format_string [nickname]

This lets you define the default logging format (without a nickname) or defines a format with a nickname for a logging format string. (See the example in the description of CustomLog above.)

Some examples are the following:

```
LogFormat "%h %l %u %t \"%r\" %>s %b \"%{Referer}i\" \"%{User-Agent}i\"" combined
LogFormat "%h %l %u %t \"%r\" %>s %b" common
```

```
LogFormat "%{Referer}i -> %U" referer
LogFormat "%{User-agent}i" agent
LogFormat "%C" cookielog
```

LogLevel

Usage: `LogLevel level`

This allows you to set how much information is logged to the error log. The error levels are `emerg`, `alert`, `crit`, `error`, `warn`, `notice`, `info`, `debug`, in the order of increasing verbosity and information.

Error Directives

There are a number of directives that allow you to control what action should occur and what content to display when an error is encountered.

ErrorDocument

Usage: `ErrorDocument error-code file|url`

This sets what content to display or action to take should an error occur, depending upon what the error code is. The options for error handling are:

❑   Static file is served, such as an HTML file with a blurb about failure

❑   A message, as defined, is displayed

❑   Redirect to either a local URL path or remote URL

Some examples are

❑   HTML file:

```
ErrorDocument 410 /errors/410.html
```

❑   mod_perl handler:

```
ErrorDocument 400 /error_handler/400
```

❑   Redirect:

```
ErrorDocument 500 http://howdyougethere.com/error
```

There are even more clever ways of handling errors to be able to dynamically handle various errors, and in various languages. Several distributions use an approach of type-map files to handle errors for multiple languages:

```
<IfModule mod_include.c>
<Directory "/usr/share/apache2/error">
        AllowOverride None
```

```
        Options IncludesNoExec
        AddOutputFilter Includes html
        AddHandler type-map var
        Order allow,deny
        Allow from all
        LanguagePriority en es de fr
        ForceLanguagePriority Prefer Fallback
    </Directory>

    ErrorDocument 400 /error/HTTP_BAD_REQUEST.html.var
    ErrorDocument 401 /error/HTTP_UNAUTHORIZED.html.var
    ErrorDocument 403 /error/HTTP_FORBIDDEN.html.var
    ErrorDocument 404 /error/HTTP_NOT_FOUND.html.var
    ...
</IfModule>
```

The type-map error file `/error/HTTP_BAD_REQUEST.html.var` has entries for each language (only German is displayed here):

```
----------cs--

Content-language: de
Content-type: text/html; charset=ISO-8859-1
Body:----------de--
<!--#set var="CONTENT_LANGUAGE" value="de"
--><!--#set var="TITLE" value="Fehlerhafte Anfrage!"
--><!--#include virtual="include/top.html" -->

    Ihr Browser (oder Proxy) hat eine ung&uuml;ltige Anfrage
    gesendet, die vom Server nicht beantwortet werden kann.

<!--#include virtual="include/bottom.html" -->
----------de-
```

As you can see, type-map files make it so the proper language is displayed based upon what language the server detects from the client. In this case, the message that is displayed is German.

ServerSignature

Usage: `ServerSignature On|Off|Email`

This sets whether or not a footer line is displayed in server-generated documents such as error messages. Having this directive turned on is especially useful if you have proxy servers, so that the server where the error message was generated can be discerned.

Access Control, Authentication, and Authorization

You will have to set values for access control to your web server, and Apache has several directives to accomplish this that you will often see while administering your web server. The directives listed here are the common ones you'll see in several default Apache configuration files for different operating system distributions.

There is first the means of blocking access to your site or directories within your site: this can be accomplished by the Order directive. Authentication and authorization have to do with specific users having access to your site and its resources. Understanding just what each is can be useful in determining how you want to configure your server.

Access Control

Access control is the mechanism that checks the host or IP address of the client making the request against that list. You enable it using the directive Order from within a <Directory> section, or by using an .htaccess file to allow or disallow certain hosts. This functionality is provided by mod_authz_host.

Authentication

Authentication is the mechanism that checks your credentials when you log in. This would be the functionality that takes the input of a user logging in and compares it to the authentication information (username and password) stored in a file or database. The two types of authentication available to use with Apache are these:

❑ **Basic:** Allows for a browser to supply a username and password, transmitted in base-64 to retain the integrity of the HTTP protocol data encoding (in particular because passwords could contain special characters that break the HTTP protocol data). This is not very secure because the data is plaintext, and base-64 can be converted back to the actual data value. The Apache module that provides this is mod_auth_basic.

❑ **Digest:** Doesn't pass a username and password over the network. Instead, it uses two MD5 hash values: one called "HA1," which is an MD5 of username, realm, and password; and another MD5 hash called "HA2," which is an MD5 of method (such as GET) and the URI being requested. When access to the restricted resource is attempted, the response contains a *nonce* — a number only used once. In turn, the client creates another MD5 hash called "response" that comprises HA1, the nonce that was retrieved in the initial request from the server (as well as other data), and HA2. This is the response that's sent back to the server that then authenticates based on that response key. The Apache module that provides Digest authentication is mod_auth_digest.

The Apache modules that provide authentication can be broken up into two categories:

❑ **Authentication types:** This is the mechanism of how the authentication credentials are negotiated with the server. The Apache modules that provide this are named mod_auth_<type>.

  ❑ Basic: As has been discussed. Provided by mod_auth_basic.

  ❑ Digest: As has been discussed. Provided by mod_auth_digest.

❑ **Authentication provider:** This is the mechanism determining where the authentication information is stored on the server. The Apache modules that provide this are named mod_authn_<type> and are listed below:

  ❑ File, using .htaccess – mod_authn_file.

  ❑ DBM files. Provided by mod_authn_dbm.

  ❑ DBD/Database, using a database such as MySQL. Provided by mod_authn_dbd.

  ❑ LDAP (Lightweight Directory Access Protocol), using an LDAP server. Provided by mod_authn_ldap.

❑ Anonymous access, allows anonymous user access, similar to the concept of anonymous FTP. Provided by `mod_authn_anon`.

❑ Fallback, default, if authentication type is not configured, this is used. Provided by `mod_authn_default`.

Authorization

Authorization is the mechanism that gives you access to resources once the user is authenticated. Think of this functionality as a bouncer or Rottweiler of a web server resource within a protected directory. Authorization functionality is provided by `mod_authz_<type>` modules. The different types of authorization you can use are the following:

❑ User authorization, based upon the user name of an authenticated user. Provided by `mod_authz_user`.

❑ Group membership, based upon entries of membership of an authenticated user to a group in a group file. Provided by `mod_authz_group`.

❑ Group membership, based upon entries of membership of an authenticated user to a group in a DBM file. This performs better for larger numbers of users than a regular text file that `mod_authz_group` provides. This DBM functionality is provided by `mod_authz_dbm`.

❑ User ownership of a file. If the authenticated user owns the file or directory being accessed, they are authorized to that resource. Provided by `mod_authz_owner`.

❑ LDAP. Provided by `mod_authz_ldap`.

❑ Default, fallback in case authorization is not configured.

Both authentication and authorization directives are found either in the Apache configuration file — in the file itself only on `<Directory>` configuration section container directives, or in an included configuration file — or within an `.htaccess` file. Because there are so many configurations available, and to keep the scope of this book to something a little less encompassing than an encyclopedia, this next section will only describe the directives more commonly seen in typical default Apache configuration files.

Order

Usage: `Order ordering`

This is probably the first access control directive you will see throughout an Apache configuration. It determines the default access policy and the order in which it is evaluated, allowed, or denied. For instance, if the ordering is `deny`, `allow`, then all the `deny` directives are evaluated first and then all the `allow` directives are evaluated, if there is a match. With the `Allow` directive, if there are no matches of any of the `Allow` directives, the request is rejected. With the `Deny` directive, if there *is* a match, the request is rejected. For example, this:

```
Order Allow, Deny
Allow from all
Deny from foo.scriptkiddie.com
```

... would mean that every host is allowed except for `foo.scriptkiddie.com`.

Whereas this:

```
Order Deny, Allow
Deny from all
Allow from patg.net
Allow from wrox.com
```

... would mean that everyone *except* `patg.net` and `wrox.com` is permitted.

`Order` is provided by `mod_authz_host`.

Require

> Usage: `Require entity-name [entity-name] ...`

This sets requirement of which user can access a directory or resource. This can be a user, user ID, group, valid-user, or other entity.

```
<Directory /var/www/mysite/book>
    AuthUserFile /etc/apache2/ht/htpasswd-wrox
    AuthType Basic
    AuthName "Wiley/Wrox Stuff"
    Require user wrox
</Directory>
```

AuthName

> Usage: `AuthName realm`

This is the name of the authorization realm, and is used within a `<Directory>` section. This is simply a name for that realm, authentication credentials being specific for each realm. In terms of user experience, this is the name that the user is presented with on a login prompt when authenticating on a directory that requires it. An example would be:

```
<Directory /rahasya>
    ... other auth directives...
    AuthName "Sunya"
</Directory>
```

AuthType

> Usage: `AuthType Basic|Digest`

This sets the authentication type used; the two choices are `Basic` or `Digest`.

AuthBasicProvider

> Usage: `AuthBasicProvider file`

This sets what type of provider (an `htpassword` file, DBM, or whatever type of storage is used for the authentication information), will be used when using basic authentication.

AuthUserFile

Usage: `AuthUserFile file-path`

This sets the name of the file containing usernames and passwords, and is created by the utility `htpasswd`. An example would be:

```
AuthUserFile /etc/apache2/ht/htpasswd-global
```

AuthGroupFile

Usage: `AuthGroupFile file-path`

This sets the name of the file used to store authorized user groups. The format of this file is this: group name, colon, followed by the list of users in the group. An example would be this:

```
pandavas: arjuna bhima yudhistira
```

AuthDBMType

Usage: `AuthDBMType type`

This sets the type of database file if using DBM to store usernames and passwords for authentication.

AuthDBMUserFile

Usage: `AuthDBMUserFile file-path`

This sets the name of the DBM file containing usernames and passwords, and is created by the utility `dbmmanage`.

.htaccess File Directives

The file `.htaccess`, which can be named whatever you want using the `AccessFileName`, is a file that performs the same functions as a `<Directory>` directive that doesn't contain regular expressions, for the directory it exists in. These files can be very convenient if you don't have access to the main server configuration. For instance, you may have your web site at a hosting company that only gives you regular user access. In that case, `.htaccess` files let you set your own configuration for the directory that the `.htaccess` file is contained in. You can also configure what can and can't be done within `.htaccess` `AllowOverride`.

If you do have access to the main Apache configuration file, you should avoid an `.htaccess` file because there is a performance penalty for each file that Apache has to read.

Just as you would see within a `<Directory>` sectional directive, you could also have the `.htaccess` file in your home directory `/home/capttofu/public_html/private` containing the following:

```
AuthUserFile /home/capttofu/web_pass_files/passwd.txt
AuthType Basic
AuthName "CaptTofu Private"
Require user capttofu
```

AccessFileName

Usage: `AccessFileName filename`

This allows you to set the name of `.htaccess` files to something other than default. An example would be:

```
AccessFileName .myconfig
```

Instead of looking for `.htaccess`, Apache would instead use `.myconfig`. On Windows, this directive is useful in that it can use `"AccessFileName htaccess"` to get around issues of having a dot on a filename.

AllowOverride

Usage: `AllowOverride All|None|directive-type [directive-type] ...`

This sets which directive types are permitted to be overridden from the main Apache server configuration within an `.htaccess` file. Directive types are:

❑   `AuthConfig`: Authorization directives such as `AuthName`, `AuthType`, `Require`, etc.

❑   `Action`

❑   `FileInfo`: Directives that handle the following:

   ❑   Document types such as `ErrorDocument`, `SetHandler`, etc.

   ❑   Meta-data such as `BrowserMatch`, `CookieName`, `Header`

   ❑   `mod_rewrite` directives

Indexing Directives

There a several directives that control various aspects of how a request for a URL that is a directory, meaning a URL not containing a specific filename, is handled. These would include which specific icons to use for specific file types in directory listings. Also, of these directory index directives, there is the `IndexOptions` directive that provides numerous options on how a directory index is displayed, influencing column widths, sorting order, and precedence per column.

DirectoryIndex

Usage: `DirectoryIndex file [file] ...`

This specifies the filename to use when a client requests a URL that ends in a directory, without a specified file. For instance, if the URL requested is `http://somesite.com/info` and the `DirectoryIndex` value is `index.html`, the actual file served out will be `http://somesite.com/info/index.html`.

HeaderName

Usage: `HeaderName filename`

This causes the file filename to be included at the top of a directory listing.

IndexOptions

Usage: `IndexOptions [+|-] option [ [+|-] option] ...`

This sets which options to use for directory indexing. It provides numerous options, more than most users would ever need, for adjusting how directory indexes are displayed.

The various options for use with `IndexOptions` are listed in the following table:

Option	Description
FancyIndexing	Turns on the sorting of files based on column headers in the index display. Options that can be used with `FancyIndexing` are: ❏ `HTMLTable`: Use a table for displaying directory index. ❏ `FoldersFirst`: List directories first. ❏ `IconsAreLinks`: Makes it so icons are links to the filename or directory listed. ❏ `ScanHTMLTitles`: Scan title elements of HTML documents used for display in directory listing. ❏ `SuppressDescription`: Turns off file descriptions in directory listing. ❏ `SuppressIcon`: Turns off display of icons in directory listing. ❏ `SuppressLastModified`: Turns off last modification date in directory listing. ❏ `SuppressFileSize`: Turns off file size in directory listing.
IconHeight, IconWidth, =pixels	The dimensions (height or width) of the directory index icons.
IgnoreCase	Sorts directory contents in order regardless of case.
IgnoreClient	Ignores query variables from client.
NameWidth	Sets the width of the filename column.
ShowForbidden	Shows files that would otherwise be hidden due to `HTTP_FORBIDDEN` or `HTTP_UNAUTHORIZED`.
SuppressHTMLPreamble	Turns off display of the HTML file specified in `HeaderName` directive.
SuppressRules	Turns off `<hr>` tags used in directory listings.

Continued

(*continued*)

Option	Description
TrackModified	Turns on Last-Modified as well as ETag (content change response header) for directory listings.
VersionSort	Turns on sorting of files by filename version number.
XHTML	Turns on the printing of the directory index using XHTML instead of HTML.

An example would be:

```
IndexOptions FancyIndexing VersionSort
```

IndexOrderDefault

Usage: `IndexOrderDefault Descending|Ascending Name|Date|Size|Description`

Sets which column the directory index is ordered by when it is displayed.

HeaderName

Usage: `HeaderName file`

This defines a file that is prepended to directory listing. This is one way you could put design into directory indexes, or some sort of logo for your site that shows up on directory listings.

And example of this would be:

```
HeaderName /header.html
```

AddIcon

Usage: `AddIcon icon-name file-name|file-extension [icon-name file-exension] ...`

This sets the icon to use in directory indexing, with `FancyIndexing` enabled, for the given file or directory name, or filename glob. You can customize your site's directory listing by simply making your own icons and setting them with `AddIcon`.

Examples would be the following:

```
AddIcon /icons/hand.right.gif README
AddIcon /icons/folder.gif ^^DIRECTORY^^
AddIcon /icons/blank.gif ^^BLANKICON^^
AddIcon /icons/dvi.gif .dvi
AddIcon /icons/script.gif .conf .sh .shar .csh .ksh .tcl
AddIcon /icons/bomb.gif core
```

AddIconByEncoding

Usage: `AddIconByEncoding icon MIME-encoding [MIME-encoding] ...`

This sets the icon to use in a directory listing per the MIME content encoding of the file, with `FancyIndexing` enabled. Here is an example of compressed files being set to an image representing a compressed image:

```
AddIconByEncoding (CMP,/icons/compressed.gif) x-compress x-gzip x-bzip2
```

AddIconByType

Usage: `AddIconByType icon MIME-type [MIME-type] ...`

This sets the icon to use in a directory listing per the MIME type encoding of the file, with `FancyIndexing` enabled. An example of setting the type for entire directories containing various types would be this:

```
AddIconByType (IMG,/icons/image2.gif) image/*
AddIconByType (SND,/icons/sound2.gif) audio/*
```

DefaultIcon

Usage: `DefaultIcon url-path`

This sets the default icon to use in a directory index listing, with `FancyIndexing` enabled, when there isn't an icon set for the filename being displayed. An example would be this:

```
DefaultIcon /icons/dunno.gif
```

IndexIgnore

Usage: `IndexIgnore file [file] ...`

This sets names of files or patterns of filenames that directory indexing should ignore. Use this to hide files you don't want seen by people perusing your site. An example would be this:

```
IndexIgnore .??* *~ *# HEADER* RCS CVS *,v *,t *.hg *.svn
```

CGI Directives

CGI scripting, which will be discussed more in the next chapter, has several directives for handling how to execute CGI scripts. With Apache 2.x, CGI is now provided by the module `mod_cgi`, as well as other directives provided by `mod_alias`.

The first thing you want to do to use CGI is to ensure `mod_cgi` is loaded. This is pretty much the default for most Apache installations, both source or packaged:

```
LoadModule cgi_module /usr/lib/apache2/modules/mod_cgi.so
```

The next setting you'll often see in an Apache configuration file for CGI scripts is to alias a site URL to a directory containing CGI programs:

```
ScriptAlias /cgi-bin/ /usr/lib/cgi-bin/
```

Then the actual directory has various directives to ensure CGI is executed. Here is an example:

```
<Directory "/usr/lib/cgi-bin">
  AllowOverride None
  Options +ExecCGI -MultiViews +SymLinksIfOwnerMatch
  Order allow,deny
  Allow from all
</Directory>
```

ScriptAlias

Usage: `ScriptAlias URL-directory directory`

This allows you to set a relative URL directory to be the alias, or to respond to an actual directory that may be out of your `DocumentRoot` directory (recommended). You may have your CGI scripts and programs (CGI can be written in any language, interpreted or compiled).

ScriptAliasMatch

Usage: `ScriptAliasMatch regex path`

Works just as `ScriptAlias` does except it allows you to use regular expressions to match against a requested CGI URL. An example would be:

```
ScriptAlias ^/perl/(.*) /var/www/perl-scripts/$1.pl
```

This allows execution of programs with no file extension. For instance, the URL form of `/perl/programname` will be executed with the actual file being executed `/var/www/perl-scripts/programname.pl`

User Directory Directives

You may be a site administrator or developer who has to manage a multiuser or multihosting setup. User directories allow users to have their own directory into which they can place web site content. Depending on how you, the administrator, have it set up, you can permit users to have various functionalities, such as CGI scripting, mod_perl with Apache::Registry, PHP, and other dynamic web functionalities. You can also permit users to use `.htpasswd` to set a number of settings using the `AllowOver`.

UserDir

Usage: `UserDir directory [directory] ...`

`UserDir enabled|disabled user [user] ...`

Sets these parameters:

❑ The directory path within a user's home directory that is used as a user directory, one that `http://sitename.com/~user` goes to. This can be a list of directories to attempt to use in the order that they are listed.

❑ Enable or disable for a list of particular users.

Next, we show a full-fledged example of setting up a user with a user directory to allow for the following:

❑ User directory site for documents.

❑ Disabled for the users "root," "wheel," "mysql," "ingleburt," and "engelbert humperdinck."

❑ Enabled for "patg," "capttofu," "brian," and "chandra."

❑ Allowance of GET, POST, OPTIONS methods for any client, disallowance for all other methods.

❑ CGI scripting.

```
<IfModule mod_userdir.c>
        UserDir public_html
        UserDir disabled root wheel mysql ingleburt humperdink
        UserDir enabled patg capttofu brian chandra

        <Directory /home/*/public_html>
                AllowOverride FileInfo AuthConfig Limit Indexes
                Options MultiViews Indexes SymLinksIfOwnerMatch IncludesNoExec
                <Limit GET POST OPTIONS>
                        Order allow,deny
                        Allow from all
                </Limit>
                <LimitExcept GET POST OPTIONS>
                        Order deny,allow
                        Deny from all
                </LimitExcept>
        </Directory>
        <Directory /home/*/public_html/cgi-bin>
          Options +ExecCGI
          SetHandler cgi-script
          </Directory>
</IfModule>
```

VirtualHost Directives

As from the earlier section on Apache configuration section directives, the `<VirtualHost>` directive is the tag you use to define a virtual host. What is a virtual host? As many of you reading this know, a virtual host is the means of supporting multiple web sites, each with their own domain name, on the same server.

Types of Virtual Hosting

There are two types of virtual hosting:

❑ **IP-based:** This is where the server running Apache would be configured with multiple IP addresses, using either real or virtual network interfaces, with each web server using each IP to respond to requests to particular web site DNS domain or host.domain

❑ **Name-based:** This is where Apache is configured to respond to multiple web sites with different domain names on the same IP address. Each domain has a different document root with its own set of documents being served based on the domain of the URL.

The `<VirtualHost>` configuration section directive has been covered already, but there is one more directive that is required if you use name-based virtual hosting: `NameVirtualHost`.

NameVirtualHost

Usage: `NameVirtualHost addr[:port]`

This specifies the IP address and port, if supplied, that requests for a particular virtual host will respond to. The other important piece of this is the value you supply with the `ServerName` directive:

```
NameVirtualHost 192.168.1.120
```

Or, you can even use an asterisk to allow for all network interfaces to be used:

```
NameVirtualHost *
```

Here is a simple example of a simple virtual host, using all interfaces:

```
NameVirtualHost *
<VirtualHost *>
  ServerName mysite.com
  ServerAlias www.mysite.com
  ServerAdmin webmaster@localhost
  DocumentRoot /var/www/mysite
  <Directory />
    Options Indexes FollowSymLinks MultiViews
    AllowOverride None
  </Directory>
</VirtualHost>
```

Handler and Filter Directives

An Apache handler is a functionality that handles, or processes, particular types of files, and generates some sort of content. For instance, the `perl-script` handler is a handler that processes Perl code through mod_perl, interpreting the Perl code and generating an output that is served to the client. Another example is `server-status`, an Apache status handler that provides status information for the running Apache server, which it displays on an information page.

An Apache filter is a new Apache 2.0 feature that allows for processing of both ingoing and outgoing data, independent of the Apache request phase cycle. Filters allow you to either modify the data coming in from the client in the request body or from the connection as a whole, as well as the response body.

AddHandler

Usage: `AddHandler handler-name file-extension`

This sets the handler of a file based on the file extension. A handler is a process that through Apache parses and acts accordingly to a particular file type, producing output that Apache returns to the client. For instance, `cgi-script` is a handler that causes Apache to call the Perl interpreter to run a Perl script and to return the output of the script's execution in the web server response. The following example would make it so any file in the URL /cgi-bin with a `.pl` or `.cgi` extension is handled as CGI script:

```
ScriptAlias /cgi-bin /usr/local/apache2/sites/default/cgi-bin
    <Directory /usr/local/apache2/sites/default/cgi-bin>
    AddHandler cgi-script .cgi
    AddHandler cgi-script .pl
    SetOptions +ExecCGI
</Directory>
```

SetHandler

Usage: `SetHandler handler-name|None`

This sets the handler of an entire directory or URL path and is used within `<Location>` and `<Directory>` sections:

```
<Location /server-status>
        SetHandler server-status
        Order deny,allow
        Deny from all
        Allow from localhost 127.0.0.1
    </Location>
```

In this case, `SetHandler` forces any request to the /server-status URL to be processed with the server-status handler. Another handler example is setting an entire directory so that any access to the URL /perl, will be run as an ModPerl::Registry script (ModPerl::Registry and mod_perl will be covered in more detail in a later chapter).

```
<Location /perl>
    SetHandler perl-script
    PerlHandler ModPerl::Registry
    Options +ExecCGI
    allow from all
    PerlSendHeader on
</Location>
```

AddInputFilter

Usage: `AddInputFilter filter[;filter...] file-extension`

This allows you to add a filter for input processing. For instance, you could enable PHP by using this directive with the example below:

```
<Location />
    AddInputFilter PHP .php
</Location>
```

AddOutputFilter

Usage: `AddOutputFilter filter[;filter...] file-extension`

This sets the filter that will be used for the output of data. The following is an example of making it so that `html`, `shtml`, `htm` and `php` files are processed through `mod_layout`, which is an Apache module that provides a Header and Footer directive to automatically include output from other URIs at the beginning and ending of a web page:

```
AddOutputFilter LAYOUT html
AddOutputFilter LAYOUT shtml
AddOutputFilter LAYOUT htm
AddOutputFilter LAYOUT php
```

Client Handling

Apache provides the ability to respond differently based on the request headers of the client. This is useful to avoid having problems with browsers that do not support the most recent features or that have problems with certain features.

BrowserMatch

Usage: `BrowserMatch user-agent-pattern [!]env-variable[=value] [[!]env-variable[=value]]`

`BrowserMatch response-behavior`

`BrowserMatch` sets environment variables and response behavior, depending on the browser user-agent string, as shown in the following table:

String	Function
Nokeepalive	Disable `keepalive` for this connection
downgrade-1.0	Change the HTTP protocol to conform to HTTP 1.0
force-response-1.0	Force the response to conform to HTTP 1.0
redirect-carefully	Redirect

Here is an example:

```
BrowserMatch "MSIE 4\.0b2;" nokeepalive downgrade-1.0 force-response-1.0
```

SSL Directives

Running a secure web server is a must if you are going to be building an e-commerce web site, and accordingly, you need to encrypt transactional data between your web server and the customer's browser. Additionally, you need to assure users that your site is indeed the site they wished to connect to. With the module mod_ssl, Apache has all the functionality you need to implement a secure web server. mod_ssl provides *SSL* (*Secure Sockets Layer*) and *TLS* (*Transport Layer Security*) protocols, including the functionality for the server to guarantee that it is legitimate and is the organization or entity it claims to be through the use of a signed certificate. A signed certificate is a digital certificate that a verifying organization such as Verisign digitally signs, vouching for the authenticity of your organization.

The client/server communication process using SSL/TLS is as follows:

1. **Handshake:** The client provides a list of the ciphers and hash functions it supports.

2. **Cipher and hash function selection:** From the list of ciphers and hash functions the client provided, the server picks the strongest of those that it also supports and notifies the client of the one that both the client and the server will use for the connection.

3. **Identification:** To identify itself, the server sends back its certificate containing the server's name, public key, and CA (certificate authority).

4. **Verification:** The client verifies the certificate with the CA the server provides either by verifying against its own local CA information or by connecting to the server of the CA issuer.

5. **Session key generation:** The client generates a session key comprising the encrypted server's public key with a random number and sends this session key to the server. Since this session key was created with the server's public key, only that server can decrypt it.

6. **Communication:** Of the session key components, the random number, which both the server and client possess, will be used for all subsequent information sent between the server and client.

The following section will cover some of the more common SSL directives required for running a secure server.

To use any of these SSL directives, many Apache configurations will utilize the `<IfModule>` directive only if mod_ssl is loaded:

```
<IfModule mod_ssl.c>
...SSL Directives...
</IfModule>
```

SSLEngine

Usage: `SSLEngine On|Off`

This turns SSL/TLS on or off. It is used within a `<VirutalHost>` section. Here is an example of a simple SSL-enabled site:

```
NameVirtualHost *:443
<VirtualHost *:443>
    SSLEngine On
</VirtualHost>
```

In this example, the standard secure HTTPS port of 443 is used.

SSLRequireSSL

Usage: `SSLRequireSSL`

Forces the use of SSL (HTTPS) to connect, and denies any requests to connect without SSL. This would be a directive you would use within a virtual server running SSL.

SSLCertificateFile

Usage: `SSLCertificateFile file-path`

This is the X.509 PEM-encoded certificate file used for verification of the authority of the server. Often you will create a self-signed certificate, which is fine for testing, but if you intend to run an actual secure web site, you'll have to get it signed by a signing authority such as Verisign. This file can also contain the DSA or RSA private key. If it does, it can be specified twice if you intend to have a private key for both DSA and RSA. You should, as good practice, have your private key(s) in a separate file, as specified by the directive `SSLCertificateKeyFile`.

Another issue to keep in mind: If the private key is encrypted, you will have to supply a password upon server startup. It's up to you as to whether you want to encrypt your private key. The pros for having a password are that you can be assured that your key is password protected, which if it wasn't, in the *unlikely event* (you have your system locked down, right?) someone were to hack into your web server, they could potentially use it to decrypt a TCP dump, or could possibly create false authentication certificates. This sounds bad, but is very unlikely.

The cons of having your key password protected are that you have to supply the password on startup.

For most pros, if someone hacks into your web server and obtains root access, you have bigger problems. And if they can get that far, they might even be able figure out the password to your key. Happy thoughts, happy thoughts!

Seriously, for most web system administrators, not having a key works fine. Just make sure you have good system security!

An example of `SSLCertificateKeyFile` is this:

```
SSLCertificateFile /etc/apache2/ssl/apache.pem
```

SSLCertificateKeyFile

Usage: `SSLCertificateKeyFile file-path`

This specifies the file containing the private key, if you didn't include your server's private key file in your certificate file, `SSLCertificateFile`. As stated before, if your server's private key is encrypted, you will have to supply a password every time you start your web server.

An example of SSLCertificateKeyFile is this:

```
SSLCertificateKeyFile /etc/apache2/ssl/apache.key
```

SSLSessionCache

Usage: SSLSessionCache type

Defines a session cache type that can be used among various HTTP processes for a given session. In the case that the page being served has images, this requires being able to serve multiple requests in parallel requiring multiple processes, all of which need access to the same session information. Using this cache can provide a performance gain.

The value for session cache type has a number of options:

Value	Description
None	Disabled
Nonetonull	Disabled, but enables sending of a non-null session id to the client
dbm:/path/file	Using a DBM file
shm:/path/file[size]	Using shared memory
dc:UNIX/path/socketfile	Distcache, a distributed network-based session cache

It's important to know that you cannot set this value within a <VirtualHost> section. You could do this, however, if you use a separate file that you include into your main Apache configuration file using Include. You would need to specify this at the top of the file, as shown in the following example:

```
NameVirtualHost *:443
SSLSessionCache shm:/etc/apache2/ssl/session_cache_shm
SSLSessionCacheTimeout 300
<VirtualHost *:443>
...
</VirtualHost>
```

SLSessionCacheTimeout

Usage: SLSessionCacheTimeout [seconds]

This defines how long to keep the session cache and when to expire it. The default is 300.

SSLMutex

Usage: SSLMutex [type]

This defines a mutex to use for synchronizing Apache forked processes. The mutex type can be one of the following:

Type	Description
default	Let Apache decide which type, out of all types, to use based on availability and platform/OS
none	No mutex, disabled
pthread	Posix threads
fcntl:/path/file	Lock file, using fcntl()
flock:/path/file	lock file, using flock()
posixsem	Posix semaphore
sysvsem	SystemV Unix semaphore
sem	Let Apache pick the best semaphore

Important to note is that SSLMutex directive cannot be used within a <VirtualUser> section. As with other options with this requirement, you can simply opt to include it at the top of your virtual host configuration file that you include from the main Apache configuration file, like so:

```
NameVirtualHost *:443
      ...
SSLMutex pthread
<VirtualHost *:443>
...
</VirtualHost>
```

Limitations when Using Virtual Hosts and SSL

There are some limitations with using virtual hosts and SSL that are due to how the SSL protocol works:

❑ You can not use name-based, non-IP virtual hosts due to the design of the SSL protocol.

❑ You can not use name-based virtual hosts to identify different virtual hosts.

For more information, see http://httpd.apache.org/docs/2.2/ssl/ssl_faq.html#vhosts and http://www.oreillynet.com/pub/a/apache/2005/02/17/apacheckbk.html

Clickstream Analysis

The module mod_usertrack tracks users throughout your site using a cookie, which you name. You then use CustomLog to define a log that tracks only this cookie and can then view the clickstream analysis, which is a marketing term for what URLs a user visits within your site. Follow these short steps:

1. Define a cookie log format in your main Apache configuration file:

```
LogFormat "%{cookie}n %r %t" cookielog
```

2. Define a log that uses this format in the virtual host file of the site for which you want user tracking:

```
CustomLog /var/log/apache2/patg_cookie.log cookielog
```

3. Make sure that mod_usertrack is enabled:

   ```
   LoadModule usertrack_module /usr/lib/apache2/modules/mod_usertrack.so
   ```

   With distributions like Ubuntu, you would run sudo a2enmod usertrack.

4. In either the main Apache configuration file or the virtual host configuration file, turn on CookieTracking:

   ```
   CookieTracking on
   ```

5. Restart Apache, tail the new log, and you'll see entries like these:

   ```
   10.222.182.1.1238500307149019 GET /book/ HTTP/1.1 [31/Mar/2009:09:02:12
   -0400]
   10.222.182.1.1238500307149019 GET / HTTP/1.1 [31/Mar/2009:09:02:12 -0400]
   10.222.182.1.1238500307149019 GET /back.gif HTTP/1.1 [31/Mar/2009:09:02:12
   -0400]
   192.168.1.118.1238504695026736 GET / HTTP/1.0 [31/Mar/2009:09:04:55 -0400]
   ```

With this information, you can now parse this file into some sort of site stats analysis software (let the marketing people do this for you!) Also, analyzing click stream data, or generating stats of your access_log is one way to find out about issues with you web site or web application. It's not just a marketing tool, but another useful tool in the toolbox of the web developer.

The following table shows the various Apache options for configuring the cookie used for clickstream analysis.

Option	Usage	Description
CookieTracking	CookieTracking on|off	Enables or disables user-tracking cookie.
CookieName	CookieName name	This is the name of the cookie that is used for user tracking clickstream analysis. Default name is *Apache*.
CookieDomain	CookieDomain domain	This is the domain value of the cookie that is used for user tracking, found in the cookie headers. The domain name must begin with a dot. Here is an example: CookieDomain .patg.net
CookieExpires	CookieExpires expiry	Defines the amount of time for the user-tracking cookie to expire. You can use either numeric seconds (non-quoted), or string values such as "3 months 1 week 1 day," etc. (must be years, months, weeks, days, hours, minutes, seconds). An example would be: CookieExpires "6 months"

Rewriting URLs

One of the most powerful tools for Apache is manipulating URLs using mod_rewrite, an Apache module that lets you change the incoming request URL and transparently direct the client to the new, modified URL. mod_rewrite manipulates a URL based on the pattern of the source URL, environment and server variables, as well as several other conditions. Being a Perl developer, you will especially love mod_rewrite because of its support of regular expressions to test the patterns!

To fully explain mod_rewrite would require a book of its own. There are many great resources out there for studying to become a mod_rewrite guru.

This section won't attempt to make you a guru, but will give you a taste of what you can do with mod_rewrite. Explaining the various rewrite directives will provide a framework from which to begin.

RewriteEngine

Usage: RewriteEngine On|Off

This option not surprisingly turns rewrite functionality on or off. This directive might not work in .htaccess depending on how Apache is configured.

RewriteCond

Usage: RewriteCond string regex [flags]

This defines a rule condition, which is a value of string that is matched against a regular expression, regex, used by a subsequent rewrite rule defined as RewriteRule to apply modifications to the URL based on the rule condition evaluating as true. The optional [flags] argument is used to further modify the RewriteCond condition.

The way it works is this: you have one or more RewriteCond directives to match whatever pattern you are looking for, and if all are evaluated as true (they are implicitly ANDed unless using the [OR] flag is used), the RewriteRule directive is applied, thus modifying the URL.

Essentially, you would see something like the following:

```
RewriteCond string regex1 # is this true?
RewriteCond string regex2 # is this true?
RewriteCond string regexN # is this true?
...
RewriteRule pattern <substituted URL> # all previous RewriteCond and this are true?
```

So what you often end up with are groupings of RewriteCond directives with their do-something-please RewriteRules. The more complex your site, the more of these you will have!

Test String

The value of string can be a simple value or can refer to numerous variables. Refer to the Apache documentation to learn all the variable names that are available. They are organized into the following groups:

Group	Description
Server Variables	This would be a way of matching the host of the client: `RewriteCond %{HTTP_HOST} ^(.*).somesite.com$`
Server Internals	Matching the document root's first directory name: `RewriteCond %{DOCUMENT_ROOT} ^/(\w+)/.*$`
HTTP Headers	Matching the user agent, which has all sorts of useful applications! `RewriteCond %{HTTP_USER_AGENT} "^Googlebot/"`
Connection and Request	Matching the class C networks 172.16.220.0 through 172.16.229.0: `RewriteCond %{REMOTE_ADDR} "^172\.16\.22[0-9]\."`
Date and Time	This example would be for matching date and time to December `RewriteCond %{TIME_YEAR} ^(11)$`

Special Variables	Testing for Apache version 1.x:
	
	`RewriteCond %{API_VERSION} "^1\."`
	`RewriteCond %{THE_REQUEST} "GET"`

Look-ahead	This is a feature that allows you to see how the request will resolve, or look ahead at what it will be, since rewriting occurs at a stage prior to when some variables may be set. You can use this feature with any of the variables mentioned, for instance: `RewriteCond %{LA-U:REQUEST_FILENAME} ^/memberhandler/(.*)`

Back-References

You also have access to back-references to both `RewriteRule` and `RewriteCond` matches within group parts (inside parentheses). For example, to have a back-reference in a `RewriteCond` to the grouped parts of the subsequent `RewriteRule`, you use $N back-references — with N denoting a number from 0 to 9, starting from the first grouped part. Do realize, however, that with `RewriteRule`, $0 is the URI being tested, $1 the actual first group match. For back-references to the group matches of the last matched `RewriteCond` having group matches, you would use %N, with N being a number from 1 to 9.

```
# capture the last two octets of the IP address being tested
RewriteCond %{REMOTE_ADDR} 172\.16\.([\d]+)\.([\d]+)

# Set environment variable CAPTTOFUS_COMPUTER equal to the last
# octet, captured by the second grouping in the previous RewriteCond
#  $0 is the actual URL being tested of the RewriteRule, $1 is
# the first actual group match, the base name of the Perl program.
RewriteRule ^/perl/(\w+)\.pl$ /handlers/$1 [E=CAPTTOFUS_COMPUTER:%2]
```

The previous example shows how both types of back-references work. Shown in this example are the `RewriteCond` directive and a `RewriteRule`, which will be discussed soon. Essentially these use back-references, two from the last `RewriteCond` having group matches which are referenced as %1 and %2, and a back-reference from itself, $1, which captures the base name of the Perl script. It then rewrites the URL to a mod_perl handler named the same as the base name of the Perl script, and sets the environment variable CAPTTOFUS_COMPUTER to the value of the second group match of the RewriteCond: the last octet of the IP address.

If the REMOTE_ADDR happens to be 172.16.221.183, %1 will have the value of 221 and %2 will have the value of 183. Finally, for the RewriteRule, if you're testing the URI value of /perl/user.pl, the group match will result in $1 having the value of *user*, which it then substitutes into the result URL, /handlers/user. The special action flag of [E=CAPTTOFUS_COMPUTER:%2] sets the environment variable CAPTTOFUS_COMPUTER to %2, which was 183.

Let's distill what the end result of the example : If the user accesses http://example.com/perl/user.pl, the value of the requested URL that is tested is /perl/user.pl, and the request of the user originates from 172.16.221.183, then the request is ultimately served by the mod_perl handler /handlers/user with CAPTTOFUS_COMPUTER being 183, which you would access in the Perl code as $ENV{CAPTTOFUS_COMPUTER}. The address value of http://example.com/user.pl in the address bar on the browser will *not* change. And it will appear that the user accessed the page with http://example.com/handlers/user despite that being the actual URL that served the request. This is because all this work is being done internally in Apache (internal redirect).

Now, if you want a request to end up visibly being served as http://example.com/handlers/user, you would change the previous example to the following:

```
RewriteCond %{REMOTE_ADDR} 172\.16\.([\d]+)\.([\d]+)

RewriteRule ^/perl/(\w+)\.pl$ /handlers/$1?HOST_IP=%2 [R]
```

In the previous example, the same group matches occur. The real difference is that the [R] (redirect) flag is applied, which causes an external redirect, "302 Moved Temporarily" to the substituted URL, in this case http://example.com/handlers/user?HOST_IP=183.

You will also notice the absence of the special flag to set the environment [E=HOST_IP:%2] and the addition of a query string value of HOST_IP. This is because the environment variable can only be set in the redirect rule within the same request. By redirecting, it becomes another request and the environment variable set would be lost.

One other very important thing to consider: back-references can only be used by one rule. After they are used, they are unset. The author found this out by trial and error in coming up with examples for this book, and has the logs to prove it! For instance, if you had:

```
RewriteCond %{REMOTE_ADDR} 172\.16\.([\d]+)\.([\d]+)
RewriteCond %1 221
RewriteCond %2 183
```

... the test of %1 against 221 would be true, but the test in the next rule of %2 against 183 would actually be testing "" against 183. This is because %2 is unset in the second RewriteCond. This also means that %2 in the RewriteRule is unset.

Rewrite Map Extensions

This is a feature where you can define a rewriting map file which contains named (by key) patterns, or can even be a program that the server passes data to, which can be used in RewriteRule directives. Let's look at an example:

```
RewriteMap mymap txt:/etc/apache2/maps/mymap.txt
```

... would contain an entry like this:

```
pattern1  perl|cgi|.pl
```

... and then the `RewriteCond` would be:

```
RewriteCond ${mymap:pattern1}
```

Conditional Pattern

The conditional pattern `regex` is a Perl-compatible regular expression. Since one of the main topics of this book happens to be Perl, it is assumed you are familiar with regular expressions. You can also use the following expressions:

Expression	Description
< (less than), > (greater than), =	For non-regular expression lexical comparisons
-d, -f, -s, etc,	Also, for non-regular expression lexical comparisons. You can use any of the file tests you have with Perl. These were previously discussed in Chapter 4.
-F	A flag for testing if the file is accessible via the server using a subrequest.
-U	A flag for testing if a URL is accessible via the server using a subrequest.

Flags

These flags let you further modify how `RewriteCond` behaves:

[OR] or **[ornext]**

Normally, `RewriteCond` conditions preceding a `RewriteRule` are explicitly ANDed, meaning that all conditions have to evaluate as true for the `RewriteRule` to be applied. For instance, you could have a list of specific network IP address ranges that are internal to your organization for which you don't want to have pop-up advertisements displayed. You might use an environment variable to set whether pop-up ads display. The following rewrite block would accomplish this using the [OR] flag:

```
RewriteCond    %{REMOTE_ADDR}    "^10\.17\.221\.14[0-9]\."  [OR]
RewriteCond    %{REMOTE_ADDR}    "^192\.168\.1\" [OR]
RewriteCond    %{REMOTE_ADDR}    "^172\.16\.22[0-9]\."
RewriteRule    ^.*        -            [E=SECRET_NO_POPUP_VAR:1]
```

The following are the flags you would use:

❑ **[NC]** or **[nocase]**: Allows the pattern matching of `TestString` and `CondPattern` to be case insensitive.

❏ [NV] or [novary] : Prevents an HTTP header that is being tested from being added to the Vary header of the response. The author knows of no one who uses this.

RewriteRule

Usage: `RewriteRule condition-pattern substitution [flags]`

The RewriteRule directive performs the actual directory manipulation depending on whether the condition it checks evaluates as true. When a RewriteRule is evaluated as true, whatever substitution value is defined is then performed on the condition. Whether a RewriteRule is evaluated as true is based upon how any previous RewriteCond directives were evaluated — all are required to be evaluated as true unless you use the [OR] type with the preceding RewriteCond directives. The condition RewriteRule tests is the URL being requested on the first RewriteRule, and on the output of preceding RewriteRules that it evaluated as true — meaning the manipulated value of the URL because the preceding RewriteRule modified it.

Condition-Pattern

This is a regular expression, just as you would use in Perl. As previously stated, the condition pattern test is applied to the initial URL being requested upon the first RewriteRule directive. And then the test is performed on the now-modified URL (from the preceding RewriteRule) in subsequent RewriteRule directives. For instance, the following example, which ultimately results in nothing happening, can be used to explain how this works:

❏ A RewriteCond checks the variable HTTP_HOST, which happens to be patg.net, and evaluates as true.

```
RewriteCond %{HTTP_HOST} patg\.net
```

❏ A RewriteRule tests the URL being requested, which in this case happens to be /perl/user.pl, which with the group match, captures the value user into the first grouping variable $1. It then modifies the URL to be /handlers/user:

```
RewriteRule ^/perl/(\w+)\.pl$ /handlers/$1 # value being tested is
/perl/user.pl
```

❏ Another RewriteCond rule tests the variable REMOTE_ADDR, which for this discussion happens to be 192.168.1.200, against the pattern ^192\.168\.1. It evaluates as true. This could be any RewriteCond test — the variable REMOTE_ADDR is used here only for the sake of discussion.

```
RewriteCond %{REMOTE_ADDR} ^192\.168\.1
```

❏ A RewriteRule tests the output of the last RewriteRule, which was /handers/user capturing in a group the value user. It then substitutes the value user, making the output /perl/user.pl all over again!

```
RewriteRule ^/handlers/(\w+)$ /perl/$1\.pl # value being tested is
/handlers/user
```

So, these steps resulted in nothing happening — the URL was changed to `/handlers/user`, but then changed back to the original URL of `/perl/user.pl`. This is a good way to describe how `RewriteRule`, in conjunction with `RewriteCond`, works and how the first value tested by a `RewriteRule` is the URL, and subsequent `RewriteRule` directives test the output of the last match.

Substitution

Substitution works the same as substitution using Perl regular expressions. In the following snippet:

```
$val =~ s/oldval(foo)/someval\/$1/
```

... `someval\/$1` is the substitution, and for `RewriteRule`, the same type of syntax can be used.

The types of values suitable for substitution are the following:

- ❑ File system path.
- ❑ URL path, relative to DocumentRoot.
- ❑ Absolute URL, with schema and hostname, such as `http://example.com/mydir`. If the URL is the same host as the web server host, then the URL is stripped down to a URL path. So, if it were `example.com`, it would end up as `/mydir`.
- ❑ Server variables, as shown with `RewritCond`, i.e., `${HTTP_HOST}`, `${REQUEST_URI}`,...
- ❑ Map file, `${mymap:pattern1}`.
- ❑ `$N`, with N being 0 to 9 and representing the values captured in a pattern grouping from `RewriteRule` pattern matching. Note: `$0` is the value being tested.
- ❑ `%N`, with N being 1 to 9 and representing the values captured from the previous (last) `ReewriteCond` that had a pattern match with a grouping that evaluated as true.
- ❑ `-` (dash), which means URL manipulation is not performed and no action is taken.

Flags

Just as with `RewriteCond`, you can specify flags:

Flag	Description
`[B]`	Escape back-references. Ensures that the URLs being rewritten will work with proxying.
`[C]` or `[chain]`	Works like Christmas tree lights — if one is out, then they all are out. Makes it so the next rule requires the current rule to be evaluated as true, otherwise neither will evaluate as true nor activate. Works like a logical AND where any failure of one negates all.

The following code allows you to set a cookie when evaluated as true:

```
[CO=name:value:domain[:expiration[:path[:secure[:httponly]]]]]
```

Or you can use this:

```
[cookie=name:value:domain[:expiration[:path[:secure[:httponly]]]]]
```

The fields can be described as:

Field	Description
name	String name of the cookie
domain	Domain of the cookie such as wrox.com
expiration	Numeric, in minutes
path	The path the cookie is set for, such as /handlers
secure	Forces cookie to only be used for HTTPS
httponly	Prevents JavaScript from reading the cookie

Here is how this useful feature could be applied to the previous example:

```
RewriteRule ^/perl/(\w+)\.pl$ /handlers/$1
[E=HOST_IP:%{REMOTE_ADDR},CO=REDIR:%{REMOTE_ADDR}:%{HTTP_HOST}:600:/handlers]
```

Along with setting the environment variable HOST_IP, a cookie named REDIR is set with the value of the client making the request. The domain is set to that of the web server, the path of the URI is now /handlers, and an expiration of 10 hours is established.

The following table shows you the list of special flags for substitution. These are appended as the third argument to RewriteRule directives:

Value	Description
[E:name:value] or [env:name:value]	Sets an environment variable, as previous examples have shown.
[F] or [forbidden]	Causes the server to send the code for FORBIDDEN, 403.
[G] or [gone]	Causes the server to send the code for GONE, 410.

[H=content-handler] or [handler=content-handler]	Sets a content handler. You could use this to make a matched rule respond with a cgi-handler, just for the Perl scripts — though you do have to have ExecCGI option set for the directory. An example would be this:
	
	`<Directory /var/www/apache2-default/docs>`
	`    Options +ExecCGI`
	`    </Directory>`
	`    RewriteRule /docs/\w+\.pl`
	`- [H=cgi-script]`

Value	Description
[L] or [last]	Makes the current RewriteRule that last rule. No further rewrite rules will be evaluated.
[N] or [next]	Creates a loop; the rewrite process starts over again from the first RewriteRule. This can be deadly if you don't know what you're doing because it could result in an endless loop. Luckily, Apache will detect such a thing, break out of it, and then report the problem to the browser.
[NC] or [nocase]	Makes the pattern matching case insensitive.
[NE] or [noescape]	mod_rewrite normally performs URLs escaping, modifying certain characters into hexcode equivalents. For instance, a space is converted to %20. This flag turns off this escaping behavior.
[NS] or [nosubreq]	If the current request is a subrequest, the current rewrite rule will not run.
[P] or [proxy]	Causes the substituted URL to be internally processed as a proxy request via mod_proxy. The substitution URL must have a scheme and hostname in the URI of the proxy server to which it will be sent.
[PT] or [passthrough]	Allows for the use of the output of the current RewriteRule by other modules or directives that occur after the rewrite stage. This flag works as a [L] flag, in that it causes the current rule to be the last RewriteRule processed.
[QS] or [querystring]	Allows a query string to be passed, when not redirecting. This solves a common dilemma.
[R=http_code] or [redirect=http_code]	This causes the substituted URL to be accessed via an external redirect. If the RewriteRule is: `RewriteRule /fee/foo /foo/fee [R]` ... and the domain being accessed is example.com, the URL being accessed ends up being http://example.com/foo/fee using a temporarily redirect (code 302). HYPERLINK "http://example.com/foo/fee"[R=301] or [R=permanent] must be used if the old URL shouldn't be used anymore (e.g., for SEO — Search Engine Optimization — purposes), instead of [R], [R=302], [R=temp] (the default). Also important to note is that if you set values that are per-request, such as environment variables using the [E] flag, they will be lost in the redirection.
[S=number] or [skip=number]	Causes the rewriting process to ignore the number of RewriteRules defined succeeding the current rule *if* the current rule evaluates as true.

Continued

(continued)

Value	Description
`[T=mime-type]` or `[type=mime-type]`	Allows you to set the mime type for how the server will handle a particular resource. An example of this would be where you have images that have no file extension stored in a specific URL, say for instance a directory named `/image_repo`: `RewriteRule /image_repo - [T=image/jpeg]` This `RewriteRule` would allow the url `/image_repo/img_0133` to be served as a jpeg. You certainly would have to make sure, though, that all the files in that directory were real jpegs!

Now let's look at a couple of more extensive examples (that couldn't fit in the table!).

❑ For the `[QS]` or `[querystring]` flag:

```
RewriteRule ^/perl/(\w+)\.pl$ /handlers/$1?QS_HOST_IP=%{REMOTE_ADDR} \
    [E=ENV_HOST_IP:%{REMOTE_ADDR}]
```

This would pass the environment variable ENV_HOST_IP but not pass the query string QS_HOST_IP=192.168.1.200.

The following code would be one way to pass the query string but not pass the environment variable ENV_HOST_IP since it is a redirect:

```
RewriteRule ^/perl/(\w+)\.pl$ /handlers/$1?QS_HOST_IP=%{REMOTE_ADDR} \
    [E=HOST_IP:%{ENV_REMOTE_ADDR},R]
```

However, you can have the best of both worlds! The following would pass both the query string QS_HOST_IP=192.168.1.200 *and* pass the environment variable ENV_HOST_IP.

```
RewriteRule ^/perl/(\w+)\.pl$ /handlers/$1?QS_HOST_IP=%{REMOTE_ADDR} \
    [E=HOST_IP:%{ENV_REMOTE_ADDR},QS]
```

❑ For the `[S=number]` or `[skip=number]` flag:

```
RewriteRule /abc /def  [S=2] # if evaluated as true, then

RewriteRule /cba /ihg # is ignored

RewriteRule /ihg /lkj # is ignored

RewriteRule /def /xyz # is evaluated, and happens to be true
```

Think of this block in terms of pseudo code:

```
unless ( uri matches '/abc' ) {
    if ( uri matches '/cba' ) {
        substitute to /ihg
```

```
        }
        if ( uri matches '/ihg' ) {
            substitute to /lkj
        }
    }
    if ( uri matches '/def' ) {
        substitute to /xyz
    }
```

This gives you a quasi-ability to have if-else blocks in your rewrite rules. Using [S] flag and the flag [N] for next (looping) and provided you know what you are doing, you can truly realize your Rewrite Fu!

RewriteLog

Usage: RewriteLog file-path

RewriteLog is your best friend when it comes to creating rewrite rules. It allows you to see what you're doing wrong and why you are at the end of your rope trying to get your rewrite rules to work. Without this log, you would be in the dark and in great despair trying to determine whether a RewriteRule does what you think it should. RewriteLog logs the actions of the rewrite engine.

The entries in the log with the debug level set to 9, the highest, would appear like the following code:

```
192.168.1.200 - - [01/Feb/2009:11:50:07 --0500]
[www.example.net/sid#7ee638][rid#c4ff68/initial]
(3) applying pattern '/perl/(\w+)\.pl' to uri '/perl/user.pl
```

The information you really want to use for debugging and finding out how your rewrite rules work is the latter half of the previous line:

```
[rid#c4ff68/initial] (3) applying pattern '/perl/(\w+)\.pl' to uri '/perl/user.pl
```

This tells you that this is an initial request, and was testing the pattern indicated.

If you had the following directives from a previous example:

```
RewriteCond %{REMOTE_ADDR} 192\.168\.([\d]+)\.([\d]+)
RewriteCond %2 200
RewriteRule /perl/(\w+)\.pl /handlers/$1?HOST_IP=%{REMOTE_ADDR}
[E=HOST_IP:%{REMOTE_ADDR},CO=REDIR:%{REMOTE_ADDR}:%{HTTP_HOST}:600:/handlers/$1,
QSA,S=2]
   RewriteRule .* - [E=SKIP1:1]
   RewriteRule .* - [E=SKIP2:1]
   RewriteRule .* - [E=SKIP3:1]
```

... and then stripped out everything but the action in the log, you can see what the rewrite engine does to make these rules work:

```
   (2) init rewrite engine with requested uri /perl/user.pl(3) applying pattern
'/perl/(\w+)\.pl' to uri '/perl/user.pl'
```

```
(4) RewriteCond: input='192.168.1.200' pattern='192\.168\.([\d]+)\.([\d]+)'
    => matched(4) RewriteCond: input='200' pattern='200' => matched
(2) rewrite '/perl/user.pl' -> '/handlers/user?HOST_IP=192.168.1.200'(5)
                    setting env variable 'HOST_IP' to '192.168.1.200'
(5) setting cookie 'REDIR=192.168.1.200; path=/handlers/user;
        domain=www.example.net; expires=Mon, 02-Feb-2009 03:00:38 GMT'(3) split
uri=/handlers/user?HOST_IP=192.168.1.200 -> uri=/handlers/user,
args=HOST_IP=192.168.1.200
(3) applying pattern '.*' to uri '/handlers/user'(5)
                        setting env variable 'SKIP3' to '1'
(3) applying pattern '/docs/\w+\.pl' to uri '/handlers/user'(2) local path result:
/handlers/user
(2) prefixed with document_root to /var/www/apache2-default/handlers/user(1)
go-ahead with /var/www/apache2-default/handlers/user [OK]
```

The messages are very useful for debugging and ensuring that your rewrite rules work. Once you feel confident that they work, you can turn the log's debug level down, or else turn off RewriteLog altogether.

RewriteLogLevel

Usage: RewriteLogLevel number

This sets the verbosity level of the RewriteLog. It's recommended that you not exceed this (or turn off the RewriteLog altogether) if you are running in a production environment. However, if you are debugging your rewrite rules, you will want to set this to a higher level.

Apache Reverse Proxying

Another functionality you will have a good chance to work with and take advantage of as a web developer is *reverse proxying* using mod_proxy. In addition to mod_rewrite covered in the previous section, you definitely want to become savvy in reverse proxying.

A reverse proxy server simply forwards client requests to another server. This allows a client to transparently connect to one front-end web server — requesting a resource that may be on yet another internal, nonpublicly accessible server — and have that resource retrieved without considering its ultimate source. Apache provides this functionality through mod_proxy and related submodules such as mod_proxy_http, mod_proxy_ftp, etc. This is especially useful when dividing up functionality among servers.

Every type of web application has its own resource requirements for running optimally. Some applications require a web server configured to provide them ample memory, while not requiring as many processes to deal with requests as a static web site (which simply serves out static content such as documents and images). If you have a busy site with a lot of requests for static pages, you wouldn't necessarily want to force your more memory-intensive application to have to work with the settings that are optimal for a static sever. Conversely, you wouldn't want to have to limit your static site with the settings your web application needs. Additionally, you wouldn't want to load all the code into memory that is needed for the application to run on a site that has numerous requests for mostly static content because this would make for a slow server.

With reverse proxying, servers can be split out by application. For instance, you may have an Apache Tomcat server running a huge Java application, and another server you have designated for PHP applications using FastCGI, and a virtual server running mod_perl applications. With `mod_proxy`, you can configure your sever to proxy to these servers based on the URL being requested. Furthermore, along with `mod_proxy`, you can have very clever setups that proxy to the appropriate server based even on a file extension.

Another security benefit of reverse proxying is that these application-specific servers can be on a protected internal network so they can never be directly accessed from the outside. Figure 11-6 below shows how reverse proxying can be set up:

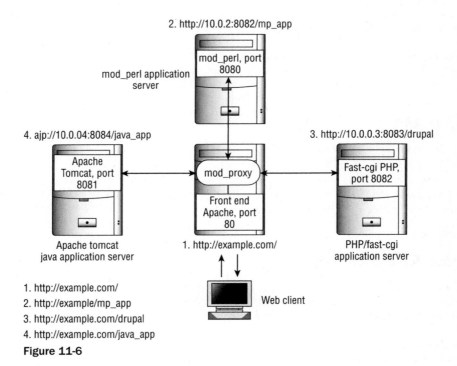

1. http://example.com/
2. http://example/mp_app
3. http://example.com/drupal
4. http://example.com/java_app

Figure 11-6

Three servers are shown in this figure. The main server runs a front-end Apache on the normal HTTP port of 80. This front-end server would be tuned for static pages. Also shown are three other specialized application servers running on an internal, private network:

❑ An Apache server running mod_perl applications at the IP address of 10.0.0.2 (arbitrary; only used for an example) port 8082.

❑ An Apache server running at the IP address 10.0.0.3, port 8083, specifically for PHP applications using fast-cgi, a common configuration for hosting companies to run PHP applications for multiple users.

❑ An Apache Tomcat server running at the IP address 10.0.0.4, port 8084, for some sort of Java application servlet or JSP pages. Also of importance is that the protocol used is `ajp` (Apache JServ Protocol, requiring `mod_proxy_ajp`) as opposed to `http`.

Figure 11-6 also shows the URLs a client would use to access different web site applications:

1. A client would use `http://example.com` to access the main front-end server without any proxy.

2. A client would use `http://example.com/mp_app`, which would in turn, through `mod_proxy` directive configuration, connect transparently and internally to `http://10.0.0.2:8082/mp_app`. User interaction to `http://example.com/mp_app` would appear to be running on the same server seamlessly, with the user experiencing it as if it were running on the main front-end server.

3. A client would use `http://example.com/drupal` through yet another `mod_proxy` directive, and would be proxied to `http://10.0.0.3:8083/drupal` (internal network IP address).

4. A client would use `http://example.com/java_app`, which would proxy to `ajp://10.0.0.4:8084/java_app`.

This is just one example of how you can use reverse proxying to divide your functionality among several servers. You could have any number of back-end servers including `mod_python`, regular CGI, PHP through mod_php/libphp5 (instead of what's shown here with FastCGI), or even a back-end Microsoft IIS server!

Enabling mod_proxy

You may need to make sure the loadable module for mod_proxy is enabled. This is critical because mod_proxy provides the actual proxying functionality, as well as the protocol module for mod_proxy, mod_proxy_http and any other modules that handle any back-end server protocols. Some prepackaged OS distribution Apache configurations have mod_proxy and its other protocol modules already configured to load. Other distributions, such as Ubuntu, require that you enable it. For Ubuntu, you would enable both modules with these commands:

```
sudo a2enmod proxy
sudo a2enmod proxy_http
```

Then restart Apache:

```
sudo /etc/init.d/apache2 restart
```

Other configurations will require that you edit the Apache configuration file and add the following two lines:

```
LoadModule proxy_module modules/mod_proxy.so
LoadModule proxy_http_module modules/mod_proxy_http.so
```

. . . to the Apache configuration file. Or, if you like, you can add them to a module-specific configuration file using the `Include` directive.

It's important to load mod_proxy.so first, then any subsequent proxy modules afterward since they contain symbols that are defined in mod_proxy.so. If mod_proxy.so is not loaded, those symbols won't resolve.

mod_proxy Directives

There are many mod_proxy configuration directives available for some really advanced setups, such as load balancing, remote proxying, running an intranet proxy — and more! For this book, only the ones required for a simple reverse proxy setup (for splitting applications between servers, as already explained) will be covered.

ProxyPass

Usage: `ProxyPass local-url !|remote-url [ key=value key=value ...]`

This is the main mod_proxy directive, used to map a remote server to a URL. When it is requested, this results in the server handling the request to interact with the remote server so that the local server appears to be the remote server in terms of the objects and functionality it provides — this happens transparently.

The first local URL, if accessed, will be proxied to the remote URL. The key/value parameters are optional and give you fine control on various settings, such as timeout values, min and max connections, etc. Do consult the Apache manual for specific information on these settings because there are many. The defaults should work just fine.

To understand how ProxyPass works, start with this example:

```
ProxyPass /internal/ http://127.0.0.2:8080/
```

This simply means that any access to the URL `/internal/` will be proxied to `http://127.0.0.2:8080/`. For instance, if a user accesses your site `http://example.com/internal`, then through the magic of proxying, the front page of the internal server will be displayed as `http://example.com/internal`. All interactions with the URL `/internal` as the base URL will be proxied to that internal server. For instance, `http://example.com/internal/otherdir`, will be proxied to `http://127.0.0.2:8080/otherdir`. But the user will never know!

The use of `!` prevents the proxying of a URL that may be in the same path of what would otherwise be proxied. For example:

```
ProxyPass /internal/foo/ !
ProxyPass /internal/ http://127.0.0.2:8080/
```

If the requested URL is `http://example.com/internal/foo`, the result will be a NOT FOUND. This works to ensure you don't proxy parts of the internal site that you want to remain inaccessible. Note that the negation proxy rule is — and must be — listed before the main proxy rule.

Proxying — it's that simple.

ProxyPassReverse

Usage: `ProxyPassReverse local-url remote-url`

This is the companion directive to `ProxyPass`, and is something you want to use to ensure that reverse proxying works for you. `ProxyPassReverse` ensures that redirection works. The issue with redirection is that if the internal server to which you are proxying issues a redirect, the redirect headers will be referencing internal URLs that will not work outside the front-end proxy.

So, for completeness you would have:

```
ProxyPass /internal/ http://127.0.0.2:8080/
ProxyPassReverse /internal/ http://127.0.0.2:8080/
```

ProxyPassReverseCookieDomain

Usage: `ProxyPassReverseCookieDomain internal-domain public-domain`

This ensures that the domain of a cookie set by the internal server is the correct public-domain of the front-end server. Here is an example:

```
ProxyPassReverseCookieDomain backend.example.net example.net
```

ProxyPassReverseCookiePath

Usage: `ProxyPassReverseCookieDomain internal-url external-url`

This ensures that the cookie path is a path of the external front-end server and not a back-end server path:

```
ProxyPassReverseCookiePath / /internal/
```

ProxyPreserveHost

Usage: `ProxyPassReverseCookieDomain`

This ensures that the `HTTP_HOST` environment variable retains the host value of the front-end server. This is an *extremely* useful feature; the author can attest to this.

Disclaimer: This is a story involving PHP in a Perl book

I was assigned a project for `Tripod.com` to implement the ability for Tripod members to have PHP and MySQL functionality. I had to implement PHP in such a way that PHP code execution was contained within each member's directory (limiting by using the php.ini setting `open_basedir`). This project required that each user's PHP programs would run separately without interference from other users' PHP programs. This further required the front-end web servers to proxy through to back-end web servers running FastCGI to execute PHP. Many PHP applications such as Wordpress, Joomla, Gallery, etc., initially broke using this setup because they were designed to use the PHP server variable `$_SERVER[HTTP_HOST]` for constructing application URLs, and this needed to be the value of the hostname of the front-end web server. However, the server variable `$_SERVER[HTTP_HOST]` takes on the value of its own hostname, as it should. In this case the value was the hostname of the back-end server, which of course

---

was not accessible from the outside — regardless of the hostname of the front-end server that the proxy request came from.

The front-end server was Apache 1.3, which doesn't have the Apache 2.2 mod_proxy directive `ProxyPreserveHost`, so I employed another trick to work around this issue — I used `auto_prepend_file` to prepend a PHP file that would overwrite various PHP server variables, including `$_SERVER[HTTP_HOST]`, to take on the value of `$_SERVER[HTTP_X_FORWARDED_HOST]`, which does contain the front-end web server hostname.

The Apache manual says that `ProxyPreserveHost` should normally be turned off. It really depends on your needs. If you are doing any type of work involving web site hosting where you employ `mod_proxy` to divide up server functionality, you will probably want to use this setting.

Apache Server Control

Several arguments that you supply to the script to restart the Apache `httpd` daemon are worth explaining:

Argument	Description
`apachectl start`	Starts Apache, obviously.
`apachectl stop`	Sends a kill to the parent Apache process; immediately kills all the children.
`apachectl graceful`	Apache parent process initiates the termination of its children to terminate once they are finished servicing their current request, or immediately if they are idle. The parent will then reread the configuration file and reopen its log files. As each child started from the previous configuration file dies off, the parent replaces it with a new child with the new configuration settings.
`apachectl restart`	The Apache parent process is sent a HUP or restart signal, which in turn sends a term to its children regardless of the state of any requests they are serving. The parent then rereads its configuration files and reopens its log files. It then starts up another batch of children that will have the new configuration settings.

Apache Configuration Schemes

In the course of configuring servers, in particular web servers, you will come across a wide variety of pre-configured Apache setup schemes. Each one has its merits and philosophy behind why it's set up the way it is. Some operating system vendors take advantage of Apache's modular capabilities. Others, such as the source install, leave it to you to start with a stock configuration and slice and dice it however you like.

This section will cover some of the more common operating system vendor configuration schemes for Apache.

Source Install

The source install is very much about letting you determine how you want to tweak your own system. The place where you install Apache (defined when you run "./configure –prefix=/path" when you first build it) is where every component of Apache will reside. In this book, the directory chosen is /usr/local/apache2

❏ **Configuration files:** There is a single httpd.conf file, which is not set up to be modular in the way that various operating system vendors package their Apache. httpd.conf is found in /usr/local/apache2/conf. It includes files in the modules that loaded directly, rather than including them as separate configuration files for each module. Although you can change this if you like.

❏ **Document root:** Found in /usr/local/apache2/htdocs. If you're running virtual hosts, which is a great possibility, you will probably end up changing ApacheRoot to /usr/local/apache2/htdocs, and then each site will have a document root found in this parent directory.

❏ **CGI:** Found in /usr/local/apache2/cgi-bin. Like document root, you may also want to divvy this up or even specify a site-specific CGI directory for each virtual server.

❏ **Loadable modules:** Found in /usr/local/apache2/modules. This is fine where it is.

❏ **Binary files:** These include the Apache server, httpd, as well as other programs and are found in /usr/local/apache2/bin.

Ubuntu/Debian

The Ubuntu/Debian package installation uses a very modular approach to setting up Apache (the two may vary). This is intended to make your server and web sites easier to develop and maintain.

Configuration Files

Configuration files are found in /etc/apache2. The main configuration file apache2.conf, which is very modular, uses the Include directive to include other "sub-configuration" files. Then there are subdirectories within /etc/apache2:

❏ conf.d/: By default, this contains a single file charset that defines what character set. Apache will use using the line:

```
# Include generic snippets of statements
Include /etc/apache2/conf.d/
```

❏ mods-available/: Contains configuration files for all available modules, though this directory is not used with an Include directive.

❏ mods-enabled/: This directory has links to the modules you want to load. They link to the configuration files in mods-available:

```
ls -l mods-enabled/
lrwxrwxrwx 1 root root 28 2009-01-25 10:23 alias.conf -> ../mods-
available/alias.conf
lrwxrwxrwx 1 root root 28 2009-01-25 10:23 alias.load -> ../mods-
available/alias.load
...
```

All the files in this line are included with the use of a wildcard in the `Include` directive:

```
# Include module configuration:
Include /etc/apache2/mods-enabled/*.load
Include /etc/apache2/mods-enabled/*.conf
```

❑   `sites-available/`: All of the virtual hosts that are available, but not specified in an `Include` directive in `apache2.conf`. These files contain virtual host configuration, one virtual host per file. All sites (even the local, default site) are set up as virtual hosts in this directory. By default, Ubuntu includes a default site configuration file in `sites-available` called, interestingly enough, `default`.

❑   `sites-enabled/`: Just as with the `mods-enabled/` directory, this directory contains links to its sibling directory, `mods-available/`, which takes you to the sites you want working upon your start of Apache. The mechanism for this to work is an `Include` directive specifying the whole directory, which loads any file in the directory:

```
# Include the virtual host configurations:
Include /etc/apache2/sites-enabled/
```

Other configuration files that are included in the Ubuntu/Debian package installation are these:

❑   The file `/etc/apache2/httpd.conf`. You might think for a second that this is the main Apache configuration file. You'll find it is empty. This file can be used for compatibility with other software so that it may exist or any other miscellaneous configuration parameter. You can probably ignore it!

```
# Include all the user configurations:
Include /etc/apache2/httpd.conf
```

❑   The ports configuration file `ports.conf`, which specifies the port that Apache will run on:

```
# Include ports listing
Include /etc/apache2/ports.conf
```

It contains:

```
NameVirtualHost *:80
Listen 80

<IfModule mod_ssl.c>
    # SSL name based virtual hosts are not yet supported, therefore no
    # NameVirtualHost statement here
```

```
        Listen 443
</IfModule>
```

Documents, Content

The standard document root on Ubuntu/Debian for web site documents is /var/www, and the default site is located in /var/www as well. However, as you add virtual hosts, you may want to put each site's documents in /var/www/<sitename>. For instance, the default site that comes included with the Apache installation could be changed from having /var/www as the document root to instead having /var/www/default, otherwise the default site would contain the directories of other virtual hosts.

Apache Modules

Note the following concerning the Apache modules:

The actual Apache loadable modules are installed in /usr/lib/apache2/modules/.

Binary Files

❑   The binary files are located in /usr/sbin.

❑   The Apache binary on Ubuntu/Debian is called apache2 instead of httpd.

❑   Apache startup script apache2ctl.

❑   The Apache benchmarking utility ab.

Also specific to Ubuntu is the Perl utility a2enmod. As seen in the mod_perl and Apache request/libapreq2 installation sections, this utility was used for Ubuntu/Debian and is for enabling mod_perl and libapreq2. All this utility does is create a link from mods-available to mods-enabled for the module you specify.

Apache Server Control

There are two server control utilities available:

```
sudo /etc/init.d/apache2 <start|stop|other options...>
sudo /usr/sbin/apache2ctl <start|stop|other options...>
```

Centos/Redhat Variants

On Centos/Redhat variants, the Apache configuration is set up modularly.

Configuration Files

The configuration files reside in /etc/httpd. The main configuration file is /etc/httpd/conf/httpd.conf and has Include directives to sub-configuration files:

❑ conf/: This direc tory contains the main httpd.conf as well as a file called magic, which is for the mod_mime_magic Apache module. The mod_mime_magic module determines file type using the first few bytes of a file to differentiate the proper mime type.

❑ conf.d/: This directory contains any configuration files, both for virtual sites as well as Apache modules. All files in this directory must be named with the extension of .conf in order to be loaded. These files are included in the httpd.conf file using the Include directive:

```
Include conf.d/*.conf
```

❑ logs/: A link to /var/log/httpd, where the Apache logs go.

❑ modules/: A link to /usr/lib64/httpd/modules or /usr/lib/httpd/modules (depending on architecture) where the Apache loadable modules are located.

❑ run/: A link to /var/run, where the PID file for Apache resides.

Binary Files, Server Control

/usr/sbin is where the binary files such as httpd, apachectl, ab and apxs are found.

Documents, Content

The following is a list of document files:

❑ /var/www/html is the main document root. You would then give your virtual hosts that you define with conf.d/<virtualhost>.conf their own document roots located in /var/www/<sitename>.

❑ /var/www/cgi-bin is the default CGI directory.

❑ /var/www/icons is the location of icons the Apache server uses to display things like directories.

❑ /var/www/manual is the Apache manual, in HTML form.

SUSE

Just as other Linux variants, SUSE 11.x has a modular configuration. It is probably the most modular of all distributions — modularity taken to another level! However, this provides a very convenient organization; you easily know exactly where to set any part of the Apache installation.

Anything that could be construed as a component or section in an httpd.conf has its own file.

Configuration Files

The configuration figures for SUSE are located in the directory /etc/apache2 and are shown in the table that follows:

File	Description
httpd.conf	The main configuration file, which doesn't contain a lot of settings itself, but does contain a lot of <Include> directives.
charset.conv	Lookup table of character-set types by abbreviated language name, such as "en" for English.
default-server.conf	A global configuration file that all virtual hosts will inherit. Specifies the main document root, icon directory, cgi-bin, etc. for the entire server.
errors.conf	Defines all of the error documents, which are found in errors as variables so that the appropriate error message according to language will be displayed.
listen.conf	Defines the default ports used by Apache — both secure SSL server and non-secure server.
magic	Used by mod_mime_magic for setting proper mime type according to file type.
mime.types	Defines all available mime types.
mod_autoindex-defaults.conf	Configuration file for directory indexing module. You can control all of the settings for how directory indexes are displayed in this file.
mod_info.conf	Configuration file for mod_info, which is used for Apache's /server-info handler.
mod_log_config.conf	Configuration file for how logging is configured.
mod_mime_defaults.conf	Configuration file for associating meta information with files by filename extensions.
mod_perl-startup.pl	Perl startup script that is executed to load Perl modules upon the startup of Apache.
mod_status.conf	Configuration file for mod_status, which gives Apache's /apache-status handler.
mod_userdir.conf	Configuration file for user web directories (public_html).
mod_usertrack.conf	Configuration file for mod_usertrack, which is an Apache module that provides logging for clickstream analysis.
server-tuning.conf	Configuration file for Apache tuning settings, grouped by whether the server is a threaded or forking server. The settings are StartServers, MinSpareServers, MaxSpareServers, ServerLimit, MaxClients, MaxRequestPerChild, etc.
ssl-global.conf	SSL settings configuration file, if running SSL.

Configuration directory subdirectories, located in /etc/apache2, are listed in the following table:

Subdirectory	Description
ssl.crl/	Contains PEM-encoded X.509 Certificate Revocation Lists (CRL) for SSL.
ssl.crt/	Contains SSL certificates.
ssl.csr/	Contains PEM-encoded X.509 Certificate Signing Requests for SSL.
ssl.key/	Contains RSA private keys for SSL.
ssl.prm/	Contains DSA parameter files for SSL.
sysconfig.d	Contains files created whenever Apache is restarted; shows run-time settings of Apache.
uid.conf	Sets the user and group Apache runs as.
vhosts.d/	Contains configuration files for each virtual host.
conf.d/	This directory contains various files for different modules such as mod_perl, PHP, GitWeb, Nagios, etc. — anything that isn't a core module or component of Apache.

Binaries

Binaries, such as the server binary ab, are located in /usr/sbin. The Apache daemon is httpd-prefork or httpd-worker, which is linked to by httpd2. Also found in this directory is apache2ctl.

Modules

The Apache modules are found in /usr/lib/apache2-<prefork|worker>.

Documents, Content

The base directory is /srv/www, and it contains the subdirectories htdocs, cgi-bin, as well as perl-lib (a location for Perl libraries).

Apache Server Control

There are two utilities available for server control. This one:

```
/etc/init.d/apache2 <various options>
```

Or this:

```
/usr/sbin/apache2ctl <start|stop|graceful|gracefull-stop|stop|various options>
```

Windows

Windows has its own particular setup. As with so many windows programs, the Apache installation is installed in C:\Program Files in a folder called by default *Apache Software Foundation*. The overall structure is somewhat Unix-like.

Apache is fully threaded on Windows, and features a MPM winnt server module.

Configuration

To begin Apache configuration on Windows, select Apache HTTP Server 2.2 from the start menu, as shown in Figure 11-7.

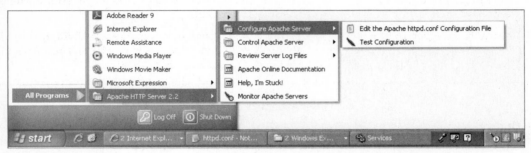

Figure 11-7

This will open up a Notepad window where you can edit your Apache configuration file.

Configuration Files

The directory, C:\Program Files\Apache Software Foundation\Apache2.2\conf\ is where the Apache configuration files belong. They are split up as shown in the following table:

File	Description
httpd.conf	Main Apache configuration file
magic	Mime types file
charset.conv	Charset information file
extra\httpd-autoindex.conf	Autoindexing configuration
extra\httpd-default.conf	This contains the default httpd settings for the entire Apache server
extra\httpd-languages.conf	This contains settings for hosting different languages
extra\httpd-mpm.confq	Server pool management for a threaded server. On Windows, Apache is threaded
extra\httpd-ssl.conf	SSL configuration file
extra\httpd-vhosts.conf	Virtual hosts configuration file
extra\httpd-dav.conf	Distributed authoring configuration file
extra\httpd-info.conf	Configuration file for the server-status handler

File	Description
`extra\httpd-manual.conf`	Configuration file for the included Apache documentation, which is in a directory in the server root, `/manual`. This configuration is set up to automatically serve the manual pages in whatever language is detected using the type-map handler
`extra\httpd-multilang-errordoc.conf`	Configuration file for serving out the proper error document according to language
`extra\httpd-userdir.conf`	Configuration file for user directories. On UNIX, this is `public_html`, but on Windows, it will be `C:/Documents and Settings/*/My Documents/My Website`

Other Files

The files in the following table are the other files required for a Windows setup:

File	Description
Binaries	`C:\Program Files\Apache Software Foundation\Apache2.2\bin\` is the directory that contains binaries such as the server httpd.exe, `htpasswd.exe`, etc. It also contains library files for APR, APR dbd and the zlib compression library
Modules	`C:\Program Files\Apache Software Foundation\Apache2.2\modules` contains modules. You might think that these would be `.dll` files, but they have the `.so` extension just as they have in UNIX
CGI	`C:\Program Files\Apache Software Foundation\Apache2.2\cgi-bin` is the directory that contains a single `printenv.pl`, which works if you have Perl installed
Error Pages	`C:\Program Files\Apache Software Foundation\Apache2.2\error` contains the error page messages for each language
Manual	`C:\Program Files\Apache Software Foundation\Apache2.2\manual` contains the entire Apache manual, which can be browsed
Logs	`C:\Program Files\Apache Software Foundation\Apache2.2\logs` contains Error and Access logs

Apache Administration on Windows

You can use the service manager to start and stop the Apache daemon, as shown in Figures 11-8 and 11-9.

From the control panel, select "Administrative Tools." This will give you a window of administrative tool applications. Click "Services." Once launched, you will see Apache listed among other services as shown in Figure 11-8.

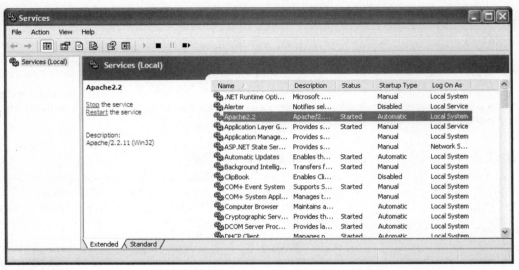

Figure 11-8

If you click Apache, you will be given a "Properties" window that allows you to edit the Apache service, as shown in Figure 11-9.

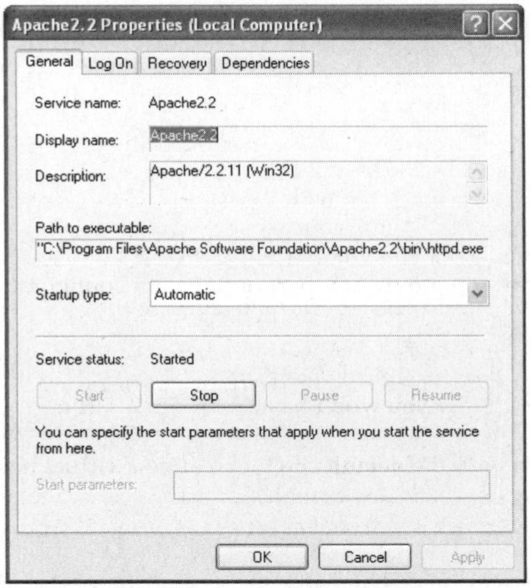

Figure 11-9

Common Apache Tasks

This section is devoted to showing you how to accomplish certain Apache tasks — these are commonplace things you have to do when you are a web developer. This section will also build on the configuration information provided in previous sections, showing you some practical examples to put that information into action.

Configuring a Name-Based Virtual Host

Configuring a virtual host is amazingly simple with Apache 2.2. It basically involves configuring an Apache configuration file with a `<VirtualHost>` section and the correct directives. You then ensure that you have all the directories created for the virtual host.

Step 1: Modify Your Apache Configuration File

You can add the `<VirtualHost>` section to your main Apache configuration file if you want, but to be more organized, it's recommended that you take advantage of a modular configuration scheme. Some operating system distributions already have Apache set up this way. For this example, a source install of Apache will be used so you can appreciate the prepackaged setups!

As mentioned earlier, the source install of Apache located in `/usr/local/apache2`, has a single configuration file `/usr/local/apache2/conf/httpd.conf` for the entire configuration. It's your job to break it up into smaller pieces! To do so, follow these steps:

First, make a directory:

```
cd /usr/local/apache2
mkdir conf.d
```

Next, edit `conf/httpd.conf`. Add this line to it:

```
include conf.d/*.conf
```

This will make it so any configuration file with the file extension `.conf` in the `conf.d` directory will be included in the Apache configuration for your server. Currently, you have none, but you can modularize your configuration as much as you want. If you desire it, you could create separate configuration files in the `conf.d` directory containing any part of the main configuration file that you see, starting a `<IfModule>` tag and including everything up to the close tag `</IfModule>`. For instance, you could create a file called `log.conf` with the contents from the main file, starting with and including `<IfModule log_config_module>` to `</IfModule>`. Just cut from the main, paste into the new `log.conf` file, and when you restart it will be loaded. Now you won't have to navigate through a monolithic file.

You probably want to start with the default site for creating a virtual host configuration file. Many configurations have the configuration for the default site contained in the main Apache server configuration file. For the sake of good organization, it makes sense to have the default site served as a virtual host.

For an example, let's suppose your site's main URL is `http://example.com`.

Edit a file, `conf.d/default_site.conf`. In it, have the lines:

```
NameVirtualHost *:80
<VirtualHost *:80>

  ServerName example.com
```

```
    ServerAlias www.example.com

DocumentRoot /usr/local/apache2/sites/default/
<Directory /usr/local/apache2/sites/default/>
  Options FollowSymLinks
  AllowOverride None
  Options Indexes FollowSymLinks MultiViews
  AllowOverride None
  Order allow,deny
  allow from all
</Directory>
ScriptAlias /cgi-bin /usr/local/apache2/cgi-bin
<Directory /usr/local/apache2/cgi-bin>
  Options +ExecCGI
</Directory>
</VirtualHost>
```

This is a very minimal virtual host, but it will work just fine. You can customize it and modify it as much as you want for your particular site needs. There are some assumptions in this file, particularly where your document root is, as well as what port you're running Apache on. As you can see, the document root is set to `/usr/local/apache2/sites/default/`, and `cgi-bin` is in the directory `/usr/local/apache2/cgi-bin`.

Step 2: Create the Virtual Host Directories

Create the directories needed for the virtual host. This can be accomplished in one step with the `mkdir` command (assuming that the working directory is to be already within the directory `/usr/local/apache2`):

```
mkdir -p /usr/local/apache2/sites/default/{cgi-bin,www}
```

This creates all the directories using the `-p` command — the main virtual host directory as well as the site's document root and its `cgi-bin`. Make sure the ownership is set to the same ownership as the user Apache runs as. In this example, both the user and group are *apache*:

```
chown -R apache:apache /usr/local/apache/sites
```

Step 3: Restart Apache

Now restart Apache, then access your new site at `http://www.example.com`!

Adding Other Virtual Hosts

To add another virtual host, you would create another virtual host configuration file for that site, named in a fashion that indicates what site it's for. For instance, if the site's name were `otherexample.com`, you would perhaps name it `otherexample.conf`. If you are creating a site that will run on port 80, just as the default site does, you could simply use the default site's configuration file as a template. Then all you would have to change is this:

```
ServerName othersite

DocumentRoot /usr/local/apache2/sites/othersite
```

You would also want to create document root directory and other necessary directories for the site, as specified in the file just created. It should have the same the permissions as the user Apache runs as. Of course, you can add whatever other specific settings you want for this additional site.

Setting Up HTTP Basic Authentication

How many times have you needed to add a password on a web site or a directory in a web site? Despite being the web guru you are, sometimes even you forget the trick for doing this. You do it only once in a while, so you have to look online every time you set it up because you forget how. The following task description will refresh your memory and distill it into simple steps that even a marketing person with shell access could do. OK, maybe not that simple.

Step 1: Modify the Apache Configuration

This can be accomplished within your configuration file or with an `.htaccess` file. Avoid the latter if you can because having `.htaccess` files scattered all about your file system adds to your management overhead and can affect the performance of Apache.

If, for instance, the directory you wish to place authentication requirements on happens to be the URL `http://example.com/private`, using the configuration you set up in the previous section, you will need to place an authentication requirement on the directory `/usr/local/apache2/sites/default/private`. Do this in a `<Directory>` section:

```
<Directory /usr/local/apache2/sites/default/www/private>
  AuthUserFile /use/local/apache2/auth/password.txt
  AuthType Basic
  AuthName "Secret Directory"
  Require user patg john
</Directory>
```

This configuration is using Basic Authentication. The realm is called "*Secret Directory*" and the two users allowed are `patg` and `john`.

Step 2: Adding Users to the Password File

The command `htpasswd` is what you use to add users to the password file. The password file, as shown from the previous basic HTTP authentication example, needs to be named `/usr/local/apache2/auth/password.txt`.

The file isn't created yet, but by using the `-c` flag when adding the first user `patg`, the file is created. It will prompt you to verify the password for the user:

```
htpasswd -c passwd.txt patg
New password:
Re-type new password:
Adding password for user patg
```

When adding the user `john` you don't need or want to use the `-c` flag because the password file is already created. It will ask you to verify the password just as you did for the first user:

```
htpasswd passwd.txt john
```

Step 3: Restart Apache

Next, restart Apache. Then attempt to access the directory `http://example.com/private`. You should be prompted with a login window to supply credentials. When you enter the correct username and password, you will be granted access to that directory.

Setting Up Digest Authentication

Most often, Basic Digest Authentication is used, but Digest is just as easy to set up and provides a better security algorithm than does Basic.

Step 1: Modify Your Apache configuration

For this example, you will be putting an authentication requirement on `http://example.com/private2`, which corresponds to the directory `/usr/local/apache2/sites/default/www/private2`. This requires you to add the following changes to your configuration file — which in this example is `default.conf`, as shown in the virtual host example.

```
<Directory /usr/local/apache2/sites/default/www/private2>
  AuthType Digest
  AuthName "Secret Directory 2"
  AuthDigestDomain /private2/
  AuthDigestProvider file
  Require valid-user
  AuthUserFile /usr/local/apache2/auth/ht_passwd
  </Directory>
```

First, `AuthType` is set to `Digest` and the realm for this will be `"Secret Directory 2,"` and the directive `DigestDomain` is set to the URL `/private2/`. The type of provider is a file, and to access this directory requires a valid user versus specific users, since Digest Authentication specifies authentication by realm.

Step 2: Create Digest Users

The command to do this is the command `htdigest`. The arguments are:

```
htdigest [-c] passwordfile realm username
```

Just as with the `htpassword` command, the first user you create will also generate the digest file with the `-c` flag. You will also be prompted for your password. One primary difference is that you have to supply the realm name that you specified in your Apache configuration file, as shown in the code snippet above.

```
htdigest -c ht_passwd "Secret Directory 2" patg
Adding password for patg in realm Secret Directory 2.
New password:
Re-type new password:
```

Step 3: Restart Apache

Now you can restart Apache. Then access `http://example.com/secret2`. You should be prompted with a login panel asking you for your credentials. Once you enter them, you will be permitted to access `/secret2`

Configuring a Secure Server

Another task that you have to do every so often is setting up a secure server. This is a very simple task, yet the steps are easily forgotten over time! This section will distill it down to three simple steps:

Step 1: Create a Self-Signed Certificate

For this example, a self-signed certificate and key will be created. A self-signed certificate won't suffice if you are running an e-commerce site, but will provide you with a secure server you can use internally in your organization. In this example, the URL for this secure virtual site is assumed to be secure.example.com.

In this example, the certificate and key will be stored in /usr/local/apache2/ssl, so first and foremost you need to create this directory and change it, like so:

```
mkdir /usr/local/apache2/ssl
cd /usr/local/apache2/ssl
```

Next, create the certificate using openssl. You will be prompted with organizational information questions:

```
openssl req -new -x509 -days 365 -sha1 -newkey rsa:1024 -nodes -keyout example.key
-out example.crt
Generating a 1024 bit RSA private key
...............++++++
.............++++++
writing new private key to 'example.key'
-----
You are about to be asked to enter information that will be incorporated
into your certificate request.
What you are about to enter is what is called a Distinguished Name or a DN.
There are quite a few fields but you can leave some blank
For some fields there will be a default value,
If you enter '.', the field will be left blank.
-----
Country Name (2 letter code) [AU]:US
State or Province Name (full name) [Some-State]:NH
Locality Name (eg, city) []:Sharon
Organization Name (eg, company) [Internet Widgits Pty Ltd]:Example Inc.
Organizational Unit Name (eg, section) []:
Common Name (eg, YOUR name) []:Patrick Galbraith
Email Address []:someemail@address.com
```

You should now have two files: example.key and example.crt.

Step 2: Add the Secure Virtual Host

Just as you did with the default virtual host and any other virtual hosts you added, you will now add a secure server configuration file for this secure virtual web site. As with other sites, you probably want to name it so you know that the configuration file is for your secure site. In this example, it's called secure.conf:

```
NameVirtualHost *:443
```

497

```
SSLSessionCache shm:/usr/local/apache2/ssl/session_cache_shm
SSLSessionCacheTimeout 600
SSLMutex pthread
<VirtualHost *:443>

ServerName secure.example.com
ServerAdmin someemail@address.com

SSLEngine On
SSLCertificateFile /usr/local/apache2/ssl/example.crt
SSLCertificateKeyFile /usr/local/apache2/ssl/example.key

DocumentRoot /usr/local/apache2/sites/secure
<Directory /usr/local/apache2/sites/secure>
  SSLRequireSSL
  Options Indexes FollowSymLinks MultiViews
  AllowOverride None
  Order allow,deny
  allow from all
</Directory>
</VirtualHost>
```

You will also want to create the virtual site's document root directory and ensure correct permissions:

```
mkdir /usr/local/apache2/sites/secure
chown apache:apache /usr/local/apache2/sites/secure
```

Step 3: Restart Apache

Restart Apache. Browse to the URL `https://secure.example.com`. You may be asked by your browser to make an exception for the unsigned certificate.

Settin Up a Secure Server with a Valid Secure Certificate

If you want to get a certificate signed by an authorized certificate authority, the steps are the same as in the last section "Configuring a Secure Server" except:

Step 1: Create a Key and Certificate Request

For this example, you will create a key and certificate request. You'll keep the key stored on your server and you'll use the certificate to submit a request to a signing authority. The URL that will be used for this secure virtual site in this example will be `secure.example.com`.

In this example, the certificate, which is yet to be obtained, and key will be stored in `/usr/local/apache2/ssl`. So first and foremost you will have to create this directory and change it to:

```
mkdir /usr/local/apache2/ssl
cd /usr/local/apache2/ssl
```

Next, create the key and certificate request using `openssl`. You will be prompted with organizational information questions — *do not enter the email* or challenge password.

```
openssl req -new -sha1 -newkey rsa:1024 -nodes -keyout example.key -out example.csr
```

Step 2: Obtain a Certificate Using the Certificate Request

Whatever you use to obtain a certificate (Verisign, RapidSSL), you must follow the steps of selecting what certificate product you want. You will eventually be given a form to enter your certificate request. You need to cut and paste everything in the `example.csr file` — everything including:

```
-----BEGIN CERTIFICATE REQUEST-----
....Request contents...
 -----END CERTIFICATE REQUEST-----
```

Depending on the signing authority, it may have you provide a phone number. The authority's system will call that number to prove you are who you say. Once the process is complete, you'll receive your certificate. If the certificate is in an email, just cut and paste the entire key's contents into `example.crt`, which is stored (for this example) in `/usr/local/apache2.ssl`.

Step 3: Set Up a Virtual Host

This step is exactly the same as Step 2 in the section "Configuring a Name-Based Virtual Host" earlier in this chapter.

Step 4: Restart Apache

After restarting Apache, you can access your secure site and verify that your site uses a valid certificate now.

Setting up a Reverse Proxy with Two Virtual Hosts

The section "Apache Reverse Proxying," that appeared earlier in this chapter, gave you insight into how a reverse proxy works and how you can use it to split up servers by task. It also explained the various settings. This section will show you how to put that information into action by setting up a back-end server, which for this discussion will have the URL `http://backend.example.com:8080` (running on port 8080) and a front-end server configured to proxy to the back-end server from the URL `http://example.com/internal`.

Step 1: Set Up the Internal Virtual Host

The internal virtual host will be set up to run on an internal IP address 127.0.0.2 and on port 8080. You won't need to create an IP alias for this address since it is a 127.x.x.x address. You will, as with other virtual hosts, create a virtual host configuration file. For this example, it will be called `backend.conf`, and will be stored in `/usr/local/apache2/conf.d` with the other virtual server configuration files. It will contain the following:

```
NameVirtualHost 127.0.0.2:8080
Listen 127.0.0.2:8080
<VirtualHost 127.0.0.2:8080>
  ServerName backend.example.com

  DocumentRoot /usr/local/apache2/sites/backend/www
  <Directory /usr/local/apache2/sites/backend/www>
    Options FollowSymLinks
    AllowOverride None
    Options Indexes FollowSymLinks MultiViews
```

```
        AllowOverride None
        Order allow,deny
        allow from all
    </Directory>

    ScriptAlias /cgi-bin /usr/local/apache2/sites/backend/cgi-bin
    <Directory /usr/local/apache2/sites/backend/cgi-bin>
        Options +ExecCGI
    </Directory>
</VirtualHost>
```

This is set up pretty much like the main site, including a cgi-bin directory for running scripts and other applications. The main difference is that the configuration file uses the address 127.0.0.2 on port 8080 using the NameVirtualHost, Listen, and <VirtualHost> directives.

You will also want to create the site's document root and cgi-bin directories:

```
mkdir -p /usr/local/apache2/sites/backend/{www,cgi-bin}
chown -R apache:apache /usr/local/apache2/sites/backend
```

Also, place a simple HTML file in /usr/local/apache2/sites/backend:

```
<html>
  <head><title>Backend Server</title></head>
  <body><h1>This is the backend server</h1></body>
</html>
```

This will come in handy when you test to see if it works — hopefully you'll see this file!

Step 2: Add Proxy Directives to the Front-End Server Configuration

Next, add the ProxyPass and ProxyPassReverse — which are the only required directives for this to work — as well as other optional Proxy*XXX* directives to the front-end site's configuration file (which in this case was default.conf):

```
ProxyPass /internal/ http://127.0.0.2:8080/
ProxyPassReverse /internal/ http://127.0.0.2:8080/
ProxyPassReverseCookieDomain backend.example.com example.com
ProxyPassReverseCookiePath / /internal/
ProxyPreserveHost On
```

Also, you will need to ensure that the proxy server is permitted to connect to the front-end server. Specify the IP address of the back-end proxy server:

```
<Location />
    Allow from 127.0.0.2
</Location>
```

Step 3: Restart Apache

Now restart Apache. You should be able to access http://example.com/internal and see the "This is the backend server" message from the file added to the document root of the internal server in Step 1. This will prove that your reverse proxy works!

Summary

This chapter introduced you to the Apache HTTP Server, the world's most popular web server. Its popularity is due in large part to how powerful, how configurable, how extendable, and, last but not least, how *free*, it is! Also in this chapter you had an overview of the HTTP protocol and how Apache works. You were shown how to install and configure Apache, including some standard Apache configurations for several Linux distributions and for Windows. Also shown in this chapter were several common Apache tasks, such as setting up a secure web server, virtual hosts, and a reverse proxy. Another section covered one of the most powerful tools for Apache, mod_rewrite, which allows you to rewrite or manipulate URLs.

12

Contact List Application

You've read about MySQL and everything you'd want to know about it. You've also read about both memcached and Apache. Now, you'll see just how all of these can fit together in a way for you to build a practical web application — with MySQL for the data store and memcached to provide a caching layer for this application.

This chapter shows you the complete implementation of a contact list application, which allows you to add or edit contacts through an HTML form, save the contact, and then provide a listing of the existing contacts. In this chapter, this application will be a CGI application using both MySQL and memcached. It will use basic HTML design and style sheets to present a clean, simple user interface. The following chapter will show how you can turn this CGI application into a mod_perl application.

Using MySQL and memcached Together

The purpose of showing you this application's implementation is to demonstrate how you can use MySQL and memcached together to provide data to a web application, with the focus being how to implement caching. The application looks simple on the surface, but there is some complex functionality at a lower level that ensures that caching is working properly.

Also, this application will introduce you to handling CGI and web programming, particularly how to process submitted form values. For this application, the CGI.pm Perl module will be used to provide a means of obtaining those submitted form values, as well as showing you some of its content generation methods.

Another Perl module demonstrated in this application is DBIx::Password, which provides a means of having a global file for storing database passwords. With this you do not have to provide database connection specifics such as the database user and password in your application code. This is always a hot debate: where to store the password for database connections. The author presents one solution for doing this; you might have your own preference.

A common issue in developing web applications is a lack of understanding about what is involved. You might have what appears on the surface to be a simple application that your employer thinks is simple to implement and should take only a fairly short amount of time to develop. However, you have no way of explaining intricate technical details about what is actually involved and have to translate those details into terms they can understand.

A CGI Program

Before there was light, there were web servers with static pages. Web site developers wanted to provide a means to process data input by users. The web site developers looked around and said "let there be dynamic pages," hence CGI was created.

CGI stands for *Common Gateway Interface* and is a standard way in which a web server runs an external program. As previously mentioned, a web server's purpose in life is to receive requests from web clients (browsers) for certain resources — HTML, XML, text pages, images, videos, audio files, etc. — and then to respond accordingly and deliver these resources. These are all examples of static resources. They don't change. The client requests them and the server responds with the content. In order for a web server to offer interactive content, you want it to be able to do something other than simply display data, to be dynamic based on some sort of user action or input. For that to happen, you need some sort of executable program or engine. CGI is the very mechanism that made this possible.

CGI defines a standard means for the web server to interact with an external program. It provides that program with web server environment variables as well as request headers containing submitted form values, file uploads, and any content from the client for processing. It then returns the output of the program as a web server response. That output consists of response headers, which could include content specifications as well as cookies, and the response body, which contains the output of the program organized within HTML. The client then receives this output and displays it to the user.

CGI Apache Setup

The first thing you want to do is ensure that CGI can run. From the previous chapter, you saw in the Apache configuration file how this was done.

```
ScriptAlias /cgi-bin /usr/local/apache2/sites/default/cgi-bin
  <Directory /usr/local/apache2/sites/default/cgi-bin>
    Options +ExecCGI
  </Directory>
```

That's all you really need to run CGI scripts. What this says is to alias the URL /cgi-bin to /usr/local/apache2/sites/default/cgi-bin as well as make it so that URL is handled by mod_cgi. Setting Options +ExecCGI provides the Apache option that gives permission for CGI to be executed. Since it is the only option listed, only running CGI is permitted.

Your Basic CGI Program, and Then Some

So many other texts start out with "hello, world" examples. Such examples may be great for learning theory, but if you are anything like the author in terms of how you learn something, working examples are the best lesson. This chapter will show you a fully functional CGI program including some of the components that have been covered thus far in this book — a simple contact list application that stores and displays user data, using MySQL and memcached, written in Perl of course, and running on Apache.

Understanding the Application's Functionality

The functionality of this application will be split up in stages:

❑ **Design.** You will see how to come up with an interface concept before coding the more internal functionalities.

❑ **Data storage requirements.** The schema for this application is very simple, but the purpose here is to focus on caching more than on any particular schema in MySQL, other than a simple table to store contact data.

❑ **Application requirements.** This provides a guide to knowing the basic program flow and what sort of subroutines and methods will be provided. The concept of how to divide presentation functionality and logic from data storage and retrieval (back-end) functionality will be shown by splitting the code between a fairly small CGI script and a larger Perl module/class that the CGI script instantiates.

❑ **Application functionality.** This gives you a good idea how to write a web application with similar applications with similar requirements using memcached and MySQL.

Conceptualizing

The first thing to do is come up with an idea and design for a simple application. What features do you plan to implement? For this simple contact list application, it will store eight fields or attributes of data per contact — a unique username, unique email address, first name, surname, phone number, city, address, and state.

This application will provide the following user interface functionality:

❑ Display a form for contact data to be entered and saved.

❑ Display a listing of any contacts already in the database.

❑ Save a new contact while preventing the use of a username and email that already exists in the database.

❑ Allow a contact to be edited and saved for an update. This application must not allow the user to change the contact username attribute.

❑ Allow a contact to be displayed.

❑ Allow one or more contacts to be deleted at a time from the contact listing.

❑ Display error messages when the following things happen:

    ❑ A user tries to save a contact that doesn't exist.

    ❑ A user does not provide required form inputs (which will be all fields in this example).

    ❑ Any database or system errors occur.

There are a lot of other user interface features for which this application could provide a demonstration — it could certainly have more fields of data — but the purpose of this particular application is to show simple, core functionality and how to implement it using a Perl CGI program. This shows you how to get started implementing a Perl-MySQL web application sooner rather than later! Adding more to it would be rather pointless since its functionality will be locked down.

Program Requirements

Next, you want to define internal design requirements:

❑ The application will provide connections to MySQL and memcached. MySQL is required and crucial for the application; memcached is optional and provides the performance benefits of caching.

❑ The application must provide methods that retrieve, add, update, and delete users.

❑ The application must have logic to display the appropriate functionality.

❑ The application must provide error handling for incorrect user input. Also, the application must do something — at least display an error message — if it cannot connect to MySQL.

The trickiest but most beneficial functionality is the caching of data to reduce database accesses as much as possible. The application must provide caching through the use of memcached. The application should always try to utilize memcached for obtaining data whenever possible in order to avoid database accessing.

The application must ensure that memcached is updated whenever MySQL is updated — on any data modification operation (INSERT, UPDATE, DELETE) — to ensure that when it does use memcached to obtain data instead of MySQL, the data it retrieves is the same as what is stored in durable storage in MySQL

The application must cache objects in such a way that they are cataloged as having been stored in memcached so the functionality that obtains data from memcached has a reliable accounting of *what* it can find in memcached.

User Interface

You also want to have an HTML design for your page. The requirements for the design follow the program design:

❑ As stated, the application needs to display a listing of users.

❑ As stated, the functionality calls for listing users and providing a form to input new users. The form needs to have four input text fields.

❑ Additionally, you want to be able to delete one or more users. That would require checkboxes, or some other means of selecting each user, and a Delete button to delete all checked users selected for deletion.

❑ A number of style sheet attributes should also be defined to give the form a useful yet aesthetically pleasing interface. If you are more of a developer than a designer, it can help to have a friend help you create an interface design (just as the author does)!

So the following HTML will be split into the various parts, and the names in italics listed here will be the name of the functions that will be assumed.

❑ A *header* display function, which will be HTML containing the title, style sheets, JavaScript if any, and any other things that would exist between the beginning of the document and the main body.

❑ A *mainform* display function, the default display when no particular operation has been selected. This will display a list of users in tabular form with a main Delete button at the bottom. In each list entry, there will be a link for viewing and a link for editing the user, as well as a delete checkbox that, when selected, will include the user in the user deletion when the Delete button is clicked. Also in this display is a link to create a new contact entry.

❑ A *userform* display function that provides a form for the user to enter a new user, or edit and existing contact. You would access this from the link from the *mainform* display or the *viewuser* display.

❑ A *viewuser* display function that will display data for the contact selected from the *mainform* user listing, per contact.

❑ An optional *footer* display function that will display the bottom of the page, depending on how much data there is.

Having this breakdown of display functions will help you to come up with an HTML design and get a better idea of the program's flow. You'll also find it useful to mock up the HTML before you write the code, putting in HTML comments where each part of display functionality begins and ends. First and foremost would be the delineation of different sections of the entire page. Then you would consider any iteration within the application that produces a list or table — and for this application that would be the user listing. You would have it so more than one contact is displayed, and add HTML comments to the beginning and end of each table row.

Then you can cut and paste later!

The Main User Form, User Listing

The interface for the *mainform* will look like Figure 12-1.

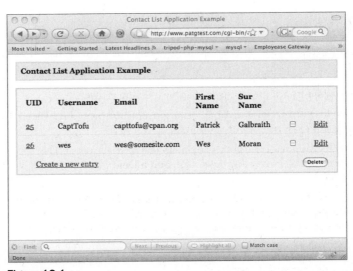

Figure 12-1

As you can see, this is a simple, clean interface that provides a tabular display consisting of four columns of the eight contact attributes for each contact, as well as the user id UID. Also included for each row are the following:

❑   The UID is a link to a page to view the contact.

❑   The last column is a link to edit the contact.

❑   A check box allows you to select a contact. You can select the contact on a particular row and click the Delete button at the bottom right corner to delete the selected contacts.

❑   A link in the bottom left corner allows you to create a new contact.

In order for the page to appear as it does in the design shown, the *header* display function will display the HTML header portion of the entire document, which includes CSS styling information that controls the look and feel of the document.

```
<!DOCTYPE HTML PUBLIC "-//W3C//DTD HTML 4.01//EN"
 "http://www.w3.org/TR/html4/strict.dtd">
<html>
  <head>
    <title>Contact List Application Example</title>
    <style type="text/css">
      body
        {
            font-family: Georgia, "Times New Roman", Times, serif;
            margin: 1em;
            color: black;
            background-color: #fff;
        }
      p.msg
        {
            font-weight: bold;
            padding: .5em;
            border: .2em solid #fcc;
            background: #fdd;
        }
      table.userlist th, table.userlist td
        {
            text-align: left;
            padding: .5em 1em;
            margin: 0;
            border-bottom: .1em solid #ddd;
        }
      table.userlist th
        {
            border-bottom: .2em solid #ddd;
        }
      table.userlist
        {
            background-color: #eee;
            border: .2em solid #ccc;
            margin: 0 0 1em;
        }
      table.userlist tfoot td
```

```
            {
                text-align: right;
                border: none;
            }

            form label
            {
                display: block;
            }
        </style>
    </head>
    <body>
    <!-- end of header() content -->
```

As you can see, most of the style information is intended for the *userlist* HTML table, which is the most "complex" part of the display. The next portion of the page includes the HTML for the *mainform* display function. This includes the table where each contact or user is listed. It might make sense to have a function that creates this table, so comments are used in this code sample to delineate where the *userlist* begins and ends.

```
    <!-- begin mainform -->
        <p class="msg">Contact List Application Example</p>
        <p>
            <!-- begin userlist -->
        <form action="/cgi-bin/app.pl" name="delete_user_form"
        id="delete_user_form" method="POST">
        <table class="userlist">
          <thead>
           <tr>
             <th>UID</th>

             <th>Username</th>
             <th>Email</th>
             <th>First Name</th>
             <th>Sur Name</th>
             <th colspan="2"> </th>
             </tr>
          </thead>
          <tbody>

            <!-- row for uid 25 -->
            <tr>
              <td><a href="/cgi-bin/app.pl?view=25">25</a></td>
              <td>CaptTofu</td>
              <td>patg@patg.net</td>
              <td>Patrick</td>
              <td>Galbraith</td>

              <td><input type="checkbox" name="25" id="25"></td>
              <td><a href="/cgi-bin/app.pl?edit=25">Edit</a></td>
              <!-- only reason for this is to have nice message -->
              <input type="hidden" name="username_25" value="CaptTofu">
            </tr>
            <!-- end row for uid 25 -->
```

```
        <!-- row for uid 26 -->
        <tr>

          <td><a href="/cgi-bin/app.pl?view=26">26</a></td>
          <td>wes</td>
          <td>wes@osdn.com</td>
          <td>Wes</td>
          <td>Moran</td>
          <td><input type="checkbox" name="26" id="26"></td>

          <td><a href="/cgi-bin/app.pl?edit=26">Edit</a></td>
          <!-- only reason for this is to have nice message -->
          <input type="hidden" name="username_26" value="wes">
        </tr>
        <!-- end row for uid 26 -->
      </tbody>
      <tfoot>
        <tr>

          <td colspan="2">
          <a href="/cgi-bin/app.pl?edit=0">Create a new entry</a>
          </td>
          <td align="right" colspan="5">
          <input type="submit" name="delete_user" id="delete_user" value="Delete">
          </td>
        </tr>
      </tfoot>
    </table>
    </form>

    <!-- end userlist -->

    </p>
    <!-- end mainform -->
```

Each row (there are two) also has a comment at the beginning and end of the row. This will be an HTML fragment that you will end up putting in the portion of the code that displays each contact row from a database result set.

Next is the immense *footer* content

```
  <!-- footer -->
    </body>
  </html>
```

You may find this comedic, but there may be a need for adding more design content to this footer. You might was well make this a functional unit now so that if you do end up adding more content, the logic for it is separated out.

User Edit Form

The next page that this application will display is a form for editing existing contacts and adding new contacts. Figure 12-2 shows how this page will appear:

Figure 12-2

The contact edit page, which for discussion can be referred to as *userform*, contains form elements for all contact attributes, including a pull-down selection for states. If you recall in a previous chapter, there was code that cached a table of state attributes. That code will be scavenged and reused for this application.

The HTML code that follows shows the *userform*, including four elements in the pull-down for states, which also is delineated with comments. The same style attributes apply, as this page and others will use the header function containing the style sheet.

```
<!-- begin userform -->
  <p class="msg">Editing new user</p>
  <p><a href="/cgi-bin/app.pl">Back to main page</a></p>
  <p>
  <form action="/cgi-bin/app.pl" name="appform" method="post">
    <fieldset>
      <p>
        <label for="username">Username:</label>
        <input type="text" name="username" id="username" size="16"
        value="CaptTofu">
      </p>
      <p>
```

```
        <label for="email">Email:</label>
        <input type="text" name="email" size="16" value="capttofu@cpan.org">
    </p>
    <p>
        <label for="firstname">First Name:</label>
        <input type="text" name="firstname" size="16" value="Patrick">

    </p>
    <p>
        <label for="surname">Sur Name:</label>
        <input type="text" name="surname" size="16" value="Galbraith">
    </p>
    <p>
        <label for="phone">Phone Number:</label>
        <input type="text" name="phone" size="16" value="2923582908">

    </p>
    <p>
        <label for="address">Address:</label>
        <textarea name="address" rows="3"
        columns="30">1333 Elm Ave.</textarea>
    </p>
    <p>
        <label for="city">City:</label>

        <input type="text" name="city" size="16" value="Marlow">
    </p>
    <p>
        <label for="state">State:</label>
        <! - this will be generated -->
        <select name="state" >
          <option value="AK">Alaska</option>
          <option value="AL">Alabama</option>
          <option selected="selected" value="NH">New Hampshire</option>
          <option value="WV">West Virginia</option>
          <option value="WY">Wyoming</option>
        </select>

        <!-- end generated state list -->
    </p>
    <p>
<!-- this hidden element for uid will be conditional -->
        <input type="hidden" name="uid" id="uid" value="25">
        <input type="submit" id="save_user" name="save_user" value="Save">
    </p>

</form>
</p>
<!-- end userform -->
```

At the bottom, also notice that there is a hidden element *uid*. This is used as a toggle for the subroutine or method to know if the form being submitted is for an existing or new contact. For an existing contact, it will be included and have the contact's uid. For a new contact, it will not be displayed. When the contact is saved, the system will create a uid for the new contact through MySQL's auto increment.

Contact View Page

The design for the next page — the page that will display a contact — is shown in Figure 12-3:

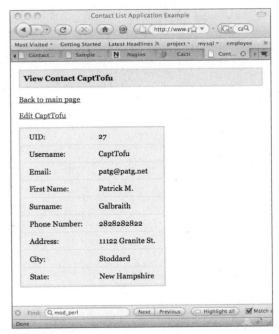

Figure 12-3

The contact view page, which can be referred to as *viewuser*, displays all the contact fields. This page uses a simple table to display all contact attributes for a given contact, taking advantage of the same styling as was illustrated for the contact list *userlist*, making for a clean interface. It also offers the ability to edit the current user being viewed, as well as a link to return to the front page. This *viewuser* contact view page will be accessible from the front page from the contact list for each listed contact. This page is just for viewing.

Database Storage Requirements

As stated, what you'll store will be a contact consisting of eight text fields. So the table must have these eight fields. You should also add to them a contact ID field, uid, which the database will use as an auto_increment column to automatically set its value — the application you are creating won't set this, but it will display it. The following table shows the various columns in the list:

Column	Description
uid	Integer, primary key, auto-increment
Username	Text, unique, should be at least 16 characters
Email	Text, unique, make it 32 characters to be safe. Anything beyond 32 is insane.
First Name	Text, 32 characters
Surname	Text, 32 characters
Phone	No, this won't be an integer. Make it a `varchar` 32.
Address	255 characters should be sufficient.
City	24 characters
State	This app will use state abbreviations, only 2 characters are needed.

The schema definition would then need to be:

```
CREATE TABLE users (
    uid int(8) NOT NULL auto_increment,
    username varchar(16) NOT NULL default '',
    email varchar(32) NOT NULL default '',
    firstname varchar(32) NOT NULL default '',
    surname varchar(32) NOT NULL,
    phone varchar(16) NOT NULL default '',
    address varchar(255) NOT NULL default '',
    city varchar(24) NOT NULL default '',
    state varchar(2) NOT NULL default '',
    PRIMARY KEY  (uid),
    UNIQUE KEY username (username),
    UNIQUE KEY email (email)
) ENGINE=InnoDB
```

To satisfy the requirements for uniqueness, what is shown in the previous code is a table with three unique indexes — uid is a primary key (which happens by design to be unique), username and email. The purpose of these unique indexes is to ensure that a user with the same username or email address cannot be inserted into the users table. The value of uid is assigned through the mechanism of auto_increment, so you don't have to worry about collisions through user input. But with email and username you do. With the UNIQUE constraints on the indexes for those columns, however, you won't have to worry about duplicated data — at the database level.

Even though the table has these constraints placed upon these columns, your application should not rely on the database for enforcing them. Nor should the database be used to indicate whether a value being inserted is for a duplicate user because it will result in an error from the database about a duplicate record. The constraints are a last-ditch effort to prevent duplicate data from being inserted. You should provide logic at the application level to check for a duplicate record even before an attempt is made to insert the user into the database, possibly resulting in an error.

The other table, which is a stripped-down version of a similar table from an earlier chapter, is *states*. It will only contain three columns, two of which are needed for this application:

```
CREATE TABLE states (
    state_id int(4) NOT NULL auto_increment,
    state_abbr varchar(3) NOT NULL default '',
    state_name varchar(32) NOT NULL default '',
    PRIMARY KEY  (state_id),
    KEY state_abbr (state_abbr),
) ENGINE=InnoDB;
```

This table will contain the state abbreviations and full state names used for dynamically generating the pull-down states menu in the contact edit form.

Program Flow

The next step is to plan how to implement the program. This means figuring out the flow of the program. What does the program need to do to deliver the functionality required? How will it handle errors, how will it function based on user input, and what sort of decision process will there be?

Start with a skeletal frame.

First Things First

You want to think about the first things the program will need to do:

- ❏ Connect to MySQL
- ❏ Connect to memcached
- ❏ Parse submitted form data, if any
- ❏ Generate error messages, should any error occur
- ❏ Print a response HTML header
- ❏ Print the HTML page header
- ❏ Display the appropriate page according to user input or lack thereof. This will require some sort of decision maker, or *dispatcher*
- ❏ If there is no user input, display the default page — in this case the *userlist*
- ❏ If there is user input, is it a contact view, edit form, contact creation, contact modification, or contact deletion?
- ❏ If a contact edit of new or existing users, display the edit form *userform*
- ❏ If a contact is being saved, new or existing, save the contact, then display the main page *mainform*
- ❏ If contacts are being deleted, delete those contacts, then display the main page *mainform*
- ❏ If the contact is merely being viewed, then display *viewuser*
- ❏ Display the *footer*

This also brings up another issue in design and organization; since this is an application utilizing MySQL and memcached for data storage and caching, it will contain a lot of non-display functionality as well as SQL statements and interactions with memcached. It might be useful to divide the display logic from the non-display logic. The main CGI script could contain all the display logic, and the non-display and database functionality can be implemented in a Perl class.

For this application, the CGI script will be called app.pl and for the Perl class, another incarnation of the ones oft-used in this book, `WebApp.pm`.

Since the HTML design for this application has already been determined, the CGI will be the first thing to sketch out.

Program Implementation

With the program flow and basic logic decided, you can now begin to implement your program.

Getting Started

So, to get started, the first things you will have to have in the code are various declarations and module importations:

```
#!/usr/bin/perl

use strict;
use warnings;

use CGI qw(:cgi :html);
use CGI::Carp qw(carp confess);
use Data::Dumper;
```

First and foremost, be strict on yourself with warnings and use strict pragma to ensure good coding from the start. You also need the ability to process submitted form values, so take advantage of the CGI Perl module.

CGI.pm, written by Lincoln Stein, is a mainstay in Perl web development that provides an API with a plethora of useful methods to enable you to do just about everything you need to write feature-rich Perl web applications. There are probably billions of lines of code running web sites throughout the Internet using this module. For this application, only the set of methods provided by :cgi and :html will be required.

The examples in this book will give you an idea of how CGI.pm is used, although do realize these examples show only the tip of the iceberg. CGI::Carp is also another useful module because it can provide as little or as much logging information as you want. CGI::Carp's subroutine carp works like a warning; confess gives you a full stack trace. Your Apache error log will love you for it.

Also, you can use Data::Dumper while you're developing. There are more elegant ways of debugging available, but the author prefers printing errors and Perl objects with Data::Dumper to the error log with the print statement or carp to give insight into what is being processed. This is useful for making sure data is what you expect it to be within different parts of the code. At least, the author thinks so.

Next, instantiate a CGI object.

```
# CGI object
my $cgi= new CGI();

# URL of program, used in form submit url, other parts of code
my $url = $cgi->url(-absolute=>1);
```

The HTML forms in this program will have an action to a given URL to submit to, its own good self, which can be obtained through the CGI method url() using the --absolute parameter. So, if the full URL is www.yoursite.com/cgi-bin/app.pl, the value would end up being /cgi-bin/app.pl, which is what you want. Then, of course, you want to define a database handle variable to use. Defining all of these variables outside any subroutine will make them available to all subroutines.

Already discussed was the need for having a Perl class implement all the back-end, non-display, database/memcached functionality. In this example, this will be WebApp.pm. So, without further ado, instantiate a WebApp object:

```
# WebApp
my $webapp= WebApp->new();
```

Since WebApp implements the functionality that interacts with MySQL and memcached by design, instantiation will also cause connections to MySQL and memcached to be made. These previous steps have taken care of the initial setup of objects that the application needs to proceed.

The next thing you want to do is run actual display functionality. To containerize this application, a main() subroutine will be used. This is the function from which all the primary display functions will in turn be called:

```
# call main subroutine
main();
```

main() Subroutine

In the introduction to this section, the basic functionality of what needs to happen was laid out. This is the functionality main() will call.

```
#
# main
#    run all other primary display subroutines
#
#    arguments:
#      none
#
#    returns:
#       nothing
#
sub main {
  my $msg;
  print $cgi->header('text/html');
  print header();
```

```
        dispatcher(\$msg);
        print footer();
    }
```

The steps to follow are:

1. Define a scalar string, $msg, which will be passed around by reference to the dispatcher, which will in turn pass it to other subroutines by reference (fast to pass by reference).

The HTML response header is printed. This tells the browser to expect HTML for this application. Every CGI program, mod_perl application, and anything interactive has to perform this step.

2. Print the HTML page header, shown in the previous code, from the HTML mock-up.

3. The decision processor is the dispatcher. This is the "brain" of the program. From it, all primary decision and display logic of what the program does is performed.

4. The footer is printed. Most important part!

header() Subroutine

The first subroutine, header(), is very simple. It just returns the HTML of the header as shown in the code that follows. The CSS information is omitted for brevity's sake, avoiding redundancy and saving trees. You will also notice the use of comments at the top of each program to provide the purpose and arguments to each subroutine. For modules, you could also make this POD.

```
#
# header
#    prints the header of the page, including style sheet
#
#    arguments:  none
#
#    returns:
#       HTML code
#
sub header {

return <<EOHTML;
<!DOCTYPE HTML PUBLIC "-//W3C//DTD HTML 4.01//EN"
  "http://www.w3.org/TR/html4/strict.dtd">
<html>
  <head>
    <title>Contact List Application Example</title>
    <style type="text/css">

... style contents as shown in HTML mockup from above ...

</style>
  </head>
  <body>
  <!-- end of header() content -->
EOHTML

}
```

dispatcher( ) Subroutine

Next, comes the real functionality. This is the `dispatcher()` subroutine that handles the top-level decision making. This is a fairly long subroutine because it must provide form processing and decision
making.

```
#
# dispatcher
#    process the form values and controls main program logic,
#    calling appropriate pages
#       + If submitted, and calls appropriate function based on the submission value.
#       + Supplies functions with required arguments.
#       + Handles missing arguments
#       + display appropriate page
#
#    arguments:
#       $msg  - scalar ref for writing the error or success message to
#
#    returns:
#       1   - success or some action taken
#       0   - no action or error
#
sub dispatcher {
    my ($msg) = @_;
    my $delete_ids;
    my $user = {};
    my $saved = 0;
    # WebApp
    my $webapp = WebApp->new();
```

The following steps explain how the `dispatcher()` subroutine works:

1.   First, several variables are declared. `$delete_ids` will be used to assume the list of contact
     IDs, uids, for deletion should the operation be contact deletion. `$user` is used to retrieve a
     single user hash reference should the operation be a contact edit or view page. `$saved` will
     be used to contain the value of failure or success upon an attempt to save a contact. It is then
     used to determine whether to redisplay the edit form where the information was entered
     that the caused the error.

```
    # if fatal is set, just print the form with the error
    unless (defined $webapp->{dbh}) {
        # obtain whatever error message was set
        $$msg ||= $webapp->{msg};
        print mainform($user,$webapp, $msg);
        return;
    }
```

2.   A check determines if the `$webapp` attribute dbh is defined. If it is not defined, this means the
     database could not be connected to due to some sort of error condition. If the database con-
     nection is not made, the `mainform()` immediately displays along with the message produced
     from the error. This ensures the application at least does something — in particular, displays
     the error message if the database is down.

```
# get all submitted form values into a hashref
my $form = $cgi->Vars();
```

3. This next stage of the program deals with obtaining the submitted form values, saving, or deleting contact data. The `$cgi->Vars()` method provides a hash reference containing the form values, keyed by the names of the form elements submitted. The hash reference `$form` is used to obtain the output of `$cgi->Vars()`. The first decision is to determine if the form value `save_user` is set, which is the name of the submit button element that would have been submitted when the Save button is selected.

```
# if save_user operation - create or update
if (defined $form->{save_user}) {
  my $not_set = 0;
```

4. `$WebApp::REQUIRED_COLS` is a class variable of WebApp (which will be discussed later) that provides an array reference of the contact attribute names that are required to be set in the contact edit form. Each required contact attribute name is used to check the submitted form values in `$form`. It checks to see if `$form` member is defined has string length. If both requirements are not satisfied, then it would mean that the `$form` member is not set. A simple `$not_set` variable is then incremented. If `$not_set` is true, the checking loop ends and there will be no attempt to save the contact, resulting in the user form being redisplayed with an error message indicating to the user which required contact field is not filled out. If `$not_set` is false, the user is saved, and the variable `$saved` is set to be used in later decision making.

```
# check all fields for being set - this means "required"
for (@$WebApp::REQUIRED_COLS) {
  # both defined and containing a value with a length
  unless (defined $form->{$_} && length($form->{$_})) {
    # create a message
    $$msg = "Error: the field for '\u$_' is not set!";
    $not_set++;
    last;

  }
}
# if all required fields, saveUser
unless ($not_set) {
  $saved = $webapp->saveUser($form);
}
}
```

5. The next test determines if a delete operation is being requested. Then a loop is used to obtain all form values in `$form` that are completely numeric. These numeric values are the user IDs (uids) that are to be deleted. These user IDs are "collected" into a hash reference `$delete_ids`. If there are one or more of these user IDs at the end of the loop, a call to `$webapp->deleteUsers()` is made, passing these IDs.

```
#
# delete of one or more users
#
```

```
      elsif (defined $form->{delete_user}) {
        # check all form values
        for my $param (keys %$form) {
          # if the param is completely numeric, that is the uid
          if ($param =~ /^(\d+)$/ && $form->{$param} eq 'on') {
            # create hash ref keyed by uid, value username which will be
            # used to build both a list of uids to delete as well as a message
            $delete_ids->{$param}= $form->{"username_$param"};
          }
        }
        # if there are no ids to delete, don't bother
        if (keys %$delete_ids) {
          $webapp->deleteUsers($delete_ids);
        }
      }
```

Now comes the final act of dispatcher(): it displays the appropriate page, depending on the operation being set by user action:

6. The scalar reference $msg assumes, if not set already, any messages in the $webapp object handle that were generated during the previous steps. These messages will be displayed in whatever page ends up being displayed.

7. The page display logic begins with a check for the $form parameter save_user and the value of $saved. If $saved is false and the $form parameter save_user is set, this indicates that the previous attempt to submit the contact editing form, with either a new or existing contact, failed and the user form userform() should again be displayed. The difference between this error condition and editing a user is that $form is passed to userform() instead of to $user, which is not set due to the error. Also, $form will contain the parameter values that were submitted in the failed attempt to save the user that might have caused the failure.

8. The next two tests determine whether there should be a view or edit operation. Many web applications could possibly use an "op" form value, but for the sake of convenience, either the value edit or view $form members are used for a true or false test, as well as for supplying the uid. Also, both edit and view are set with a GET as opposed to a POST, so having a single form parameter makes for a cleaner URL to have as few variables as possible passed in a query string. In either case, $webapp->getUser() is called supplying the user ID uid, depending on whether the action is an edit or view and the $user hash reference — a hash reference with the data for the contact — is retrieved for displaying in either the user editing form edituser or user display page viewuser.

9. Finally, if no particular action is being requested, the default contact listing page, mainform(), is displayed.

```
    #
    # if no previous message, set to whatever WebApp created
    $$msg||= $webapp->{msg};
    if (!$saved && defined $form->{save_user}) {
      # edit form
      print userform($form,$webapp, $msg);
    }
    elsif (defined $form->{edit}) {
      # edit form
      $user= $webapp->getUser({ uid => $form->{edit}});
```

```
                    print userform($user,$webapp,$msg);
                }
                elsif (defined $form->{view}) {
                    # view page
                    $user= $webapp->getUser({ uid => $form->{view}});
                    print viewuser($user,$webapp, $msg);
                }
                else {
                    # default, print user list
                    print mainform($user,$webapp, $msg);
                }
                return;
            }
```

This completes the `dispatcher()` subroutine, and the application displays the appropriate page. The subroutines that were called from within `dispatcher()` will be discussed next.

mainform() Subroutine

As you saw in `dispatcher()`, when no submission or contact lookup for either editing or viewing is initiated by the user, the default display `mainform()` displays its content. `mainform()` has the purpose of displaying the list of contacts as well as displaying the message returned from any previous action. When implementing this, it was possible to utilize the sections of HTML from the mock-up, as shown by the HTML comments.

```
#
# mainform
#    prints the main form of the page, when no user action
#    printing out the list of users
#
#    arguments:
#       $msg - scalar ref containing error or success messages
#
#    returns:
#       HTML code
#
sub mainform {
  my ($user, $msg)= @_;
  my $ulist= '';

  #
  # obtain the contact list HTML
  # do not attempt to obtain the contact list HTML if a fatal condition,
  # such as the database not being able to be connected to is set
  #
  $ulist = userlist($$msg) unless $webapp->{fatal};

  $$msg||= "Contact List Application Example";

  return <<EOHTML;
    <!-- begin mainform -->
    <p class="msg">$$msg</p>
    <p>
    $ulist
```

```
    </p>
    <!-- end mainform -->
EOHTML
}
```

`mainform()` obtains the content for the contact list table from a call to `userlist()`, passing along `$msg` by reference to assume any messages generated in other subroutines or from the `WebApp` object.

userlist() Subroutine

The subroutine `userlist()`, called by `mainform()`, generates the HTML display that consists primarily of a table containing rows for each contact. Each of these rows provides the ability to view, edit, or delete the contact. For deletion, a checkbox for each contact is provided. The Delete button below the table will delete the contacts that are checked.

```
#
# userlist()
#    builds an HTML table containing the list of users who exist
#    or print a message that there are no users
#
#    arguments:
#       $msg  - scalar ref for writing the error or success message to
#
#    returns:
#       $data - HTML table with list of users or messages stating that
#                users can be added
#
sub userlist {
  my $msg= shift;
  # start out with empty string
  my $data= '';

  # not looking for a specific user, specified in first argument
  # so pass empty hashref
  my $uref= $webapp->getUsers({});
```

The call to the method `$webapp->getUsers()` returns a hash reference, `$uref`, where each key is the uid for each user, pointing to yet another hash reference for each user, keyed by user attributes. The table header is started in advance of iterating through each contact entry of `$uref` — if, of course, `$uref` has any records. If `$uref` has no data, then an alternative to the table must be generated, notifying the user that there are no contacts yet in the database.

```
    # if there is data and no error, build a table
    if (defined $uref && keys %$uref) {
      # table header
      $data= <<EOHTML;
    <!-- begin userlist -->
    <form action="$url" name="delete_user_form"
                    id="delete_user_form" method="POST">
      <table class="userlist">
        <thead>
         <tr>
           <th>UID</th>
```

```
<th>Username</th>
        <th>Email</th>
        <th>First Name</th>
        <th>Sur Name</th>
        <th colspan="2"> </th>
      </tr>
    </thead>
    <tbody>
EOHTML
```

This is where the iteration of each hash reference member, a contact hash reference, is iterated over. Seven columns are displayed: uid with a link to view the contact, username, email, firstname, surname, a checkbox that uses the user id as the checkbox's form element name, and the final column that is a link with the contact uid as the value to the edit parameter. Also included is a hidden form element with the form element name of the concatentation of username_ and the contact uid value. This is so any subsequent messages generated can utilize this value in messages.

```
# build up the row with each row of the result set
for my $uid (sort keys %$uref) {
  my $row= $uref->{$uid};

  # encode any entities to prevent HTML injection
  $webapp->encodeUserData(\$row);

  # for each row, build the <tr>...</tr>
  $data .= <<EOROW;
    <!-- row for uid $row->{uid} -->
    <tr>
      <td>
      <a href="$url?view=$row->{uid}" title="View contact $row->{uid}">
      $row->{uid}
      </a></td>
      <td>$row->{username}</td>
      <td>$row->{email}</td>
      <td>$row->{firstname}</td>
      <td>$row->{surname}</td>
      <td>
        <input type="checkbox" name="$row->{uid}" id="$row->{uid}">
      </td>
      <td><a href="$url?edit=$row->{uid}">Edit</a></td>
      <!-- only reason for this is to have nice message -->
      <input type="hidden" name="username_$row->{uid}"
                                     value="$row->{username}">
    </tr>
    <!-- end row for uid $row->{uid} -->
EOROW
    }
```

Finally, the bottom of the table is generated, along with the Delete button to submit a deletion for whatever checkboxes in each contact row for the uid values of the contacts selected for deletion.

```
# table footer
$data .= <<EOHTML;
```

```
            </tbody>
            <tfoot>
              <tr>
                <td colspan="2"><a href="$url?edit=0">Create a new entry</a></td>
                <td align="right" colspan="5">
                <input type="submit" name="delete_user" id="delete_user" value="Delete">
                </td>
              </tr>
            </tfoot>
          </table>
          </form>
          <!-- end userlist -->
    EOHTML

      }
      # otherwise, let the user know there aren't any contacts, give them
      # link to create some
      else {
          $data= '<p class="msg">You have no users in your contact list currently</p>';
          $data.="<p><a href=\"$url?edit=0\">Create a new entry</p>";
      }
      return $data;
    }
```

If `$userlist` didn't have any contact rows, then an alternative display notifying the user that there were not any contacts in the database is generated.

Finally, the generated contact list data or alternative notification message is returned to the calling subroutine, `mainform()`.

userform() Subroutine

The `userform()` subroutine has the purpose of displaying the contact editing form elements either for entering data to add a new contact or for editing an existing contact. The form fields for user data that can be entered are all contact attributes except the contact id, `uid`.

Additionally, there needs to be some logic to disable the `username` form element for editing an existing contact since this is one attribute, at least in the design of this application, that cannot be changed.

```
    #
    # userform
    #    generates the contact edit form.
    #
    # args
    #    $user - hash reference of user attributes
    #    $msg - scalar reference for messages
    #
    # returns
    #    contact editing HTML data
    sub userform {
      my ($user, $msg)= @_;
      my $hidden_uid_element;
```

A test is made to determine if $msg has a value. If it does, that means an error occurred. If it does not have a value, then it will construct a message depending upon whether this is a new or existing contact being edited.

```
unless ($$msg) {
  $$msg= "Editing ";
  $$msg.= $user->{uid} ? "$user->{username}" : " New Contact" ;
}
```

A call to the $webapp->getStates() method returns a hash reference keyed by state abbreviates and the values of the full state names.

```
my $states= $webapp->getStates();
```

The logic to test whether a user is being edited either sets the scalar string value $readonly with a read-only attribute or with an empty string:

```
# make read-only if user edit existing user
 my $readonly= $user->{uid} ? 'readonly="1"' : '';
```

Next, a pop-up menu form element is created using the CGI method popup_menu(). This is just one of the many useful form generation methods CGI provides that can make building dynamic HTML quite simple for you.

For this application, the state abbreviations are stored in the database for each contact instead of the full state name. So in addition to the keys of $states – the value of the -values argument to popup_menu() which in turn provides popup_menu() a list of the values it will contain — the argument -labels is provided the full $states hash reference to map the state abbreviations. The abbreviations are the value of each option to a label display value, the full state name. This makes it so the user selects a state name for a contact, but when the data is saved, the state abbreviation will be the value used.

To ensure that the user interface has some indication that a state value must be selected, another member called default is added to $states along with a label of *Select a state*, which in turn will result in that option being provided in the pop-up menu. The mechanism for setting *Select a state* is provided by a check for the value of the contact id uid upon assignment to the -default argument to popup_menu(). This is the argument to determine which pop-up menu option is the selected option. If uid is set, then the argument to -default is the state abbreviation, which results in the value of the state for the contact being edited to become the selected value. If uid is not set, the option selected by default is the default, displaying as *Select a state*.

```
# add a default select option to the states hashref
      $states->{default}= 'Select a state';

 my $states_select= popup_menu(
                       -name     => 'state',
                       -values   => [sort keys %$states],
                       -default  => $user->{uid} ? $user->{state} : 'default',
                       -labels   => $states);
```

A scalar string $hidden_uid_element is set either to the value of a hidden form element named uid or to an empty string, depending on whether the contact id uid value for $user is set. This makes is so a contact id value `uid` is available upon the submission of a form for an existing user being edited. If the submission of the form is for a new user, there will not yet be a contact id `uid` value, but one will be created as soon as the contact is inserted.

```
# set this if the user exists - a $user->{uid} existing.
$hidden_uid_element=
    '<input type="hidden" name="uid" value="'. $user->{uid} . '">' if $user->{uid};
```

Finally, the entirety of the form, along with the pregenerated form elements, is returned to the calling subroutine `dispatcher()`, which prints this returned content. The form values are all set with `$user`, which is unset by default when the form is displayed.

```
# encode HTML entities
$webapp->encodeUserData(\$user);

return <<USERFORM;
    <!-- begin userform -->
    <p class="msg">$$msg</p><p><a href="$url">Back to main page</a></p>
    <p>
    <form action="$url" id="appform" name="appform" method="post">
      <fieldset>
        <p>
          <label for="username">Username:</label>
          <input type="text" $readonly id="username" name="username"
          size="16" value="$user->{username}">
        </p>
        <p>
          <label for="email">Email:</label>
          <input type="text" id="email" name="email" size="16" value="$user->{email}">
        </p>
        <p>
          <label for="firstname">First Name:</label>
          <input type="text" id="firstname" name="firstname" size="16"
          value="$user->{firstname}">
        </p>
        <p>
          <label for="surname">Sur Name:</label>
          <input type="text" id="surname" name="surname" size="16"
          value="$user->{surname}">
        </p>
        <p>
          <label for="phone">Phone Number:</label>
          <input type="text" id="phone" name="phone" size="16" value="$user->{phone}">
        </p>
        <p>
          <label for="address">Address:</label>
          <textarea id="address"
          name="address" rows="3" columns="30">$user->{address}</textarea>
        </p>
        <p>
          <label for="city">City:</label>
          <input type="text" id="city" name="city" size="16" value="$user->{city}">
        </p>
        <p>
```

```
            <label for="state">State:</label>
              $states_select
          </p>
          <p>
            $hidden_uid_element
            <input type="submit" id="save_user" name="save_user" value="Save">
          </p>
      </form>
      </p>
      <!-- end userform -->
  USERFORM
```

viewuser( ) Subroutine

The viewuser() subroutine displays a user for the uid value supplied by the parameter value of view, which if set is what results in viewuser() being called from within dispatcher().

```
  #
  # viewuser
  #   prints the contact view page
  #
  #   arguments:
  #     $msg - scalar ref containing error or success messages
  #
  #   returns:
  #     HTML code
  #
  sub viewuser {
    my ($user, $msg)= @_;
    my $hidden_uid_element;

    my $statename = $webapp->getState($user->{state});
```

A call is made to the method, $webapp->getState(), supplying the argument with the state member of $user, which is a state abbreviation. The full state name will be returned, which will in turn be displayed in the subsequent page.

Next, the WebApp method encodeUserData() is used to encode any HTML entities in the user data to prevent HTML injection in the page about to be displayed.

```
  # encode HTML entities, prevent HTML injection
    $webapp->encodeUserData(\$user);
```

Then the page itself, a simple table with a row for each contact attribute is retuned and printed by the calling subroutine dispatcher().

```
  return <<USERFORM;
      <!-- begin viewuser -->
      <p class="msg">View User $user->{username}</p>
      <p><a href="$url">Back to main page</a></p>
      <p><a href="$url?edit=$user->{uid}">Edit $user->{username}</a></p>
      <table class="userlist">
        <tbody>
```

```
        <tr><td>UID:</td><td>$user->{uid}</td></tr>
        <tr><td>Username:</td><td>$user->{username}</td></tr>
        <tr><td>Email:</td><td>$user->{email}</td></tr>
        <tr><td>First Name:</td><td>$user->{firstname}</td></tr>
        <tr><td>Surname:</td><td>$user->{surname}</td></tr>
        <tr><td>Phone Number:</td><td>$user->{phone}</td></tr>
        <tr><td>Address:</td><td>$user->{address}</td></tr>
        <tr><td>City:</td><td>$user->{city}</td></tr>
        <tr><td>State:</td><td>$statename</td></tr>
      </tbody>
  </table>
<!-- end viewuser -->
USERFORM

}
```

WebApp Class Methods

Now that all the front-end display logic functionality, as implemented in the main CGI script app.pl, has been explained, this section will explain the methods that app.pl utilized for data retrieval, storage, modification, and deletion:

1. First of all, there is a package declaration for setting the namespace of this module, and importation of strict and warning pragmas for the sake of being picky. Also, other modules necessary for use within WebApp are imported.

   ```
   package WebApp;

   use strict;
   use warnings;

   use CGI::Carp qw(carp confess);
   ```

2. Use of CGI::Carp provides several types of error display. For this application, you have the choice of carp() or confess(). carp() provides a print-out similar to what warn() would provide; confess() provides a full stack trace.

3. DBIx::Password is a very useful module that inherits from DBI.

   ```
   use DBIx::Password;
   ```

   Developed by Brian Aker, this module provides a way to connect to the database without having to provide full connection credentials, thereby keeping all database connection values stored in a single location. This is a common database application developer dilemma: where one should store database connection information for an application. DBIx::Password has the concept of a virtual database user, which is implemented with the use of a hash reference, keyed by this virtual username and containing the connection meta-data as the hash members. Wherever your Perl library is, DBIx::Password will contain this connection information. When you want to add a new database user, you can add to this file another virtual user by adding another hash member to the $virtual hash reference, as shown in the file /usr/lib/perl5/site_perl/5.8.8/DBIx/Password.pm

```
my $virtual1 = {
                        # this is the virtual user
                        'webuser' => {
                                'port'          => '',
                                'username'      => 'webuser',
                                'host'          => 'localhost',
                                'database'      => 'test',
                                'password'      => 'webpass',
                                'attributes'    => {},
                                'connect'       =>
                                'DBI:mysql:database=test;host=localhost',
                                'driver'  => 'mysql'
                        },

                        # this is where you would enter other virtual
                        # database users, having their own
                        # same attributes as shown here with webuser
}
```

4. Next import `Cache::Memcached::libmemcached`, which will be used for caching data to memcached, as well as `Data::Dumper`, which you will remove after testing!

    ```
    use Cache::Memcached::libmemcached;
    use Data::Dumper;
    ```

5. Finally, the Perl module HTML::Entities is imported. This module provides methods for encoding and decoding HTML entities. This will be used in WebApp to filter user data for display in HTML pages to prevent HTML injection.

    ```
    use HTML::Entities;
    ```

There are declarations of various package-scoped variables shown in the code that follows:

❑ $MEMC_DEFAULT_SERVERS is the default memcached server list connect to.

❑ $DB_VIRTUAL_USER is the default virtual user unless specified otherwise in instantiation.

❑ $USER_COLS is the list of contact attributes that will be used throughout the code, particularly for building dynamic SQL statements and value verification.

❑ $REQUIRED_COLS is used in various parts of the code to provide a list of contact attributes that must be specified when entering data.

```
# memcached server list, can be overridden upon instantiation
our $MEMC_DEFAULT_SERVERS= ['127.0.0.1:11211'];

# virtual user for DBIx::Password
our $DB_VIRTUAL_USER= 'webuser';

# when to expire the cache catalogue
our $MEMC_CATALOGUE_EXPIREY= 300;

# all columns except primary key for the user, which auto_increment sets
```

```
our $USER_COLS = [ qw(username email firstname surname phone city state address)];

# required columns for submissions
our $REQUIRED_COLS = [ qw(username email firstname surname)];
```

Instantiation with the new() Method

The new() method is for instantiating the WebApp object. Its purpose in life is first and foremost to return a blessed object reference to itself, as well as set class attributes for $DB_VIRTUAL_USER and $MEMCACHED_SERVERS, and to establish a connection with MySQL and memcached for the rest of the class's methods to use.

$MEMC_CATALOGUE_EXPIREY is a class variable that determines when the object that contains a list of the contact IDs uids is expired in memcached. This is used to control the frequency of how often the cache users are reloaded in memcached.

It takes two arguments:

❑ $caller is a reference to another WebApp object or the scalar string value of its name set upon instantiation.

❑ $opts provides a means of overriding class attributes — in this case $DB_VIRTUAL_USER and $MEMCACHED_SERVERS.

One other thing new() does is to set an attribute msg to an empty string, which is where messages (either errors or success operation notifications) will be stored.

```
=head2 new()

instantiates a new WebApp object

=item args

=over

$caller - class name

$opts - for overriding default values

=back

=item returns

=over

$self - object reference

=back

=cut

sub new {
  my($class, $opts) = @_;
```

```
    my $self = {
      memc_servers          => $MEMC_DEFAULT_SERVERS,
      db_virtual_user       => $DB_VIRTUAL_USER,
      db_virtual_user_ro    => $DB_VIRTUAL_USER_RO,


      # set the message to empty string
      msg => '',
    };
    $self->{$_} = $opts->{$_} for keys %$opts;

    bless($self, $class);
```

Of course, the connections are made to MySQL and memcached, and each connection handle is stored in the class attribute $self->{dbh} and $self->{memc} respectively. Connecting to MySQL is crucial for this application to function, so if the connection to MySQL fails, then WebApp must immediately return the instantiated class reference. This will result in app.pl simply displaying a message saying that the database cannot be connected to.

```
  # connect to MySQL
    return $self unless $self->_connectDB();

    # connect to memcached
    $self->_connectMemcached();

    return $self;
  }
```

Finally, the constructor new() will return a blessed object reference.

Connection to MySQL

The _connectDB() method provides a simple means to connect to MySQL. This is different than previous database connection subroutines or methods discussed in this book in that it is using DBIx::Password. As was already mentioned, DBIx::Password provides an abstraction to the connection specifics of DSN, user and password, storing the database connection credentials in one place. All that is needed to connect is *virtual user* that exists in Password.pm (found in your system's Perl library). Since DBIx::Password inherits from DBI, all DBI methods are available via the handle you instantiate.

Also different about this connection is the number of tests performed to ensure the database connection is working. This is the one method that is crucial to the application working at all. The class attribute dbh, which if not set, means the database connection could not be established and is used in app.pl to indicate that a major error has occurred and to display the error message. You might think that upon such an error you would want to return undefined, but in order for the script using WebApp to obtain the database error message, you need to return the object reference so the script can print the database error message that was set when the connection failed, or at least have access to it.

The attribute PrintError is set to cause the error to be printed as a warning to the Apache error log.

```
  =head2 _connectDB()

    connects to MySQL, sets the object attribute "dbh", database handle
```

```
=item arguments

=over

$self - object reference

=back

=item returns

=over

1 - success

0 - failure

=back

=cut

 sub _connectDB {
  my ($self)= @_;

  eval {$self->{dbh}= DBIx::Password->connect(
                      $self->{db_virtual_user}, {PrintError => 1})};
  if ($@) {
    $self->{msg}= "Database ERROR: $@ $DBI::errstr\n";
    confess $self->{msg};
    return 0;
  }
  unless (defined $self->{dbh}) {
    $self->{msg}= "Database ERROR: $@ $DBI::errstr\n";
    return 0;
  }
  return 1;

}
```

Connection to memcached

The method _connectMemcached() connects to the memcached cluster specified in the array reference list of $self->{memc_servers}. The default is ["127.0.0.1:11211"], but can be specified to override the default upon WebApp instantiation. _connectMemcached() also has logic to test the connection by attempting to set a simple value. If it fails it sets a message and returns 0. If successful, the class attribute $self->{memc} is available to use for calling Cache::Memcached::libmemcached methods, and a 1 is returned.

With error handling, the app only needs to log a warning that it cannot connect to memcached. This application must be able to work without memcached.

```
=head2 _connectMemcached()

connects to Memcached, sets the object attribute "memc", database handle
```

```
=item arguments

=over

$self - object reference

=back

=item returns

=over

1 - success

0 - failure

=back

=cut
 sub _connectMemcached {
  my ($self)= @_;

  $self->{memc}= new Cache::Memcached::libmemcached({
      servers             =>  $self->{memc_servers},
      compress_threshold  => 10_000 });

  unless ($self->{memc}->set('memcached_alive', 1)) {
    # don't need to display message, just log the error
    carp "ERROR: memcached unable to connect!";
    $self->{memc}= undef;
    return 0;
  }
  return 1;
}
```

The getUsers() Method

The getUsers() method is the first method shown in the previous section covering app.pl display logic. The call, as you will remember, was made from the userlist() subroutine to obtain the list of contacts.

```
# not looking for a specific user, specified in first argument
# so pass empty hashref
my $uref= $webapp->getUsers({});
```

getUsers() returns one or more contact records in a hash reference keyed by uid, which in turn is used to generate an HTML table listing the contacts. In doing so, getUsers() also caches to memcached the hash reference of users so that subsequent retrievals of contacts obtain data from memcached as opposed to MySQL.

```
=head2 getUsers()

select and retrieve an arrayref of users from the database
```

```
=item arguments

=over

$self - object reference

$uref -  user ref containing one or more keys

$reload_cache - used to cause the cached users to be reloaded

=back

=item returns

=over

return arrayref containing result set

=back

=cut
 sub getUsers  {
   my ($self, $uref) = @_;
   my $userlist_ref;
   my @bind_values;
```

The first argument to getUsers() is the object hash reference to its own class. This provides access to all class attributes and methods, as well as the msg class attribute. The second argument, which is optional, is a hash reference containing lookup contact attributes such as uid, username, or email (each being a unique attribute). Any of these could be used for the lookup of a single contact. This makes it so getUsers() can be used for either single- or multiple-contact retrieval.

The variable $userlist_ref will be used to store the contacts retrieved from either memcached or MySQL. @bind_values will be used to contain any bind values used to satisfy placeholder values upon database query execution, should the data not be found in memcached and need to be retrieved from MySQL.

An attempt is made to obtain the contact list into $userlist_ref from memcached. If it is found in memcached, $userlist_ref is simply returned, and no data retrieval $userlist_ref from MySQL is attempted.

There is one major assumption in all of this that if not done correctly would be fraught with peril. This is the assumption that memcached contains an up-to-date representation of the contact database, matching what is stored in MySQL. In order for this to work, it's absolutely important to make sure when you update MySQL that you also update everything that needs to be set in memcached. There are other tricks and mechanisms you can use to ensure memcached has one-to-one data correlation with MySQL.

One possible method would be to store a value in memcached that expires within a given time, forcing data to be retrieved from MySQL on some regular basis, thus helping to lessen the chances of data being missing from memcached that is in MySQL, as well as the chances of having data in memcached that has since been deleted from MySQL. You could also have a regularly scheduled cron job to reload all contacts from the database into memcached. It all depends on what lets you sleep at night!

For this application, every write operation will ensure that whatever write action — DELETE, INSERT, UPDATE — that is performed in MySQL is also performed in memcached. Also, a hash reference of all contact IDs, uid, or every contact in MySQL is stored in memcached. This is a *catalogue* value and it will be called user_uid_list, and will be set with an expiration of 5 minutes, forcing it to be reloaded from the database every 5 minutes. This provides a little extra CYA.

Remember, this is a simple contact list application, and the object of this example is to show how you can reduce the requirements of having to obtain data from MySQL using memcached.

```
# obtain from cache, use if there are entries
$userlist_ref= $self->getUsersFromCache();
return $userlist_ref if keys %$userlist_ref;
```

If $userlist_ref is not in memcached, proceed to obtain it from MySQL. Also, you will use this opportunity to reload the contact list in the database.

```
# not in memcached, procede to check the database

#
# this check is here to make sure something happens so the page will
# print, as well as provide an error message
#
unless (defined $self->{dbh} && $self->{dbh}->ping) {
   $self->{msg}= "Unable to connect to MySQL";
   carp $self->{msg};
   return undef;
}

# start a query
my $query= 'SELECT * FROM users';
```

Next, the database query is constructed and bind values are gathered for each user attribute — only if they are defined in $uref.

```
#
# if the $uref hashref has any keys specified, then construct
# a WHERE clause
#
if (keys %$uref) {
   $query .= ' WHERE ';
   # here, we want the uid
   for my $key('uid', @$USER_COLS) {
      if (defined $uref->{$key}) {
         $query .= "$key = ? AND ";
         push(@bind_values, $uref->{$key});
      }
   }
   # chop off trailing ' AND '
   $query= substr($query, 0, -5);
}
```

Then the query is executed. If there is an error, set $self->{msg} to that error, which will be displayed to the user. This is also something you have to consider — that you may not necessarily want to display database error messages to the end user. This is all your decision. You may want to euphemize the gory details of database errors with a more benign message to the end user. For this example, the audience is you, and you like database error messages!

```
    my $sth= $self->{dbh}->prepare($query);
    $sth->execute(@bind_values);
    if ($self->{dbh}->err) {
      # build a message
      $self->{msg}= "ERROR: $DBI::errstr";
      # print to log
      carp $self->{msg};
      return undef;
    }
  # force results into arrayref of hashrefs
    $userlist_ref= $sth->fetchall_hashref('uid');
```

Upon successfully obtaining the data for the list of contacts, immediately cache that data into memcached, and return it to the caller.

```
    $self->cacheUsers($userlist_ref);
    return $userlist_ref;
}
```

The getUser() Method

The getUser() method is all about code reuse. Its first argument $self is an object reference to its own class. The second argument is the hash reference $uref, which contains the attributes and values of those attributes for a specific contact, namely the uid value of that contact that will be used as a lookup value.

getUser() simply uses the method getUsers(), specifying the specific user with whatever attributes happen to be found in $user. In most cases, because of caching, it will not require a database access to obtain them, and instead will be simply provided by the hash keying of the main user list. If it were not for memcached, getUser() would initiate a database query obtaining the correct user since it is specifying the uid.

```
=head2 getUser()

obtains a user hashref, using getUsers to do the heavy lifting
taking the list of hashrefs returned (which there should only be one)
and returning a single user hashref obtained by user key uid

=item arguments:

=over

$self - object reference

$uref - hashref with uid, username , email or other lookup value

=back

=head returns:
```

```
=over

hashref representing a user keyed by user fields

undef - no user or an error, msg will be set

=back

=cut

  sub getUser  {
    my ($self, $uref)= @_;
```

$users is a multilevel hash reference containing keys that are the uid value of yet other hash references for each contact. The goal of getUser() is to then return the correct hash reference. Since a uid is being specified with $uref being passed to getUsers(), there should be only one member in $users, that single contact hash reference per uid.

```
    # get the big user ref, keyed by uid
    my $users= $self->getUsers($uref);
```

Hashes/hash references are the greatest things in the programming world! This is why we love Perl! The specified user is returned using the uid value of $uref to return yet another hash ref that that uid points to in $users. This single-contact hash reference, containing the attributes and values of those attributes, is returned.

```
    # return a single hashref obtained using uid
    return $users->{$uref->{uid}};
  }
```

The saveUser() Method

The next method that was used from app.pl is saveUser(). It takes as its first argument an object reference to its own class. The second argument is a hash reference, $user, which contains contact attributes and values of those attributes. saveUser() has the task of saving a contact, whether the contact being saved is new (an insert) or existing (an update). This logic is tricky, because it has to test a number of conditions, as well as handle attempts to insert duplicate contacts or change existing contacts to having values for unique attributes that other contacts already have.

```
=head2 saveUser()

either inserts or updates the user specified by $user into both
MySQL and memcached

=item arguments

=over

$user - hashref representing a user keyed by user fields

$msg  - scalar ref for writing the error or success message to
```

```
=back

=item returns

=over

1 - success

0 - error

=back

=cut

  sub saveUser {
    my ($self, $user) = @_;
```

Note these steps:

1. saveUser() takes a single argument, a hash reference containing the contact attributes, which will be the data that saveUser() will attempt to save. The first check is to see whether $user has the attribute uid. If it does it means that what is being saved is an existing contact.

```
#
# if $user has a uid update
#
if ($user->{uid}) {
  my $update_user;
```

2. Check to ensure that the contact does in fact exist. $check_user assumes the hash reference value of the contact, if the existing contact is currently stored, or an empty hash reference if not.

```
# check if the user is in the database, even though a uid is specified
# this $check_user ref will be used to see what columns actually were
# changed
my $check_user= $self->getUser({ uid => $user->{uid}});


#
# if the user's email address changed, make sure the address they are
  changing
# it to is not already existing.
#
if ($check_user->{email} ne $user->{email}) {
```

3. A comparison is then made of the email address of the contact being saved to determine if the user is changing their email address. If the email address is different, then that means the user is changing their email address. The value of $exists_uid is obtained from userExists() using the email address as a lookup argument, which is different from the contact's existing email address. userExists() will either return a valid uid value of the contact being checked (true) or a 0 (false), indicating whether the contact exists or not. The return value of -1 means there was a systemic failure of `userExists()` — a database or some other error, and if this happens `saveUser()` then returns a 0.

4.   If `$exists_uid` is set *and* `$exists_uid` is different than `$user->{uid}`, the uid of the contact being saved, this means that there is an existing contact with this same email address, hence this email address value the user is trying to use for this existing contact cannot be used. An error message is set to notify the user that there is a conflict, and 0 is returned to the caller.

```
my $exists_uid= $self->userExists({email => $user->{email}});
return 0 if $exists_uid == -1;

# let the user know they have to use a different email address
if ($exists_uid && $exists_uid != $user->{uid}) {
    $self->{msg}=
    "ERROR: You cannot use $user->{email} as an email address, it's
being
    currently used";
    return 0;
}
}
```

Otherwise, those checks/tests have passed.

5.   The next check is to test whether the user is changing the `username`. This will not happen in the example because of the way the application is designed, since the form has the `username` form element set to read-only. But, if that form wasn't set to read-only, this check would prevent the user from changing the contact's `username`. It's good to check this anyway because a web application must always assume it can be called via a script, and hence never rely on restrictions coded in HTML (or JavaScript).

```
# for this application, do not allow the user to change their username
if ($check_user->{username} ne $user->{username}) {
    $self->{msg}= "ERROR: You cannot change your username!\n";
    return 0;
}
```

6.   A hash reference is used to "collect" only the attributes (database columns) for the contact that have changed. This is not really necessary, but since the data in `$check_user` is available, you might as well put it to good use. It can't hurt to update only those attributes/columns that have changed. Also, if none of the attributes have been changed, then there will be no attempt made to update the user, thus saving a trip to MySQL and memcached.

```
# use the user columns as the mapping
    for my $key (@$USER_COLS) {
        # tmp user ref for storing changed keys
        # only update keys that are changed
        if ($user->{$key} ne $check_user->{$key}) {
            $update_user->{$key}= $user->{$key}
        }
    }
```

7. The uid value is added to $update_user. This is required to pass to the method updateUser(), which must have a uid value to know what contact to update. Then if there are any keys in $update_user, that means the contact changed and can be updated. The update is then performed by the method updateUser(). If updateUser() returns a true value, the method saveUserToCache() is called to set the user in memcached.

```
# if $update_user has keys, something changed with the user, so update
if (keys %$update_user) {
  #
  # the uid has to be in $update_user in order by the WHERE clause to
    work
  #
  $update_user->{uid}= $user->{uid};

  if ($self->updateUser($update_user)) {

    $self->{msg}= "Updated $user->{username}\n";

    # save user in cache
    $self->saveUserToCache($user);

    return 1;
  }
}
} # end of saving existing user
```

8. If the hash reference $user doesn't have a uid, then that means the contact being saved is a new contact. The method userExists() is called, performing a lookup using both the email address and username for the new contact. If the user doesn't exist, a call is made to the method insertUser() within the unless block, and if successful, the contact is subsequently saved into memcached using the method saveUserToCache().

If either the email or username is used for the new contact, then the default value of 0 at the end of the program is returned. The message indicates that the contact's email or username is set already through userExists():

```
#
# otherwise, no uid, must be a new user
#
  else {

    # make sure user doesn't exist and no error
    unless ($self->userExists($user)) {

      # insert the suer
      $user->{uid}= $self->insertUser($user);

      #
      # if there is a $user->{uid}, then the insert was successful, so
      # store in memcached too
      #
      if ($user->{uid}) {
```

```
            $self->saveUserToCache($user);

            $self->{msg}= "Created contact $user->{username}\n";
            return 1;
        }
    }

    }
    # default return 0, if errors, msg contains error message
    return 0;
}
```

Database Methods

These are the methods that will insert, update, and delete contacts in MySQL. For the most part, the logic for storing data in memcached is separated from MySQL, except in the case of the method deleteUsers(), which has an iterative step that cannot be resisted for being made useful!

The insertUser() Method

The insertUser() method inserts the contact into the database as well as into memcached. Its first argument is the object reference to itself, the second argument is the contact being saved, $user, which is a hash reference with contact attributes as the keys and the values for those attributes.

```
=head2 insertUser()

insert the user into MySQL

=item args

=over

$self - object reference

$user - user hash reference

=back

=item returns

=over

insert id containing new user uid

0 failure

=back

=cut
 sub insertUser   {
  my ($self, $user)= @_;
```

The values of $USER_COLS provides a mapping to the attributes and values of $user, which is used to build the SQL statement fields.

```
# build up the columns specification
my $query = 'INSERT INTO users (' . join(',', @$USER_COLS) . ')';
```

It is also a nice trick to build the VALUES portion of the statement with the correct number of placeholders:

```
# build up the placeholders
$query .= ' VALUES ( ' . join( ',', ( '?' ) x @$USER_COLS ) . ')';


# remove the trailing comma
chop($query);my $sth= $self->{dbh}->prepare($query);
```

Finally the query is executed, using the hash slice to provide the bind values to satisfy the placeholders in the previously prepared statement. As you can see, the order in which the fields were appended to the SQL statement is in the same order of the bind values because $USER_COLS was used for both operations!

```
#
# use hash slice to provide the bind values,
# which will be in the correct order
#
$sth->execute(@{$user}{@$USER_COLS});
```

If there is an error, the message is set to that error — again, remember that you may not want to display database error messages to the user.

```
if ($self->{dbh}->err) {
  $self->{msg}= "Database Error: $DBI::err_str";
  return 0;
}
```

Lastly, the last insert id is returned to the caller, which happens to be the new uid of the contact.

```
# return the new uid
return $self->{dbh}->{mysql_insertid};
}
```

The updateUser() Method

The updateUser() method updates an existing contact. Its first argument is an object reference to its own class. Its second argument is a hash reference, $user, which contains the keys as the contact attributes for the contact being updated, and the values for those attributes. Like the insertUser() method, it also uses both the $user hash reference and the $USER_COLS array reference to dynamically generate the SQL statement used to update the contact. The difference with updateUser() is that $user will have a uid attribute set.

```
=head2 updateUser()
```

```
update the user in MySQL, make sure there is a uid

=item args

=over

$self - object reference

$user - user reference

=back

=item returns

=over

number of rows on update - should be 1 on success

0 on failure

=back

=cut

 sub updateUser {
   my ($self, $user)= @_;
   my @bind_values;
```

Note the following steps:

1. The first pre-update check is to test if the uid attribute is the only attribute in $user, in which case no update will be performed, an informational message is set, and 0 is returned.

```
# no need to update if all there is is a uid
if ($user->{uid} && keys %$user == 1) {
  $self->{msg}= "Contact unchanged, not updated";
  return 0;
}
```

2. The second check tests if there is no *uid* attribute, in which case an error message is set and 0 returned.

```
# no uid, set error, return
unless ($user->{uid}) {
    $self->{msg}= "ERROR: uid not set!";
  carp $self->{msg};
  return 0;
}
```

3. Next comes the generation of the UPDATE statement. Each attribute of the package variable, array reference $USER_COLS, is used to build the column specification and placeholders of the update statement and populate the @bind_values for each placeholder for only those attributes that are defined in $user.

```
my $query = "UPDATE users SET " ;
# construct a query
for my $key (@$USER_COLS) {
  if (defined $user->{$key}) {
    $query .= "$key = ?,";
    push(@bind_values, $user->{$key});
  }
}
# chop off trailing ,
chop($query);
```

Also, the WHERE clause specifying the uid has to be appended to the statement and the value pushed into @bind_values — all of which are in the same order as listed in the UPDATE statement.

```
# where clause
$query .= " WHERE uid = ?";

# value for where clause
push(@bind_values, $user->{uid});
```

4. Finally the query is prepared, and then executed with @bind_values providing the values. If there is a database error, the message is set and 0 is returned. If the update was successful, the number of rows, which is one, will be returned.

```
my $sth= $self->{dbh}->prepare($query);
$sth->execute(@bind_values);
if ($self->{dbh}->err) {
  $self->{msg}= "Database Error: $DBI::err_str";
  return 0;
}
# return 1 - since uid specified, only one row should be updated
return $sth->rows();
}
```

The deleteUsers() Method

The deleteUsers() method deletes one or more contacts at a time. Its first argument is an object reference to its own class. The second argument is a hash reference having as the keys the uids to be deleted and the usernames as the values.

Since the interface provides checkboxes for each contact row displayed in the contact listing, it's possible to select one or more contacts at a time to be deleted with the submission of the Delete button. The idea of deleteUsers() is to have a means to accept a list of uids and construct an SQL DELETE statement using the WHERE uid IN (...) to delete the selected contacts.

Also, it would be a bonus to have a useful message indicating back to the user which uids were deleted:

```
=head2 deleteUsers()

deletes one or more users specified by uid in $delete_ids
```

545

```
=item arguments

=over

$self - object reference

$delete_ids - hashref keyed by uid, values usernames

=back

=item returns

=over

1 - success

0 - no deletion or error

=back

=cut

 sub deleteUsers {
  my ($self, $delete_ids) = @_;
  # no ids, don't bother
 keys %$delete_ids or return 0;
```

Note the following steps:

1. The SQL DELETE statement is built, particularly the WHERE IN (?, ?, ...) clause, which is simple enough to accomplish by appending placeholders for each uid to be deleted and calling the method deleteUserFromCache() for each uid, which deletes that contact from memcached.

   ```
   # start the query
   my $query = 'DELETE FROM users WHERE uid IN (';

   # put together placeholder list
   for my $uid(keys %$delete_ids) {
      $self->deleteUserFromCache($uid);
            }
   ```

2. The following is the join that builds the WHERE IN (?, ?, ?. ...) clause:

   ```
   # build up placeholders list
   $query .= join( ',', ( '?' ) x keys %$delete_ids );


   $query .= ')';
   ```

3. The query is executed. Since the statement used $delete_ids was used to construct the WHERE IN clause, its keys can be used for the bind values.

```
        my $sth= $self->{dbh}->prepare($query);

        # keys are the ids
        $sth->execute(keys %$delete_ids);

        if ($self->{dbh}->err) {
          $self->{msg}= "Database Error: $DBI::err_str";
          return 0;
        }
```

4. After the `DELETE` statement is successfully executed, an informational message is con-
    structed using the values of the `$delete_ids` hash reference — this is the whole reason for
    `$delete_ids` being a hash reference, which satisfies the need for providing both the list of
    uids to delete as well as the usernames for the message, as opposed to an array reference.

    deleteUsers() returns the number of rows deleted using $sth->rows()

```
        #
        # if any rows were deleted from the database
        # create a success message
        #
        if ($sth->rows()) {
          warn "deleted: " . $sth->rows() ."\n";

          # values are the usernames. Make a nice message
          $self->{msg}= sprintf("Deleted contacts: \u%s",
                                join(', ', values %$delete_ids));

          return $sth->rows();
        }
        return 0;
    }
```

The userExists() Method

The userExists() method is used to return the uid value of a contact if found using either the *email*
or *username* contact lookup attributes. The first argument of userExists() is $self, the object reference
to its own class. The second argument is $user, a hash reference with either *email* or *username* as the key
attributes and the values of the email address and username for that contact. Each of these will be used
to perform a query to the database to see if the contact exists. If the contact exists, the uid for that contact
will be returned.

Since userExists() does perform two queries against MySQL, it does perform the lookup against memcached first to avoid these database accesses if possible.

```
=head2 userExists()

checks to see if a user exists by either the username or email address

=item arguments

=over
```

```
$user - hashref representing a user keyed by user fields

=back

=item returns

=over

uid > 1 - user exists
0 - user doesn't exist
-1 - error

=back

=cut

sub userExists {
  my ($self, $user)= @_;
  my @bind_values;
```

Check memcached first. If the uid is found, return it without further ado.

```
  # try memcached first before hitting the database
  my $uid= $self->userExistsInCache($user);
  return $uid if $uid;
```

Next, query MySQL uses both the `email` and `username`:

```
  # ok, not in memcached, check MySQL

  # now attempt to see if in MySQL, using username or email
  for my $key(qw (username email)) {
    #
    # have to run a separate query for each column
    # otherwise there is no way to tell the user which column
    # there is a duplicate on
    #
    if (exists $user->{$key}) {
      my $query= "SELECT uid FROM users WHERE $key = ?";
```

The single `uid` value is then returned to the caller, if found.

```
      my $exists= $self->{dbh}->selectcol_arrayref($query, {}, $user->{$key});
      if ($exists->[0]) {
        $self->{msg}= "Error the \u$key $user->{$key} exists already";
        return ($exists->[0]);
      }
    }
  }
```

If no `uid` values are found, 0 is returned.

```
  return 0;
}
```

Caching Methods

The other part of data storage for this application is caching contact data in such a way that the data is available and reliable for retrieval to reduce the necessity of obtaining it from MySQL as much as possible.

When developing an application that uses memcached, you may find that you are repeating certain caching retrieval and modification steps. This is where it's helpful to abstract this functionality into methods that hide the details of how that cache is maintained.

For this application, a memcached object, referred to from this point on as *uid_list*, is what will be used to ensure an accounting of what contacts are stored in memcached. It will be a simple hash reference with the keys the memcached key values used to store or retrieve the hash references for each contact. Not only will this provide a "catalog" or inventory of cached contact uid for lookup of single contacts, but it can also be used as the key list argument to Cache::Memcached::libmemcached method get_multi() to automatically provide the list of keys needed to fetch all stored contacts at once.

It is crucial to ensure that this uid_list is accurate and reflects the contact uids of the contacts currently stored in MySQL. With painstaking logic, this is achieved by updating the list in both MySQL and memcached whenever a contact is inserted, updated or deleted. Also, the expiration for uid_list is set to 5 minutes whenever this uid_list is stored. This will cause the cache to be reloaded at least every 5 minutes with the full contact list, or whenever the user loads the contact listing page.

Most importantly, all of these methods must immediately return to the caller a false or undefined value (depending on what is being expected) in case there was no connection to memcached established — $self->{memc} being undefined. This is so that the application can function without using memcached.

The saveUserToCache() Method

The saveUserToCache() method has an easier job to perform than saveUser with memcached — particularly the Cache::Memcached::libmemcached set() method, which sets a value whether or not that value already exists. That behavior is the reason saveUserToCache() can simply store the values that it needs to.

The saveUserToCache() method takes two arguments. The first, $self, is an object reference, and the second, $user, is the hash reference of contact attributes, with the keys being the contact attribute (database columns) names and the values being those for the attributes. The values saveUserToCache() stores in memcached are the contact hash references stored using the memcached key "uid_$user->{uid}"; If $user->{uid} is 22, the key would be uid_22. It also stores the contact id $user->{uid}, using both the email and username as keys. This will provide a means of lookup by email and username.

```
=head2 saveUserToCache()

stores a user into cache, insert or update since 'set' doesn't care

=item args

=over
```

```
$self - object reference

$uref - user hash ref

=back

=item returns

=over

1 on success

0 failure

=back

=cut
 sub saveUserToCache {
   my ($self, $user)= @_;
   return 0 unless defined $self->{memc};
```

saveUserToCache() also must update the uid_list, which again is a hash reference stored in memcached that provides an inventory of contacts stored in memcached. For it to work, any method that modifies data in memcached must also update this list. This is what the calls to the method updateMemcUIDList() provide.

```
#
# ensure uid_list is updated - this is vitally important
# for this app to work properly!
#
$self->updateMemcUIDList($user->{uid});

# store the user
$self->{memc}->set("uid_$user->{uid}", $user);


#
# other lookup keys - mail and username
# used in userExists/userExistsInCache
#
$self->{memc}->set($user->{email}, $user->{uid});
$self->{memc}->set($user->{username}, $user->{uid});
}
```

The cacheUsers() Method

The cacheUsers() method does what it says it does. It caches all contacts stored in MySQL. Its first argument, $self, is an object reference to its own class. The second argument, $users, is the result set from selecting all contacts as returned from the DBI method, fetchall_hashref(). This is a multiple-level hash reference having as keys the uid values of each contact the key is pointing to. cacheUsers() iterates through each key of $users and stores each contact hash reference in memcached.

```
head2 cacheUsers()

stores the complete user reference of users to memcached
```

```
=item args

=over

$self - object reference

$uref - hashref of user hash refs

=back

=item returns

=over

success if stored

=back

=cut

 sub cacheUsers {
  my ($self, $users)= @_;
  defined $self->{ memc } or return 0;
  my $uid_list;
```

This `for` loop will iterate over each `uid` for each contact hash reference in `$users`. Within the loop, it first creates the key value (found in `$key`) by creating a string of "uid_<uid>". So, if the current uid being iterated over is 22, the key will be uid_22. This key will be used to store the contact in memcached and be added to the hash reference `$uid_list`.

Then the following will be stored within this loop:

❑ The current contact hash reference containing the keys for the attributes of the contact and the values for those attributes, stored with the key `$key`. So if the uid value is 22

❑ The `uid` value of the contact, keyed by the `email`, used for email lookup of the contact in memcached

❑ The `uid` value of the contact, keyed by the `username`, used for username lookup of the contact in memcached:

```
for my $uid (keys %$users) {
    # first, set the entire user, keyed by uid_<uid>
    my $key= "uid_$uid";
    $self->{memc}->set($key, $users->{$uid});
    # if new, add it to the list, otherwise no effect
    $uid_list->{$key} = $uid ;

    # then by email
    $self->{memc}->set($users->{$uid}{email}, $uid);

    # then by username
    $self->{memc}->set($users->{$uid}{username}, $uid);

    }
```

The last thing `cacheUsers()` does is to call `setMemcUIDList()`, which properly caches `uid_list`:

```
# so we know what keys we have without asking the database!
$self->setMemcUIDList($uid_list);
return;
}
```

The getUsersFromCache() Method

The `getUsersFromCache()` method returns the cached contacts from memcached. Its first and only argument is `$self`, an object reference to its own class. `getUsersFromCache()` returns all the hash references for every contact stored in memcached. The purpose is to return the same data structure that MySQL would return by using the DBI method `fetchall_hashref()`, which happens to be a multilevel hash reference consisting of hash keys the `uid` values pointing to contact hash references. This is the hash reference that will inevitably be used to generate the HTML table containing the contact list.

```
=head2 getUsers()

select and retrieve an arrayref of users from the database

=item arguments

=over

$self - object reference

$uref -  user ref containing one or more keys

$reload_cache - used to cause the cached users to be reloaded

=back

=item returns

=over

return arrayref containing result set

=back

=cut

sub getUsersFromCache {
  my ($self)= @_;
  my $users = {};
  return $users unless defined $self->{memc};
```

`$uid_list` is set to the value of `uid_list`, which is returned from a call to `$self->{memc}->get()`:

```
# get the list of keys for multiple fetching
my $uid_list= $self->{memc}->get('uid_list');

#
```

```
# if empty, Cache::Memcached::libmemcached returns an empty string
# so test whether it's a ref or not as well as being defined
# if this isn't set, then return, which will in turn
# force the data to be re-cached
#
ref $uid_list or return {};
keys %$uid_list or return {};
```

Besides providing an accounting of what contacts are stored in memcached, uid_list has another use: to provide an automatic list of keys for every contact stored in memcached. It is important to note however, that these contacts were stored with the key uid_$uid, so to get the data structure so that the keys are only the $uid value, some processing is required:

```
# the key values of $uid_list from uid_list provides
# the list of keys to get
$users= $self->{memc}->get_multi(keys %$uid_list);
```

The following for loop iterates over all the contacts retrieved from memcached. Each key is "uid_$uid" ($uid is used here for discussion to mean a numeric-only key with the uid value for the contact), and what is needed is to convert $users into a hash reference keyed by just $uid. To do this, the numeric part of the "uid_$uid" key is parsed and then in turn used to create another key in $users pointing the hash reference for the current contact, then original key "uid_$uid" is deleted. At the end of the loop, $users is now keyed by $uid.

```
# what is needed is for it to be keyed by UID
for my $uid(keys %$users) {

    # parse out the numeric part of the key
    $uid =~ /uid_(\d+)/;

    $users->{$1}= $users->{$uid};
    delete $users->{$uid};

}

return $users;
}
```

Finally, the converted $users hash reference is returned to the caller.

The userExistsInCache() Method

The userExistsInCache() method is used to perform the same operation as the similarly named database access method, userExists. userExistsInCache() has as its first argument $self, which is an object reference to its own class. The second argument, $user, is a hash reference containing lookup attributes for a contact such as email and username. Because when a contact is cached, the email and username values are also used to store the $uid value to provide a cache lookup to return a fast uid value, userExistsInCache() will attempt a lookup with either of these attributes. If a contact hash reference is found with either of those keys, it is returned to the caller.

```
=head2 userExistsInCache()
```

```
=item args

=over

$self - object reference

$user - user hashref

=back

=item returns

=over

uid value, if exists

0 if not

=back

=cut

 sub userExistsInCache {
  my ($self, $user)= @_;
  return 0 unless defined $self->{memc};
  # over-assuming I am
  $self->{msg}= "ERROR: The ";
```

The following loop is where the lookup to memcached is attempted. A loop that iterates over the strings email or username is used to look up the contact based on the value either of email or username of $user. If found, the value of the memcached object is returned, which happens to be the $uid for the particular contact.

```
    #
    # try to see if in memcached, using username or email
    # which are two possible storage keys
    #
    for my $key(qw (username email)) {
        exists $user->{$key}) or next; # pre-condition
        my $uid= $self->{memc}->get($key);
        $uid or next; # pre condition for following code

        # provides a message showing column and value
        $self->{msg} .= "\u$key $user->{$key} exists already.";
        return $uid;
    }
```

The deleteUserFromCache Method

The deleteUserFromCache() method deletes a contact hash reference from memcached. Its first argument is $self, an object reference pointing to the current class. The second argument is $uid, the uid value for the contact to be deleted.

```
=head2 deleteUserFromCache()

deletes a user from memcached - any entry in memcached for the user
including the email, username, as well as from the list of user uids

=over args

$self - object reference
$uid - user id

=back

=over

=item returns

no value

=back

=cut

sub deleteUserFromCache {
    my ($self, $uid)= @_;
    return 0 unless defined $self->{memc};
```

First, `deleteUserFromCache()` creates the memcached lookup key "uid_$uid"

```
    my $key= 'uid_' . $uid;
```

Then the contact is retrieved from memcached for the sole purpose of obtaining the username and email attributes which will be used to delete the username and email lookup entries for the contact. The first deletion is the contact hash reference, then the email and username lookup values.

```
    # obtain the user - why? Need the email address and username
    my $user= $self->{memc}->get($key);

    # delete entry keyed by email
    $self->{memc}->delete($user->{email});
    # delete entry keyed by username
    $self->{memc}->delete($user->{username});

    # now delete the user
    $self->{memc}->delete($key);
```

Finally, `deleteMemcUIDList()` deletes from the user_list the contact id of the contact that was just deleted.

```
    # take user out of uid list
    $self->deleteMemcUIDList($user->{uid});
}
```

The setMemcUIDList() Method

The setMemcUIDList() method is a convenience method, which means it merely is used to abstract some of the details of setting the user_list in memcached. In particular, it automatically sets the expiration value determined by $MEMC_CATALOGUE_EXPIREY at the top of the class, unless a different value is used upon instantiation of WebApp with the option memc_catalogue_expirey. The first argument to setMemcUIDList(), $self, is an object reference to itself. The second argument, $uid_list, is the actual hash reference that will be stored in memcached indicating the uids of the contacts stored in memcached.

```
=head2 setMemcUIDList()

convenience method to set the uid_list object in memcached

=item args

=over

$self - object reference

$uid_list - hash reference of UIDs

=back

=item returns

=over

true - success

false - failure

=back

=cut

sub setMemcUIDList {
  my ($self, $uid_list)= @_;

  return 0 unless defined $self->{memc};

  $self->{memc}->set("uid_list", $uid_list, $self->{memc_catalogue_expirey});

}
```

The updateMemcUIDList Method

The updateMemcUIDList() method is another method to hide the details of how the user_list is updated. Its first argument, $self, is an object reference to its own class. Its second argument, $uid, is the $uid that is to be acted upon within the list. The third argument, $delete_flag, is used to toggle deletion of the $uid value from user_list.

```
head2 updateMemcUIDList()

convenience method used to either insert, update or delete (if flag set)
a UID into/from the hashref stored as uid_list and re-stored in  memcached

=item args

=over

$self - object reference

uid -  UID

$delete_flag - 1 delete, 0 no delete

=back

=item returns

=over

true - success

false - failure

=back

=cut

 sub updateMemcUIDList {
  my ($self, $uid, $delete_flag)= @_;

  return 0 unless defined $self->{memc};

  # if no uid supplied, error
  unless ($uid) {
    $self->{msg}= "ERROR: No UID value for updateMemcUIDList";
    carp $self->{msg};
  }

  # get the uid_list
  my $uid_list= $self->getMemcUIDList;
```

At this point, the variable $uid_list should contain a current inventory of uids, which if $delete_flag is set, deletes then the hash member with the value of "uid_$uid." If $delete_flag is not set, then the value of "uid_$uid" is set into $uid_list. This either sets an existing hash member or creates it — it doesn't matter — the point is that the uid_list is updated.

```
  # if the delete flag was set, then delete the uid from the list
  if ($delete_flag) {
    delete $uid_list->{"uid_$uid"};
  }
```

```
    # otherwise, add the uid
    else {
      # this will do nothing if there ....? , add if not
      $uid_list->{"uid_$uid"}= $uid;
    }
```

Lastly, the modified hash reference $uid_list is stored back in memcached as uid_list and provides an up-to-date inventory of uids.

```
    # store it back in there
    $self->setMemcUIDList($uid_list);
  }
```

The deleteMemcUIDList() Method

The deleteMemcUIDList() method is a convenient method that uses the updateMemcUIDList() to do the dirty work. All deleteMemcUIDList() does is to call updateMemcUIDList() with its second argument, $uid, the uid to be removed from the uid_list, as well as passing a 1 (true) as the $delete_flag, the third argument of updateMemcUIDList().

```
=head2 deleteMemcUIDList()

convenience method to updateMemcUIDList, passing the delete flag,
resulting in the UID being removed from uid_list and re-stored in
memcached

=item args

=over

$self - object reference

$uid -  UID

=back

=item returns

=over

true -  success

false - failure

=back

=cut
 sub deleteMemcUIDList {
   my ($self, $uid)= @_;

   return 0 unless defined $self->{memc};

   $self->updateMemcUIDList($uid, 1);
```

```
      return;

  }
```

The getMemcUIDList Method

The getMemcUIDList() method obtains the uid_list from memcached. Its first and only argument, $self, is an object reference to its own class. getMemcUIDList() ensures that the uid_list hash reference is up to date with an accurate accounting of the uids of contacts stored in memcached, and then returns uid_list.

```
=head2 getMemcUIDList()

convenience method used to retrieve the UID hashref
stored as uid_list in memcached, ensuring if it isn't
stored either due to expiration or restart of a memcached server,
it is re-cached, then returned to the caller

=item args

=over

$self - object reference

=back

=item returns

=over

hashref

=back

=cut
sub getMemcUIDList {
  my ($self)= @_;

  return {} unless defined $self->{memc};

  # try to obtain the uid_list
  my $uid_list= $self->{memc}->get('uid_list');
```

First, an attempt is made to obtain $uid_list from memcached. If this is not found — either due to the memcached server being restarted (who did it!?) or expiring, or LRU causing it to be replaced — the method getUsers() is called. This will result in the contact list being reloaded into memcached, which in turn will cause uid_list to be reloaded into memcached as well.

```
  # force re-caching of users if the list is not there
  unless (ref $uid_list) {
    $self->getUsers({});

    # now get the $uid_list again, should be there ;)
```

```
        $uid_list= $self->{memc}->get('uid_list');

    }

    return $uid_list;
}
```

Finally, the `$uid_list` hash reference is returned, supplying the inventory of cached contacts to the caller.

Other Methods

The two other methods worth discussing are `getState()` and `getStates()`. These provide the state data. For this application, that means the data for the pulldown menu that lists the states in the contact edit form. Since state data hardly ever changes, these methods don't have to have any functionality to deal with the consistency of the number of states stored (which was required with the contacts, where each contact is stored separately). You know there are a fixed number of states, and that number is not huge, so it's just as easy to store all the state data in memcached once. If it's there in memcached, it can be used, otherwise `getState()` and `getStates()` will reload the cache.

The getStates() Method

The `getStates()` method has the simple task of returning the entire hash reference consisting of keys of the state abbreviations: the values the state names. `getStates()` takes a single argument, `$self`, the `blessed` object reference to its own class.

```
=head2 getStates()

    method to obtains a hash reference of states - keyed by state
    abbreviation, value the state name

=over args

$self - object reference

=back

=over returns

hash reference of states keyed by state abbr, value state name

=back

=cut

  sub getStates {
    my ($self)= @_;

        my $states;
```

First, `getStates()` for checks to see if `$states` are stored in memcached already. If `$states` are found in memcached, it returns `$states`.

```
# a simple true/false to indicate that cities have been cached
$states= $self->{memc}->get('states_cached') if defined $self->{memc};

# return if in memcached
return $states if ref $states;
```

Otherwise, getStates() obtains the state data from MySQL and then maps that data from an array reference of hash references for each state record into the hash reference required — a simple hash reference of state_abbr for the keys and state_name for the values. Then it stores the $states hash reference in memcached with the key states_ cached then returns $states.

```
# define the base query
my $query= 'SELECT state_abbr, state_name FROM states';

my $sth= $self->{dbh}->prepare($query);

$sth->execute();


# fetch the states data
my $sref= $sth->fetchall_arrayref({});

# map into hashref of keys the state abbreviation values the state names
$states->{$_->{state_abbr}} = $_->{state_name} for @$sref

# cached $states and indicate that $states have been cached
unless ($self->{memc}->set('states_cached',$states)) {
   $self->{msg}= "ERROR: setting 'states_cached'\n";
}
return $states;

}
```

The getState() Method

The getState() method takes two arguments: $self, a blessed object reference to its own class, and $state_abbr, a scalar string containing the value of state abbreviations. getState() is a simple convenience/lookup method that simply uses the getStates() to provide the hash reference of states, referred to as $states. This then returns a member of $states keyed by $state_abbr. The getState() method is used to provide a state name for display of contact data in the *viewuser* page since the value stored for a contact in the database is a state abbreviation.

```
=head2 getState

returns a full state name given a state abbreviation, using
the state ref returned by getStates()

=item args

=over

$self - object reference
```

```
$state_abbr - scalar string state abbreviation value

=back

=item returns

=over

scalar string state name, success

undef on failure

=back

=cut

sub getState {
  my ($self, $state_abbr)= @_;

  my $states= $self->getStates();

  return $states->{$state_abbr};
}
```

The encodeUserData() Method

The `encodeUserData()` method encodes any HTML entities found in each user attribute. This prevents *HTML injection* — also known as *cross-site scripting,* where HTML entities (or even JavaScript) alter the page that displays to the end user. For an excellent description of cross-site scripting, see `http://www.cgisecurity.com/xss-faq.html`.

An example of `encodeUserData()`:

```
=head2 encodeUserData()

Encodes any HTML entities which might be contained in each
user attribute to prevent HTML injection in any forms or pages
that print out this data

=item arguments

=over

$self - object reference

$user - reference to user hash reference

=back

=item returns

=over
```

```
does not return a value since it modifies $user passed as a reference

=back

=cut

sub encodeUserData {
    my ($self, $user)= @_;

    # encode any HTML entities if defined
    for my $attr (@$USER_COLS) {
        if (defined $$user->{$attr}) {
            $$user->{$attr}= encode_entities($$user->{$attr}) ;
        }
    }
    return;
}
```

Testing

Now that the application code is completed, you should be able to use this application. You will want to perform some usability tests to make sure it works as you have intended it to work. Here is what you should be able to see in testing:

- ❑ Save a new contact, start by clicking on the "Create a New Contact" link from the contact listing page.
- ❑ Supply completely new data for a contact, no existing email address.
- ❑ Supply an existing username or email address. When you save it, the program should display an error stating that one of those attributes is already being used for an existing contact.
- ❑ Supply incomplete data, particularly username, email, firstname or lastname. The application should display an error and return you to the contact edit form to complete the form.
- ❑ Edit an existing contact from the contact list.
- ❑ Modify an existing contact successfully, see the modified values displayed in the contact listing, contact view and contact edit pages.
- ❑ Attempt to use an email address of an existing contact other than the contact being edited. Upon submission, an error should be displayed along with the edit form for the user to try a different email address.
- ❑ Attempt to submit empty values for required fields such as email address, first name, and last name.
- ❑ Delete one or more contacts from the contact list.
- ❑ Delete one or more contacts by selecting from the checkboxes for each contact in the contact list. Upon submission by the Delete button, the list should be redisplayed along with a message that those contacts were deleted and are absent from the list.
- ❑ Delete all contacts. The contact listing page should indicate that there are no contacts and should not display any contacts.

❑   View a contact. Selecting a contact to view should display that contact.

❑   When you shut down memcached, the application should still function.

❑   When you shut the database down, the application should at least display an error.

Summary

This chapter showed you a fully functional contact list application. This application is a CGI application, but as you will see in Chapter 13, you can use it as a mod_perl ModPerl::Registry application or convert it to a mod_perl handler. On the surface, this application is simple in terms of user functionality, but it's fairly complex internally, especially in how it implements that functionality, particularly the caching.

This chapter discussed the following:

❑   The stages of conceptualization, design, and implementation.

❑   A comprehensive listing of every subroutine and method of the application.

❑   How to divide up functionality between front-end display logic and back-end data storage logic.

❑   In the example application, you saw how you can use memcached to cache application data to reduce database access to MySQL.

❑   A listing of user interface testing, showing you what functionality you have to test to ensure that all of the code you wrote results in the application functioning correctly.

This application provided you with an idea that can be built upon for other web applications. From here this book can go on to explain other concepts, such as mod_perl, templating and web applications that use Ajax, which you will read about in the next several chapters.

13

mod_perl

In Chapter 12, you learned about programming a Perl CGI application. As was stated, CGI is a standard for web servers to be able to execute external programs. It provides both input data to the program, and receives data back from the program. In the case of the contact application in Chapter 12, the Perl interpreter `perl`, running the Perl code in `app.pl` was the external program. This requires that in addition to each Apache child or thread, for whatever number of requests call this program, an equal number of external processes also are executed. Secondly, and key to this discussion, the state of the program execution — the interpreted Perl code, database connections, are all created and then destroyed for each CGI URL request and have to be re-created every time the program runs again.

This is where mod_perl steps in. mod_perl is an Apache module that loads a persistent Perl interpreter into each Apache process. This allows Perl applications to be parsed and compiled by this persistent Perl interpreter once so that each request to the application will receive the benefit of precompiled code.

Having a persistent Perl interpreter loaded into the Apache server is certainly a big benefit to using mod_perl. Most importantly, and the primary advantage of using mod_perl, is that mod_perl provides you complete access to the Apache API. This lets you write mod_perl handlers, and — just as can be done with regular Apache modules — this allows you to implement them in any stage of the Apache life cycle, including the HTTP request phase cycle. When you develop web applications using several other programming languages, you are developing functionality only within the last part of the HTTP request phase cycle, the response phase.

In addition to being able to write handlers that have the same access that C modules have, there are also Perl language bindings into Apache's request library, libapreq2. This library is the Apache subproject `httpd-apreq` that includes the Perl modules Apache2::Request, Apache2::Cookie, and Apache2::Upload, and provides you, the Perl developer, with methods for parsing cookies, file uploads, and POST and GET form data.

Essentially, mod_perl gives you all the access that C developers have to the Apache API, but with Perl you can significantly expedite the development process. This is an incredibly compelling reason to use mod_perl.

The purpose of this chapter is to cover mod_perl in a general sense, showing you some of what you can accomplish with it. In the chapters following this one, you will see practical demonstrations of these concepts that you can use!

New mod_perl 2.0 Features

There are some new features and changes in mod_perl 2.0 worth mentioning:

❑ Namespace for the modules has changed from Apache to Apache2.

❑ Naming conventions for mod_perl handler phase names have changed.

❑ Threads support — now mod_perl uses a thread-safe Perl interpreter known as ithreads or Interpreter Threads. There is a pool of Perl interpreters used instead of one interpreter per thread.

❑ Two APIs: Apache API and Apache Portable Runtime (APR) API.

❑ Better Windows support.

❑ Filters that interface to Apache's filtering API using either streaming or bucket brigades.

❑ Protocol modules that make the web server behave like another type of server, such as an IMAP server.

❑ Apache::Registry is now ModPerl::Registry.

The API has changed significantly enough that if you have code written for mod_perl 1.x, you will want to review the mod_perl web site documentation at `http://perl.apache.org` to see all that has changed and modify your code. The effort will be worth it.

For more on installing Apache, see Chapter 11, which also covers the installation of mod_apreq2.

Configuring mod_perl

The first thing is to load the mod_perl shared library from your Apache configuration file (shown in Chapter 11):

```
LoadModule perl_module modules/mod_perl.so
```

Also, load libapreq2:

```
LoadModule apreq_module modules/mod_apreq2.so
```

With these added, after restarting Apache, your web server will have mod_perl and libapreq2 loaded so you can start using mod_perl.

To easily begin, use the module ModPerl::Registry. This instantly turns your CGI scripts into mod_perl applications by compiling the contents of your script into a handler routine and into memory, thus making what was a one-time-only script persistent. It also provides a tremendous performance gain for your old CGI applications.

So, to turn the CGI contact application example from Chapter 12 into a mod_perl application, you first have to think about how it will behave if it becomes persistent. For the most part, it should run out of the box, with no changes required. However, there are certain caveats.

In the original version, the CGI module was instantiated at the top of the script as a lexical global variable, making it available to the other various methods, prior to main() being called.

```perl
use strict;

use CGI qw(:standard);
use WebApp;

# CGI object
my $cgi = new CGI;

# URL of program, used in form submit url, other parts of code
my $url = $cgi->url(-absolute=>1);

# WebApp
my $webapp= new WebApp();

# call main subroutine
main();

exit();
```

This was so you didn't have to pass the instantiated object hash reference around explicitly. However, since this is an object having to do with request parsing, etc., it can cause problems to scope it as a global variable. You would have to change the instantiation of the $cgi object reference to main():

```perl
sub main {
   my $msg;

   my $cgi = new CGI;

   # URL of program, used in form submit url, other parts of code
   $url = $cgi->url(-absolute=>1);

   print $cgi->header('text/html');
   print header();

   dispatcher($cgi, \$msg);

   print footer();
}
```

You would leave $url scoped as a global variable at the top of the script, but not set it to anything until $cgi is instantiated. Also, notice that you would pass $cgi to dispatcher(), which uses it to get the submitted form values:

```perl
sub dispatcher {
   my ($cgi, $msg)= @_;
```

```
...
# get all submitted form values into a hashref
my $form = $cgi->Vars();

...
}
```

You may need to make other tweaks, but these should be sufficient changes for the script to be persistent.

Next, you would simply add to your Apache configuration file:

```
PerlModule ModPerl::Registry
PerlModule Apache::DBI

PerlPostConfigRequire /usr/local/apache2/perl-conf/startup.pl

  Alias /perl/ /usr/local/apache2/sites/default/perl/

  <Location /perl>

      SetHandler perl-script

      PerlResponseHandler ModPerl::Registry

      PerlOptions +ParseHeaders

      Options +ExecCGI

  </Location>
```

You would create a file /usr/local/apache2/perl-conf/startup.pl that contains the following:

```
#!/usr/bin/perl

use lib '/usr/local/apache2/perl-lib';
use WebApp

my $webapp = new WebApp();

$webapp->getUsers();


1;


1;
```

Make sure WebApp.pm is in /usr/local/apache2/perl-lib, and then, as long as your CGI script is in the newly configured directory, restart Apache. Then run the application as normal, except much more efficiently!

What you see in the previous examples are the various mod_perl configuration directives, which will be explained in more detail later in this chapter. The purpose here was to show you just how simple it is to set up and use mod_perl, particularly with ModPerl::Registry; as a developer you might not delve deeper into the full capabilities that mod_perl offers. The author can certainly attest to this!

The directives in the previous Apache configuration file simply mean this:

- ❑ `PerlModule ModPerl::Registry`: This is just like having `use ModPerl::Registry` in your source code. It imports the Perl module ModPerl::Registry into mod_perl.

- ❑ `PerlModule Apache::DBI`: This is a very useful module that buys you a lot with hardly any effort. Apache::DBI basically intercepts all DBI database connection requests, caching database handles.

- ❑ `PerlPostConfigRequire = /usr/local/apache2/perl-conf/startup.pl`: This causes `startup.pl` to load whenever Apache is started. It runs whatever is in `startup.pl`, which can be a convenient way to load modules, preconnect to databases. In this example, all that `startup.pl` currently has is:

  ```
  #!/usr/bin/perl

  use lib '/usr/local/apache2/perl-lib';

  use WebApp

  my $webapp = new WebApp();

  $webapp->getUsers();


  1;
  ```

  This allows for WebApp to be imported for either ModPerl::Registry scripts or mod_perl handlers. Also notice that `$webapp->getUsers()` is called — this caches all the users when Apache is started! These are just a few mod_perl features and configuration directives.

- ❑ `Options +ExecCGI`: This causes whatever file is being accessed within this URL location to be executed instead of being served as a static file.

mod_perl Configuration Directives

Just as the main Apache server has configuration directives, so too does mod_perl. These directives are set the same way Apache directives are set.

<Perl> Sections

Usage: `<Perl> ... Perl code ... </Perl>`

Just as you saw with the `PerlPostConfigRequire` directive in the previous section, to run the startup Perl script, `startup.pl`, you can do this with `<Perl>` sections. A `<Perl>` section allows you to write Perl code directly into your Apache configuration file and configure your server as a whole, if you so desire.

This is useful when you have many virtual hosts and could actually use a database connection to provide information about each virtual host, dynamically creating what would normally require numerous virtual host configuration files with Perl code.

An example of how to implement both the startup script above and configure the /perl directory to run ModPerl::Registry scripts is accomplished by the following code:

```
<Perl>
use Apache::DBI;
use ModPerl::Registry;
use lib qw(/etc/apache2/perl-lib);

use WebApp;


my $webapp= new WebApp();

$webapp->getUsers();
$webapp->cacheBannedIPs();
$webapp->cacheUsersByMD5();

$Alias= "/perl /var/www/apache2-default/perl";

$Location{"/perl"} = {
  SetHandler       => "perl-script",
  PerlHandler      => "ModPerl::Registry",
  PerlSendHeader   => "On",
  PerlOptions      => "ParseHeaders",
};


</Perl>
```

Each Apache directive becomes a Perl variable having the same name. Nesting is accomplished with hash references. If an attribute has multiple values, an array reference is used:

```
DirectoryIndex => [qw(index.html index.htm index.shtml index.php)]
```

PerlModule

Usage: `PerlModule ModuleName [ModuleNameN, [...]]`

This imports a Perl module, the same as:

```
Use ModuleName
```

You can also specify that you want the module to be automatically loaded at Apache startup by having a plus (+) sign in front of the module:

```
PerlModule +MyLib::MyModule
```

PerlLoadModule

Usage: `PerlLoadModule ModuleName [ModuleNameN, [...]]`

This is the same as `PerlModule`, except it causes Perl to start up earlier than the default, which is normally after the configuration phase of the Apache server life cycle.

SetHandler perl-script

Usage: `SetHandler perl-script`

This sets the handler for a `<Location>` or `<Directory>` to be handled by mod_perl. This is used with ModPerl::Registry scripts so that they are run through mod_perl. It allows you to take your CGI scripts and run them as mod_perl handlers. It also automatically sets several things:

- ❏ `PerlOptions +GlobalRequest` for `PerlResponseHandler` handlers (including ModPerl:: Registry).
- ❏ `PerlOptions +SetupEnv` so your CGI scripts automagically have the `$ENV{XXX}` variables available to them, otherwise they would break if they had to rely on these `$ENV` values being set .
- ❏ Ties `$r` (Apache2::RequestRec) object to `STDERR` and `STDOUT`.
- ❏ Saves the Perl global variables such as `@INC`, `%ENV`, `STDOUT`, `STDERR`, etc., before the response handler, the script, is called. Then it restores them afterward.

SetHandler modperl

Usage: `SetHandler modperl`

This is the same as perl-script, except without much of the setup that perl-script provides for CGI compatibility. `SetHandler modperl` has:

- ❏ No `PerlPassEnv`: Does not pass `$ENV` variables. The only variables available are what you define with `PerlSetEnv` as well as `MOD_PERL` and `MOD_PERL_API_VERSION`.
- ❏ No preservation of `$ENV` variables before and after the response phase.

PerlSetEnv

Usage: `PerlSetEnv ENV_VARIABLE_NAME value`

This is a very useful feature that allows you to set an environment variable that is accessible via `$ENV` in your mod_perl script or handler.

Here is an example:

```
PerlSetEnv VIRTUAL_DB_USER webuser
```

Then, in the code you would have:

```
my $dbh= DBIx::Password->connect($ENV{VIRTUAL_DB_USER});
```

PerlPassEnv

> Usage: `PerlPassEnv VARIABLE`

This causes environment variables set on your system to be passed to your ModPerl::Registry scripts or handlers. This is particularly useful for ModPerl::Registry scripts. You may have CGI code that you migrated to mod_perl that depends on environment variables being set. This ensures that those specified environment variables are available from mod_perl as `$ENV{VARIABLE}`.

PerlSetVar

> Usage: `PerlSetVar name value`

This allows you to set a variable that you can retrieve using the Apache2::RequestRec method `dir_config()` in your mod_perl code. In your Apache configuration file you would have:

```
PerlSetVar ADMIN_USER CaptTofu
```

Then in the code you would use:

```
my $admin_user= $r->dir_config(`ADMIN_USER')
```

PerlAddVar

> Usage: `PerlAddVar name value (...)`

This has the same effect as using the Perl `push()` function. This allows you to set array configuration variables available via `$r->dir_config`.

An example would be in your Apache configuration file:

```
PerlAddVar MEMCACHED_SERVERS `127.0.0.1:11211"
PerlAddVar MEMCACHED_SERVERS `192.168.10.33:11211"
PerlAddVar MEMCACHED_SERVERS `172.16.221.130:11211"
```

Then, in your code, you could connect with this array to memcached:

```
my @servers= $r->dir_config('MEMCACHED_SERVERS');

my $memc= new Cache::Memcached::libmemcached({
                        servers            => \@servers,
                        compress_threshold => 10_000});
```

PerlPostConfigRequire

Usage: `PerlPostConfigRequire file-path [file-path [...]]`

This works just like `require` in Perl.

```
PerlPostConfigRequire /etc/apache2/perl-lib/startup.pl
```

The above is the same as this:

```
require `/etc/apache/perl-lib/startup.pl´;
```

... which causes the file specified to be loaded at Apache startup. You can use this to set up whatever you need to — paths, variables, database connections, etc., so they are already set up for use later.

PerlRequire

Usage: `PerlRequire file-path [file-path [...]]`

Same as `PerlPostConfigRequire`, except there is no way to control when the file specified is loaded. Use `PerlPostConfigRequire` instead.

PerlOptions

Usage: `PerlOptions option [option [...]]`

PerlOptions works similarly to the regular Apache options:

Option	Description
`Enable`	Used to disable or enable mod_perl. For instance, `PerlOptions -Enable` would disable mod_perl for the server or virtual host it is set for.
`Clone`	Allows a virtual host to have its own Perl interpreter pool.
`InheritSwitches`	Allows the virtual host to inherit the PerlSwitches settings of the parent server.
`Parent`	Creates a new parent Perl interpreter and interpreter pool for the virtual host.
`Perl*Handler`	Allows you to specify which handler phases you can run handlers for, using the phase part of the handler name. For instance, if you wanted to allow `PerlResponseHandler`, `PerlAuthenHandler`, and `PerlAuthzHandler` but no others, you would have: `PerlOptions none +Authz +Authen +Response`

Continued

(continued)

Option	Description
AutoLoad	Loads modules at Apache startup. This can also be accomplished with using the plus (+) sign in front of the module, as in: `PerlAuthenHandler +WroxHandlers::AuthTestHandler`
GlobalRequest	Sets up the global request object, $r, as the first argument to any ModPerl::Registry script or a mod_perl handler.
ParseHeaders	Scans the output of a response handler — mainly for ModPerl::Registry scripts — for HTTP headers. Required if these scripts manually print the HTTP header.

MergeHandlers	Causes mod_perl handlers that are defined within <Directory> or <Location> sections to be merged with mod_perl handlers that are defined in the main configuration file. For instance:
	
	`PerlLogHandler WroxHandlers::LogHandlerMain`
	`<Location /mydir>`
	`        PerlOptions +MergeHandlers`
	`        PerlLogHandler`
	`WroxHandlers::LogHandlerMyDir`
	`</Location>`
	
	Normally, requests to `/mydir` would result in only using `LogHandlerMyDir`, but `+MergeHandlers` will cause `/mydir` to have both `LogHandlerMain` and `LogHandlerMyDir` to handle the logging phase.

SetupEnv	Causes all environment variables to be populated within mod_perl. This allows CGI scripts to be migrated to ModPerl::Registry easily, which would otherwise break due to relying on environment variables to function. If you do have scripts that use environment variables, it might be worth it to modify the code to use other means, as there is a performance cost to using `SetupEnv`.

PerlSwitches

Usage: `PerlSwitches switch`

Allows you to set any Perl switch that you would set in your code, such as `-w`:

```
PerlSwitches -w
```

This would make your code run with the `-w` flag.

POD

You can use Perl's POD tokens `=pod`, `=over`, and `=cut` in your Apache configuration file if mod_perl is enabled:

```
NameVirtualHost *
<VirtualHost *>
=pod
```

```
Welcome to the apache configuration file. You can add
documentation this way

=over mysite

  ServerName example.net
  ServerAlias www.example.net
  ServerAdmin webmaster@localhost

=back

That was the value that set which hostname this virtual host will answer

=cut
```

mod_perl Handler Directives

These directives are listed as other directives. For instance, the most common handler directive you will use is `PerlResponseHandler`. The usage for this would be:

```
PerlReponseHandler WroxHandlers::TestHandler
```

As was mentioned in Chapter 12, handlers are a unit of functionality that performs a certain task in the web server. That chapter also discussed Apache 2.2's various phases of processing a connection and how the Apache API provides *hooks* for modules to access those phases with callbacks, or handlers that can "hook" into the particular request phase. This enables modules to alter or extend the default functionality of Apache. mod_perl can use all those same hooks by means of different types of handlers.

Handler Scope

With mod_perl 2.0, you can employ handlers at any part of the request phase cycle, as well as during the connection to the web server itself. Since these mod_perl handlers can be applied at any phase of the connection or request cycle, they have a particular scope:

❑   SRV: Server-wide. This means either in the main configuration file or within a `<Virtualhost>` sectional directive. This will run for every connection to the server.

❑   DIR: The handler will only run within a particular `<Directory>`, `<Location>` or `<Files>` sectional directive.

Handler Type

Handlers can be *stacked*, which means you can assign more than one handler to an Apache phase. All handler types are executed in the order they are defined or registered and their type is determined by how it behaves with regard of the return value of the previously defined handler in a stacked group for that phase.

❑   VOID: All handlers in the grouping will run regardless of the value returned, though these handlers need to and are expect to return OK.

❑ RUN_FIRST: All handlers will be executed as long as every handler returns DECLINED. Apache will move on to the next phase if one of these handlers in the grouping returns the value of OK, and any other return value will cause execution of the cycle to abort and be logged.

❑ RUN_ALL: All handlers will be executed as long as every handler returns either DECLINED or OK.

Handler Category

mod_perl handlers are categorized by the scope of when they run: The full scope is the entire Apache server. The other possibilities are the connection loop or the request phase cycle.

In Chapter 11, the Apache request phase cycle was described as having four primary phases:

❑ Request parsing
❑ Security
❑ Preparation
❑ Handler

Each of these primary Apache phases has steps or hook names, as described in Chapter 11 of this book and in the Apache documentation (http://httpd.apache.org/docs/2.0/developer/request.html). In the mod_perl 2.0 documentation (http://perl.apache.org/docs/2.0/user/handlers/intro.html), some of the steps or hooks in these four phases are themselves considered to be phases. The mod_perl manual lists 12 phases. The following table correlates mod_perl phases (in the mod_perl documentation) to the steps or hooks shown in the Apache documentation:

mod_perl Request Phase Handler Name	Apache Server Steps
PostReadRequest	Unescape URL, strip ../ and ./ from path, initial URL \<Location\> walk, post_read_request
Trans	translate_name
MapToStorage	map_to_storage
	Second URI location walk
HeaderParser	header_parser
Access	access_checker
Authen	check_user_id
Authz	auth_checker
Type	type_checker
Fixup	fixups Insert_filter
Response	response/handler
Cleanup (mod_perl only)	
Log	log_transactions

Apache Life Cycle Overview

The following table gives an overview of the category, name, scope, and type of the Apache life cycle phase name, or hook name, and the name of the mod_perl handler type you would use for declaring a handler for the given phase.

Apache Phase Name	Apache Step/ Hook Name	mod_perl Phase, Handler Name	Scope	Type
Server Life Cycle	open_logs	PerlOpenLogsHandler	SRV	RUN_ALL
	post_config	PerlPostConfigHandler	SRV	RUN_ALL
	child_init	PerlChildInitHandler	SRV	VOID
	child_exit	PerlChildExitHandler	SRV	RUN_ALL
Protocol, connection	pre_connection	PerlPreConnectionHandler	SRV	RUN_ALL
	process_connection	PerlProcessConnectionHandler	SRV	RUN_FIRST
Filters	Connection or request phase	PerlInputFilter	DIR	VOID
	Connection or request phase	PerlOutputFilter	DIR	VOID
Request phase, HTTP protocol	post_read_request	PerlPostReadRequestFilter	SRV	RUN_ALL
	translate	PerlTransHandler	SRV	RUN_FIRST
	map_to_storage	PerlMapToStorageHandler	SRV	RUN_FIRST
	post_read_request or header_parser	PerlInitHandler	SRV or DIR	RUN_ALL
	header_parser	PerlHeaderParserHandler	DIR	RUN_ALL
	access_checker	PerlAccessHandler	DIR	RUN_ALL
	check_user_id	PerlAuthenHandler	DIR	RUN_FIRST
	auth_checker	PerlAuthzHandler	DIR	RUN_FIRST
	type_checker	PerlTypeHandler	DIR	RUN_FIRST
	fixups	PerlFixupHandler	DIR	RUN_ALL
	handler	PerlResponseHandler	DIR	RUN_FIRST
	log_transaction	PerlLogHandler	DIR	RUN_ALL
		PerlCleanupHandler	DIR	RUN_ALL

Server Life Cycle Phase Handlers

These phases pertain to the entire scope of a parent process starting up, spawning children, and the shutting down of child processes. In a prefork MPM, the parent spawns a child. The connection loop of that child begins, which is where it serves a given number of requests as determined by the configuration parameter `MaxRequestsPerChild`. With the threaded model, the connection loop is served by threads.

❑ `PerlOpenLogsHandler`: This phase is when the Apache parent process is first executed, the `open_logs` phase. During this, Apache opens the primary log files that it will log to, such as the main access and error logs, and SSL logs. Scope is SRV; type is RUN_ALL.

❑ `PerlPostConfigHandler`: This phase immediately follows the reading of the configuration files but happens prior to any child processes, and is known as the `post_config` phase. At this stage, it's possible to set settings that all subsequent child processes will share. Scope is SRV; type is RUN_ALL.

❑ `PerlChildInitHandler`: This phase occurs immediately following the spawning of child processes (not thread), and is known as the `child_init` phase. Scope is SRV; type is RUN_ALL.

❑ `PerlChildExitHandler`: This phase provides access immediately prior to the shutdown of a child process (not thread), as known as the `child_exit` phase. Scope is SRV; type is RUN_ALL.

Connection Cycle Phase Handlers

This phase pertains to the connection as a whole, which will be served by a particular protocol such as HTTP. A connection will serve one or more *requests*. At this level, you can rewire Apache to use whatever protocol you want — SMTP, IMAP, FTP, etc. — in addition to HTTP. With the new filter interface, you also have the ability to apply filters to a connection.

Connection Cycle Phase Handler Template

The connection cycle phase handler template is pretty simple. It declares the package name, imports various pragmas to force good behavior, and imports the constants you need within the body of your handler, such as return values.

```
# the name of your package
package WroxHandlers::ConnectionHandlerTemplate;

# good practice
use strict;
use warnings;

use Apache2::Connection ();
use Apache2::Const qw(OK FORBIDDEN ...);

# import other modules here
```

Connection handlers take as their first argument an Apache2::Connection object reference. This is an object reference that provides methods and attributes for various values you will use in your handler. For more information, see `perldoc Apache2::Connection`:

```
sub handler {
    # the first argument is the Apache2::Connection object reference
    my ($c)= @_; # connection
```

Then, you return either a success or failure value provided by Apache2::Const.

```
    # an error might be
    #    return FORBIDDEN;

    return OK;
}

1;
```

Connection Cycle Phase Handler Names

There are two connection handler phases for implementing connection handlers:

❑ PerlPreConnectionHandler: This phase occurs immediately after Apache accepts the connection, prior to being handed off to a protocol such as HTTP, and is known as the pre_connection phase. At this point, you can set what protocol you want to serve the connection. This is also where you would insert input connection filters. Scope is SRV; type is RUN_FIRST.

❑ PerlProcessConnectionHandler: Incoming connections are processed at this phase, the process_connection phase, and can be used to assign protocol handlers, replacing the default HTTP protocol with another protocol handler if desired. Scope is SRV; type is RUN_FIRST.

Filter Handlers

Filters are a new feature in Apache 2.2 and mod_perl has the ability to take advantage of them. They can be applied in scope to either the connection or the request/response phases, and were developed in response to the need for an Apache module to modify the output of another Apache module. Filters are applied to *buckets*, which are segments or chunks of data connected in a set of *bucket brigades* — which, as a whole, are used to store data from the network. Filters act upon each bucket in the bucket brigade one at a time, and are able to replace, remove, and modify from first bucket in the brigade to the last. Additionally, filters can be chained. The output of one filter is the input to another.

Filter Handler Template

In some ways, filters resemble handlers in terms of the handler method they use. However, filters work differently in that a filter is run against chunks of the page being filtered, and the processing part of the filter can run several times, depending on how large the document is.

The first argument, shown in the template code that follows, is $f, which is an Apache2::Filter object reference. The documentation (perldoc Apache2::Filter) provides information on what methods and attributes are available to this object.

```
package WroxHandlers::TestFilter;

use strict;
use warnings;

use Apache2::Filter ();
use Apache2::RequestRec ();
use APR::Table ();
use Apache2::Const qw(OK);
use Data::Dumper;
```

```
use constant BUFFER_LENGTH => 1024;

#
# FilterTemplate - a template for Apache mod_perl filters
#
sub handler {
    my ($f)= @_;
```

The code here happens at least once, usually at the beginning. This is the filter initialization.

```
    unless($f->ctx) {
        $f->r->server->warn('filter start.');
        $f->r->headers_out->unset('Content-Length');
        $f->ctx(1);
    }
```

This is where the processing of the filter occurs, where the real work is done:

```
    while ($f->read(my $buffer, BUFFER_LENGTH)) {
        # code here happens as many times as necessary per the
        # size of the document
        $f->r->server->warn('filter apply.');
        $f->print($buffer);
    }
```

This is the finalization of the filter. This is where you would perform any cleanups or flushing of data:

```
    if ($f->seen_eos) {
        # this happens when last, the EOS bucket brigade is detected
        $f->r->server->warn('filter end.');
    }

    return OK;
}
```

Filter Handler Type Descriptions

The following lists the two handler directives available for filter handlers:

❑   PerlInputFilterHandler: These act upon input data as it is being processed at the start of either the connection or HTTP request phase cycle. Scope is DIR; type is VOID.

❑   PerlOutputFilterHandler: Acts upon output data from a content generator, from the output of the connection or HTTP request phase cycle. Scope is DIR; type is VOID.

HTTP Request Cycle Phase Handlers

These are the handlers you are probably most familiar with if you have done any mod_perl programming before. They provide hooks into the various phases of the HTTP request phase cycle, of which the response is part. The best known part of this is the response phase, which is where actual content generation occurs. This is the realm in which other web programming approaches and languages such as CGI, PHP, Python, etc., primarily exist.

HTTP Request Cycle Handler Template

The basic template for HTTP request cycle phase handlers is shown in the following code. You would give your handler some sort of name with the package declaration. The next thing to know is that the default method name for a mod_perl handler is handler(), but you can use any name you want if you set the particular name of the method in your Apache configuration file when declaring a handler for a given <Location> directive.

```
# named to whatever naming scheme you need
package WroxHandlers::HandlerTemplate;

# good practice
use strict;
use warnings;

# list of return values you want to use
use Apache2::Const qw(OK DENIED REDIRECT ...);

# any list of modules to import can go here
# use WebApp

#
# this is an Apache HTTP Request Phase Cycle template
#
```

The next thing to know is that the handler will obtain as its argument the Apache2::RequestRec object reference. This is a handle to the Apache request record where you have access to numerous methods and attributes. This is a very powerful object reference. To see how to use it, you can read the documentation by running perldoc Apache2::RequestRec, which provides good information, as is the case for all Apache* Perl modules.

```
sub handler {
    #
    # this is the Apache2::RequestRec object.
    # "perldoc Apache2::RequestRec" to see how to use it!
    my ($r) = @_;

    #
    # handler implementation
    #
```

A handler returns various values for which you can obtain descriptions with perldoc Apache2::Const:

```
    # if everything goes well
    return OK;

    # if there are problems, you would return an error code
    #
    #   return DECLINED ... etc. "perldoc Apache2::Const" to
    #   obtain a list of return values and what they mean
#
}
# you need to include this
1;
```

HTTP Request Cycle Handler Phase Names

The follow table shows the 13 handler names for the different HTTP request cycle phases. These are the names you specify when defining a mod_perl handler for a given phase in your Apache configuration file.

Phase Name	Description
`PerlPostRead RequestHandler`	This is the handler name used for the phase immediately following when the server reads the request and the headers are parsed. This is known as the `post_read_request` phase (as shown in the mod_perl documentation). This handler is used in the main server directory and within `<VirtualHost>` directives. The handler at this stage has access to the request headers and can implement useful functionality, such as blocking of certain clients based on the type of user agent being used. This handler has server-wide scope, meaning that it runs for the entire server or within a `<VirtualHost>` sectional directory, and you cannot confine its functionality to a particular directory or URI. Scope is SRV; type is RUN_ALL.
`PerlTransHandler`	This is the handler name where the request URI can be manipulated, also known as the `translate_name` Apache hook. You could implement similar functionality to rewrite at this phase. Scope is SRV; type is RUN_FIRST.
`PerlMapToStorageHandler`	This is the handler name for the Apache hook `map_to_storage`, where the URL is mapped to the file on disk by reading the directory starting from the document root, which, depending on how deep the directory structure is, carries with it some overhead. mod_perl response handlers are implemented within the Apache `<Location>` sectional directive and there is no corresponding file for the URI of the handler. If you had a mod_perl application-only server that never had to worry about mapping URI to a file, this step would be unnecessary and could be bypassed using a *PerlMapToStorageHandler* handler. Scope is SRV; type is RUN_FIRST.
`PerlInitHandler`	This handler name is an alias to either `PerlPostReadRequestHandler` or `PerlHeaderParserHandler`, depending on where it is declared. If it is server-wide, global configuration including within `<VirtualHost>`, then it is an alias to `PerlPostReadReqestHandler`. If this handler is directory-scoped, meaning within a container directive such as `<Directory>`, `<Location>`, etc., then it is an alias to `PerlHeaderParserHandler`, in which case it is the first handler to serve a request. The scope of this handler is either server-wide or directory-based. Scope is SRV or DIR; type is RUN_FIRST.

Phase Name	Description
PerlHeaderParser Handler	This is the handler name used for the header_parser Apache hook that immediately follows the URI mapping phase, which, if the resource was for a file, was mapped to the resource on disk. This handler has access to the request headers where it can implement functionality to make a decision at an early stage in the request cycle, similar to PerlPostReadRequestHandler, though after URI mapping. Scope is DIR; type is RUN_ALL.
PerlAccessHandler	This is the handler name used for the access_checker Apache hook that is used to check the source IP or host of a request, as well as any nonuser-specific attributes that would be used for access control. You could, for instance, implement a handler to permit or reject client access from a given IP address at this stage. Scope is DIR; type is RUN_ALL.
PerlAuthenHandler	This is the handler name used for the auth_checker Apache hook. This is where access is either granted or denied on a directory that requires user authorization. Authentication succeeds for a user depending on whether or not the user credentials (user id) and password supplied match the username and password values from the password file or other user/password storage scheme. You could implement a handler at this stage that uses a MySQL database table as the user credential source. The user would have to supply a username and password that match what is stored in the table, which could further be tied into an entire user account application. Scope is DIR; type is RUN_FIRST.
PerlAuthzHandler	This is the handler name used for the Apache hook check_user_id. This happens after authentication. If authentication was required for a given resource or directory and the user was successfully authenticated, that user is then either authorized or not to a given access to the resource. This is the stage where you could implement a handler that further limits the access to a directory based on a username. For instance, you could have the requirement of "valid-user" required for a given directory, and then further control which users have access to specific subdirectories within that protected directory. Scope is DIR; type is RUN_FIRST.
PerlTypeHandler	This is the handler name for the Apache hook type_checker. This is where the MIME headers "Content-type" is set. This is one stage that is not commonly implemented with mod_perl handlers because when you override the default handler for this stage you are also required to set the handler for the response phase. *Caveat emptor*. Scope is DIR; type is RUN_FIRST.
PerlFixupHandler	This is the handler name used for the Apache hook fixups. This happens just prior to the response phase. At this stage, you can implement handlers to perform any functionality prior to the content being generated. You could, for instance, set any variables the response handler utilizes or even short-circuit the default handler based on a subdirectory or file extension of the <Directory> or <Location> for which this is in effect. Scope is DIR; type is RUN_ALL.

Continued

(continued)

Phase Name	Description
PerlResponseHandler	This is the handler name that you will most often use. This corresponds to the handler Apache hook. This is the one that every web developer is the most familiar with: the response phase. This is where the actual response content is generated and displayed to the client. Most mod_perl handlers are written for this phase, as are ModPerl::Registry scripts and other web programming approaches such as PHP, CGI, Python, Ruby, etc. Most of what you will develop in terms of web applications has to do with producing output, which is why this will be the most important stage to you. Scope is DIR; type is RUN_FIRST.
PerlLogHandler	All paths lead to this phase — you've got to get in to get out. Seriously, this is the log_transaction phase that will always be executed, regardless of whether all other handlers succeeded or failed. It logs information about the request and response. You could implement a handler to log to a MySQL database at this phase. Scope is DIR; type is RUN_ALL.
PerlCleanupHandler	This is a mod_perl-specific phase; there is no corresponding Apache phase. This is where you would implement cleanup code, which runs immediately following the response being generated by the PerlResponseHandler handler. Scope is DIR; type is RUN_ALL.

Figure 13-1 gives you a visual idea of when in both the server life and request cycles handlers can be implemented. It's pretty amazing to see just how encompassing mod_perl is, in terms of where within the Apache server life cycle you can implement Perl handlers. This is especially true when you consider various other web programming approaches or languages that are confined to the response phase!

Every type of handler is displayed, pointing to where within the server life cycle or request life cycle they exist. The server life cycle image shows all the various stages of the Apache process, including the HTTP request phase cycle, which is further expanded in the image to the right. The four primary phases of the request phase cycle as described in the Apache manual are shown in the HTTP request phase cycle block. The HTTP request phase cycle block displays them grouped by the four primary phases listed in the Apache documentation, as well as the twelve phases that mod_perl is concerned with.

Also of particular interest is where the filter handlers can be implemented, either on the input or output of a connection or response.

This is power that mod_perl gives you for developing web applications — not just page generation applications, but server applications.

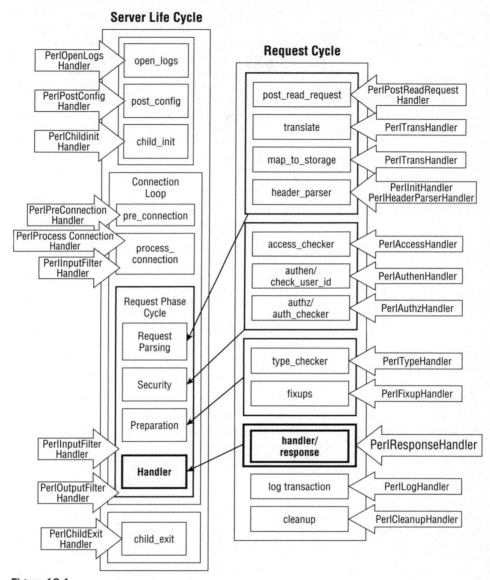

Figure 13-1

Perl Apache2 Modules

Available to you as a mod_perl developer are a number of Apache2 Perl modules, as well as the APR modules. You can always read any Perl module `perldoc` page for detailed information about these. For brevity, this section will cover the ones you will use the most.

It's extremely useful to have a good understanding of these modules for developing mod_perl applications. Virtually every part of Apache can be accessed from mod_perl, and each of these Apache2 modules are categorized by what type of Apache component they provide an API for (as shown in the following table).

Module	Description
Constants	Provides constant values needed for proper return codes.
Request/Request Record	A Perl object that provides you with access to the Apache `request_rec` data structure (in C), which contains everything pertaining to the current web client request.
Connection Record	A Perl object that provides you with access to the Apache `conn_rec` data structure (in C), which represents the current connection.
Filter Record	A Perl object that provides you with access to the Apache `ap_filter_t` structure, which is a C data structure containing information for a filter chain.
Server Record	A Perl object that provides you with access to the Apache `server_rec` structure, which is a C data structure containing information for each virtual server.
Logging	The `server_rec` structure has a file descriptor, `error_log`, used for logging messages to the Apache error log.
Server Configuration	Allows you to access information about your Apache configuration settings by means of your Apache configuration file.
Performance	Allows you to see thresholds of how many resources or how much memory processes can consume.
Status	Provides you with status information about mod_perl as it is running with your Apache server.

Apache2 Constants and Request Record Perl Modules

The Apache request record (`request_rec`) is an object that is at the core of your mod_perl development. There are a number of Apache2 Perl modules you will use in the course of development that provide you with different APIs for the request record.

Also, you will want a Perl interface for Apache constants, which Apache2::Const provides.

Apache2::Const

Apache2::Const provides constants to use within your code, particularly for return values in the mod_perl handlers you write. Its usage is simple:

```
use Apache2::Const qw(OK REDIRECT);
```

This would make it so you can have the following in your handler:

```
sub handler {
        my ($r)= @_;
        ... do some processing ...
        return OK;
}
```

In this example, OK is imported into your handler code's namespace. There is a memory requirement for this, so to save memory you could instead use:

```
use Apache2::Const -compile => qw(OK REDIRECT);

sub handler {
        my ($r)= @_;
        ... do some processing ...
                return $Apache2::Const::OK;
}
```

But then you have to use the fully qualified name for each constant, for example $Apache2::Const::OK and $Apache2::Const::Redirect.

Apache2::Request

Apache2::Request provides API methods for processing GET or POST form data. Usage is pretty much the same as with CGI.pm. You can use this to obtain either single form values, or set a hash reference to all values.

```
sub handler {
      my ($r)= @_;
      my $form;

      # obain the request object
      my $req= new Apache2::Request($r);

      # map all the keys that were submitted to $form hashreference
      $form->{$_} = $req->param($_) for $req->param();

      # code body, print header, etc...
      $r->print("<p>" . $req->param('item1') . "</p>");
      $r->print("<p>" . $form->{item2} . "</p>");

       # code body
}
```

You can also use it for uploads:

```
my $upload= $req->upload('file');

$upload->link("/uploaddir/$newfile");
```

For a full listing of all the methods Apache2::Request provides, run perldoc Apache2::Request.

Apache2::RequestRec

Apache2::RequestRec is the primary API you will work with using mod_perl. This is the request record object that is the first argument to a mod_perl handler. It has accessor methods for everything you would need. Some of the methods and simple usage are shown in the handler code here:

```
sub handler {
        my ($r) = @_;
        $r->content_type(`text/html');
        $r->print("<html><head><title>test</title></head><body>");
        $r->print("<h1>test this<h1>");
        $r->print("<p> IP " . $r->connection->remote_ip() . "</p>");
        $r->print("<p> METHOD " . $r->connection->method() . "</p>");

        $r->print("<p> HOST " . $r->hostname() . "</p>");

        $r->server->warn("warned you");
        $r->print("</body></html>");
}
```

Apache2::RequestUtil

Apache2::RequestUtil provides API methods for request record utilities. Examples of some of the methods are:

❑ Obtain a variable set with `PerlSetVar MY_VAL "foo"` in the Apache configuration file:

```
my $var= $r->dir_config(`MY_VAL');
```

❑ Get the document root of the server:

```
my $doc_root = $r->document_root();
```

❑ Get an array reference of registered handlers for a given phase:

```
my $access_handlers = $r->get_handlers(`PerlAccessHandler') ;
```

❑ Set new handlers for a given phase:

```
$r->set_handlers(`PerlResponseHandler', [ `WroxHandlers::MyNewHandler']);
$r->set_handlers(`PerlResponseHandler', \&hander_code_ref);
```

❑ Set an HTTP config value:

```
$r->add_config(['require valid-user']);
```

See `perldoc Apache2::RequestUtil` for a full listing of methods for this API.

Apache2::RequestIO

Apache2::RequestIO provides API methods for accessing the raw IO of an Apache request record. You will use one of its methods extensively: print(). Some of the other methods it provides are shown here:

❑   Reading

```
my $buffer;
my $len = 1024;
$r->read($buffer, $len);
```

❑   You can also send/print the contents of a file to the output of your handler:

```
$r->sendfile('/tmp/foo.txt');
```

❑   Of course print():

```
$r->print("<p>this is a test</p>");
```

❑   And printf():

```
$r->printf("<b>test %s %d</b>\n", "this", 2);
```

To see all the methods available with Apache2::RequestIO, run perldoc Apache2::RequestIO.

Apache2::Response

Apache2::Response provides an API for request record response methods, such as setting response headers, content-length header, last-modified, keepalive, custom response headers, etc. Run perldoc Apache2::Response for API usage details.

Apache2::Access

The Apache2::Access module provides an API that has methods you would use for handlers you use in the access, authentication and authorization phases. An example of the usage of one of the methods is:

❑   Get the password from the request headers:

```
my ($status, $password) = $r->get_basic_auth_pw;
```

❑   Note failure of authentication:

```
$r->note_basic_auth_failure;
```

Apache2::URI

The Apache2::URI module provides an API for processing URI strings via the Apache::RequestRec object, $r. This also includes methods for constructing and analyzing components of URI strings.

Apache2::Util

The Apache2::Util module provides two utility methods:

❑   escape_path(): Converts an OS path to URL path.

❑   ht_time(): Converts a numeric time value to a string of a specified format.

Apache2 Connection and Filter Record Modules

Also available are Apache2 Perl modules for both the connection record and filter object, which are used for writing connection and filter handlers respectively.

Apache2::Connection

This module provides an API for the Apache connection record object. This object is available as the first argument in mod_perl connection handlers and also is a member of the Apache2::RequestRec (request record) object in HTTP request phase cycle handlers.

Simple usage examples are:

```
# get the connection record from the request record
my $c= $r->connection();
# client remote IP
my $ip= $c->remote_ip();
# client host
my $host= $c->remote_host();
```

Apache2::Filter

The Apache2::Filter module provides an API for the Apache filter object. This is the first argument in a filter handler, $f, as shown here:

```
sub handler {
    my ($f)= @_;

    # filter handler body
}
```

The filter API provides numerous methods and attributes for working with the filter object, such as the following:

❑   Request record object:

```
my $r = $f->r;
```

❑   Server object:

```
my $server = $f->server;
```

❑   Connection record object:

```
my $c = $f->c;
```

❑   Read and set filter context:

```
my $context = $f->ctx;
$f->ctx(1);
```

❑   print():

```
$f->print($buffer);
```

But these are just some of the methods it provides. For a more complete list (and this is a topic in itself), see perldoc Apache2::Filter.

Apache2 Server Record Modules

For developing server handlers, or even having access to the error log file descriptor, you should use the Apache2::ServerRec server record.

Apache2::ServerRec

The Apache2::ServerRec Perl module provides an API for the Apache server record. It can be accessed via the request record. Some of the methods are shown here.

```
sub handler {
    my ($r) = @_;
    my $server = $r->server
    my $servername = $s->server_hostname();
    my $process_id = $s->process();
    # handler body
}
```

You can run perldoc Apache2::Server for more details on the API.

Apache2::ServerUtil

The Apache2::ServerUtil module provides a Perl API to the server record utilities. You can obtain a server record object from the request object:

```
my $server = $r->server;
```

❑   This sets a value for the server as you would with PerlSetVar:

```
$server->add_config([`ReloadDebug off´]);
```

❑   This gets a value:

```
my $debug_off = $server->dir_config(`ReloadDebug´);
```

❑   This gets the server version:

```
my $server_version = Apache2::ServerUtil::get_server_version();
```

For a full description and details, run perldoc Apache2::ServerUtil.

Apache2::Log

The Apache2::Log module provides an API for logging methods. It gives you the ability to log messages to the Apache error log at various logging levels (see Chapter 11 for information about the various Apache logging levels). Just as is the case with the server record, this is available via the Apache::Server object:

```
$r->server->log_error(`ERROR! You have problems.");
```

```
$r->server->warn(`I am warning you...");
```

Apache2 Configuration Modules

Several Apache2 Perl modules can be used to access and modify Apache configuration settings.

Apache2::Directive

The Apache2::Directive provides an API for accessing information about your Apache configuration file. It basically parses your Apache configuration file, which is an SGML file, into a DOM-like tree structure so that you can manipulate it to retrieve any directive's value, or other configuration values.

For instance, to obtain the value of your server's error log:

```
my $tree = Apache2::Directive::conftree();
my $error_log = $tree->lookup(`ErrorLog');
```

... which would be:

```
/var/log/apache2/error_log
```

To access one of your servers as a hash, which would take the same format as it would need for Perl sections (<Perl>), you would use:

```
my $conf_ref = $tree->as_hash();
```

This would give you a hash reference that would show your entire Apache configuration file in the same format that <Perl> sections would require. For instance, a truncated view of an entire dump (using Data::Dumper) of the reference for an Apache configuration file would be the following:

```
$VAR1 = {
  Listen' => [
              '80',
              '443',
              '127.0.0.2:8080'
              ],
  ],
  'NameVirtualHost' => [
                        '*',
                        '127.0.0.2:8080',
                        '192.168.1.118:443',
                        '*'
                        ],
```

```perl
  'MaxSpareServers' => '10',
  'DefaultType'     => 'text/plain',
  'MaxClients'      => '20',
  'VirtualHost'     => {
        '127.0.0.2:8080'    => {
              'DocumentRoot'    => '/usr/local/apache2/sites/default-backend',
              'ServerSignature' => 'On'
              'ErrorLog'        => '/var/log/apache2/error-backend.log',
              'ServerName'      => 'backend.someexample.net',
              'CustomLog'       => '/var/log/apache2/access-backend.log combined',
              'LogLevel'        => 'warn',
              'ScriptAlias'     => '/perl /usr/local/apache2/sites/default/perl',
              'ServerAdmin' => 'webmaster@localhost',
              'Directory' => {
                  '/' => {
                      'Options'       => 'FollowSymLinks',
                      'AllowOverride' => 'None'
                  },
                  '/usr/local/apache2/sites/default-backend' => {
                      'Order'         => 'allow,deny',
                      'Options'       => 'Indexes FollowSymLinks MultiViews',
                      'Allow'         => 'from all',
                      'AllowOverride' => 'None'
                  }
              },
              'Location' => {
                      '/' => {
                          'Order'   => 'allow,deny',
                          'Allow'   => 'from all'
                      },
                      '/perl' => {
                          'Options'    => '+ExecCGI',
                          'SetHandler' => 'cgi-script'
                      }
              },
        },
        '*' => {
              'DocumentRoot' => '/usr/local/apache2/sites/default',
              'ErrorLog'     => '/var/log/apache2/error.log',
              'ServerName'   => 'someexample.net',
              'ScriptAlias'  => '/cgi-bin/ /usr/lib/cgi-bin/',
              'Directory' => {
                  '"/usr/lib/cgi-bin"' => {
                  'Order'         => 'allow,deny',
                  'Options'       => '+ExecCGI -MultiViews +SymLinksIfOwnerMatch',
                  'Allow'         => 'from all',
                  'AllowOverride' => 'None'
                  },
              }
              # ... more directives ...
        }
  }
};
```

As you can see, this would get quite huge — especially considering that even this example has been truncated in order to save some trees!

You can also see that each directive, having no children, is a scalar. Whereas if there are children or a list of settings, these are found as hash references to yet more configuration parameters or array references for lists of settings.

Apache2::MPM

This module provides an API for accessing Apache MPM (Multi-threaded Processing Module). This has not been discussed much here because it is beyond the scope of this book. But you should know it provides methods for accessing information from your server if you are using a threaded server. For instance, if you wanted to test to see if your server is threaded using Perl, you would use the following:

```
my $is_threaded = Apache2::MPM->is_threaded;
```

To read more about this module, run `perldoc Apache2::MPM`.

Apache2::PerlSections

Apache2::PerlSections provides the ability to completely configure your Apache web server using Perl, as was shown earlier in this chapter under the heading "mod_perl Configuration Directives" and the subheading "Perl Sections" (`<Perl>` ... `</Perl>`.). You can read more about Perl Sections by running `perldoc Apache2::PerlSections`.

Apache2 Resource/Performance, Status, and Other Modules

A number of Perl modules relate to performance and you will probably want to become familiar with them. These modules provide features such as database handle caching, displaying mod_perl system status, and making mod_perl handler development easier by not requiring you to have to restart Apache to see changes to your application.

Apache2::Reload

Apache2::Reload is a Perl module that provides you with the ability to force your mod_perl handlers to be reloaded by mod_perl if the underlying code has changed. This is very useful for development; you don't have to restart your web server every time you want to see the results of changes you have made to your code. To use it, you just need to add the following to your Apache configuration file:

```
PerlModule Apache2::Reload
PerlInitHandler Apache2::Reload
```

You can set other variables as well, such as whether to check all loaded Perl code or specify particular modules to be reloaded. In this example, only the modules with the name `WroxHandlers` will be reloaded.

```
PerlSetVar ReloadAll Off
PerlSetVar ReloadModules "WroxHandlers::*"
```

You can also turn on debugging:

```
PerlSetVar ReloadDebug On
```

Doing so will make it so you can see in your error log what modules Apache2::Reload is reloading:

```
[Mon Feb 16 10:29:46 2009] -e: Apache2::Reload: Checking mtime of
WroxHandlers/TestResponseHandler.pm
```

Make sure when you are done with the development stage and ready to release your code into production that you don't use this setting. Apache2::Reload is something you would set up on a development server. When you are ready to move your code to a QA or live server, those servers will not be using Apache2::Reload.

Apache::DBI

This provides persistent database connections. This is one of the easiest modules you will ever have to use!

The module does not use the Apache2 namespace, but works just as well with mod_perl 2.0.

DBI will forward a database connection request to Apache::DBI, which will first try to see if there is a cached database handle already available (meaning it is still connected to the database). If so, it will summarily return that one. Otherwise, it will create a new database handle, which it keeps in the cache for subsequent requests to take advantage of.

To use it, simply have this:

```
PerlModule Apache::DBI
```

. . . or this:

```
Use Apache::DBI;
```

. . . in your Apache configuration file Perl sections or in your startup file.

Apache2::Resource

Apache2::Resource allows you to limit resources used by Apache children. For instance, the following code would limit the address space for a child process to a soft limit of 16MB and a hard limit of 32MB:

```
PerlSetEnv PERL_RLIMIT_AS 16:32
```

See perldoc Apache2::Resource for more usage details.

Apache2::SizeLimit

Apache2::SizeLimit allows the server to kill off child processes that exceed a certain value. You use it by including it in either your startup script that you included with PerlPostConfigRequire, or within Perl sections. You would use the following code to limit the max process size to 15MB, minimum shared to 8MB, and unshared to 6MB:

```
$Apache2::SizeLimit::MAX_PROCESS_SIZE  = 15000;
$Apache2::SizeLimit::MIN_SHARE_SIZE    = 8000;
$Apache2::SizeLimit::MAX_UNSHARED_SIZE = 6000;
```

You can also use Apache2::SizeLimit in both your mod_perl handlers and ModPerl::Registry scripts.

❏   For ModPerl::Registry scripts:

```
Use Apache2::SizeLimit;
...
Apache2::SizeLimit::setmax(15000);
Apache2::SizeLimit::setmin(8000);
Apache2::SizeLimit::setmax_unshared(6000);
```

❏   For mod_perl handlers:

```
use Apache2::SizeLimit;
sub handler {
        my $r= (@_);
        Apache2::SizeLimit::setmax(15000, $r);
        Apache2::SizeLimit::setmin(8000, $r);
        Apache2::SizeLimit::setmax_unshared(6000, $r);
        # code body
}
```

For a full description of how you can take full advantage of Apache2::SizeLimit, see `perldoc Apache2::SizeLimit`.

Apache2::Status

This Perl module provides a very comprehensive view into the status of mod_perl for your server. To use it, simply add to your Apache configuration file the following:

```
<Location /perl-status>
  SetHandler modperl
  PerlOptions +GlobalRequest
  PerlResponseHandler Apache2::Status
</Location>
```

The interface you will see (shown in Figure 13-2) is a top-level menu that takes you to other informational pages, such as those in the following table:

Page	Description
Environment	Displays the environment variables.
Loaded Modules	Shows which modules are loaded.
Inheritance Tree	Provides a tree view showing module inheritance.

Page	Description
Perl Configuration	Shows how mod_perl is configured for the server including perl version, compile flags, platform information, and anything you might need to know about your specific installation of mod_perl.
Compiled Registry Scripts	Shows a listing of ModPerl::Registry scripts that have been compiled.
Required Files	Shows all files either required from included modules or from `PerlPostConfigRequire`.
Signal Handlers	Shows a listing of all signals such as `KILL`, `ALRM`, and `IO` and their current values.
Symbol Table Dump	Shows a listing of all symbols for all Perl code loaded by mod_perl. This will even show you the actual code, deparsed, for each method or subroutine of every piece of code loaded, as well as view variables for each.

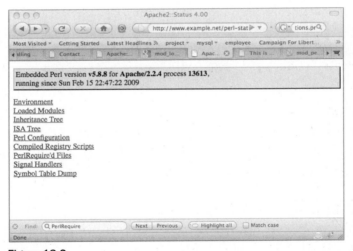

Figure 13-2

If for instance, you select Loaded Modules, you will see a long list of the modules that are loaded for your Apache server, as shown in Figure 13-3.

Figure 13-3

There are many configuration settings provided for using Apache2::Status. For more information, read the `perldoc` for Apache2::Status.

Summary

This chapter introduced you to mod_perl 2.0, an Apache module that embeds a Perl interpreter into the Apache web server and allows significant improvement to Perl web application performance over using CGI. This is because with mod_perl, you are using a built-in interpreter within the web server, rather than an external execution of a Perl interpreter. Thus, mod_perl 2.0 is able to provide persistence to Perl web applications, which is a great improvement over Perl web applications using CGI, where every time the CGI script runs it must reparse and recompile the Perl code. mod_perl instead parses and compiles the Perl code once when it's first loaded, and thereafter the compiled code is available for subsequent requests. This persistence is of great benefit to web applications, particularly for objects such as database handles and memcached connections.

This chapter also discussed how easy it is to run your existing Perl CGI scripts and mod_perl applications using ModPerl::Registry, a Perl module that results in your CGI application being compiled into the body of Perl subroutine that is compiled once and stored in memory, breathing persistent life into your Perl CGI code.

You also explored an overview of the various mod_perl configuration directives that let you specify various settings controlling how mod_perl functions for your server, as well as the 12 different handler directives, each with an Apache life cycle in addition to processing cycles within the Apache life cycle, such as the HTTP request phase cycle connection loop.

Finally, filters, one of several new Apache 2 features, were explained. Filters differ from regular handlers in that they act on brigades, which are groupings of data chunks known as buckets, forming a bucket brigade.

Upon finishing this chapter, you should have a good idea of just how powerful mod_perl is!

14

Using mod_perl Handlers

In Chapter 13, you learned what mod_perl is and how it can be used, what different types of mod_perl handlers there are, and what stages of the Apache life cycle and the HTTP request phase cycle they can be implemented for.

You probably are curious to see just what this really means. If you are like the author, you thought more in terms of writing Perl code to implement a web application, displaying content, processing input, and displaying other content based on user input. This all happened at the HTTP request response phase. mod_perl is about much more than just implementing functionality at the response phase. It's about having complete access to the Apache life cycle and HTTP request cycle. This is what the various handlers are for. They take advantage of Apache 2.0/2.2 *hooks*, which provide modules with the ability to alter the way Apache runs at given phases of its life cycle. mod_perl gives you the same ability to do what Apache module developers do.

This chapter will show you some simple, practical examples that give you a hint of how powerful mod_perl handlers can be. Also, these examples will use MySQL and memcached to show you how you could theoretically build an entire system around Apache using mod_perl that has access to the same database.

PerlResponseHandler Example

The first handler you probably want to see is a `PerlResponseHandler`, since this would be the most common handler you would implement for your various web application requirements.

The following example is a little bit more involved and somewhat odder than your usual *Hello, World!* example. The idea here is to show you a little taste of programming with mod_perl handlers, particularly the response handler since that's the phase you most likely are curious about.

Also, if you are familiar with Apache 1.3/mod_perl 1.x, you'll see in this example that things have changed a bit in your write handlers. Hopefully the code shown in this chapter will give you ideas of what you need to do in your own code to migrate to mod_perl 2.0.

This example shows a few concepts:

❏ Form parsing with Apache2::Request

❏ Printing debug to the error log with $r->server (Apache2::ServerReq)

❏ Setting the log level in order to print debug messages

❏ Redirecting internally or externally to a URL of the user's choice

❏ Setting HTTP headers

Initial Handler Setup

This first thing is to create the handler file. As you recall, there is a directory on this server (your own will vary on your own setup): /usr/local/apache2/perl-lib. In this directory there is already a startup.pl and WebApp.pm. In this example, the handler will be called TestResponseHandler, and since there will be other handlers, it will be stored in a directory that will be called WroxHandlers as TestResponseHandler.pm, so its package name will be WroxHandlers::TestResponseHandler.

```
package WroxHandlers::TestResponseHandler;

use strict;
use warnings;
use Apache2::Const -compile => qw(OK REDIRECT LOG_DEBUG);
use Apache2::Request;
```

The line -compile => (OK REDIRECT LOG_DEBUG) is used to make the Apache2::Const constants available. Also, for this example, to have access to the Apache2::Request object (obtaining form parameters), that module is imported.

The next thing to do is to define the handler() method. This is the default name entry method to mod-_perl handlers, though you can use other names, as you will see later.

The only argument to this handler method is $r, which is an Apache::RequestRec object reference. Next, the $url of the script is obtained with $r->uri. This provides the URL of itself to be used in the form that will soon be printed.

```
sub handler {
    # Apache2::RequestRec object reference.
    my ($r)= @_;
    my $url= $r->uri;

    # scalar to hold the html list of arguments
    my $table;
```

Log Messages Using the Server Object and Form Parsing

Next, $s is set to the value of $r->server, an object reference to the Apache2::ServerRec object. For the example, this will be used for logging debug messages to the error log.

```
    # Apache2::ServerRec object
    my $s = $r->server;
```

An Apache2::Request object reference is obtained to use with $req. This will be used to obtain the submitted form values — which will work for both a POST and GET:

```
# obain the request object
my $req = new Apache2::Request($r);

# a hashref for the submitted form keys/values
my $form = {};
```

The Apache2::Request method is $req->param() with no arguments provided. It returns a list of all the submitted form value names. With these names, you can then obtain all the values for those named form parameters. That is what the mapping and assignment to the hash reference variable $form achieves:

```
# map all the keys that were submitted to $form
$form->{$_} = $req->param($_) for $req->param();
```

Setting the Log Level and Printing the HTTP Header

The log level is set to LOG_DEBUG. This is required to set the log level equal to or greater than the type of logging level you wish to print at. In this case printing at debug level is desired. Without this, Apache will not log these debug messages because the default debug level for Apache is warn, which is not high enough for a debug level message.

```
# set the apache log level to debug
# needed in order to user r->log->debug()
$s->loglevel(Apache2::Const::LOG_DEBUG);
```

This prints out a debug message in the Apache error log.

```
# print a nice debug message
$r->log->debug("--> WroxHandlers::TestResponseHandler::handler");
```

These previous lines of code that set up printing debug messages could be abstracted into your own logging module, if you did not want to implement these details in your web applications. You need some method of printing to the Apache error log easily while you are still developing your application.

Next, the HTTP header needs to be printed out. This prints out the MIME type for this handler, which is HTML:

```
# print mime header
$r->content_type('text/html');
```

Redirection

The following logic tests the pattern of the submitted form value $form->{redirect}. This is a crude test and is not by any means bulletproof. It is used to show how you can achieve an internal or external redirect.

If $form->{redirect} starts with a forward slash (/), then it most likely needs to be an internal redirect. To call an internal redirect (subrequest) to the internal URL requires the constant Apache2::Const::OK to be returned:

```
# just to show you how redirect works
if (defined $form->{redirect} && length($form->{redirect})) {

    # if no scheme, this is an internal redirect
    if ($form->{redirect} =~ /^\//) {

        # subrequest to the internal URI
        $r->internal_redirect($form->{redirect});

        # make sure to print exit debug statement
        $r->log->debug("<-- WebPub::TestHandler::handler (internal redirect)");

        # return OK - no REDIRECT
        return Apache2::Const::OK;
    }
```

If it does not start with a forward slash, perform an external redirect. To do this, the location header is set. Print a debug before you redirect. Then return from the handler the `Apache::Const::REDIRECT` constant:

```
    # otherwise, external redirect
    else {
        # set the Location header
        $r->headers_out->add('Location' => $form->{redirect});

        # make sure to print exit debug statement
        $r->log->debug("<-- WebPub::TestHandler::handler (external redirect)");

        # return REDIRECT
        return Apache2::Const::REDIRECT;
    }
}
```

Print the Document Header

Next, an HTML header is printed:

```
$r->print(q(
<html>
    <head>
        <title>Test Handler</title>
    </head>
    <body>
    ));
```

The following code shows the printing of the form, which has various form values for the purpose of having something to submit. In this case, the method will be POST. But this form will also process GET if you use a query string when accessing this handler:

```
        $r->print("\t\t<h1>This is the Test (TM) handler</h1>");
    $r->print(qq(
```

```
<form action="$url" method="POST" id="testform" name="testform">
    <fieldset>
        <p>
            <label for="item1 ">item1</label>
            <input type="text" id="item1" name="item1" size="16">
        </p>
        <p>
            <label for="item2">item2</label>
            <input type="text" id="item1" name="item2" size="16">
        </p>
        <p>
            <label for="item3">item3</label>
            <input type="text" id="item1" name="item3" size="16">
        </p>
        <p>
            <label for="lifes_options">Life's options</label>
            <select name="lifesoptions" id="lifesoptions">
            <option value="savemoney">Save Money</option>
            <option value="spendanddebt">Spend Money</option>
            <option value="monk">Live like a monk</option>
            <option value="mooch">Mooch off of Mom and Dad</option>
            </select>
        </p>
        <p>
            <label for="redirect">Redirect to:</label>
            <input type="text" id="redirect" name="redirect" size="16">
        </p>
        <p>
            <label for="myfile">File upload:</label>
            <input type="file" id="myfile" name="myfile" size="40">
        </p>
        <input type="submit" value="Press me" id="pressme" name="pressme">
    </fieldset>
</form>));
```

Next, a table is built to display the submitted form values, and the Apache::RequestRec method `$r->method()` shows what method was used:

```
# build up a table
    if (keys %$form) {

        # print the method
        $r->print("\t\t<p>method was: " . $r->method() . "</p>\n");

        # table header prior to row generation
        $table= <<'EOHEAD';
        <p>
        <table>
            <thead>
                <tr>
                    <th>Argument Name</th><th>Value</th>
                </tr>
            </thead>
```

```
            <tbody>
EOHEAD

        # use the keys of the form to print the table
        for my $key (keys %$form) {
            $table.= "\t\t\t<tr><td>$key</td><td>$form->{$key}</td></tr>\n";

        }
        $table.= "\t\t</tbody></table><p>\n";

        # print the table
        $r->print($table);
    }

    # print the rest of the document
    $r->print("\n\t</body>\n</html>");
```

The debug return message is printed to indicate that this handler is done executing. OK is returned, as required to indicate success:

```
        $r->log->debug("<-- WroxHandlers::TestResponseHandler::handler");
        return Apache2::Const::OK;

    }
    1;
```

To use this handler, you would need to add the following change to your Apache configuration file:

```
PerlPostConfigRequire /usr/local/apache2/perl-lib/startup.pl
  <Location /test>
    SetHandler perl-script
    PerlResponseHandler WroxHandlers::TestResponseHandler
</Location>
```

Then you would need to restart Apache.

With mod_perl handlers, you will need to restart the server for changes to take effect every time you make a change. This can get old fast. There is fortunately, an answer to this problem — the perl module Apache2::Restart. To use this module, set it to run as a PerlInitHandler in your Apache configuration file. It causes mod_perl to check if the handler or handlers you define to be checked using ReloadModules or ReloadAll have changed on disk. If so, it reloads that file from disk. This allows you to be able to develop mod_perl handlers without having to restart Apache every time you make a change. This will certainly help your sanity and ensure better relations among developers!

The following lines show you how you can possibly use Apache::Reload:

```
PerlModule Apache2::Reload
PerlInitHandler Apache2::Reload

PerlSetVar ReloadAll Off
PerlSetVar ReloadModules "WroxHandlers::*"
PerlSetVar ReloadDebug On
```

The handler WroxHandlers::TestReponseHandler is accessible for you at the /test URL. If example.net were the site in question, this would be http://example.net/test. If you enter values into the various fields and hit the Submit button, you should see a form such as the one shown in Figure 14-1.

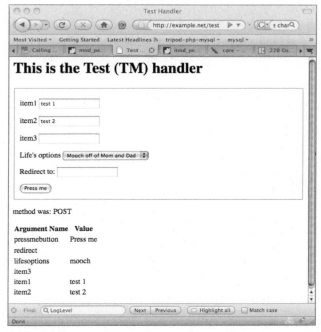

Figure 14-1

This figure shows the resulting form after a submission — the values shown in the form, which have already been submitted to show you what was submitted.

Also, if you look in your error log, you will see that the logging in the code works as well:

```
[Sat Feb 14 19:33:34 2009] [debug] TestResponseHandler.pm(32):
[client 192.168.10.3] --> WroxHandlers::TestResponseHandler::handler
[Sat Feb 14 19:33:34 2009] [debug] TestResponseHandler.pm(129):
[client 192.168.10.3] <-- WroxHandlers::TestResponseHandler::handler
```

This handler, though basic, is a good testing tool to see how mod_perl handlers work. You can extend it or use it as a skeleton for other applications.

Connection mod_perl Handlers

As stated, these are mod_perl handlers that act upon the connection of a client. The connection phase happens prior to requests being served and responded to. The two handlers for this phase are *PerlPre-ConnectionHandler* and *PerlProcessConnectionHandler*. This is the phase where you can utilize connection input filters as well as do useful things like banning abusive IP addresses.

PerlPreConnectionHandler Example

The next example shows you how you can use MySQL, memcached, and a PerlPreConnectionHandler to deny a malicious IP address at the earliest possible stage in a connection — at the connection level, before even attempting to serve a request.

This could be part of an overall system you design, which would also include a PerlResponseHandler web application to enter miscreant IP addresses, ban or unban those addresses, and to store the data in MySQL.

The following application will use the startup script in perl-lib, startup.pl, to load the full result set of a MySQL table called *banned_ips* into memcached, with each IP address stored with the IP address as the memcached key and the value of the banned value. The startup script will utilize the Perl module from the previous example in Chapter 12, WebApp.pm, since it already has the database and memcached connection in place and adding other methods to it is easy to do.

The table will be defined as:

```
CREATE TABLE banned_ips (
    id int(3) NOT NULL auto_increment,
    ip_address int(10) unsigned not null default 0;
    banned tinyint(1) default '0',
    PRIMARY KEY  (id),
    KEY ip_address (ip_address),
    KEY banned (banned)
) ENGINE=InnoDB;
```

This table will contain records that have three columns, two of which are the following:

❑   ip_address for the IP address. This will be an unsigned integer. The MySQL function inet_aton() will be used to store the string value of the IP address as an integer in this column.

❑   banned, a Boolean column that indicates whether the IP address is banned or not.

The next step is to create the handler module, which will be called *WroxHandlers::DenierHandler*, with the filename WroxHandlers/DenierHandler.pm. This handler will act upon a connection object reference to Apache2::Connection, as opposed to acting on a request object. For this handler, the two constants that are needed are the constants Apache::Const::OK and Apache::Const::FORBIDDEN. One of these will be returned. Also, this handler is using WebApp, which will provide a connection to memcached and the method for checking the IP address.

```
package WroxHandlers::DenierHandler;

use strict;
use warnings;
use Apache2::Connection ();
use Apache2::Const -compile => qw(OK FORBIDDEN);
use WebApp ();

sub handler {
    my ($c)= @_; # connection

    # instantiate WebApp
```

```
    my $webapp= new WebApp();
     # obtain the IP address
     my $ip_address= $c->remote_ip;

     # check if the IP address is allowed to connect
     if ($webapp->isDenied($ip_address)) {
         # if denied, return forbidden
         warn "The IP address $ip_address is not welcome here. SCAT!";
         return Apache2::Const::FORBIDDEN;
     }
     # otherwise, they are permitted to connect
     warn "The IP address $ip_address is welcome at this site.";
     return Apache2::Const::OK;
 }
```

The IP address is checked with the WebApp method `isDenied()`, which will return a true or false as to whether or not the IP address will be denied/banned. In order to do this, `isDenied()` checks memcached for the value stored by the IP address being checked. For this, the UDF `memc_get()` will be used along with the MySQL function `inet_aton()` to convert the IP address string value to an integer, which is how the IP address is stored in memcached.

If the value is true, the handler needs to return `$Apache::Const::DENIED`, denying the connection to the client. If the value is false, the handler will return `$Apache::Const::OK` and allow the client to connect.

To `WebApp.pm`, you would add two methods. One to cache the *banned_ips* table by select all the data and caching each in memcached by IP address:

```
=head2 cacheBannedIPs()

cache the banned_ips table

=over

=item args

$self - object reference

=back

=over

=item returns

no value

=back

=cut

sub cacheBannedIPs {
    my ($self)= @_;

    # fetch all data from banned_ips
    my $query = 'SELECT ip_address, banned FROM banned_ips';
```

```perl
        my $bref= $self->{dbh}->selectall_arrayref($query);

        # cache by IP address
        $self->{memc}->set($_->[0], $_->[1]) for @$bref;

        return;
    }
```

With just loading the data on startup, this might not be completely sufficient to ensure complete representation of the list of banned IP addresses, but the application that enters or modifies the list could update memcached as well. You get the idea!

Also, the method you called in the handler in the previous code, isDenied(), uses MySQL, through the UDF memc_get() and the function inet_aton(), to check if the IP address is stored in memcached. The reason the UDF is used here instead of the Perl memcached client is to be able to use the inet_aton() MySQL function within the UDF function memc_get() to retrieve the value stored by numeric IP address.

There are three return values from isDenied:

❑ undef if the value is not found in memcached, in which case the user is not banned.

❑ 0, if the value is found in memcached but the IP address has the banned column as false, in which case the user is not banned.

❑ 1, if the value is found in memcached and the banned column is true, in which case the user is banned and cannot connect.

```perl
=head2 isDenied()

Returns true or false whether a given IP address is banned or not.
It uses memcached to fetch the object from memcached for the
IP address value, returning the 1 or 0 that it was stored with

=over

=item args

$ip_address - the IP address being checked

=back

=over

=item returns

1 or 0, banned or not

=back

=cut

sub isDenied {
    my ($self, $ip_address)= @_;
```

```
    # set the memcached server to use
    $self->{dbh}->do("select memc_servers_set('127.0.0.1:11211')");

    # obtain the value from memcached, using inet_aton to convert to int
    my $sth = $self->{dbh}->prepare("select memc_get(inet_aton(?))");

    $sth->execute($ip_address);

    my $ip_ref= $sth->fetchrow_arrayref();

    return($ip_ref->[0]);
}
```

Next, you would set the PerlPreConnectionHandler to this handler in your Apache configuration file:

```
PerlPreConnectionHandler WroxHandlers::DenierHandler
```

The other piece required for this handler to function properly is the means to load memcached with the list of banned IP addresses from MySQL. This is done with the startup perl script (set with PerlRequire in your Apache configuration file) startup.pl. This will instantiate the WebApp class (as was shown when explaining ModPerl::Registry) and call cachedBannedIPs(). startup.pl (or <Perl> section) would then be seen as:

```
use lib qw(/usr/local/apache2/perl-lib);
use WebApp;

use strict;
use warnings;

my $webapp= new WebApp();

$webapp->getUsers();

$webapp->cacheBannedIPs();


1;
```

This calls cacheBannedIPs(), which simply selects all rows out of *banned_ips* and stores each one, by IP address, into memcached upon Apache startup.

To test, you can add an entry into the *banned_ips* table to ban the IP of your choice (use yours for testing!). Notice that you must use the MySQL function inet_aton() to properly set the numeric value of the IP address.

```
insert into banned_ips (ip_address, banned) values (inet_aton('192.168.1.123'), 1);
```

Finally, you must restart Apache.

Now, when a banned client attempts to connect to your site, they will see the unwelcoming message shown in Figure 14-2.

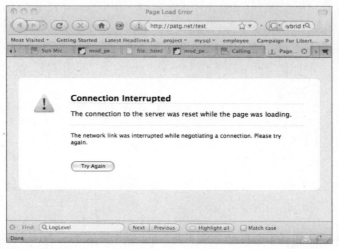

Figure 14-2

The beauty of this is that you get to ban a malicious IP before you spend any more CPU cycles serving a request. This demonstrates the power of mod_perl and how you have access to the Apache life cycle using the Perl programming language, as well as using MySQL and memcached together to provide the cached banned IP data.

Finally, before moving on to other sections, one thing you might want to do is un-ban your IP address!

```
update banned_ips set banned = 0 where ip_address = inet_aton('192.168.1.123');
```

Other HTTP Request Cycle Phase Handlers

You saw above the use of a `PerlResponseHandler` mod_perl handler to serve up a simple form application. This is the most common phase in the HTTP Request Cycle where you would implement mod_perl handlers. However, there is much more to the HTTP request cycle phase in terms of the functionality you can implement with mod_perl handlers.

There are 12 phases of the HTTP request cycle loop to chose from in which to implement a mod_perl handler. The previous section explained what each of those phases does and gave you a sense of what you can implement in each of those phases. This section will make manifest some practical examples that give you a better sense of what having access to all these phases means.

PerlAccessHandler Example

You just saw how to ban a client IP address at the connection level. The next three mod_perl handlers will deal with the access, authentication, and authorization phases. The first of which will take the `PerlPreConnectionHandler` example, `DenierHandler.pm`, and modify it somewhat to work as a `PerlAccessHandler` handler.

The easiest way to do this is to copy over `DenierHandler.pm` to a new filename called `AccessTestHandler.pm`.

The first thing to do would be to rename the package:

```
package WroxHandlers::AccessTestHandler;
```

All the various module imports will remain the same, but you will add the constant `Apache2::Const::LOG_INFO` for printing `[info]` to the error log for a successful access:

```
use strict;
use warnings;
use Apache2::Connection;
use Apache2::RequestRec;
use Apache2::Const -compile => qw(OK FORBIDDEN LOG_INFO);
use WebApp;
```

Handlers for the HTTP request cycle phase take a request record object (instead of a connection record object, as was used in the `PerlPreConnectionHandler` example), so simply change $c to $r, and then obtain $c from $r->connection, which is a connection record. The rest of the code will simply work!

```
sub handler {
    my ($r) = @_; # connection

    # obtain connection from request object
    my $c= $r->connection;

    # obtain the IP address
    my $ip_address= $c->remote_ip;

    # get a webapp object
    my $webapp= new WebApp();

    # check if the IP address is allowed to connect
    if ($webapp->isDenied($ip_address)) {
        # if denied, return forbidden
        $r->server->warn("The IP address $ip_address is not welcome here. SCAT!");
        return Apache2::Const::FORBIDDEN;
    }
```

The only other change to mention here is that the code will use `LOG_INFO` log level to print `[info]` to the error log when the login is successful.

```
    # otherwise, they are permitted to connect
    $r->server->loglevel(LOG_INFO);

    $r->log->info("The IP address $ip_address is welcome at this site.");
    return Apache2::Const::OK;
}
```

Also, change your Apache configuration file. Make sure to comment out the `PerlPreConnectionHandler` directive if you want to test that this bans a banned IP address, otherwise the `PerlPreConnection Handler` will deny the IP address before your `PerlAccessHandler` has a chance to deny it!

```
#PerlPreConnectionHandler WroxHandlers::DenierHandler
```

Then add this:

```
PerlPostConfigRequire /etc/apache2/perl-lib/startup.pl

  <Location /test>

    PerlAccessHandler WroxHandlers::AccessTestHandler

    SetHandler perl-script
    PerlResponseHandler WroxHandlers::TestResponseHandler

  </Location>
```

Also remember that `PerlAccessHandler` is per `<Directory>` or `<Location>`, which is different than how `PerlPreConnectionHandler` was for the entire server, so it will only be applied to the /test URL in this example.

You already have the caching of banned IP addresses happening with your changes to `startup.pl` from the previous example of the `PerlPreConnectionHandler`, so that part is already taken care of. All you have to do now is set the IP address you want to test to being banned:

```
update banned_ips set banned = 1 where ip_address = inet_aton('192.168.1.123')
```

Then restart Apache!

When you access the URL `http://example.net/test` (whatever your domain is), you see a page like the one shown in Figure 14-3.

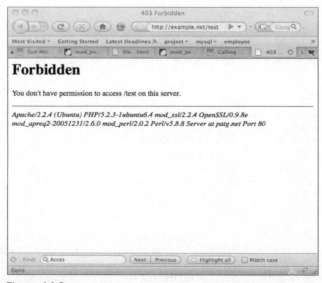

Figure 14-3

PerlAuthenHandler Example

Another good handler example is one that implements authentication using a mod_perl handler. Not only that, but using a mod_perl handler that uses both MySQL and memcached for the source of data to verify authentication.

The following example, `WroxHandlers::AuthenTestHandler`, will use basic authentication to verify user-supplied credentials that are stored in both memcached and MySQL. The handler will, of course, attempt to check memcached first, and then MySQL. If neither sources have the user stored, then authentication will return unauthorized, denying the user from the protected resource. Again, the WebApp class will be used to provide the database and memcached connection.

The user database table is the same as the *users* table as shown for the `app.pl` CGI application, except with a `password` column added:

```
alter table users add (password char(32) NOT NULL default '');
```

A `UNIQUE` index on `username` and `password` should also be added. You would first need to drop the existing index on `username`:

```
alter table users drop index username;
alter table add unique index username (username, password);
```

The table definition ends up being:

```
CREATE TABLE users (
    uid int(8) NOT NULL auto_increment,
    username varchar(16) NOT NULL default '',
    firstname varchar(32) NOT NULL default '',
    surname varchar(32) NOT NULL,
    email varchar(32) NOT NULL default '',
    phone varchar(16) NOT NULL default '',
    state varchar(3) NOT NULL default '',
    address varchar(255) NOT NULL default '',
    city varchar(24) NOT NULL default '',
    password char(32) NOT NULL default '',
    PRIMARY KEY  (uid),
        UNIQUE KEY username (username,password),
        UNIQUE KEY email (email)
) ENGINE=InnoDB;
```

If you already had an existing user, you would simply update that user to now have a password. In this example, this will be the user with the `uid` of 5:

```
update users set password = md5('foo') where uid = 5;
```

Or, insert a new user:

```
Insert into users (username, firstname, surname, email, password)
values ('someuser', 'Test', 'User', 'user@example.com', md5('s3kr1t'));
```

Additionally, for extra credit, you can modify the contact list application to have a password field with minimal effort and have means to update these contacts/users!

The password is a hexidecimal representation of the MD5 digest of the password the user enters when being authenticated, as well as when he or she sets his or her password in whatever application manages the account. The method of looking up the user in memcached is to store the user's *uid* value using the key `username-md5password`. The method of looking up the user in MySQL is to look up the user by username and password. The application must supply a MD5 hex value of the password in the lookup.

```
package WroxHandlers::AuthTestHandler;

use strict;
use warnings;

use Apache2::Access;
use Apache2::RequestUtil;
use Apache2::Const -compile => qw(OK DECLINED HTTP_UNAUTHORIZED LOG_INFO);
```

In this example, `WebApp.pm` will again provide connectivity to memcached and MySQL. Additionally, the constant `Apache2::Const::HTTP_UNAUTHORIZED` will be required. Also, the constant `Apache2::Const::LOG_INFO` will be used to demonstrate using the info logging level.

```
use Digest::MD5 qw(md5_hex);
use WebApp;

#
# AuthTestHandler will authenticate a user using memcached and MySQL. It will
# attempt to find the user in memcached, if not, then in MySQL. If not found,
# authentication for the user will fail and they will not have access to the
# restricted resource.
#
sub handler {
    my ($r)= @_;
```

The method `$r->get_basic_auth_pw` returns the status and password, unencrypted, from the user-supplied credentials. If the status was anything other than OK, then that status is returned. Next, the `$username` is set to the value of the user id with `$r->user`.

```
    # get the password from the request headers
    my ($status, $password)= $r->get_basic_auth_pw;

    # return if $status not OK
    $status == Apache2::Const::OK or return $status;
    # instantiate a WebApp
    my $webapp= new WebApp();

    # obtain the username
    my $username= $r->user;
```

Now that the `$username` and `$password` values are set, they can be checked with `isAuthorized()`, which returns 1 (true) or 0 (false). If the return value from `isAuthorized()` is true, then a log message of the appropriate level of info is printed to the Apache error log, and then OK is returned, resulting in the user being authenticated and allowed to access the protected resource. If the returned value is false, then the user is not authorized and the constant `Apache2::Const::HTTP_UNAUTHORIZED` is returned.

```
    # check if the user is authentcated, if so, return OK
    if ($webapp->isAuthenticated($username, $password)) {

        $r->server->loglevel(Apache2::Const::LOG_INFO);
        $r->log->info("User $username is authenticated");
        return Apache2::Const::OK;
    }
```

The method $r->note_basic_auth_failure sets up the client headers so the client will know how to authenticate itself the next time.

```
    # default is to return un-authenticated
    $r->note_basic_auth_failure;
    $r->server->warn("User $username is not authenticated");
    return Apache2::Const::HTTP_UNAUTHORIZED;


}
```

The WebApp method isAuthenticated() has a simple interface where a $username and $password are supplied. If the username and password are found, it will return a 1 or 0. The first attempt to find the user entry (which is the uid value in memcached) is using a key derived from concatenating the username with a hyphen and the MD5 password and is made against memcached. If this is found in memcached, 1 (true) is returned immediately before even attempting to connect to MySQL. If this is not found in memcached, an attempt is made to check in MySQL. If the information is found in MySQL, then 1 (true) is returned. If the user cannot be found, a 0 is returned. This 0 means the user will not be authenticated.

Digest::MD5 will have to be used to obtain the hexadecimal representation of the MD5 digest using md5_hex. So, to the top of WebApp.pm, add:

```
    use Digest::MD5 qw(md5_hex);
```

Then implement isAuthenticated() like so:

```
    =head2 isAuthenticated

    A method used to check if the user and password are in the database,
    as supplied when prompted when accessing an <Location> or <Directory>
    that requires it using md5 digest

    =over

    =item Arguments

    $self - object reference

    $username - username supplied at prompt

    $password - password, in non-md5 form, from prompt

    =back
```

```
=over

=item Returns

The UID value or undef

=cut

sub isAuthenticated {
    my ($self, $username, $password)= @_;

    # create a hex password using md5_hex, which is how the password is stored
    my $digest = md5_hex($password);

    # create a memcached key by username and hex password
    my $memc_key= $username . '-' . $digest;
    my $uid= $self->{memc}->get($memc_key);
    return($uid) if $uid;

    # user and password must match
    my $query= 'SELECT uid FROM users WHERE username = ? AND password = ?';

    my $resref= $self->{dbh}->selectrow_arrayref($query,
                                                 {},
                                                 ($username, $digest));
    # return uid or undef
    return $resref->[0];
}
```

Another requirement for this to function properly is to ensure memcached is preloaded with the users is to add caching of users from the *users* table using the `startup.pl` script or `<Perl>` section in your Apache configuration file. For the previous example, this now appears as:

```
!/usr/bin/perl

use lib qw(/usr/local/apache2/perl-lib);
use WebApp;

my $webapp= new WebApp();

$webapp->getUsers();

$webapp->cacheBannedIPs();

$webapp->cacheUsersByMD5();

1;
```

Since passwords are already MD5-hexed, there is no need to do anything other than select all records from users, keyed in memcached by `username-MD5`.

To use this module, you need to add the handler directive to your Apache configuration. Since this directive is of type DIR, you will add it within a `<Directory>` or `<Location>` sectional directive. For this example it will be added to the `<Location>` of the test response handler:

```
<Location /test>

    PerlAccessHandler WroxHandlers::AccessTestHandler

    PerlAuthenHandler WroxHandlers::AuthTestHandler
    AuthType Basic
    AuthName TestAuth
    require valid-user

    SetHandler perl-script
    PerlResponseHandler WroxHandlers::TestResponseHandler

</Location>
```

Once you restart Apache and try to access the URL, you will find you need to supply the credentials for whatever user you created or updated with a new password. If everything works correctly, and you authenticate correctly, you will see in your Apache error log:

```
[Sat Feb 14 22:57:15 2009] [info] [client 192.168.1.1] User someuser
is authenticated
```

PerlAuthzHandler Example

Now that you have a working example of a PerlAuthenHandler example, you can easily use much of that code to implement a `PerlAuthzHandler`. This is a handler that would check the user id after the user has made it past the authentication phase, and apply yet one more layer of credential checking to the access control.

In this example, a handler named *WroxHandlers::AuthZTestHandler* will check memcached and MySQL for a user's admin status. If the user has the admin parameter set, then they will be granted access.

First of all, you will need to add yet another column to the *users table*, admin, which will be a simple Boolean true or false value:

```
alter table users add (admin tinyint(1) NOT NULL DEFAULT 0);
```

You can then set the appropriate value of admin for the users you want to give admin privileges to:

```
update users set admin = 1 where uid = 3;
```

You can basically copy over `AuthenTestHandler.pm` to `AuthZTestHandler.pm` and rename the package. You can use the same imports that you used in the last example as well.

```
package WroxHandlers::AuthZTestHandler;

use strict;
use warnings;

use Apache2::Access;
use Apache2::RequestUtil;
```

```
use Apache2::Const -compile => qw(OK HTTP_UNAUTHORIZED LOG_INFO);

use WebApp;
```

`AuthZTestHandler` only has to check the username since the user and password have already been authenticated at this point. A WebApp object reference will be instantiated and will establish the connection to both MySQL and memcached. Next, simply pass the username to `$webapp->isAdmin()`, which will return a 1 or 0, depending on whether the user is an admin or not:

```
#
# AuthZTestHandler will authorize a user using memcached and MySQL. It will
# attempt to find the user in memcached, if not, then in MySQL. If found,
# it will check if the user 'admin' attribute is 1 or 0. If 1, then the
# user is authorized. If 0 or if not found, authorization for the user will fail
# and they will not have access to the restricted resource.
#
sub handler {
    my ($r)= @_;

    # obtain the username
    my $username= $r->user;

    my $webapp= new WebApp();
```

If a 1 (or true) is returned, then that user is authorized, otherwise he or she is not and the constant `Apache2::Const::HTTP_UNAUTHORIZED` is returned, just as in the previous `PerlAuthenHandler` example.

```
    # check if the user is authorized, if so, return OK
    if ($webapp->isAdmin($username)) {
        $r->server->loglevel(LOG_INFO);
        $r->log->info("User $username is authorized");
        return Apache2::Const::OK;
    }

    # default is to return unauthorized
    $r->note_basic_auth_failure;

    $r->server->warn("User $username is not authorized");
    return Apache2::Const::HTTP_UNAUTHORIZED;

}

1;
```

The `isAdmin()` method is added to `WebApp.pm`. It uses `getUser()` to obtain the `$user` hash reference that contains all the user attributes for the user specified by `$username`, including the admin attribute. If the user is found *and* that user has the admin attribute set to 1, then 1 is returned, and the user is an admin user. Otherwise, 0 is returned, and the user is not an admin user.

```
=head2 isAdmin()

This method returns 1 or 0, representing if the user is
an admin user or not
```

```
=over

=item args

$self - instantiated object ref to itself

$username - the username to check

=back

=over

=item returns

1 - is admin

0 - is not admin

=back

=cut

sub isAdmin {
    my ($self, $username)= @_;
    my $user= $self->getUser({username => $username});
    return defined $user ? $user->{admin} : 0;
}
```

Next, add the PerlAuthZHandler directive for WroxHandlers::AuthZTestHandler to your Apache configuration file:

```
<Location /test>

    PerlAccessHandler WroxHandlers::AccessTestHandler

    PerlAuthenHandler WroxHandlers::AuthTestHandler

    PerlAuthzHandler WroxHandlers::AuthZTestHandler

    AuthType Basic
    AuthName TestAuth
    require valid-user

    SetHandler perl-script
    PerlResponseHandler WroxHandlers::TestResponseHandler

</Location>
```

The final piece to this has already been taken care of. startup.pl called getUsers() upon startup, caching all the users and ensuring that the user will be retrieved from memcached as often as possible, with as few cache misses as possible. So, after the previous examples, it now appears as:

```
#!/usr/bin/perl
```

```
use lib qw(/etc/apache2/perl-lib);
use WebApp;

my $webapp= new WebApp();

$webapp->getUsers();

$webapp->cacheBannedIPs();

$webapp->cacheUsersByMD5();

1;
```

Restart Apache, clear your authenticated sessions (depending on the web browser you use), and attempt to log in. Just as before, you will be presented with a login panel. Upon a successful login, you will see the following in your Apache error log:

```
[Sun Feb 15 10:16:55 2009] [info] [client 192.168.3.4] User someuser is authenticated
[Sun Feb 15 10:16:55 2009] [info] [client 192.168.3.4] User someuser is authorized
```

You can see that both the authentication and authorization phases are being served by mod_perl handlers.

PerlLogHandler Example

The logging HTTP request cycle phase is also another phase of interest for implementing mod_perl handlers. There are a few Apache modules that can log to a database (such as mod_log_mysql). But it's worth seeing just how you can alter the logging phase to log things however you want with a mod_perl handler.

This next example will show how you can set up logging to log to the <Location> where you have implemented the other handlers.

1. The first thing to do is define a MySQL table for logging to. In this example, the weblog table will be created. It will use the archive storage engine, which is used in many cases for storing logs and data warehousing:

    ```
    CREATE TABLE weblog (
        created timestamp,
        uri varchar(32) not null default '',
        hostname varchar(32) not null default '',
        ip_address int(10) unsigned NOT NULL default '0',
        method  varchar(5) not null default '',
        userid varchar(16) not null default '',
        useragent varchar(64) not null default '',
        filename varchar(64) not null default '',
        last_modified  datetime,
        status varchar(16) not null default ''
        ) ENGINE=archive;
    ```

This handler will be called `WroxHandlers::LogTestHandler`. This will resemble the other handlers in that it also accepts the `$r Apache2::RequestRec` object. First, it will define a hash reference called `$logref`, which will have various attributes that will be logged to MySQL. The hash reference is then simply passed to `$webapp->weblog()`. The return value is OK:

```
package WroxHandlers::LogTestHandler;

use strict;
use warnings;

use Apache2::RequestRec;
use Apache2::Connection;
use Apache2::Const -compile => qw(OK);
use Data::Dumper;

use WebApp;

#
# LogTestHandler will log various request parameters to a MySQL
# database table using the WebApp method weblog()
#
sub handler {
    my ($r) = @_;
    my $webapp = new WebApp();

    # obtain the username
    my $logref = {
        uri             => $r->uri,
        hostname        => $r->hostname,
        ip_address      => $r->connection->remote_ip,
        method          => $r->method,
        userid          => $r->user,
        useragent       => $r->headers_in->{'User-Agent'},
        filename        => $r->filename,
        last_modified   => $r->mtime,
        status          => $r->status,
    };

    $webapp->weblog($logref);

    return Apache2::Const::OK;
}

1;
```

2. The method `weblog()` is added to WebApp. This method will take the second argument `$logref`, which it will then use to construct an SQL INSERT statement to insert the log contents.

```
=head2 weblog()

A method that is used to log apache log entries to MySQL
```

```
=over

=item Args

$self              - object reference

$logref            - a hash reference containing the following:

=over

uri                - the URI of the request

hostname           - the hostname of the client

ip_address         - the ip address of the client

method             - the request method

user               - the user id of the client, if set

filename           - the mapped filename of the URI

useragent          - the user-agent value

last_modifed       - last modification date of the resource

status             - status of response

=back

=back

=over

=item Returns

1 for inserted, 0 for not

=back

=cut

sub weblog {
    my ($self,$logref)= @_;
```

3. An array, @logfields, is created to use as a map to ensure order when building up both the fields, placeholders, and bind variables inevitably passed to DBI execute(). It might even make sense to make this a class variable, depending on whether you want to have access outside this method to the list of fields.

```
#
# $logfields is used from the mapping of field value in query
# generation and bind values to placeholder
#
```

```
my @logfields =    qw(
                      uri
                      hostname
                      ip_address
                      method
                      userid
                      useragent
                      filename
                      status
                      last_modified
                      );

my $insert = 'INSERT INTO weblog (';
```

4. Build up the fields:

```
# build up the fields list
$insert .= join(',',@logfields);
$insert .= ') VALUES (';
```

5. Build the values (placeholders) — it's important to note the following about the last two fields: ip_address and last_modified:

❏   ip_address is an IP address string value that needs to be converted to an integer using the MySQL function inet_aton(), so the mapping that creates a comma-separated string of placeholders must stop at two less than the number of elements to let the value ' inet_aton(?) , ' to be appended to the insert statement string.

❏   The value for last_modified is in epoch time and needs to be converted to a regular date-time value using the MySQL function from_unixtime(), which will be appended as ' from_unixtime(?) ' to the insert statement string:

```
#
# build up the placeholders
# using -2 because inet_aton and from_unixtime need to be used
#
$insert .= '?,' x (scalar @logfields - 2);
$insert .= ' inet_aton(?), ';
$insert .= ' from_unixtime(?) )';

my $sth= $self->{dbh}->prepare($insert);
```

6. Next, execute the INSERT statement. Pass the bind values by using a hash slice. @logfields provides the mapping of $logref members to obtain the values of the $logref in the correct order, cast as an array, which is what the DBI execute() expects. This will insert the row into MySQL:

```
#
# use a hash slice to pass the bind variables- the values of
# $logfields ensures order of placeholders and their values
#
```

```
        my $inserted = $sth->execute(@{$logref}{@$logfields});

        return $sth->rows();

    }
```

7. Next, add to your Apache configuration file the `PerlAccessHandler` directive:

```
<Location /test>

    PerlAccessHandler WroxHandlers::AccessTestHandler

    PerlAuthenHandler WroxHandlers::AuthTestHandler

    PerlAuthzHandler WroxHandlers::AuthZTestHandler

    AuthType Basic
    AuthName TestAuth
    require valid-user

    SetHandler perl-script
    PerlResponseHandler WroxHandlers::TestResponseHandler

    PerlLogHandler WroxHandlers::LogTestHandler

</Location>
```

You'll soon realize you have infiltrated the HTTP request phase cycle with mod_perl handlers doing your bidding! Now you must restart Apache.

If you want to have all logging for the entire site use this handler, just specify this with the following in your Apache configuration file:

```
<Location />
...
PerlLogHandler WroxHandlers::LogTestHandler

</Location>
```

Now, after accessing the URL `http://example.net/test` with three different browsers, you will see that there are now rows in the database for those accesses. You now have log messages being stored to MySQL for this URL, which will allow you perform data analysis of web site accesses using MySQL, and you won't have to crunch through text logs.

```
mysql> select created,uri,hostname,inet_ntoa(ip_address),
    -> method,userid,useragent,last_modified,status from weblog;\G
*************************** 1. row ***************************
       created: 2009-02-15 12:54:28
           uri: /test
      hostname: example.net
    ip_address: 192.168.1.1
        method: GET
```

```
          userid: sam
       useragent: Mozilla/4.0 (compatible; MSIE 5.23; Mac_PowerPC)
        filename: /usr/local/apache2/sites/default/test
   last_modified: 1969-12-31 19:00:00
          status: 401
*************************** 2. row ***************************
         created: 2009-02-15 12:54:33
             uri: /test
        hostname: example.net
      ip_address: 192.168.1.44
          method: GET
          userid: CaptTofu
       useragent: Mozilla/5.0 (Macintosh; U; Intel Mac OS X 10.5; en-US; rv:1.9.0.
        filename: /usr/local/apache2/sites/default/test
   last_modified: 2009-02-14 12:44:39
          status: 200
*************************** 3. row ***************************
         created: 2009-02-15 12:54:39
             uri: /test
        hostname: www.example.net
      ip_address: 192.168.1.203
          method: GET
          userid: wes
       useragent: Mozilla/5.0 (Macintosh; U; Intel Mac OS X 10_5_4; en-us) AppleWe
        filename: /usr/local/apache2/sites/default/test
   last_modified: 2009-02-14 12:44:39
          status: 200
```

Perl Filter Handler Example

Filters are altogether different from anything you might have come across previously. They are applied to either the input of the connection or request, or the output of the connection or request. They are applied to data chunks known as *buckets*. Filters work on the principle of *bucket brigades*, which are groupings of sequential buckets of data that the filter processes one at a time until all the data in the document or other content has been processed. This is then indicated by an EOS (end of stream) brigade.

It takes a little bit of thinking to figure out how you might want to use a filter. It's not a response handler. It is a filter. It *filters* content, as opposed to producing content as a response handler does. It filters the content of whatever you set it up to filter in your Apache configuration file, such as HTML. It can even be set to trigger something such as PHP being run. Of interest, the following code shows how you could use a filter to execute PHP (yes, this is a Perl book, I know):

```
<Location />
 AddInputFilter PHP .php
 Allow from 127.0.0.2
 </Location>
```

This would, of course, cause files ending in .php to be filtered by the PHP filter. If you think about it, this makes sense because with PHP the code is embedded in the document that is then parsed or filtered, then interpreted based on what tags are found in the document. This makes PHP an ideal candidate for filtering.

Filters are a topic that is worthy of a book in and of itself, so this section won't attempt to try to make you an expert with filters. However, it will give you a simple idea of what you can accomplish with filters.

The following section will show a mod_perl filter handler example. It's a very simple, and maybe not entirely practical, filter that filters HTML documents, uppercasing HTML tags using regular expressions for those who like their HTML that way. (Of course XML requires it be lowercase, but that's yet another topic.) The idea here is to show a simple implementation of a filter — you can always build on the idea!

This is an output filter, using the simple streaming interface, without attempting to shuffle, slice, and dice bucket brigades, an activity which would be best suited for a gray, rainy Sunday afternoon.

It also ensures that the word *mysql* is properly formatted to *MySQL*, and *sql* is changed to *SQL*. Furthermore, it prepends the DTD (document type definition) to the HTML document.

This filter is called, interestingly enough, TestFilter:

```
package WroxHandlers::TestFilter;

use strict;
use warnings;

use Apache2::Filter;

use Apache2::RequestRec;
use APR::Table;
use Apache2::Const -compile => qw(OK);
use constant BUFFER_LENGTH => 1024;
```

The only argument to this filter is $f, an Apache2::Filter object reference, which is a Perl object reference that provides you with access to the Apache ap_filter_t structure, a C data structure containing information for a filter chain. This provides you with access to filter methods and attributes, including references to the Apache2::RequestRec and Apache2::Server objects. You can run perldoc Apache2::Filter for more information.

```
#
# LogTestHandler will log various request parameters to a MySQL
# database table using the WebApp method weblog()
#
sub handler {
    my ($f)= @_;
```

This is the filter initialization part of the code. It is run once for each request. This is where you implement code that you want to run at the beginning of the filter execution. You can use this as a point where you return the constant Apache2::Const:DECLINED if, for instance, the filter is turned off.

```
    unless($f->ctx) {

        # obtain the value for ApplyFilter
        my $apply_filter= $f->r->dir_config->get('ApplyFilter');

        # if ApplyFilter is Off, return DECLINED so filter is not applied
```

```
        return Apache2::Const::DECLINED
            unless defined $apply_filter && $apply_filter eq 'On';

        $f->r->server->warn('filter start.');

    $f->r->headers_out->unset('Content-Length');

        # a DTD at the beginning of the document
        my $doctype=
        '<!DOCTYPE HTML PUBLIC "-//W3C//DTD HTML 4.01  Transitional//EN">';
        $f->print($doctype);
        $f->print("\n");
        $f->ctx(1);
    }
```

Apply the regular expressions to uppercase HTML tags. This makes <BR> tags conform to HTML 4.01 as well as ensure that instances of the term *mysql* are changed to *MySQL* in the following code, for each chunk of the document until EOS (end of stream):

```
    while ($f->read(my $buffer, BUFFER_LENGTH)) {
        $f->r->server->warn('filter read.');
        $buffer =~ s/<([\w^\s]+)>/<\U$1>/g;
        $buffer =~ s/<\/(\w+)>/<\/\U$1>/g;
        $buffer =~ s/<([\w^\s]+)\s/<\U$1 /g;
        $buffer =~ s/\s([\w]+=)/ \U$1/g;
        $buffer =~ s/<BR>/<BR \/>/gi;
        $buffer =~ s/mysql/MySQL/gi;
        $buffer =~ s/sql/SQL/gi;

        $f->print($buffer);
    }
```

This happens on the last bucket brigade, known as an EOS (end of stream) brigade:

```
    if ($f->seen_eos) {
        $f->r->server->warn('filter end.');
        $f->print('<!-- END OF DOCUMENT -->');
    }

    return Apache2::Const::OK;
}
1;
```

The settings that are required for your Apache configuration file to activate this filter are both to set a variable with `PerlSetVar` for `ApplyFilter` as well as to have the filter process all HTML documents with either the `.html` or the `.htm` extension.

```
PerlSetVar ApplyFilter On
<FilesMatch "\.htm*">

    PerlOutputFilterHandler WroxHandlers::TestFilter

</FilesMatch>
```

So, to test this filter, create an HTML file. For instance, the file containing the following:

```
<html>
  <head><title>This is a test</title></head>
  <body>
    <h1>This is a test</h1>
    <p><a href="http://mysql.com">mysql</a></p>
    <p>I use sql all the time</p>
  </body>

</html>
```

... will be filtered to have the following output:

```
<!DOCTYPE HTML PUBLIC "-//W3C//DTD HTML 4.01 Transitional//EN">
<HTML>
  <HEAD><TITLE>This is a test</TITLE></HEAD>
  <BODY>
    <H1>This is a test</H1>
    <P><A HREF="http://MySQL.com">MySQL</A></P>
    <P>I use SQL all the time</P>
  </BODY>

</HTML>
<!-- END OF DOCUMENT -->
```

So, what you can do with filters is limited only by your imagination. The Apache documentation contains many snippets of code as well as extensive information on filters.

Summary

This chapter showed how you can use mod_perl handlers at various phases of the Apache server life cycle and the HTTP request phase cycle. The handlers shown were:

❑   PerlResponseHandler — WroxHandlers::TestResponseHandler. This is a response phase mod_perl handler that presented the user with a form that he or she can submit. You saw how to process form inputs and log messages to the error log at different levels.

❑   PerlPreConnectionHandler — WroxHandlers::DenierHandler: A preconnection connection handler that uses the WebApp module to obtain information from memcached to determine if an IP address was banned or not. If the IP address is banned, it blocks the IP address at the connection level, long before a request would be read.

❑   A PerlAccessHandler — WroxHandlers::AccessTestHandler. This handler is an access request cycle phase handler that uses essentially the same code as WroxHandlers::DenierHandler, which uses the WebApp module to obtain information from memcached to determine whether an IP address is banned or not. If the IP address is banned, it denies access to the IP address for the <Location> tag specified (/test) within the response phase cycle.

❑   PerlAuthenHandler — WroxHandlers::AuthTestHandler. This handler uses the WebApp module to determine if credentials supplied by the user match those in memcached, or MySQL if not cached for the specified <Location>. If the user credentials match, authentication is passed, allowing access. If the user is not authenticated, he or she is not permitted to access the directory specified by the `<Location>` tag in the Apache configuration file.

❑ A PerlAuthzHandler — WroxHandlers::AuthZTestHandler. This handler uses the WebApp module to determine if a user is an admin user for the specified `<Location>`. This is determined by looking in memcached if cached, or in MySQL for an admin flag for that user. If the user has the admin flag, authorization is granted. If not, he or she is denied.

❑ PerlLogHandler — WroxHandlers::LogTestHandler. This handler uses the WebApp module to log Apache requests for the specified `<Location>` to a MySQL database.

❑ PerlOutputFilterHandler — WroxHandlers::TestFilter. This handler is used to filter HTML files to have uppercase tag names and to make instances of the term *"mysql"* always be printed as *MySQL*.

Having seen some practical examples of just how much functionality you have with mod_perl, you should now have a better appreciation of how it can be used to extend Apache's overall functionality and be used for much more than content generation for the HTTP response. The HTTP life cycle response phase.

15

More mod_perl

In Chapter 14, you saw just how versatile mod_perl handlers are and how they can be used within the various phases of the server life cycle as well as HTTP request phase cycle. Most often, you will be most concerned with developing applications for the HTTP response phase. This chapter focuses on providing examples for this phase.

mod_perl Handlers or ModPerl::Registry?

You saw in Chapter 14 how to easily use ModPerl::Registry to convert the contact list CGI application to mod_perl application. In most cases, if you have a lot of code written as a ModPerl::Registry program, this should suffice for what you want to do. ModPerl::Registry essentially turns your script into a mod_perl handler, though it's worth considering the steps that that ModPerl::Registry has to perform. These steps include the following:

❏   Create a namespace derived from the filename.

❏   Check if the script should be compiled, depending on whether it is in the cache, as well as whether it was modified. If there is no need for it to be compiled, skip to execution.

❏   If it is not in cache, a check is made to determine if the script was allowed to be executed and can be compiled (if `Options ExecCGI` is set, which is the Apache configuration file for the directory the script is in).

❏   The process changes its current working directory from the server root directory to the directory where the script exists.

❏   Read in the script, stripping various components, including the options in the shebang `#!/usr/bin/perl` line of the script, as well as the code body.

❏   Generate a Perl package name based on the URI of the script

❑ Compile the code read by eval (as an expression), cache, and set a timestamp on this compiled code.

❑ The process changes its current working directory from the directory where script exists back to the server root directory.

❑ Execute the handler code.

    ❑ Change to the directory of the script.

    ❑ Check to see if the %INC hash needs to be changed.

    ❑ Set return code to Apache::Const::OK.

    ❑ eval the compiled code as a block { ...code...}.

    ❑ Checks for any errors; if any, set return code to the error.

❑ Flush the namespace

❑ Return to the server root directory

❑ Just as any mod_perl does, return the return code. This would be Apache::Const::OK if there were no errors.

With today's hardware capabilities, this complex process isn't so much an issue as it once was. However, these steps do translate into CPU cycles. So why not cut out any steps that negatively affect performance?

There are several benefits to using ModPerl::Registry scripts:

❑ You can make changes to your program and not have to restart the server.

❑ The Apache configuration file can be set up so that regular non-root users don't need access to the Apache server configuration file to run their applications. If ModPerl::Registry is set up for regular users to run, they can run their Perl web applications in the same manner that PHP developers can easily write applications that don't require modifying the Apache configuration. This can be a boon to encouraging development of Perl applications that are easy to install, just like the various PHP applications that exist.

❑ Depending on how the ModPerl::Registry scripts are coded, you can run them on the command line, which could be used to generate static content (Slashdot) or for testing.

So, what do you choose to use? Ultimately, you go with whatever works for your development organization. You would certainly want to run tests for your hardware and compare both mod_perl handlers and ModPerl::Registry scripts.

For this and the next chapter, the examples will be mod_perl handlers. The same code could work with ModPerl::Registry.

Using ModPerl::RegistryLoader

You can use ModPerl::RegistryLoader to preload your Apache Registry scripts. Doing so can help with performance in that it eliminates the step of compilation for every Apache child process. The parent process runs the compilation of the Perl code, to which each child is given a copy. When the script is initially accessed, it will be ready for execution.

In your startup.pl or <Perl> sections, you would have, for instance:

```
use ModPerl::RegistryLoader;

my $registry= ModPerl::RegistryLoader->new(package=> 'ModPerl::Registry');

$registry->handler('/perl/app.pl', '/var/www/apache2-default/perl/app.pl');
$registry->handler('/perl/contact.pl', '/var/www/apache2-default/perl/contact.pl');
$registry->handler('/perl/bench.pl', '/var/www/apache2-default/perl/bench.pl');
$registry->handler('/perl/user.pl', '/var/www/apache2-default/perl/user.pl');
```

. . . for each script you want to have precompiled.

Converting a ModPerl::Registry Script to a mod_perl Handler

Now you're familiar with the contact list application. This is a simple application that could be used to store contacts or manager users. It's simple enough, but it could be extended to be more specific:

❑   The main idea is to show you how to write an application that stores, lists, and provides a means to edit data.

❑   The other purpose is to show you how you can use memcached to reduce the number of database accesses. This next section will show you how easy it is to convert the contact list application to a mod_perl handler.

You already know from the previous chapter that by default, a mod_perl handler has the subroutine handler() as the entry point to the program. You can, however, have any subroutine name you want. For contact.pl, the subroutine main() was used as the top-level call. For this chapter's example code, the top-level call won't be changed.

For a mod_perl handler, the code is implemented in a package file with a .pm extension. So, for a start, you could copy contact.pl into a directory containing your mod_perl handler code. In this example, the handlers are stored in the apache root (/usr/local/apache2) under perl-lib/WroxHandlers. For this example, the handler name will be ContactHandler, so the filename would be ContactHandler.pm, which is the file you would copy contact.pl to.

The next thing to do would be to decide what URL you want the handler to respond as. For this example, http://example.com/contact is what will be used. The entry will be:

```
PerlModule WroxHandlers::ContactListHandler
    <Location /contact>
    SetHandler perl-script
    PerlResponseHandler WroxHandlers::ContactListHandler->main
    </Location>
```

You'll notice that that this handler is registered differently than those you saw in the previous chapter, in that main() is called as a class method. This allows the use of main() as the entry point to the handler. It also makes it so that there are two arguments passed to the handler instead of the usual one: the calling object or class, and the request object.

Now you can begin editing ContactHandler.pm. The first thing is to give it a package name.

The code currently at the top appears like so:

```
#!/usr/bin/perl

use strict;
use warnings;

use CGI qw(:standard);
use lib qw(/etc/apache2/perl-lib);
use WebApp;

# package scoped so other subroutines have access
my $url;

# call main subroutine
main();
```

You would remove the #!/usr/bin/perl line — that is no longer needed. Replace it with the package name:

```
package WroxHandlers::ContactHandler;
```

Since the WroxHandlers directory where ContactHandler.pm resides is a subdirectory of the Perl include path perl-lib, the package name has to include *WroxHandlers*, hence the package name WroxHandlers::ContactHandler.

Also, this program will need to import the modules needed:

```
use Apache2::Const -compile => qw(OK);
use Apache2::RequestRec ();
use Apache2::RequestIO ();
```

The first module, Apache2::Const, provides constant values you will need for your handler. For this example, only the OK constant is needed. This will be the return value that is returned at the end of handler process to provide a response to the client.

The other two modules, Apache2::RequestRec and Apache2::RequestIO (which were described in Chapter 14), are needed to provide methods for the Apache request object. You will next see this is what you will use throughout the handler for a number of purposes.

Since the handler is registered in the Apache configuration file with this:

```
PerlResponseHandler WroxHandlers::ContactListHandler->main
```

main() will be the entry point to this handler. You no longer need to call main() explicitly. Remove that call.

The top of the program now looks like this:

```
package WroxHandlers::ContactListHandler;

use strict;

use Apache2::Const -compile => qw(OK);
use Apache2::RequestRec ();
use Apache2::RequestIO ();
use CGI qw(:standard);
use WebApp;

my $url;
```

The next thing to modify is the top-level subroutine main(). The current implementation of main() in contact.pl is this:

```
sub main {
  # CGI object
  my $cgi= CGI->new();

  # URL of program, used in form submit url, other parts of code
  $url = $cgi->url(-absolute=>1);

  # print the HTML mime header
  print $cgi->header('text/html');

  print header();

  dispatcher($cgi);

  print footer();
}
```

As is shown, a CGI object is instantiated to provide various functionality, such as parsing submitted form variables, obtaining the URI of the program, printing the HTTP content-encoding response header, etc. Simple print statements are used to print content from the other subroutines. The real processing is accomplished with a call to dispatcher(). The object reference variable $cgi is passed to provide form variable parsing, which is processed in dispatcher().

For this handler, CGI will still be used for variable processing, but won't be required for printing the HTTP as it will instead be accomplished using the request object to do instead.

The implementation of main() for the handler now becomes the following:

```
sub main {
    my ($class, $r) = @_;

    # print the HTML mime header
    $r->content_type('text/html');
```

```
        $r->print(header());

        dispatcher($r);

        $r->print(footer());

        # return OK, response
        return Apache2::Const::OK;
    }
```

Since this handler was registered with main being called as a class method, it is passed two arguments, the class object and the request object. Also notice is that CGI is no longer instantiated in main(). CGI will still be used, but its instantiation will be moved to dispatcher(), which will be shown later. Instead of using the CGI method header() to print the HTTP content-encoding response header, the request object's (Apache2::RequestRec) content_type() method is used. The printing of each section of the page is implemented using the request object's print() method. Finally, the response constant Apache2::Const::OK is returned.

The next piece to modify is dispatcher(). The current incarnation of dispatcher(), as it is in contact.pl is (highlighted code shows changes):

```
sub dispatcher {
    my ($cgi, $msg) = @_;
    my $delete_ids;
    my $user = {};
    my $saved = 0;

    # WebApp
    my $webapp = WebApp->new();

    unless (defined $webapp->{dbh}) {
        $$msg ||= $webapp->{msg};
        print mainform($user, $webapp, $msg);
        return;
    }

    # get all submitted form values into a hashref
    my $form = $cgi->Vars();

    # if save_user operation - create or update
    if (defined $form->{save_user}) {
        my $not_set = 0;
        # check all fields for being set - this means "required"
        for (@$WebApp::REQUIRED_COLS) {
            # both defined and containing a value with a length
            unless (defined $form->{$_} && length($form->{$_})) {
                # create a message
                $$msg = "Error: the field for '\u$_' is not set!";
                $not_set++;
                last;
            }
        }
    }
```

```perl
        # if all required fields, saveUser
      unless ($not_set) {
        $saved= $webapp->saveUser($form);
      }
    }
    # delete of one or more users
    elsif (defined $form->{delete_user}) {
      # check all form values
      for my $param (keys %$form) {
        # if the param is completely numeric, that is the uid
        if ($param =~ /^(\d+)$/ && $form->{$param} eq 'on') {
          # create hash ref keyed by uid, value username which will be
          # used to build both a list of uids to delete as well as a message
          $delete_ids->{$param}= $form->{"username_$param"};
        }
      }
      # if there are no ids to delete, don't bother
      if (keys %$delete_ids) {
        $webapp->deleteUsers($delete_ids);
      }
    }
    # if no previous message, set to whatever WebApp created
    $$msg||= $webapp->{msg};
    if (!$saved && defined $form->{save_user}) {
      # edit form
      print userform($form,$webapp, $msg);
    }
    elsif (defined $form->{edit}) {
      # edit form
      $user= $webapp->getUser({ uid => $form->{edit}});
      print userform($user,$webapp,$msg);
    }
    elsif (defined $form->{view}) {
      # view page
      $user= $webapp->getUser({ uid => $form->{view}});
      print viewuser($user,$webapp, $msg);
    }
    else {
      # default, print user list
      print mainform($user,$webapp, $msg);
    }
    return;
}
```

There isn't much to change with dispatcher(), really. The changes in the highlighted areas that follow show what needs to be changed with dispatcher():

```perl
sub dispatcher {
  my ($r)= @_;
    my $delete_ids;
```

```perl
my $user= {};
my $saved= 0;

# CGI object
my $cgi = CGI->new($r);


# WebApp
my $webapp= WebApp->new();

unless (defined $webapp->{dbh}) {
    $$msg||= $webapp->{msg};
    $r->print(mainform($user,$webapp, $msg));

    return;
}

# get all submitted form values into a hashref
my $form = $cgi->Vars();

# if save_user operation - create or update
if (defined $form->{save_user}) {
  my $not_set = 0;
  # check all fields for being set - this means "required"
  for (@$WebApp::REQUIRED_COLS) {
    # both defined and containing a value with a length
    unless (defined $form->{$_} && length($form->{$_})) {
      # create a message
      $$msg= "Error: the field for '\u$_' is not set!";
      $not_set++;
      last;
    }
  }
    # if all required fields, saveUser
  unless ($not_set) {
    $saved= $webapp->saveUser($form);
  }
}
# delete of one or more users
elsif (defined $form->{delete_user}) {
  # check all form values
  for my $param (keys %$form) {
    # if the param is completely numeric, that is the uid
    if ($param =~ /^(\d+)$/ && $form->{$param} eq 'on') {
      # create hash ref keyed by uid, value username which will be
      # used to build both a list of uids to delete as well as a message
      $delete_ids->{$param}= $form->{"username_$param"};
    }
  }
  # if there are no ids to delete, don't bother
  if (keys %$delete_ids) {
    $webapp->deleteUsers($delete_ids);
  }
}
# if no previous message, set to whatever WebApp created
```

```
$$msg||= $webapp->{msg};
if (!$saved && defined $form->{save_user}) {
  # edit form
  $r->print(userform($form,$webapp, $msg));
}
elsif (defined $form->{edit}) {
  # edit form
  $user= $webapp->getUser({ uid => $form->{edit}});
  $r->print(userform($user,$webapp,$msg));
}
elsif (defined $form->{view}) {
  # view page
  $user= $webapp->getUser({ uid => $form->{view}});
  $r->print(viewuser($user,$webapp, $msg));
}
else {
  # default, print user list
  $r->print(mainform($user,$webapp, $msg));
}
return;
}
```

As you can see, the request object $r is now passed instead of $cgi, which is instead instantiated within dispatcher(). Any printing is now handled by the request object's method $r->print().

The next changes you have to make are — wait! There are no other changes to make! Since the code was implemented in such a way that the content generated in the various subroutines, such as userform(), viewuser(), and mainform(), was simply returned and didn't print anything in the response, and because dispatcher() performs all of the printing for the application, only the methods main() and dispatcher() needed to be change.

This code is now a handler! The last small thing you should do is to add:

```
1;
```

... to the end of ContactHandler.pm. Of course, you now need to restart Apache. Then you can access this handler at http://example.com/contact and it should function just as it did when it was a Mod-Perl::Registry script.

Converting a mod_perl Handler to a ModPerl::Registry Script

OK, what is the meaning of this? You just went through the steps of converting your ModPerl::Registry script to a mod_perl handler! Seriously, the purpose of this very short section is to point out a couple things about using ModPerl::Registry for writing applications. There really is no significant change. You can run the handler code that you just converted in the last example with this:

```
#!/usr/bin/perl

use strict;
```

```
use warnings;

use lib qw(/etc/apache2/perl-lib);
use WroxHandlers::ContactHandler;

my $r = defined $_[0] ? $_[0] : Apache2->request; # or you could have used shift
return WroxHandlers::ContactHandler->main($r);
1;
```

That's all there is to it! In this example, you are simply using the WroxHandlers::ContactHandler module as you would any other module, as well as passing it the request object that it expects. The first argument to any ModPerl::Registry script (which above is accessed as $_[0]) is the request object. This works because the code is wrapping in a sub {} block.

Another approach would have been to copy the handler module file, ContactHandler.pm, back as a Perl script and simply add the calling of main() at the top of the file, before any subroutine definitions:

```
main($_[0]);
```

This makes it so you can actually use all the same functionality you have in a handler within a Mod-Perl::Registry script. The following simple code snippet shows you how:

```
#!/usr/bin/perl

use strict;
use warnings;

use Apache2::RequestRec ();

main($_[0]);

sub main {
    my ($r)= @_;

    $r||= Apache2->request;

    $r->content_type('text/html');

    my $page= <<'EOHTML';
<html>
    <head><title>Test Code</title></head>
    <body>
    <p>This is a test</p>
    <pre>
EOHTML


    $page .= "$_ => $ENV{$_}\n" for keys %ENV;

    $page .=<<EOHTML;
    </pre>
    </body>
</html>
```

```
EOHTML
    $r->print($page);
}
1;
```

You'll see that you have to squint for a second, because this almost looks like a mod_perl handler. The point is, you can use either mod_perl handlers or ModPerl::Registry scripts and have code that works with both.

> **Bomb alert/IMPORTANT:** There are a couple issues you must be aware of with using ModPerl::Registry scripts. The first and foremost is never name a subroutine in your code `handler()`! This is because the way ModPerl::Registry works is to load your script into a method called `handler()`. You can imagine what happens if `handler()` has yet another subroutine called `handler()`!
>
> The other issue is that if you use the request object methods, they may not work if you run your script by command line.

Dealing with Cookies

One of the most important things you'll have to understand as a web developer is cookies. You probably already know what a cookie is. In the simplest of terms possible, a cookie is strings of text that are exchanged between the web client and web server. The text is passed via the request headers as the header *Cookie* from the client to the server, and via the response headers as the response header *Set-Cookie* of the server. Your web browser stores these cookie values for a given web site and presents them when accessing the site they were created by.

Cookies are used for a number of purposes:

❑ **User tracking:** Both within the web site and between web sites. An application of this would be ad systems where cookies are used to determine how many or what type of advertisements a user has seen on a web site.

❑ **Session ids:** For instance, keeping track of items you have selected for purchase from a shopping cart.

❑ **Access control:** Using the cookie to determine if you have been authenticated or not.

CookieTestHandler

This section will show you a very simple mod_perl handler that allows you to set and unset a cookie using a form.

The first thing, of course, is to define the package name as well as some variables used throughout the code.

```
package WroxHandlers::CookieTestHandler;

use strict;
```

```
use warnings;

use Apache2::Const -compile => qw(OK);
use Apache2::Request;
use Apache2::Cookie;

# package scoped scalar to store URL
my $url;

# package scoped scalar to store message
my $msg;

# global scoped scalar to store submit button value
my $submit;

# the name of the cookie this example will use
my $cookiename       = 'wroxcookie';

# expiration time of the cookie
my $expires          = '+3M';

# negative expiration used for deleting the cookie
my $delete_expires   = '-3M';

# the domain of the cookie
my $cookiedomain     = '.example.com';

# the path the cookie is set for
my $cookiepath       = '/';
```

The various module importations are defined. The Perl modules in particular you will want for this are Apache2::Request for parsing the submitted form (you could also use CGI), and Apache2::Cookie, which has the methods you will use for processing cookies.

The variables defined are globally scoped so all subroutines have access to them.

❏   The first two variables are $msg and $submit. $msg is used to display the message of whatever action has occurred, and $submit is used to toggle the value of what the Submit button does — either create or delete a cookie.

❏   The other package-scoped variables include (as the comments indicate) values for the name, expiration, domain, and path of the cookie. For this example, the expiration will be 3 months. The cookie name will be *wroxcookie*, and to allow all example.com domains, ".example.com" is used.

❏   Additionally, there is a $delete_expires variable. This is used to set an expiration of the cookie to 3 months ago, which will be used for cookie deletion. When you set a cookie's expiration in the past, your browser will automatically delete that cookie from its stored cookies.

> **If you intend for a cookie to work for all hosts of your domain — for instance, `example.com`, `www.example.com`, `otherhost.example.com`, use ".example.com" as the cookie domain value.**

❑ The main handler body is very simple and calls first the `handle_cookie()` subroutine, which performs the processing for setting the cookie and setting the values, such as the Submit button value and message that will be displayed when the page is displayed.

❑ `handle_cookie()` is called first, particularly before content response is generated because it needs to read the *Cookie* request header from the client, as well as set the *Set-Cookie* response header from the server. This must be set prior to page content response.

```
sub handler {
    my ($r)= @_;

    # this subroutine processes cookies
    handle_cookies($r);

    $r->content_type('text/html');

    $r->print(header());
    $r->print(form());
    $r->print(footer());

    return Apache2::Const::OK;
}
```

❑ The `handle_cookies()` subroutine does all the work for processing cookies. The first thing it does is instantiate an Apache2::Request. This will be used for parsing the submitted form values. Then an Apache2::Cookie::Jar object is instantiated. This provides you with access to all the cookies for this domain if you don't specify a cookie name. For this application, you only want the particular cookie defined in `$cookiename`, which is *wroxcookie*, so this scalar is passed.

❑ Next, a default value for the Submit button is set. Then the cookie is tested to see if it exists and has an actual value. If it does, that means the cookie is set. With the cookie known to be set, the message and Submit button values are changed to indicate this.

❑ A test is made to determine if the form submitted was set to delete the cookie. If the cookie is to be deleted, then a new Apache::Cookie object is instantiated. This particular cookie will be used to unset and delete the existing cookie. This is accomplished by both setting the cookie value to an empty string and setting the expiration date to the past, in this case 3 months ago.

❑ The call to `$cookie->bake()` sets the *Set-Cookie* response header with this cookie. When the browser reads this cookie and sees that it's set for 3 months in the past, it will delete it from its cookie list. The Submit button and message variables are set to indicate that the cookie is deleted and the Submit button is then set to create a cookie since the old cookie no longer exists.

```
sub handle_cookies {
    my ($r)= @_;

    # obtain the request object
    my $req = Apache2::Request->new($r);

    # obtain the cookie jar object
    my $j = Apache2::Cookie::Jar->new($r);

    # get the particular 'wroxcookie' cookie
    my $cookie = $j->cookies($cookiename);
```

```perl
        # set up the text for the submit button and message to a default value
        $submit = "Create";
        $msg = "Cookie is not set";

        # if a cookie exists
        if (defined $cookie && $cookie->value()) {
            # change button message
            $submit = "Delete";
            $msg = "Cookie is set";

            # if a delete, then set a cookie which expires 3 months ago, with
            # and empty value
            if ($req->param('cookie_action') eq 'Delete') {
                my $delcookie = Apache2::Cookie->new($r,
                    -name    =>  $cookiename,
                    -value   =>  '',
                    -expires =>  $delete_expires,
                    -domain  =>  '.patg.net',
                    -path    =>  $cookiepath,
                    );
                # this sends the cookie via response headers
                $delcookie->bake($r);

                # set the submit button back to the appriate message
                $submit = "Create";
                $msg = "Cookie was deleted";
            }
            # no need to create if existing
            elsif ($req->param('cookie_action') eq 'Create') {
                $msg= "No need to create. You already have a cookie";
            }
        }
        # if a cookie doesn't exist, then create one
        elsif ($req->param('cookie_action') eq 'Create') {

            # create a new cookie
            my $newcookie = Apache2::Cookie->new($r,
                -name    =>  $cookiename,
                -value   =>  'thisisset',
                -expires =>  $expires,
                -domain  =>  $cookiedomain,
                -path    =>  $cookiepath,
                );

            # set the cookie via response headers
            $newcookie->bake($r);

            # set the message and submit button value
            $msg= "Cookie was created";
            $submit= "Delete";

        }
    return;
}
```

❑ If the value is made to create a cookie, a new Apache2::Cookie object is instantiated. This cookie will have an expiration of 3 months from now. $newcookie->bake() sets the *Set*-Cookie response header for this cookie.

❑ Finally, the form is printed. It prints out the form with the message and Submit buttons set according to whatever action has occurred.

```
sub form {
    return <<"COOKIEFORM";
    <!-- begin cookieform -->
    <p class="msg">$msg</p>
    <p>
    <form action="$url" id="cookieform" name="cookieform" method="post">
      <fieldset>
        <label for="cookie_action">$submit cookie</label>
        <p>
          <input type="submit" name="cookie_action"
                 id="cookie_action" value="$submit">
        </p>
    </form>
</p>
    <p><a href="$url">Reload page</a></p>
    <!-- end cookieform -->
COOKIEFORM

}
```

❑ Next, the needed handler registration is made in the Apache configuration file:

```
PerlModule WroxHandlers::CookieTestHandler
  <Location /cookietest>
   PerlOptions +GlobalRequest
  SetHandler perl-script
  PerlResponseHandler WroxHandlers::CookieTestHandler
  </Location>
```

Apache is restarted, and the test begins:

1. First, the page when it is first loaded shows that there is not yet a cookie, as in Figure 15-1.

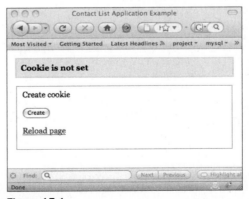

Figure 15-1

2. When you click on Create, it will create a cookie, as shown in Figure 15-2. At this point, the client header is passed, as are numerous other headers left out for brevity's sake.

```
POST /cookietest HTTP/1.1
Host: example.com
User-Agent: Mozilla/5.0 (Macintosh; U; Intel Mac OS X 10.5; en-US;
rv:1.9.0.4)
Gecko/2008102920 Firefox/3.0.4
...
Cookie: inventory=Cacti=ab8a174bb44b59b130b3e7bf62f939b8
Content-Type: application/x-www-form-urlencoded
Content-Length: 20
cookie_action=Create
```

You'll see that there is one cookie for Cacti (a monitoring application) already existing. Also, you'll see the POST data, which has a length of 20 and a value of cookie_action=Create, which the handler will parse.

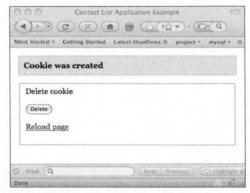

Figure 15-2

3. The server then responds with a Set-Cookie header with the new cookie:

```
HTTP/1.x 200 OK
Date: Wed, 25 Feb 2009 19:24:41 GMT
...
Set-Cookie: wroxcookie=thisisset; path=/; domain=.example.com;
expires=Tue, 26-May-2009 19:24:41 GMT
```

This is where the cookie gets set. Notice all the values you expected are set — particularly the expiration date 3 months from February 25.

4. Then delete the cookie by clicking the Delete button. The client headers as a result of the deletion are these:

```
POST /cookietest HTTP/1.1
Host: example.com
Cookie: inventory=Cacti=ab8a174bb44b59b130b3e7bf62f939b8;
wroxcookie=thisisset
```

```
Content-Type: application/x-www-form-urlencoded
Content-Length: 20
cookie_action=Delete
```

You can see the cookie set prior to this is presented in the request headers. However, considering the POST data this time is `cookie_action=Delete`, that won't be the case for long!

The server's response is quick and painless:

```
HTTP/1.x 200 OK
Date: Wed, 25 Feb 2009 19:24:42 GMT^M
...
Set-Cookie: wroxcookie=; path=/; domain=.patg.net; expires=Thu,
27-Nov-2008 19:24:42 GMT
```

The browser reads in the new cookie which has an expiration date set for 3 months in the past and acts accordingly, deleting the cookie from its cookie inventory. Figure 15-3 below shows the resulting page after deleting a cookie.

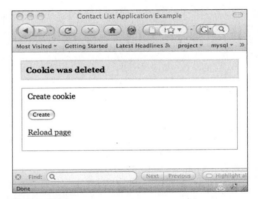

Figure 15-3

The handler displays the form with the appropriate information.

As you can see, this application is very simple. But it serves to show you that working with cookies with mod_perl, and, in particular, Apache2::Cookie is very easy.

Tools for Testing Cookies and Headers

Having the tools to troubleshoot what cookies you have or view what client request and server response HTTP headers are being passed is invaluable to debugging issues with cookies and sessions in web development. There are a various tools for this. The first tool, which you can use to see what cookies you have stored is built right into Firefox. You access it by selecting Preferences ➪ Privacy ➪ Show Cookies. The *Cookies* tool is shown in Figure 15-4.

Firefox also has numerous "add-ons" to do any number of tasks, such as viewing headers, debugging JavaScript, blocking ads, downloading managers, photo tools, the NHL Vancouver Canuck Hockey Toolbar and Theme, etc.

Figure 15-4

Two add-ons you will particularly find useful in web development are these:

❑ **Firebug:** This allows you full access to the CSS, JavaScript, DOM of the loaded page, headers, cookies, and many other features, of the pages you load. This is the tool for debugging not only server-side web programming, but AJAX, JavaScript, etc. Figure 15-5 shows the cookies tab in action.

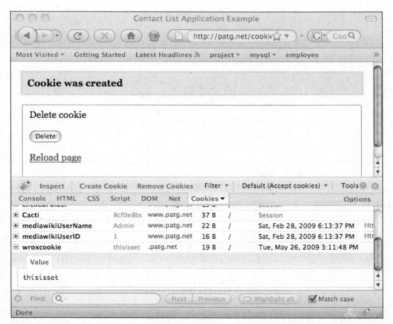

Figure 15-5

❑ **LiveHTTPHeaders:** This is a fairly simple but extremely useful tool that displays both the client request and server response HTTP headers. Figure 15-6 shows you the output of a HTTP POST operation.

Figure 15-6

Generic Database Methods

Before this chapter digs deep into sessions, there are some things that can be done to make data storage and retrieval easier, which is something that makes implementing session saving a lot easier. These methods would have to be implemented one way or the other. It's better to implement generic methods so any code that is subsequently implemented will be able to take advantage of methods that work, regardless of the table being used.

The same module that has been used in previous chapters (for which there already is code) can be reused for this endeavor. WebApp.pm requires only a couple of changes that will be discussed next.

WebApp.pm already has various methods for storing data, however, these methods have been for specific tables. There was a need to store data for various types of entities, yet the methods all performed similar steps that you end up implementing over again, such as building SQL statements for INSERT, UPDATE, DELETE, and SELECT. Take, for instance, the snippet from the method insertUser():

```
# build up the columns specification
my $query = 'INSERT INTO users (' . join(',', @$USER_COLS) . ')';
# build up the placeholders
$query .= ' VALUES ( ' . join( ',', ( '?' ) x @$USER_COLS ) . ')';

$query .= ')';
```

This is something find yourself having to implement for every type of data or table you access or insert in order to be able to pass hash references to database methods and have them automatically stored. What is needed are more *generic* data access methods. The other big benefit of this is that you will confine the methods that have SQL queries in them to these methods. Thus, there will no longer be a need to have SQL strewn about your application code.

Though there are some CPAN modules available, such as DBIx::Class, that provide this generic database functionality out of the box, the intention of this section is for you to see how you can implement this type of functionality by writing a simple API. You can use this to abstract database calls and dynamically generate SQL statements based on the data you are either reading (SELECT) or writing (INSERT, UPDATE, DELETE) from the database.

dbGetRef()

This method is used to obtain a hash reference containing one or more records that you select. As you'll see, it is a generic method that has code you've seen elsewhere, particularly when constructing database queries off hash references you pass to it.

```
=head2 dbGetRef()

Retrieves an array reference of hash references for each record
retrieved from a query specified by list of columns being
selected, a hashref containing the column names and values
used to construct a WHERE clause

=over 4

=item Arguments

$self    object reference

$table   table name

$fields  scalar, comma separated list of columns being selected

$where   hashref, keys column names, values the conditions.

=item Return value

Array reference of hash references for each record

=back

=cut

sub dbGetRef {
    my ($self, $table, $fields, $where, $options) = @_;
    my $rows;
    $fields||= '*';

    my $query = "SELECT $fields FROM $table ";

    # build up the where clause
    $query .= $self->whereClause($where) if defined $where;
```

```
    # run the query, obtain statement handle
    my $sth = $self->runQuery({
        'sql'       => $query,
        'values'    => [values %$where]}, \$rows);

    return $sth->fetchall_arrayref({});
}
```

Using this is very simple (which is why it was written):

```
    my $ref= $webapp->dbGetRef('users', '*', {uid => 27, username => 'capttofu'});
```

You'll notice that the $where variable, the third argument to dbGetRef, is what determines what the WHERE clause will specify. In this case, it specifies uid of 27, username of capttofu.

This would return a hash reference:

```
    {
                    'admin' => '1',
                    'firstname' => 'Patrick',
                    'uid' => '27',
                    'phone' => '2828282822',
                    'state' => 'NH',
                    'surname' => 'Galbraith',
                    'username' => 'CaptTofu',
                    'email' => 'patg@patg.net',
                    'city' => 'Stoddard',
                    'password' => 'acbd18db4cc2f85cedef654fccc4a4d8',
                    'address' => '11122 Granite St.'
    },
```

dbInsert()

The method dbInsert() is a generic insertion method that allows you to insert a hash reference, corresponding to a record in the database, of a given table. This hash reference contains hash keys that are the columns of the table, the values the value being inserted. It returns the insert id of the inserted column if the table has an auto_increment column, or the number or rows inserted if there is no auto_increment column.

```
=head2 dbInsert()

Inserts a single hash reference, which represents a particular entity into
the named table. You are responsible for providing the correct name and
number of columns

=item Arguments

$self -- object reference

$table -- name of the table to be inserted to

$dataref -- hashref, keys column names value values, to be inserted

$options -- any particular options such as IGNORE

=item Returns
```

```
    Id of item inserted from insert id

    =cut

    sub dbInsert {
        my ($self, $table, $dataref, $options) = @_;

        # this would cause INSERT IGNORE to be used
        my $ignore= $options->{IGNORE} ? 'IGNORE' : '';

        # build up the SQL INSERT statement
        my $sql = "INSERT $ignore INTO $table " . $self->buildInsert($dataref);

        # run the query
        my $sth = $self->runQuery({
                'sql'       => $sql,
                'values'    => [values %$dataref]}, \$rows);

        return(0) unless $sth;

        # return last insert id
        return($sth->{mysql_insertid} ? $sth->{mysql_insertid} : $sth->rows());
    }
```

You'll see here that it uses a method called `buildInsert()` to build up the columns and values part of the SQL statement. The implementation details of `buildInsert()` will be shown later.

Usage of `dbInsert()` would be this:

```
    my $newuser = { 'admin'    => '1',
                    'firstname' => 'Dharma',
                    'phone'     => '5558881818',
                    'state'     => 'AZ',
                    'surname'   => 'Vidya',
                    'username'  => 'dharma',
                    'email'     => 'dharma@somesite.com',
                    'city'      => 'Tucson',
                    'password'  => 'acbd18db4cc2f85cedef654fccc4a4d8',
                    'address'   => '1 River St.'};

    my $id = $webapp->dbInsert('users', $newuser);
```

dbUpdate()

The method `dbUpdate()` updates one or more records of the table specified with the variable $table. $fields_ref is a hash reference containing keys for the column that will be updated; $where contains the keys and values that are used to build up the WHERE clause.

```
    =head2 dbUpdate()

    Updates a particular record in the table specified. Uses a hash
    reference to supply the values that will be updated, as well as
    another hash reference to supply the WHERE clause

    =item Arguments
```

```
$self -- object reference

$table -- the table being updated

$fields_ref -- hash reference containing the keys the columns
and values being updated

$where -- hash reference containing the keys as the columns and values
that will be used in the where clause

=item Returns

number of rows updated

=cut

sub dbUpdate {
    my ($self, $table, $fields_ref, $where, $options) = @_;
    my $rows;

    my $query = "UPDATE $table ";

    # build the SET part of the UPDATE statement
    $query .= $self->buildUpdate($fields_ref) if defined $fields_ref;

    # build the SET part of the UPDATE statement
    $query .= $self->whereClause($where) if defined $where;

    my $sth = $self->runQuery({
        'sql'       => $query,
        'values'    => [values %$fields_ref,values %$where]
        }, \$rows);

    return ($sth->rows());
}
```

You'll notice that dbUpdate() uses two helper methods to build up the different parts of the UPDATE statement. The first is buildUpdate(), which builds the SET col1= `value2´, col2 = `value3´, etc., based on the value of $fields_ref, which contains the column names and values of the table being updated. The second method used, whereClause (also used in dbGetRef()), builds up the WHERE clause.

The use of dbUpdate() is just as simple as the other new methods have been:

```
my $ref= $webapp->dbUpdate('users', {
                'firstname' => 'Sara', surname => 'Smith'},
            { username => 'Sjones'} );
```

dbDelete()

The method dbDelete() deletes one or more records in the table specified by $table, and uses the same convention as dbGetRef() and dbUpdate. The $where hash reference argument specifies the WHERE clause columns and values.

```
=head2 dbDelete()

Deletes one or more records specified in $where
```

```
=item Arguments

$self -- object reference

$table -- table variable

$where -- hash reference used to specify WHERE clause

$options -- any specific options, none for this method yet

=item Returns

Number of rows deleted

=cut

sub dbDelete {
    my ($self, $table, $where, $options) = @_;
    my $rows;

    my $query = "DELETE FROM $table ";

    # use whereClause to build the WHERE clause from $where
    $query .= $self->whereClause($where) if defined $where;

    my $sth = $self->runQuery({
        'sql'         => $query,
        'values'      => [values %$where]}, \$rows);

    return ($sth->rows());

}
```

Usage of dbDelete() is the following:

```
$webapp->dbDelete('users', { uid => 44});
```

In this example, the resulting query would be 'DELETE FROM users WHERE uid = 44'

whereClause()

This is the helper method used to build the WHERE clause. This is the type of database query building code that you would often end up duplicating. What was done in the following code was to make it non-table specific as well as non-query specific — meaning this method can be used to build a WHERE clause for SELECT, DELETE, or UPDATE.

This whereClause() method is a helper method. All it does is take a hash reference, $fields_ref, which has the keys that represent the table column names, and the values of this hash reference (the values specified in the WHERE clause), and it builds up a string containing the WHERE clause.

Please note, this method will use placeholders '?' and not the actual values, unless the column names are specified with a dash in front of them. In this case, the key is deleted from $fields_ref, which is the very hash reference that will be also used in the actual query execution to supply the bind values. This is important to know because whereClause() ensures the order of both the fields and values in the string it produces is passed in the query execution and must correspond to the bind values being passed or an error will occur.

The code that handles whether to use a placeholder or a literal value is shown in the highlighted block that follows:

```
=head2 whereClause()

Builds up a WHERE clause for a SELECT, DELETE, UPDATE
statement based off of a Perl hash reference containing
the column names with the values of the WHERE condition

=item Arguments

$self - object reference

$fields_ref - hash reference. Fields are columns of the
where clause, values the values of the where condition
This will build up the where clause with either placeholder
or literals. If literal, it removes that column from
the hashref so it won't be used in passing placeholders

=item Returns

String, WHERE clause

=cut
sub whereClause {
    my ($self, $fields_ref)= @_;
    return unless ref $fields_ref && keys %$fields_ref;
    my $where;

    # loop through the reference
    for (keys %$fields_ref) {
        # if the key contains a dash, translate as a literal
        if ($_ =~ /^-/) {
            my $actual_col = $_;
            # need to make sure to strip off hyphen/dash from column name
            $actual_col =~ s/^-//;

            $where .= " $actual_col = ". $fields_ref->{$_} . ' AND ';

            # since this won't be used for a place-holder, remove it
            delete $fields_ref->{$_};

            $_ =~ s/^-//;
        }
        # or append a placeholder
        else {
            $where .= " $_ = ? AND ";
        }
    }
```

```
        # remove the trailing AND
        if (defined $where && length($where) ) {
            $where= substr($where, 0, -5);
            $where = "WHERE $where" ;
        }
        return $where;
    }
```

Just so you will understand the whereClause() a bit more, two snippet examples demonstrate usage:

```
$where_string= $self->whereClause({
                                        'name' => 'John',
                                        'age'   => 33 });
```

$where_string would be this:

```
WHERE name = ? AND age = ?
```

And the values passed in query execution will be values %$fields_ref, which would pass ('John', 33), to satisfy both placeholders in the WHERE clause.

```
$where_string = $self->whereClause({
`name´ => `John´,
`-age´ => 33 }) ; # notice the dash `-` for -age
```

$where_string would be:

```
WHERE name = ? AND age = 33
```

The age key would have been deleted from %fields_ref, so the value passed in query execution would be only (`John´), for the single placeholder in the WHERE clause.

You would support literal values in cases where you don't want to use a placeholder — for instance, if you want to use something like "colname = now()" in your WHERE clause.

buildUpdate()

This is another helper method, just like whereClause(), that builds up a string based off a hash reference of keys, the table column names, and the values of the placeholder or literal value, depending on how the column names are referenced. A dash '-' prepended to the key denotes a literal value is to be used. This also results in the removal of that member from the hash reference, which will inevitably be used in query execution for the bind values.

```
=head2 buildUpdate()

Helper method to construct the SET part of an UPDATE statement. This method
uses a hash reference $fields_ref to construct the column names and values
specified in the SET part of an UPDATE statement. Like whereClause, this also
allows you to specify literals so the default placeholder isn't appended for
that column as well as deleting the  value for that column from fields_ref
which is inevitably used for the query execution
```

```
=item  Args

$self - object reference
$fields_ref - hash reference containing the columns and values for the SET

=item Returns

SET string

=cut
sub buildUpdate {
    my ($self, $fields_ref)= @_;
    return unless ref $fields_ref && keys %$fields_ref;
    my $set;

    for (keys %$fields_ref) {
        if ($_ =~ /^-/) {
            # need to make sure to strip off hyphen/dash from column name
            my $actual_col = $_;
            $actual_col =~ s/^-//;

          $set .= "$actual_col = " . $fields_ref->{$_} . ',';

            delete $fields_ref->{$_};
            $_ =~ s/^-//;
        }
        else {
            $set .= "$_ = ?,";
        }
    }
    chop($set);    # remove trailing comma

    return " SET  $set ";
}
```

Usage for buildUpdate() is similar to that of whereClause(). If you have, for instance, this:

```
$set_string= $self->buildUpdate({ `name' => `John', `-age' => 33, `state' => `NH'});
```

. . . then $set_string will be this:

```
SET name = ? AND age = 33 AND state = ?
```

$fields_ref will only have `name' and `state' remaining, so the values supplied to the query execution will be (`John', `NH')

buildInsert ()

This is another helper method that constructs SQL statement components. buildInsert() constructs the string "(col1, col2, col3) VALUES (value1, value2, valueN)" part of the SQL INSERT statement. It has the same ability to allow you to specify literals, otherwise it appends placeholders.

```
=head2 buildInsert()

This is a helper method that constructs the fields and values of an INSERT
```

SQL statement. It builds the string based off of the keys and values
of the $fields_ref hash reference

```
=item Args

$self -- object reference
$fields_ref -- hash reference used to construct the string

=item Returns

String of the form
"(field1,field2,fieldN...) VALUES (value1, value2, valueN..)"

=cut

sub buildInsert {
    my ($self, $fields_ref)= @_;
    my ($values, $fields);

    for (keys %$fields_ref) {
        if ($_ =~ /^-/) {
            $values .= $fields_ref->{$_} . ',';
            delete $fields_ref->{$_};
            $_ =~ s/^-//;
        }
        else {
            $values .= '?,';
        }
    }
    chop($fields);
    chop($values);

    return '(' . $fields . ') VALUES (' . $values . ')';
}
Usage is just like whereClause() and buildInsert() my $insert_string
$self->buildInsert({
                                    'name'   => 'John',
                                    'age'    => 33,
                                    '-state' => 'NH');
```

The value of $insert_string would be this:

```
(name, age, state) VALUES (?, ?, `NH´)
```

Other Changes to WebApp

Some other convenient changes were made to WebApp. Since every handler has had to obtain the submitted form values, this is something that will automatically be done by instantiating WebApp and passing it the request object. The changes to the constructor method for WebApp, new(), are shown in the highlighted code:

```
sub new {
  my($class, $opts) = @_;
```

```perl
my $self = {
  memc_servers       => $MEMC_DEFAULT_SERVERS,
  db_virtual_user    => $DB_VIRTUAL_USER,
  db_virtual_user_ro => $DB_VIRTUAL_USER_RO,


  # set the message to empty string
  msg => '',
};
$self->{$_} = $opts->{$_} for keys %$opts;

bless($self, $class);


if ($self->{r}) {
    $self->{req}||= new Apache2::Request($self->{r});
    $self->{form}->{$_} = $self->{req}->param($_) for $self->{req}->param();
}


# connect to MySQL
return undef unless $self->_connectDB();

# connect to memcached
$self->_connectMemcached();

return $self;
}
```

So now, if you pass a request object to WebApp upon instantiation, you will automatically be able to have access to submitted form values (stored as $self->{form}), as well as the Apache2::Request object, stored as $self->{req} .

There is also now an accessor method, getForm() :

```perl
=head2 getForm()

Returns a hash reference containing the submitted form values

=item Args

$self -- object reference

=item Returns

hash reference with form values

=cut
sub getForm {
    my $self= $_[0];
    return $self->{form};
}
```

... which you would now be able to use from within your handler, by using the following code:

```
my $webapp = WebApp->new({r => $r});
my $form = $webapp->getForm();
```

Also added is an export list:

```
our @EXPORT = qw(
    randomString );
```

This allows the use of the `randomString` method without instantiation:

```
$random_string = randomString();
```

This is a method that you will use to create a random session key value.

Session Management

Now that the mechanics and basic details of cookie management have been explained and demonstrated with the simple cookie handler from an earlier section, it's time to add some flesh to the concept.

Also, there are now database methods that make storing data much simpler.

The cookie is one part of session management. What you do with the cookie is what can give you the ability to implement many things. For this section, you'll see how to use a cookie for session management.

Essentially, the session will be implemented by using a cookie that has a value that can be used to look up information in memcached, if cached, and in MySQL, if it is not in memcached. When this cookie is created, an entry into a database table for sessions will be made. In this sessions table, Perl objects can be serialized and stored. Also, any data stored in sessions will have data stored in memcached. Since the Perl drivers for memcached, Cache::Memcached or Cache::Memcached::libmemcached, both serialize Perl objects, the same data stored in the sessions table will also be stored in memcached. This will make it so that all sorts of information for that session can be stored. And since that information is stored in memcached, accessing that information won't result in accesses to MySQL, thus helping with the site's overall performance. This is especially true considering that in order to store serialized Perl objects, you will most likely have to use a table with a BLOB column to store this information, which can carry with it a performance penalty.

For instance, sessions can be used for shopping carts. A user comes to a site and a session is created for that user after they have logged in to the site, or even if they remain anonymous. The user selects several products. Each product has some sort of ID or other identifier that is stored in that session. If the user is distracted, depending on how long that session exists, the user can come back and resume shopping. This is just one such application where sessions are useful.

The first thing to do is to plan how the session will work. The steps are these:

1. When the user accesses a page, the session cookie for that user is checked. Does the user have a session cookie? If so, then check both memcached and MySQL for the session id of the cookie read.

2. If the session doesn't exist in the database or in memcached, then delete their session cookie, and have the user log back in.

3. If session does exist in the database or in memcached, then the user is allowed access to the page, and their session data is made available.

4. If the user doesn't have a cookie, the user is presented with a login form. They will enter their username and password and submit the form.

5. If the user credentials are satisfied, then a session cookie is created, and an entry in both the database as well as in memcached is inserted.

6. If the user credentials are not satisfied, then the login form is presented again.

Furthermore, this can be implemented in such a way that the session checking code will use redirection to send the user to the login form if they need to log in. When you redirect them to that login form, also use a GET parameter to set the URL that the user was trying to access when they failed to have a session cookie.

Implementing the mod_perl Handler LoginHandler

The first place to start is the mod_perl handler implementation that allows the user to log in. This handler will also demonstrate how you can store session values — such as for applications like shopping carts:

1. First, define a package name and import the necessary modules. This handler will be called LoginHandler:

```
package WroxHandlers::LoginHandler;

use strict;
use warnings;

use Apache2::Const -compile => qw(OK REDIRECT);
use Apache2::Request;
use WebApp;
my $url;
```

2. Next come the handler implementation details. This handler is like many other handlers you have seen so far, except this one will use the WebApp method getSession(), which will perform all the steps of checking for the existence of the session cookie and determining if there is an existing session for the user:

```
sub handler {
    my ($r) = @_;
    my $msg;

    $url = $r->uri;
    my $webapp = WebApp->new({ r => $r });
    my $form = $webapp->getForm();

    # this is the URL that the user came from, so when they are
    # given a session, they will return to that page
```

```
        my $returnto= $form->{returnto};

        my $path_info= substr($r->path_info, 1, length $r->path_info);
        my $headers= $r->headers_in();
```

3. The line below is where the session is checked. If a session exists, the `$sessionref->{sessionid}` and `$sessionref->{uid}` will be set. This is the piece of code you can use in any handler you wish to make it so a session is required for access:

```
        # obtain the session
        my $sessionref= $webapp->getSession(\$msg);
```

4. Next, a check is made to determine if the submission is trying to also store session values; if so, store those values like so:

```
        # if they are storing session values
        if ($form->{save} && $sessionref->{sessionid}) {
            $sessionref= $webapp->storeSession($sessionref->{sessionid},
                    { $form->{fieldname} => $form->{fieldvalue}});
        }
```

5. Then, a check is made to see if a `returnto` value is set. If so, and they have a session set, the user is redirected to the page they came from:

```
    # if the user has a session id and the returnto value is set
        # then redirect them back to that page
        if ($sessionref->{sessionid}) {
            if ($returnto) {
                $r->headers_out->add('Location' => $returnto);
                return Apache2::Const::REDIRECT;
            }

        }
```

6. Finally, print out the content. The `body()` subroutine will make a determination of what form to display, depending on whether the user is logged in or not:

```
        $r->content_type('text/html');
        $r->print(header());
        $r->print(body($sessionref, $returnto, $msg));
        $r->print(footer());

        return Apache2::Const::OK;
    }
```

The body subroutine prints out the appropriate form, depending on the state of the session. If a session is set, and the user hasn't already been redirected, call the `sessionInfo()` subroutine, which displays information about their session and provides a way to set session values (for the purpose of showing how to save sessions):

```
sub body {
    my ($sessionref, $returnto, $msg) = @_;
```

```
        warn $returnto;
        my $data= '';

        # default messages
        # leave room for unauthenticated sessions (those without uid)
        $msg||= ($sessionref->{sessionid} && $sessionref->{uid}) ?
            "User UID $sessionref->{uid} is logged in" :
            "Login Form";

        # if there is a session and user is logged in
        if ($sessionref->{sessionid}) {
            $data= sessionInfo($sessionref, $msg);
        }
        # if there is not a session, user is not logged in
        else {
            $data= loginForm($returnto, $msg);
        }

        # handy reload to test page
        $data.= qq(\t\t<p><a href="$url">Reload page</a></p>\n);
        return $data;
    }
```

The `sessionInfo()` subroutine is an informational page that shows you that your session works, what is stored in the session, and provides you with a form to insert a session name and value. It then calls the `sessionVariablesTable()` subroutine to return a table containing the current session information:

```
sub sessionInfo {
    my ($sessionref, $msg)= @_;

    my $table= sessionVariablesTable($sessionref);

    return <<"EOPAGE";
        <p class="msg">$msg</p>
        <!-- begin sessionInfo form -->
        <p>
        <form action="$url" id="loginform" name="loginform" method="post">
            <p>Add a session field and value:</p>
            <fieldset>
                <label>Field Name</label>
                <p><input type="text" name="fieldname" /></p>
                <label for="fieldvalue">Field Value</label>
                <p><input type="text" id="fieldvalue" name="fieldvalue" /></p>
                <input type="submit" name="save" value="Save" />
            </fieldset>
        </form>
        </p>
        $table
        <p>
        <form name="logout" method="POST" action="$url">
            <fieldset>
              <input type="submit" name="logout" value="Log out" />
            </fieldset>
        </form>
```

```
            </p>
            <!-- end sessionInfo form -->
    EOPAGE

    }
```

The `sessionVariablesTable()` subroutine loops over all the session variables as stored in the `$sessionref` hash reference. If one of the session variables has a reference itself — this would be if you stored in the session previous form submissions, shopping cart items, etc. — then Data::Dumper will be used to print it out:

```
sub sessionVariablesTable {
    my ($sessionref)= @_;
    my $table='';

    # if the session has values, display what they are
    if (scalar keys %$sessionref) {
        $table .= <<EOTABLE;
        <p class="msg">Session data for $sessionref->{uid}</p>
        <table class="userlist">
            <thead>
            <tr><th>Key</th><th>Value</th></tr>
            </thead>
            <tbody>
    EOTABLE

        for my $key (keys %$sessionref) {
            my $value;
            if (ref($sessionref->{$key})) {
                $value= Dumper $sessionref->{$key};
                $value= '<pre>' . $value . '</pre>' ;
            }
            else {
                $value= $sessionref->{$key};
            }

            $table .="
                <tr><td>$key</td><td>$value</td></tr>\n";
        }

        $table .="
            </tbody>
        </table>
        </p>\n";
    }

    return $table;
}
```

The `loginForm()` subroutine is the form displayed if the user does not have a session, so that they have the opportunity to log in and thereby create a session:

```
sub loginForm {
    my ($returnto, $msg)= @_;
```

```
    if ($returnto) {
        $returnto = encode_entities($returnto);
        $returnto = qq(<input type="hidden" name="returnto" value="$returnto">);
    }
    return <<EOPAGE;
    <!-- begin loginform -->
    <p class="msg">$msg</p>
    <p>
    <form action="$url" id="loginform" name="loginform" method="post">
      <fieldset>
        <label for="username">Username</label>
        <p>
          <input type="text" name="username" id = etc.>
        </p>
        <label>Password</label>
        <p>
          <input type="password" name="password">
        </p>
        $returnto
        <input type="submit" name="login" value="Login">
    </form>
    </p>
    <!-- end loginform -->
EOPAGE
}
```

Understanding the WebApp Class

Now that LoginHandler handler details are fleshed out, it is time to explain the WebApp methods that LoginHandler uses. These will show you the inner workings of how sessions can be implemented.

1. First, some package imports and package variables are added to WebApp. These are required for the session cookie to be properly set:

```
use Apache2::Cookie;
use Apache2::Request;
use Storable qw(nfreeze thaw);

our $COOKIENAME = 'websession';
our $COOKIEDOMAIN = '.example.net';
our $COOKIEPATH= '/';
```

Apache2::Cookie is for processing cookies, as you saw in the last chapter. Storable is used for the methods nfreeze() and thaw(), which are the same methods the Cache::Memcached::libmemcached module uses internally to serialize Perl data objects. nfreeze() is used particularly because it will allow session data to be stored on either 32-bit or 64-bit machines interchangeably because it always stores bytes in the network order (big-endian), for portability regardless of machine used.

2. The session cookie name will be websession, the domain for example.net, and the path the root of the web site.

3. The method getSession() is the top-level method that handles setting up a session. First, the Apache2::Cookie::Jar object is instantiated. Then the cookie, if it exists, is retrieved for the cookie $COOKIENAME, which as you saw above is websession:

```
sub getSession {
    my ($self, $msg) = @_;

    my $j = Apache2::Cookie::Jar->new($self->{r});
    my $cookie= $j->cookies($COOKIENAME);
```

4. If the cookie is defined and has a value, call the method digestCookieValue(), which produces a hash reference containing the user's uid and session id, which was encoded in the cookie value:

```
if ($cookie && $cookie->value()) {
    my $cookieref= digestCookieValue($cookie->value());
```

5. memcached both action was for a logout, then delete the cookie and session from the database and memcached both.

```
if ($self->{form}{'logout'}) {
    unsetCookie($self->{r});
    $self->deleteSession($cookieref->{sessionid});
    $$msg= 'User is logged out';
    return {};
}
```

6. Otherwise, the user has a session, so obtain the session data (a hash reference of anything saved for that user for that session). Then there is a check to make sure that there is actually a session id set. If not, it deletes the session cookie, resulting in the user having to log in to have a session created:

```
else {
    my $sessionref= $self->getSessionData($cookieref->{sessionid});
    unless ($sessionref->{sessionid}) {
        unsetCookie($self->{r});
        return {};
    }
    return $sessionref;
}
}
```

7. If the operation is a login, then the login credentials are checked. If they are satisfied, then a session id is created, the session is inserted in the database and in memcached, and the cookie for that session is set:

```
elsif ($self->{form}{login}) {
    if (my $uid= $self->isAuthenticated(
                        $self->{form}{'username'},
                        $self->{form}{'password'})) {

        # get a session id
        my $sessionid= $self->makeSessionId($uid);

        # initial entry in the sessions database table
        my $sessionref= $self->insertSession($sessionid, $uid);
```

```
                    # set the cookie
                    setCookie($self->{r}, encodeCookieValue($uid, $sessionid));

                    $$msg= "Session was created";

                    return $sessionref;
                }
```

8. If, on the other hand, the login credentials supplied did not satisfy isAuthenticated(), then it returns an empty hash reference that will result in the user having to resubmit the login with the correct credentials:

```
                # otherwise, force the user to log in again
                else {
                    $$msg= "User " . $self->{form}{username} .
                                " not authenticated. Try again";
                    return {};
                }
            }
        }
```

9. Next comes the setCookie() method. This method will look very familiar to you, except here it has a little more functionality than before. There is an optional $value argument, which is then checked for its length. If the length is zero, this means that the cookie needs to be deleted, so then the expiration value is set to 3 months in the past, which will result in the cookie being deleted by the browser. If the value has a length, the expiration will be set 3 months in the future:

```
        sub setCookie {
            my ($r, $value)= @_;

            # if no value, then this means a delete cookie
            my $expires= length($value) ? '+3M' : '-3M';

            my $cookie = Apache2::Cookie->new($r,
                -name    =>  $COOKIENAME,
                -value   =>  $value,
                -expires =>  $expires,
                -domain  =>  $COOKIEDOMAIN,
                -path    =>  $COOKIEPATH,
                );
            $cookie->bake($r);
        }
```

10. All unsetCookie() does is to call setCookie() with an empty string, which you know from above means that the cookie will be set with an expiration value in the past, resulting in its deletion:

```
        sub unsetCookie {
            my ($r)= @_;
            setCookie($r, '');
        }
```

11. The method `makeSessionId()` creates a unique session id key. It appends both the random eight-character string returned from `randomString()` with the value of `localtime()` and then converts that to an MD5 string. This could also be done using MySQL to generate a UUID or CPAN module Data::UUID:

```perl
sub makeSessionId {
    my ($uid)= @_;
    my $value= randomString();
    $value.= localtime;
    $value= md5_hex($value);
    return $value;
}
```

12. The method `encodeCookieValue()` is used to hide the details and store separate strings of the cookie value — which is the `$id` and `$value` passed in separated by ':::'. This can be used to provide both the session id, `sessionid` and the user `uid` without having to even access the database or memcached just from the cookie's value. It does this by converting the value to a hexadecimal string:

```perl
sub encodeCookieValue {
    my ($id, $value) = @_;
    $value = $id . ':::' . $value;
    $value =~ s/(.)/sprintf("%%%02x", ord($1))/ge;
    return $value;
}
```

13. The method `digestCookieValue()` allows you to read the value of the cookie as encoded by `encodeCookie()`, returning a hash reference with the id and `sessionid` decoded from the cookie value:

```perl
sub digestCookieValue {
    my ($value) = @_;
    $value =~ s/%([a-fA-F0-9][a-fA-F0-9])/pack('C', hex($1))/ge;
    my ($id, $sessionid) = split(/:::/, $value, 2);
    return({
        id          => $id,
        sessionid   => $sessionid});
}
```

Storing Session Data

The next set of methods to show you are those that store the session data in the database and in memcached. To first understand what is being stored, a look at the *sessions* table:

```sql
CREATE TABLE sessions (
  sessionid        char(32) not null default '',
  uid              int(8) not null default 0,
  stored_session   blob,
  primary key sessionid (sessionid),
  key uid (uid)
) ENGINE = InnoDB ;
```

❏   The *sessions* table is pretty simple. It has two columns: sessionid, using fixed number of 32 characters since the MD5 session id will always be 32 characters; and stored_session, which is a BLOB where the serialized Perl object will be stored.

❏   The other table you will need is the *users* table, which is the same table as the one used for the contact list application. This *users* table can be used for this application as well; you'll just need to add a password column to it:

```
ALTER TABLE users ADD (password char(32) NOT NULL default '');
```

❏   Then set a password for the user:

```
UPDATE users SET password = md5('password') WHERE username = 'CaptTofu';
```

You could modify the contact application to have a password field, as well as a check for whether you are an administrative user. You could even extend the contact list application to become a web site user administrative tool! All the pieces are there.

The method insertSession() is used to create an initial session entry in the *sessions* table and in memcached. The initial session, as stored as $sessionref, will contain a session id, and a hash reference for the user, as returned from the method getUser(). You'll also notice the use of the nice shiny, new method dbInsert()! This makes inserting data so much easier; you do not have to write a database query. Also notice the use of Storable's nfreeze() method to serialize $sessionref to be stored in the *sessions* table. For storing $sessionref in memcached, it is not necessary to serialize $sessionref because Cached::Memcached::libmemcached automatically serializes data, using the same technique used here for the database.

After inserting this hash reference into the *sessions* table, the hash reference is returned to the caller:

```
sub insertSession {
    my ($self, $sessionid, $uid)= @_;

    my $sessionref = {
        uid          => $uid,
        sessionid    => $sessionid,
        user         => $self->getUser({ uid => $uid})
        };

    $self->dbInsert('sessions', {
            sessionid       => $sessionid,
            uid             => $uid,
            stored_session  => nfreeze($sessionref),
            }
        );
    $self->{memc}->set($sessionid, $sessionref);
    return $sessionref;
}
```

The method storeSession() is used to store session data. Since insertSession() is always used to create an initial entry into the *sessions* table, storing a session will always be an update, which will be accomplished using the other new database method, dbUpdate(). With this method, the existing session hash reference has to be retrieved; the method getSessionData() will provide it either from memcached or from MySQL. The new session hash reference values are mapped into the existing session hash reference; new values overwrite the old ones. The same idea of storing the session hash reference that you saw in insertSession() is applied — nfreeze() serializes the hash reference and then updates the existing session with the new session data using dbUpdate(). Also, the session data (stored in memcached) is updated as well:

```perl
sub storeSession {
    my ($self, $sessionid, $newsession)= @_;

    # obtain the existing session
    my $existingsession= $self->getSessionData($sessionid);

    # map new values into exiting, new values overwrite old
    @{$existingsession}{keys %$newsession}= values %$newsession;


    # update the existing session record in sessions
    $self->dbUpdate('sessions',
            { stored_session => nfreeze($existingsession)},
            { sessionid      => $sessionid});

    $self->{memc}->set($sessionid, $existingsession);
    return $existingsession;
};
```

The method getSessionData() obtains an existing session from either memcached or MySQL. If it is able to obtain it from memcached, it returns it immediately. If not, it obtains the session from MySQL, using the new database access method dbGetRef(), and then writes back to memcached what it just read from MySQL (read-through caching):

```perl
sub getSessionData {
    my ($self, $sessionid)= @_;
    my $sessionref;

    # check in memcached
    $sessionref= $self->{memc}->get($sessionid);

    # return if in memcached and has a session id
    return $sessionref if $sessionref->{sessionid};

    # otherwise, obtain from database
    my $sref= $self->dbGetRef('sessions', 'sessionid, uid, stored_session',
                                     { sessionid   => $sessionid, });

    # if nothing, return empty hash ref
    return {} unless defined $sref && scalar @$sref;

    # de-serialize
    $sessionref= thaw($sref->[0]{stored_session});

    # write to memcached on the way out
    $self->{memc}->set($sessionid, $sessionref);
```

```
    # finally, return the session ref
    return $sessionref;
}
```

Finally, the method `deleteSession()` deletes the session from both MySQL and memcached:

```
sub deleteSession {
    my ($self, $sessionid)= @_;
    $self->dbDelete('sessions', {sessionid => $sessionid});
    $self->{memc}->delete($sessionid);
}
```

So, the appropriate entry is made in the Apache configuration file:

```
PerlModule WroxHandlers::LoginHandler
<Location /login>
      SetHandler perl-script
      PerlResponseHandler WroxHandlers::LoginHandler
   </Location>
```

Restart Apache, and then you can test this handler.

The first thing in testing would be to access `http://example.com/login`. You will see the login form as shown in Figure 15-7.

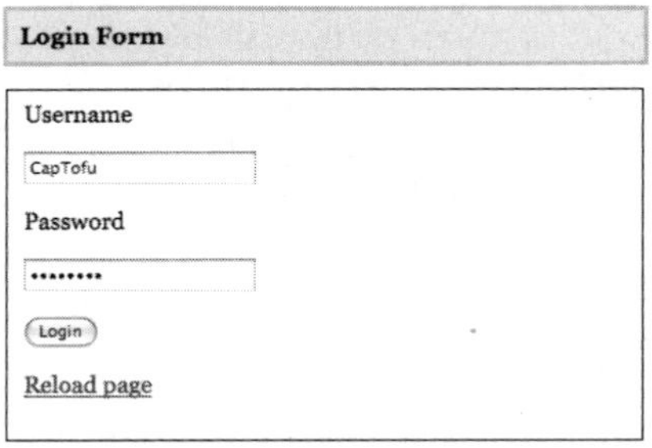

Figure 15-7

Upon submitting the login form (Figure 15-7) with the correct credentials, you will then see the session information page. This page has two parts to it. The top half is a form, as shown in Figure 15-8; it is where you can submit a value in both *"Field Name"* and *"Field Value"* input text fields, which correspond to a key and value stored in the session. This form shows you how you can store values for a given session.

The second half of the form, the lower half, as shown in Figure 15-9, is where the contents of the current session are displayed. As you can see, these values can be scalars or any Perl data type. In this instance, you'll see the hash reference for the session user. At the very bottom of this form is a button to log out. If you then press this button, you will be logged out of your session.

The form shown in Figure 15-10 shows what is displayed after you log out. Since your session has been deleted, this form is automatically displayed.

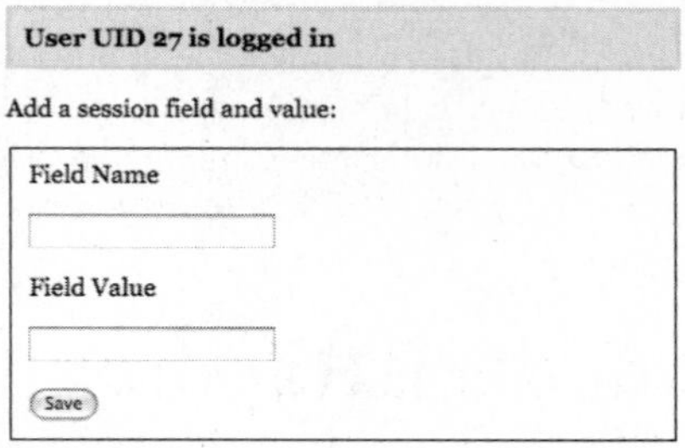

User UID 27 is logged in

Add a session field and value:

Field Name

Field Value

(Save)

Figure 15-8

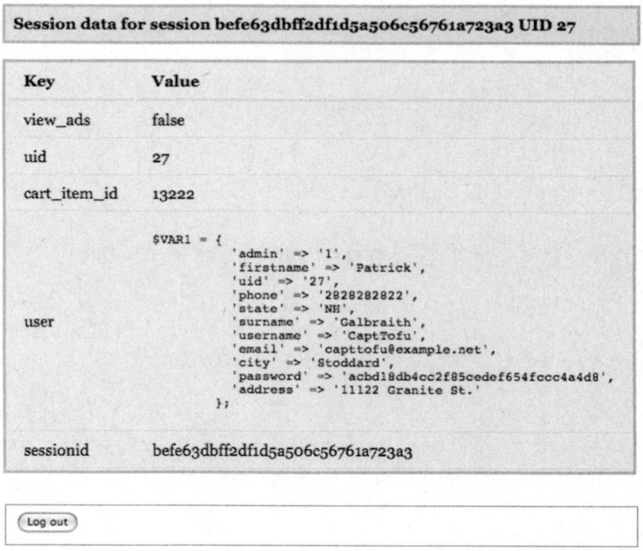

Session data for session befe63dbff2df1d5a506c56761a723a3 UID 27

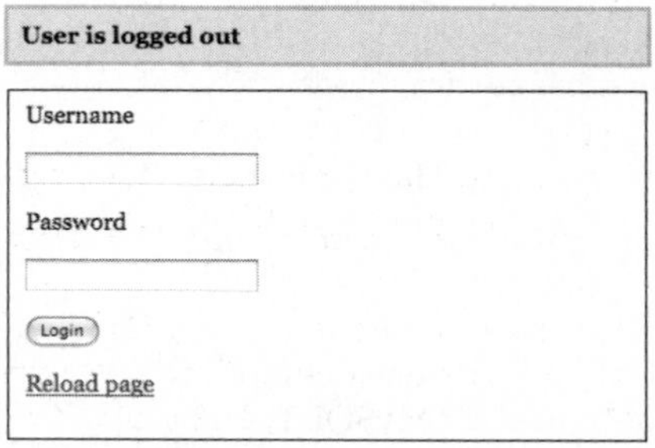

Key	Value
view_ads	false
uid	27
cart_item_id	13222
| user | ```
$VAR1 = {
          'admin' => '1',
          'firstname' => 'Patrick',
          'uid' => '27',
          'phone' => '2828282822',
          'state' => 'NH',
          'surname' => 'Galbraith',
          'username' => 'CaptTofu',
          'email' => 'capttofu@example.net',
          'city' => 'Stoddard',
          'password' => 'acbd18db4cc2f85cedef654fccc4a4d8',
          'address' => '11122 Granite St.'
        };
``` |
| sessionid | befe63dbff2df1d5a506c56761a723a3 |

(Log out)

Figure 15-9

User is logged out

Username

Password

(Login)

Reload page

Figure 15-10
```

This concludes the section on session management. As you can see, there are a lot of pieces required to make session management work. The functionality that is implemented for session management is something that's taken for granted; it seems to simply work. As a web developer, though, it helps to understand what exactly is required for it to work. That's what this section on session management hoped to achieve.

File Upload mod_perl Handler

Another common web application functionality that's worth looking at is how to handle file uploads. This is what allows you to develop applications that perform a number of functions:

- ❑ Image gallery
- ❑ Web publishing
- ❑ Web site hosting
- ❑ File manager application

Luckily, mod_perl has just the tools for handling file uploads. It's easier than you would think.

Storing Files in the Database or Not?

The following handler shows you how to perform file uploads. It's a very simple application that allows you to upload a file. It stores that file's location in MySQL, but not the file's contents. The file is stored on disk, and the database provides a "legend" or map to where the file is.

There is a debate over whether or not to store files (images, text, etc.) in databases. Certainly, MySQL is capable of storing BLOBs, which is where you would store the file contents, regardless of file type.

The pros of storing a file in the database are the following:

- ❑ All your data, including the file contents, are stored in one place.
- ❑ You don't have to provide functionality to map a file's actual location to where it is on disk.
- ❑ Backups of the database include the files.

The cons of storing a file in the database are these:

- ❑ It has an impact on performance. Having to fetch a blob requires memory.
- ❑ Cost of database disk space is higher than regular file-system disk space.

The performance issue is the clincher — having to select a BLOB, or multiple BLOBs, requires memory. The official dogma about what should be done doesn't always correspond to reality. It's not that difficult to have a scheme that maps a file on disk. MySQL is especially fast with meta-data. Just remember, it's best to let MySQL do what it's good at doing, and let the filesystem do what it's good at — storing files.

Database Table

The database table that will be used to store the file meta-data is, not surprisingly, called `files`. This table stores various parameters, some of which won't be used for the following handler example, but are included to give an idea of the type of data you might want to store for a given file.

```
CREATE TABLE files (
    id int(8) NOT NULL auto_increment,
    filename varchar(32) NOT NULL default '',
    fileurl varchar(80) NOT NULL default '',
    filetitle varchar(64) NOT NULL default '',
    filecomment varchar(128) NOT NULL default '',
    filepath varchar(128) NOT NULL default '',
    created timestamp NOT NULL default CURRENT_TIMESTAMP on update CURRENT_TIMESTAMP,
    fileid varchar(16) NOT NULL default '',
    filesize int(8) NOT NULL default '0',
  filetype varchar(32) NOT NULL default '',
    uid int(8) NOT NULL default '0',
    PRIMARY KEY  (id),
    UNIQUE KEY filename (uid,filename),
    KEY uid (uid)
) ENGINE=InnoDB DEFAULT CHARSET=utf8;
```

mod_perl Handler Implementation

Next, you'll see a mod_perl handler that implements the core of file uploading, using MySQL for the file information. Once you have file uploading, it could be extended into a number of applications. The following handler will demonstrate:

❑   How to handle file uploads

❑   How to ensure the directory path where the uploaded file resides is set up

❑   How to store meta-data for the file in MySQL for a given user

❑   Display the list of files for a given user

Set Up the Uploads Directory in the Apache Configuration

To have a directory where this handler will upload its files, you need to set up an "uploads" directory. You will want to set this outside your document root and not allow directory indexes within this directory and its subdirectories to prevent peeking into these directories — only the upload application, which is about to be implemented, provides a means of viewing what is contained within. You can do this using the Alias Apache directive along with a <Directory> directive in your Apache configuration file:

```
Alias /uploads/ "/var/uploads/"
<Directory /var/uploads>
  AllowOverride None
```

```
    Order allow,deny
    Allow from all
</Directory>
```

Implement the mod_perl Handler

Create the handler file. You will declare a namespace for the package and import the various Apache2 packages. The key module here is Apache2::Upload. It implements methods for file uploads, as well as HTML::Entities:

```
package WroxHandlers::UploadHandler;

use strict;
use warnings;

use Apache2::Const -compile => qw(OK REDIRECT :log);
use Apache2::Upload ();

use Apache2::RequestRec ();
use HTML::Entities;
use WebApp();
```

The handler() Subroutine

Implement the handler() subroutine. The main body of the handler implementation is defined. In this example, the new session functionality from the last chapter will be used. This will allow files to be owned by particular users and only viewable by them. Also, a WebApp object is instantiated. The Apache request object is passed upon instantiation. WebApp will then provide access to an Apache2::Request object through $webapp->{req}, which has access to the file being uploaded:

```
sub handler {
    my ($r) = @_;
    my $msg = '';

    # obtain the main URL
    my $url = $r->uri;

    # instantiate a webapp object
    my $webapp = WebApp->new({ r => $r});
```

❑   This is where the session is obtained, if set. If not set, then a redirection to the /login URL (LoginHandler) is made so the user can log into the application. Note also that the *returnto* value is set upon redirection. That of course is how the login handler can redirect the user back to the page that originally sent them from to log in:

```
    # get the session
    my $sessionref = $webapp->getSession();

    # if no session, redirect to login page
    unless ($sessionref && $sessionref->{uid}) {
        $r->headers_out->add('Location' => "/login?returnto=$url");
```

```
            return Apache2::Const::REDIRECT;
        }

        # print mime header
        $r->content_type('text/html');
```

❑   The subroutine saveUpload() handles the uploaded file and stores it in the database:

```
        # call saveUpload() which will process any file that is uploaded
        saveUpload($r, $webapp, $sessionref->{uid}, \$msg);
```

❑   The file upload form is printed. This is the form that will allow the user to upload files. It gives the user the ability to give the file a title as well as select the file to be uploaded. An additional checkbox is provided to give the user the ability to overwrite an existing file. A message displays the status of the file being uploaded — whether it was saved or not, if this is defined:

```
        # print the HTML header
        $r->print(q(
    <html>
        <head>
            <title>File Upload Handler</title>
            <link type="text/css" href="/css/webapp.css" rel="stylesheet"></style>
        </head>
        <body>
        ));

        my $msg_block =  qq(<p class="msg">$msg</p>) if length($msg);
        # print main form of the document
        $r->print(qq(
            <h1>File Upload handler</h1>
            $msg_block
            <form action="$url" id="uploadform" name="uploadform"
            method="POST" enctype="multipart/form-data" name="testform">
                <fieldset>
                    <p>
                        <label for="filetitle">File title:</label>
                        <input type="text" name="filetitle" size="20">
                    </p>
                    <p>
                        <label for="upload_file">File upload:</label>
                        <input type="file" name="upload_file">
                        Overwrite: <input type="checkbox" name="overwrite">
                    </p>
                    <input type="submit" value="Upload" name="pressmebutton">
                </fieldset>
            </form>));
```

❑ Display any files the user owns. This is accomplished by looping over the results of the query to obtain the user's files. Also notice that the loop provides an HREF link displayed in the loop. You will be able to access the files you upload:

```
# obtain the array reference of files
my $files= $webapp->getFiles($sessionref->{uid});

# only attempt printing the table if there are any files to begin with
if (scalar @$files) {
    $r->print(qq(
    <table name="filelist" id="filelist" class="userlist">
        <thead>
            <tr>
                <th>Title</th>
                <th>Date entered</th>
                <th>Size</th>
                <th>Link</th>
            </tr>
</thead>
        <tbody>
    ));

        # variable for accumulating the rows of the table
        for (@$files) {
            # encode any HTML entities for file title and name
            $_->{filetitle} = encode_entities($_->{filetitle});
            $_->{filename}  = encode_entities($_->{filename});

            $rowcontent.= <<EOROW
                <tr>
                    <td>$_->{filetitle}</td>
                    <td>$_->{created}</td>
                    <td>$_->{filesize}</td>
                    <td><a href="$_->{fileurl}">$_->{filename}</a></td>
                </tr>
EOROW
        }
        $rowcontent.= <<EOTAB;
            </tbody>
        </table>
EOTAB

        $r->print($rowcontent);
    }
```

❑ After the list of files is printed, the rest of the document is displayed, and OK is returned.

```
# print the rest  of the document
$r->print(qq(
```

```
        </body>
</html>)
);

        return Apache2::Const::OK;

}
```

The saveUpload() Subroutine

Implementation of the subroutine, saveUpload(), processes the uploaded file. It stores the file on disk, and stores the file's meta-data in MySQL table called *files*. The submitted form values are obtained with getForm():

```
sub saveUpload {
    my ($r, $webapp, $uid, $msg)= @_;
    my $saved = 0;
    my $filepath;

    my $form = $webapp->getForm();
```

1. First, the upload directory value is obtained.

```
        # obtain the value of the directory in which  files will be uploaded
        $upload_dir= $r->dir_config('UploadDir');
```

2. Then an Apache2::Request object — accessed via the attribute req of $webapp — is used to call the method upload() for parsing the submitted file from upload form element *upload_file*. Then a check is made to ensure that the upload exists and, if so, to set the path information of where the file will be stored and the file meta-data is stored in MySQL.

```
        # obtain the upload,if there was an upload
        my $upload= $webapp->{req}->upload('upload_file');

        # if there is an upload, process it
        if ($upload) {
```

3. Each user has their own subdirectory, specified by the $uid value and obtained by looking up the uid from the database when given the session id from the session cookie. For instance, if the path is /var/uploads, and the user's uid is 27, the full path to the user's upload directory will be /var/uploads/27:

```
            # append the uid to the path
            $filepath = $upload_dir . '/' . $uid;
```

4. This is where the base directory /var is stripped from the full file path to provide a URL path which the Alias directive in your Apache configuration specified. For instance, the URL from the path above after substitution would end up being /uploads/27.

```
        # strip out /var to obtain the url
        my ($fileurl) = $filepath =~ /\/var(.*)/;
```

5.   Then the filename value is obtained from the `$upload` handle (an Apache2::Upload object reference). It should be noted that this might be a good place to implement filtering of the filename. This example won't show the implementation of this for the sake of simplicity, but it's definitely something worth mentioning since the filename comes from user input and can contain anything.

```
# filename
my $filename= $upload->filename();

# full path on disk
$filepath = "$filepath/$filename";
        # url path
        $fileurl = "$fileurl/$filename";
# build the fileinfo hash reference which will be inserted
my $fileinfo = {
    uid             => $uid,
    fileid          => $webapp->randomString(),
    filename        => $filename,
    filesize        => $upload->size(),
    fileurl         => $fileurl,
    filepath        => $filepath,
    filetitle       => $form->{filetitle},
};
```

6.   The next line is a call to the method `fileExists()` to determine if this meta-data for the file already exists in the database. If the meta-data exists, another check is made to determine if the user checked the *overwrite* checkbox. If the file's meta-data exists and the user checked the *overwrite* checkbox, then the file meta-data will be updated by the method `saveFileInfo()`. If not, then an error message is set and the subroutine returns.

```
if ($webapp->fileExists($fileinfo)) {
    if ($form->{overwrite}) {
        $saved = $webapp->saveFileInfo($fileinfo);
        $$msg = "File $fileinfo->{filename}, saved and
overwritten"
                                            if $saved;
    }
    else {
        # exists error
        $$msg = "File $fileinfo->{filename} already exists, not \
overwriting";
        return -1;
    }
}
```

7.   If the meta-data for the file doesn't exist, then it is inserted by the method `saveFileInfo()` and a message indicating success is set.

```
else {
    $saved = $webapp->saveFileInfo($fileinfo);
    $$msg = "New file $fileinfo->{filename} saved." if $saved;
}
```

8. If the file meta-data was either successfully inserted or updated, the value of $saved should be true. In that case, the file can be linked into the upload directory. A check is made to ensure that the user's upload directory exists, and if not, it creates one. If $saved is false, then an error message is set and displayed back in the upload form page. Whatever is the value of $saved is returned. If there was no uploaded file at all, 0 is returned.

```
        if ($saved) {
            # if the upload directory doesn't exist, create it
            unless(-e $filepath) {
                mkdir($filepath);
            }
            # this creates the file on disk
            $upload->link($filepath);
        }
        else {
            $$msg = "Unable to save $fileinfo->{filename}";
        }
        return $saved;
    }
    return 0;

1; # end of handler file
```

Methods That Need to be Added to WebApp

The database methods previously shown in the upload handler implementation need to be implemented in WebApp. These are very straightforward and are required for storing and retrieving file meta-data methods.

getFiles() Method

The method getFiles() obtains an array reference, using dbGetRef, of the specified user's files. This is the data that is displayed in the previous handler when listing the files.

```
=head2 getFiles()

Returns an array reference containing hash references for each
file's meta-data saved in the files table

=item arguments

=over

$self - object reference

$uid - the user ID of the files owner

=back

=item returns

=over
```

```
Array reference containing hash references of meta data for every file

=back

=cut

sub getFiles {
    my ($self, $uid) = @_;
    return $self->dbGetRef('files', '*', { uid => $uid});
}
```

fileExists() Method

The method fileExists() is used to determine if meta-data for a given filename and user id exists. If it exists, the file id for that meta-data entry is returned, if not, then 0 is returned.

```
=head2 fileExists()

Returns an either the file id of the entry for a given file's
meta-data or zero, if not exists. The look-up for the data is
done using the file name (filename) and the user id (uid)

=item arguments

=over

$self - object reference

$fileinfo - hash reference of file meta data

=back

=item returns

=over

file id - success
0       - failure

=back

=cut


sub fileExists {
    my ($self, $fileinfo)= @_;

    my $file_exists= $self->dbGetRef('files', 'id', {
        uid         => $fileinfo->{uid},
        filename    => $fileinfo->{filename}});

    # file id, primary key of file
    return(defined $file_exists->[0]{id} ? $file_exists->[0]{id} : 0 );
}
```

saveFileInfo() Method

The method saveFileInfo() will insert a file meta-data hash reference if it exists. It uses the previously mentioned fileExists() method to determine if there is an existing entry for the file's meta-data. If the file's meta-data exists, the return value from fileExists() is a valid file id. This is then used to update the existing record for the file meta-data. If the file's meta-data doesn't exist, then it is inserted with dbInsert().

```
=head2 saveFileInfo()

Either updates or inserts a given file's meta data, depending on
whether the meta-data entry already existed or not

=item arguments

=over

$self - object reference

$fileinfo - hash reference of file meta data

=back

=item returns

=over

$rows
> 0       - success
0         - failure

=back

=cut

sub saveFileInfo {
    my ($self, $fileinfo)= @_;
    my $file_id= $self->fileExists($fileinfo);
    my $rows;

    warn "file_id $file_id";
    # if file exists, update
    if ($file_id) {
        $rows = $self->dbUpdate('files', $fileinfo, { id => $file_id });
    }
    # otherwise update
    else {
        $rows = $self->dbInsert('files', $fileinfo);
    }
    return $rows;
}
```

Using the mod_perl Upload Handler

Now let's use this handler and upload some files! Set the appropriate settings to declare the handler in your Apache configuration file:

```
PerlModule WroxHandlers::UploadHandler
<Location /uploadhandler>
  PerlSetVar UploadDir /var/www/apache2-default/uploads
  SetHandler perl-script
  PerlResponseHandler WroxHandlers::UploadHandler
</Location>
```

Restart Apache, and upload some files! The interface for this handler will appear as shown in Figure 15-11. Notice the clean table displaying the list of files that were uploaded, with each one providing a link to the file.

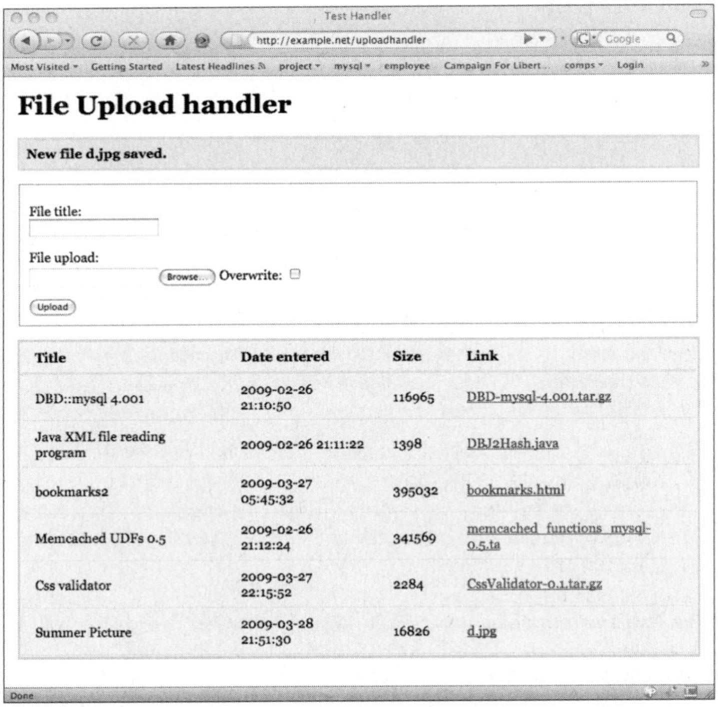

Figure 15-11

This completes the section showing you how to work with file uploads. This simple example is something you could easily extend. For instance, you could make an image sharing program with this. You would just need to limit the files being uploaded to image type, preventing uploads of other types of files, and creating thumbnails of the image when the image is created in the upload directory.

Templating

The other big question in mod_perl development specifically, and web application development in general, is what templating system you should use. Up until this section, all the Perl handlers shown have been implemented using the simple printing of HTML from within the handler code. This section will show you how templating can be used to separate code from content. Perl, which always has a way to solve a problem (sometimes numerous ways), also has a number of templating systems.

This section will show you three of the many templating solutions available for Perl. Each has its own philosophy and implementation details.

The two philosophies or approaches are outlined here:

❑ Have code to perform the processing in either a ModPerl::Registry script or a mod_perl handler, and then use the template to display the content.

❑ Similar to the philosophy of PHP; have a template with tags that allow you to embed Perl code into the template. The tags also allow you to separate the code from the content.

Of the three template solutions presented in this section, the first two take the former approach. The third is like the latter. The three templating solutions are:

❑ Template Toolkit: As described on its own web site, "The Template Toolkit is a fast, flexible and highly extensible template processing system." Template Toolkit has its own presentation language, specifically for displaying data that you provide to the template when you call it to be processed.

❑ HTML::Template: "HTML::Template is a new solution to an old problem — Perl CGI development," as described on its web site. Its focus is to completely separate the tasks of developers from those of designers. HTML::Template keeps the template language very simple, offering the ability to display variables, use conditionals, loop, and include another template.

❑ HTML::Mason: The Mason web site states, "Mason is a powerful Perl-based web site development and delivery engine. With Mason you can embed Perl code in your HTML and construct pages from shared, reusable components." Mason's aim is content management of large sites, but it is also fine for small sites. Its markup language is simple enough to use and designers can edit without having to learn Perl.

The first two are solutions that allow you to process and display the template from within the code. The HTML::Mason template has code embedded in it that is indicated with tags.

The following examples will all perform the same basic functionality, but each uses a different templating system.

Template Toolkit

Template Toolkit, also referred to as Template, has its own presentation language. This language is similar to other programming languages and has all the conditionals, variables, loops, etc. Template::Toolkit was written in such a way that the back-end is Perl-specific and aimed at developers, whereas the front-end template presentation language is aimed at the designer.

The web site for Template Toolkit, `http://template-toolkit.org`, is a wealth of information. It includes a tutorial, installation information, and other reference manuals. It should be noted that Template Toolkit also has a Python version.

Features

Template Toolkit has a number of features that it is known for, including these:

❑ Full support for all Perl data types

❑ Clear separation between content and application code, making it easy for designers to work with

❑ Good balance — front-end is designer-centric, back-end is programmer-centric

❑ Templates are precompiled into Perl code and cached for performance

Plug-Ins to Template Toolkit

Template Toolkit has a good number of plug-ins available via CPAN and as shown on `http://template-toolkit.org/docs/manual/Plugins.html`. These plug-ins provide functionality extensions to Template Toolkit, such as database connectivity, an iteration abstraction object, a string class, filtering, and much more.

Template Toolkit Syntax

The language uses the opening and closing square brackets and percent symbol (`[%` and `%]`) to enclose tags that contain directives and variables. Here is an example:

```
<h1>[% main_message %]</h1>
```

This will interpolate the variable `$main_message` in between the h1 tags. If `$main_message` was equal to "Hey, I'm here," the value displayed would be this:

```
<h1>Hey, I'm here</h1>
```

You can also use filtering. The example that follows shows you that you can filter a string through an HTML filter to translate HTML entities, which is something you want to do to avoid HTML injection. If `main_message` contains "Up & running," like so:

```
<h1>[% main_message | html %]</h1>
```

... it would result in the following being displayed:

```
<h1>Up &amp; running</h1>
```

More complex data is accessed using the dot(.) notation operator. The following is a Perl array reference:

```
my $list_of_things = [`patram`, `pushpam`, `toyam`, `phalam`];
```

In the Template Toolkit syntax, when passed to the template, it would appear like this:

```
[% list = ['patram', 'pushpam', 'toyam', 'phalam'] %]
```

And it would be accessed as this:

```
[% list = ['patram', 'pushpam', 'toyam', 'phalam'] %]
<p>[% list.0 %]</p>
<p>[% list.1 %]</p>
<p>[% list.2 %]</p>
<p>[% list.3 %]</p>
<p>size [% list.size %]</p>
```

... which would produce in the resulting HTML:

```
<p>patram</p>
<p>pushpam</p>
<p>toyam</p>
<p>phalam</p>
<p>size 4</p>
```

To print out all the elements, you can then loop over this array with the following:

```
[% FOREACH word = list %]
<p>[% word %]</p>
[% END %]
```

Hashes are accessed similarly:

```
[%
  states = {
    NH => "New Hampshire",
    VT => "Vermont",
    WA => "Washington"
  }
%]

<p>[% states.NH %]</p>
<p>[% states.VT %]</p>
<p>[% states.WA %]</p>
<p>size of states [% states.size %]</p>
```

This would result in the display of this:

```
<p>New Hampshire</p>
<p>Vermont</p>
<p>Washington</p>
<p>size of states 3</p>
```

To loop over the hash, an example would be:

```
[% FOREACH abbr = states.keys %]
  <p>Abbr [% abbr %] Name [% states.$abbr %]
[% END %]
```

And here is a more complex data structure, a hash reference of hash references:

```
[% FOREACH uid = userlist.keys %]
        <tr>
            <td>[% userlist.$uid.uid | html %]</td>
            <td>[% userlist.$uid.username | html %]</td>
            <td>[% userlist.$uid.firstname | html %]</td>
            <td>[% userlist.$uid.surname | html %]</td>
        </tr>
    [% END %]
```

Whereas Perl would use `$userlist->{$uid}{username}`, Template Toolkit's language uses the dot notation, and would refer to the former as `userlist.$uid.userame`.

The INSERT directive is used to insert the contents of an external file at the location in the page specified. No interpolation of the file will be attempted.

```
[% INSERT .signature %]
```

... would insert the contents of the `.signature` file.

The INCLUDE directive includes and processes the template named at the location in the page specified:

```
<html>
[% INCLUDE header title = title %]
<body>
... Content ...
[% INCLUDE footer %]
</html>
```

... which would include the contents of the *header* and *footer* templates. For instance, the *header* template may have something like this:

```
<head>
<title>[% title %]</title>
        <link type="text/css" href="/css/webapp.css" rel="stylesheet">
</head>
```

You can also use the PROCESS directive, along with defining a BLOCK:

```
<html>
[% PROCESS header title = title %]
<body>
... content ...
</body>
</html>
[% BLOCK header %]
<head><title>[% title %]</title></head>
[% END %]
```

In this example, the BLOCK directive is used to define a component block within the current page that will provide the header content. The block also contains a title variable.

A mod_perl Handler Example Using Template Toolkit

Now that you've seen some examples of the template language, you will now see how to use Template Toolkit with a mod_perl handler. As stated, all these templating examples will print out exactly the same page — a listing of contacts/users from the *users* table. The object here is to try to use various features of Template Toolkit to show you how it works.

Handler Declaration in the Apache Configuration File

This is just like any other handler declaration, with the addition of specifying the template path that the mod_perl handler will obtain with dir_config().

> It should be noted that **/var/www** is not the document root, and that you should not put your templates in a subdirectory of the document root.

```
PerlModule WroxHandlers::TemplateToolkitHandler
   <Location /userlisttemp>
    SetHandler perl-script
    PerlSetVar TEMPLATE_PATH "/var/www/templates"
    PerlResponseHandler WroxHandlers::TemplateToolkitHandler
   </Location>
```

Handler Body

The handler works similarly to the other handlers you've seen in this book, except that there is no display logic in the code — no HTML or other content. This handler works by preparing the data required for the template to function properly. This includes any variables that are used within the template.

```perl
package WroxHandlers::TemplateToolkitHandler;

use strict;
use warnings;

use Apache2::Const -compile => qw(OK REDIRECT SERVER_ERROR);
use Apache2::Request;
use Template;
use WebApp;
sub handler {
    my ($r)= @_;
    my $msg;
    my $url= $r->uri;
    my $template_path;

    # instantiate a WebApp object
    my $webapp= WebApp->new({ r => $r});

    # get the submitted form values
    my $form= $webapp->getForm();

    my $sessionref= $webapp->getSession(\$msg);

    # if no session, redirect to login page
    unless ($sessionref && $sessionref->{uid}) {
```

```
$r->headers_out->add('Location' => "/login?returnto=$url");
return Apache2::Const::REDIRECT;
}
```

To understand this code, note the following:

1. The first thing that is needed is the path to where the templates exist. This can be set, as shown here, in the Apache configuration file. This is a base directory where templates are located. Whatever template name you use, it must exist in that directory.

```
# obtain the template path
$template_path= $r->dir_config('TEMPLATE_PATH');
```

2. The next step is to instantiate a template object. Several parameters are provided here upon instantiation and each has a particular effect on how the object is instantiated, as indicated by the comments for each.

```
# instantiate a new Template object
my $template = Template->new({
    INCLUDE_PATH => $template_path, # where to look for templates
    INTERPOLATE  => 0, # expansion of Perl variables in plain text
    POST_CHOMP   => 1, # removal of whitespace
    EVAL_PERL    => 0, # evaluate [%Perl%] code blocks
});
```

3. The hash reference $userlist is obtained, which is a result set of the *users* table. This and other parameters are specified in the hash reference $tparams, which will be passed to the template. These variables will be accessible in the template using the Template Toolkit language syntax.

```
# get the userlist reference
my $userlist= $webapp->getUsers();

# set up template parameters
my $tparams = {
    msg          => $msg,
    url          => $r->uri,
    userlist     => $userlist
};
```

The template name is set.
```
# set up the template name
$url =~ s/^\///;
my $tname= $url . '.tt2';
```

4. The content generation, which first includes printing out the HTTP Content-type header, and is then followed by the Template Toolkit method process(). process() takes two arguments: the name of the template file, and the parameters passed in the hash reference $tparams. This produces output based on the template and the variables supplied to it.

```
$r->content_type('text/html');

# this will process the template
$template->process($tname, $tparams) ||
```

```
              do {
                  # if an error, return SERVER_ERROR
                  $r->server->warn($template->error());
                  return Apache2::Const::SERVER_ERROR;
              };
          return Apache2::Const::OK;
  }

  1;
```

5. The template code is shown next. Here you can see a template included called dtd. This contains the document type declaration. Then the title is set with the SET directive. Also seen here are conditional checks for the msg variable, then a PROCESS directive to include the looping over the userlist hash reference to display the table rows.

```
[% INCLUDE dtd %]
[% SET title = "Template Toolkit Test" %]
<html>
  <head>
    <title>[% title %]</title>
    <link type="text/css" href="/css/webapp.css" rel="stylesheet">
  </head>
  <body>


[% IF msg %]
    <p class="msg">[% msg | html %]</p>
[% END %]
    <p class="msg">URI [% url %]</p>
    <table class="userlist">
      <thead>
          <tr>
            <th>UID</th>
            <th>Username</th>
            <th>First Name</th>
            <th>Surname</th>
          </tr>
      </thead>
[% PROCESS userloop userlist = userlist %]
      <tbody>
      </tbody>
    </table>
  </body>
</html>

[% BLOCK userloop %]
  [% FOREACH uid = userlist.keys %]
<tr>
            <td>[% userlist.$uid.uid | html %]</td>
            <td>[% userlist.$uid.username | html %]</td>
            <td>[% userlist.$uid.firstname | html %]</td>
            <td>[% userlist.$uid.surname | html %]</td>
        </tr>
  [% END %]
[% END %]
```

Caching Templates

Template::Toolkit has many optimizations to how it compiles and caches templates, but you can take a step further and cache your templates in memcached.

First, you want to import the File::Slurp to WebApp. File::Slurp has the subroutine `read_file()` for reading in the contents of the template.

```
use File::Slurp;
```

The following method is added to WebApp. It will read in a template file directly into memcached, which the mod_perl handler can easily use to obtain a cached template instead of having to read from disk:

```perl
sub cacheTemplate {
    my ($self, $template_path, $template_name)= @_;

    # set the content to an empty string
    my $template_content = '';

    # construct a key with namespace and template name
    # for memcached lookup
    my $template_key = "templates:$template_name";

    # check memcached first, if it's there, return it
    $template_content = $self->{memc}->get($template_key);

    # otherwise,
    if ($template_content) {
        return $template_content;
    }

    $template_content = read_file("$template_path/$template_name");

    # cached the template contents
    $self->{memc}->set($template_key,$template_content);
    return $template_content;
}
```

Now to use this new method, just add the following to your mod_perl handler:

```perl
# obtain the contents of the template, only the first time will
# it need to be read from disk, then subsequently from memcached
my $template_cached= $webapp->cacheTemplate($template_path,$tname);

if ($template_cached) {
    $tname = \$template_cached;
}
```

The first time the handler is executed, the template will have to be read and cached, but in subsequent requests it will be obtainable from memcached. The template will display one way or another — either if $tname is a scalar reference to the template contents, or if $tname is a template name.

HTML::Template

HTML::Template is another templating solution available for Perl web applications. Written by Sam Treger, the templating syntax is very simple and includes a few directives. It doesn't have as much syntax features as Template Toolkit, but depending on your needs and preferences, it may work just fine for you. It does have in common with Template Toolkit the concept of dividing design from the code, passing variables that are prepared prior to display, and then processing the template, which is in turn printed in a CGI script or mod_perl handler.

Tags

HTML::Template has what they refer to as "HTML-esque" tags. The name indicates the variable name, and the variable name can be quoted or not and still work either way.

`<TMPL_VAR NAME=VARNAME>` when displayed is converted to the variable value of VARNAME. If, for instance, you had a variable $foo with the value of "hello world," the following line:

```
<p><TMPL_VAR name=foo><p>
```

. . . would, when displayed, be:

```
<p>hello world</p>
```

To escape HTML entities, preventing HTML injection, for HTML::Template you can use:

```
<TMPL_VAR ESCAPE=HTML NAME=foo>
```

To be able to use conditionals (if, else, unless), you use the following:

* `<TMPL_IF somevariable>` begins an if block

* `</TMPL_IF>` ends an if block

* `<TMPL_ELSE>` begins an else block

* ended by `</TMPL_IF>`

An example is:

```
<TMPL_IF testflag>
<p>Test flag set</p>
<TMPL_ELSE>
<p>Test flag not set</p>
</TMPL_IF>
```

The `<TMPL_UNLESS>` is the opposite of `<TMPL_IF>`, and to use the tag, you would have this:

```
<TMPL_UNLESS "somevariable">
      some variable is set to the value of <TMPL_VAR somevariable>
<TMPL_ELSE>
```

```
some variable is not set
</TMPL_UNLESS>
```

`<TMPL_LOOP somearrayref>` iterates over an array reference of hash references. This requires you to prepackage anything you want to loop over to a hash reference.

So if you have in your Perl code, prior to display, a hash reference variable `$aref`:

```
my $aref= [
    { one  => `eins´, two => `zwei´,  lang => `German´},
    { one  => `uno´,  two => `dos´,   lang => `Spanish´},
    { one  => `ek´,   two => `do´,    lang => `Hindi´},
    { one  => `ekam´, two => `dva´,   lang => `Sanskrit´}
];
```

You would iterate over this as:

```
<TMPL_LOOP aref>
<p>English: one is <TMPL_VAR name=one>  is in <TMPL_VAR name=lang> </p>
<p>English: two is <TMPL_VAR name=two>  is in <TMPL_VAR name=lang> </p>
</TMPL_LOOP>
```

You can also include other templates with `<TMPL_INCLUDE="filename.tmpl">`, which would cause the display of `filename.tmpl` at the location in the template that this tag was specified.

A mod_perl Handler Example Using HTML::Template

The following shows an example of how to use HTML::Template to print out the hash reference result set of the *users* table. This will resemble the steps that were used with Template Toolkit, in that the data that the template requires is set up prior to display.

1. First, the Apache configuration:

```
PerlModule WroxHandlers::HTMLTemplateHandler
    <Location /userlist>
     SetHandler perl-script
     PerlResponseHandler WroxHandlers::HTMLTemplateHandler
     PerlSetVar TEMPLATE_PATH "/var/www/templates"
    </Location>
```

You'll notice the same directory that was used for Template::Toolkit is used here for HTML::Template to find its templates as well.

2. Then comes the handler code, itself:

```
package WroxHandlers::HTMLTemplateHandler;

use strict;
use warnings;

use Apache2::Const -compile => qw(OK REDIRECT);

use HTML::Template;
```

```
use WebApp;


sub handler {
    my ($r)= @_;
    my $url= $r->uri;
    my $tpath;
```

3. The template path is obtained as set in the Apache configuration file. This could also have been set with the environment variable HTML_TEMPLATE_ROOT.

```
    # obtain the template path
    $tpath= $r->dir_config("TEMPLATE_PATH");

    # instantitate WebApp
    my $webapp = WebApp->new({ r => $r});

    my $sessionref= $webapp->getSession();

    # if no session, redirect to login page
    unless ($sessionref && $sessionref->{uid}) {
        $r->headers_out->add('Location' => "/login?returnto=$url");
        return Apache2::Const::REDIRECT;
    }
```

4. Here is where the template variables are prepared. Initially, $tparams only has msg and url members.

```
    # set up the template parameters that will be passed
    my $tparams = {
        msg     => "Session " . $sessionref->{sessionid} . " logged in",
        url     => $r->uri,
    };
```

5. Next, the result set of users is obtained. This is a hash reference, so it needs to be organized into an array reference in order to be used in the template with a <TMPL_LOOP> tag. An iterative loop is used to construct an array reference for the users into the $tparams userloop member:

```
    # get the user list ref
    my $users= $webapp->getUsers();

    # build up an array reference of hash references for each
    # user. This is what the template requires for <TMPL_LOOP>
    for my $uid (keys %$users) {
        push(@{$tparams->{userloop}}, {
            uid             => $uid,
            username        => $users->{$uid}{username},
            firstname       => $users->{$uid}{firstname},
            surname         => $users->{$uid}{surname},
            });
    }
```

6. The template name is specified and then an HTML::Template object is instantiated. Its sole argument is the template name passed as a hash member `filename`.

```
# set up the template name
$url =~ s/^\///;
my $tname= $url . '.tmpl';

my $template = HTML::Template->new(
    filename => $tpath . '/' . $tname);
```

7. The `param()` method sets the parameters that the template will use.

```
$template->param($tparams);
```

8. Finally, the HTTP Content-type is set, then the document is printed by calling `print()` with a call to `$template->output()`, displaying the template.

```
$r->content_type('text/html');

$r->print($template->output());

return Apache2::Const::OK;
}

1;
```

HTML::Template template

The template for displaying the userlist table is fairly straightforward. The main thing to notice here is the use of the tag `<TMPL_VAR>` to display the message and the URL. Also, the loop over the `userlist` array reference containing the result set of the *users* table, which was then mapped to an array reference:

```
<html>
  <head>
    <title>HTML::Template test</title>
    <link type="text/css" href="/css/webapp.css" rel="stylesheet">
  </head>
  <body>
    <p class="msg"><TMPL_VAR ESCAPE=HTML name="msg"></p>
    <p class="msg">URI <TMPL_VAR name="url"></p>
    <table class="userlist">
      <thead>
        <tr>
          <th>UID</th>
          <th>Username</th>
          <th>First Name</th>
          <th>Surname</th>
        </tr>
      </thead>
      <tbody>
<TMPL_LOOP NAME="userloop">
        <tr>
```

```
            <td><TMPL_VAR ESCAPE=HTML name="uid"></td>
            <td><TMPL_VAR ESCAPE=HTML name="username"></td>
            <td><TMPL_VAR ESCAPE=HTML name="firstname"></td>
            <td><TMPL_VAR ESCAPE=HTML name="surname"></td>
        </tr>
</TMPL_LOOP>
        </tbody>
      </table>

    </body>
</html>
```

So, as you can see, HTML::Template is pretty simple to use. For more information about how to use HTML::Template, please see http://search.cpan.org/~samtregar/HTML-Template-2.9/Template.pm.

HTML::Mason (Mason)

HTML::Mason, or just Mason, takes a different approach to that of Template::Toolkit and HTML::Template. Developed by Jonathan Swartz, Dave Rolsky, Ken Williams, and John Williams, Mason is a "a powerful Perl-based web site development and delivery engine," as stated on the Mason web site. Indeed, it does give you a lot of functionality and flexibility. It is targeted for large, dynamic, high-load web sites, but can be used just as well for any sized web site, even your own person web site.

Mason uses the concepts of *components*, which are files containing HTML, Perl, and Mason commands. Generally, you would have a top-level component such as the main page, then smaller components that are embedded in the larger components.

Mason is run in such a way that it is set as a mod_perl handler to interpret files in a given directory, site-wide, or with a particular extension using the Apache <LocationMatch> sectional directive, as shown in the following code:

```
PerlModule HTML::Mason::ApacheHandler
    <LocationMatch "\.(mhtml|mtxt)$">
        SetHandler perl-script
        PerlResponseHandler HTML::Mason::ApacheHandler
        PerlAddVar  MasonCompRoot  "main => /var/www/apache2-default"
        PerlAddVar  MasonCompRoot  "datadir => /etc/apache2/mason"
    </LocationMatch>
```

So instead of having a mod_perl handler that prepares data for a template that has a display method to display the template, you simply write the code in the Mason component, and the server interprets it if it meets the criteria for being interpreted. In the case of the previous code, that would mean any files with .mhtml or .mtxt extensions on the web site will be interpreted.

Mason Syntax

Mason has a syntax that is very easy to understand because, for the most part, it uses Perl syntax. However, there are a couple of things to know.

In-Line Perl Sections

There are three primary types of in-line Perl Sections:

❑   Using the block form of `<% $variable %>`. If you have for instance `<b><% $variable %></b>` and `$variable` is of the value "Hey!" then what would be interpreted would be: `<b>Hey!</b>`.

An entire line is treated and interpreted as Perl if it begins with the percentage sign (%). Anything between open tag `<%perl>` and close tag `</%perl>` is interpreted as Perl. This is case-sensitive.

An example of all of these in use would be the following:

```
% my $msg = "This is a test";
<html>
  <head>
    <title><% $msg |h %></title>
    <link type="text/css" href="/css/webapp.css" rel="stylesheet">
  </head>
  <body>
    <p class="msg"><% $msg |h %></p>
    <p class="msg">URI <% $r->uri %></p>
% if ($r->method() eq 'POST') {
    <p>This was a POST</p>
% } else {
    <p>This was a GET<p>
% }

<%perl>
my $aref= ['one', 'two', 'three'];
</%perl>

    <ul>Numbers
% for (@$aref) {
        <li><% $_ %></li>
% }
    </ul>
  </body>
</html>
```

In this example, all three types of in-line Perl sections were used. The message variable was set at the top of the file with a % line sectional directive, then displayed in a block as `<% $msg|h %>`, with the `|h` providing HTML entity escaping. As you can see, the Apache request object, `$r`, is available. The line sectional directive was then used for an if/else block to display text based on whether the request was a GET or POST. Next, the `<%perl>` sectional block was used to set an array reference that was then iterated over in a *for* loop with a line sectional directive to print out an unformatted list. The HTML produced from the above example (using GET) would be this:

```
<html>
  <head>
    <title>This is a test</title>
    <link type="text/css" href="/css/webapp.css" rel="stylesheet">
  </head>
  <body>
```

```
    <p class="msg">This is a test</p>
    <p class="msg">URI /mason_basic.mhtml</p>
    <p>This was a GET<p>

<ul>Numbers
    <li>one</li>
    <li>two</li>
    <li>three</li>
</ul>


    </body>
</html>
```

Mason Objects

As stated above, you have available to you the Apache request object $r. You also have available $m, which is the Mason request object for accessing Mason's API for features not available using the syntactic tags described above. This is a full API that is worthy of a book of its own, and the details of it are well documented on the Mason web site. Some later examples will show some examples of how it is used.

Mason Components

Mason components can be called by other components, the top-level page itself being a component. In these component calls, you can pass variables to the component being called. A component is called using the <& ... &> tag. This tag takes two arguments: the first argument lets you specify the path and name of the component, the second argument lets you set parameters to the template in name => value pairs.

No arguments:

```
<& header &>
```

Specifying a $msg and $color parameter:

```
<& header, msg => $msg, color => $color &>
```

The following example shows how you could use components and have a top-level Mason document:

```
% my $msg = "This is a test";
<& mason/dtd &>
<& mason/header, msg => $msg |h &>
<& mason/body &>
<& mason/footer &>
```

Then, each component, as found in the subdirectory "mason":

❑   mason/dtd

```
    <!DOCTYPE HTML PUBLIC "-//W3C//DTD HTML 4.01//EN"
      "http://www.w3.org/TR/html4/strict.dtd">
```

❏   mason/header

```
<%args>
$msg
</%args>
<html>
  <head>
    <title>This is a test</title>
    <link type="text/css" href="/css/webapp.css" rel="stylesheet">
  </head>
  <body>
    <p class="msg"><% $msg |h %></p>
    <p class="msg">URI <% $r->uri %></p>
```

❏   mason/body

```
<p>This is the body</p>
```

❏   mason/footer

```
  </body>
  </html>
```

The entire document would appear like so:

```
<!DOCTYPE HTML PUBLIC "-//W3C//DTD HTML 4.01//EN"
 "http://www.w3.org/TR/html4/strict.dtd">

<html>
  <head>
    <title>This is a test</title>
    <link type="text/css" href="/css/webapp.css" rel="stylesheet">
  </head>
  <body>
    <p class="msg">This is a test</p>
    <p class="msg">URI /main_mason.mhtml</p>

<p>This is the body</p>

  </body>
</html>
```

You can also include components using the Mason request object, $m, from within a Perl code block. For instance:

```
% $m->comp('/mason/dtd');
```

You will also notice the <%args> section. This is used to read in the variables passed to a component. The example for the header above could have alternatively used this:

```
% my ($msg) = @_;
```

This is also how you would read in form parameters from a POST or GET. The following example shows you a simple form and the page that it posts to:

```html
<html>
  <head><title>Mason form</title></head>
  <body>
    <form action="/mason_post.html" method="POST">
      <label>Var1</label>
      <input type="text" name="var1">
      <label>Var2</label>
      <input type="text" name="var2">
      <input type="submit" name="varsubmit" value="Submit">
    </form>
  </body>
</html>
```

Two form elements, var1 and var2, are submitted by this form, and then read by mason_post.html:

```
<%args>
$var1
$var2
</%args>
<html>
  <head><title>form post</title></head>
  <body>
  var1: <% $var1 |h %>
  var2: <% $var2 |h %>
  </body>
</html>
```

> Since Mason reads the **GET** or **POST** parameters, you cannot use Apache2::Request to read them.

Initialization and Cleanup

There are sections that define code that will execute at specific times:

❑ <%init>: Executes as soon as the component is called.

❑ <%cleanup>: Executes just prior to the exit of the component.

❑ <%once>: Executes only once when the component is loaded; all variables declared here are available to the entire component and any subcomponent for the lifetime of the component.

❑ <%shared%>: Runs once per request; all variables declared are available to the entire component and subcomponents, however, only per request.

An example of an <%init> section will be shown later in the component called *webapp_load*:

```
<%init>
use WebApp;
my $webapp = WebApp->new({ r => $r });
return $webapp;
</%init>
```

This will be used in the following example to load the WebApp object.

Userlisting Page in Mason

You have now seen how to implement this page that lists users in both Template Toolkit and HTML::Template. Now you will see how it is implemented with HTML Mason.

This works just like the other examples; both mod_perl examples with and without templating. The WebApp object is instantiated with the mason/webapp_load component. Then the session is obtained, variables declared, and the variable $url set.

If there is no session, then the Mason request object, $m, is used to perform a redirect — this is how you do redirects with Mason. The list is created by the component specified in the variable $page, which happens to be 'userlist'. The *userlist* component takes the argument $webapp, which it uses to obtain the result set of users.

```
% my $webapp= $m->comp('mason/webapp_load');
% my $session= $webapp->getSession();
% my $msg = $webapp->{msg};
% my ($page, $title);
% my $url= $r->uri;
%
%
% if ($session->{sessionid}) {
%    $page= 'userlist';
%    $title= 'User Listing with HTML::Mason';
% }
% else {
%    $m->redirect("/login?returnto=$url");
% }
<& mason/dtd &>
<html>
  <head>
    <title>HTML::Mason Example</title>
    <link type="text/css" href="/css/webapp.css" rel="stylesheet">
  </head>
  <body>
% if ($msg) {
    <p class="msg"><% $msg |h %></p>
% }

    <p class="msg">URI <% $url %></p>
    <& "mason/$page", webapp => $webapp, url => $url &>
    <a href="/login?logout=1">Log out</a>
  </body>
</html>
```

The *userlist* template is passed both the $url and $webapp variables, as shown in the <%args> section as having been passed. It then calls getUsers() to obtain the $users hash reference, which it then loops over and displays.

```
<%args>
$webapp
$url
</%args>
% my $users= $webapp->getUsers();
```

```
    <table class="userlist">
        <thead>
            <tr><th>Username</th><th>First Name</th><th>Surname</th></tr>
        </thead>
        <tbody>
% for my $uid(keys %$users) {
        <tr>
            <td><% $uid %></td>
            <td><% $users->{$uid}{username} |h %></td>
            <td><% $users->{$uid}{firstname} |h %></td>
            <td><% $users->{$uid}{surname} |h %></td>
        </tr>
% }
        </tbody>
    </table>
```

The Apache configuration settings for this example are the following:

```
PerlModule HTML::Mason::ApacheHandler
    <LocationMatch "\.html">
        SetHandler perl-script
        PerlResponseHandler HTML::Mason::ApacheHandler
        PerlAddVar MasonAllowGlobals $url
        PerlAddVar MasonAllowGlobals $msg
        PerlAddVar MasonAllowGlobals $webapp
        PerlAddVar  MasonCompRoot  "main    => /var/www/apache2-default"
        PerlAddVar  MasonCompRoot  "datadir => /etc/apache2/mason"
    </LocationMatch>
    <Location /mason>
        SetHandler perl-script
        PerlInitHandler Apache2::Const::NOT_FOUND
    </Location>
```

Any file on this web server ending in either .html or text will be processed by Mason. The setting *MasonAllowGlobals* is required to pass the variables specified to the components. *MasonCompRoot* defines the top-level directory of your component hierarchy, and it must be a directory that is readable by the user that the web server process runs as. In this case, it's the document root of the site. The parameter *datadir* specifies a writable directory that Mason uses for various features and optimizations.

The second <Location> sectional directive is used to prevent your component directory from being accessible. You could alternatively set up an alias to a directory outside the document root to avoid this.

Summary

This chapter covered various common functionalities that a web developer will want to be familiar with — cookies, sessions, file uploads, and templating. The discussion included the following:

❑   Whether to write mod_perl apps using ModPerl::Registry. This chapter covered how it works internally, and showed you that there are more steps required to run a mod_perl registry script than a mod_perl handler.

❑ How to convert the contact list/user list application to a mod_perl handler. The primary changes were to use the Apache request object instead of CGI for parsing form variables and also to print out the HTTP content-type header and the document content. You then saw that ModPerl::Registry scripts, since they are essentially mod_perl handlers, have access to all the same variables mod_perl handlers have, namely the Apache request object. To demonstrate this, you were shown how a mod_perl handler could be used with ModPerl::Registry.

❑ How to handle cookies. You learned what a cookie is, and then how to process cookies using the Apache2::Cookie Perl module, via a simple mod_perl handler example that let you set and delete a cookie assigned to your browser. You also saw tools you can use with web development for debugging cookies such as Firebug and Live HTTP Headers. These show you everything you'd want to know about the cookies your browser has stored.

❑ An entire session management application that uses MySQL and memcached for storing session data. To make this application easier to implement, simple generic database methods were added to WebApp.pm. You saw how each works internally and how to use these new methods to make data storage and retrieval much easier for web applications, removing the need for calling SQL statements in the higher-level application code.

❑ The session application was shown in detail — everything from the new cookie creation and processing methods, a *sessions* database table, new database and memcached data storage methods, and how to use this new session code, which will provide user session functionality for the remainder of the book.

❑ How to implement file uploads. A mod_perl application that handled file uploads and stored the file upload information in MySQL was shown in detail, providing you with a good understanding of how to implement applications that perform file uploads, as well as a skeletal concept that could be extended to have more features such as a photo upload system.

❑ Three templating systems: Template Toolkit, HTML::Template, and Mason. Numerous code examples were provided, including two mod_perl handlers for Template Toolkit and HTML::Mason. Both implement the same functionality as shown in a previous non-template mod_perl handler, which prints out the list of users. Then Mason was explained in detail, and a Mason component was demonstrated that also implemented the user listing functionality.

16

Perl and Ajax

Web development has changed a lot since 2000. Web applications used to work in such a way that a user would enter information and submit the form. The server would check the form, and then create a reply of success or error, which required loading a new page, thus sending the entire page contents as a reply. Now things are different. Now web developers not only eliminate the need for requiring an entire page submission, but they also reduce the amount of data between client and server. This is a phenomenal development in that it allows web applications to behave more like traditional desktop applications.

This chapter gives an overview of how you can develop applications with Apache/mod_perl using Ajax. This book covers so many topics, and it should be noted that Ajax and JavaScript programming are entire worlds in and of themselves, in terms of information. Therefore, this chapter is meant to at least pique your interest, so you may dig deeper. For those of you who want to delve deeper, there are some excellent books on the topic, including *Professional Ajax*, by Nicholas C. Zaka, Jeremy McPeak, and Joe Fawcett (Wiley Publishing, 2007).

What Is Ajax?

Most of you who are reading this book probably know what Ajax is. But some developers, particularly those who focus more on the "back-end" of web development, may still think of web applications in terms of how they were implemented in the past. The author is one such person. But with many late nights studying, coding, pulling out hair, and cursing at JavaScript and cross-browser Hades, he has come to really appreciate what Ajax and JavaScript add to the arsenal of tools a web developer can use to make really useful and feature-rich applications.

Ajax, or AJAX, is an acronym for *Asynchronous JavaScript and XML*, although it is now more commonly referred to as *Ajax* because it doesn't necessarily comprise the components that the acronym stands for. Ajax provides the ability for your web application — the page itself, which is the client, to asynchronously send and retrieve information to and from the web server, without having the page itself reload. This functionality is a fundamental change in web application development because now web applications can be implemented in such a way that they behave like a desktop application. It also reduces the amount of information that has to be passed back and forth between client and server.

The core of Ajax functionality is implemented using an `XMLHttpRequest` object. This `XMLHttpRequest` object is what serves to transfer data back and forth between the web page and the server. It is a DOM (*Document Object Model*) API object that is responsible for sending XML or other data such as JSON (*JavaScript Object Notation*), HTML, or plain text.

Since Ajax allows web applications to behave more like desktop applications, companies such as Google (with both Gmail and Google Maps), Google Suggest, Writely.com, Amazon's A9, and others are aggressively pushing the idea of replacing desktop applications with Ajax web applications. This will dramatically change the way we compute. For example, there used to be a concern of what desktop mail client to use. Now with web applications like Gmail and Hotmail, a mail application is more often thought of as a web application versus some application you download to your PC.

mod_perl Applications and Ajax

Perl, as usual, has a number of ways for developing web server applications that can work with Ajax web clients. This section will show you a number of examples of how you can write your own mod_perl web applications for serving Ajax clients.

Basic Ajax Examples

The following section introduces you to some very simple Ajax web applications that use mod_perl handlers to exchange information between the client and server, as well as how to instantiate a simple Ajax request. The first several examples show specific details of how an Ajax request object is created without using any of the newer JavaScript libraries (such as the Prototype JavaScript Framework, which hides many of the details and makes using Ajax much easier). The assumption is that you are a Perl programmer and you like to dig into the details and guts of the code, and want a more in-depth idea of how an Ajax request is created. The example will also help you appreciate the convenience newer libraries give you.

Example 1

Here is an example: You are introduced to the instantiation of an `XMLHttpRequest` object. This is the object you will issue Ajax requests through. This example is a simple application that reads a message from the server application — the mod_perl handler — and then displays what it reads from the server in a `<div>` tag.

The first JavaScript function listed, `doMsg()`, instantiates an `XMLHttpRequest` object based on the type of browser being used. The first try block tries to instantiate using `XMLHttpRequest()`, which is for all browsers other than Microsoft's. The catch block attempts instantiation of Microsoft's `XMLHttpRequest` object, which is an ActiveX control and has a number of versions that need to be tested.

```
<html>
  <head><title>Ajax test</title>
  <link type="text/css" href="/css/webapp.css" rel="stylesheet">
  <script type="text/javascript">

function doMsg()
{
  var xmlHttp;
```

```
try
{
  // Firefox, etc
  xmlHttp = new XMLHttpRequest();
}
catch (e)
{
  // Microsoft IE Latest
  try
  {
    xmlHttp = new ActiveXObject("Msxml2.XMLHTTP");
  }
  // IE 5.0
  catch (e)
  {
    try
    {
      xmlHttp = new ActiveXObject("Microsoft.XMLHTTP");
    }
    catch (e)
    {
      alert("No Ajax for YOU!");
      return false;
    }
  }
}
```

In the following lines of code, *onreadystatuschange* is an xmlHTTPRequest object property that sets or retrieves the event handler used for the Ajax request. This means that when the request is completed, this is the function that will be called, resulting in the code of this anonymous function, listed as function(), being executed. In this case, a status message is set in the *msg* <div> tag having the id *msg*, which will appear to the user. In the old days, to see a message, you would have had to wait for the server to display it; the server had to generate it. In contrast, now the client generates it.

The other property, *readyState*, is an integer value indicating the state of the xmlHTTPRequest object. The values are:

❏   0 (Uninitialized): The object has been created but not initialized.

❏   1 (Open): The object is opened though no data sent.

❏   2 (Send): Data has been sent but not yet received. Neither the body (*responseText*) nor the response header (*responseData*) data is yet available.

❏   3 (Receiving): Data is in the process of being received, though still neither *reponseText* nor *responseData* is available.

❏   4 (Loaded): All data has been received and both *responseText* and *responseData* are now available.

```
xmlHttp.onreadystatechange = function()
  {
    document.getElementById("msg").innerHTML="processing...";

    if (xmlHttp.readyState == 4)
```

```
            {
                document.getElementById("msg").innerHTML=xmlHttp.responseText;
            }
        }
```

Here, you see that the HTTP GET request is made to the mod_perl /ajax_handler URL, which is a mod_perl handler that prints out a message that the Ajax client reads. Nothing is sent, hence null is passed to the send() method.

```
    xmlHttp.open("GET", "/ajax_handler", true);
    xmlHttp.send(null);

}
</script>

</head>
```

In the body of the HTML page, an onclick() event is set to call doMsg(). Clicking this button will result in doMsg() being called and the Ajax GET request being made to the mod_perl handler.

```
<body>
    <form name="myForm">
        <input type="button" onclick="doMsg();" value="Message"/>
    </form>

    <p class="msg" id="msg">Message</p>

</body>
</html>
```

This example was very simple, but it gives you a foot in the door of Ajax.

mod_perl Handler for Example 1

The mod_perl handler for the first example is a very short piece of code. All it does is print out a random string value using WebApp::randomString(). You'll also notice one line that performs a 7-second sleep. This is to simulate a load on the remote server, or provide a delay so you can see the Ajax functionality and just what it means to say it is *asynchronous*.

```
package WroxHandlers::Ajax;

use strict;
use warnings;

use Apache2::Const -compile => qw(OK );
use WebApp;

sub handler {
    my ($r)= @_;
    sleep 7;

    $r->content_type('text/html');
    print "Ajax Reply: " . WebApp::randomString();
    return Apache2::Const::OK;

}

1;
```

Ajax Example 2: Display Returned HTML Table

This Ajax example builds on the previous example and displays in a <div> tag a preformatted HTML table returned from the mod_perl handler. Also shown here is the previous implementation of an xmlHTTPRequest object instantiation being moved to an external JavaScript file, xmlhttp.js with a single function, getXmlHttp(). This function simply performs all the aforementioned steps and returns the instantiated xmlHTTPRequest object to the caller. This also reduces how many trees are required for this book you are reading!

In this example, the <div> tag that is written to has the id *userlist* within the DOM.

```html
<html>
  <head><title>Ajax test</title></head>
  <link type="text/css" href="/css/webapp.css" rel="stylesheet">
   <script language="javascript" type="text/javascript"
                   src="/javascript/xmlhttp.js"></script>

  <script type="text/javascript">
  <! —


function userList()
{
  var xmlHttp = getXmlHttp();

  xmlHttp.onreadystatechange = function()
  {
    document.getElementById("msg").innerHTML="processing...";

    if (xmlHttp.readyState == 4)
    {
      document.getElementById("userlist").innerHTML=xmlHttp.responseText;
    }
  }
  xmlHttp.open("GET", "/ajax_handler", true);
  xmlHttp.send(null);
}
</script>

</head>

<body>
  <form name="myForm">
    <input type="button" onclick="userList();" value="Userlist"/>
  </form>

  <div id="userlist" name="userlist"></div>

</body>
</html>
```

mod_perl Handler for Example 2

The mod_perl handler in this example will use Template Toolkit to print out the table. The data required for the list of users to be printed out is obtained with the WebApp method getUsers() that you have seen in several chapters now. This hash reference, $userlist, is passed to the template, which will then print it out in a table.

```perl
WroxHandlers::AjaxExample2

use strict;
use warnings;

    use Apache2::Const -compile => qw(OK REDIRECT SERVER_ERROR);
use Template;
use WebApp;


sub handler {
    my ($r)= @_;
    my $template_path;

    sleep 7;

    $r->content_type('text/html');

    my $webapp= new WebApp({r => $r});
    my $userlist= $webapp->getUsers();

        $template_path= $r->dir_config('TEMPLATE_PATH'),

    my $template = Template->new({
        INCLUDE_PATH => $template_path,
        POST_CHOMP   => 1,

    });

    # set up template parameters
    my $tparams = {
        msg         => "User list",
        url         => $r->uri,
        userlist    => $userlist
    };

    $template->process('userlist_ajax.tt2', $tparams) ||
        do {
            $r->server->warn($template->error());
            return Apache2::Const::SERVER_ERROR;
        };

    return Apache2::Const::OK;

}

1;
```

Example 2: Template Code

The Template Toolkit template, `userlist_ajax2.tt2`, is a very short template, since it only has to build a table. The only argument passed to it, as shown in the previous template example, was the `$userlist` hash reference.

```
<table class="userlist">
    <thead>
        <tr>
            <th>UID</th>
            <th>Username</th>
            <th>First Name</th>
            <th>Surname</th>
        </tr>
    </thead>
    <tbody>
[% FOREACH uid = userlist.keys %]
        <tr>
            <td>[% userlist.$uid.uid %]</td>
            <td>[% userlist.$uid.username %]</td>
            <td>[% userlist.$uid.firstname %]</td>
            <td>[% userlist.$uid.surname %]</td>
        </tr>
[% END %]
    </tbody>
</table>
```

More Examples Using the JSON Perl Module

The Perl modules, JSON, JSON::XS and JSON::PP all work the same way, and are different only in how they are implemented internally. JSON::XS is written in C, whereas JSON::PP is a pure Perl implementation. The modules essentially provide a way to display JSON, encoding a Perl hash reference into JSON (JavaScript Object Notation) and from JSON to Perl. You can, for instance, convert a database result set to a JSON object that you return to the client via Ajax. Then you can utilize it like any other JavaScript variable in your JavaScript functions. This will be shown in the next example.

You should use the JSON::XS Perl module if at all possible. By simply using JSON, it should by default use JSON::XS. The method overview is in the following blocks of code.

Perl to JSON:

```
$json_text = to_json($perl_obj);
```

JSON::XS will require:

```
$json_text = encode_json($perl_obj);
```

JSON to Perl:

```
$perlvar = from_json($json_text);
```

JSON::XS will require:

```
$perlvar = decode_json($json_text);
```

It's not enough that you just read the JSON text value. You will have to *eval* it as well within your JavaScript code for it to be brought to life.

Ajax Example 3: Building the Table on the Client

You can also build a table using JavaScript from the JSON response from the server provided by the mod_perl handler. In this example, it is introduced as a new Perl module, JSON::XS. All the same setup is performed.

This example also introduces another JavaScript concept, which is disabling the button that was pressed to activate the Ajax request, thus preventing the user from resubmitting the button multiple times. The button is disabled in the calling function, userList(), and in the *onreadystatechange* function, re-enabled. Thus the button is disabled for the duration of the Ajax requests. In this case, since the mod_perl handler emulates a load with a 7-second sleep, the button will be disabled for that amount of time.

You can also employ this idea to keep abusive resubmission, for instance on a blob, from occurring. You just wouldn't re-enable the button. Just keep in mind that when the page is reloaded, the button is enabled again.

```
<html>   <head><title>Ajax test</title></head>
    <link type="text/css" href="/css/webapp.css" rel="stylesheet">
    <script language="javascript" type="text/javascript"
                        src="/javascript/xmlhttp.js"></script>

    <script type="text/javascript">

function userList()
{
    var xmlHttp = getXmlHttp();

    document.getElementById('ajaxtest').setAttribute("disabled", "disabled");
    button.setAttribute("disabled","disabled");
```

The onreadystatechange event handler function is where all the display logic is implemented. It takes the JSON object string returned from the mod_perl handler that was returned from the xmlHTTPRequest object and performs a JavaScript eval on this string, making this JSON object response an actual object that can be utilized in the page:

```
    xmlHttp.onreadystatechange = function()
    {
        document.getElementById("msg").innerHTML="processing...";

        if (xmlHttp.readyState == 4)
        {
            // deserialize the JSON text
            var response = eval( "(" + xmlHttp.responseText + ")" );

            // obtain the userlist
            var ulist = response.userlist;
```

Next, the message is set, and a table element *usertable* is created. This table is built by looping over the result set. The outer loop builds the rows and inserts them into *usertable*, while the inner loop builds the table cells and inserts them into each row. The array, `cols`, is used to control exactly which columns are displayed:

```
// set the message
document.getElementById("msg").innerHTML="Userlist: " + response.msg;

// start constructing a table
var usertable= document.createElement('table');
usertable.className = 'userlist';
document.body.appendChild(usertable);
usertable.setAttribute('id','userlist');
usertable.setAttribute('name', 'userlist');

// this is so we iterate trough only the columns we want
cols = new Array('uid', 'username', 'firstname', 'surname');
var i= 0;
for (var uid in ulist)
  {
     var urow = usertable.insertRow(i);

     for (var j = 0; j < cols.length; j++)
     {

       var ucell = urow.insertCell(j);

       ucell.innerHTML = ulist[uid][cols[j]];
     }
     i++;

  }
```

The following block of code builds the table header. By inserting the row at zero with `insertRow(0)`, this table row is placed at the top of the table and is used for the column names.

```
// build the table header
var urow = usertable.insertRow(0);
var uidcell= urow.insertCell(0);
uidcell.innerHTML = 'UID';
var unamecell = urow.insertCell(1);
unamecell.innerHTML = 'Usernamae';
var fnamecell = urow.insertCell(2);
fnamecell.innerHTML = 'Firstname';
var snamecell = urow.insertCell(3);
snamecell.innerHTML = 'Surname';
    }

  document.getElementById('ajaxtest').removeAttribute("disabled");
  }

xmlHttp.open("GET", "/ajax_handler", true);
xmlHttp.send(null);
}
</script>
```

```
    </head>

    <body>
      <form name="myForm">
        <input type="button" id="ajaxtest" name="ajaxtest"
          onclick="userList();" value="Userlist"/>
      </form>

      <p class="msg" id="msg">Status</p>
      <div id="userlist" name="userlist"></div>

    </body>
    </html>
```

Example 3: mod_perl Handler

The mod_perl handler example, repeated in this section, uses the JSON::XS Perl module to encode the Perl database result set, which was created by the retrieval of the list of users into a JSON data string using the JSON::XS method encode_json().

```perl
package WroxHandlers::Ajax;

use strict;
use warnings;

use Apache2::Const -compile => qw(OK);
use JSON::XS;
use WebApp;


sub handler {
    my ($r)= @_;

    # load emulation
    sleep 7;

    $r->content_type('text/html');

    my $webapp= new WebApp({r => $r});
    my $userlist= $webapp->getUsers();
    my $num_users= keys %$userlist;
    $r->print(encode_json({ 'msg'        => "Returned $num_users users" ,
                            'userlist'   => $userlist}));


    return Apache2::Const::OK;

}
```

The JSON is printed, which the xmlHTTPRequest object reads and then displays as shown above.

Example 4: MySQL Ajax Client

The example in this section takes the previous example a step further. It adds a text field to the form for entering SQL queries.

> **Major caveat!** This example uses a database query text field in the form and allows any query to be run on the database, which, normally, is not a good idea unless you really lock this application down. This is only being shown as a nifty example of what you can do with Ajax! You must always control what queries are executed on your database server, which means you should not run raw queries to the database. Likewise, you should always use placeholders in your SQL to prevent things such as SQL injection attacks.

With that said, this is a nifty example! It shows how the Perl JSON module can take a Perl array reference, as returned by DBI `fetchtall_arrayref()` and converts it into a JSON data structure that you can then access from the Ajax response. You use this returned JSON data structure to build an HTML table, displaying the results.

In this example, it should also be noted that there is no limitation of which columns are printed.

```
<html>
  <head><title>Ajax test</title></head>
  <link type="text/css" href="/css/webapp.css" rel="stylesheet">
  <script language="javascript" type="text/javascript" src="/javascript/xmlhttp.js">
  </script>
  <script type="text/javascript">
  <!--

 function dbList()
{
  var xmlHttp = getXmlHttp();
  document.getElementById('ajaxtest').setAttribute("disabled", "disabled");

  xmlHttp.onreadystatechange = function()
  {
    document.getElementById("msg").innerHTML="processing...";
```

The following lines of code check to see if there is an existing result set prior to creating a new one. (Otherwise it would keep adding tables to the page.) If the result set exists, it removes it.

```
if (xmlHttp.readyState == 4)
    {
      // deserialize the JSON text
      var response = eval( "(" + xmlHttp.responseText + ")" );

      // obtain the result
      var result = response.result;

      // set the message
      document.getElementById("msg").innerHTML="MySQL result set: " + response.msg;

      var existing_result = document.getElementById('result');
      if (existing_result) {
        existing_result.parentNode.removeChild(existing_result);
      }
```

```
            // start constructing a table
            var result_table= document.createElement('table');
            result_table.className = 'userlist';
            document.getElementById('result_div').appendChild(result_table);
            result_table.setAttribute('id','result');
            result_table.setAttribute('name', 'result');
```

The same mechanism used with the previous example is employed to print out the table. Then a loop is made over the JSON object, adding rows and cells iteratively.

```
    for (var i = 0; i < result.length; i++)
        {
          var j = 0;
          var urow = result_table.insertRow(i);
          for (var colname in result[i])
          {
            var ucell = urow.insertCell(j);
            if (i == -1) {
              ucell.innerHTML = colname;
            }
            else {
              ucell.innerHTML = "<pre>" + result[i][colname] + "</pre>";
            }
            j++;
          }
        }
        var j = 0;
        var urow = result_table.insertRow(0);
        for (var colname in result[0])
        {
          var ucell = urow.insertCell(j);
          ucell.innerHTML = colname;
          j++;
        }
        document.getElementById('ajaxtest').removeAttribute("disabled");
      }
    }
```

For this request, a POST is used. To do this, you need to set the Content-type request header to indicate that it is indeed a POST, in addition to setting the form content. The xmlHttpRequest method send() takes the value of the form, which causes a submission of those form values to occur.

```
    xmlHttp.open("POST", "/ajax_db", true);
    xmlHttp.setRequestHeader("Content-Type",
      "application/x-www-form-urlencoded; charset=UTF-8");
    var post = "dbquery=" + document.getElementById("dbquery").value;
    xmlHttp.send(post);

}
  // -->
</script>

</head>
```

```
<body>
  <form name="myForm">
    <fieldset>
    <label>Query</label> <input type="text" id="dbquery" name="dbquery">
    <input type="button" id="ajaxtest" name="ajaxtest"
            onclick="dbList();" value="Query"/>
    </fieldset>
  </form>

  <p class="msg" id="msg">Status</p>
  <div id="result_div" name="result_div"></div>

</body>
</html>
```

Example 4: mod_perl Handler

First and foremost, you want to add a read-only user to your database for the schema that this application will use, so that only read-only queries can be run using this application. In the SQL statement that follows, only the SELECT privilege is granted to 'webuser_ro'.

```
mysql> GRANT SELECT  ON webapp.* TO 'webuser_ro'@'localhost' IDENTIFIED BY  's3kr1t
```

Then the user is then added to DBIx::Password.(/usr/local/share/perl/5.8.8/DBIx/Password.pm):

```
'webuser-ro' => {
                    'port'       => '',
                    'username'   => 'webuser_ro',
                    'host'       => 'localhost',
                    'database'   => 'webapp',
                    'password'   => 's3kr1t',
                    'attributes' => {},
                    'connect'    => 'DBI:mysql:database=webapp;host=localhost',
                    'driver' => 'mysql'
                 },
```

This new virtual db user, 'webuser-ro', is the user the application will connect as so that you can sleep at night!

The mod_perl handler for the example reads in the submitted form value query from the Ajax request.

> When the WebApp object is instantiated, the database read-only virtual user is passed as the db_virtual_user parameter to ensure that the database connection is a read-only connection.

The form value query is passed to the selectall_arrayref() to produce a result set of an array of hash references for each record returned from the query. If there is an error, there is no result set. But you need to return one for the calling page's JavaScript to work properly. Therefore a dummy result set is created. Finally, encode_json() is called in $r->print(), which prints the JSON result back to the Ajax client. This result includes various data members, including the result set from MySQL, which is now in JSON format.

```perl
use Apache2::Const -compile => qw(OK);
use JSON::XS;
use WebApp;

sub handler {
    my ($r)= @_;

    sleep 1;

    $r->content_type('text/html');

    my $webapp = WebApp->new(
                    'r'              => $r,
                    'db_virtual_user' => 'webuser-ro',
                    });


    my $form= $webapp->getForm();
    $webapp->{dbh}{RaiseError}= 0;
    warn Dumper $form;

    my $result= $webapp->{dbh}->selectall_arrayref(
                            $form->{dbquery},
                            { Slice => {} });

    if ($webapp->{dbh}->errstr){
        $result= [{'errstr' => $webapp->{dbh}->errstr}];
    }

    my $num_results = scalar @$result;
    $r->print(encode_json({ 'msg'    => "Returned $num_results rows" ,
                        'result'=> $result}));


    return Apache2::Const::OK;

}

1;
```

Example 4 in Action

Now to see this MySQL Ajax client in action! Seeing several queries run using this application will give you an idea of how interesting this application is.

Figure 16-1 shows using this page to select the first ten rows from the *states* table.

Figure 16-2 shows this being used to run the MySQL SHOW PROCESSLIST SQL statement, displaying the processes running in MySQL. This is something any MySQL database administrator would appreciate!

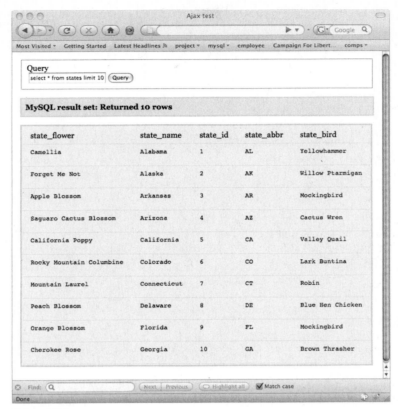

Figure 16-1

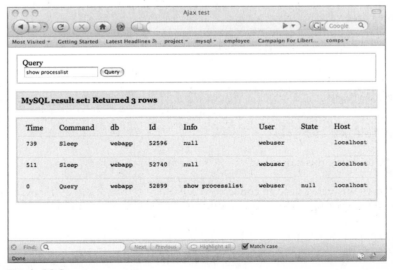

Figure 16-2

Figure 16-3 displays the status of the memcached server using the UDF call memc_stats().

Figure 16-3

This example shows some of the really clever things you can do with Ajax, JavaScript, and mod_perl handlers using the JSON Perl module.

Example 5: Reading the Raw Post Data

The example in this section shows how Ajax can send raw POST from the Request Record to JSON, which the mod_perl handler reads and then converts to a Perl data structure (a hash reference). The example still uses the same data — which in fact will be passed back and forth between the client and server. This application may not be practical, but it demonstrates how convenient it is to go between Perl and JSON, and how you can simply pass JSON back and forth, rather using form POST data.

```
<html>
  <head><title>Ajax test</title></head>
  <link type="text/css" href="/css/webapp.css" rel="stylesheet">
    <script language="javascript"
        type="text/javascript" src="/javascript/xmlhttp.js">
  </script>

  <script type="text/javascript">

function userList()
```

```
  {
    var xmlHttp = getXmlHttp();

    document.getElementById('ajaxtest').setAttribute("disabled", "disabled");
    }
    xmlHttp.onreadystatechange = function()
    {
      document.getElementById("msg").innerHTML="processing...";
```

The previous code is where the response from the server is read. The server sends the JSON response that has the userlist. That is the JSON data structure that eval will evaluate, making it available as a JavaScript variable userlist. Using the JavaScript variable userlist, a table can be constructed in an iterative loop, as was done in the previous examples (3 and 4).

```
      if (xmlHttp.readyState == 4)
      {
        // deserialize the JSON text
        var response = eval( "(" + xmlHttp.responseText + ")" );

        // obtain the userlist
        var ulist = response.userlist;

        // set the message
        document.getElementById("msg").innerHTML="Userlist." + response.msg;

        // start constructing a table
        var usertable= document.createElement('table');
        usertable.className = 'userlist';
        document.body.appendChild(usertable);
        usertable.setAttribute('id','userlist');
        usertable.setAttribute('name', 'userlist');

        // this is so we iterate trough only the columns we want
        cols = new Array('uid', 'username', 'firstname', 'surname');
          var i= 0;
          for (var uid in ulist)
          {

            var urow = usertable.insertRow(i);

            for (var j = 0; j < cols.length; j++)
            {
              var ucell = urow.insertCell(j);

              ucell.innerHTML = ulist[uid][cols[j]];

            }
            i++;
          }

        // build the table header
        var urow = usertable.insertRow(0);
        var uidcell= urow.insertCell(0);
        uidcell.innerHTML = 'UID';
```

```
          var unamecell = urow.insertCell(1);
          unamecell.innerHTML = 'Usernamae';
          var fnamecell = urow.insertCell(2);
          fnamecell.innerHTML = 'Firstname';
          var snamecell = urow.insertCell(3);
          snamecell.innerHTML = 'Surname';
      }

          document.getElementById('ajaxtest').removeAttribute("disabled");
      }
```

The following JSON string shows what will be sent to the server as a POST and decoded to a Perl data structure:

```
// This is the json string that will be sent to the server
  var json_userlist= '{"userlist":{"27":{"firstname":"Patrick","admin":"1",
"uid":"27","phone":"2828282822","username":"CaptTofu","surname":"Galbraith",
"state":"NH","email":"capttofu@example.net","password":
"acbd18db4cc2f85cedef654fccc4a4d8","city":"Stoddard","address":"11122GraniteSt."},
"28":{"firstname":"Wes","admin":"1",
"uid":"28","phone":"2324448888","username":"wes","surname":"Moran","state":"NH",
"email":"wes@somesite.com","password":"acbd18db4cc2f85cedef654fccc4a4d8",
"city":"Happy Corner","address":"18182 Moosehaven St."},"29":{"firstname":
"Jim","admin":"0","uid":"29","phone":"2929888",
"username":"Jimbob","surname":"Bob","state":"NH","email":"jimbob@unix.com",
"password":"","city":"Des Moines","address":"222 Elm St."}},
"msg":"Test Post from JSON."}';
```

```
  xmlHttp.open("POST", "/ajax_handler", true);
  xmlHttp.setRequestHeader("Content-Type", "application/x-www-form-urlencoded");
```

```
  xmlHttp.send(json_userlist);
}
</script>

</head>

<body>
  <form name="myForm">
    <input type="button" id="ajaxtest" name="ajaxtest"
                      onclick="userList();" value="Userlist">
</form>

  <p class="msg" id="msg">Status</p>
  <div id="userlist" name="userlist"></div>

</body>
</html>
```

Example 5: mod_perl Handler

Instead of reading individual parameters of POST data, the example in this section sets the variable $json to the entire POST request header by the amount specified in the request header *Content-Length*. The value of $json is then decoded using from_json() — this is where you could make use of the decoded JSON data as a Perl data structure. In this case, it's encoded back to a JSON string that the client will read in the request.

```perl
package WroxHandlers::AjaxPost;

use strict;
use warnings;

use Apache2::Const -compile => qw(OK);
use Apache2::RequestRec ();
use Apache2::RequestIO ();

use JSON;

sub handler {
    my ($r)= @_;
    my $template_path;

    # simulate a load
    sleep 7;

    my $json;
    if ($r->method() eq 'POST') {
        if ($r->can('read')){
            $r->read( $json, $r->headers_in->{'Content-length'} );
        }
    }

    my $jref = from_json($json);

    my $num_users= keys %{$jref->{userlist}};
    $r->content_type('text/html');
    $r->print(to_json({ 'msg'        => "Returned $num_users users" ,
                        'userlist'   => $jref->{userlist}}));


    return Apache2::Const::OK;

}

1;
```

Example 6: Using the Prototype JavaScript Framework

The JavaScript Prototype library is a JavaScript framework that is intended to ease web development of dynamic applications. You can download this framework from http://www.prototypejs.org/. This framework provides a lot of very useful functionality for easy Ajax and DOM manipulation. The following are the author's two favorite things about it:

❑   It features an *Ajax.Request* object that is much easier to use because you don't have to implement code to check the type of client in try/catch blocks.

❑   The prototype library provides a shorthand way to access DOM elements.

For making an Ajax request, it's very simple. This:

```
var myajax = new Ajax.Request('/perl_handler', { method: 'GET'});
```

... would create a request object to the URL /perl_handler using a GET. You can also set response callbacks for various events such as success and failure, similar to what was shown previously as *onreadystatechange* events, but with greater ease and enhanced ability to set the events that a particular event function will handle. In the following code snippet, the onMsg() function (which is a function you have coded) is set to handle a successful request, whereas the onError() function (which you have also coded) would be run upon an error condition.

```
var myajax = new Ajax.Request('/perl_handler',
                {
                  method: 'GET'},
                  onSuccess: function(transport) {
                        onMsg (transport.responseText);
                  },
                  onFailure: function() {
                        onError ("Errors encountered!");
                  }
                });
```

There are other events that are available for setting functions to handle as well, per the documentation available from the Prototype JavaScript Framework web site.

To see how the Prototype JavaScript Framework extends the DOM, look at the next simple example. It shows how to provide a "shorthand" way of accessing DOM objects when you have an element in a form with the id of userform that is also within a <fieldset> called someelement:

```
var myelement = document.userform.userfieldset.someelement;
```

... or this:

```
var myelement = document.getElementById("someelement") ;
```

Can be written as:

```
var myelement = $("somelement");
```

The following example will give you a better sense of how useful the Prototype JavaScript Framework is. This example will reuse the first example, Example 1, using the Prototype JavaScript Framework:

> **Make sure that whatever templating system you are using, or if you are printing out the HTML in your mod_perl handler, that you don't interpolate the sigils ($) characters in the JavaScript! This will give you hours of debugging enjoyment if you are not careful.**

1. Download the library file from http://www.prototypejs.org and include it in your document using the script element.

2. As you can see, instead of having to reference the element "msg" by using document .getElementById("msg"), you can now simply use $("msg").

Also, you can see the Ajax request object is instantiated to create a request to the mod_perl handler /ajax_handler, setting the function onMsg() as the event handler for a successful request — which will inevitably result in the value of the response being writing to the div element, msg.

```html
<html>
  <head><title>Ajax test</title>
    <link type="text/css" href="/css/webapp.css" rel="stylesheet">
    <script language="javascript" type="text/javascript"
                        src="/javascript/prototype-1.6.0.3.js">
    </script>

    <script type="text/javascript">

function onMsg(resptext) {

  var obj = resptext.evalJSON(true);
  $("msg").innerHTML = obj.msg;
}

function doMsg()
{
    $("msg").innerHTML="processing...";
    var ajax = new Ajax.Request('/ajax_handler',
                { method:'GET',
                  onSuccess: function(transport) {
                    onMsg(transport.responseText);
                  }
                });

}
</script>

</head>

<body>
  <form name="myForm">
    <input type="button" onclick="doMsg();" value="Message"/>
  </form>

  <p class="msg" id="msg">Message</p>

</body>
</html>
```

The mod_perl handler for this will function the same way as Example 1; it returns a random string value using WebApp::randomString().

Example 7: Account Creation with Ajax

Example 7 will show you a full-fledged application that creates an account for a user. The application will create an account that is then used in setting a session, using the application that was demonstrated in Chapter 15. This application will also show you how this application is implemented to send email to the user's email address specified during account creation.

This example will use two mod_perl handlers: one to display the account creation page, containing the account creation form; and the other to handle Ajax requests. For the Ajax and JavaScript, this example will use the JavaScript Prototype library.

Account Page mod_perl Handler

The first handler is the account page handler. This handler uses a template containing JavaScript functions to implement user interface functionality. It also has Ajax code that will send the account request to the other mod_perl handler that creates the user account.

It's important to note that the parameter INTERPOLATE is set to 0 upon instantiation of a Template Toolkit object. This is very important because you want to ensure that the Template Toolkit does not interpolate the sigils (located in the template and used by the JavaScript Prototype library) as Perl variables. You could, alternatively, omit it because INTERPOLATE will default to 0 if it is not set. The author can attest to this being an issue; he spent three hours trying to figure out why the JavaScript would not work properly!

In the following application example, a pull-down menu is required to display the list of states. The data for the states is obtained using the WebApp method getStates(). And the actual pull-down option menu is provided by the CGI popup_menu() method.

```perl
package WroxHandlers::AccountHandler;

use strict;
use warnings;

use Apache2::Const -compile => qw(OK REDIRECT SERVER_ERROR);
use Apache2::Request;
use Template;
use CGI qw(:standard);
use WebApp;


sub handler {
    my ($r)= @_;
    my $msg;
    my $url= $r->uri;
    my $template_path;

    my $webapp = WebApp->new({ r => $r});

    # get the submitted form values
    my $form= $webapp->getForm();

    my $sessionref= $webapp->getSession(\$msg);

    # obtain the template path
```

```
    $template_path= $r->dir_config('TEMPLATE_PATH'),

    # instantiate a new Template object
    my $template = Template->new({
        INCLUDE_PATH => $template_path,
        INTERPOLATE  => 0, # or simply leave out
        POST_CHOMP   => 1,
    });

    my $states= $webapp->getStates();

    $states->{default}= 'Select a state';
    my $states_select= popup_menu(
            -name     => 'state',
            -id       => 'state',
            -values   => [sort keys %$states],
            -default  => $form->{state} ? $form->{state} : 'default',
            -labels   => $states);


    my $tparams = {
        msg           => "Create an account",
        url           => $r->uri,
        states_select => $states_select,
    };


    $url =~ s/^\///;
    my $tname= $url . '.tt2';

    $r->content_type('text/html');

    $template->process($tname, $tparams) ||
        do {
            $r->server->warn($template->error());
            return Apache2::Const::SERVER_ERROR;
        };

    return Apache2::Const::OK;
}
```

Account Page Template

The template, account.tt2, contains all the JavaScript functionality. You'll notice a trend here — that functionality is moved out of the server code and now is contained on the client in the page with the various JavaScript functions.

```
<html>
  <head>
    <title>Session Example</title>
    <link type="text/css" href="/css/webapp.css" rel="stylesheet">
    <script language="javascript" type="text/javascript"
                        src="/javascript/prototype-1.6.0.3.js">
```

```
</script>
<script type="text/javascript">
<! -
```

The first function shown, createAccount(), is an onSuccess event handler. This is the function that handles what to display in the account page once the Ajax request creates an account. First, the function checks the state of the response. If no error is known to have occurred, it must re-enable the Submit button.

```
function createAccount(responseText) {
        var obj = responseText.evalJSON(true);
        var msg = obj.msg;

        if ( obj == null ) {
          // no message from response, so set one
          $("msg").innerHTML = "No response for user create " + $("username");
          // re-enable the submit button
          $("create_account").removeAttribute("disabled");
          return;
        }

        // set message from response
        $("msg").innerHTML = obj.msg;
```

If the error code is -1, this indicates that the user already has a session and is logged in, in which case, the window.location will cause a redirect to the site's base URL.

```
        /*
          if user is logged in - don't want them to create an account!
          redirect them to main site, or wherever you like
        */
        if ( obj.err == -1 ) {
          window.location = "/";
        }
```

If there is a noncritical error, then it simply re-enables the Submit button and returns a false:

```
        // if there was any non-critical error, re-enable the submit button
        if ( obj.err == 1 ) {
          // re-enable the submit button, failure
          $("create_account").removeAttribute("disabled");
          return false;
        }
```

If no errors are returned from the account creation mod_perl handler, then it will proceed. It re-enables the Submit button, and then hides the account form, which is contained in a div DOM element having the id of accountform. You then want to make another element containing a successful id message. Now, once the user's account is created, the user can't resubmit another account creation request.

```
        // Re-enable submit button, success
        $("create_account").removeAttribute("disabled");
```

```
    // Hide the form
    $("accountform").style.visibility = 'hidden';

    // make visible the message
    $("success").style.visibility = 'visible';

}
```

The next function demonstrated, `processForm()`, takes care of two primary tasks:

❏ Form validation

❏ Creation of the Ajax request to create the user account

The form elements are checked to make sure they are all set using a loop over all the element ID names, provided by the array `fields`. If any of them are empty, then the `div` element `msg` is set to contain a message to the user indicating the problem, and the function returns to allow the user to correct the error.

```
/*
  this function is used to validate the form as well as initiate
  the Ajax request
*/
function processForm()
{
  var retval = true;

  fields = new Array(
            "password", "verify", "email", "username", "firstname", "surname");

  for (var i = 0; i < fields.length; i++) {

    if ($(fields[i]).value == '') {
      console.log("field " + fields[i] + " value " + $(fields[i]).value);
      $("msg").innerHTML = "The " + fields[i] + " field is empty";
      return false;
    }
  }
```

Next, a check is made to compare the string value of the `password` form element to the string value of the `verify` form element. If they don't match, then the `msg` div element is set, telling the user. Then the function returns.

```
if ($("password").value != $("verify").value)
{
  $("msg").innerHTML="Passwords do not match.";
  return false;
}
```

Finally, when all form validation has been passed, the Ajax request can be issued. The Submit button element `create_account` is disabled, and the `msg` div element is set to indicate the processing is occurring.

```
$("msg").innerHTML = "processing...";

// disable the submit button so they can't resubmit
$("create_account").setAttribute("disabled","disabled");
```

For the Ajax request, this will be a POST. In order to post, you will need to build up your post data for each form element. This is trivial using the Prototype JavaScript Framework. Just append the text parameter names with the values provided. The request is made and the form values are posted to the mod_perl handler. The *onSuccess* event handler is the createAccount() function already shown above.

```
var ajax = new Ajax.Request('/ajax_handler',
            { method:'POST',
            parameters:
            'password=' + $("password").value + '&verify='
            + $("verify").value
            + '&email=' + $("email").value + '&username='
            + $("username").value
            + '&firstname=' + $("firstname").value + '&surname='
            + $("surname").value
            + '&address=' + $("address").value + '&phone=' + $("phone").value
            + '&city=' + $("city").value + '&state=' + $("state").value,

            onSuccess: function(transport)
            { createAccount(transport.responseText); }
        } );

}

// -->
</script>
</head>
<body>
<!-- end of header() content -->
```

Account Handler

Next, let's look at the mod_perl account creation Ajax handler, AjaxAccountHandler. This handler has quite a bit of functionality contained within it. It has two primary tasks to create the user's account, and to send the new user an email indicating that his or her account has been created.

```
package WroxHandlers::AjaxAccountHandler;

use strict;
use warnings;
use JSON::XS;

use Apache2::Const -compile => qw(OK );
use Digest::MD5 qw(md5_hex);
use WebApp;
```

The `handler()` Subroutine

First, the session is checked. If the user is logged in, he or she should not be creating an account, so set the variable, $err, which indicates the error code, to -1. This will result in the JavaScript function `createAccount()`, shown previously in the account page template code, to issue a redirect of the page.

```
sub handler {
    my ($r)= @_;
    my $msg = '';
    my $err = 0;

    my $webapp = WebApp->new({ r => $r});
    my $form = $webapp->getForm();

    # obtain the session
    my $sessionref= $webapp->getSession();

    # if the user is logged in, they do not need to create an account
    if ($sessionref->{uid}) {
        $err = -1;
    }
}
```

Next, if the user is not logged in, it performs a check on the form element `password` and `verify` to make sure they match. The JavaScript in the form already should have caught this, but it can't hurt to have another check at the server level. The message being set here in the server code will result in the same thing that the JavaScript function `processForm()` does, which is to set the message indicating an error in the `msg` div.

```
else {

    if ($r->method() eq 'POST') {
        if ($form->{password} ne $form->{verify}) {
            $msg= "Password and password verify do not match";
            $err= 1;
        }
    }
```

Next, the WebApp method `userExists()` is used to check if the user already exists. If he or she does exist, the error message and error code are set with `$msg` and `$err`.

```
my $uid= $webapp->userExists({
    username    => $form->{username},
    email       => $form->{email}});

warn "uid $uid" if $uid;

if ($uid) {
    $msg = <<EOMSG;
The user $form->{username} or email $form->{email} already exist.
Please try another value.";
EOMSG
    $err= 1;
}
```

If the user doesn't exist, the WebApp method `saveUser()` is used to save the user. As you will recall, all the functionality to make sure the user is inserted (as well as cached) is implemented in `saveUser()`; it is very convenient to include it here in this mod_perl handler.

```
        else {

            my $saved = $webapp->saveUser({
                username    => $form->{username},
                email       => $form->{email},
                password    => md5_hex($form->{password}),
                firstname   => $form->{firstname},
                surname     => $form->{surname},
                phone       => $form->{phone},
                state       => $form->{state},
                city        => $form->{city},
                address     => $form->{address} });
```

Set a success message that will be displayed in the `msg` div. Also, call the `notifyUser()` subroutine, which is a subroutine that calls a WebApp method to send mail:

```
            if ($saved) {
                notifyUser($form);
                $msg = <<EOMSG;
The account for $form->{username} has been created
and information sent to $form->{email}
EOMSG
            }
            else {
                $msg =
                "There was a problem creating the account for $form->{username}";
            }
        }
    }
}
```

Just as with the other handlers previously shown in this chapter, a sleep period is added to simulate a loaded server so you can verify things, such as the Submit button being disabled during processing. Finally, it prints out the encoded JSON, which is read as the Ajax request object and provides the calling JavaScript function `createAccount()`. The members `err` and `msg` are used for decision making and message display, respectively.

```
    # simulate a load
    sleep 7;

    $r->content_type('text/html');
    $r->print(encode_json({
            msg => $msg,
            err => $err }));

    return Apache2::Const::OK;


}
```

The notifyUser() Subroutine

Next comes the subroutine notifyUser(). This subroutine prepares the message, and sets some values in the message, such as the login URL, the user's new password, and the subject of the email the user will receive.

You may not want to send the user their password. This is a very simple example, and you would probably want to have some mechanism that would require them to change their password right away. You could alternatively send them a link that activates their account completely. It all depends on what your security requirements are.

Finally, the WebApp method sendEmail() is called, sending the message to the user's email address, from accounts@example.com.

```perl
sub notifyUser {
    my ($form) = @_;
    my $username = $form->{username};
    my $email = $form->{email};
    my $password = $form->{password};
    my $login_url = 'http://example.com/login';

    warn "sending mail for $username $email";
    my $subject= "New Account and Password information";
    my $msg = <<EOMSG;
A new account has been set up for $form->{username}
 with the email address $form->{email}


Username: $username
Password: $password

Now you can log in at: $login_url.

EOMSG

    sendEmail($email, 'accounts@example.com', $subject, $msg, 'example.com');
}

1;
```

New WebApp Method sendEmail()

The sendEmail() method, which the account mod_perl handler requires, is added to the WebApp class. This is how you can send email to a user, although you can also use it for a number of purposes other than new account creation.

This new method (or subroutine) is included in the EXPORT list so that it doesn't require instantiation or an object handle.

Required for this method is the importation of both Mail::SendMail and Email::Valid modules, which you can obtain from CPAN.

```perl
use Mail::Sendmail;
use Email::Valid;
# code body
our @EXPORT = qw(randomString buildRange sendEmail);
```

The `sendEmail()` method takes five arguments, as will be shown. It uses Email::Valid to test the address of the new user. If the address is invalid, it will not permit the email to be sent. It then organizes a Perl hash `%data`, which contains the email parameters. It then uses the hash in the method `Mail::Sendmail::sendmail()` to send the email to the user. If there is any error, 0 is returned.

```perl
sub sendEmail {
    my ($addr, $from, $subject, $content, $emailhost) = @_;
    $from= 'accounts@patg.net';
    $emailhost ||= 'patg.net';

    unless (Email::Valid->rfc822($addr)) {
      warn "Can't send mail '$subject' to $addr: Invalid address\n";
      return 0;
    }

    my %data = (
        From                => $from,
        Smtp                => $emailhost,
        Subject             => $subject,
        Message             => $content,
        To                  => $addr,
        'Content-type'      => 'text/plain; charset="us-ascii"',
        'Content-transfer-encoding' => '8bit'
        );

    if (Mail::Sendmail::sendmail(%data)) {
      return 1;
    }
    warn "Can't send mail '$subject' to $addr: $Mail::Sendmail::error\n";
    return 0;

}
```

Ajax Account Creation in Action

Now, let's see a demonstration of account creation! Figure 16-4 shows the initial form that the user has filled out, just before hitting the Submit button.

Figure 16-5 shows the message that is displayed while the account is being created. Because the page in Figure 16-5 is too long to capture in full, you can't see that the Submit button is grayed out.

Finally, the user's account is created and the success message is displayed (see Figure 16-6). At this point, the user will have an email waiting in their mailbox, informing them of their new account.

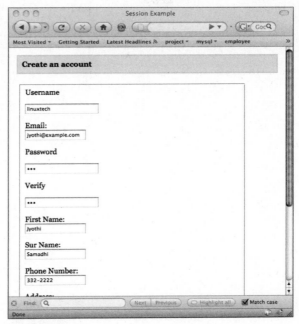

Figure 16-4

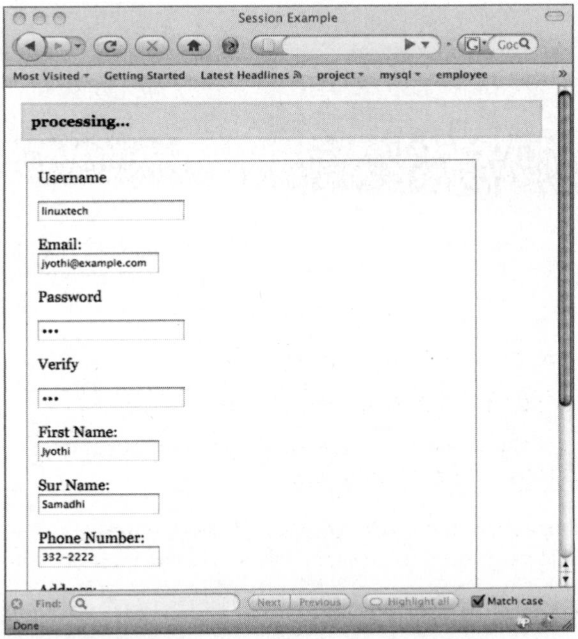

Figure 16-5

The account for linuxtech has been created and information sent to jyothi@example.com

Your account has been created, now please check your mail for verification!

Once you obtain your information, you can log in at http://example.com/login

Figure 16-6

Summary

In this chapter, you were introduced to using Ajax and mod_perl together. You may want to remember the following as you progress through the rest of the book:

❏ Ajax allows you to write applications that provide a better user experience because data is exchanged asynchronously with the web server. A page submission to the server is not required for information exchange, allowing the display of the page to remain unaffected. In this case, it means mod_perl handlers read data from a request and send responses back to the Ajax client. With Ajax and JavaScript together, it is possible to generate display content on the web client instead of having to generate it on the server.

❏ You can write both Ajax client applications and mod_perl handlers that process the information from the Ajax client using the JSON Perl module. You were shown how you can manipulate the DOM (Document Object Model) of the web page, for example, to set a response message from the server and enable or disable the Submit button.

❏ You were also shown the other piece of the session management system from Chapter 15. This new application, shown in detail, uses Ajax to provide a front-end application that creates a user account. Additionally, you saw how to send email by means of a new method added to the WebApp module.

You should now have a good understanding of how you can use mod_perl and Ajax together to develop some really useful applications.

17

Search Engine Application

In the beginning of the World Wide Web, search engine applications were one of the first types of applications implemented. Being able to collect and store data from various sources across the web and provide an interface to make that data searchable for users is a common functionality that has been implemented in a number of ways throughout the history of computing and, more recently, the Web. There are a lot of requirements for this functionality: a means of storing the data, a means of full-text indexing the data so terms or queries can be used to perform searches against that data and retrieve results, having hits that are quickly returned, and a user interface for the person performing the search.

This chapter shows you a search engine application — one that's probably implemented differently than other search engine applications you have seen before. This chapter shows you the following:

❑   How to implement a search engine from top to bottom!

❑   How to use Sphinx for a real-life application.

❑   How to use Gearman to distribute work and how to use both the Perl client and worker API for Gearman, as well as the Gearman MySQL UDFs, which you can use with triggers to further automate job assignments.

❑   A simple web client crawler implemented in Perl that is a worker to which the Gearman job server will assign work.

❑   Yet another application that takes advantage of memcached and MySQL together, and even more practical examples of using the Memcached Functions for MySQL.

This chapter will put together all the pieces of everything you've learned throughout this book into a really interesting and useful application. This is the icing on the cake!

Using Gearman to Put the Search Engine Application Together

Chapter 16 discussed all the great tools that are available for building Web Applications. Some of those discussions focused solely on a particular tool — such as MySQL, memcached, Memcached Functions for MySQL, Sphinx, Apache, or Perl itself. This section shows you how to use all of them together with an additional, incredibly useful project: Gearman.

Gearman

Gearman is a server that assigns jobs requested by clients. It was developed by the same people who brought you memcached: Danga. Gearman is "used to farm out work to other machines, dispatching function calls to machines that are better suited to do work, to do work in parallel, to load balance lots of function calls, or to call functions between languages," according to the project site. At several points in this book, the idea of splitting up functionality of the web application into other processes has been mentioned. Gearman is the ultimate tool for making this a reality.

Originally written in Perl, but recently rewritten in C by Eric Day for better performance, Gearman is at heart a job server — it receives requests for jobs and then assigns them. The basic Gearman setup consists of a client, a worker, and a job server. The client creates a job and requests that it be done. The job server delegates the job to an appropriate worker for the given job. These workers can do anything that you want them to do — fetch documents off the Web, store data in memcached, stop and restart other servers — for anything that you can code, Gearman can have that job run.

The essential idea of Gearman is shown in Figure 17-1.

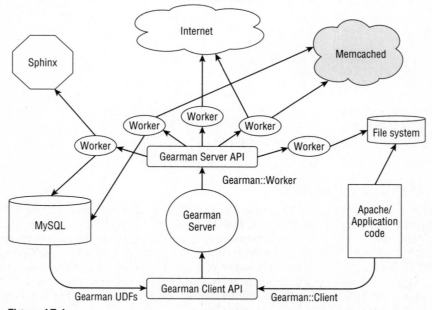

Figure 17-1

The idea here is simple: In your development using Perl and MySQL, you would issue requests for jobs through the client API either using the Perl module Gearman::Client or using the Gearman MySQL user defined functions (UDF). You would issue a particular job request that would then be assigned by the job server to the appropriate worker. This job could be anything — copying data to and from memcached to MySQL or any other data source, building Sphinx indices, fetching remote content off of a web site, or running thumbnail generation in a directory containing uploaded images. Note in Figure 17-1 that only one Gearman job server is shown. However, you could have any number of Gearman job servers, running on different hosts and dispatching workers in a distributed scheme.

Installing and Running Gearman

Installing the latest version of Gearman is a very straightforward task. You can obtain the latest source at http://www.gearman.org/doku.php?id=download. This site includes links to every component you would need to run Gearman, including the job server itself and the Gearman MySQL UDFs.

gearmand Job Server Install

To install the Gearman job server, follow these steps:

1. Download the latest source distribution for gearmand into a directory where you usually compile source code, such as /usr/local/src. The first thing is to unpack the source distribution:

   ```
   tar xvzf gearmand-0.3.tar.gz
   ```

2. Enter the gearmand source distribution directory:

   ```
   cd gearmand-0.3
   ./configure
   ```

3. Now build and install gearmand:

   ```
   make
   make install
   ```

At this point, gearmand will be installed and ready to use.

Gearman MySQL UDF Install

Also available for use with Gearman are the Gearman MySQL user defined functions or UDFs. Eric Day also wrote these UDFs (as well as the new C-based job server) and the UDFs offer even more power when you use Gearman than with just using external programs. The UDFs are themselves client programs and run internally within the MySQL server. With these UDFs, you can add jobs to the Gearman job server just as you do regular client programs, however you do so from within MySQL, rather than using an external program or from within your application code. This may sound confusing at first — running a client within a server. However, if you will recall from earlier chapters, both the example Curl UDF http_get() and the memcached UDFs are also clients.

The Gearman MySQL UDFs offer the ability to request jobs of the Gearman job server from within MySQL. This means you can have triggers on tables, so that when an UPDATE, DELETE, or INSERT occurs, a job can also be added. Think of the power this gives you!

To begin installation of the Gearman MySQL UDFs, follow these steps:

1. Download the latest UDF source into the same directory where you downloaded the Gearman job server source code:

```
tar xvzf gearman-mysql-udf-0.2.tar.gz
```

2. Enter the Gearman MySQL UDF source directory:

```
cd gearman-mysql-udf-0.2
```

3. Configure the package for compiling. The path you use depends on what distribution of MySQL you have, whether it's source or binary, etc. You will need to locate the path where mysql_config exists. You will probably have to install whatever MySQL development or community development package (yum search mysql, apt-cache search mysql, yast ...) is required.

On an Ubuntu system, it would be:

```
./configure --with-mysql=/usr/bin/mysql_config --libdir=/usr/lib/mysql/lib
```

--with-mysql is the argument that tells the configuration program where to find mysql_config, --libdir is where the shared UDF libraries will be installed and this will have to be a directory that MySQL can load the libraries from. You may have to add or edit /etc/ld.so.conf.d/mysql.conf to make sure that the path is listed, then run ldconfig.

4. Next, build and install the UDF source code:

```
make
make install
```

5. To load the UDFs, you will need to do so from within MySQL:

```
CREATE FUNCTION gman_do RETURNS STRING SONAME "libgearman_mysql_udf.so";
CREATE FUNCTION gman_do_high RETURNS STRING SONAME
"libgearman_mysql_udf.so";
CREATE FUNCTION gman_do_background RETURNS STRING SONAME
"libgearman_mysql_udf.so";
CREATE AGGREGATE FUNCTION gman_sum RETURNS INTEGER SONAME
"libgearman_mysql_udf.so";
CREATE FUNCTION gman_servers_set RETURNS STRING SONAME
"libgearman_mysql_udf.so";
```

At this point, the Gearman MySQL UDFs are installed.

Running the Gearman Job Server

Running gearmand, the Gearman job server, is the next thing you must do to use it.

To start gearmand:

1. Run (whatever path it is installed in):

```
/usr/local/bin/gearmand -d
```

This tells gearmand to run detached in the background.

2. Now, run a worker. The gearmand distribution includes both some sample worker and client programs in the directory examples/ of the source directory. To really do something, you need to run a worker program. For testing out gearmand (as well as both the workers and client to get a concept of how Gearman works as a whole), use two windows to see what exactly it does. In one window, start up the reverse worker. Do not background it by using '&':

```
./reverse_worker
```

3. Run a client program. With the Gearman job server (gearmand), you have two ways of requesting a job:

❑ Attached/callback, which will wait until the job that the job server delegates is completed and then will return a return value of that worker.

❑ Detached/backgrounded, which will let the process run at its own volition, without waiting for a return value of the worker.

For this example, the callback/attached client will run.

4. In another window, run the reverse_client_cb program:

```
./reverse_client_cb "This is a test"

Created: H:hanuman:929
Created: H:hanuman:930
Created: H:hanuman:931
Created: H:hanuman:932
Created: H:hanuman:933
Created: H:hanuman:934
Created: H:hanuman:935
Created: H:hanuman:936
Created: H:hanuman:937
Created: H:hanuman:938
Completed: H:hanuman:929 tset a si sihT
Completed: H:hanuman:930 tset a si sihT
Completed: H:hanuman:931 tset a si sihT
Completed: H:hanuman:932 tset a si sihT
Completed: H:hanuman:933 tset a si sihT
Completed: H:hanuman:934 tset a si sihT
```

```
Completed: H:hanuman:935 tset a si sihT
Completed: H:hanuman:936 tset a si sihT
Completed: H:hanuman:937 tset a si sihT
Completed: H:hanuman:938 tset a si sihT
```

If you look in the window there the worker is running, you'll see:

```
Job=H:hanuman:929 Workload=This is a test Result=tset a si sihT
Job=H:hanuman:930 Workload=This is a test Result=tset a si sihT
Job=H:hanuman:931 Workload=This is a test Result=tset a si sihT
Job=H:hanuman:932 Workload=This is a test Result=tset a si sihT
Job=H:hanuman:933 Workload=This is a test Result=tset a si sihT
Job=H:hanuman:934 Workload=This is a test Result=tset a si sihT
Job=H:hanuman:935 Workload=This is a test Result=tset a si sihT
Job=H:hanuman:936 Workload=This is a test Result=tset a si sihT
Job=H:hanuman:937 Workload=This is a test Result=tset a si sihT
Job=H:hanuman:938 Workload=This is a test Result=tset a si sihT
```

As you can see, the client requests a job from the job server, gearmand, to the *reverse* worker, which was dispatched via the job server to the workers, which in turn reversed the text and returned the result of that reversal.

Using the Gearman MySQL UDFs

Another way to make job requests to the Gearman job server is to use the Gearman MySQL UDFs. The UDFs that are offered are discussed in detail in the following sections.

gman_severs_set()

This UDF, which you *must* call before calling any of the other Gearman MySQL UDFs, sets the server that will be used for any UDF call within the client session. It takes as its first argument one or more comma-separated servers, port optional — it will default to port 4730. The second argument can be used to set a particular server to run a specific job!

```
gman_servers_set("<server list>", "<optional: job>")
```

Here is an example of a single server:

```
SELECT gman_servers_set("192.168.1.33:7004")
```

Here is an example of assigning 192.168.1.33 to run the reverse worker:

```
SELECT gman_servers_set("192.168.1.33:4730", "reverse");
```

And here is a example of assigning two servers to run the indexer worker:

```
SELECT gman_servers_set("192.168.1.88:4730,192.168.1.99:7004", "indexer");
```

Once your servers are set up, you can then request jobs from your UDF queries using the Gearman MySQL UDFs.

gman_do()

These UDFs send job requests to the Gearman job server, gearmand.

```
gman_do("<job name>", "<input value>")
gman_do_high("<job name>", "<input value>")
gman_do_background("<job name>", "<input value>")
```

gman_do() runs a normal job, and waits for the job to finish before returning a result. If there is one, gman_do_high() is a high-priority job, which waits as well, and gman_do_background() runs the job in the background at a lower priority, returning the host and job number.

> **If you want a job request to be made through a Gearman MySQL UDF using a trigger, you need to call** gman_do_background()**. Otherwise, the** INSERT **statement for the data being inserted into the table will not complete until the job is done.**

gman_sum()

This is an aggregate function used to run jobs in parallel:

```
SELECT gman_sum("wc", Host) AS test FROM mysql.user;
```

Usage Examples

Here are some examples of using the UDFs to submit a job to the reverse worker you already started:

```
mysql> select gman_servers_set('127.0.0.1');
+-------------------------------+
| gman_servers_set('127.0.0.1') |
+-------------------------------+
| NULL                          |
+-------------------------------+

mysql> select gman_do('reverse', 'This is a test');
+--------------------------------------+
| gman_do('reverse', 'This is a test') |
+--------------------------------------+
| tset a si sihT                       |
+--------------------------------------+

mysql> select gman_do_background('reverse', 'This is a test');
+-------------------------------------------------+
| gman_do_background('reverse', 'This is a test') |
+-------------------------------------------------+
| H:hanuman:940                                   |
+-------------------------------------------------+

mysql> set @a = gman_do_background('reverse', "XYZ");

mysql> select @a;
+---------------+
| @a            |
```

```
+---------------+
| H:hanuman:945 |
+---------------+

mysql> set @a = gman_do('reverse', "XYZ");

mysql> select @a;
+------+
| @a   |
+------+
| ZYX  |
+------+
```

As you can see from the output of `gman_do_background()`, it returns the name of the host and job number.

Perl and Gearman

Since Gearman was originally written in Perl, it of course has a well-supported client library. The modules you will need are Gearman::Client and Gearman::Worker, installed as one CPAN module, Gearman. The POD documentation provides information on the usage for these modules.

Perl Gearman Worker

This is a basic Perl worker that performs that same job functionality as the C-binary worker you ran earlier. It would be implemented as:

```perl
#!/usr/bin/perl

use strict;
use warnings

use Gearman::Worker;

sub my_reverse_fn {
  reverse $_[0]->arg;
}

my $worker= Gearman::Worker->new();
$worker->job_servers('127.0.0.1:4730');
$worker->register_function('reverse',
                           \&my_reverse_fn);
$worker->work() while 1;
```

Regarding usage, you will implement the following:

❑ Instantiate a Gearman::Worker object.

❑ Set the job server to use using the method `job_servers()`.

❑ Register the function to a job name — in this case "reverse."

❏ Register the function to a subroutine name — in this case `my_reverse()` — that contains the body of code that will implement the worker. This name that you register is the name of the job you will refer to when requesting what job to run.

❏ The method `work()` will run the worker in a `while` loop, just as you would run a server. In this case, the subroutine `my_reverse_fn()` is the function registered. It takes as its first argument whatever was supplied by the client program. In this case, it will be a string that it reverses.

Perl Gearman Client

A basic Perl Gearman client requires even fewer lines than the worker:

```perl
#!/usr/bin/perl

use strict;
use warnings;

use Gearman::Client;
my $client = Gearman::Client->new();
$client->job_servers('127.0.0.1:4730');
$ref = $client->do_task('reverse', 'This is a test');
print "$$ref\n";
```

You implement this client using similar steps to the Perl worker implementation:

1. Instantiate a Gearman::Client object.

2. The servers are set with `job_servers()`.

3. The method `do_task()` calls the job, which in this case is 'reverse', to run with the argument "This is a test." This inevitably results in the worker running its subroutine registered as 'reverse', shown in the worker example as `my_reverse_fn()`.

The Search Engine Application

Your curiosity should be sparked by what you just have read about regarding Gearman. Now you will really see Gearman, along with MySQL, memcached, memcached UDFs, Sphinx, Apache and Perl in action!

Search engines are applications that are most likely to have a lot of moving parts and functionality. This is required to dispense information. The search engine application for discussion in this section has a few moving parts of its own — perhaps it will seem like a Rube Goldberg contraption, but in a good way! This application will show you just how useful all these new technologies are in implementing something in a wholly different way. It is a prototype, and there may be ways of implementing it other than what is shown. The main point is to demonstrate how processing can be spread out to various jobs and across various servers, alleviating the work that a web application has to perform.

This search engine application has two major components:

❏ A data gathering system for data retrieval, storage, and creating full-text indices

❏ A search engine user application

The entire application consists of the components listed in the following table:

Component	Description
A mod_perl search handler application	Displays the search page, allowing you to enter a search term and the number of searches per page.
A mod_perl URL entry interface application	Where you enter URLs of web sites that you want to place in a queue. These are fetched from the Internet, stored in MySQL, and indexed with the full-text search engine Sphinx.
A Perl web client worker application	Given a URL, this will retrieve the page at that URL as well as a recursion of one level deep through the document at that URL, parsing any links and subsequently fetching the page content of the web page at those links. It stores content in memcached keyed by the MD5-hexed value of the URL that yet another worker retrieves from memcached and stores in MySQL to the appropriate tables. This web client worker is initiated by a database trigger on a simple table that stores the URLs and receives its URL argument from the trigger.
A Perl data storage worker	This is trigger activated. It fetches a batch of web pages from memcached if a counter object, also in memcached, is of a given value. The web pages stored in memcached are identified by the MD5 hex of the URL value. This worker both retrieves and stores these cached web pages from memcached into MySQL using the memcached UDFs. Finally, this data storage worker resets the URL storage counter object in memcached.
A Perl Sphinx indexer worker	Also trigger-activated. If a counter object in memcached has reached a given value, meaning a certain number of web pages have been stored and therefore it needs to have the index rebuilt, the index worker calls the Sphinx indexer program to re-index the Sphinx index for the table containing the retrieved web pages. It also resets the indexer counter object in memcached.
MySQL	Four database tables, two triggers.
A meta-data table	For storing information about the web page such as its URL, unique ID, date, title, status, etc.
A BLOB/text table	Has a 1:1 relation to the meta-data table that stores the actual content of the web page for the particular URL in a TEXT column.
A URL queue table	Stores the URLs of the web pages that need to be fetched from the Internet. This is the table that has a trigger on it and initiates all the other actions.
A URL inventory table	Stores the URLs of web pages that were stored in memcached by the web client worker.
Two triggers on the URL queue table	One trigger is on an INSERT; another is on an UPDATE. Both use the Gearman MySQL UDF to call gman_do_background() to call the web client worker. The other trigger will be on the URL inventory table that checks values of both URL storage counter and indexer counter. If either is exceeded, the job for whatever check is exceeded is requested to be run.
Sphinx full-text index	This is built from database table containing the web pages.
memcached	Stores the web pages retrieved as a somewhat temporary storage.

The flow of how content is fetched from a web page, parsed, stored, and then indexed follows:

1. A user enters a URL value into the URL entry page and the URL value is stored in the URL queue table.

2. The trigger on the URL queue table makes a job request to the Gearman job server for the web client worker using the Gearman MySQL UDF `gman_do_background()`.

3. The web client worker fetches the web pages' contents from the web site for the given URL provided to it from the client UDF. In addition to the content of the initial page, which through recursion at one level deep, the web client worker also fetches any URLs in the page. All retrieved web content pages are stored in memcached per columns of data (columns that will inevitably be stored in MySQL). The ID of each stored page is based off the md5 of the URL. With this, an entry is made to the URL inventory table.

4. The entry into the URL inventory table results in the activation of an INSERT trigger. This trigger will use the memcached UDF `memc_increment()` to access and increment the value of both counter objects in memcached.

5. The stored URL counter indicates the number of URLs stored to MySQL since the last retrieval and subsequent storage. If the value of the data storage counter is greater than a predetermined value (set to 5 in this example), then this trigger calls `gman_do_background()` to request the data storage worker and sets the data storage counter object back to 0.

6. The indexer counter also indicates the number of URLs stored to MySQL since the last retrieval. However, the value that the counter has to exceed in order for `gman_do_task_background()` to request the Sphinx indexer worker to run is greater than the value that needs to be exceeded for the data storage worker. This is because you don't want to be re-indexing as often as you would be storing data from memcached to MySQL. The example in this book is 20, which is really low for real-life situations but it is set to this value for demonstration purposes.

7. The data storage worker is triggered. This worker simply retrieves and deletes all the URLs from the URL inventory table. The URL values it retrieves are used to build up an MD5 value that's then used to retrieve the data from memcached. This retrieval and storage is done in a single query that provides values in either an UPDATE or INSERT statement using the memcached UDF `memc_get()`.

8. The indexer worker is triggered. This runs the Sphinx indexer program, making it so the new data in the database is indexed into the Sphinx full-text index.

As users request the search page, they can run search queries via the web search user interface that this mod_perl application provides.

Database Tables for the Search Engine Application

When building a search engine, the first thing to think about is how the data is stored. For this application, as shown in the previous section's table, there will be four database tables.

```
CREATE TABLE urls (
    id int(8) NOT NULL auto_increment,
    url_md5 char(32) not null default '',
    url varchar(128) not null default '',
```

```
        title varchar(64) not null default '',
        created date,
        last_updated timestamp,
        last_modified varchar(40) not null default '',
        status varchar(32) not null default '',
        primary key (id),
        unique url_md5 (url_md5)
);
```

The four database tables are as follows:

❑   The *urls* table will store the meta-data information for a web page retrieved. This includes fields such as title, last updated, the created date, the status of the web request, but not the actual web page content. It's good practice to keep your BLOB or text data in a separate table so that any queries for meta-data type values don't have to be retrieved from a table containing TEXT or BLOBs; combining tables would make these queries perform slower and would require more memory.

```
        CREATE TABLE urls_blob (
            id int(8) NOT NULL default 0,
            content mediumtext,
            primary key (id)
        );
```

❑   The *urls_blob* table stores the actual web page contents. It also has a primary key *id* which is a direct relation to the *urls* table id column:

```
        create table urls_queue (
            url_md5 char(32) NOT NULL default '',
            url    varchar(128) NOT NULL default '',
            last_updated timestamp,
            primary key url_md5 (url_md5)
        ) ENGINE=InnoDB;
```

❑   The *urls_queue* table is a simple, searchable table that stores a list of URLs you want Sphinx to index. The *urls_queue* could be compared to the process of priming something. In this case you're priming the search engine. Its modification — either initial INSERT or UPDATE, results in job requests for the web client worker to fetch the value of the row being inserted or modified.

```
        create table urls_stored (
            url_md5 char(32) NOT NULL default '',
            url    varchar(128) NOT NULL default '',
            primary key url_md5 (url_md5)
        ) ENGINE=InnoDB;
```

❑   The *urls_stored* is a URL inventory table of the URLs of web pages that have been stored temporarily in memcached to be subsequently stored in MySQL. This table provides a way to account for the URLs as well as a means to activate a trigger to store these web pages for the specified URLs. The trigger is set to call the data storage worker only if a certain number of URLs have been stored, which is determined by checking a counter value stored in memcached that's incremented for every row inserted into the table. For the example in this chapter, this is set to 5. If there are five or more URLs in this table, then the data storage worker updates or inserts into both the *urls* and *urls_blob* tables the values that were stored in memcached.

Database Triggers

There are three database triggers that are used for calling each of the workers, depending on whether a row is inserted or updated:

❑ The trigger *urls_queue_insert* starts the whole process into action. When a URL is inserted into this table, it sets the MD5 of the URL for the url_md5 column and then calls the Gearman MySQL UDF gman_do_background('url_fetch', NEW.url). This results in the url_fetch job being dispatched by the Gearman job server. This, in turn, fetches the web page of that URL, as well as any links in that web page, and stores them in memcached.

```
DELIMITER |
CREATE TRIGGER urls_queue_insert
BEFORE INSERT ON urls_queue
FOR EACH ROW BEGIN
  SET NEW.url_md5 = md5(NEW.url);
  SET @gd= gman_do_background('url_fetch', NEW.url);
END |
```

❑ The trigger *urls_queue_update*, performs the same action as the previously mentioned trigger, *urls_queue_insert*, but this time it happens when an UPDATE statement is run against the table *urls*. You would activate this by running a query, such as:

```
update urls_queue set last_updated=now()
    where url_md5 = '57fb6e137fed0e9d60ec31a93a5ca427';
```

This would cause this trigger to run, updating the stored web page in memcached and inserting a URL into the table *urls_stored*.

```
CREATE TRIGGER urls_queue_update
BEFORE UPDATE ON urls_queue
FOR EACH ROW BEGIN
  SET @gd= gman_do_background('url_fetch', OLD.url);
END |
```

❑ The trigger *urls_queue_update* first checks and increments (memc_increment(), returning the value it increments) the value of the urls_stored and indexer values in memcached using the memcached UDF memc_increment(). These values, if exceeding 5 and 20, respectively, will result in gman_do_background() running for either the url_process or indexer jobs, as well as resetting the counter variables in memcached to 0 using memc_set().

```
CREATE TRIGGER urls_stored_insert
BEFORE INSERT ON urls_stored
FOR EACH ROW BEGIN
  SET @count = memc_increment('urls_stored');
  SET @index_count = memc_increment('index_counter');
  IF @count > 5 THEN
```

```
        SET @gd = gman_do_background('url_process', NEW.url);
        SET @reset = memc_set('urls_stored', 0);
    END IF;
    IF @index_count > 20 THEN
        SET @gd = gman_do_background('indexer', NEW.url);
        SET @reset = memc_set('index_counter', 0);
    END IF;
END |

DELIMITER ;
```

Sphinx Setup

To index web pages stored in MySQL using the Sphinx full-text index, Sphinx also has to be set up. For this example, we will use a simple Sphinx setup with a single distributed index that uses two Sphinx agents — one for the main index, urls, and one for the delta index, urls_delta.

You have two indexes — one main, large index and a smaller delta index — for good reason: you don't want to re-index in its entirety a continually growing data set too often and have changes, or deltas, added to it. Because Sphinx has distributed index functionality, you can have two indexes — the main, large index and a smaller delta index work together as if they were a single index, while you only update the smaller delta index. Then at some interval, you merge the delta index into the main index.

The first thing to review is the MySQL table that will contain the positions of both the main and delta indices. The indexer uses this positional information in the table, *sphinx_counter*, to obtain the limits, or extents, of what the records the indices will comprise. The indexer uses this to determine what data should be selected when indexing.

The main urls index will contain all records having an id value less than the value of column, max_id, in the table *sphinx_counter*. The delete index, urls_delta, will contain records having their id value starting from the value of the column sphinx_counter.max_id with no upward limit.

Where the main index ends and the delta index starts is set only when the main index is re-indexed. The delta index grows over time, and at some point, you merge the two of them. The break point will be set to the maximum of the main index, which now contains what was previously in the delta, and the delta is rebuilt with a starting point equal to the maximum of the newly merged index.

Each index has exactly one entry in this table and the position data is updated during indexing:

```
CREATE TABLE 'sphinx_counter' (
    'id' int(11) NOT NULL,
    'max_id' bigint(20) unsigned NOT NULL,
    'index_name' varchar(32) NOT NULL default '',
    'last_updated' timestamp,
    PRIMARY KEY  (`id`),
    KEY 'index_name' (`index_name`)
) ENGINE=InnoDB;ed
```

Here is an example showing the positional data of a running setup:

```
mysql> select * from sphinx_counter;
```

```
+----+--------+------------+---------------------+
| id | max_id | index_name | last_updated        |
+----+--------+------------+---------------------+
|  1 |   1133 | urls       | 2009-03-02 11:05:30 |
|  2 |   1181 | urls_delta | 2009-03-02 11:12:12 |
+----+--------+------------+---------------------+
```

To use this to explain the topic further, the main index, urls, will contain records with the url.id value of 0 through 1133, and the delta index, *urls_delta*, will contain records with the url.id value of 1134 through 1181.

The entry in the *sphinx_counter* counter table for the delta index is not necessary really, but it has an added informational benefit to show you the state of what records your indices represent. The single entry for the main index is sufficient to delineate the extents of the main and the delta indices for indexing.

To set up Sphinx, follow these steps:

1. Define the data sources that will be used. The first source, urls, is set to use the MySQL server running on localhost on port 3306. The sql_query_pre directive defines the query that is run prior to the main document fetching query. In this case, the sphinx_counter table is updated with the max (id) value from the *urls* table, moving the positional information up to represent the index that is about to be regenerated.

2. The sql_query directive specifies the main query that will be run. The primary key or other unique identifier must always be the first column specified in this query. In this instance, it is the id column of the urls table. This makes it so when you perform a search against Sphinx, you will obtain one or more values of the primary key id that you will subsequently use to retrieve the actual data from MySQL, making for a fast lookup.

   About this query: it performs a join of urls *with* urls_blob *to obtain the actual content from the BLOB table, as well as the other columns specified after the primary key value. These columns are used to create a full text index and are therefore searchable. Sphinx has a very flexible language, allowing you to specify which columns to search on. Also, this query uses a* WHERE *clause to select records less than or equal to the value in the* sphinx_counter *table for the main index. This is the mechanism that applies an extent to the data being gathered.*

3. The directive, sql_query_info, provides a query to the search command-line program, which is good for running test queries against your index. Do note that search does not search against Sphinx through the Sphinx search daemon, searchd — rather, it searches on the index itself, so it will not work with distributed indices.

```
source urls
{
        type                    = mysql

        sql_host                = localhost
        sql_user                = webuser
        sql_pass                = webpass
        sql_db                  = webapp
```

```
               sql_port                    = 3306   # optional, default is 3306

               sql_query_pre = UPDATE sphinx_counter \
                            SET max_id = (SELECT MAX(id) FROM urls) \
                            WHERE index_name = 'urls'

        # main document fetch query
        # mandatory, integer document ID field MUST be the first selected
   column
               sql_query    = SELECT id, url_md5, url, title, \
                            UNIX_TIMESTAMP(last_updated) as ulast_updated,
   content \
                            FROM urls join urls_blob using (id) \
                            WHERE id <= \
                               (SELECT max_id FROM sphinx_counter \
                                WHERE index_name = 'urls')

        # document info query, ONLY for CLI search (ie. testing and
   debugging)
               # must contain $id macro and must fetch the document by that id
               sql_query_info  = SELECT * FROM urls JOIN urls_blob USING (id) \
                            WHERE id = $id

   }
```

4. The source for the delta index, *urls_delta*, is defined. The notation "urls_delta : urls" means that urls_delta will inherit every option/directive from the data source *urls*, unless otherwise overridden. In this case, the directive sql_query_pre and sql_query are overridden to specify a different range than what is used with the *urls* data source. For the urls_delta data source, all records *greater than* the max_id value for the data source *urls* are specified.

```
   source urls_delta : urls
   {
            sql_query_pre = UPDATE sphinx_counter SET max_id = (SELECT MAX(id) \
                         FROM urls) WHERE index_name = 'urls_delta'
            sql_query     = SELECT id, url_md5, url, title, \
                         UNIX_TIMESTAMP(last_updated) as ulast_updated, \
                         content \
                         FROM urls join urls_blob using (id) \
                         WHERE id > \
                            (SELECT max_id FROM sphinx_counter
                             WHERE index_name = 'urls')

   }
```

5. The indices are defined. The directives shown here are the most important. The directive source defines the data source that is used to build this index; in this case the source urls is used. The directive path is used to specify path and base name of the actual index files. docinfo just specifies the storage mode. min_word_length specifies the minimum size of a word that is indexed. The value of '1' specifies all words. It's important to point out that MySQL full-text indices have a limit of three, so this is yet another improvement over MySQL full-text indices.

```
   index urls
   {
            # document source(s) to index
```

```
        # multi-value, mandatory
        # document IDs must be globally unique across all sources
        source              = urls

        # index files path and file name, without extension
        # mandatory, path must be writable, extensions will be auto-
appended
        path                        = /usr/local/sphinx/var/data/urls

        # document attribute values (docinfo) storage mode
        # optional, default is 'extern'
        # known values are 'none', 'extern' and 'inline'
        docinfo             = extern

        # minimum indexed word length
        # default is 1 (index everything)
        min_word_len        = 1

        # 'sbcs' (Single Byte CharSet)
        charset_type        = sbcs
}
```

6. The delta index, `urls_delta`, inherits everything from the index `urls`, except path and source, which it overrides. Since the source for `urls_delta` is `urls_delta` — this is the data source that has a different range than `urls`, hence `urls_delta` is a smaller index comprised of a smaller range (the topmost records) of the database table *urls*.

```
index urls_delta : urls
{
        path    = /usr/local/sphinx/var/data/urls_delta
        source  = urls_delta
}
```

7. Next, the distributed index, `dist_urls`, is defined. This is the *glue* that makes the delta index and main index work together as one index. Queries run against this distributed index; the user never knows that the index is made up of parts.

```
index dist_urls
{
        type    = distributed

        agent   = localhost:3312:urls
        agent   = localhost:3312:urls_delta

        agent_connect_timeout   = 1000
        agent_query_timeout     = 3000
}
```

8. The indexer configuration is simple enough, and the directive `mem_limit` species how much memory is used for the indexer, when it runs, to generate indices.

```
indexer
{
```

```
                          # memory limit, in bytes, kiloytes (16384K) or megabytes (256M)
                          # optional, default is 32M, max is 2047M, recommended is 256M to
           1024M
                          mem_limit                          = 32M


               }
```

9.   The `searchd` daemon is configured in the following section. The `listen` directive specifies
     which port or socket the daemon will bind to. In this case, none is specified, so all interfaces
     are used. The log directive specifies the log for the *searchd* daemon — this log will log the
     status of the `searchd` daemon. The `query_log` directive specifies a log used to log the search
     queries that are run against *searchd*.

The other directives set timeout values, max number of children to run, a `pid` file, maximum number
of matches returned, and whether the *searchd* daemon can be restarted seamlessly after running the
indexer.

Also listed is the directive `seamless_rotate`. This makes it so that when you run the indexer, `searchd` is
seamlessly restarted once the indexer completes.

```
    searchd
    {
            # hostname, port, or hostname:port, or /unix/socket/path to listen on
            # multi-value, multiple listen points are allowed
            # optional, default is 0.0.0.0:3312 (listen on all interfaces, port 3312)
            #
            # listen                              = 127.0.0.1
            # listen                              = 192.168.0.1:3312
            # listen                              = 3312
            # log file, searchd run info is logged here

            log       = /usr/local/sphinx/var/log/searchd.log

            # query log file, all search queries are logged here
            query_log                   = /usr/local/sphinx/var/log/query.log

            # client read timeout, seconds
            # optional, default is 5
            read_timeout          = 5
            max_children          = 30
            pid_file              = /usr/local/sphinx/var/log/searchd.pid

            # max amount of matches the daemon ever keeps in RAM, per-index
            # default is 1000 (just like Google)
            max_matches           = 1000
            seamless_rotate       = 1
    }
```

Gearman Workers

In this application, three workers are used and they take care of various parts of the data retrieval,
caching, storage and indexing of web pages. The following sections discuss each one.

Web Client Worker

This worker accesses the URL specified, parsing through the requested document for other links, for which it fetches the pages, storing both the originally requested web page's content as well as the web page content of the URLs parsed into memcached:

```
url_fetcher_worker.pl
```

It stores the title, URL, last_modified, status, and content columns of the fetched pages — these are columns that correspond to the database table columns. Each value is stored with a key that is a composite of the md5 of the URL, separated by a ';' and the column name. After storing the data in memcached, it enters a record into *urls_stored* for that URL. Please note the following about this worker:

❏ The body of the worker begins with the various Perl module imports. For this worker, you need LWP and HTTP::Request for the web client functionality, and HTML::Strip for stripping the HTML from what you store in MySQL that will inevitably be indexed by Sphinx.

> *Sphinx also has the ability to strip HTML.*

❏ Digest::MD5 will be used for calling md5_hex to create a url_md5 value. Encode provides the encode_utf8() method for encoding values that will be stored in memcached, which would otherwise give an error. Gearman::Worker, of course, provides the methods for this program to be a Gearman worker program.

```
#!/usr/bin/perl

use strict;
use warnings;

use LWP;
use HTTP::Request;
use HTML::Strip;
use Digest::MD5 qw(md5_hex);
use Gearman::Worker;
use Encode qw(encode_utf8);
use LWP::UserAgent;

use lib qw(/etc/apache2/perl-lib);
use WebApp;
my $webapp= new WebApp();
```

❏ The entry point into this worker, and the subroutine registered to the job url_fetch is url_fetch(), which then calls fetch_remote_doc(), is as follows:

```
sub url_fetch {
    fetch_remote_doc($_[0]->arg, 1);
}
```

❏ The fetch_remote_doc() subroutine does all the work of fetching the remote document. It takes as its first argument a URL and as the second argument a flag that determines if links within the web page fetched will need to be parsed and subsequently fetched. The way the worker is set up for this example is to use only one level of recursion. If there was no limit on recursion, it would end up running for a very long time!

```
sub fetch_remote_doc {
    my ($local_url, $recurse)= @_;

    my $last_modified;
```

❑ The next check that follows is here to obtain a Last-Modified response value if the web page has already been stored and to use this in the web page request. This will save having to fetch and store the web page if there has been no modification to the page since it was stored.

```
    my $if_modified = get_if_modified($local_url);
```

❑ Next, the User-Agent request header is set up. This creates a web client; this one will have the user agent string 'WroxClient/0.1'

```
    # Create a user agent object


    my $ua = LWP::UserAgent->new;

    $ua->agent("WroxClient/0.1 ");
```

❑ An HTTP request is created for the URL.

```
    # Create a request
    my $req = HTTP::Request->new(GET => $local_url);

    my $res = $ua->request($req); #, 'If-Modified-Since' => $if_modified);
```

❑ If the request is successful, then processing continues. The content is obtained and stored in the variable $html. This currently includes the entire content of the web page, including HTML tags, style sheets, and any sort of information.

```
    if ($res->is_success) {
        my $html = $res->content;
```

❑ The title of the web page is parsed. This will be the value for the title column.

```
        my $title= parse_title($html);
        $title ||= $local_url;
```

❑ Any links in the web page are parsed and stored in the array reference $urls. Then the web page content in $html is stripped of HTML tags, as well as any occurrences of two or more spaces being replaced with one space. The tags are not needed because Sphinx only needs to only index the actual text values of the web page, as well as reduce the data storage requirements.

```
        my $urls = parse_links($html);

        my $hs = HTML::Strip->new();
        my $plain_text = $res->content ? $hs->parse( $res->content) : '';
```

```
$hs->eof;
$plain_text =~ s/\s{2,}/ /g;
$plain_text =~ s/\W/ /g;

$last_modified = defined $res->header('Last-Modified') ? '';
```

❏ The Content-Type response header value is checked. For this worker, only HTML, plain text, or XML is allowed. If the web page is this type, then a hash reference is used to organize the data into a structure that will be stored in memcached using store_page():

```
my $content_type= $res->header('Content-type');
if ($content_type =~ /^text\//) {
    my $pageref = {
        'last_modified' => $last_modified,
        'title'         => $title,
        'url'           => $local_url,
        'content'       => $plain_text,
        'status'        => $res->status_line,
    };

    store_page($pageref);
}
```

❏ If the recursion flag $recurse is set, then the list of URLs obtained in the previous code block is used in an iterative loop to call fetch_remote_doc() from within itself, however with the recursion flag set to false. This worker could be modified to allow deeper levels of recursion using a global/package-scoped variable that is decremented for every time fetch_remote_doc() is called.

```
if ($recurse) {
    for my $murl (keys %$urls) {
        fetch_remote_doc($murl, 0);
    }
}

}

}
```

❏ The store_page() subroutine stores the web page in memcached, with each member of the $pageref hash reference being stored as a separate memcached value, keyed by the value of $url_md5 prepended to ":<column name>". You might wonder why the whole $pageref hash reference isn't simply stored. This is so it's possible to obtain the actual values and not a serialized object using the memcached UDFs, which are used in other parts of the code.

❏ The memcached UDF memc_servers_set(), and the Gearman MySQL UDF are called. This is to ensure that the insert trigger, urls_stored_insert, on the urls_stored table, reads counter values from memcached to determine if it should either request from Gearman the data storage worker or the Sphinx indexer worker.

```
sub store_page {
    my ($pageref)= @_;
```

```
    my $url_md5 = md5_hex(encode_utf8($pageref->{url}));

    $webapp->{dbh}->do("SELECT memc_servers_set('127.0.0.1:11211')");
    $webapp->{dbh}->do("SELECT gman_servers_set('127.0.0.1:4730')");
```

❑   The URL being stored is checked to see if it already exists in *urls_stored* because there is no
    reason to store it again since the *urls_stored* table is also a queuing table that is simply there
    to provide a list of URLs for the data storage worker to know what to retrieve from memcached
    and store in MySQL.

```
    my $exists= $webapp->dbGetRef('urls_stored', 'url_md5',
                                      { url_md5 => $url_md5});

    unless (scalar @$exists) {
        $webapp->{memc}->set("$url_md5:url", encode_utf8($pageref->{url}));
        $webapp->{memc}->set("$url_md5:status", encode_utf8($pageref-
    >{status}));
        $webapp->{memc}->set("$url_md5:title", encode_utf8($pageref-
    >{title}));
        $webapp->{memc}->set("$url_md5:last_modified",
                                  encode_utf8($pageref->{last_modified}));
        $webapp->{memc}->set("$url_md5:content",
                                  encode_utf8($pageref->{content}));
```

❑   After setting the web page in memcached, a row is inserted into the *urls_stored* table. This
    will result in the trigger, *urls_stored_insert*, being activated. It increments and checks two
    counter values in memcached: one for determining if the *urls_stored* job should run, and the
    other for determining if the *indexer* job should run. If these counters have values greater than 5
    and 20 respectively (these can be increased), then either the data storage worker or the indexer
    worker are requested with the Gearman MySQL UDF, gman_do_background('urls_process'),
    or gman_do_background('indexer'), respectively.

```
        $webapp->dbInsert('urls_stored', {
            url          => $pageref->{url},
            url_md5      => $url_md5,
            });
    }


    }
```

❑   The subroutine get_if_modified() obtains the Last-Modified value from the *urls* table, if set.
    This in turn will be used in the web client request to return the document only if it has changed
    since that value.

```
    sub get_if_modified {
        my ($url)= @_;

        my $uref= $webapp->dbGetRef('urls', 'last_modified', {url => $url});
        return $uref->[0]{last_modified};
    }
```

❑   This very short subroutine, is_junk(), is used to filter out URLs that are most likely nonsense.
    The author created this subroutine because he noticed that there were a ton of Viagra links!

Though a very sparse subroutine, this can be fleshed out to use values from a table from the database that supply a list of keywords to filter on to avoid acquiring nonsense, spam, or rubbish web pages.

```perl
sub is_junk {
    my ($url)= @_;
    return 1 if $url =~ /viagra/i;
    return 0;
}
```

❏ The subroutine `parse_title()` parses from the web page content URL links into an array reference that are then returned to the calling method. This provides a list of more URLs to fetch.

```perl
sub parse_title {
    my ($html)= @_;

    my   ($title) = $html =~ /\<title\>([\w\W\r\n]+)\<\/title\>/gi;
    $title =~ s/\r|\n|//g;
    $title =~ s/\s{2,}/ /g;

    return $title;
}
```

❏ The `parse_links()` subroutine splits the web page into an array for each line of the web page, then loops through each line, parsing any links and storing any found in the regular expression into an array `@url_list`. An iterative loop of `@url_list` is then used to check if the URL should be rejected using the subroutine `is_junk()`, and then it is keyed into the hash reference `$urls`, which is simply used to collect all the URLs parsed. Incrementing the keyed value of this hash reference simply avoids collecting duplicate URL values. Note: You could also parse links using the convenient CPAN module HTML::LinkExtor.

```perl
sub parse_links {
    my ($html)= @_;
    my $urls;
    my @doc= split("\n", $html);
    for my $line(@doc) {
        my @url_list= $line =~ /href=\"([^"]+)\"/gi;
        for my $url(@url_list) {
            is_junk($url) or $urls->{$1}++
        }
    }
    return $urls;
}
```

❏ The bottom of `url_fetcher_worker.pl` has the necessary code to implement the Gearman worker part of this program. A Gearman::Worker object is instantiated, then the Gearman job server is set with the subroutine `job_servers()`, and the subroutine `url_fetch()` is registered as the job `url_fetch`. Last but not least, the method `work()` is run in a `while` loop that is always set to true, making this worker run until it is stopped.

```
my $worker= Gearman::Worker->new();
$worker->job_servers('127.0.0.1:4730');
$worker->register_function('url_fetch',
                                    \&url_fetch);
$worker->work() while 1;
```

Data Storage Worker

The data storage worker, url_store_worker.pl, when requested by the action of the trigger url_queue_insert or url_queue_update, selects the url and url_md5 columns from the urls_stored table for all records currently stored, and then deletes those records, within a transaction. With the list of URLs it now has, it either inserts or updates the urls and urls_blob tables with the contents of what is stored in memcached in a single SQL statement that sets the values of the tables with the output of the memcached UDF memc_get().

❑   The url_process() subroutine is the entry point for this worker and the subroutine that is registered with the job url_process.

```
sub url_process {
    $webapp->{dbh}->do("SELECT memc_servers_set('127.0.0.1:11211')");
    $webapp->{dbh}->do("SELECT gman_servers_set('127.0.0.1:4730')");

    my $count= $webapp->{memc}->get('urls_stored');

    store_urls();
}
```

❑   The subroutine, store_urls(), is where all the work happens. The first thing it does within a transaction is to select all the URLs from urls_stored. Then it immediately deletes them, using the SQL statement WHERE IN clause, which is built from the list of URLs it obtained.

```
sub store_urls {
    my $pageref;

    $webapp->{dbh}->do('BEGIN WORK');
    my $urls = $webapp->dbGetRef('urls_stored', 'url, url_md5');
    unless (scalar @$urls) {
        $webapp->{dbh}->do('COMMIT');
        return;
    }

    # build up SQL statement WHERE url_mdt IN (id1, id2, idN...)
    my $where_in = ' WHERE url_md5 IN ( ';
    $where_in .= join(',', map { $webapp->{dbh}->quote($_->{url_md5}) } @$urls);
    $where_in .= ') ';


    $webapp->dbDelete('urls_stored', $where_in);

    $webapp->{dbh}->do('COMMIT');
```

❑ Using the list of URLs it obtained in `parse_links()`, it then checks to see if each URL currently exists in the *urls* table. The `where` clause that was utilized for the deletion is now used to obtain a result set of `id` and `url_md5` values from the *urls* table. This result set is mapped to another hash reference to provide a quick lookup to see if the ID for the `url_md5` exists, and if so signifies an UPDATE.

```
my $pages_exist = {};


    my $pref= $webapp->dbGetRef('urls', 'url_md5,id', $where_in);
    $pages_exist->{$_->{url_md5}}= $_->{id} for @$pref;

for my $url (@$urls) {
    my $url_md5 = $url->{url_md5};

    my $file_id= $pages_exists->{id};
```

❑ Both the UPDATE and INSERT statements use the memcached UDF function `memc_get()` to provide the values being inserted from memcached. This may seem simplistic in its approach because there is no checking to ensure the value for each column exists in the first place. However, the point here is to show the concept of using it in a single statement to both obtain values from memcached and insert or update those values.

```
                    # if the file id exists, perform an update
                    if ($file_id) {
                            $webapp->dbUpdate('urls, urls_blob', {
                                '-status'         => "memc_get('$url_md5:status')",
                                '-title'          => "memc_get('$url_md5:title')",
                                '-last_modified'  =>
        "memc_get('$url_md5:last_modified')" ?
                                    "memc_get('$url_md5:last_modified')"
                                        : '',
                                '-content'        => "memc_get('$url_md5:content')" },
                            { '-urls.id'          => 'urls_blob.id',
                                'urls.id'          => $file_id });
                    }
                    # otherwise insert
                    else {
                        my $id= $webapp->dbInsert('urls', {
                            url_md5        => $url_md5,
                            '-title'       => "memc_get('$url_md5:title')",
                            '-url'         => "memc_get('$url_md5:url')",
                            '-status'      => "memc_get('$url_md5:status')",
                            -last_modified' => "memc_get('$url_md5:last_modified')" ?
                                    "memc_get('$url_md5:last_modified')"
                                        : '',
                            '-created'     => 'now()'
                            });

                        $webapp->dbInsert('urls_blob', {
                            id        => $id,
                            '-content' => "memc_get('$url_md5:content')"
                            });
```

```
            }
        }
    }
```

❑ At the bottom of url_worker.pl is the standard declaration for the job servers to use. It registers the job *url_process* with the url_process() subroutine, then the while loop has the program wait.

```
my $worker= Gearman::Worker->new();
$worker->job_servers('127.0.0.1:4730');
$worker->register_function('url_process',
                           \&url_process);
$worker->work() while 1;
```

Indexer Worker

The indexer worker, index.pl, has a very simple implementation when triggered in that it needs only to run the Sphinx indexer program. This worker runs as the Sphinx user, which gives it the ability to run the indexer in the first place — since the Sphinx indexes are owned by the Sphinx system user (for this particular Sphinx setup). There is a little extra debugging shown in this example so when the worker is run, it prints out the count of the indexer counter to verify that it's correctly being run on the count specified in the trigger:

```
#!/usr/bin/perl

use strict;
use warnings;
use Gearman::Worker;

use lib qw(/etc/apache2/perl-lib);
use WebApp;
my $webapp= new WebApp();

sub indexer {
    my $count= $webapp->{memc}->get('index_counter');
    warn "Count $count";
    warn "indexing!";
    my $retval = system('/usr/local/sphinx/bin/indexer --rotate -all');

    return $retval;
}

my $worker= Gearman::Worker->new();
$worker->job_servers('127.0.0.1:4730');
$worker->register_function('indexer',
                           \&indexer);
$worker->work() while 1;
```

Running the Workers

For the Gearman job server, gearmand, to assign jobs to specific workers, you need to run these workers. You can run them backgrounded or not, depending if you are testing them — once you know they are working properly, you would probably want to run them backgrounded. In the following example, you will see that if they are run without backgrounding them, you can observe that they are working properly. Follow these steps:

1. Run the `url_fetch` job, which will cause all other jobs to run:

    ```
    mysql> select gman_do_background('url_fetch', 'http://timesofindia.com');
    +------------------------------------------------------------+
    | gman_do_background('url_fetch', 'http://timesofindia.com') |
    +------------------------------------------------------------+
    | H:hanuman:14                                               |
    +------------------------------------------------------------+
    ```

2. Start each of the workers, non-backgrounded, and you'll see the following output for each:

    ❏   URL fetching worker:

    ```
    root@hanuman:/etc/apache2/perl-lib/gearman# ./url_fetcher_worker.pl
    [Thu Mar  5 14:57:53 2009] url_fetcher_worker.pl: processing url
     http://timesofindia.com
    [Thu Mar  5 14:57:59 2009] url_fetcher_worker.pl: processing url
     http://timesofindia.com
    [Thu Mar  5 14:58:00 2009] url_fetcher_worker.pl: trying to store
     72f3babec2c8a24779088b2dab9addf2 http://timesofindia.com
    [Thu Mar  5 14:58:00 2009] url_fetcher_worker.pl: storing
     72f3babec2c8a24779088b2dab9addf2:title
    [Thu Mar  5 14:58:00 2009] url_fetcher_worker.pl: processing url
     http://ecoomictimes.indiatimes.com/quickieslist/4113930.cms
    [Thu Mar  5 14:58:00 2009] url_fetcher_worker.pl: trying to store
     b5a61ade1bfcedf55846ecfa9436255f
    http://economictimes.indiatimes.com/quickieslist/4113930.cms
    [Thu Mar  5
    14:58:00
    2009] url_fetcher_worker.pl: storing
    b5a61ade1bfcedf55846ecfa9436255f:title
    ...
    ```

    ❏   URL storage worker:

    ```
    root@hanuman:/etc/apache2/perl-lib/gearman# ./url_store_worker.pl
    update 015d674703f19ec8fa363a41d045cd4a
    update 02a691d73124d48df446d87df9e96e2e
    insert 034a6f0160a80723fcdc176f33635dca
    update 035420c9c4dc689f10a6cfe6c145fea8
    insert 03f6d3d7072608e733b79d47f7dd0123
    insert 0436220c092fd3fded9422267778ec5b
    update 04dd23d3b35c5e4e01b793d45fc6e064
    update 062b292265b5b1003532edde3fb3052c
    ...
    ```

    ❏   Indexer worker:

    ```
    sphinx@hanuman:~$ ./bin/index_worker.pl
    [Fri Mar  6 09:23:44 2009] index_worker.pl: Count  at
    ```

```
./bin/index_worker.pl
line 16.
[Fri Mar  6 09:23:44 2009] index_worker.pl: indexing! at
./bin/index_worker.pl
 line 17.
Sphinx 0.9.9-rc1 (r1566)
Copyright (c) 2001-2008, Andrew Aksyonoff

using config file '/usr/local/sphinx/etc/sphinx.conf'...
indexing index 'urls_delta'...
collected 227 docs, 1.8 MB
sorted 0.3 Mhits, 100.0% done
total 227 docs, 1796327 bytes
total 0.178 sec, 10071751.00 bytes/sec, 1272.76 docs/sec
total 7 reads, 0.0 sec, 150.8 kb/read avg, 0.2 msec/read avg
total 13 writes, 0.0 sec, 188.8 kb/write avg, 0.7 msec/write avg
rotating indices: succesfully sent SIGHUP to searchd (pid=26238).
...
```

mod_perl Handler Web Applications

There are two mod_perl handlers used in this application:

❏ **The search engine application page and the URL queue page**. This is where searches are performed and results are displayed.

❏ **URL queue administrative page**. This is where a user, most likely an administrative user, would enter URLs that results in the urls_queue table being inserted into that starts the entire content-fetching phase.

The following sections delve into each handler in more detail.

Search Application

This application provides the interface for performing searches and viewing results, so you would first want a design for how you want the page to appear. For this application, Template Toolkit is used for the display functionality, so this is where all the design interface features will be implemented.

Search Template

From Chapter 15, you are familiar with Template Toolkit enough to understand how this template works. The following template provides the actual form for the URL queue:

```
[% INCLUDE dtd %]
[% SET title = "Search Page" %]
<html>
  <head>
    <title>[% title %]</title>
    <link type="text/css" href="/css/search.css" rel="stylesheet">
  </head>
  <div id="header">
  <h1 id="resume-title">Search Page</h1>
```

```
<p id="description">
  Sphinx-Memcached-MySQL-Memcached-UDF-Gearman-Perl-Apache Powered!
</p>
</div>


[% IF msg %]
    <!-- [% msg %] -->
[% END %]

  <div id="content">
  <div id="main">
   <div id="main2">
     <form action="/search" method="POST" name="searchform">
       <fieldset>
         <label for="query">Search term</label>
         <input type="text" id="query" name="query" value="">
         <input type="submit" id="search" name="search" value="Search">
```

❏   The template variable res_pp_select is a popup menu/select box that is created in the
    mod_perl handler by using the CGI method popup_menu. This pull-down select will use an
    onChange() JavaScript event to resubmit the page. It will select how many results to display
    per page, and when selected, the page will be resubmitted. It will contain the number of results
    selected to be displayed.

```
        <label for="results_per_page">Results per page</label> [%
        res_pp_select %]

        [% IF sinfo.sresults %]
```

❏   The following part of the page will provide useful query information about a search result set,
    such as how many searches there were, the amount of time it took for the search to complete, as
    well as pagination.

```
        <p>Total Found : [% sinfo.total_found %] Time: [% sinfo.time %]
```

This condition checks for the existence of sinfo.range, a Perl array reference containing a list
of sets with beginning and end values for the record limits of the given page — the subscript of
this array reference corresponding to the search result set page number. For instance, if there are
100 results, and the value for results-per-page is 10, then the first set/array will contain 1–10, the
second 11–20, and so on.

❏   The sets are looped over, and the links to the search page with this start and stop values are spec-
    ified in a query string of the URL. Note: for print display, this had to be broken, but it is a single
    line starting from <a>... to </a> in the actual template.

```
            [% IF sinfo.ranges.max > 1 %]
            Pages:
                    [% FOREACH i = [ 1 .. sinfo.ranges.max] %]
                    [% page = i + 1 %]
            <a
            href=
```

```
                    "/search?start=[% sinfo.ranges.$i.0 %];
                    stop=[% sinfo.ranges.$i.1 %];query=[% form.query %]"
                >
              [% page %]</a>
                      [% END %]
          [% END %]
      [% END %]
```

❏ The following hidden field provides the query value to the mod_perl search handler when the form is resubmitted if the JavaScript action changes when the results-per-page select box (res_pp_select) is selected.

```
<input type="hidden" name="hquery" value="[% form.query | html %]">
        </fieldset>
        </form>
```

❏ If there are any results, contained in the hash reference sinfo.sresults, these results are iterated over, resulting in their being printed on the page.

```
[% IF sinfo.sresults %]
  [% FOREACH item = sinfo.sresults %]
      <div class="post" id="[% item.id %]">
          <h3 class="post-title">
          <a href="[% item.url | html%]" alt="[% item.url %]"
           target="_new">[% item.title | html %]</a>
          </h3>
          <div class="post-body">[% item.excerpt %]</div>
          <h2 class="date-header">Last updated: [% item.last_updated
%]</h2>
        </div>
  [% END %]
[% END %]
      </div>
    </div>
    </body>
</html>
```

The mod_perl Search Handler

The mod_perl Search handler implementation is called WroxHandlers::SearchHandler. In addition to Perl modules with which you are already familiar, it will use Sphinx::Search, which is the Perl client library for Sphinx, specifically a Perl client API for the searchd server.

Main Handler Method

First, of course, is the importation of various modules as well as the implementation of the main handler method:

```
package WroxHandlers::SearchHandler;

use strict;
use warnings;

use Apache2::Const -compile => qw(OK REDIRECT SERVER_ERROR);
```

```
use Apache2::Request;
use Template;
use Sphinx::Search;
use lib qw(/etc/apache2/perl-lib);
use WebApp;
use CGI qw(:standard);

sub handler {
    my ($r)= @_;
    my $msg;
    my $url= $r->uri;

    my $sinfo;

    # instantiate a WebApp object
    my $webapp = WebApp->new({ r => $r});

    # get the submitted form values
    my $form = $webapp->getForm();
```

Note the following concerning the previous code:

❑   Some defaults are set up. If the form value results_per_page is not set, then a default of 10 results per page is set. This is hard-coded to '10' here, but you could set this in your Apache configuration file with PerlSetVar/dir_config. The start form result value is set to 1 if not set; the end form value is set to 10.

> *Note that the* $form *members are being overwritten since* $form *is going to be passed to the template. It makes a convenient way to set default values prior to the display of the page.*

```
# defaults
$form->{results_per_page} = $form->{results_per_page} ?
                        $form->{results_per_page} : 10;

$form->{start} ||= 1;
$form->{end}   ||= 10;
```

❑   The CGI popup_menu() method is used to construct the *results_per_page* select pull-down. The default selections are set with the array reference being passed to the popup_menu() attribute –values and are 10, 25, 50, and 100 results per page.

```
my $res_pp_select = popup_menu(
                    -name     => 'results_per_page',
                    -values   => [10, 25, 50, 100],
                    -onchange => 'this.form.submit();',
                    -default  => $form->{results_per_page} ?
                            $form->{results_per_page} : 10);
```

❑   The session is obtained and checked to see if the user is allowed to use this page. If this is a public search engine, you will probably not need this, or you could at least modify the session code to create automatically an "anonymous" session for user tracking or allowing the user to save search results — the sky is the limit!

```
my $sessionref = $webapp->getSession(\$msg);
# if no session, redirect to login page
unless ($sessionref && $sessionref->{uid}) {
    $r->headers_out->add('Location' => "/login?returnto=$url");
    return Apache2::Const::REDIRECT;
}

# obtain the template path
my $template_path= $r->dir_config('TEMPLATE_PATH');
```

❑   The following is the functionality that allows the *results_per_page* select pull-down to resubmit the form without the user having supplied a search term to the *query* text field of the search form. This line simply ensures that the value of $form->{query}, which will be passed to the search() subroutine (which will be explained next), is set so that the search is re-run with the new results per page setting.

```
# allow select box to resubmit when results per set changes
$form->{query} = $form->{hquery}
        unless defined $form->{query} && length $form->{query};
```

❑   A check is made for whether the method is a POST or a GET. If it is a POST, the user submitted a search either by search term or by selecting the *results_per_page* select menu. If it is a GET, the user clicked on the URL containing the query string to access a page from the pagination links. In either case, a GET or POST means that a search must be performed and therefore the subroutine search() is called, passing in the Apache request object, the WebApp object handle, as well as the submitted form values hash reference $form.

❑   The value returned from search(), $sinfo, is a reference to a hash containing various other data structures, including the search result set, as well as values pertaining to the search result set.

```
# if the user has submitted a search, get the results
if ($r->method() eq 'POST'
    || $r->method() eq 'GET'
    && length($form->{query})) {
    $sinfo = search($r, $webapp, $form);
}
```

❑   A check is made to first determine if the hash result set reference $sinfo is set at all, then if the result sets $sinfo->{results} is set, and finally if it contains any results. If so, then the WebApp method buildRange() is called and it supplies an array reference of begin and end sets (each also an array reference, the first subscript the being value of the range, the second value the end of the range).

```
if (defined $sinfo &&
    defined $sinfo->{sresults} &&
    scalar @{$sinfo->{sresults}}) {
        $sinfo->{ranges}= buildRange(
                    $form->{results_per_page},
                    $sinfo->{total_found});
}
```

❑ Next, the Template Toolkit object is instantiated.

```
# instantiate a new Template object
my $template = Template->new({
    INCLUDE_PATH => $template_path,  # where to look for templates
    POST_CHOMP   => 1, # removal of whitespace
});
```

❑ The template parameters that will be passed to the template are set up. This includes the search result set hash reference $sinfo, the submitted form values hash reference $form, and the select box that was built with the CGI method popup_menu().

```
# set up template parameters
my $tparams = {
    msg            => "Session " . $sessionref->{sessionid} . "
logged in",
    url            => $r->uri,
    sinfo          => $sinfo,
    form           => $form,
    res_pp_select  => $res_pp_select,
};
```

❑ Finally, the content is generated, displaying the search form and results, if any!

```
# set up the template name
$url =~ s/^\///;
my $tname= $url . '.tt2';

$r->content_type('text/html');

$template->process($tname, $tparams) ||
    do {
        $r->server->warn($template->error());
        return Apache2::Const::SERVER_ERROR;
    };

return Apache2::Const::OK;
}
```

The search() Subroutine

The search() subroutine implements the actual search functionality using the Perl module Sphinx::Search methods. This is a fairly straightforward API that this subroutine will give you a basic idea of how to use.

```
sub search {
    my ($r, $webapp, $form)= @_;
    my $sinfo;
    my $cref;
    my $docs = [];
```

Regarding this subroutine, note the following:

❑ First, some Sphinx server information values set in the Apache configuration file are obtained. These include which host, search index, port, and excerpt index to use.

What Is an Excerpt?

An excerpt is a smaller fragment of the entire raw text of the document found in a search and retrieved from the database given the ID returned from the original search result. The raw text is reprocessed through Sphinx in order to highlight the search term within the text with predefined HTML elements such as <b> or <em>. The highlighting points out the term being searched, which is what you end up seeing on the search results page.

It's important to realize that excerpts cannot be generated against a distributed index, which is the reason for specifying a separate index for excerpts. It can be any index. You only need to supply a construct for building excerpts against. Excerpt building doesn't use the index itself other than to search on the key word you want highlighted in the excerpt.

❑ Next, several variables specifying the name of the main search index, excerpts index, search host, and port are set:

```
my $search_index    = $r->dir_config('SEARCH_INDEX');
my $excerpts_index  = $r->dir_config('EXCERPT_INDEX');
my $search_host     = $r->dir_config('SEARCH_HOST');
my $search_port     = $r->dir_config('SEARCH_PORT');
```

❑ A Sphinx::Search object is instantiated.

```
my $sphinx = Sphinx::Search->new();type="general"
```

Some Sphinx::Search Methods

The following table provides a brief listing and description of some of the methods you will use when setting up a search using Sphinx::Search:

Method	Description
SetServer($host, $port)	Sets the Sphinx server $host and $port (where searchd is running).
SetRankingMode($mode)	Sets how results will be ranked. The ranking modes available are set with the following constants for $mode: ❑ SPH_RANK_PROXIMITY_BM25: Default, phrase proximity the major factor and Okapi BM25 the minor factor (sorting by relevance to given search query) ❑ SPH_RANK_BM25: BM25 ranking only.

Method	Description
	❏ SPH_RANK_NONE: No ranking at all. All matches given a weight of 1.
	❏ SPH_RANK_WORDCOUNT: The ranking is done using a weighted sum of per-field keyword occurrence counts.
SetLimits($offset, $limit)	Allows you to set a LIMIT just as you would in MySQL — and this is where the values of the pagination URLs are used.
SetMatchMode($mode)	Sets what types of matches are used. The search modes you can set are set using the following constants, for the argument $mode:
	❏ SPH_MATCH_ALL: Matches all words.
	❏ SPH_MATCH_ANY: Matches any words.
	❏ SPH_MATCH_PHRASE: Exact phrase match.
	❏ SPH_MATCH_BOOLEAN: Matches using AND (&), OR (|), NOT (!,-) and grouping with parentheses.
	❏ SPH_MATCH_EXTENDED: An extended match that includes Boolean syntax as well as including field, phrase, and proximity operators.
SetSortMode($mode, $sortby)	Sets the way results are sorted such as by relevance of time. The $mode can be one of the constants available:
	❏ SPH_SORT_RELEVANCE: Sort by relevance.
	❏ SPH_SORT_ATTR_DESC: Sort by attribute descending order; $sortby specifies the sorting attribute.
	❏ SPH_SORT_ATTR_ASC: Sort by attribute ascending order; $sortby specifies the sorting attribute.
	❏ SPH_SORT_EXTENDED: Sort using SQL-like syntax; $sortby specifies the sorting attribute.
	❏ SPH_SORT_TIME_SEGMENTS: Sort by time segments (last hour, day, week, or month) in descending order, then by relevance in descending order; $sortby specifies the sorting attribute.
	❏ SPH_SORT_EXPR: Sort expression.

❑ Next, the host and search port of the Sphinx search server to connect to is set, as well as the ranking mode, the limits (start and stop range) of the IDs of the records to return, the match mode, and sort mode (not used in this handler, but shown for an example).

```
# set search directives
$sphinx->SetServer($search_host, $search_port);
$sphinx->SetRankingMode(SPH_RANK_PROXIMITY_BM25);
$sphinx->SetLimits($form->{start}, $form->{end});

# other options for extending functinality, shown for posterity ;)
# $sphinx->SetMatchMode(match_mode);
# $sphinx->SetSortMode(sort_mode,sortby)
```

❑ Finally, the Query() method is called, passing the search term and index_name to run the query against. This returns a comprehensive Perl data structure hash reference, $hits, that contains all the information about the result set.

```
my $hits= $sphinx->Query($form->{query}, $search_index);
```

❑ One of the $hits members is total_found, which is the value of the total number of results found. In the conditional that follows, if there are no results found, then an empty hash reference is returned to the caller, in this case back to the mod_perl search handler.

```
$hits->{total_found}) or return {};
```

❑ If there is a result set, then the hash reference that is being used to return the values that are needed for the search handler is set:

1. First, $sinfo->{hits} and $sinfo->{time} are obtained from $hits — these are values printed on the search interface after a successful search.

2. The results are obtained from the subroutine get_results_from_db(), which uses the primary key values from the results in $hits to retrieve the actual data from MySQL.

```
$sinfo->{$_} = $hits->{$_} for qw (total_found time);

$sinfo->{sresults} = get_results_from_db($webapp, $hits);

my $warning = $sphinx->GetLastWarning;
$r->server->warn($warning) if $warning;
```

❑ The search term is "cleaned up," stripping any Sphinx-specific search syntax. This cleaned-up term will be used for obtaining excerpts. The ~1 in particular is a Sphinx proximity search operator, in this case, meaning the term is found within one word of each other.

```
my $term= $form->{query};
$term =~ s/[|()"]/ /g;
$term=~s/\~1//g;
$term =~ s/\s{2,}/ /g;
```

❑ The result set of content from the database is looped through in order to build up the excerpts. This is where you set various parameters to BuildExcerpts() to control how the excerpt is generated. Since the content column is the only data we are concerned with generating content for excerpts, a quick mapping of the database results is used to generate an array reference containing the content that will then be passed to build excerpts as the first argument.

❑ The second argument to BuildExcerpts() is the index that will be used to construct the excerpt against, providing lexing, stemming, and case folding. Important to note is that this has to be a physical and not a distributed index.

❑ The third argument is the actual search term (this is the *needle,* and the content, the *haystack*!).

❑ The fourth argument to BuildExcerpts() is a hash reference containing various parameters:

    ❑ before_match and after_match specify the HTML tag that is placed before and after the search term within the excerpt.

    ❑ around specifies how many words will be highlighted around each match, in this case four.

    ❑ single_passage specifies if the single best passage is used for the excerpt or not. In this case it is set to false.

```
if (scalar @{$sinfo->{sresults}}) {
        # only want content to generate excerpts
        push(@$cref, $_->{content}) for @{$sinfo->{sresults}};
        my $excerpts = $sphinx->BuildExcerpts(
                                        $cref,
                                        $excerpts_index,
                                        $term,{
                                        before_match    => '<em><b>',
                                        after_match     => '</em>',
                                        around          => 4,
                                        single_passage  => 0,
                                        limit           => 180}
        );
```

❑ At this point, there are now excerpts, so these need to be added to the result set in $sinfo->{sresults} as $sinfo->{sresults}[$i]{excerpt}, which will inevitably be passed to the search template.

❑ After the excerpts are generated and set into $sinfo, $sinfo is returned to the handler.

```
        # add in the results
        for my $i (0 .. $#{$sinfo->{sresults}}) {
            $sinfo->{sresults}[$i]{excerpt}= $excerpts->[$i];
            delete $sinfo->{sresults}[$i]{content};
        }
        # stash the search results
        #$sinfo->{results} = $sresults
    }
    return $sinfo;
}
```

The get_results_from_db() Subroutine

The subroutine get_results_from_db() simply "glues" the search result ID values to results from the database. Sphinx has kindly provided a list of primary key values for use to construct a WHERE IN clause. This is then used to obtain the results from MySQL.

```
sub get_results_from_db {
    my ($webapp, $hits)= @_;

    # build up WHERE .. IN
    my $where = 'WHERE id IN (';
    $where .= join(',', map { $_->{doc} } @{$hits->{matches}});
    $where.= ')';
```

Here, a formatted string is set for the date function date_format(). It will be used in the query to provide a data string that will inevitably be printed in the search results for every result.

```
    my $time_format=
      q(date_format(last_updated, '%W, %m/%d/%y %H:%i:%s') as last_updated);

    my $sresults= $webapp->dbGetRef('urls join urls_blob using (id)',
               "urls.id as id, title, $time_format, url, content", $where);

    return $sresults;
}

1;
```

Before proceeding further, it should be noted that get_results_from_db() *could in fact be extended to try to obtain the content from memcached before checking MySQL, especially considering that the data has been stored there by the* url_fetcher *Gearman worker. This would make your searches even faster! The key to doing this is to ensure that the data stored in memcached has the same IDs as the database.*

Paginating the Search Application

There is one new method added to WebApp.pm: buildRange(). This is a common problem to be solved with any web application that produces an arbitrary number of results — pagination.

As already mentioned, this method constructs sets of ranges based on the total number of results found and the user-selected results_per_page. It uses a simple algorithm to loop through the total number of results, adding each range to the @ranges array until the last range is found.

```
sub buildRange {
    my ($results_per_page, $total) = @_;
    my @ranges;
    my $start = 1;
    while ( $start + $results_per_page < $total ) {

       push @ranges, [ $start, $start + $results_per_page - 1 ];
       $start += $results_per_page;
    }

    # this handles the last range
    $start > $total or push @ranges, [ $start, $total ];

    return \@ranges;
}
```

Taking this snippet of code and printing the output of the $ranges array can help to explain this. In the printout that follows, the test shows a result set total of 47, with results per page at 10. You can see the ranges are correctly set for each page set:

```
Total 47, results_per_page 10
$VAR1 = [
            [
              1,
              10
            ],
            [
              11,
              20
            ],
            [
              21,
              30
            ],
            [
              31,
              40
            ]
          ];
```

Using the Search Application

Finally, you can see the end result of all of this work! The search, empty, before a search is submitted appears in Figure 17-2.

Figure 17-2

Then, you see it performing a search using the term `'Perl Programming'` (see Figure 17-3).

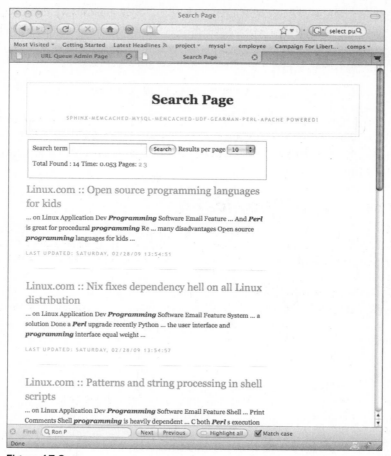

Figure 17-3

URL Queue Application

The URL queue application is a fairly simple application. All it does is INSERT, UPDATE, or DELETE URLs from the *urls_queue* table. These values control what the entire data gathering process is going to do. They are listed as follows:

❑ INSERT: An insert of a URL causes data retrieval to occur using the INSERT trigger on *urls_queue*, *urls_queue_insert*, which is executed. In turn, this causes all the other actions using Gearman and its workers to gather, store, and then index the data retrieved. If the user attempts an insertion of an already existing URL, it will instead update the timestamp of that

URL. This is one behavior this application can have, although you could also issue an error if that was your choice.

❑ UPDATE: Updates the `last_updated` column on `urls_queue`, causing the `urls_queue_update` trigger to execute, which in turn causes the same process to occur in the same manner that occurs upon an `INSERT`.

❑ DELETE: The URL is deleted from the `urls_queue` table.

This URL queuing application will consist of two mod_perl handlers:

❑ `URLHandler`: For displaying the URL queue page, an Ajax application page, containing all the JavaScript and Ajax code for processing user input and displaying of data.

❑ `URLQueueHandler`: For processing requests from the Ajax client to insert, delete, or update a URL from the `urls_queue` table.

URLHandler — AJAX Application

The URLHandler mod_perl handler will provide user interface functionality for the user to manage their URLs. It is an Ajax application that will make calls to another mod_perl handler, `URLQueueHandler`, at the URL of `/url_queue`. URLHandler will utilize Template Toolkit to display the user interface.

The Main handler() Subroutine

As with other mod_perl handlers shown previously, the `handler()` subroutine is implemented:

```
package WroxHandlers::URLHandler;

use strict;
use warnings;

use Apache2::Const -compile => qw(OK REDIRECT SERVER_ERROR);
use Apache2::Request;
use Template;
use Digest::MD5 qw(md5_hex);
use WebApp;
```

❑ As with other handlers shown in this book, this handler will use the WebApp object.

```
sub handler {
    my ($r)= @_;
    my $msg;
    my $url= $r->uri;
    my $template_path;
    my $sresults;

    my $webapp= new WebApp({ r => $r});

    my $form= $webapp->getForm();
```

❑   For this application, a session will be required. If there is no session, then the user is redirected to the login page.

```
my $sessionref = $webapp->getSession(\$msg);

# if no session, redirect to login page
unless ($sessionref && $sessionref->{uid}) {
    $r->headers_out->add('Location' => "/login?returnto=$url");
    return Apache2::Const::REDIRECT;
}

$template_path= $r->dir_config('TEMPLATE_PATH');
```

❑   Next, a list of the URLs is obtained from the *urls_queue* table. This will be displayed in tabular form in the template page with an iterative loop over the result set.

```
# obtain the list of urls in urls_queue
my $urls = $webapp->dbGetRef('urls_queue', 'url,url_md5');


# instantiate a new Template object
my $template = Template->new({
    INCLUDE_PATH => $template_path,
    POST_CHOMP   => 1,

});

# set up template parameters
my $tparams = {
    msg          => "Session " . $sessionref->{sessionid} . " logged in",
    url          => $r->uri,
    urls         => $urls,
};

$url =~ s/^\///;
my $tname= $url . '.tt2';

$r->content_type('text/html');

$template->process($tname, $tparams) ||
    do {

$r->server->warn($template->error());
        return Apache2::Const::SERVER_ERROR;
    };

    return Apache2::Const::OK;
}

1;
```

URLHandler JavaScript

The URLHandler application will require JavaScript to implement the Ajax functionality. For this, a new file will be created that the template will end up using: url_queue.js.

The JavaScript functions required for URLHandler include the following:

❑ onChange(): This is the Ajax *onSuccess* event handler for updating and deleting URLs. It takes care of removing the rows for a given URL from the table for the URL being deleted.

❑ onQueue(): This is the Ajax *onSuccess* event handler for inserting URLs. It takes care of inserting into the existing table the new rows for the newly inserted URL.

❑ processUrl(): This is a function that that is activated from an onClick() event from a link within the table rows of each URL for either UPDATE or DELETE. It takes a single argument, op, which determines which of those two operations it will perform.

❑ saveUrl(): This is a function that is activated by an onSubmit() event from the Submit button to save a URL. It will then be inserted by the Ajax request, which will use its onSuccess event handler onQueue().

JavaScript Functions

The following shows the implementation of the JavaScript functions listed previously.

❑ First listed is the onChange() function. It takes a single argument, op, which determines if the operation being performed is either deletion or an update. All the usual steps of checking the Ajax response are made. In this example, a -1 for the obj.err value indicates that the user did not have a session, so it redirects to the front page of the site.

```
function onChange(responseText, op) {
    var obj = responseText.evalJSON(true);
    var msg = obj.msg;
    var url_md5 = obj.url_md5;

    if ( obj == null ) {
        // no message from response, so set one
        $("msg").innerHTML = "No response from server for url process";

        // re-enable the submit button
        $("addurl").removeAttribute("disabled");

        return;
    }

    /*
        if user is not logged in
        redirect them to main site, or wherever you like
    */
    if ( obj.err == -1 ) {
        window.location = "/";
    }
    // set message from response
    $("msg").innerHTML = obj.msg;
```

❑ If the operation being performed is a deletion, remove the row with the document ID of the url_md5 value that was deleted. This will result in the row being removed from the table — all without reloading the page! Also, it will re-enable the Submit button.

```
    if (op == 'delete') {
      // remove the row
      $(url_md5).parentNode.removeChild($(url_md5));
    }
    // re-enable the submit button
    $("addurl").removeAttribute("disabled");

  }
```

❑ The onQueue() function handles a URL insertion. This function has to do a bit more work than the previous function. It has to insert into the table the row representing the URL that was inserted into the *urls_queue* table. It does this all through DOM manipulation, as you will see.

```
function onQueue(responseText) {
  var obj = responseText.evalJSON(true);
  var msg = obj.msg;
  var url_md5 = obj.url_md5;
  var url       = obj.url;
  var updated = obj.updated;
```

❑ The same error checks that were made in the onChange() function are also made in onQueue().

```
if ( obj == null ) {
  // no message from response, so set one
  $("msg").innerHTML = "No response from server for url process";

  // re-enable the submit button
  $("addurl").removeAttribute("disabled");

  return;
}
/*
  if user is not logged in redirect them to main site,
  or wherever you like
*/
if ( obj.err == -1 ) {
  window.location = "/";
}

// set message from response
$("msg").innerHTML = obj.msg;

/*
  if there was any non-critical error, re-enable the submit button
*/
if ( obj.err == 1 ) {
  // re-enable the submit button, failure
  $("addurl").removeAttribute("disabled");
  return;
}

// Re-enable submit button, success
$("addurl").removeAttribute("disabled");
```

❑ The mod_perl handler is intelligent such that if you try to insert an existing URL, it will instead simply update that URL, and then return in the JSON response to Ajax a parameter called updated. This may seem a little bit odd, but it is just a choice to use what would otherwise be an error to instead trigger the update of the data for this URL. As shown in this conditional check, if updated is zero, then the row for that URL will be inserted into the table.

```
if (updated == 0) {
```

❑ A <tr> element, a row, is created. This row is given the id of the url_md5 for the row that was inserted. It then creates a <td> element, the cell for that row — the cells displaying the URL — update link, and delete link. For the update and delete link, these cells each have their own <a> element. For each, this <a> element has to be built to have onClick attributes set to the JavaScript function processUrl(). processUrl() needs to be called with the correct value for the op argument in order to handle either an update or deletion. Also, for each <a> element, the href attribute is set to load to '#'.

```
var urow = document.createElement('tr');
urow.setAttribute('id', url_md5);

var url_td = document.createElement('td');

// Cell node containing the the URL value
url_td.innerHTML= url;

// append to the row
urow.appendChild(url_td);

// Cell containing updater link
var up_td = document.createElement('td');

// create  the link node
var up_aref = document.createElement('a');

// set the value
up_aref.setAttribute('href', '#');

// create an onclick value
up_aref.onclick= function () {
  processUrl(url_md5,'update'); return false;
}

// create the text
var update_txt = document.createTextNode('[Update]');

// now append the text
up_aref.appendChild(update_txt);
```

❑ Once the <a> link element is created, it is then appended to the cell. Then each <td> element (the actual table cells) is appended to the row.

```
up_td.appendChild(up_aref);

urow.appendChild(up_td);
```

```
var del_td = document.createElement('td');

var del_aref = document.createElement('a');
del_aref.setAttribute('href', '#');
del_aref.onclick= function () {
  processUrl(url_md5, 'delete'); return false;
}
var delete_txt = document.createTextNode('[Delete]');
del_aref.appendChild(delete_txt);
del_td.appendChild(del_aref);
urow.appendChild(del_td);
```

❑ The `<tr>` element, the row, is then appended to the table. This will result in it being displayed to the user dynamically!

```
    $("urllist_body").appendChild(urow);
  }

}
```

The `processUrl()` function, which is executed on an `onClick()` event on both the "Update" and "Delete" links in the URL queue listing table, performs form validation, and creates the Ajax request to post either a deletion or an update to the mod_perl handler. It takes two arguments: `url_md5`, a variable containing the MD5 value of the URL that is being updated or deleted, and the string variable `op`, which is either 'delete' or 'update'.

```
/*
   this function is used to validate the form as well
   as initiate the Ajax request
*/
function processUrl(url_md5, op)
{
  // set message
  $("msg").innerHTML = "processing...";

  // disable the submit button so they can't submit
  $("addurl").setAttribute("disabled","disabled");
```

❑ Here, the Ajax request object is instantiated. This will be a POST to the mod_perl handler `/url_handler`. The POST data is set as well, and it is constructed using the variables `op` and `url_md5` concatenated with the string values to create a valid POST. The *onSuccess* event handler is set to be the function `onChange()`. The request is made, posting the data to the mod_perl handler. `onChange()` will then be executed.

```
// create Ajax request
var ajax = new Ajax.Request('/url_handler',
            { method:'POST',
              parameters:
              op + '=1&url_md5=' + url_md5,
              onSuccess: function(transport)
              { onChange(transport.responseText, op); }
```

```
            } );

        }
```

❑ The saveUrl() function is run on an onSubmit() event — the submission of the *add url* Submit
button. It performs form validation and creates the Ajax request object to post the action for the
insertion of a URL into the *urls_queue* table via the mod_perl handler.

```
/*
  this function is used to validate the form as well
  as initiate the Ajax request
*/
function saveUrl()
{

  var url = $("url").getValue();
  if (url == "")
  {
    $("msg").innerHTML ="You need to supply a URL.";
    return false;
  }
```

❑ As with other Ajax applications previously shown, the Submit button is disabled once the form
is submitted, during the sending of the POST data and response, and will be re-enabled when
there is a response. Also shown here is that the text field for the URL is cleared. This makes it so
the text field is clear after submitting the form, otherwise the same URL value that was already
submitted will remain.

```
// disable the submit button so they can't resubmit
$("addurl").setAttribute("disabled","disabled");

// set message
$("msg").innerHTML = "processing...";

// Empty the text field
$("url").setValue("");

// create Ajax request
var ajax = new Ajax.Request('/url_handler',
            { method:'POST',
              parameters:
              'create=1&url=' + url,
              onSuccess: function(transport)
              { onQueue(transport.responseText); }
            } );

        }
```

URLHandler Template

Next, you see the template implementation that this handler requires, url_queue.tt2. This template uses
the JavaScript file shown in the previous section: url_queue.js.

The main template body is shown. You'll see the iterative loop where the table is built, and within each row, a `tr` DOM element having an element ID of the MD5 hex of the URL listed. This is the very thing that makes it possible to perform the removal or addition of rows, which you saw above, using JavaScript DOM manipulation.

```
[% INCLUDE dtd %]
[% SET title = "URL Queue Admin Page" %]
<html>
  <head>
    <title>[% title %]</title>
    <link type="text/css" href="/css/webapp.css" rel="stylesheet">
    <script language="javascript" type="text/javascript"
        src="/javascript/prototype-1.6.0.3.js">
    </script>
    <script language="javascript" type="text/javascript"
          src="/javascript/url_queue.js">
    </script>
  </head>
  <body>
    <p class="msg" id="msg">[% msg %]</p>
  <form action="#" method="post" id="urlform" name="urlform"
      onsubmit="saveUrl(); return false;" />
    <fieldset>
    <label>Add a URL to the queue</label>
    <input type="text" length="50" id="url" name="url"/>
    <br />
    <input type="submit" id="addurl" name="addurl" value="addurl" />
    </fieldset>
  </form>
  <br />
[% IF urls %]
    <table class="userlist" id="urllist" name="urllist">
      <thead id="urllist_head">
          <tr>
            <th>URL</th>
            <th>Update</th>
            <th>Delete</th>
          </tr>
      </thead>
      <tbody id="urllist_body">
  [% FOREACH url = urls %]
        <tr id="[% url.url_md5 %]">

              <td>[% url.url %]</td>
<td><a href="#"
            onclick="processUrl('[% url.url_md5 %]', 'update');
              return false;">[Update]</a></td>
            <td><a href="#"
            onclick="processUrl('[% url.url_md5 %]', 'delete');
              return false;">[Delete]</a></td>
        </tr>
  [% END %]
      </tbody>
    </table>
```

```
[% END %]
    </body>
</html>
```

URLQueueHandler mod_perl Handler

The URLQueueHandler is the mod_perl handler that will handle Ajax requests for the URLHandler application. Depending on the message from the Ajax client, it will either insert, update, or delete a URL in the *urls_queue* table. It will be able to determine what action to take based on the POST data it parses. As you recall, a variable called op was used in the Ajax request that had the value of CREATE, DELETE, or UPDATE. URLQueueHandler will test for these values in the POST data.

URLQueueHandler will use the perl module JSON::XS to create a JSON response using the method json_encode(). Also, the module Digest::MD5 will be used run md5_hex() to MD5-encode the URL. This is the unique identifier for every URL in this system and it is the primary key for the *urls_queue* table. As you've seen, it is also used in the client JavaScript code for DOM manipulation to be able to remove and insert rows dynamically into an HTML table.

```
package WroxHandlers::URLQueueHandler;

use strict;
use warnings;
use JSON::XS;

# list of return values you want to use
use Apache2::Const -compile => qw(OK );
use Digest::MD5 qw(md5_hex);
use WebApp;
```

URLQueueHandler handler() Subroutine

The handler body for URLQueuHandler will be implemented as shown in the following code and steps:

```
sub handler {
    my ($r)= @_;
    my $msg = '';
    my $err = 0;
```

1. The variable $updated is set to 0 initially. Because the application works in such a way that if you try to insert an already existing URL, it automatically updates that URL's timestamp, this variable (which is inevitably returned to the Ajax client in JSON) is then used in the JavaScript function Ajax onSuccess event handler onQueue() (as shown in the template code above) to determine if the submission of what was intended to be an insert was actually an update.

```
    my $updated = 0;

    my $webapp = new WebApp({ r => $r});
    my $form = $webapp->getForm();
```

2. The URL is MD5 hex encoded. Next, the hexadecimal representation of the MD5 digest of the URL is calculated.

3. The session is obtained and checked to see if the user is logged in. This is where you might also add a check for an admin flag for the session, considering this is an administrative interface for this application and you would probably not want to make it available to regular users.

4. If the user is not logged in, set `$err` to -1. This will result in a redirection to the main site URL.

```
my $url_md5 = $form->{url_md5};
$url_md5 ||= $form->{url} ? md5_hex($form->{url}) : '';


# obtain the session
my $sessionref= $webapp->getSession();

# if the user is logged in, the JavaScript function will redirect them
# to log in
$sessionref->{uid} or $err = -1;
```

5. The request method is checked to see if it was a POST, and if it was, then a query is made to the `urls_queue` table to obtain the list of URLs. This list will be passed to the template to be displayed in a table.

6. There are checks made to see what operation was requested. First, the form parameter `create` is checked to see if it exists. If so, then a check is made to see if it already exists. If the URL already exists, then its timestamp is updated. If the URL does not yet exist, then the URL is inserted.

```
else {
    if ($r->method() eq 'POST') {
        if ($form->{create}) {
            if ($form->{url}) {
                my $urls = $webapp->dbGetRef('urls_queue',
                    'url,url_md5', { url_md5 => $url_md5});

                if (scalar @$urls) {
                    $updated= $webapp->dbUpdate('urls_queue',
                        { '-last_updated' => 'now()'},
                        { url_md5          => $url_md5 });

                    $msg = "Updated $form->{url}";
                    $updated = 1;
                }
                else {
                    $webapp->dbInsert('urls_queue',{
                        url      => $form->{url},
                        url_md5  => $url_md5});

                    $msg = "Inserted $form->{url} into the queue";
```

```
                }
            }
            else {
                $msg = "Missing URL value";
                return 1;
            }
        }
```

7. The form parameter `delete` is checked. If set, then the record for the specified URL is deleted using the variable of `$url_md5` as the value for the primary key. Also, the message that will be returned to the client is set.

```
elsif ($form->{'delete'}) {
    my $deleted= $webapp->dbDelete('urls_queue',
        { url_md5 => $url_md5});
    $msg = "Deleted $url_md5 from the queue";
}
```

8. The form element `update` is checked. If set, then the `last_updated` column of the record for the specified URL is updated using the variable of `$url_md5` as the value for the primary key. Also, the message is set.

```
elsif ($form->{'update'}) {
    my $updated= $webapp->dbUpdate('urls_queue',
        { '-last_updated' => 'now()'},
        { url_md5 => $url_md5 });
    $msg = "Updated $form->{url}";
    $updated = 1;
}
        }
    }
```

9. Finally, the result is sent back to the Ajax client, as shown in the following code snippet:

```
$r->content_type('text/html');
    $r->print(encode_json({
            url_md5 => $url_md5,
            msg     => $msg,
            url     => $form->{url},
            updated => $updated,
            err     => $err }));

    return Apache2::Const::OK;

}

1;
```

10. The JSON that is sent contains several members shown in the following table:

Member	Description
url_md5	The MD5 hex value of the URL being acted upon; it passes back to the calling JavaScript function.
url	The actual URL that was submitted and is passed back in this response so the JavaScript function onQueue() has access to this value. onQueue() will be used to display the URL in the row that is inserted.
Msg	The message that is displayed in the msg div element.
Updated	The updated variable used to determine if an update occurred or not in the function onQueue().
Err	Err is used for printing an error message.

URLQueue Interface

The following three figures (17-4, 17-5, and 17-6) show this URLQueue interface in action — the addition of a single URL. Figure 17-4 shows the interface before any user input.

Figure 17-4

In Figure 17-5, http://timesofindia.com is submitted. The form indicates processing is occurring.

In Figure 17-6, you can see the row is added for http://timesofindia.com. This all happened without a page reload! This is where the utility of Ajax is made obvious.

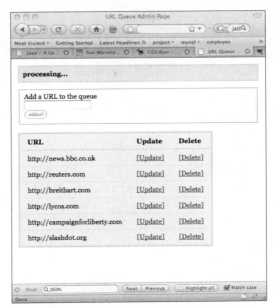

Figure 17-5

Figure 17-6

If all your triggers shown earlier are set up properly, whenever you add or update a URL, a data-gathering process is triggered to gather the content for that URL. You will probably want to set up a cron job to run also, because user-triggered events aren't sufficient enough to keep a site up-to-date. The cron job would only have to update the `last_updated` column of `urls_queue` to do this. You might also want to modify the URL fetching worker to allow more recursion. It all depends on how much data you want to gather.

The important thing to know is that with Gearman, MySQL, memcached, and the code shown, plus a little ingenuity, you have just the right tools for spreading out the processing of data retrieval!

Summary

This chapter showed you an entire search engine application. This example put together all of the examples you have read about throughout the book — Apache, mod_perl/Perl, memcached, Memcached Functions for MySQL, the MySQL server itself, Sphinx, and a new system called Gearman. Gearman includes a job server, known as gearmand, and a client/worker library that is used by clients to request jobs through the job server. The jobs are then assigned to workers. In this case, both clients and workers are written in Perl.

This search engine example was chosen to demonstrate data retrieval and storage, as well as full-text indexing jobs. The application showed you the following:

❑ How to install and set up the new C-based Gearman job server, gearmand, as well as how to write three different gearman Perl workers.

❑ How to set up the Gearman MySQL UDFs, which allow you to request jobs from Gearman from within MySQL. In the case of this application, these were run via database triggers.

❑ How to setup Sphinx to utilize a delta index to provide full-text search capability for data it indexes from a MySQL table. The MySQL table was where the web pages were retrieved and stored by the Perl workers.

❑ An Ajax application that is used with this example search engine application to insert, update, or delete the URLs stored in a table that are used to trigger the data retrieval process.

Installing MySQL

The ease of installing MySQL is one of the primary reasons for its adoption among web developers. Regardless of platform or OS versions, getting MySQL up and running and ready for use is one of the easiest installations of any database available.

This appendix explains how to install and configure MySQL for various operating systems and package formats.

The basic steps of installing MySQL involve determining what package you need to download for your particular operating system type, version, and hardware platform, as well as determining what version of MySQL you need to support the features your web application requires.

You also want to determine the minimum system requirements to run a particular version and configuration of MySQL.

Choosing a MySQL Version

Product-wise, MySQL offers a "community" server that is under the GPL (General Public License) and MySQL Enterprise — a commercial license. Businesses who want support and add-ons for things such as monitoring and backup may want to choose the commercial product. Individuals or businesses willing to take on the responsibility of maintaining their own database installation, administration, and monitoring can use the community server.

The next question is which version of MySQL to use. This depends on what features are needed and the level of acceptance (or aversion) you have for the possibility that some features might still need maturation. The versions available are summarized in the following table:

Version	Description
MySQL 5.1	Currently a release candidate, meaning that it is almost at the stage of being generally available with the caveat that it should not be installed on production level systems or systems with critical data.
MySQL 5.0	The version considered generally available, meaning production ready, that a business can depend on.
MySQL 4.1	Also commonly used, but no longer supported by MySQL.
MySQL 4.0	There are even some who still use this version, just as there are some people still using old Linux distributions because what they are using is "good enough."

Because MySQL 5.1 is due to release when this book prints, this will be the version used in the following installation demonstrations, as well as throughout this book.

Choosing a MySQL Package Type

You choose the package type depending on which OS, OS distribution, or platform you're installing MySQL on, and on the level of MySQL knowledge the person performing the installation has:

❏ Advanced users often prefer source installations because they can determine exactly how to tailor the MySQL build to suit their needs — such as what storage engines to include, what features to support or disable, operating system-specific settings, MySQL server variable default overrides, etc.

❏ Other users may want a standard installation, the configuration of which is determined by the operating system packager (as is the case with Linux distributions like Debian, Ubuntu, CentOS, Redhat, and SUSE). Packaged installations of MySQL can be installed during the time of operating system installation, or after through software package management utilities such as Yast, Yum, and apt-get.

The thing to keep in mind is that with older Linux distributions, depending on default package, installations of MySQL can contain bugs that have since been fixed. Please refer to your operating system's documentation, particularly regarding which software packages are included in the distribution.

There is a balance between bleeding edge versus stability. With open source software, bugs are fixed sooner rather than later, particularly with MySQL. So it is a good practice to determine ahead of time which version of MySQL will be installed if you're using an operating system distribution packaged MySQL (see the previous section for a description of the various versions). The release notes for the various versions of MySQL can be found at http://dev.mysql.com/doc and they are a good source of information about what features, enhancements, and fixed bugs a particular version contains.

The following sections will first detail a Windows installation, followed by both RPM-based and Debian-based (apt-get) Linux installations, and will finally detail a MySQL source installation.

Installing MySQL on Windows

Installation of MySQL on Windows is a very simple, guided process. The steps are essentially:

1.   Determine what installation package to use.

2.   Download that package.

3.   Start the install program.

4.   Give input to a number of dialogs.

The installation program is called the *Setup Wizard*. It will take care of all the underlying details of installing the MySQL server where it needs to be and ensuring it will run properly after installation.

The very first thing you'll do is navigate the download page to the list of download package types at `http://dev.mysql.com/downloads/mysql/5.1.html`. You will see in that list Community Server.

Depending on release of 5.1, you may have to explicitly select 5.1 download.

On the following page, select Windows (as opposed to Windows 64-bit).

Figure A-1 shows the three Windows download options. These options are:

❑   **Windows Essentials:** This file contains the essential files needed to run MySQL on windows with the Installation Wizard.

❑   **Windows ZIP/Setup.EXE (x86):** This is the full installation package, including the Installation Wizard. It is also a ZIP file, so the unzip utility is required. Unzipping comes standard with Windows XP and higher.

❑   **Without Installer (unzip in C:\):** This download is the MySQL package for windows without the installer. For this book, the first file is the one that should be chosen. The Windows installer (with `.msi` extension) is the installer for Windows 2000 and newer versions. Written using WIX (Windows Installer XML), it makes Windows installations a lot simpler than in previous versions.

Windows downloads (platform notes)				
Windows Essentials (x86)		5.1.25	24.3M	Pick a mirror
	MD5: bc62420722f1c4bc2bb377992da7d4d8	Signature		
Windows ZIP/Setup.EXE (x86)		5.1.25	82.1M	Pick a mirror
	MD5: f4677b923e6314a7947555efb80c9333	Signature		
Without installer (unzip in C:\)		5.1.25	98.4M	Pick a mirror
	MD5: dc17e1e7c1d4df8de6b0af49d213e944	Signature		

Figure A-1

The following steps show how to install MySQL on Windows:

1.   Download the first of these files (`.msi`) into the folder of choice, usually defaulting to the Desktop.

2. Log in with an account that has Administrator rights.

3. Click the downloaded file, named `mysql-essential-5.1.x-win32.msi`. Figure A-2 shows the MySQL Installation Wizard, which will guide you through the installation, prompting input for various questions.

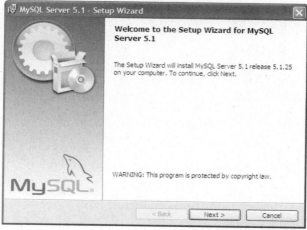

Figure A-2

4. Click Next. Figure A-3 shows an Installation Wizard dialog for installation types.

❑ **Typical** installs the basic options required for having a working MySQL installation and this is the choice that this book will use.

❑ **Complete** installs all program features.

❑ **Custom** allows the custom selection of specific server components and other settings.

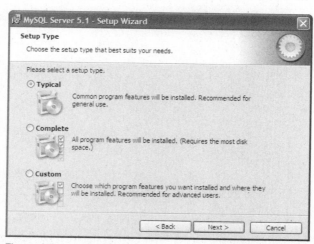

Figure A-3

5. Chose Typical, and click Next. The Summary dialog appears as shown in Figure A-4. This dialog displays the settings that will be used for the installation. At this point, it is possible to go back and change any installation settings if needed.

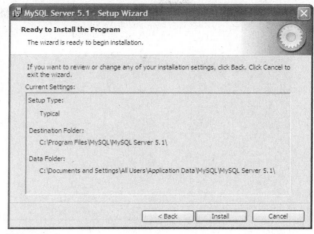

Figure A-4

6. Click Install. A screen appears showing the installation status dialog, after which the Installation dialog presents information about MySQL Enterprise, the commercial version of MySQL.

7. Click Next to continue. Finally, the dialog shown in Figure A-5 appears. It states that the installation is complete, with the Configure the Server Now check box.

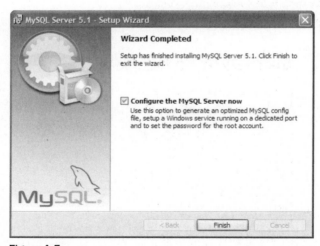

Figure A-5

8. Leave this "Configure the Server Now" box checked, and click Finish. After the installation dialogs are completed, another dialog appears, as shown in Figure A-6. This dialog is for the

MySQL Server Instance Configuration Wizard. This is the start of various steps to configure the newly installed server.

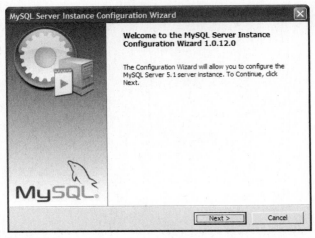

Figure A-6

9.   Click Next. Figure A-7 shows a choice between Detailed and Standard Configuration. The default is Detailed Configuration.

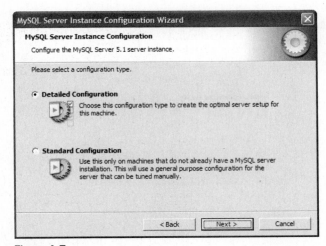

Figure A-7

10.   Leave the default checked and click Next. Figure A-8 shows a dialog for selecting what type of server is going to be run. The choices displayed are for Developer, Server, or Dedicated MySQL Server Machine. Developer Machine is selected by default.

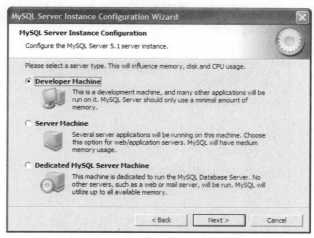

Figure A-8

11. Leave the default checked and click Next. Figure A-9 gives the selection of what type of database will be used. The choices are for Multifunctional Database, Transactional Database Only, or Non-Transactional Database Only. This means that the first includes MyISAM and InnoDB, the second InnoDB by default (while still including MyISAM), and the third MyISAM only. (Chapter 3 of this book covers the differences between MyISAM and InnoDB.)

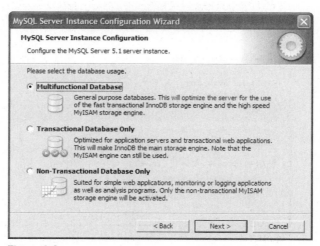

Figure A-9

12. Leave the default (Multifunctional Database) selected, and click Next. Figure A-10 allows for selecting the choices of where to set up InnoDB tablespace file(s).

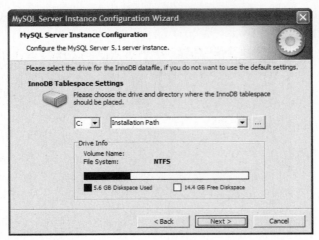

Figure A-10

13. Some database administrators choose to have their tablespace files in a different directory than default, or even on a separate disk for performance benefits. Choose a different location if you wish or the default, which is Installation Path, and then click Next. Figure A-11 shows the dialog that appears for selecting the number of concurrent connections the database installation will support. The default is the first check box. Depending on what the plans are and what this server installation will require, the selection can be made here.

For example, if the server is for a busy web site, the Online Transaction Processing (OLTP) option may be appropriate. If this server is for testing development of web applications for MySQL, Decision Support (DSS/OLAP) will work well. If the administrator is familiar enough with MySQL to know the appropriate number of connections to allow for the application in question, the Manual Settings option allows for whatever value is desired.

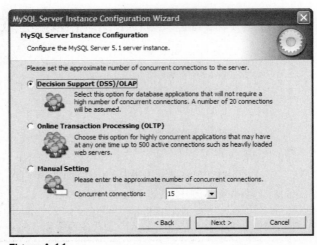

Figure A-11

14. After making the appropriate selection, click Next. Figure A-12 is a dialog for choosing TCP options.

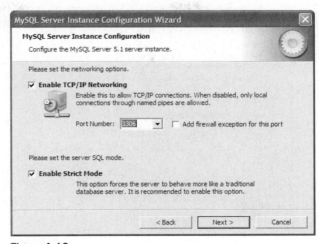

Figure A-12

The TCP choices are:

❏ Enable TCP/IP networking, including what port to run MySQL, with a check box labeled "Add firewall exception for this port."

❏ Enable Strict Mode

The defaults should suffice. You may want to also enable the firewall exception, depending on your firewall settings on your Windows server. Click Next.

15. Select a default character set (Figure A-13). Your choice will depend on your locale, or if the web application using this database needs to be able to work internationally. For instance, if the application needs to support numerous character sets, UTF8 would be the appropriate choice. Choose the character set and then click the Next button.

Figure A-13

16. Select how MySQL will start up (Figure A-14). The choices are Install As Windows Service or Include Bin Directory in Windows PATH. Most users find it convenient for MySQL to be started as a service, so leave the defaults set, and click the Next button.

Figure A-14

17. Select the root password (Figure A-15). Enter a root password of your choice. It's recommended that you not check the (default) box labeled "Enable root access from remote machines"; also leave "Create An Anonymous Account" unchecked (default). Click the Next button. Also, readers might want to check the box labeled "Include Bin Directory in Windows PATH" in order for the various utilities such as the MySQL command-line client, mysqldump, and others to work from a command prompt.

Figure A-15

18. The Summary dialog, shown in figure A-16, appears. It shows that the Configuration Wizard is about to execute the final steps of the configuration. Click Execute to complete.

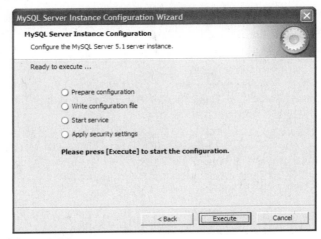

Figure A-16

19. Figure A-17 is the final dialog. It says everything is completed. Click Finish.

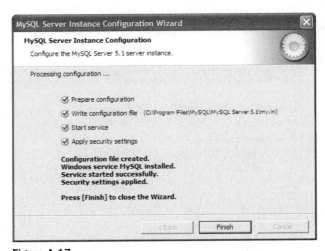

Figure A-17

MySQL is now installed on your Windows box!

Installing MySQL on RPM-based Linux Systems

Various RPM-based Linux distributions — SUSE, Redhat Enterprise, Centos, Fedora Core, etc. — allow for you to install MySQL during OS installation and each have installation instructions available. For these systems, it is also possible to install MySQL at any time after installation.

The various system management tools you can install MySQL from are:

❑ **Yast:** SUSE's system management utility allows you to select software installation sources as well as packages. You can do this either via the command line as Yast, or from the windowed environment under Administrator Settings.

❑ **Yum:** Available on various RPM-based Linux systems such as Redhat, Centos, Fedora Core, Yellow Dog Linux, and others. Yum, invoked as yum from the comment line, works similarly to apt-get on Debian-based systems, and is essentially a means of installing the appropriate RPMs for a package, taking care of dependencies. An example of running yum to get a list of packages having to do with MySQL is this:

```
yum search mysql
```

In this case, you would get a pretty big list of packages. The ones that would most likely install the server and other packages that you would list (among a big list of others) are as follows:

```
mysql-devel.i386 : Files for development of MySQL applications.
mysql-server.x86_64 : The MySQL server and related files.
innotop.noarch : A MySQL and InnoDB monitor program
mysql-bench.x86_64 : MySQL benchmark scripts and data.
mysql.x86_64 : MySQL client programs and shared libraries.
mysql-connector-odbc.x86_64 : ODBC driver for MySQL
mysql.x86_64 : MySQL client programs and shared libraries.
mysql-connector-odbc.x86_64 : ODBC driver for MySQL
perl-DBD-MySQL.x86_64 : A MySQL interface for perl
mysql-proxy.x86_64 : A proxy for the MySQL Client/Server protocol
perl-DBIx-DBSchema.noarch : Database-independent schema objects
```

❑ **RPM:** This involves simply obtaining the RPM from MySQL's download site and installing the package. There are various RPM packages for MySQL: server, client, shared libraries, shared compatibility packages, etc. In most cases, server and client (and perhaps shared libraries) should suffice. An example of installing an RPM is:

```
[root@localhost ~]# rpm -ihv MySQL-server-community-5.1.26-0.rhel5.ia64.rpm
```

❑ The RPM installations usually install MySQL binaries in /usr/bin, and data files in /var/lib/mysql.

Installing MySQL on Ubuntu

If MySQL wasn't installed during the Ubuntu installation, it's easy enough to install using the apt-* tools commonly available on Debian-derived Linux distributions. Follow these steps:

1. Update the package list. Run the command:

    ```
    sudo apt-get update
    ```

    All the sources will be fetched from an update list and displayed when this command is run.

2. Run this as follows:

    ```
    sudo apt-cache search mysql|grep ^mysql-
    ```

    ```
    mysql-admin - GUI tool for intuitive MySQL administration
    mysql-gui-tools-common - Architecture independent files for MySQL GUI Tools
    mysql-navigator - GUI client program for MySQL database server
    mysql-proxy - proxy for high availability, load balancing and query
    modification
    mysql-query-browser - Official GUI tool to query MySQL database
    mysql-doc-5.0 - MySQL database documentation
    mysql-client - MySQL database client (meta package depending on the latest
    version)
    mysql-client-5.0 - MySQL database client binaries
    mysql-common - MySQL database common files
    mysql-server - MySQL database server (meta package depending on the latest
    version)
    mysql-server-5.0 - MySQL database server binaries
    ```

    You want to use grep to filter out only the primary MySQL installation packages. Without grep, apt-cache returns any package with the string mysql included.

3. The packages that are needed are mysql-server, mysql-common, and mysql-client. Install each by entering these commands:

    ```
    sudo apt-get install mysql-common
    sudo apt-get install mysql-client
    sudo apt-get install mysql-server
    ```

4. When the mysql-client package is installed, there will be a message prompt for the inclusion of more packages:

    ```
    sudo apt-get install mysql-client
    Reading package lists... Done
    Building dependency tree
    Reading state information... Done
    The following extra packages will be installed:
      libdbd-mysql-perl libdbi-perl libmysqlclient15off libnet-daemon-perl
    libplrpc-perl
      mysql-client-5.0
    Suggested packages:
      dbishell libcompress-zlib-perl mysql-doc-5.0
    The following NEW packages will be installed:
      libdbd-mysql-perl libdbi-perl libmysqlclient15off libnet-daemon-perl
    libplrpc-perl
      mysql-client mysql-client-5.0
    ```

```
0 upgraded, 7 newly installed, 0 to remove and 191 not upgraded.
Need to get 11.2MB of archives.
After this operation, 27.3MB of additional disk space will be used.
Do you want to continue [Y/n]? Y
```

5.   'Y' is the default, as shown. Press Enter. These are all packages that will be needed for the examples of this book, so the more the merrier.

```
sudo apt-get install mysql-server
Reading package lists... Done
Building dependency tree
Reading state information... Done
The following extra packages will be installed:
  mysql-server-5.0
Suggested packages:
  mysql-doc-5.0 tinyca
Recommended packages:
 · libhtml-template-perl mailx
The following NEW packages will be installed:
  mysql-server mysql-server-5.0
0 upgraded, 2 newly installed, 0 to remove and 191 not upgraded.
Need to get 0B/28.1MB of archives.
After this operation, 89.3MB of additional disk space will be used.
Do you want to continue [Y/n]?
```

6.   Likewise with the installation of mysql-server: 'Y' is the default again. Press Enter.

Figure A-18 shows the prompt asking for a password for the MySQL *root* user. This prompt is to set the password for the *root* database user. The *root* user is the default administrative user for the database. Even though the name is the same as the operating system *root* user, this user is only for MySQL and any changes you make to this user are only within the database. Enter a password (make sure to remember this password!) and press Enter. Another prompt will ask the password to be repeated; enter the password again and press Enter. When this is completed, MySQL will be installed, running, and ready to use.

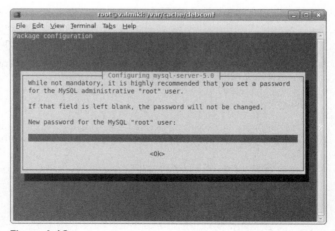

Figure A-18

Installing MySQL from Source on UNIX Systems

Many developers and database administrators prefer to install MySQL from source. This gives them the ability to compile MySQL with exactly the features they want. If you are comfortable with compiling source code on a UNIX system, the following instructions will guide you through this process.

The steps of installing MySQL from source on UNIX systems are pretty much the same regardless of UNIX variant. Before you attempt compilation of the MySQL source code, you should ensure that the prerequisite tools are installed. These tools are the following:

- ❑ gcc/g++ or commercial compiler
- ❑ gnu make or commercial make
- ❑ lexx/yacc
- ❑ automake
- ❑ autoconf
- ❑ libtool
- ❑ libncurses

To install, you follow these steps:

1. In working with MySQL source code, it can be very helpful to create a directory from within the home directory.

   ```
   cd ~
   mkdir mysql-build
   ```

2. Of course, you want to download the source distribution. This can be obtained from the URL http://dev.mysql.com/downloads/.

3. From there, navigate to the appropriate source package and download it via the web browser, saving the tar.gz file to the directory listed above, or wherever is convenient.

4. Next, as root or using the program sudo, create the mysql group and user:

   ```
   sudo groupadd mysql
   sudo useradd -d /usr/local/mysql -g mysql -m mysql
   ```

5. Then use the tar program to unarchive and decompress the downloaded file:

   ```
   tar xvzf  mysql-5.1.x.tar.gz
   ```

6. Enter the directory of the MySQL source to build:

   ```
   cd mysql-5.1.x
   ```

7. There are two ways to build MySQL.

   ❑ The `configure` script can be used to specify default options to include or exclude from the server:

   ```
   /configure -prefix=/usr/local/mysql -with-this -without-that
   ```

   You can find out what all the various options `configure` *affords you by typing:*

   ```
   /configure -help | less
   ```

   Once you run configure with the options you chose, you can now run the build: `make`.

   ❑ Optionally, and lesser-known but also very convenient, there are build scripts found in the `BUILD` directory that are named according to architecture, inclusiveness of features, compiler, debug or not, etc., of the build:

   ```
   /BUILD/compile-pentium-debug-max
   /BUILD/compile-solaris-sparc
   /BUILD/compile-amd64-valgrind-max
   ```

   The build scripts with `debug` *or* `valgrind` *are built specifically for debug purposes and are not good choices for performance, but are good for using debuggers to trace how the server runs for the inquisitive mind.*

8. Once a build script has been chosen, all that needs to be done is to run the script. It runs everything to perform the build — both `configure` with the options specified (defaulting to `prefix=/usr/local/mysql`) and `make`.

9. Should there be a problem with the build process, useful information on how to deal with a variety of issues can be found at `http://dev.mysql.com/doc/refman/5.1/en/compilation-problems.html`.

10. Once the compilation is complete, the next step is to install MySQL from the compiled source:

    ```
    sudo make install
    ```

    Once this command is completed, all the files are installed in the directory specified, in this case `/usr/local/mysql`.

11. To begin setting up MySQL as `root` user:

    ```
    sudo su -
    ```

12. Change to this directory:

    ```
    cd /usr/local/mysql
    ```

13. Set up permissions for this directory and its subdirectories:

    ```
    chown -r mysql .*
    ```

14. Install the system database tables:

```
/mysql_install_db -user=mysql
```

This script creates the *data directory* and `mysql` schema containing system tables. The data directory is the directory where database schemas are found, including the new `mysql` schema. The `mysql` schema contains tables required for system functionality such as user database, tables, column privileges, time zones, general logging, slow queries log, and help information. Also, whenever you create a new schema, a new directory with the same name as the schema will be created in the data directory. In each schema's directory, MySQL will store all files and actual data (except for InnoDB, which stores one or more tablespace files in the data directory directly).

15. Change the data directory to have user permissions to both `mysql` user and group:

```
chown -R mysql:mysql ./var
```

16. To make it so the newly installed MySQL binary programs are readily executable and do not need to be explicitly run with the full path, add the directory to the PATH variable so it contains these programs in `/etc/profile` by adding this line:

```
export PATH=$PATH:/usr/local/mysql/bin
```

Another option is for this line to be added to each individual's `.bash_profile` if it's not necessary for every user to be able to run MySQL binary programs. With it added to `/etc/profile`, the next time the system is restarted, all logins to the system will have this directory in their path. For this session, this same command will set the PATH variable correctly.

17. MySQL can now be started with the command:

```
/usr/local/mysql/bin/mysqld_safe -user=mysql &
```

Unix Post Install

If the UNIX variant being used is the System 5 (SYSV) variant, there is a MySQL daemon start/stop script available in the source directory where MySQL was compiled:

```
support/mysql.server
```

This script most likely will need to be edited for the specific system settings. Once it's ready to use, it can be set up in `/etc/init.d/` and linked to the appropriate run-level directories so that the MySQL daemon is started and stopped according to the system's running state, either when the system is being started or shut down.

Also included in the support directory are different MySQL `my.cnf` configuration files. With the source build of MySQL, there is no `my.cnf` installed and the running MySQL server uses default settings. The various `my.cnf` configuration files in this directory are provided with settings for installations of several sizes and are named accordingly:

```
my-huge.cnf
my-medium.cnf
my-small.cnf
```

Whichever type of MySQL deployment is being planned, one of these files can be chosen and edited according to any system specifics and copied as /etc/my.cnf. The next time MySQL is restarted, it will use the settings of this new configuration file.

B

Configuring MySQL

Now that you have a running MySQL installation, as an administrator, you can make some configuration setting changes and perform some administrative tasks. The first thing to do is set up a schema and privileges to allow web applications to access that schema. Other tasks are to set various MySQL command options for optimal performance.

Running MySQL for the First Time

The first thing to do is to change the password for the root user. The root user is the default administrative user for the database. Even though the name is the same as the operating system root user, this root user is only a MySQL user, and any changes you make to this user are only made within the database. By default, this user has no password, though you can only connect to the database from the same host that the database is running on. Despite this, it is still a good idea to change it so the root user has an actual password. To change the root user's password, start the MySQL command line client:

```
mysql -user=root
```

Then set the user password with the following SQL statements:

```
mysql> SET PASSWORD FOR root@localhost=PASSWORD('rootpass');
mysql> SET PASSWORD FOR root@127.0.0.1=PASSWORD('rootpass');
mysql> SET PASSWORD FOR root@myhost=PASSWORD('rootpass');
```

Of course, replace the word *rootpass* in the previous code with the desired password. The reason for running this three times for the same user but different hosts is because database users are specified with user@host; in order for the *root* user to connect to MySQL running on the local server, you must have an entry for root@localhost, root@127.0.0.1, and root@myhost (with "myhost" being the name of your server). All of these are possible host values of the local server that MySQL is running on.

Setting Up Privileges and Creating a Schema

The second administrative task that should be performed is to create the user that will connect to the schema where the web application database objects will be located.

```
mysql> GRANT ALL PRIVILEGES ON webapps.* TO 'webuser'@'localhost'
    -> IDENTIFIED BY 'mypass';
```

Again, replace `"mypass"` in your code with the password of your choice.

This entry is just for the WebApp user to connect to the local database. There may be other database hosts from where this user will need the privileges to connect from:

```
mysql> GRANT ALL PRIVILEGES ON webapps.* TO 'webuser'@'www.example.com'
    -> IDENTIFIED BY 'mypass';
```

Whatever the hostname is, or IP address that the `webuser` user will be connecting from, the name of that host will replace `www.example.com`, which is a database schema that contains all database objects that the web application requires. For this book, the name *webapp* is used. To create a database schema, the following command is run:

```
mysql> CREATE DATABASE webapp
```

Alternatively, the command `mysqladmin -u root -p create webapp` *can also be used. MySQL client programs, including the* `mysqladmin` *client program, are explained in Chapter 2.*

MySQL Server Configuration File

After installing MySQL, there are some server command options that can be set, depending on what hardware you have available and what your application may require.

The file, `my.cnf`, or on Windows, `my.ini`, is a file containing various MySQL server command options that the server reads upon starting up. It usually resides in `/etc` on UNIX systems, although some GNU/Linux distributions such as Debian and Ubuntu place it in `/etc/mysql`. Individual users can also have their own specific settings stored in a file `.my.cnf`, located in the user's home directory. The `my.cnf` file has a general format for sections, indicated like such:

```
[client]
```

The `[client]` option group would be used to specify command options for MySQL client programs.

```
[mysqld]
```

The `[mysqld]` option group would be used to specify command options for the main server.

There are several sections that can be contained within `my.cnf`: `mysqld`, `mysqld_safe`, `mysqld_multi`, `client`, `mysql`, `mysqldump`, etc. Within each of those sections are the different server command options "`name = value`". These are the values for the program of that section, such as this:

```
[client]

port = 3306

[mysqld]

datadir = /usr/local/mysql/var
```

In the previous example, this means that MySQL client programs such as `mysql` command line client, `mysqldump` and `mysqladmin` will expect to connect to the server on port 3306 and `mysqld`, the MySQL server itself, uses the directory `/usr/local/mysql/var` as the place where schemas are located.

To see all the different command options that MySQL uses, issue the following command (the path to `mysqld` may vary according to installation):

```
shell> /usr/local/mysql/libexec/mysqld --verbose --help
```

This will print not only `mysqld` options that can be specified, but the also the values of the settings it is using.

There are some basic command options that are worth setting immediately after installing MySQL, before the database populates with application data and is used as a production server. The following types of command options are those that specify where data is stored on the filesystem (`datadir`) as well as InnoDB tablespace configuration. These command options are easier to set prior to populating your database with application data because you don't yet have to concern yourself with losing any crucial data. Also, data files are relatively small at this time — so if you wanted to set your data directory variable to a separate disk and you needed to move your data files to that disk, it would be much easier to do with small data files.

Basic Command Options

This section covers the basic command options for configuring MySQL. These options are used for setting MySQL system values, such as where to store the database data and index files, network settings, where temporary tables will be created, as well as the user id that MySQL will run as.

datadir

As mentioned before, this setting specifies the base directory where MySQL schemas are located. A schema in MySQL is stored in its own directory. Each table created has a set of one or more files, depending upon the type of storage engine set. For instance, say you have a schema named *webapps*, and there are three tables *t1* (MyISAM), *users* (InnoDB), and *history* (Archive), and the `datadir` is defined as `/usr/local/mysql/var`. The files that you would see are the following:

```
ls -l /usr/local/mysql/
total 112
-rw-rw----   1 mysql  mysql    65 Jun 23 09:17 db.opt
-rw-rw----   1 mysql  mysql  8642 Jun 23 09:18 history.ARZ
-rw-rw----   1 mysql  mysql  8554 Jun 23 09:18 history.frm
-rw-rw----   1 mysql  mysql     0 Jun 23 09:18 t1.MYD
-rw-rw----   1 mysql  mysql  1024 Jun 23 09:18 t1.MYI
```

```
-rw-rw----   1 mysql  mysql  8554 Jun 23 09:18 t1.frm
-rw-rw----   1 mysql  mysql  8554 Jun 23 09:18 users.frm
```

For every table, regardless of storage engine type, there will always be an .frm file. This is the table definition file. Then, with *t1*, which uses the MyISAM storage engine, it has two additional files: *t1.MYD* and *t1.MYI*. The first is the data file where actual data is stored, and the second is the index file, which contains the indexes for *t1*. The history table, on the other hand, has just one other file: history.ARZ. This is a gzip-compressed data file. The Archive storage engine doesn't support indexes, so there is no index file for the *history* table. The *users* table has its sole .frm file, but its actual data and indexes are stored in an InnoDB tablespace file. Chapter 4 explains in more detail the specifics of each storage engine.

As mentioned in Appendix A, some administrators choose to set the datadir value to a separate disk than the operating system disk, having all IO for the database on its own disk partition. An example of this would be to have a separate disk partition that is mounted on /data, and to set datadir to this value:

```
datadir = /data
```

tmpdir

MySQL has a feature known as temporary tables. These are tables that can be used to temporarily store the results of one query for use in a subsequent query. Temporary tables are also used internally by MySQL for sorting and other operations when using system memory isn't possible due to the amount of data being processed. This value defaults to the directory /tmp but can also be set to a separate disk or even set to RAM disk, making it so temporary tables are created in memory instead of on disk.

Examples of setting tmpdir are as follows:

```
tmpdir = /tmp
```

```
tmpdir = /disk2/tmp
```

user

This command option is used to set the system user (UID) the MySQL daemon mysqld will run as. The default is "mysql," but this can be set to any value the administrator chooses. An example is:

```
user = mysql
```

port

The port setting is to specify what port MySQL will run on. The default is 3306, but in some situations, another port may be used. It's possible to run multiple instances of MySQL on a single system. (The section "Replication" that appears later in this appendix explains this in more detail.) In order to run multiple instances of MySQL on a single system, you would have in your my.cnf multiple [mysqld] sections such as the following:

```
[mysqld1]

datadir = /usr/local/mysql/var/data1
```

```
port = 3306

[mysqld2]

datadir = /usr/local/mysql/var/data2

port = 3307
```

socket

The socket setting is to specify what socket MySQL will use. The default can depend on whether it was specified during compilation, or what the package for MySQL was set to by the operating system vendor. As with the port setting, the socket setting can also be used to accommodate running multiple MySQL instances on the same system. An example of this setting would be:

```
socket = /tmp/mysqld.sock
```

InnoDB Path and Tablespace Command Options

The InnoDB storage engine has its own particular command options that pertain specifically to the performance and data file configuration. The tablespace settings can be changed at any time, even after you have a full data set loaded, but they're much easier to change in the beginning. If you plan on using the InnoDB storage engine, and have included in your plan some of the requirements for your application, it can certainly help to configure the InnoDB settings from the start. The settings listed here are those types of settings.

```
innodb_data_home_dir
```

This is similar to the `datadir` command option except it only pertains to the InnoDB storage engine. InnoDB employs for its storage what is known as a tablespace file. This file contains both the data and indexes for tables. This tablespace file can be configured to contain all tables, or one tablespace per table. Like `datadir`, administrators can define this to be any location, or even a separate disk. Moreover, the InnoDB storage engine can even use a raw partition of an entire disk.

```
innodb_data_home_dir = /usr/local/mysql/var
innodb_data_home_dir = /innodata
```

innodb_data_file_path

This command option specifies the tablespace file configuration. It specifies the initial size of the tablespace file or files, whether the tablespace file can autoextend, and can be used to set the actual path of the tablespace. The basic usage is this:

```
innodb_data_file_path=datafile_spec1[;datafile_spec2]...
```

Here is a simple example of a single tablespace file that automatically grows when the initial size is exceeded:

```
innodb_data_file_path=ibdata1:10M:autoextend
```

The autoextend attribute allows for the tablespace file to grow when the initial size of the tablespace is exceeded. It will grow by 8MB increments by default. Another example that would allow for good capacity and growth is to use two tablespace files:

```
innodb_data_file_path = ibdata1:100M;ibdata2:100M:autoextend
```

Explicitly defining the path is done by leaving the previous innodb_data_home_dir an empty string and specifying the actual path:

```
innodb_data_home_dir =
innodb_data_file_path=/innodata/ibdata1:100M;/innodata/ibdata2:100M:autoextend
```

As already mentioned, it's possible even to use a raw partition. This means the tablespace is not a file but an entire disk partition and that the disk partition is not using an operating system filesystem format, but rather InnoDB's own format. Another feature of using raw disk partitions is that you can perform non-buffered I/O on Windows and on some UNIX variants. To use raw partitions, this can be achieved with the settings:

```
innodb_data_home_dir =
innodb_data_file_path = /dev/sdb1:3Gnewraw;/dev/sdb2:2Gnewraw
```

The previous example means that two partitions will be used: One is 3 gigabytes, and the second is 2 gigabytes. It's important to note that the keyword in the example, newraw, should only be used the first time that MySQL is started after adding the new configuration using raw partitions. MySQL processes this newraw keyword and initializes the new partitions. After you start and run MySQL, these keywords should be removed.

innodb_file_per_table

This setting allows each InnoDB table to have its own tablespace file (<tablename>.ibd) versus one or more tablespaces for all tables. This makes it convenient to move tables from one disk to another, and also has some performance benefits. Another benefit using innodb_table_per_file: using single tablespace files for each table (multiple tablespaces) allows for disk space to be freed up when OPTIMIZE TABLE is performed on the given table, whereas with single tablespace files for multiple tables, the tablespace file will not decrease even when running OPTIMIZE TABLE. Multiple tablespace files are by default auto-extending, meaning they will automatically grow according to data storage needs. Single tablespace files have a given size as specified in the parameter innodb_data_file_path, which can also specify the single tablespace file as being auto-extending. innodb_file_per_table is definitely one setting you want to make sooner rather than later, before you have a lot of data in your database. The process to switch to using this setting is to simply add this to the my.cnf:

```
[mysqld]
innodb_file_per_table
```

Existing InnoDB tables will remain in the single tablespace(s). One way to switch existing tables to using file-per-table is to simply run ALTER TABLE:

```
ALTER TABLE t1 ENGINE=InnoDB;
```

The existing InnoDB table will be recreated with its own .ibd tablespace file. The one problem with this is if the existing single tablespace(s) are large. Once you convert to using innodb_file_per_table, it's unnecessarily a large size since it will no longer contain the table data.

> Note that the previous statement assumes you're converting every single table.

The one way to change InnoDB to use a smaller tablespace file is this:

1. Convert *every* InnoDB table to temporarily use MyISAM, making sure no clients are allowed to connect to the database before this step because there will be no ACID compliance after the ALTER has completed:

   ```
   ALTER TABLE t1 ENGINE=MyISAM
   ```

2. Stop the MySQL server.
3. Move (back up) the existing tablespace file(s).
4. Change settings for innodb_data_file_path to the desired reduced size.
5. Start the MySQL server.
6. Convert *every* table you converted to MyISAM back to InnoDB:

   ```
   ALTER TABLE t1 ENGINE=InnoDB
   ```

There are many other command options pertaining to InnoDB (and MySQL in general) that are beyond the scope of this appendix. More information about these options can be found at http://dev.mysql.com/doc/, MySQL's documentation web site.

Backups

Backing up your database is one of the most important administrative tasks you need to perform. Doing so will give you assurance that your data won't be lost — and that you can sleep at night! Also, being able to quickly restore your database from a backup is crucial in an effective backup and restoration procedure.

With MySQL, there are a number of tools and strategies for backing up and restoring your data. This section will cover some of the more common ones.

Replication Backup Slave

One common strategy is to use a slave that is used solely for running backups. This allows you to run backups on a live database, regardless of how large it is, without affecting any applications using the main database. You can even use features such as the MySQL global variable slave_replication_delay (see http://bugs.mysql.com/bug.php?id=28760) to make it so the backup slave is lagging the master by a given amount of time so you can have "lagged" backups of your data. This might be useful in the case where you want backups that represent your system's data state at a time somewhat in the past — say, for instance, there was some catastrophic data loss (God forbid) at a particular time near the time of your backups. This might result in your backup process adversely being affected. This would give you both a live server to use (you would immediately shut down replication), as well as create a backup from it.

mysqldump

The MySQL client tool, mysqldump, is the most commonly used method to create backups. To see how to use mysqldump, as well as a list of options available, you can run this:

```
mysqldump --help
```

To produce a simple backup of a schema, in this case called webapp, connect as the user username, which should be whatever user has access to the webapp schema. The output of mysqldump contains SQL statements that recreate the tables in webapp and insert the data. These statements are outputted to the file webapp.sql.

```
mysqldump --user=username --password=pass webapp > webapp.sql
```

If you wanted to dump only the schema files (create tables), you could use the flag -d or --no-data.

```
mysqldump --user=username --password=pass --no-data webapp > webapp_schema.sql
```

One way to produce backups of your database is to produce a separate schema creation file and data file. For specifying that you want to exclude schema creation information — no CREATE TABLE statements — you use the following:

```
mysqldump --user=username --no-create-info webapp > webapp_data.sql
```

To restore your database from a backup created by mysqldump, you simply need to run that backup file with the MySQL command line client, mysql. The following would reload the entire dump file of the webapp schema:

```
mysql --user=root webapp < webapp.sql
```

Scripting mysqldump Backups with Perl

You can also automate your backups, as well as perform your backups from a MySQL slave dedicated to providing backups. The following Perl script, which would be automated as a cron job, does this by making sure the slave is up-to-date before performing the dump, and attempts to let the slave catch up within a defined number of tries (seconds in this case due to using a sleep).

This script timestamps the dump and removes any dumps older than a week. This script also obtains the current position of the slave (the data that has been read from the master) and writes it to a file that contains the CHANGE MASTER statement that would be run if you were to restore a database with a dump produced from this script.

```
!/usr/bin/perl

use strict;
use warnings;

use Carp qw(croak);
use DBI;
use Getopt::Long;
```

```
our $dbh;
our $dump_dir = '/var/backups/mysql';
our $mysqldump = '/usr/local/mysql/bin/mysqldump';

our $opt_schema;

# always connect
sub BEGIN {
  $dbh= DBI->connect('DBI:mysql:webapp', 'root', '');
}

# make sure to start the slave io_thread even if failure
sub END {
  $dbh->do('start slave io_thread');
}

GetOptions(
  "s|schema=s" => \$opt_schema
);

# always assume 'webapp' unless otherwise specified
$opt_schema = 'webapp' unless defined $opt_schema;

# clear out anything older than a week
`find . -name '*.sql' -mtime +7 -exec rm -f \{\} \\;`;

get a data stamp
my $dump= `date +%d%m%y`;
chomp($dump);
$dump= 'webapp-' . $dump . '.sql';
chdir($dump_dir) or croak "Unable to chdir $!\n";

# stop the slave from being updated
$dbh->do('stop slave io_thread');
my $up_to_date = 0;
my $sth = $dbh->prepare('SHOW SLAVE STATUS');

my $row;

# total number of attempts (seconds) to see if slave is up to date
my $max_tries = 100;
my $tries= 1;
while (!$up_to_date && $tries < $max_tries) {
  $sth->execute();
  $row= $sth->fetchrow_arrayref();
  # if the columns are equal, then this means the slave has caught up
  if ($row->[6] == $row->[21]) {
    $up_to_date= 1;
  }
  sleep 1;
  $tries++;
}

if ($tries == $max_tries) {
```

```
        $dbh->do('start slave io_thread');
        warn "slave too far behind, exiting.";
        exit;
}
create change master string
my $change= 'CHANGE MASTER TO MASTER_HOST=\" . $row->[1] .
            '\', MASTER_LOG_FILE=\" . $row->[5] .
            '\', MASTER_LOG_POS=' . $row->[6] . ';';
my $fh;
open($fh, '>', 'change_master.txt') or die "unable to open change_master_txt" ;
print $fh $change;
close($fh);

# run the backup
my $retval = system("$mysqldump -u root --master-data=2 $opt_schema > $dump");

# restart the slave IO thread
$dbh->do('start slave io_thread');

1;
```

Creating a Backup by Copying Data Files

If you are using only MyISAM as the storage engine for a given schema or tables, you can simply copy data from the data directory to a backup directory. Of course, you have to issue LOCK TABLES to ensure these tables aren't being written to while copying. You will need two terminal windows for this.

1. In one terminal window, as a user with the proper privileges, connect to the schema you want to back up, in this case, webapp:

```
mysql --user=root --password=pass webapp
```

2. Then in another terminal window (this is important), issue a write lock on the tables. Don't leave this screen until you're done with the file copying in the next step!

```
mysql> FLUSH TABLES WITH READ LOCK;
```

3. Then, from within the data directory, copy the files to the backup directory:

```
cd /var/lib/mysql/webapps

cp *.MYD *.MYI *.frm /var/backups/mysql/
```

4. Now you can unlock the schema in the other terminal window.

```
mysql> UNLOCK TABLES;
```

To restore the database with these files, or even create a slave with this data, you would want to shut down the database you are restoring and simply copy these files to the appropriate data directory. Then restart the database.

mysqlhotcopy

mysqlhotcopy is a Perl backup utility originally written by Tim Bunce (creator of DBI) for backing up MyISAM and Archive tables only. It automatically performs a backup using the file copy method, as just shown in the previous section. It is a standard client utility that is part of the MySQL distribution. An example of performing a backup of the webapps schema is shown in the snippet below:

```
mysqlhotcopy --user=root webapp /var/backups/mysql/
```

After running this, you would find all of the MYD, MYI and .frm files for the webapp schema located in /var/backups/mysql/webapp. You could use these to either restore a database or build a new one.

Snapshots Using LVM

LVM, or *Logical Volume Manager*, is a logical volume manager available for Linux for managing disk drives or partitions. LVM offers the ability to create snapshots, which are images or blocks devices, that represent an exact copy of the logical volume at the point in time when the snapshot was taken. It gives a pointer to the data at that time, and once created, it accrues a delta (of sorts) that provides a path of restoration back to the state of the logical volume the moment the snapshot was made. Over time, this delta grows, so it's important to mount the snapshot as soon as possible after its having been made, copy all the data of that mounted snapshot to a backup disk, unmount the snapshot, and then destroy it.

Some commands for seeing your logical volume setup are:

❑ pvs: This shows physical volumes that comprise an LVM volume:

```
root@vidya:~# pvs
  PV         VG   Fmt  Attr PSize    PFree
  /dev/sdb1  data lvm2 a-   372.54G       0
  /dev/sdb2  data lvm2 a-   326.09G 296.80G
```

❑ vgs: This lists logical LVM volume groups:

```
root@vidya:~# vgs
  VG   #PV #LV #SN Attr   VSize   VFree
  data   2   1   1 wz--n- 698.63G 296.80G
```

❑ lvs: This lists logical volumes:

```
root@vidya:~# lvs
  LV                  VG   Attr   LSize  Origin     Snap% Move Log Copy%
  dbbackup_2008-09-22 data swi-a- 29.30G mysql_data 40.84
  mysql_data          data owi-ao 372.54G
```

The commands used for creating and removing snapshots are:

❑ lvcreate: Creates a snapshot.

❑ lvremove: Removes an existing snapshot.

An example of removing a snapshot using `lvremove` is shown here:

```
root@vidya:~# lvremove /dev/data/dbbackup_2008-09-22
Do you really want to remove active logical volume "dbbackup_2008-09-22"? [y/n]: y
   Logical volume "dbbackup_2008-09-22" successfully removed
```

Also important to know is that when you create the snapshot, you must lock the database with this:

```
FLUSH TABLES WITH READ LOCK;
```

Locking it prevents writes, but allows reads, which was discussed in the previous section on data file copying for backups. The snapshot is created very quickly, so the database doesn't have to be locked for any more than a minute at most. Then issue:

```
UNLOCK TABLES;
```

The following sample Perl code snippet shows how this could be scripted:

```
# connect to the database
my $dbh = DBI->connect('DBI:mysql:webapp', 'root', 'root');
$dbh->do('flush tables with read lock');

# obtain a date string for yesterday and today
my $query = 'select date(date_sub(now(), interval 1 day)),date(now()) from dual';
my $dref = $dbh->selectall_arrayref($query);
my ($yesterday,$today)= @{$dref->[0]};

# remove previous day snapshot
print "removing old backp yesterday $yesterday\n";
my $remove= '/sbin/lvremove -f /dev/data/dbbackup_$yesterday`;
print "output of /sbin/lvremove -f /dev/data/dbbackup_$yesterday : $remove\n";

# create new snapshot
print "creating today's ($today) backup\n";
my $create= '/sbin/lvcreate -L30000M -s -n dbbackup_$today /dev/data/mysql_data`;
print "output lvcreate -L30000M -s -n dbbackup_$today /dev/data/mysql_data:$create\n"
;
print "created backup, unlock tables\n";
$dbh->do('unlock tables');
```

An even better solution is to use Lenz Grimmler's excellent LVM backup utility, `mylvmbackup`, which you can find out about at `http://www.lenzg.org/mylvmbackup/`.

InnoDB Hotbackup, ibbackup

InnoDB Hotbackup, `ibbackup`, is a commercial tool available from InnoBase Oy, a subsidiary of Oracle. `ibbackup` allows you to back up a live database that is using InnoDB as the storage engine, without requiring any locks or affecting normal database operation. It provides you with a consistent copy of your database for a given point in time. It can also be used to create snapshots of data for creating slaves.

Also available is a Perl backup utility for creating hot backups of both InnoDB (using `ibbackup`) and MyISAM tables.

`ibbackup` is a commercial product, so you will have to purchase it from the InnoBase. For more information, visit InnoBase's web site at `http://www.innodb.com/hot-backup/`.

Monitoring

Knowing the status of your web application system, including the health of the database and operating systems — both the running status as well as performance over a given period of time — can help you to ensure maximum up-time and the best performance for the application as a whole. There are many tools out there to give you this ability, two of which will be discussed here.

Nagios

Nagios is an industry standard, open source system and network monitoring software application. It can be used to monitor a number of systems and services, including databases, web servers, SSH, and virtually anything you want to keep an eye on. It can also send alerts via email — which can be set to dial a pager (so you can be awakened from sleep at 3 A.M.!) when there are problems. Nagios also provides you with a means of problem remediation, proactive planning (scheduling downtime, capacity planning), and reporting.

Nagios can also be used in conjunction with nrpe, which is an add-on that allows for the execution of plug-ins to return status of a remove server to the Nagios server.

Nagios has a web interface (CGI), as shown in figure B-1, that provides numerous overview and summary pages organized by hosts and services, as well as a status map. This is also the interface you will use to schedule downtime.

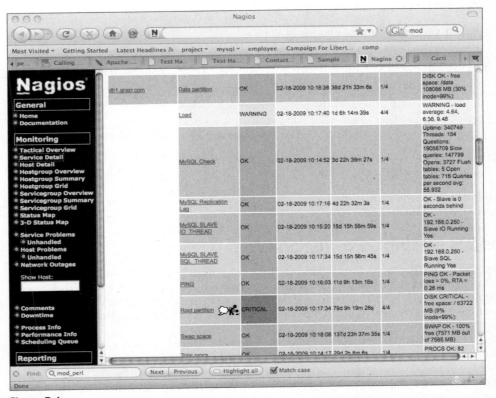

Figure B-1

For more info on Nagios, visit the Nagios project web site. It has information and documentation about everything you would ever want to know about Nagios at http://www.nagios.org/.

Cacti

Cacti, an extremely useful tool, gives you insight into numerous systems by providing a complete network graphing solution that uses RRDTool (Round Robin Database). With Cacti, you can graph both networking and database performance. With its web interface, an administrator can configure Cacti itself, as well as devices, data sources, graphs, polling, and other components.

Figure B-2 shows one of many graphs that Cacti produces, in this case, system load average.

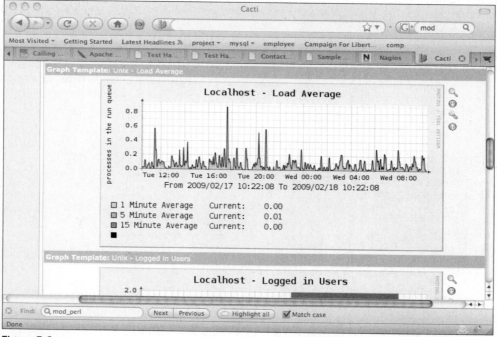

Figure B-2

Additionally, you can find some excellent templates, developed by Baron Schwartz of Percona, for graphing MySQL performance — graphs for numerous InnoDB and general MySQL statistics, as well as memcached and Apache. For more information, visit the site at http://www.xaprb.com/blog/2008/05/25/screenshots-of-improved-mysql-cacti-templates/. The templates can be found at http://code.google.com/p/mysql-cacti-templates/.

MySQL Enterprise Monitor

The MySQL Enterprise Monitor is a commercial, distributed web application available from MySQL/Sun that continually monitors your database systems, sending alerts when there are problems. It also provides a consolidated view of your database system. Other features include auto-detection of your replication topology, a replication monitor that provides a view of real-time master-slave performance, the MySQL query analyzer that you can use to improve application performance, as well as many other features. The Enterprise Monitor is available under MySQL Enterprise subscription levels Silver, Gold, and Platinum. For more information, see `http://www.mysql.com/products/enterprise/monitor.html`.

my.cnf Sample File

Chapter 3 demonstrates how to set up replication, with each step explained. The following code is the my.cnf file used for that demonstration, in its complete form. This my.cnf is set to run on a MacBook Pro, with 2GB RAM.

```
#
# Sample my.cnf for running with mysqld_multi
#
# The path settings in this file pertain to a
# MySQL source install where mysql is installed
# in /usr/local/mysql
#

[mysqld_multi]
mysqld         = /usr/local/mysql/bin/mysqld_safe
mysqladmin     = /usr/local/mysql/bin/mysqladmin
# mysqld_multi runs as root so it can start up the servers
# which will themselves run as the mysql user
user           = root

[client]
port           = 3306
socket         = /tmp/mysql.sock

[mysqld1]
mysqld         = /usr/local/mysql/bin/mysqld_safe
mysqladmin     = /usr/local/mysql/bin/mysqladmin
user           = mysql
port           = 3306
socket         = /tmp/mysql.sock
# don't leave this on for production, performance hit
log            = /tmp/sql1.log
datadir        = /usr/local/mysql/var/data1

server-id          = 1
log-bin            = /usr/local/mysql/var/data1/bin.log
```

```
log-slave-updates
binlog-do-db            = webapps

master-host             = localhost
master-user             = repl
master-password         = repl
master-port             = 3307

report-host             = slave-3306
report-port             = 3306
replicate-wild-do-table = webapps.%
relay-log               = /usr/local/mysql/var/data1/relay.log
relay-log-info-file     = /usr/local/mysql/var/data1/relay-log.info
relay-log-index         = /usr/local/mysql/var/data1/relay-log.index

auto-increment-increment = 2
# this will be the odd ID server
auto-increment-offset    = 1

key_buffer              = 64M
max_allowed_packet      = 20M
table_cache             = 64
sort_buffer_size        = 1M
net_buffer_length       = 16K
read_buffer_size        = 512K
read_rnd_buffer_size    = 1M
myisam_sort_buffer_size = 16M

# innodb settings. Adjust according to your hardware
innodb_file_per_table
innodb_data_home_dir            = /usr/local/mysql/var/data1
innodb_data_file_path           = ibdata1:10M;ibdata2:10M:autoextend
innodb_buffer_pool_size         = 64M
innodb_additional_mem_pool_size = 10M
innodb_log_file_size            = 5M
innodb_log_buffer_size          = 8M
innodb_flush_log_at_trx_commit  = 1
innodb_lock_wait_timeout        = 50

[mysqld2]
mysqld              = /usr/local/mysql/bin/mysqld_safe
mysqladmin          = /usr/local/mysql/bin/mysqladmin
user                = mysql
port                = 3307
socket              = /tmp/mysql2.sock
# don't leave this on for production, performance hit
log                 = /tmp/sql2.log
datadir             = /usr/local/mysql/var/data2

# replication settings
server-id           = 2
log-bin             = /usr/local/mysql/var/data2/bin.log
binlog-do-db        = webapps
log-slave-updates
```

```
# replication settings
master-host          = localhost
master-user          = repl
master-password      = repl
master-port          = 3306

report-host          = slave-3307
report-port          = 3307
replicate-wild-do-table = webapps.%
relay-log            = /usr/local/mysql/var/data2/relay.log
relay-log-info-file  = /usr/local/mysql/var/data2/relay-log.info
relay-log-index      = /usr/local/mysql/var/data2/relay-log.index

auto-increment-increment = 2
# This will be the even ID server
auto-increment-offset    = 2

key_buffer           = 64M
max_allowed_packet   = 20M
table_cache          = 64
sort_buffer_size     = 1M
net_buffer_length    = 16K
read_buffer_size     = 512K
read_rnd_buffer_size = 1M
myisam_sort_buffer_size = 16M

innodb_file_per_table
innodb_data_home_dir              = /usr/local/mysql/var/data2
innodb_data_file_path             = ibdata1:10M;ibdata2:10M:autoextend
innodb_log_group_home_dir         = /usr/local/mysql/var/data2
innodb_buffer_pool_size           = 64M
innodb_additional_mem_pool_size   = 10M
innodb_log_file_size              = 5M
innodb_log_buffer_size            = 8M
innodb_flush_log_at_trx_commit    = 1
innodb_lock_wait_timeout          = 50
```

Sample sphinx.conf

Chapter 3 also provides a demonstration of installing and configuring the Sphinx search engine. The following is the sphinx.conf used in that demonstration, in its entirety:

```
#
# Sphinx configuration file sample
#
# WARNING! While this sample file mentions all available options,
# it contains (very) short helper descriptions only. Please refer to
# doc/sphinx.html for details.
#

#############################################################################
## data source definition
#############################################################################
```

```
source sakila_main
{
        type            = mysql
        sql_host        = localhost
        sql_user        = webuser
        sql_pass        = mypass
        sql_db          = sakila
        sql_port        = 3306  # optional, default is 3306
        sql_sock        = /tmp/mysql.sock

        sql_query       = SELECT film_id, title, description FROM film_text
        sql_query_info  = SELECT * FROM film_text WHERE film_id=$id
}

#############################################################################
## indices
#############################################################################

index film_main
{
        source          = sakila_main
        path            = /usr/local/sphinx/var/data/film_main
        charset_type    = utf-8
}



index sakila_dist
{
        type            = distributed
        agent           = localhost::3312::film_main
}

#############################################################################
## indexer settings
#############################################################################

indexer
{
        mem_limit       = 32M
}

#############################################################################
## searchd settings
#############################################################################

searchd
{
        address         = 127.0.0.1
        port            = 3312
        log             = /usr/local/sphinx/var/log/searchd.log
```

```
query_log       = /usr/local/sphinx/var/log/query.log
read_timeout    = 5
max_children    = 30
pid_file        = /usr/local/sphinx/var/log/searchd.pid
max_matches     = 1000
seamless_rotate = 1
}
```

Index